COMPUTER GRAPHICS

Volume 18 • Number 3 • July 1984
A quarterly report of ACM SIGGRAPH

SIGGRAPH '84 Conference Proceedings
July 23-27, 1984, Minneapolis, Minnesota
Edited by Hank Christiansen

Sponsored by the Association for Computing Machinery's
Special Interest Group on Computer Graphics

The Association for Computing Machinery, Inc.
11 West 42nd Street
New York, New York 10036

Copyright© 1984 by the Association for Computing
Machinery, Inc. Copying without fee is permitted provided
that the copies are not made or distributed for direct
commercial advantage and credit to the source is given.
Abstracting with credit is permitted. For other copying of
articles that carry a code at the bottom of the first page,
copying is permitted provided that the per-copy fee
indicated in the code is paid through the Copyright
Clearance Center, 21 Congress Street, Salem MA 01970.
For permission to republish write to: Director of
Publications, Association for Computing Machinery. To
copy otherwise, or republish, requires a fee and/or
specific permission.

ISBN 0-89791-138-5

Sponsored by the Association for Computing Machinery's
Special Interest Group on Computer Graphics in
cooperation with the IEEE Technical Committee on Com-
puter Graphics, Eurographics, the Minneapolis College of
Art and Design, the University of Minnesota, the Science
Museum of Minnesota and the Institute for Media Arts.

Additional copies may be ordered prepaid from:
ACM Order Department   Price:
P.O. Box 64145   Members: $30.00
Baltimore, MD 21264   All Others: $40.00
ACM Order Number: 428840

Manufactured By K Graphics, Inc.

Printed in the U.S.A.

Computer Graphics Achievement Award
Dr. James H. Clark

Dr. James H. Clark has been designing and implementing both hardware and software for special-purpose computer graphics and computer-aided design systems since 1970. He holds a MS degree in Physics and was awarded a Ph.D. in Computer Science from the University of Utah in 1974. He then spent three years at the University of California, two years consulting and the last four years as an Associate Professor at Stanford University, Computer Systems Laboratories. He is the author of fifteen technical articles in the fields of Computer Graphics, IC Computer-Aided Design, and Solid Geometric Modeling. He founded Silicon Graphics, Inc., in November, 1981 to produce advanced high performance geometric processing workstations based upon his past work in these fields.

The Computer Graphics Achievement Award is being presented to Dr. Clark for his work on the development of the "Geometry Engine," which brought custom silicon capabilities to the highly demanding area of real time computer graphics. In doing so, Dr. Clark refined and structured the algorithms needed for 3D display to the point where they could be encapsulated in silicon. The work on refining the algorithms is considered by some to be as significant as the construction of the silicon Geometry Engine itself. This work has provided one of the first examples of compiling high level graphics functionality into custom silicon thereby demonstrating the benefit of using custom integrated circuitry to realize hitherto unattainable cost performance ratios.

Preface

This issue of Computer Graphics (Volume 18, Number 3) contains the proceedings of the Eleventh Annual Conference on Computer Graphics and Interactive Techniques (SIGGRAPH' 84) held July 23-27, 1984 in Minneapolis, Minnesota.

This year's call for papers resulted in the on time submission of one hundred eighteen papers and five papers which arrived too late to be included in the review process. Immediately following the deadline, the papers were read by Turner Whitted, Tom Sederberg, or myself for the purpose of selecting an appropriate member of the Technical Program Committee to serve as the senior reviewer. The papers were then sent to the senior reviewers and on to more than one hundred additional reviewers. The names and affiliations of these reviewers are listed with the conference committees. Following the collection of the reviews, the Technical Program Committee met at Evans and Sutherland Computer Corporation in Salt Lake City to select the final program. I feel that the thirty papers published here represent the state of the art in computer graphics research and applications. There were a large number of very high quality papers submitted. The only thing more impressive, to me, than the quality of the papers was the effort of the Committee to make appropriate selections.

I would like to express my appreciation to the Technical Program Committee and the reviewers which they selected for their very considerable efforts. Also, I wish to thank Peter Seitz for taking responsibility for negotiations with prospective printers and for the selection of the cover images.

There are a few other people to whom I wish to add a special note of appreciation. Foremost among these is Turner Whitted. In addition to serving as a senior reviewer, Turner made a mid-winter trip to Utah to help us select the most appropriate senior reviewers for each paper. Turner's knowledge of the field is astonishing and his dedication to SIGGRAPH is most impressive. It must be possible to complete the review process without Turner, but I note that no one has tried it for a long time and I am most grateful for his continued service.

I am very much in the debt of Dixie Seegmiller who served as the Secretary to the Technical Program Committee. Dixie is simply the best secretary I have ever known. She certainly deserved the ovation which she was accorded by the Technical Program Committee. I have also enjoyed the association with Bob Kushner of K Graphics. We are indeed fortunate to be working with a printer that is so devoted to producing a quality product.

Finally, may I add a thank you to Evans and Sutherland Computer Corporation for their assistance to the Technical Program Committee, to Peter Tanner, my predecessor who was most helpful in sharing his experiences, and to Dick Mueller and Dick Weinberg for giving me this opportunity.

Hank Christiansen
Technical Program (Papers)
Proceedings Editor

For me, the preparation for SIGGRAPH '84 began at the '83 Conference when two events occured that clearly set in motion a thought process that has lead to Bob Dunn's keystone panel. I was struck by the feeling that more than 90%, it seemed to me, of those attending the SIGGRAPH reception were under 28 years old. Second, while attending a breakfast meeting of the Graphic Pioneers, an organization whose membership is restricted to those who have been active in computer graphics for over 15 years, I was struck by just how much perspective and insight this group could offer to the young and enthusiastic membership of SIGGRAPH.

Thus began Bob Dunn's effort to bring together a most impressive group of major graphic contributors including Dave Evans, my early mentor at the University of Utah during a very exciting time for our industry in the mid to late sixties. I'll never forget my own excitement in 1965 when Dave first exposed me to that wonderful mix of computers, CRT's and geometry. I'm confident the whole panel will be just as exciting an experience for all at Minneapolis—young and old (er).

The other ten panels span a fairly typical range of SIGGRAPH interests, I believe, and some new areas as well. There's an excellent standards panel that asks some hard questions about the reality of where we are today.

Henry Fuchs has organized a group of experts to discuss the fast-paced world of hardware—semiconductor hardware, that has the promise to benefit vendor and user alike.

Few of us who watch television or go to the movies are not impressed with the visual contribution computer graphics is making there. Carl Rosenthal's panel will not only dazzle the audience with pretty pictures but also attempt to critically review the nature of the penetration of computer graphic techniques in commercial broadcast production. A very exciting and topical area. Dick Weinberg's panel will discuss the off-the-shelf and special computer systems needed to make all those pretty pictures.

In attempting to cover the growing business of computer graphics I have included back-to-back sessions on the international aspects of the process in terms of both the development of non-USA sources of technology and markets. Again, on an international theme, we have two panel sessions featuring Japanese contributors. One panel will illuminate the not-so-well known research taking place at Japanese universities while the other will be more application oriented, covering the Japanese specialty—computer integrated manufacturing. A final international group will explore the trends and issues at the intersection of graphics and text.

A panel organized by Howard Pearlmutter rounds out the sessions. He has brought together a group of individuals involved with an explosive, but hitherto somewhat unrepresented, area of computer graphics—microcomputer graphics. This panel will, interestingly enough, be one of the only to use and demonstrate, given the small size of these devices, a real live unit during its session. I can't help but catch some of the spirit and enthusiasm this group has shown concerning their speciality. What they lack in traditional graphics functionality they make up in inventiveness.

I've enjoyed the process of putting these panels together. It's now up to the panel members to entertain and educate and, hopefully, we've all had another worthwhile SIGGRAPH experience. My thanks to Jeff Possdamer at Washington University for helping to review panel proposals.

David A. Luther
Panels Chair

Conference committee

Conference co-chairs
Richard M. Mueller
Control Data Corporation

Richard A. Weinberg
Fifth Generation Graphics, Inc.

SIGGRAPH conference planning committee
Robert A. Ellis, chair
Calma Company

John C. Beatty
University of Waterloo

Kellogg S. Booth
University of Waterloo

Pat Cole
Atari Inc.

Raymond L. Elliott
Los Alamos National Laboratory

Ellen Gore
ISSCO

Robert Heilman
Gould Inc.

Richard M. Mueller
Control Data Corporation

Elaine L. Sonderegger

Richard A. Weinberg
Fifth Generation Graphics, Inc.

Committee chairs
Lee B. Anderson
Student coordinator
University of Minnesota

Michael Bailey
Courses
Purdue University

Maxine D. Brown
Electronic theater
Maxine Brown Associates

Hank Christiansen
Technical program
Brigham Young University

John French
User groups
Exxon Production
Research Company

Ellen Gore
Slide sets
ISSCO Graphics

Susan Hartwig-Hood
Advertising
Cipher Data Corporation

Michael Herman
Merchandising
University of Waterloo

Wayne Huelskoetter
Exhibits
DICOMED Corporation

Cal Kirchhof
Omnimax film
DICOMED Corporation

Cheryl Landman
Public relations
Seiko Instruments U.S.A., Inc.

John Lehman
Treasurer
University of Minnesota

David A. Luther
Panels
Lexidata Corporation

Sally Rosenthal
Audio/Visual
Independent

Richard P. Sonderegger Jr.
Registration
Summagraphics Corporation

Carol Stenborg
Conference administration
University of Minnesota

Steve Van Frank
Local arrangements
Purdue University

Patrick Whitney
Design arts show
Institute of Design, IIT

Technical program committee
Brian A. Barsky
University of California at Berkeley

John Brewer
Louisiana State University

Bruce Brown
The Quail Group

Edwin Catmull
Lucasfilm Ltd.

Jim Clark
Stanford University

John Dill
Computer-Aided Design Instructional Facility

Jose Encarnacao
FG Graphisch—Interaktive Systeme

Dick Gordon
University of Manitoba

Ian Hirschsohn
Superset, Inc.

Larry McCleary
Naval Ocean Systems Center

Bary W. Pollack
Vulcan Systems

Richard Riesenfeld
University of Utah

Gary Rogers
Superset, Inc.

Tom Sederberg
Brigham Young University

Maureen Stone
Xerox Palo Alto Research Center

Turner Whitted
University of North Carolina at Chapel Hill

Technical sessions reviewers
Kurt Akeley
Silicon Graphics

Mike Bailey
Purdue University

Richard Bartels
University of Waterloo

Rich Beach
Xerox PARC

John C. Beatty
University of Waterloo

Mike Blake
Digital Equipment Corporation

Jim Blinn
Jet Propulsion Laboratory

John Blunden
Lawrence Livermore National Laboratories

Wayne Brodland
University of Manitoba

K. Brodlie
University of Leicester

Robert Burton
Brigham Young University

Loren Carpenter
Lucasfilm Ltd.

Peter Chen
Louisiana State University

Elizabeth Cobb
University of Utah

James Cobb
University of Utah

Elaine Cohen
University of Utah

Robert L. Cook
Lucasfilm Ltd.

George R. Cross
Louisiana State University

Frank Crow
Xerox PARC

Tom Davis
Silicon Graphics

Atam Dhawan
University of Manitoba

Larry Dickson
Superset, Inc.

D.A. Duce
Rutherford & Appleton Labs.

Tom Duff
Lucasfilm Ltd.

G. Enderle
Kernforschungszentrum Karlsruhe

Dan Field
University of Waterloo

Russell Fish
University of Utah

Connie Fisher
University of Utah

Eugene Fiume
University of Toronto

Alain Fournier
University of Toronto

Todd Fugua
University of Utah

Vanessa Fuson
University of Utah

Ron Goldman
Control Data Corporation

Julian Gomez
Ohio State University

Gerard Gouw
Children's Hospital, Winnipeg

Eric Grant
University of North Carolina

Don Greenberg
Cornell University

Roy Hall
Robert Abel & Associates

Pat Hanrahan
New York Institute of Technology

Ostap Hawaleska
University of Manitoba

Paul Heckbert
New York Institute of Technology

Randy Heiland
University of Utah

Franz Herbert
ETH-Zurich

Jeff Hoel
Imagen Corporation

F.R.A. Hopgood
Rutherford & Appleton Labs.

George Joblove
Joblove/Kay, Inc.

J.Q. Johnson
Cornell University

Robert Judd
Lawrence Livermore National Laboratories

Jeff N. Jortner
Louisiana State University

Lewis Knapp
University of Utah

Jim Kajiya
California Institute of Technology

Dave Kasik
Boeing

Jeff Lane
Vulcan Systems

Waldemar Lehn
University of Manitoba

Bruno Leps
Informart

Jeffrey A. Levin
Superset, Inc.

Steve Levine
Digital Equipment Corporation

Marc Levoy
Hanah-Barbara

Rich Littlefield
Battelle N.W.

Henry A. Long
Louisiana State University

Don Marcynuk
University of Manitoba

Bruce McLean
Spectragraphics

Andrew J. McPhate
Louisiana State University

Gary Meger
Cornell University

Henry Moreton
Silicon Graphics

Tim Mueller
University of Utah

John Peterson
University of Utah

G.E. Pfaff
Tech. U. Darmstadt

Ken Pier
Xerox PARC

Rob Pike
Bell Labs.

Michael Plass
Xerox PARC

Thomas Porter
Lucasfilm Ltd.

Michael Postmesil
Bell Labs.

Art Quanbury
Rehab. Center Children, Winnipeg

Rangaraj Rangayyan
University of Manitoba

Bill Reeves
Lucasfilm Ltd.

Rocky Rhodes
Silicon Graphics

John Roese
Naval Oceans Systems Center

David F. Rogers
US Naval Academy

Lynn Ruggles
Stanford University

David Salesin
Lucasfilm Ltd.

Sidney H. Sanderson
Louisiana State University

Ray Sarraga
GM Research Labs.

Stephen R. Scott
Louisiana State University

Kim Shelley
Robert Abel & Associates

Seymour Shlien
University of Manitoba

Ed Shwedyk
University of Manitoba

Siafulla Sikandar
Louisiana State University

Alvy Ray Smith
Lucasfilm Ltd.

Mat Smith
Superset, Inc.

Dick Stanford
Superset, Inc.

Paul Stay
University of Utah

James J. Thomas
Battelle N.W.

Spencer Thomas
University of Utah

David E. Thompson
Louisiana State University

Gary Thomson
Naval Oceans Systems Center

Don Vickers
Lawrence Livermore National Laboratories

D. David Vicknair
Engineering Systems Corp.

Herb Voelcker
University of Rochester

Van Warren
University of Utah

Kevin J. Weiler
General Electric

Lance Williams
New York Institute Technology

Paul I. Wolf
Superset, Inc.

Sally Wood
Cornell University

Jonathon Yen
University of Utah

Course committee
Sheldon Applegate
Sandia National Laboratories
General Courses

Frank Bliss
Ford Motor Company
CAD/CAM/CAE courses

Kevin Borg
AT&T
Notes and audio/visual

Laura Carey
Motorola, Microsystems Division
Visual synthesis courses

Barbara Duncan
Tektronix, Inc.
Graphics applications courses

Design arts show curatorial committee
Del Coates
Santa Fe State University

Muriel Cooper
Visible Language Workshop-MIT

William Mitchell
University of California-Los Angeles

Electronic theater committee
Doris Kochanek
National Film Board of Canada

Nelson Max
Lawrence Livermore National Laboratory

Electronic theater jury
Loren Carpenter
Lucasfilm Ltd.

Louise Etra
General Electronics Systems, Inc.

Kenneth Knowlton
Via Video, Inc.

Electronic theater performance committee
Ed Arroyo
Second Genesis

Joan Collins
Laser Media

Art Durinski
Omnibus Computer Graphics

Ed Emshwiller
California Institute of the Arts

Denise Gallant
Synopsis Video

Ron Hays
Ron Hays Music-Image

Andy Rosen
Ruxton Ltd.

James Seligman
Videowave

Tom Seufert
Visual Music Productions

Peter Sorensen
Second Genesis

Vibeke Sorensen
Art Center College of Design

Registration/Merchandise committee
Adele Newton
University of Waterloo

Staff listing

ACM liaison
Roberta Bukar

Audio/Visual management
Video Research Consultants
Phil Morton
Mark Fausner
Cynthia Neal
Harland Snodgrass

Conference management
Smith, Bucklin and Associates, Inc.
Ellen Frisbie
Sheila Hoffmeyer
Paul Jay
Joy Lee
Jodie A. Misch
Cynthia Stark
Lynn Valastyan

Courses executive assistant
Martha Schlegel
Purdue University

Decorator
Andrews-Bartlett and Associates Inc.
Bob Borsz
Betty Fuller
Ken Gallagher
Barby Patronski
John Patronski

Exhibition management
Robert T. Kenworthy, Inc.
Robert Kenworthy
Hank Cronan
Barbara Voss

Graphic design
Seitz Yamamoto Moss Inc.
Peter Seitz
Hideki Yamamoto
Miranda Moss
Joanne Biron
Sherice Bowers
Beth Garland
Aimee Hucek
Barbara Schubring

Exposition Exhibitor List

Adage, Inc.
Addison-Wesley Publishing Co., Inc.
Adds/Data-Type, Inc.
Advanced Color Technology, Inc.
Advanced Electronics Design, Inc.
Altek Corporation
AMF Logic Sciences, Inc.
Amtron Corporation
Ann Arbor Terminals, Inc.
The Anderson Report
Antics Enterprises
Apollo Computer Inc.
Artronics Inc.
Association for Computing Machinery
Association for Women in Computing
Auscom, Inc.
AutoCad
AVL
Barco Industries, Inc.
Benson, Inc.
Charles Besseler Company
Robert Bosch Company
Business Computing
CalComp
Celco
Cohu, Inc.-Electronics Division
Computer-Aided Engineering
Computer Arts, Inc.
Computer Decisions
Computer Design Magazine
Computer Graphics News
Compute Graphics World
Computer Pictures
The Conference Book Service, Inc.
Conrac Division-Conrac Corporation
Control Data Corporation
Control Systems
CPT Corporation
Cray Research, Inc.
CSP, Inc.
Cubicomp Corporation
CW Communications, Inc.
Daikin Industries, Ltd.
Datacopy Corporation
Datacube, Inc.
Dataplotting Services
Dataram Corporation
Decision Images, Inc.
DIC Americas Inc.
DICOMED Corporation
Digigraphic Systems Corporation
Digital Design
Digital Engineering, Inc.
Digital Equipment Corporation
DIPIX, Inc.

Dubner Computer Systems
DYNAIR Electronics, Inc.
Eastman Kodak Company
EDN Magazine
EIKONIX Corporation
Elector USA, Inc.
Electrohome Limited
Electronic Business Magazine
Electronic Imaging
Electronic News
Electronic Systems Products
Elographics, Inc.
Engineering Automation Systems, Inc.
Equitable Life Leasing Corp.
Eutectic Electronics Inc.
Ferranti International Controls
Fibronics International, Inc.
Floating Point Systems, Inc.
Florida Computer Graphics, Inc.
FutureNet Corporation
W.W. Gaertner Research Inc.
General Electric Company
Genisco Computers Corp.
GIXI, Inc.
Gould Inc., Imaging and Graphics Division
Graphic Controls Corporation
Graphon
Grinnell Systems Corporation
GTCO Corporation
Harris Corporation, Computer Systems Division
Hewlett-Packard Company
Hitachi America, Ltd.
Hitachi/Denshi America Ltd.
Houston Instrument
IBIS Systems, Inc.
ID Systems Corporation
IGC, Inc.
IEEE Computer Society
Ikegami Electronics (U.S.A.), Inc.
IMAGEN Corp.
Imaging Technology, Inc.
ImagiTex, Inc.
IMI Corporation
Imtec Equipment, Inc.
Infinite Graphics Incorporated
INMOS
Intecolor Division, Intelligent Systems Corporation
International Imaging Systems
Intran Corporation
ISSCO
Ithaca InterSystems, Inc.
James River Graphics
Japan Computer Corporation
Japan Radio Company
JVC (Victor Company of Japan)

Kloss Video Corporation
KMW Systems Corporation
KURTA Corporation
Lang Systems, Inc.
Lexidata Corporation
LogE Dunn Instruments
LogEtronics
Machine Design
Management Graphics, Inc.
MASSCOMP
Masterbyte Computers (U.S.A.), Inc.
Matrix Instruments, Inc.
Matrox Electronic Systems Ltd.
McDonnell Douglas Corporation
MCI/Quantel
Mead Corporation
Measurement Systems, Inc.
Megatek Corporation
MegaVision Inc.
Mercury Computer Systems
Metheus Corporation
Micro Control Systems
Mini-Micro Systems
Minnesota Trade Office
Modgraph, Inc.
Moniterm Corporation
Mosaic Technologies, Inc.
Motorola Semiconductor
Multiwire Division
New GEA Corporation
New Media Grapics Corp.
Nicolet Computer Graphics Division
Northern Micrographics Inc.
Nova Graphics International Corporation
Number Nine Computer Corporation
Numelec
Numonics Corporation
OCLI
Omnicomp Graphics Corporation
The Optical Publishing Co., Inc.
Panasonic Industrial Co./ Computer Components Div.
Panasonic Industrial Company/Optical Disc Department
Parallax Graphics
PennWell Publishing/Advanced Technology Group
Peritek Corporation
PERQ Systems
Photographic Sciences Corp.
Photonics Spectra
Picture Element Limited
Polaroid Corporation
Precision Visuals, Inc.
Printronix, Inc.
PRIVAC Inc.
Quality Micro Systems, Inc.
Ramtek Corporation
Raster Technologies, Inc.
Recognition Concepts, Inc.
Ridge Computers
River Electronics Corporation
Saber Technology Corporation
Schoeller Technical Papers
Scientific Calculations, Inc.
Scriptel Corporation
Secapa Informatique
Seiko Instruments U.S.A., Inc.
Seillac Company Ltd.
Silicon Graphics, Inc.
Sogitec
Spring Systems
SPSS Inc.
Stereographics Corporation
Stobe, Inc.
Sumitomo Corporation of America
Summagraphics Corporation

Sun Microsystems
Superset, Inc.
Symbolics Inc., Graphics Division
Systems Research Laboratories, Inc.
Talaris Systems Inc.
T&W Systems
Technology & Business Communications, Inc.
Tektronix, Inc.
Telex Communications, Inc.
Texas Instruments
Tigre S.A.
Time Arts Inc.
Trilog, Inc.
UNIRAS, Inc.
Universal Data Systems
Universal Technical Graphics
Vector Automation, Inc.
Vectrix Corporation
Versatec, Inc.
Visual Intelligence Corp.
Western Graphtec, Inc.
Westward Technology Inc.
Xtar Electronics, Inc.

Contents

Friday, July 27, 1984

PLANTS, FRACTALS, AND FORMAL LANGUAGES

Alvy Ray Smith

Computer Graphics Project
Computer Division
Lucasfilm Ltd.

ABSTRACT.   Although fractal models of natural phenomena have received much attention recently, there are other models of complex natural objects which have been around longer in Computer Imagery but are not widely known.   These are procedural models of plants and trees.   An interesting class of these models is presented here which handles plant growth, sports an efficient data representation, and has a high "database amplification" factor.   It is based on an extension of the well-known formal languages of symbol strings to the lesser-known formal languages of labeled graphs.   It is so tempting to describe these plant models as "fractal" that the similarities of this class of models with fractal models are explored in an attempt at rapprochement.   The models are not fractal so the common parts of fractal theory and plant theory are abstracted to form a class of objects, the *graftals*.   This class may prove to be of great interest to the future of Computer Imagery.   Determinism is shown to provide adequate complexity, whereas randomness is only convenient and often inefficient.   Finally, a nonfractal, nongraftal family of trees by Bill Reeves is introduced to emphasize some of the paper's nongrammatical themes.

CR CATEGORIES AND SUBJECT DESCRIPTORS:
    F.4.3 [**Mathematical Logic and Formal Languages**]: Formal Languages - *Classes defined by grammars or automata*; I.3.5 [**Computer Graphics**]: Computational Geometry and Object Modeling; I.3.7 [**Computer Graphics**]: Three-Dimensional Graphics and Realism; J.5 [**Arts and Humanities**]: *Arts, fine and performing*.

ADDITIONAL KEY WORDS AND PHRASES: plant, tree, graftal, fractal, particle system, parallel graph grammar, L-system, database amplification, Computer Imagery.

Permission to copy without fee all or part of this material is granted provided that the copies are not made or distributed for direct commercial advantage, the ACM copyright notice and the title of the publication and its date appear, and notice is given that copying is by permission of the Association for Computing Machinery. To copy otherwise, or to republish, requires a fee and/or specific permission.

© 1984   ACM   0-89791-138-5/84/007/0001 $00.75

INTRODUCTION

Two of the newest contributions to Computer Imagery are the adaptive, "fractal" technique of Fournier, Fussel, and Carpenter‡[7], and the particle systems of Reeves[19]. Both of these are displayed in the *Genesis Demo*[20], the growing mountains realized by fractals and the fires by a particle system. Another example is the picture *Road to Point Reyes*[2], the mountains again being fractal and the grasses particulate. They are both departures from traditional computer graphics which takes the "cubist" approach of constructing models from geometric primitives, now the domain of CAD/CAM. *Computer Imagery* is used to refer to the newer, more flexible and subtle state of the art of computed pictures.

A main purpose of this paper is to present another class of complex renderable objects. Members of this rich class will be interpreted as plants or trees. The class shares characteristics with fractals and particle systems; another purpose of the paper is to make the relationships clear. The definitions from Benoit Mandelbrot's inspiring book[14] apparently do not allow the plants presented here to be described as fractals (see his Chapter 16 in particular) because the notion of fractal is strongly geometrical and defined only in the limit. What may prove to be of as much or more interest is structural rather than geometrical and becomes sufficiently intriguing far below the limit. This paper is concerned with formal language techniques, instances of which implicitly underlie many of Mandelbrot's examples and, as will be shown below, other Computer Imagery techniques.

The key idea is contained in the nature of formal languages. The plants presented are words in a formal language - in particular, a *parallel graph grammar*[13] language. These languages are not the well-known Chomsky hierarchy[10] languages but the lesser known *L-systems*[9,12]. It is suggested that the parallel graph grammar languages - the *graftals* - have more potential for Computer Imagery than fractals because they are less restrictive.

Graftals share with fractals the attribute of "the closer you get, the more it looks the same" when a scaling geometry is imposed. Fractals have been explored by investigating the special cases of strict and statistical self-

---

‡ But it is the *locally* adaptive technique of Carpenter which is emphasized here.

similarity which permit actual computation of the Hausdorf-Bescovitch dimension. This is of only limited usefulness in Computer Imagery. What will be shown to be more useful is a relaxed "self-similarity" which is an ability to generate detail preserving the nature of an object without strictly copying it. This attribute is forced by the finiteness of a formal grammar. "Fractality" is thus a special characteristic achieved by only some graftals. Those fractals generated with true random processes - e.g., fractional Brown fractals - are not graftals. Although the random fractals can be used to generate beautiful still pictures[14,23] their computational practicality is yet to be demonstrated, particularly in the context of animated sequences.

An advantage of the graftal approach is its intrinsic locality. Locality admits adaptive subdivision which has proved valuable in Computer Imagery for its computational savings in patch rendering and spline computation.

An implication of the finiteness of grammars is that randomness is not allowed. Surprisingly, evidence will support the acceptability of this restriction. In fact, it is computationally more efficient to avoid random number generators when objects as complex as plants are rendered.

In addition to the plant models which are the primary focus of this paper, several other models are discussed including two grammars from Mandelbrot, mountains by Carpenter, and particle system trees by Reeves in order to elucidate the functions of locality, randomness, and formal grammars in systems designed to generate complex images from small databases, a property called *database amplification*.

ALGORITHMIC PLANTS

Lindenmayer[12] introduced the notion of parallel rewriting grammars for the modeling of developing biological systems. The grammars are similar to those of conventional formal language theory[10] except productions are applied simultaneously, and there is no distinction between terminal and non-terminal symbols. All strings generated from an initial string, or axiom, are considered to be words in the language of the grammar. The axiom is typically an element of the grammar's alphabet, but this is not a requirement here. An extensive literature[8] has developed on these so-called *L-systems*, particularly for the context-free subset (the *0L-systems*, for zero neighbors) and for the two simplest context-sensitive subsets (the *1L-systems*, for a one-symbol, nearest-neighbor context and the *2L-systems*, for the two-symbol, nearest-neighbors context).

Lindenmayer also introduced the notion of *bracketed* L-systems which extend an L-system alphabet by the set {[,]}. This allows the representation of trees with strings. The brackets contain branches which are attached at the symbol just left of the left bracket. A simple example is the (context-free) 0L-system with alphabet {0, 1, [,]}, axiom 0, and production rules {0→1[0]1[0]0, 1→11, [→[,]→]}. The first three steps (generations) are 0, 1[0]1[0]0, and 11[1[0]1[0]0]11[1[0]1[0]0]1[0]1[0]0. An equivalent graphic presentation of the system above is presented in Figure

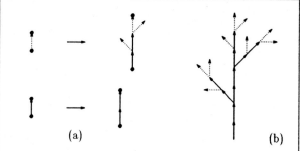

Figure FREETREE. (a) Production rules. (b) Generation $n = 2$.

FREETREE. Notice that affine transformations of the graphical statements of the rules are required and that dots are used to show corresponding connections before and after replacements. Notice also that two kinds of branching, left and right, have been used rather than just the one of the string representation. Another set of bracket symbols could represent this extension; so the branching rule becomes 0→1[0]1(0)0. Representing diversity with larger alphabets will receive further mention when the role of randomness is discussed.

The (geometric) trees generated are considered to be data structure maps, not necessarily the final image. A postprocessing step, called an *interpretation*, expands this map, assumed to have only a finite amount of information at each node (finite alphabet), into the final image. Thus all trees structurally equivalent to the data structure tree under finite interpretation can be considered to be words generated by the grammar. Notice that finite interpretation does not allow randomness.

Notice also that the string representation of these plants is quite concise. Any language - e.g., C - which has character or byte manipulation operators permits easy, speedy implementation.

Finally, notice that if $T(n)$ is the n-th generation, then the $(n+1)$-th generation can be expressed recursively in string notation as

$$T(n+1) = 1^{2^n}[T(n)]1^{2^n}[T(n)]T(n) .$$

In the terminology of Mandelbrot ([14] pp. 152-3), the tree is a *subfractal* (seems like a fractal but isn't) which is not *self-similar* but has a *residue* which corresponds to the progeny of the 1's in the trunk of generation $n=1$. In formal language terminology, the residue is the consequence of another symbol in the alphabet. In the example above, the production rule for the solid arrow is not very interesting, so "residue" is perhaps appropriate, but in general its rule could be as interesting as that of any other symbol.

Plate CARTOON.TREE is a 2-dimensional representation of the 7th generation of this system. Since the string representation of a plant is referred to as its *gene*, or *genotype*, it follows that the plant is the *phenotype* of the string. The phenotype in this example is obtained from the genotype by representing each 0 or 1 with an antialiased line segment. At the end of each branch - thus at each] in the gene - a "leaf" is drawn which, in this simple case, is just an antialiased disk.

The program used, called **Gene**, gives control over color of stem and leaf, provides a dropped shadow for each primitive, does depth darkening, and provides separate width controls for stems and leaves. It also generates a 3-dimensional database for full rendering with hidden surfaces removed; the 2-dimensional versions are simply speedy sketches and color studies. There is no reason the leaves or stems could not be more complex, but the simple shapes used so far - lines and disks in 2-D or cylinders and spheres in 3-D - have yielded surprisingly pleasing results (Plate WHITE.SANDS). Notice that the branches get smaller with distance from the root and the leaves get larger. These attributes are not part of the grammar but are variations modeling global gravitational, chemical, or electromagnetic tropisms. They are added during interpretation of the word generated by the grammar. Kawaguchi[11] gives many examples of the beauty which can be obtained at the interpretation step of a simply generated word.

The program **Gene** also allows the use of an arbitrarily large (or small) finite set of angles or a random set if so desired. It will be demonstrated that randomness is not required for pleasing results, but just one angle and its negative do not suffice, as demonstrated by Plate CARTOON.TREE. The addition of more complexity in the form of context is studied next.

Hogeweg and Hesper[9] studied the *propagating, deterministic* bracketed 2L-systems, where "propagating" means there are no erasing rules and "deterministic" means no two distinct rules share the same left side. With these systems they obtained a wide variety of plant-like species. Their paper, plus the books of Stevens[22] and Mandelbrot[14], are the principal inspirations for my work here. Hogeweg and Hesper were restricted to simple black-and-white line drawings and only 25 generations (successive applications of all applicable productions). I have been able to apply full-color 3-D Computer Imagery techniques to their results, add flowers and leaves, and use much deeper generation trees (35-45 generations typically suffice) to make stills, growth movies, and a hologram.

An example of a bracketed 2L-system has the alphabet {0, 1, [,]}, the axiom 1 and the production rules 0.1[1].1.1.0.11.1.0, where the dots separate the images of the eight binary triples in numeric order, left to right. Thus 001 maps to 1[1], meaning that wherever a 0 occurs in a string with a 0 to its left and a 1 to its right, it is replaced at the next step (generation) with the string 1[1]. There are assumed to be invisible 1's at the unattached ends of all branches. Only the 0's and 1's are replaced, the brackets being structural markers only. The left neighbor of a branch is the 0 or 1 just left of the branch - e.g., in the string 0[1], the left and right neighbors of the 0 are two invisible 1's and those of the 1 are the 0 and another invisible 1, respectively. The first 11 generations of the bracketed 2L-system above are shown in Table 1. An equivalent description of the system is graphical, Figure SENSTREE. The left-side symbol to be replaced by the right side of a rule is surrounded by a dashed box. All productions not shown leave a symbol unchanged. From this inauspicious beginning arises - after 35 generations and less restrictive branching - the plant of Plate

n	L(n)
0	1
1	0
2	11
3	00
4	01[1]
5	111[0]
6	000[11]
7	001[1][10]
8	01[1]1[0][111]
9	111[0]0[11][000]
10	001[11]11[10][001[1]]

Table 1. 11 generations of the 2L-system 0.1[1].1.1.0.11.1.0.

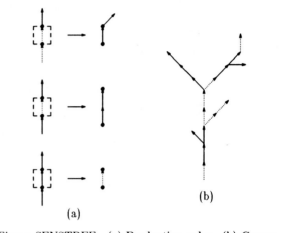

Figure SENSTREE. (a) Production rules. (b) Generation $n = 11$.

WITH.WITHOUT which shows the same plant, in two dimensions, with and without flowers to reveal its beautifully intricate branching structure.

By rendering successive generations in successive frames, a plant's growth can be animated. See Plate WISP.GROWTH. To ensure coherence between successive generations, an angle must be "nailed" to its branch once it has been selected. Plates GARDEN, GARDEN.DROP and BUSHES demonstrate a variety of related graftals with and without flowers or leaves. Plates GREEN.FLAME and VITA.PLANTS illustrate application of **Gene**'s controlling parameters.

If a geometry is forced on a plant grammar, so that a production rule requires the same space be occupied before and after replacement, then the grammar has the property that "the closer you get, the more it looks the same". Thus, as we zoom in on a plant generated by such a grammar, we cause further invocation of the replacement rules to generate more detail. This detail will resemble the overall plant since it is generated by the same small set of rules. So the plants have a form of "self-similarity" which is much looser than that associated with fractals.

CARPENTER MOUNTAINS

Loren Carpenter has shown that a grammar with the rule shown in Figure CARPENTER suffices to turn a database (axiom) of a small set of triangles into a rich mountain at the 10th generation, more or less. Plate FOUR.FRACTAL is the 5th generation in a Carpenter grammar with one triangle as the axiom. Clearly, database amplification is one of the benefits of this grammar. We have apparently been quite lax in applying the production rule of the Carpenter grammar since in no case is its left side literally (geometrically) satisfied even allowing affine transformations. Our formal language must allow topological deformation in the sense that any deformation required of a left side to make it apply must be applied as well to the right side before replacement. The rule must apply to any triangle.

There is a problem with shared edges here. How is the common edge between two triangles to be replaced identically as the result of two separate applications of the production rule, each requiring a different deformation? There is no way to solve this problem in the style of this paper if any kind of infinity is involved - for example, if arbitrary real displacements of the midpoint are allowed. The usual way the algorithm has been stated has been with a random number generator determining the displacements. In practice, however, only small tables of random numbers have been used to avoid the speed sacrifice involved in using a random number generator millions of times. In fact, as Plate FOUR.FRACTAL shows, only three different numbers suffice for good-looking mountains. If a random number generator is used at all, its only role is to provide a nice spread to the finite set of numbers to be used repeatedly. Plate THREE.THISTLE shows a similar result for graftal plants, the system 0.1.0.1[1].0.11.0.0 in this case.

A small (finite) number of different displacements with only local effect suggests formal language theory again. We can expand the one rule in Figure CARPENTER to a finite set of rules corresponding to one left side for every possible triple of symbols, each of which represents one of the allowed displacement factors. A midpoint displacement becomes a function of its two nearest node labels, so shared edges are forced to behave the same way.

These mountains suffer from a defect known as the "creasing problem". The midpoint displacements are in height only to avoid foldover and self-intersection. Thus the initial database lines are never broken out of recognition by the subdivision process, especially if observed along their initial directions. In formal language terminology, as Loren Carpenter has pointed out to me, the problem with his language is that it is context-free. Information internal to an original database triangle is never passed to neighboring triangles. An open question is whether a context-sensitive grammar exists for mountains which avoids the creasing problem. Loren believes so and has designed a context-sensitive grammar which he is currently testing. Of course, a context-sensitive neighborhood must be finite (cf. local); it is already known that a global approach will work[23], but our goal is to find a

Figure CARPENTER. The production rule for a Carpenter mountain.

Figure KOCH. The production rule for a Koch (or Cesàro) curve.

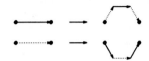

Figure SIERPINSKI. The production rules for a Sierpiński arrowhead.

computationally more satisfactory approach. As anyone can testify who lives near the edge of a tectonic plate, creases in landscapes are natural. The problem is to bring them under control.

LANGUAGES IN MANDELBROT'S BOOK

Mandelbrot's book is filled with formal language examples informally presented. At first glance they appear to be of a very simple kind. An example is the production rule for the so-called Koch curve shown in Figure KOCH. If the axiom is an equilateral triangle, then the first generation is a Star of David in this language (cf. [14], p. 42). Arrowheads have been added to the line segments in the production rules whenever direction is important.

All of the languages in Mandelbrot use only one symbol in the production rule, a solid line segment, but the production rules are frequently augmented with non-grammatical rules such as "the generator‡ must be made to alternate between the left and the right". These additional remarks can be handled entirely by a formal language if additional symbols are allowed. Figure SIERPINSKI shows the two production rules on two symbols replacing the one rule on one symbol plus additional stipulation in [14], p. 142. Directionality is important. The use of two symbols and arrows readily captures the notion of swapping from left to right in successive generations. Of course, in the final interpretation of a word, arrowheads are removed and dotted lines replaced with solid lines.

PARALLEL GRAPH GRAMMARS

There are several approaches we might take for defining the class of languages suggested in the preceding sections. The class chosen must answer to the following observations:

---

‡ Mandelbrot calls the axiom an "initiator" and the right-hand side of a production rule a "generator".

The context-free plant productions require the form tree-replaces-segment. There must be a way of specifying connectivity during replacement. Several symbols must be allowed. Directionality is important. Preservation of branching is important, but the actual angles taken and the lengths of branch segments are immaterial to the language generation; they matter greatly at the interpretation step, of course. Thus the tree topology is important but the geometrical scaling of parts is not important. Similarly, the production rules are applied to segments of any length and rotation, and hence are topological. The context-sensitive plant productions require the same form but require a mechanism for specifying context of the replaced segment.

The Carpenter mountain language requires a graph-replaces-graph form, with attachment information for before and after replacement. It is context-free, however. The geometry is derived from the finite alphabet of displacement factors in an interpretation postprocessing step. Only the topology of the language is important. Directionality is not important in this case.

Directionality is important for most of the languages in Mandelbrot's book. The replacement rules are of the form graph-replaces-arc, although tree-replaces-arc usually suffices. Geometry is always important in these languages. In analogy with the other languages in this paper, I have used a grammar to generate the data *representation* and assumed a postprocessing step for data *interpretation*. For the languages in Mandelbrot, the interpretation step is mostly cosmetic - removing arrowheads and substituting solid lines for dotted lines. The geometry is carried with the production rules which means that they must work under affine transformation. These grammars might be most appropriately described as *parallel picture grammars* which are parallel graph grammars with an enforced geometry.

It is difficult to find a single formal grammar definition that will capture all of the aspects above, so my intention is to give an intuitive definition for graftals indicating a possible form for the formal definition of the representation. Formalization of the crucial interpretation step must await further work.

There have been several attempts at extending 1-dimensional L-systems to graphs[4,5,15,16,18]. It turns out to be quite difficult to do concisely. The general notion is based on a picture being a bounded subset of E^2 or E^3 that may have color. It is replaced with another picture, perhaps empty, with the same bounds. The rules are translation, scale, and rotation invariant. Thus whenever the left side of a rule is found to apply to a picture - by thinking of it as a template which is moved about over a "word", or another bounded, colored subset of space, by affine transformation - it is replaced by the right side of the rule transformed by the same transformation required for the template match.

The replacement rules are easy to specify in the context-free case. In the context-sensitive case, a neighborhood is defined to be a picture as above, and only a subset of it, its *kernel*, is replaced by a right-side picture. The kernel and the right-side picture must have the same

bounds. The entire neighborhood (including the kernel) must match as a template before the kernel is eligible for replacement.

Graph grammars use graphs instead of pictures. Templates are replaced by "coverings" of labeled nodes by labeled nodes and labeled arcs by labeled arcs, so matches are determined on the basis of connectivity and label matches. The main difficulty in defining how the replacement rules work is that of defining the connectivity before and after. We have shown how to solve this problem for very simple graphs in the examples of this paper.

A very general approach, based on the "push-out" construction of category theory, is presented in Ehrig and Kreowski[4] which generalizes the pioneering paper of Ehrig, Pfender, and Schneider[3] to the parallel case. The restriction of the general case to injective mappings, or embeddings, might suffice for our purposes. An even more restrictive approach which works for all examples here except the Carpenter mountains is the "handle substitution parallel graph grammars" of Ehrig and Rozenberg[5], where a "handle" is a graph arc together with its source and target nodes. Two paper collections[1,13] and, in particular, the two surveys by Ehrig[6] and Nagl[17] are good starting points for graftal investigations.

PARTICLE SYSTEM PLANTS

Bill Reeves has written a program for generating trees, the output of which is shown in Plates ASPEN.SPRUCE, MEADOW, and MAXFIELD[21]. These form another class of rich, complex, natural objects which are related to particle systems in their use of thousands of randomly controlled particles, or leaves, and to graftals in their use of small initial descriptions which are used to generate elaborate tree structures of high complexity. A major difference is the use of randomness throughout (but we shall not be surprised if finite sets of well-selected numbers work as well). Each tree is essentially a data structure with many elements, each of which controls one of the random processes used to realize the tree at rendering time. These include height, width, branching angles, bending factors, number of branches, and coloring. For example, an aspen tree is specified with about 120 parameters. Another difference is the lack of an obvious way to obtain plant growth.

So far as similarities are concerned, besides sharing the database amplification property with graftals, these trees have the "closer you get, the more you see" property in common with them due to the recursive leaf generation feature which causes more leaves to be rendered as the screen space occupied by the tree gets larger.

The lighting model, derived in conjunction with Tom Duff and Rob Cook, approximates the extensive self-shadowing of plants by darkening from the surface toward the trunk, modulated by branch density. This is in addition to the surface lighting obtained by assuming the outer envelope of the tree is shaded by conventional models. Neighboring trees also cast shadows determined from their envelopes - e.g., ellipsoids or cones. These lighting techniques go through for the graftals if an approximating envelope can be extracted.

SUMMARY

A rich class of plant models is presented here. The models gain their interest from great visual complexity approaching that of Nature's plant kingdom. The complexity is gained with little human effort by the exploitation of the database amplification property of formal languages, generalized from strings to graphs. These plants can be represented with efficient data structures, and they can be made to grow and flower in time.

Failure of the plants to qualify as fractals, plus the fact that they share much of the spatial complexity of fractals, led to the definition - intuitive, so far - of the graftals, a family of objects generated by parallel graph grammars and including many of the well-known fractals. They do not, however, have to be fractal - i.e., have Hausdorf-Bescovitch dimension greater than topological dimension. Because they are, in general, not strictly self-similar, the Hausdorf-Bescovitch dimension is difficult to compute. It is suggested that fractality itself is not the important property of fractals for Computer Imagery but that it is their well-controlled database amplification property that is of such great usefulness. This is a feature of the graftal family in general, the amplification being controlled by a finite - sometimes surprisingly small - set of grammar rules.

The particle system plants of Bill Reeves were introduced to emphasize that neither graftals nor fractals cover the gamut of natural form generation systems. What all these systems have in common is the database amplification property which is very important for the construction of satisfyingly complex scenes in reasonably short times. They all also share a loose notion of "space filling" with "self-similar" constructions but not strictly enough (in the nonfractal cases) to jump into higher dimensionality.

It has been demonstrated that randomness is not necessary for pictures of interesting complexity. Randomness is just a convenient way of generating a well-dispersed set of numbers, instead of doing it by hand. Tom Duff has pointed out that the pseudo-random number generators used in computer science are based on a related principle: From a small set of generating rules, they supply strings of sufficient length and complexity to simulate true randomness. There are measures of how close to random these finite sequences are. This raises the question of what is sufficient complexity to satisfy perceptual and esthetic requirements of human beings.

It is well-known that a set recognized by a Turing machine is equivalent to a language generated by a type 0 grammar. Thus the operation of a computing machine is strongly related to the generation of language by a formal grammar. The formal language approach advocated here renders the computational processes of such a machine as objects - the state of a computation is frozen and called a picture. Strictly speaking, it is a data representation of a picture. The representation and the thing represented are kept separate. After the machine has done its work, the artist may step in and modulate the computed form with esthetic judgment, thus becoming the composer of the image.

ACKNOWLEDGEMENTS

My colleagues in the Graphics Project have aided me with their usual zest. Specifically, Loren Carpenter and Bill Reeves contributed important comments and pictures to the work, Rodney Stock and David Salesin discussed the creasing problem with me at length, and Rob Cook and Tom Porter are authors of the principal rendering software used. Ed Catmull, Tom Duff, and Andrea Kaufman were helpful critics as well.

REFERENCES

1. Claus, Volker, Hartmut Ehrig, and Grzegorz Rozenberg (Editors), *Lecture Notes in Computer Science No. 73: Graph-Grammars and Their Application to Computer Science and Biology,* Springer-Verlag, Berlin/Heidelberg/New York (1979). Proceedings of the conference held at Bad Honnef, West Germany, October 30-November 3, 1978.

2. Cook, Rob, Loren Carpenter, Thomas Porter, William Reeves, David Salesin, and Alvy Ray Smith, *Road to Point Reyes,* By the Lucasfilm Computer Graphics Project. Title page picture for SIGGRAPH '83 Proceedings. July 1983.

3. Ehrig, Harmut, M. Pfender, and H. J. Schneider, "Graph-Grammars: An Algebraic Approach," pp. 167-180 in *Proceedings of 14th Annual Symposium on Switching & Automata Theory* (October 1973). Now known as the Symposium on the Foundations of Computer Science.

4. Ehrig, Harmut and H.-J. Kreowski, "Parallel Graph Grammars," pp. 425-442 in *Automata, Languages, Development,* ed. Aristid Lindenmayer and Grzegorz Rozenberg, North-Holland Publishing Company, Amsterdam/New York/Oxford (1976).

5. Ehrig, Harmut and Grzegorz Rozenberg, "Some Definitional Suggestions for Parallel Graph Grammars," pp. 443-468 in *Automata, Languages, Development,* ed. Aristid Lindenmayer and Grzegorz Rozenberg, North-Holland Publishing Company, Amsterdam/New York/Oxford (1976).

6. Ehrig, Hartmut, "Introduction to the Algebraic Theory of Graph Grammars (A Survey)," pp. 1-69 in *Lecture Notes in Computer Science No. 73: Graph-Grammars and Their Application to Computer Science and Biology,* ed. Volker Claus, Hartmut Ehrig, and Grzegorz Rozenberg, Springer-Verlag, Berlin/Heidelberg/New York (1979).

7. Fournier, Alain, Don Fussel, and Loren C. Carpenter, "Computer Rendering of Stochastic Models," *Communications of the ACM* **25**(6), pp. 371-384 (June 1982).

8. Herman, Gabor T. and Grzegorz Rozenberg, *Developmental Systems and Languages,* North-Holland Publishing Company, Amsterdam/New York/Oxford (1975).

9. Hogeweg, Pauline and B. Hesper, "A Model Study on Biomorphological Description," *Pattern Recognition* **6**, pp. 165-179, Pergamon Press (1974).

10. Hopcroft, John E. and Jeffrey D. Ullman, *Formal Languages and Their Relation to Automata,* Addison-Wesley Publishing Company, Menlo Park, California (1969). The latest edition of this book is entitled *Introduction to Automata Theory, Languages, and Computation,* 1979, and includes a small section on L-systems.

11. Kawaguchi, Yoichiro, "A Morphological Study of the Form of Nature," *Computer Graphics* **16**(3), pp. 223-232 (July 1982). SIGGRAPH '82 Proceedings.

12. Lindenmayer, Aristid, "Mathematical Models for Cellular Interactions in Development, Parts I and II," *Journal of Theoretical Biology* **18**, pp. 280-315 (1968).

13. Lindenmayer, Aristid and Grzegorz Rozenberg (Editors), *Automata, Languages, Development,* North-Holland Publishing Company, Amsterdam/New York/Oxford (1976). Proceedings of the conference held at Noordwijkerhout, The Netherlands, March 31-April 6, 1975.

14. Mandelbrot, Benoit, *The Fractal Geometry of Nature,* W. H. Freeman and Company, San Francisco (1983). The 1983 printing differs from the 1982 printing by the addition of a small section at the end.

15. Mayoh, Brian H., "Another Model for the Development of Multidimensional Organisms," pp. 469-485 in *Automata, Languages, Development,* ed. Aristid Lindenmayer and Grzegorz Rozenberg, North-Holland Publishing Company, Amsterdam/New York/Oxford (1976).

16. Nagl, Manfred, "On a Generalization of Lindenmayer-Systems to Labelled Graphs," pp. 487-508 in *Automata, Languages, Development,* ed. Aristid Lindenmayer and Grzegorz Rozenberg, North-Holland Publishing Company, Amsterdam/New York/Oxford (1976).

17. Nagl, Manfred, "A Tutorial and Bibliographical Survey on Graph Grammars," pp. 70-126 in *Lecture Notes in Computer Science No. 73: Graph-Grammars and Their Application to Computer Science and Biology,* ed. Volker Claus, Hartmut Ehrig, and Grzegorz Rozenberg, Springer-Verlag, Berlin/Heidelberg/New York (1979).

18. Paz, Azaria, "Multidimensional Parallel Rewriting Systems," pp. 509-515 in *Automata, Languages, Development,* ed. Aristid Lindenmayer and Grzegorz Rozenberg, North-Holland Publishing Company, Amsterdam/New York/Oxford (1976).

19. Reeves, William T., "Particle Systems - A Technique for Modeling a Class of Fuzzy Objects," *ACM Transactions on Graphics* **2**(2), pp. 91-108 (April 1983).

20. Smith, Alvy Ray, Loren Carpenter, Pat Cole, Tom Duff, Chris Evans, Thomas Porter, and William Reeves, "Genesis Demo," in *Star Trek II: The Wrath of Khan,* Paramount (June 1982). Created by the Lucasfilm Computer Graphics Project for Industrial Light and Magic.

21. Smith, Alvy Ray, Loren Carpenter, Ed Catmull, Rob Cook, Tom Duff, Craig Good, John Lasseter, Eben Ostby, William Reeves, and David Salesin, *André and Wally B.,* Created by the Lucasfilm Computer Graphics Project. July 1984.

22. Stevens, Peter S., *Patterns in Nature,* Little, Brown and Company, Boston (1974).

23. Voss, Richard F., *Fractal Lunar Mist,* Cover picture for SIGGRAPH '83 Proceedings. July 1983.

Plate ASPEN.SPRUCE.   Aspen and spruce trees by Bill Reeves. These are related to particle systems and graftals.

Plate BUSHES.   Several context-sensitive species without flowers or leaves.

Plate CARTOON.TREE. A 2-D rendering of the context-free grammar in Figure FREETREE.

Plate GARDEN. Several context-sensitive graftal species showing the variety easily obtained.

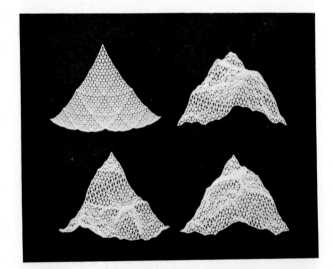

Plate FOUR.FRACTAL. The upper left mountain results from only one subdivision factor. It is unsatisfactory. The upper right mountain resulted from three carefully chosen factors, and the lower left from five. They both work. The lower right mountain is generated using random factors. It is clear that deterministic mountains (e.g., the upper right one) suffice.

Plate GARDEN.DROP. Several more examples of flowering species, with dropped shadows.

Plate GREEN.FLAME.   Several 2-D renderings of the grammar in Figure SENSTREE, varying the parameters of the rendering program **Gene**.

Plate MEADOW.   More computer generated aspen and spruce trees, seen against a meadow handpainted by John Lasseter.

Plate MAXFIELD.   Computer generated aspen and spruce trees, with coloring inspired by Maxfield Parrish, in a fern-covered glen painted by John Lasseter with a computer painting program.

Plate THREE.THISTLE.   The plant on the left has only one elevation angle (actually two, but one is the negative of the other); this plant is unsatisfactorily regular. It has only one azimuth angle also. The center plant has only two elevation angles and two azimuth angles. It works. The plant on the right is fully random. Every angle (azimuth and elevation) is distinct. It works too. But the principal result illustrated is that fully deterministic plants (e.g., the center one) suffice.

Plate VITA.PLANTS. Several variations obtained with the **Gene** program.

Plate WISP.GROWTH. Frames 20, 40, 60, 80, and 120 from a growing plant movie. The plant is also slowing rotating.

Plate WHITE.SANDS. Several 3-D renderings of the context-sensitive grammar 0.0.0.11.1.1[1].1.0 mixed with particle system grasses.

Plate WITH.WITHOUT. A 2-D rendering of the grammar in Figure SENSTREE, showing the 35th generation with and without flowers.

Simulation of Natural Scenes Using Textured Quadric Surfaces

Geoffrey Y. Gardner

Grumman Aerospace Corporation
Research & Development Center
Bethpage, New York   11714

ABSTRACT

Because of the high complexity of the real
world, realistic simulation of natural scenes is
very costly in computation. The topographical
subtlety of common natural features such as trees
and clouds remains a stumbling block to cost-
effective computer modeling. A new scene model,
composed of quadric surfaces bounded with planes
and overlaid with texturing, provides an efficient
and effective means of representing a wide range
of natural features. The new model provides a
compact and functional data base which minimizes
the number of scene elements. Efficient hidden
surface algorithms for quadric surfaces bounded by
planes are included. A mathematical texturing
function represents natural surface detail in a
statistical manner. Techniques have been
developed to simulate natural scenes with the
artistic efficiency of an impressionist painter.

CR Categories: I.3.3 [Computer Graphics]:
Picture/Image Generation - display algorithms;
I.3.5 [Computer Graphics]: Computational Geometry
and Object Modeling - curve, surface, solid and
object representations; geometric algorithms,
languages and systems; I.3.7 [Computer Graphics]:
Three-Dimensional Graphics and Realism - color,
shading, shadowing, and texture; visible
line/surface algorithm; J.7 [Computers in Other
Systems]: Military, real time.

1. INTRODUCTION

Realistic simulation of natural scenes is one
of the greatest challenges facing computer graphics. Exact mathematical representation of the
extreme complexity of nature is generally not
cost-effective because of the high computation
load. Nonetheless, a wide range of applications,
including training, scientific modeling, and
entertainment, have created a demand for effective
and efficient computer techniques for simulating
natural scenes. In attacking the problem, the
choice of data base is critical. A great deal of
effort has been applied employing a wide range of
data bases including points, planar surfaces, and
curved surfaces.

Permission to copy without fee all or part of this material is granted
provided that the copies are not made or distributed for direct
commercial advantage, the ACM copyright notice and the title of the
publication and its date appear, and notice is given that copying is by
permission of the Association for Computing Machinery. To copy
otherwise, or to republish, requires a fee and/or specific permission.

© 1984   ACM   0-89791-138-5/84/007/0011 $00.75

The point is mathematically the simplest data
base primitive. Dungan [6] and Spooner, et al
16 have developed techniques to generate perspective images of Defense Mapping Agency elevation data points. Csuri, et al [5] have used
points to model smoke, and Reeves [13] has used
points to model fire and grass. The problem with
the point data base is that very large numbers of
scene elements have to be transformed to a
perspective projection, producing extremely high
computation loads.

The next simplest data base primitive, and
the most commonly used, is the planar face bounded
by straight edges [17]. Because of its mathematical simplicity this linear approach has
allowed real-time implementation and is widely
used in flight simulation [15]. An elegant
application of the linear data base has been the
construction of fractal surfaces to model terrain
with unprecedented realism [7,9]. Marshall, et al
[10] have also used a linear data base to model
trees with great detail. Like the point data
base, however, the linear data base requires very
large numbers of scene elements to represent the
nonlinear complexity of the real world. The
realism of fractal surface images is achieved only
by rendering hundreds of thousands of planar
faces, and a single linear tree requires thousands
of faces. The number of scene elements is critical to the efficiency of the image generation
approach. The greater the number of scene elements, the greater the number of surfaces and
boundaries that must be computed, resulting in
greater computation costs for sorting, priority
determination, and antialiasing. Limiting the
number of scene elements limits the realism of the
linear model. For this reason, current flight
simulation systems have been criticized for being
too cartoonish.

Various approaches to scene simulation using
curved surfaces have been developed. Quadric
surfaces have been used effectively by the
Mathematical Applications Group, Inc. (MAGI) [8]
and the New York Institute of Technology (NYIT)
[18] to model complex man-made objects. MAGI also
used a large number of quadric surfaces to model a
tree. In a landmark application of computer image
image generation, Blinn used quadric surfaces with
texture maps to model Jupiter and its moons for
the Voyager flyby [2]. Quadrics have also been
used to model molecules and are common data base
primitives in CAD/CAM. None of these applications, however, has exploited the potential of
quadric surfaces for modeling a wide range of
natural features.

More complex curved surfaces, in particular
bicubic surfaces, have been studied extensively
[1,3,4]. Such surfaces provide great modeling
flexibility because they allow for continuity of
slope between adjoining surfaces. However,
despite the development of several clever image
generation algorithms, the mathematical complexity
of these surfaces results in severe computation
loads for complex scenes.

2. AN EFFICIENT DATA BASE FOR SIMULATING NATURAL SCENES

In selecting a data base for simulating
natural scenes, we must contend with the inevi-
table tradeoff between realism and computation
load. We must define a level of realism that we
desire and then choose the data base that will
produce this level of realism most efficiently.
Efficiency is particularly important when our goal
is to generate long sequences of images to produce
dynamic presentations. To achieve real-time image
generation, efficiency is critical. In defining a
desired level of realism which would reduce the
computation problem to manageable proportions, we
have adopted an approach used successfully by
impressionist painters: to represent the essence
of natural scenes as simply as possible. An
impressionist painter produces a very effective
picture of a tree by representing the shape and
texture of its foliage without expending effort on
precise delineation of individual twigs and
leaves. With this modest level of realism, the
painter quickly produces a strong impression of
the essence of a tree. A similar result can be
produced by a computer using simple curved
surfaces and texture patterns. Quadric surfaces,
in particular, lend themselves to this approach
because a single quadric surface can be used to
model a natural scene feature such as a tree, a
hill, or a rock. This simplifies scene modeling
and reduces the number of scene elements required
to model complex scenes. Furthermore, quadaric
surfaces are mathematically the simplest form of
curved surface and therefore provide an efficient
means of representing natural topographical
curvature without piecewise-linear approximation.

Texture patterns can be mapped onto quadric
surfaces to simulate natural scene detail. The
most commonly used technique in texture mapping is
to store images of texture patterns [1,3]. This
approach is inefficient for simulating natural
scenes because too much storage would be required
to represent the wide variety of patterns necessary. In addition, arbitrary views of natural
scenes require perspective manipulation and
antialiasing of the texture patterns. Furthermore, in dynamic presentations it is desirable to
include complex motion of texture patterns to
simulate flowing rivers and blowing trees. To
provide on-line control of perspective validity,
antialiasing, and dynamics, we produce texturing by
means of a mathematical texturing function which
can be mapped onto scene surfaces in such a way as
to modulate surface shading and translucence.
Because only 25 parameters are required to define
a natural-looking texture pattern, a wide variety
of patterns can be stored.

2.1 The Geometric Data Base

A geometric data base composed of quadric
surfaces only would not provide the topographical
variety required for natural scenes. To provide
greater flexibility in our topographical model and
to allow for adjoining quadric surfaces, we
include in our geometric data base the option of
bounding each quadric with a finite number of
planes. We then define the geometric data base to
be a set of discrete convex objects, with each
object defined by one quadric surface and N
bounding planes, where N can be zero. This avoids
the costly computation of intersections between
quadrics and ensures that all surface boundaries
will be at most second-order, allowing for scan-
line intercept determination in closed form.

We define a three-dimensional scene coordi-
nate space (X_s, Y_s, Z_s), with the X_s axis pointing
east, the Y_s axis pointing north, and the Z_s axis
pointing vertically up. We define a ground plane
$(Z_s = 0)$, and a unit light vector. For each two-
dimensional image of the three-dimensional scene,
we define an eyepoint and look angle. The
coefficients of the quadric surface and bounding
planes for each object are defined in scene coordinates and must be transformed to eye coordinates
(X, Y, Z), centered at the eyepoint $(0,0,0)$, with
the Y axis pointing in the direction the eye is
looking (Fig. 1).

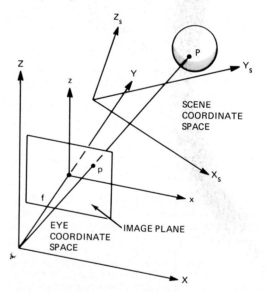

Fig. 1 Transformation From Scene to Eye
Coordinates & Projection Onto Image
Plane

For each quadric, we get an equation in eye
coordinates of the form

$$Q(X,Y,Z) = Q_1 X^2 + Q_2 Y^2 + Q_3 Z^2 + Q_4 XY + Q_5 YZ + Q_6 XZ$$
$$+ Q_7 X + Q_8 Y + Q_9 Z + Q_0 = 0 \qquad (1)$$

For each plane, we get an equation of the
form

$$P(X,Y,Z) = B_1 X + B_2 Y + B_3 Z + B_4 = 0 \qquad (2)$$

The surface geometry of a quadric surface bounded by an arbitrary number of planes can be quite complex. Generating an image of such an object requires exact determination of which surface is visible at each pixel, but testing each surface at each pixel is inefficient. We can make use of area coherence and scan line coherence by noting that a given surface will cover many pixels and many scan lines. We can greatly reduce visibility computation by noting that there are far fewer boundary points than there are surface points in a typical image, and that boundary information can be used to determine surface visibility. The key to efficient processing of the geometric data base is, then, to determine which portions of the boundary curves are visible in the image.

We define an image plane with coordinates (x,z) parallel to the XZ plane a distance f in front of the eyepoint such that the Y axis pierces the coordinate axes origin. We also define the image x axis to be parallel to the eye coordinate X axis and the image z axis to be parallel to the eye coordinate Z axis (Fig. 1). Then the transformation from eye coordinates to image coordinates can be represented as

$$X = kx$$
$$Y = kf$$
$$Z = kz \qquad (3)$$

Our strategy will now be to use Eq (1), (2), and (3) to project all surface boundaries onto the image plane. We will then determine all key points on each boundary, that is points at which boundary visibility, and therefore surface visibility, changes across scan lines. We will then use the key points to determine a scan line list of visible boundaries and surfaces.

The most important image curve is the limb curve, defined as the projection of the quadric silhouette (Fig. 2). The limb curve can be derived by substituting Eq (3) into Eq (1) to obtain a quadratic equation in k,

$$Ak^2 + Bk + C = 0 \qquad (4)$$

where A is a second-order expression in the image coordinates, x and z, B is a linear expression in x and z, and C is a constant. (Algebraic expansions will be omitted for the sake of brevity.) The parameter k relates to the distance from the eye, varying from a value of 0 at the eyepoint to a value of 1 at the image plane, and increasing along the ray out into the eye coordinate space. In general, a ray will intersect a quadric surface at two points, giving two distinct values of k from Eq (4). By definition, the limb curve is the set of image points for which the rays are tangent to the quadric surface. For these points k is single valued, so the discriminant of Eq (4) is zero.

$$B^2 - 4AC = 0 \qquad (5)$$

This then gives the limb curve as

$$f(x,z) = a_1 x^2 + a_2 z^2 + a_3 xz + a_4 x + a_5 z + a_6 \qquad (6)$$

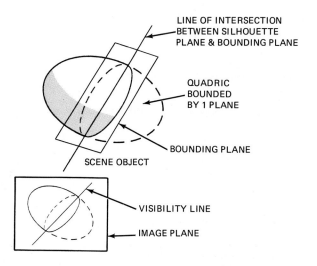

Fig. 2 Limb Curve, Intersection Curve and Visibility Line

where the coefficients are expressions containing only the quadric surface coefficients, and f, the distance from the eye to the image plane.

The remaining image curves will be intersection curves, that is, projections of the curves of intersection between the quadric and its bounding planes (Fig. 2). To solve for the coefficients of an intersection curve, we must satisfy Eq (1), (2), and (3) simultaneously. Substituting Eq (3) into Eq (2), we get

$$k = -B_4/(B_1 x + B_2 f + B_3 z) \qquad (7)$$

Then substituting for k in Eq (3) and using the result in Eq (1), we get the intersection curve as

$$g(x,z) = e_1 x^2 + e_2 z^2 + e_3 xz + e_4 x + e_5 z + e_6 = 0 \qquad (8)$$

where the coefficients are all expressions containing the quadric surface coefficients, the bounding plane coefficients, and f.

Given a quadric surface with one or more bounding planes, we must determine which boundary curve segments are visible. To do this, we introduce the concept of a visibility line. We define a visibility line for each bounding plane as the projection on the image plane of the line of intersection between the quadric silhouette plane and the bounding plane (Fig. 2). Since the visibility line will be used to partition a particular curve into visible and invisible segments, its definition must include a sense or sign determined from the sense of the bounding plane. Rewriting Eq (2) as an inequality to include the bounding plane sense, we have

$$P(X,Y,Z) = B_1 X + B_2 Y + B_3 Z + B_4 > 0 \qquad (9)$$

Substituting Eq (3) into Eq (9) gives

$$k(B_1 x + B_2 f + B_3 z) + B_4 > 0 \qquad (10)$$

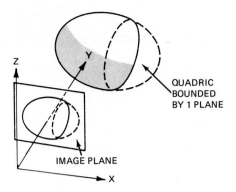

a. Bounding Plane Not Visible

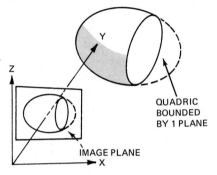

b. Bounding Plane Visible

Fig. 3 Intersection Curve Visibility

The equation for the silhouette plane can be determined from Eq (4) and (5) to be

$$kB + 2C = 0 \qquad (11)$$

Since B is a linear expression in x and z, and C is a constant, Eq (10) and (11) can be combined to give the visibility line as

$$v_1 x + v_2 z + v_3 > 0 \qquad (12)$$

where the coefficients are expressions in the quadric surface and bounding plane coefficients and f.

The visibility line defined by Eq (12) can be used to determine the visibility of any point on the limb curve relative to a particular bounding plane. If the limb point satisfies Eq (12), it is defined to be visible relative to the plane used to define the line. If more than one bounding plane is used in the object definition, a limb point must satisfy the visibility line for each in order to be visible in the image.

The visibility line for each bounding plane can also be used to determine the visibility of any point on the intersection curve related to that plane. This visibility test is only necessary when the plane faces away from the eye, that is, when the eye is on the same side of the plane as the defined part of the quadric surface (Fig. 3a). When the eye is on the other side of the plane, no visibility test is necessary because

the whole intersection curve is visible (Fig. 3b). To determine which case applies, we simply substitute the eyepoint $(X,Y,Z) = (0,0,0)$ into Eq (9) to get

$$B_4 > 0 \qquad (13)$$

If Eq (13) is satisifed, the eye is on the object side of the plane and a visibility test for the intersection curve is required. Figure 2 shows that in this case, the visible portion of the intersection curve lies on the opposite side of the visibility line as the visible portion of the limb curve. Therefore, for a point on the intersection curve to be visible, it must fail to satisfy Eq (12).

Thus, the visibility line can be used to determine portions of the limb curve defined to be visible as well as portions of the intersection curve whose visibility depends on eye position in the scene.

Images of objects with more than one bounding plane may include linear boundaries resulting from the intersection of two planes. We introduce the concept of an intersection line, which we define as the image of the intersection between two bounding planes. The intersection line will define that portion of the intersection curve of one bounding plane defined to be visible relative to the other (Fig. 4). In this sense, the intersection line is analogous to the visibility line with the first intersection curve replacing the limb curve. With a derivation similar to that used for the visibility line, we get the intersection line for two bounding planes as

$$x_1 x + x_2 z + x_3 > 0 \qquad (14)$$

where the coefficients are in terms of the coefficients of the two bounding planes.

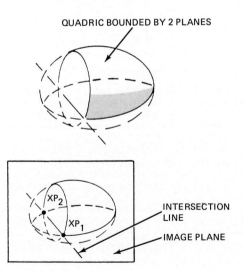

Fig. 4 Intersection Line Defines Intersection Curve Visibility Relative to Intersecting Bounding Plane and Contains Intersection Points XP_1, XP_2

In addition to its function as a visibility criterion, an intersection line may also be a visible image boundary. In order for a point on an intersection line to be visible it must satisfy the appropriate form of Eq (14) for all other intersection lines produced by a common bounding plane.

Having computed the equations for all image boundary curves and lines, we must now determine which boundary segments are visible. We note that boundary segments are generally visible over many scan lines and that their state of visibility changes only at certain key points. Determining these key points and restricting visibility tests to a few sample scan lines will greatly reduce visibility computations. The key points of boundary visibility are curve extrema (minimum and maximum z), contact points, intersection points, and triplet points.

Curve extrema can be computed from Eq (6) and (8) in the standard manner. Since curves don't exist on scan lines outside their extrema, they clearly are potentially visible only on scan lines in between.

We define a contact point as a point of tangency between the limb curve and an intersection curve. In general, two contact points exist for each intersection curve and can be determined from the intersection of the relevant visibility line and the limb curve (Eq (12) & (6)). Contact points are points of potential change of visibility state for limb and intersection curves.

We define an intersection point as a point of intersection between an intersection line and an intersection curve related to a common plane (Fig. 4). Intersection points are points of potential change of visibility for intersection curves and intersection lines.

We define a triplet point as the image point of the corner intersection of three bounding planes. Triplet points can be computed as the intersection of two intersection lines and are points of potential change of visibility for intersection lines.

Once we have computed all the potentially visible curves, lines, and key points for the image of an object, we are prepared to perform visibility tests. In determining what tests to make for particular boundaries, the following rules apply. Any image point relating to a point on the quadric surface must be tested against all visibility lines. Any image point relating to a point on a particular bounding plane must be tested against all intersection lines related to that plane (except for the line producing the point) and, if the plane is not visible, the visibility line related to that plane.

We begin the visibility testing by testing all key points, since only visible key points affect visibility changes in the boundaries. Editing out invisible key points, we compile a list of visible key points sorted on z in scan-line order. We call this a z-band list because it defines regions in the image z direction (vertical) in which boundary visibility remains constant from scan line to scan line.

Within each z-band in the list, an average z value is computed to represent a typical scan line on which all boundary curve and intersection line intercept points are computed. These intercept points are tested for visibility, and codes for all visible boundary intercepts are entered in the z-band, sorted from left to right based on the intercept x value. Boundary curve intercepts are coded to define leftmost or rightmost intercept. Finally the sorted visible boundary intercepts are used to determine the visible surfaces in between. The surface between two boundary intercepts is assumed to be the quadric surface unless both boundaries are related to a common bounding plane.

The resulting object visibility list, consisting of sorted z-bands, each with x-sorted boundary intercept and surface codes, provides a very efficient image "blueprint" for directing scan-line surface shading of the object. As the image is generated, scan line by scan line, a particular object is considered only if the scan line falls within the z-band list. For each such object, the pertinent z-band is referenced, and, proceeding from left to right, boundary codes are referenced, intercepts computed, and surfaces shaded on pixels in between. Figure 5 shows how this approach simplifies the image generation of a complicated object by reducing a maze of potentially visible boundaries to a manageable list of visible boundaries and surfaces. Figure 5a shows the limb and intersection curves, and the intersection and visibility lines in an image of a sphere bounded by 6 planes. Figure 5b shows the z bands indicated by horizontal lines drawn through all visible key points. Note how within each z band the visibility of boundaries and surfaces remains constant. Figure 5c shows the final shaded object with hidden surfaces removed.

In addition to streamlining intraobject visibility, that is, the determination of visible surfaces for a single object, the visibility list simplifies interobject visibility, the determination of priority between different objects. Because our geometric data base includes only convex objects, we need not compute the distance to the visible object surface at every pixel. Instead, we can use the z-band lists to compute the leftmost and rightmost surface distance on a scan line and use linear interpolation in between. Then, when two objects overlap on a scan line we can use the interpolated distances to determine priority within the overlap region.

2.2   The Texture Data Base

We can simulate textural detail efficiently by modulating surface shading intensity in a defined manner. In so doing, we must take care to assure perspective validity by making the texture intensity depend on the scene coordinates of the surface being textured. For any given image we are interested in texturing visible surfaces only. Thus it would be inefficient to produce texture intensity values for all scene surface points. The most practical approach is to produce texture values only for visible scene surface points corresponding to image sample points. Since the image sample points depend on the viewing perspective, we must be able to produce

a. All Curves & Lines

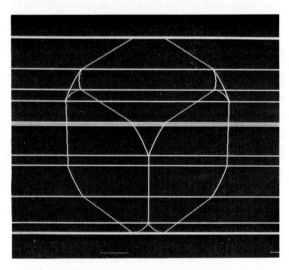

b. Visible Boundary Segments & Z Bands

c. Shaded Visible Surfaces

Fig. 5 Visibility Determination for Sphere With 6
Bounding Planes

texture values for arbitrary scene points. For
this reason we have chosen a mathematical function
to produce texture. A mathematical texturing
function offers the additional advantage of
requiring a minimal data base to produce a wide
variety of texture patterns, each of which can
cover an unlimited region in the scene. The
control inherent in a mathematical function,
computed during image generation, also provides
for straightforward antialiasing of texture
patterns and allows implementation of complex
texture motion.

In choosing the exact form of our texturing
function, we decided that it would be most efficient to represent real-world detail at a statistical level. An effective way to do this is to
use the principle of Fourier expansion, [11, 14].
After investigating different expressions of
various waveforms, we found a very effective
texturing function to be defined as

$$T(X_s, Y_s, Z_s) = \sum_{i=1}^{n} c_i \frac{[(\text{Sin}(\omega_i X_s + PX_i) + 1]}{2} \times$$

$$\sum_{i=1}^{n} c_i \frac{[(\text{Sin}(\omega_i Y_s + PY_i) + 1]}{2} \qquad (15)$$

Where PX_i and PY_i represent phase shift functions
to avoid a tartan-like regularity of the pattern.
We have found that defining PX_i as a sinusoidal
function of Y_s and PY_i as a sinusoidal function of
X_s produces natural-looking patterns for low
values of n (Fig. 6).

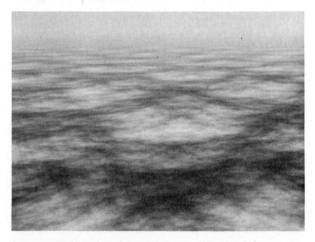

Fig. 6 Texture Pattern on Ground Plane From
Texture Function Eq (15) With n = 7

The primary use of the texturing function is
to simulate surface detail by modulating shading
intensity. This is done by computing a weighted
average of the surface shading intensity and the
texture function value at each visible point. A
texture weighting parameter is defined for each
object to provide flexibility in scene modeling.
A secondary use of the texture function is to
simulate boundary irregularity and amorphousness
of certain natural features, such as trees and

clouds. We accomplish this by treating locally
dark texture regions on an object's surface as
though they were holes in the object. This effect
is achieved quite simply by assigning a threshold
value for the texture function and defining an
object to be translucent at any image point where
the texture function falls below the threshold.
The artificial boundaries produced between the
visible and invisible portions of the texture
surface can be softened by varying the translucence linearly as the texture function crosses
the threshold. This technique is demonstrated in
Fig. 7, which shows a sky plane textured with
variable translucence to simulate a cloud layer.

a. Scene Without Texture Function

Fig. 7 Cloud Layer Simulated by Texture Function
        Modulating Shading & Translucence

b. Scene With Texture Function

Fig. 8 Mountains Modeled by Hyperboloids

   The texturing function greatly enhances the
realism of objects defined by the geometric data
base. Figure 8a shows mountains modeled by the
geometric data base only, and Fig. 8b shows the
same scene enhanced by the texturing function. In
addition to adding simulated topographical detail,
the texturing blends surface shading across boundaries between abutting objects. This unifying
effect is due to the fact that all objects, as
well as the ground plane, are textured with the
same texture function parameters so that the
texturing function maps the same pattern continuously across all scene surfaces as a function
of scene coordinates.

   The combination of the geometric and texture
data bases is particularly effective in simulating
amorphous objects, such as trees and clouds, whose
boundaries are both complex and subtle (Fig. 9).
The trick of simulating such features so efficiently is to control the translucence at an
object's silhouette. This capability is provided
as much by the geometric data base as by the
texturing function, for it is the definition of
the limb curve (Eq 6) that allows us to vary the
threshold of the texturing function to increase
translucence in a straightforward manner at image
points near the object boundary. Because the
translucence can be increased smoothly and continuously, the image will have soft boundaries
which will require no antialiasing.

   The control inherent in the mathematical
texturing function has two more advantages over
less flexible texturing techniques, such as stored
texture maps. Antialiasing of texture patterns
can be achieved simply by testing sine wave
frequencies and dropping those that exceed the
image sampling frequency (projected into scene
space). In addition, any of the texturing function image parameters can be varied from frame to
frame, allowing the simulation of a wide range of
dynamic effects. Thus it would require little
additional frame computation to simulate trees
blowing, smoke rising, clouds drifting, or rivers
flowing.

   The texture data base required to implement
this simulation capability is extremely modest. A
natural-looking texture pattern can be defined by
25 parameters, including sine coefficients and
frequencies, phase shifts, and translucence
thresholds. A given texture pattern can be used
for any number of objects covering any region in
the scene. Thus, all trees of a particular type
could be simulated using one pattern, all rivers
using another pattern, etc. We have found that
complex and varied natural scenes can be simulated
effectively using only 10 texture patterns. This
compactness of the texture data base simplifies
both scene modeling and image generation.

2.3 Data Base Construction for Complex Scenes

The new data base simplifies the modeling of complex scenes because it conveniently partitions the model into two levels of topographical detail. The geometric data base can be used to model major topographical features, such as hills, explicitly, and the texture data base can be used to represent secondary topographical variations statistically. The compactness of each of these data bases permits a straightforward specification of the parameters of size, shape, position, and frequency content, which are the essential characteristics of natural scene features.

To facilitate the modeling of complex natural scenes, we developed procedural algorithms to generate clusters of scene features. Only two types of quadric surfaces are required to produce a wide variety of scene features. Hyperboloids of two sheets are very effective in simulating hills and mountains, and ellipsoids are efficient for modeling trees, rocks, and clouds. For each feature cluster, we define a region on the ground plane over which the cluster, will be generated. We also define a typical spacing between features in the cluster as well as size, shape, and color parameters for a typical template object. The algorithm places the template object within the defined region at positions determined from the defined spacing. As the object modeling each feature is generated, the algorithm perturbs its position, size, shape, and color parameters randomly to produce natural statistical variations within the cluster. Adjacent objects are tested for intersection, and bounding planes are computed for abutting objects. This permits the modeling of topographic structures, such as rolling terrain, mountain ranges, and forests, which are too complex to be simulated by isolated objects. The algorithm also allows us to define features in a cluster as "terrain objects" upon which other scene objects will lie. Terrain objects are generated first so that the objects composing subsequent clusters can be raised to the appropriate terrain elevation after they are positioned on the ground plane. The simplicity of quadric surface shape and position definition makes this process quite straightforward. Similarly, clusters can be defined to be positioned at a fixed altitude above the ground plane, a capability useful in modeling clouds.

To use the mathematical texturing function to model secondary topographical variations we must define sets of function parameters, with each set chosen to simulate a desired texture pattern. The individual parameters in each set can be determined from an analysis of the spatial frequency content of features being modeled. In general, natural features have a power spectrum whose amplitude decreases as frequency increases. Natural-looking texture patterns can be generated using from 3 to 7 sine waves whose frequencies increase by a factor of approximately 2 and whose amplitudes decrease by a factor of approximately one half the square root of 2. The complete texture data base is defined by a list of parameter sets. As clusters of scene features are generated, each object is assigned a specified texture parameter set number. A particular texture pattern can be assigned to any number of clusters, minimizing the size of the overall data base.

The clustering algorithm can be extended to generate clusters of clusters. Using the extended clustering algorithm, we can quickly generate and change models of complex natural scenes. Figures 10 and 11 show two examples of complex natural scenes simulated using these algorithms.

3. CONCLUSIONS

We have described efficient hidden surface algorithms for complex curved objects composed of quadric surfaces bounded by planes. We have demonstrated the effectiveness of a texturing function which modulates the shading intensity and translucence of scene surfaces. We have shown how these tools can be incorporated in procedural algorithms to simulate complex natural scenes efficiently.

Textured quadric surfaces provide a means of bridging the gap between computationally cheap, but cartoonish, scene simulation and highly realistic, but costly, scene simulation. Textured quadric surfaces produce a compact, functional data base related directly to the most significant topographical characteristics of scene features. This approach reduces image generation computation because it reduces the number of scene elements that must be processed. Textured quadric surfaces allow us to represent the essential realism of natural scenes as an impressionist painter would, thus avoiding the costly replication of unimportant details. The new scene model is particularly effective for modeling amorphous objects, such as trees and clouds, which continue to be stumbling blocks for other approaches. The new model is, however, comprehensive because it can model man-made as well as natural features. The inclusion of bounding planes even permits modeling linear features, such as buildings.

As a quantitative measure of the computational efficiency of this approach, the images in Figs. 10 and 11 took 10 min. 29 sec. and 9 min. 40 sec., respectively, to generate on a dedicated Data General Eclipse S/250 16-bit minicomputer with 512 KBYTE memory and floating point accelerator. Image resolution is 480 scan lines by 640 pixels by 24 bits. The image generation routines were programmed in Fortran V using floating point arithmetic. (Runs for figure 10 at 512 x 512 resolution took 5 min. 34 sec. on a VAX 11/760 and 6.49 sec. on a CRAY 1M.) The current programs are in no way claimed to be optimal. On the contrary, there is much room for improvement in both computation time and image quality, and the author hopes that this paper will stimulate others to explore and extend this technology.

Scene simulation using textured quadric surfaces has application in many diverse fields, including art, entertainment, advertising, scientific simulation, and training. At Grumman we have used it in a public relations film to show an advanced concept, forward-swept-wing aircraft in flight before it was built (Fig. 12). We have also applied the technology to pattern recognition research in target tracking by a missile [12]. We

Fig. 9   Trees, Clouds & Hills Modeled by Textured
          Quadric Surfaces

Fig. 12   Frame From X-29 Promotional Film. The
          X-29 aircraft is modeled by 40 quadric
          surfaces without texturing. The clouds
          are modeled by quadric surfaces with
          texturing.

are currently investigating real-time implementation of the algorithms for flight simulators.

4. ACKNOWLEDGEMENTS

Significant contributions to this work were
made by Tom Jacquish, Ed Berlin, Jr, Bob Gelman,
and Mike Gershowitz. I am indebted to my wife
Joan for pointing out that hyperboloids make
better mountains than paraboloids.

The research described in this paper was
sponsored in part by the Air Force Human Resources
Laboratory (AFHRL) under contract F33615-79-C-
0029.

Fig. 10   Clusters of Hills & Trees Generated With
          Cluster Algorithm

5. REFERENCES

1. Blinn, J., Computer display of curved sur-
    faces, PhD Thesis, Computer Science.
    Department, U. of Utah (Dec 1978).

2. Blinn, J., Voyager 2. SIGGRAPH Video Review,
    Issue 1, May 1980.

3. Catmull, E., A subdivision algorithm for
    computer display of curved surfaces. UTEC-
    CSc-74-133, PhD Thesis, Computer Science
    Department, U. of Utah (Dec 1974).

4. Clark, J., Designing surfaces in 3-D. Comm.
    ACM 19, 8 (Aug 1976), 454-460.

5. Csuri, C., Hackathorn, R., Parent, W.,
    Carlson, W., and Howard, M. Towards an
    interactive high visual complexity animation
    system. Computer Graphics 13, 2 (Aug 1979),
    289-299.

6. Dungan, W., Jr., A terrain and cloud computer
    image generation model. Computer Graphics 13,
    2 (Aug 1979), 143-147.

Fig. 11   Clusters of Hills, Trees & Clouds
          Generated With Extended Cluster
          Algorithm

7. Fournier, A., Fussell, D., and Carpenter, L., Computer rendering of stochastic models. Comm. ACM 25, 6 (June 1982), 371-384.

8. Goldstein, R. A., and Nagel, R., 3-D visual simulation. Simulation 16, 1 (Jan 1971), 25-31.

9. Mandelbrot, B. B., Fractals: Form, Chance and Dimension. Freeman, San Francisco, (1977).

10. Marshall, R., Wilson, R., and Carlson, W., Procedure models for generating three-dimensional terrain. Computer Graphics 14, 3 (July 1980), 154-159.

11. Max, N., Vectorized procedural models for natural terrain: waves and islands in the sunset. Computer Graphics 15, 3 (Aug 1981) 317-324.

12. Mendelsohn, J., and Leib, K. G., Optical correlation module design study. Air Force Systems Command Contract AF 33615-82-C-1727 Final Report (Sept 1983).

13. Reeves, W. T., Particle systems - a technique for modeling a class of fuzzy objects. Computer Graphics 17, 3 (July 1983), pp 359-376.

14. Schacter, B. J., Long-crested wave models. Computer Graphics and Image Processing 12 (1980), 187-201.

15. Schacter, B. J., Computer Image Generation. Wiley-Interscience, New York, 1983.

16. Spooner, A. M., Breglia, D. R., and Patz, B. W., Realscan - a CIG system with increased image detail. Proc 2nd Interservice/Industry Training Equipment Conf, Salt Lake City, Utah (Nov 1980) 110-116.

17. Sutherland, I. E., Sproull, R. F., and Schumacker, R. A., A characterization of ten hidden surface algorithms. ACM Computing Surveys 6, 1 (May 1974), 1-55.

18. Williams, L., Casting curved shadows on curved surfaces. Computer Graphics 12, 3 (Aug 1978), 270-274.

GLOBAL AND LOCAL DEFORMATIONS
OF SOLID PRIMITIVES

Alan H. Barr
Computer Science Department †
California Institute of Technology
Pasadena, California

Abstract

New hierarchical solid modeling operations are developed, which simulate twisting, bending, tapering, or similar transformations of geometric objects. The chief result is that the normal vector of an arbitrarily deformed smooth surface can be calculated directly from the surface normal vector of the undeformed surface and a transformation matrix. Deformations are easily combined in a hierarchical structure, creating complex objects from simpler ones. The position vectors and normal vectors in the simpler objects are used to calculate the position and normal vectors in the more complex forms; each level in the deformation hierarchy requires an additional matrix multiply for the normal vector calculation. Deformations are important and highly intuitive operations which ease the control and rendering of large families of three-dimensional geometric shapes.

KEYWORDS: Computational Geometry, Solid Modeling, Deformation

Introduction

Modeling hierarchies are a convenient and efficient way to represent geometric objects, allowing users to combine simpler graphical primitives and operators into more complex forms. The leaf-nodes in the hierarchy are the hardware/firmware commands on the equipment which draws the vectors, changes the colors of individual pixels, and operates on lists of line segments or polygons. With the appropriate algorithms and interfaces, users can develop a strong intuitive feel-ing for the results of a manipulation, can think in terms of each operation, and are able to create the objects and scenes which they desire.

In this paper, we introduce globally and locally defined deformations as new hierarchical operations for use in solid modeling. These operations extend the conventional operations of rotation, translation, Boolean union, intersection and difference. In section one, the transformation rules for tangent vectors and for normal vectors are shown. In section two, several examples of deformation functions are listed. A method is shown in section three to convert arbitrary local representations of deformations to global representations, for space curves and surfaces. Finally, in section four, applications of the methods to the rendering process are described, opening future research directions in ray-tracing algorithms. Appendix A contains a derivation of the normal vector transformation rule.

Deformations allow the user to treat a solid as if it were constructed from a special type of topological putty or clay, which may be bent, twisted, tapered, compressed, expanded, and otherwise transformed repeatedly into a final shape. They are highly intuitive and easily visualized operations which simulate some important manufacturing processes for fabricating objects, such as the bending of bar stock and sheet metal. Deformations can be incorporated into traditional CAD/CAM solid modeling and surface patch methods, reducing the data storage requirements for simulating flexible geometric objects, such as objects made of metal, fabric or rubber.

Permission to copy without fee all or part of this material is granted provided that the copies are not made or distributed for direct commercial advantage, the ACM copyright notice and the title of the publication and its date appear, and notice is given that copying is by permission of the Association for Computing Machinery. To copy otherwise, or to republish, requires a fee and/or specific permission.

© 1984   ACM   0-89791-138-5/84/007/0021 $00.75

† Previous address, Raster Technologies Inc., N. Billerica, Mass.

Although it is possible to use these techniques to accurately model the physical properties of different elastic materials with the partial differential equations of elasticity and plasticity theory, simpler mathematical deformation methods exist. These simpler methods have reduced computational needs, are widely applicable in modeling, and are described in the examples section. It is beyond the scope of this paper to formulate the mathematical details of exact mechanical descriptions of physical deformation properties of materials.

1.0 Background and Derivations.

A **globally specified deformation** of a three dimensional solid is a mathematical function $\underline{F}$ which explicitly modifies the global coordinates of points in space. Points in the undeformed solid are called (small) $\underline{x}$, while points in the deformed solid are called (capital) $\underline{X}$. Mathematically, this is represented by the equation

$$\underline{X} = \underline{F}(\underline{x}). \qquad [Equation \quad 1.1a]$$

The x, y, and z components of the three dimensional vector $\underline{x}$ are designated x_1, x_2, and x_3. (For notational convenience, x_1, x_2, and x_3 and x, y, and z are used interchangably. A similar convention holds for the upper case forms.)

A **locally specified deformation** modifies the tangent space of the solid. Differential vectors in the substance of the solid are rotated and/or skewed; these vectors are integrated to obtain the global position. The differential vectors can be thought of as separate chain-links which can rotate and stretch; the local specification of the deformation is the rotation and skewing matrix function. The position of the end-link in the chain is the vector sum of the previous links, as shown in section three.

Tangent vectors and normal vectors are the two most important vectors used in modeling — the former for delineating and constructing the local geometry, and the latter for obtaining surface orientation and lighting information. Tangent and normal vectors on the undeformed surface may be transformed into the tangent and normal vectors on the deformed surface; the algebraic manipulations for the transformation rules involve a single multiplication by the Jacobian matrix $\underline{J}$ of the transformation function $\underline{F}$. In this paper, the term "tangent transformation" substitutes for "contravariant transformation" and is the transformation rule for the tangent vectors. The term "normal transformation" substitutes for "covariant transformation" and is the transformation rule for the normal vectors.

The Jacobian matrix $\underline{J}$ for the transformation function $\underline{X} = \underline{F}(\underline{x})$ is a function of $\underline{x}$, and is calculated by taking partial derivatives of $\underline{F}$ with respect to the coordinates x_1, x_2, and x_3:

$$\underline{J}_i(\underline{x}) = \frac{\partial \underline{F}(\underline{x})}{\partial x_i} \qquad [Equation \quad 1.1b]$$

In other words, the ith column of $\underline{J}$ is obtained by the partial derivative of $\underline{F}(\underline{x})$ with respect to x_i.

When the surface of an object is given by a parametric function of two variables u and v,

$$\underline{x} = \underline{x}(u, v), \qquad [Equation \quad 1.1c]$$

any tangent vector to the surface may be obtained from linear combinations of partial derivatives of $\underline{x}$ with respect to u and v. The normal vector direction may be obtained from the cross product of two linearly independent surface tangent vectors.

The **tangent vector transformation rule** is a restatement of the chain rule in multidimensional calculus. The new vector derivative is equal to the Jacobian matrix times the old derivative.

In matrix form, this is expressed as:

$$\frac{\partial \underline{X}}{\partial u} = \underline{J}\frac{\partial \underline{x}}{\partial u} \qquad [Equation \quad 1.2a]$$

This is equivalent in component form to:

$$X_{i,u} = \sum_{j=1}^{3} J_{ij}x_{j,u} \qquad [Equations \quad 1.2b]$$

In other words, the new tangent vector $\partial \underline{X}/\partial u$ is equal to the Jacobian matrix $\underline{J}$ times the old tangent vector $\partial \underline{x}/\partial u$

The **normal vector transformation rule** involves the inverse transpose of the Jacobian matrix. A derivation of this result is found in Appendix A.

$$[Equation \quad 1.3]$$

$$\underline{n}^{(X)} = \det \underline{J}\,\underline{J}^{-1T}\underline{n}^{(x)}$$

Of course, since only the direction of the normal vector is important, it is not necessary to compute the value of the determinant in practice, although it sometimes is implicitly calculated as shown in Appendix A. As is well known from calculus, the determinant of the Jacobian is the local volume ratio at each point in the transformation, between the deformed region and the undeformed region.

2.0 Examples of Deformations.

Example 2.1: Scaling. One of the simplest deformations is a change in the length of the three global components parallel to the coordinate axes. This produces an orthogonal scaling operation :

$$X = a_1 x$$
$$Y = a_2 y \qquad [Equation \quad 2.1a]$$
$$Z = a_3 z$$

The components of the Jacobian matrix are given by

$$J_{ij} = \frac{\partial X_i}{\partial x_j},$$

so

$$\underline{\underline{J}} = \begin{pmatrix} a_1 & 0 & 0 \\ 0 & a_2 & 0 \\ 0 & 0 & a_3 \end{pmatrix} \qquad [Equation \quad 2.1b]$$

The volume change of a region scaled by this transformation is obtained from the Jacobian determinant, which is $a_1 a_2 a_3$. The normal transformation matrix is the inverse transpose of the Jacobian matrix (optionally times the determinant of the Jacobian matrix), and is given by:

$$\det J \quad \underline{\underline{J}}^{-1T} = \begin{pmatrix} a_2 a_3 & 0 & 0 \\ 0 & a_1 a_3 & 0 \\ 0 & 0 & a_1 a_2 \end{pmatrix}$$

Without the factor of the determinant, the normal transformation matrix is:

$$\underline{\underline{J}}^{-1T} = \begin{pmatrix} 1/a_1 & 0 & 0 \\ 0 & 1/a_2 & 0 \\ 0 & 0 & 1/a_3 \end{pmatrix}$$

To obtain the new normal vector at any point on the surface of an object subjected to this deformation, we multiply the original normal vector by either of the above normal transformation matrices. The new **unit** normal vector is easily obtained by dividing the output components by the magnitude of the vector.

For instance, consider converting a point $[x_1, x_2, x_3]^T$ lying on a roughly spherical surface centered at the origin, with normal vector $[n_1, n_2, n_3]^T$. The transformed surface point on the resulting ellipsoidal shape is $[a_1 x_1, a_2 x_2, a_3 x_3]^T$ and the transformed normal vector is parallel to $[n_1/a_1, n_2/a_2, n_3/a_3]^T$. The volume ratio between the shapes is $a_1 a_2 a_3$.

The scaling transformation is a special case of general affine transformations, in which the Jacobian matrix is a constant matrix. Affine transformations include skewing, rotation, and scaling transformations. When the transformation consists of pure rotation, it is interesting to note that the inverse of the matrix is equal to its transpose. For pure rotation, this means that the tangent vector and the normal vector are transformed by a single matrix. For more general affine transformations, pairs of constant matrices are required.

Example 2.2: Global Tapering along the Z Axis. Tapering is similar to scaling, by differentially changing the length of two global components without changing the length of the third. In figure 2.2, the function $f(z)$ is a piecewise linear function which decreases as z increases (from page bottom to the top). The magnitude of the tapering rate progressively increases from figure 2.2 a through figure 2.2 d. When the tapering function $f(z) = 1$, the portion of the deformed object is unchanged; the object increases in size as a function of z when $f'(z) > 0$, and decreases in size when $f'(z) < 0$. The object passes through a singularity at $f(z) = 0$ and becomes everted when $f(z) < 0$.

$$r = f(z),$$
$$X = rx,$$
$$Y = ry, \qquad [Equation \quad 2.2a]$$
$$Z = z$$

The tangent transformation matrix is given by:

$$\underline{\underline{J}} = \begin{pmatrix} r & 0 & f'(z)x \\ 0 & r & f'(z)y \\ 0 & 0 & 1 \end{pmatrix} \qquad [Equation \quad 2.2b]$$

The local volumetric rate of expansion, from the determinant, is r^2.

The normal transformation matrix is given by:

$$r^2 \underline{\underline{J}}^{-1T} = \begin{pmatrix} r & 0 & 0 \\ 0 & r & 0 \\ -rf'(z)x & -rf'(z)y & r^2 \end{pmatrix}$$

The inverse transformation is given by:

$$r(Z) = f(Z),$$
$$x = X/r,$$
$$y = Y/r, \qquad [Equation \quad 2.2c]$$
$$z = Z$$

Figure 2.2 Progressive Tapering of a Ribbon

Example 2.3: Global Axial Twists. For some applications, it is useful to simulate global twisting of an object. A twist can be approximated as differential rotation, just as tapering is a differential scaling of the global basis vectors. We rotate one pair of global basis vectors as a function of height, without altering the third global basis vector. The deformation can be demonstrated by twisting a deck of cards, in which each card is rotated somewhat more than the card beneath it.

The global twist around the z axis is produced by the following equations:

$$\theta = f(z)$$
$$C_\theta = cos(\theta)$$
$$S_\theta = sin(\theta)$$

$$X = xC_\theta - yS_\theta,$$
$$Y = xS_\theta + yC_\theta, \qquad [Equation \quad 2.3a]$$
$$Z = z.$$

The twist proceeds along the z axis at a rate of $f'(z)$ radians per unit length in the z direction.

The tangent transformation matrix is given by

$$\underline{\underline{J}} = \begin{pmatrix} C_\theta & -S_\theta & -xS_\theta f'(z) - yC_\theta f'(z) \\ S_\theta & C_\theta & xC_\theta f'(z) - yS_\theta f'(z) \\ 0 & 0 & 1 \end{pmatrix}$$

Note that the determinant of the Jacobian matrix is unity, so that the twisting transformation preserves the volume of the original solid. This is consistent with our "card-deck" model of twisting, since each individual card retains its original volume.

The normal transformation matrix is given by:

$$\underline{\underline{J}}^{-1T} = \begin{pmatrix} C_\theta & -S_\theta & 0 \\ S_\theta & C_\theta & 0 \\ yf'(z) & -xf'(z) & 1 \end{pmatrix}$$

Our original deck of cards is a rectangular solid, with orthogonal normal vectors. We can see from the above transformation matrix that the normal vectors to the twisted deck will generally tilt out of the *x-y* plane.

Figures 2.3.1 a–d show the effect of a progressively increasing twist. In these line drawings of solids, vectors are hidden by the normal vector criterion—if the normal vector (as calculated by the above transformation matrix) faces the viewer, the line is drawn, otherwise, the line segment is not drawn. Figure 2.3.3 shows an object which has been twisted and tapered, while figures 2.3.4 and 2.3.2 show the results from twisting an object around an axis not within the object itself.

The inverse transformation is given by:

$$[Equation \quad 2.3b]$$

$$\theta = f(Z),$$
$$x = XC_\theta + YS_\theta,$$
$$y = -XS_\theta + YC_\theta,$$
$$z = Z$$

which is basically a twist in the opposite direction.

Figure 2.3.1 Progressive Twisting of a Ribbon

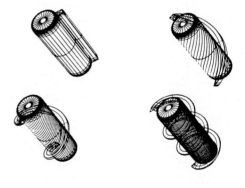

Figure 2.3.2 Progressive Twisting of Two Primitives

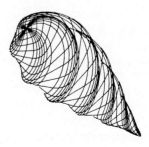

Figure 2.3.3 Twisting of a Tapered Primitive

Figure 2.3.4 Tapering of a Twisted offset Primitive

Example 2.4: Global Linear Bends along the Y-Axis. For other applications, it is useful to have a simple simulation of bending.

The following equations represent an isotropic bend along a centerline parallel to the y-axis: the length of the centerline does not change during the bending process. The bending angle θ, is constant at the extremities, but changes linearly in the central region. In the bent region, the bending rate k, measured in radians per unit length, is constant, and the differential basis vectors are simultaneously rotated and translated around the third local basis vector. Outside the bent region, the deformation consists of a rigid body rotation and translation. The range of the bending deformation is controlled by y_{min}, and y_{max}, with the bent region corresponding to values of y such that $y_{min} \leq y \leq y_{max}$. The axis of the bend is located along $[s, y_0, 1/k]^T$, where s is the parameter of the line. The center of the bend occurs at $y = y_0$—i.e., where one would "put one's thumbs" to create the bend. The radius of curvature of the bend is $1/k$.

The bending angle θ is given by:

$$\theta = k(\hat{y} - y_0),$$
$$C_\theta = cos(\theta),$$
$$S_\theta = sin(\theta),$$

where

$$\hat{y} = \begin{cases} y_{min}, & \text{if } y \leq y_{min} \\ y, & \text{if } y_{min} < y < y_{max} \\ y_{max}, & \text{if } y \geq y_{max} \end{cases}$$

The formula for this type of bending along the y

axis centerline is given by the following relations:

[*Equation   2.4a*]

$$X = x$$

$$Y = \begin{cases} -S_\theta(z - \tfrac{1}{k}) + y_0, & y_{min} \leq y \leq y_{max}, \\ -S_\theta(z - \tfrac{1}{k}) + y_0 + C_\theta(y - y_{min}), & y < y_{min} \\ -S_\theta(z - \tfrac{1}{k}) + y_0 + C_\theta(y - y_{max}), & y > y_{max} \end{cases}$$

$$Z = \begin{cases} C_\theta(z - \tfrac{1}{k}) + \tfrac{1}{k}, & y_{min} \leq y \leq y_{max}, \\ C_\theta(z - \tfrac{1}{k}) + \tfrac{1}{k} + S_\theta(y - y_{min}), & y < y_{min} \\ C_\theta(z - \tfrac{1}{k}) + \tfrac{1}{k} + S_\theta(y - y_{max}), & y > y_{max} \end{cases}$$

These functions have continuous values at the boundaries of each of the three regions for y, and in the limit, for $k = 0$. However, there is a jump in the derivative of the bending angle θ at the $y = y_{min}$ and $y = y_{max}$ boundaries. The discontinuities may be eliminated by using a smooth function for θ as a function of y, but the transformation matrices would need to be re-derived.

The tangent transformation matrix is given by:

$$\underline{\underline{J}} = \begin{pmatrix} 1 & 0 & 0 \\ 0 & C_\theta(1 - \hat{k}z) & -S_\theta \\ 0 & S_\theta(1 - \hat{k}z) & C_\theta \end{pmatrix}$$

where

$$\hat{k} = \begin{cases} k, & \text{if } \hat{y} = y \\ 0, & \text{if } \hat{y} \neq y. \end{cases}$$

The local rate of expansion, as obtained from the determinant, is $1 - \hat{k}z$.

The normal transformation matrix is given by:

$$(1 - \hat{k}z)\underline{\underline{J}}^{-1T} = \begin{pmatrix} 1 - \hat{k}z & 0 & 0 \\ 0 & C_\theta & -S_\theta(1 - \hat{k}z) \\ 0 & S_\theta & C_\theta(1 - \hat{k}z) \end{pmatrix}$$

The inverse transformation is given by:

[*Equation   2.4b*]

$$\theta_{min} = k(y_{min} - y_0)$$

$$\theta_{max} = k(y_{max} - y_0)$$

$$\hat{\theta} = -tan^{-1}\left(\frac{Y - y_0}{Z - \tfrac{1}{k}}\right)$$

$$\theta = \begin{cases} \theta_{min}, & \text{if } \theta < \hat{\theta}_{min} \\ \hat{\theta}, & \text{if } \theta_{min} \leq \hat{\theta} \leq \theta_{max} \\ \theta_{max}, & \text{if } \hat{\theta} > \theta_{max} \end{cases}$$

$$x = X$$

$$\hat{y} = \frac{\theta}{k} + y_0$$

$$y = \begin{cases} \hat{y}, & y_{min} < \hat{y} < y_{max} \\ (Y - y_0)C_\theta + (z - \frac{1}{k})S_\theta + \hat{y}, & \hat{y} = y_{min} \text{ or } y_{max} \end{cases}$$

$$z = \begin{cases} \frac{1}{k} + ((Y - y_0)^2 + (Z - \frac{1}{k})^2)^{1/2}, & y_{min} < \hat{y} < y_{max} \\ -(Y - y_0)S_\theta + (z - \frac{1}{k})C_\theta + \hat{y}, & \hat{y} = y_{min} \text{ or } y_{max} \end{cases}$$

Figure 2.4.2 Progressive Change in Bending Range of a Region

In figure 2.4.2, a constant 90° bend is produced by varying the range and the bend rate. In other words, $k(y_{max} - y_{min}) = \pi/2$ in each of the examples. In figure 2.4.3, a twisted object is subjected to a progressive bend to produce a Moebius band. Figures 2.4.4 a and b show a hierarchy of tapering, twisting, and bending, by superimposing a bend on the objects in figures 2.3.2 and 2.3.3. In figure 2.4.5, a chair is made from six primitives using seven bends. The details of the crimp in the coordinate systems is shown in figures 2.4.6 a - b.

However, the type of bending shown in the figures does not retain all of the generality that true bending requires. Some materials are anisotropic and have an intrinsic "grain" or directionality in them. Although this is beyond the scope of this paper, it is interesting to note that the tangent and normal transformation rules may still be utilized.

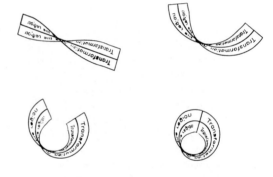

Figure 2.4.3 Moebius band is produced with a twist and a bend

Figure 2.4.4 a Bent, Twisted, Tapered Primitive

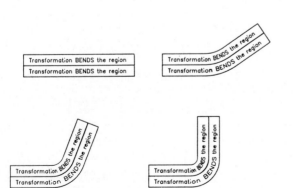

Figure 2.4.1 Progressive Bending of a Region

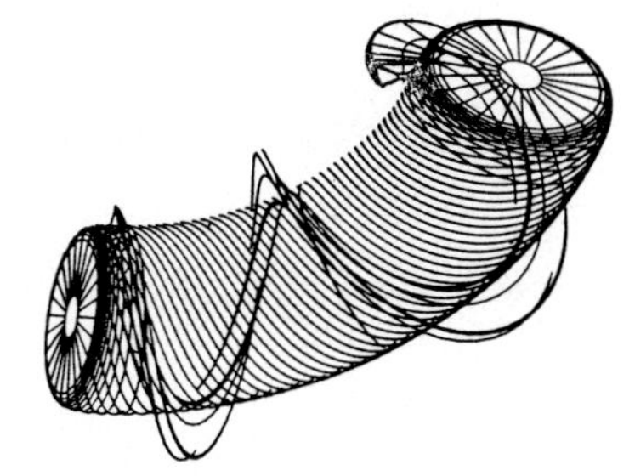

Figure 2.4.4 b Bent, Twisted Primitive

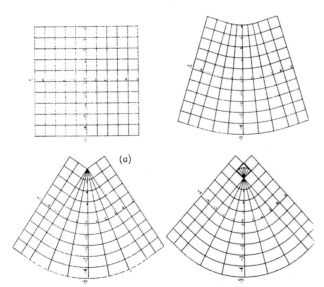

Figure 2.4.5 Chair Model, with six primitives and seven bends.

Figure 2.4.6 Details of the Bend near the Crimp

3.0 Converting Local Representations to Global Representations.

In this section, a method for generating more general shapes is addressed. The Jacobian matrix $\underline{\underline{J}}(\underline{x})$ is assumed to be known as a function of x_1, x_2, and x_3, but a closed form expression for the corresponding coordinate deformation function $\underline{X} = \underline{F}(\underline{x})$ is not known (i.e., in terms of standard mathematical functions). The basic method involves

(1) the conversion of the undeformed input shape into its tangent vectors by differentiation,

(2) transforming the tangent vectors via the tangent transformation rule into the tangent vectors of the deformed object, and then

(3) integrating the new tangent vectors to obtain the new position vectors of the deformed space curve, surface, or solid.

This "local-to-global" operation converts the local tangent vectors and Jacobian matrix into the global position vectors. The absolute position in space of the deformed object is defined within an arbitrary integration constant vector .

The above method provides a completely general description of deformation, and may be directly coupled to the output from the elasticity equations, finite element analysis, or other advanced mathematical models of deformable entities describing a profoundly general collection of shapes. The integrations outlined above need not be calculated explicitly in a ray-tracing environment: a multidimensional Newton's method can use the Jacobian matrix directly.

3.1 Transformations of Space Curves. Given a space curve, parameterized by a single variable s,

$$\underline{x} = \underline{x}(s), \quad s_0 \leq s \leq s_1$$

a new curve $\underline{X}(s)$ is desired which is the deformed version of $\underline{x}(s)$. The Jacobian matrix $\underline{\underline{J}}(s)$ or $\underline{\underline{J}}(\underline{x}(s))$ is assumed to be known, but the coordinate transformation function $\underline{X} = \underline{F}(\underline{x})$ is assumed to be unavailable. As stated above, the equation for $\underline{X}(s)$ may be derived from the fact that,

(1) by definition, the position $\underline{X}(s)$ is a constant vector plus the integral of the derivative of the position, i.e.,

[Equation   3.1a]

$$\underline{X}(s) = \int_0^s \underline{X}'(\tilde{s})d\tilde{s} + \underline{x}_0,$$

(2) the derivative of the position is obtained via the tangent transformation rule, Equation 1.2 a, so

[*Equation* 3.1*b*]

$$\underline{X}(s) = \int_0^s \underline{\underline{J}}(\underline{x}(\tilde{s}))\underline{x}'(\tilde{s})d\tilde{s} + x_0$$

where $\underline{J}(\underline{x}(s))$ is the Jacobian matrix which depends upon the value of s, and $\underline{x}'(s)$ is the arclength derivative (a tangent vector) of the input curve $\underline{x}(s)$. At each point in the untransformed curve, $\underline{x}(s)$, the tangent vectors $\underline{x}'(s)$ are rotated and skewed to a new orientation in the transformed curve: the curve can be bent and twisted with or without being being stretched. For this case, any matrix function which allows the integral to be evaluated may serve as a Jacobian, since there is only one path along which to integrate.

For inextensible bending and twisting transformations of the space curve, with no stretching at any point of the curve, the Jacobian matrix $\underline{J}(s)$ must be a varying rotation matrix function. (Even though this is not a constant affine rotation, the matrix function for the tangent vector transformation rule is identical to that used for the normal vector transformation rule.)

3.2 Transformations of 3-D surfaces and solids.
The representation of a transformed surface or solid can be obtained much in the same manner as a space curve. First, an origin $\underline{O}$ is chosen in the object to be deformed. For each point $\underline{x}$ in the surface of the object, a piecewise smooth space curve is chosen, which connects the origin $\underline{O}$ to the input point $\underline{x}$. The space curve is then subjected to the deformation as in section 3.1. If $\underline{J}(\underline{x})$ is in fact the Jacobian of some (unspecified) deformation function $\underline{X} = \underline{F}(\underline{x})$, the transformation from $\underline{x}$ to $\underline{X}$ is unique: all smooth paths connecting $\underline{O}$ and $\underline{x}$ will be equivalent. Since the equation of the surface is given by $\underline{x} = \underline{x}(u,v)$, the space curve in the surface may be obtained by selecting two functions of a single variable, say s, for u and for v. i.e.,

$$u = u(s)$$

$$v = v(s)$$

so that the space curve in the surface $\underline{\hat{x}}(s)$ is obtained by substituting the values of u and v into the equation for $\underline{x}$.

$$\underline{\hat{x}}(s) = \underline{x}(u(s), v(s))$$

This space curve is then transformed as shown above, in Equation 3.1 b. The space curve should be piecewise differentiable, so that the derivatives can be evaluated and integrated. The equation for the deformed curve is

[*Equation* 3.2.1]

$$\underline{X}(u(s), v(s)) =$$

$$\int_0^s \underline{\underline{J}}(\underline{x}(u(\hat{s}), v(\hat{s})))\underline{x}'(u(\hat{s}), v(\hat{s}))d\hat{s} + x_0$$

Expanding the above equation, using the fact that the symbol ′ means d/ds, and using the multidimensional chain rule, we obtain

$$\underline{X}(u(s), v(s)) =$$

$$\int_0^s \underline{\underline{J}}(\underline{x}(u(\hat{s}), v(\hat{s})))(\frac{\partial x}{\partial u}u'(\hat{s}) + \frac{\partial x}{\partial v}v'(\hat{s}))d\hat{s} + x_0$$

As stated before, for consistency, $\underline{J}$ must be the Jacobian matrix of some global function $\underline{F}(\underline{x})$, so that the results are independent of the path connecting $\underline{O}$ and $\underline{x}$, and so that the tangent and normal vector transformation rules apply. The test for the "Jacobian-ness" of the matrix, (in the absence of a pre-specified deformation function $\underline{F}(\underline{x})$) depends on the partial derivatives of the columns of $\underline{J}(\underline{x})$

The columns must satisfy

$$\underline{J}_{i,j} = \underline{J}_{j,i} \qquad [\textit{Equation} \quad 3.2.2]$$

In other words, the partial derivative of the ith column of $\underline{J}$ with respect to x_j must be equal to the partial derivative of the jth column of $\underline{J}$ with respect to x_i. (The underlying principle to prove this result is a multiple-integration path consistency requirement. The integrand must be an exact differential.) The values of the Jacobian may be directly related to the material properties of the substance to be modeled, and may utilize the plasticity and elasticity equations.

4.0 Applications to Rendering

To obtain a set of control points and normal vectors with which to create surface patches like polygons or spline patches, we sample the deformed surface parametrically, With the appropriate sampling, the patches can faithfully tesselate the desired object, with more detail where the surface is highly curved, and less detail where the surface is flat.

First, the object is sampled with a raw grid of parametric *u-v* values. This raw parametric sampling of the surface is then refined using normal vector criteria, as calculated by the transformation rule: the surface is recursively subdivided when the adjacent normal vectors diverge too greatly. Dot products which are far enough from unity indicate that more recursive detail is necessary in that region.

In this way, patch-oriented methods like depth-buffer and scan-line encoding schemes are effective. These algorithms are linear in terms of the total surface area and total number of patches. The direct subdivison approach is not as well-suited to ray tracing, since the total number of operations is quadratic in the number of ray comparisons and objects.

The incident ray can be intersected with the deformed primitive analytically, to reduce the number of objects. In addition, it is possible to use the inverse deformation to undeform the primitives and trace along the deformed rays. (See figures 4.1 and 4.2). This reduces the dimensionality of the parameter search from three to one, indicating a tremendous saving in numerical complexity.

The Jacobian techniques in this paper aid the traditional solution methods to find roots of non-linear ray equations (in the context of ray-tracing deformed objects), including the multidimensional Newton-Raphson method, the method of regula falsi, and the one-dimensional Newton's methods in N-space. (See [ACTON].) The analysis of rendering deformed primitives using these techniques is left to a future study.

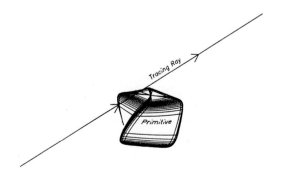

Figure 4.1 Deformed primitive, in undeformed space.

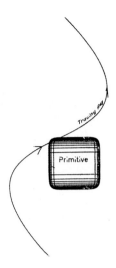

Figure 4.2 Undeformed primitive, in its undeformed coordinate system, showing path of ray

Appendix A:
Proof of the normal vector transformation rule.

A short derivation in cross product and dot product style demonstrates the normal vector transformation rule.

The surface of an undeformed object is given by a parametric function of two variables u and v, $\underline{x} = \underline{x}(u, v)$. The goal is to discover an expression for the normal vector to the surface after it has been subjected to the deformation $\underline{X} = \underline{F}(\underline{x})$.

We note that the inverse of an arbitrary three by three matrix $\underline{\underline{M}}$ may be obtained from the cross-products of pairs of its columns via:

$$[\underline{M}_1, \underline{M}_2, \underline{M}_3]^{-1} = \frac{[\underline{M}_2 \wedge \underline{M}_3, \underline{M}_3 \wedge \underline{M}_1, \underline{M}_1 \wedge \underline{M}_2]^T}{\underline{M}_1 \cdot (\underline{M}_2 \wedge \underline{M}_3)}.$$

We start the derivation using the fact that the normal vector is the cross product of independent surface tangent vectors:

$$\underline{n}^{(X)} = \frac{\partial \underline{X}}{\partial u} \wedge \frac{\partial \underline{X}}{\partial v} \qquad [Equation \quad B.1d]$$

The tangent vectors for $\underline{X}(u, v)$ are expanded in terms of $\underline{x}(s, t)$.

$$\underline{n}^{(X)} = \left(\underline{\underline{J}} \frac{\partial \underline{x}}{\partial u} \right) \wedge \left(\underline{\underline{J}} \frac{\partial \underline{x}}{\partial v} \right)$$

Matrix multiplication is expanded, yielding

$$\underline{n}^{(X)} = \left(\sum_{i=1}^{3} \underline{J}_i x_{i,u} \right) \wedge \left(\sum_{j=1}^{3} \underline{J}_j x_{j,v} \right)$$

The summations are combined together:

$$= \sum_{i=1}^{3} \sum_{j=1}^{3} \left(\underline{J}_i \wedge \underline{J}_j \right) x_{i,s} x_{j,t}$$

Since the cross product of a vector with itself is the zero vector, and since for any vectors $\underline{b}$ and $\underline{c}$, $\underline{b} \wedge \underline{c} = -\underline{c} \wedge \underline{b}$, this expands to:

$$\underline{n}^{(X)} = \left(\underline{J}_2 \wedge \underline{J}_3, \underline{J}_3 \wedge \underline{J}_1, \underline{J}_1 \wedge \underline{J}_2 \right) \begin{pmatrix} x_{2,u} x_{3,v} - x_{3,u} x_{2,v} \\ x_{3,u} x_{1,v} - x_{1,u} x_{3,v} \\ x_{1,s} x_{2,v} - x_{2,u} x_{1,v} \end{pmatrix}$$

Thus,

$$\underline{n}^{(X)} = [\underline{J}_2 \wedge \underline{J}_3, \underline{J}_3 \wedge \underline{J}_1, \underline{J}_1 \wedge \underline{J}_2] \underline{n}^{(x)}$$

Since $\det \underline{\underline{M}} = \underline{M}_1 \cdot (\underline{M}_2 \wedge \underline{M}_3)$ for an arbitrary matrix $\underline{\underline{M}}$,

$$\underline{n}^{(X)} = \det J \underline{\underline{J}}^{-1T} \underline{n}^{(x)}$$

In other words, the new normal vector $\underline{n}^{(X)}$ is expressed as a multiplication of matrix $\underline{\underline{J}}^{-1T}$ and the old normal vector $\underline{n}^{(x)}$.

Since only the direction of the normal vector is important, it is not necessary to compute the value of the determinant in practice, unless one needs the local volume ratio between corresponding points in the deformed and undeformed objects.

The fact that the normal vector follows this type of transformation rule makes it less expensive to calculate, increasing its applicability in a variety of modeling circumstances.

Acknowledgements

I would like to thank Dan Whelan, of the California Institute of Technology, and Olin Lathrop, of Raster Technologies Inc., for technical help with the typography and the illustrations.

Bibliography

1. Acton, F.S., Numerical Methods that Work, Harper and Row, 1970.

2. Barr, A.H., "Superquadrics and Angle-Preserving Transformations," IEEE Computer Graphics and Applications, Volume 1 number 1 1981.

3. Buck, R. C., Advanced Calculus, McGraw-Hill, 2nd edition, 1965

4. Faux, I.D., and M.J. Pratt, Computational Geometry for Design and Manufacture, Ellis Horwood Ltd., Wiley and Sons, 1979.

5. Franklin, W.R., and A.H. Barr, "Faster Calculation of Superquadric Shapes," IEEE Computer Graphics and Applications, Volume 1 number 3, 1981.

6. Kajiya, J.T., "Ray Tracing Parametric Patches," SigGraph 82 Conference Proceedings, Computer Graphics, Volume 16, Number 3, 1982.

7. Segel, L.A., Mathematics Applied to Continuum Mechanics, Macmillan Publishing Co., 1977.

8. Solkolnikoff, I.S., Mathematical Theory of Elasticity, McGraw Hill, 1956.

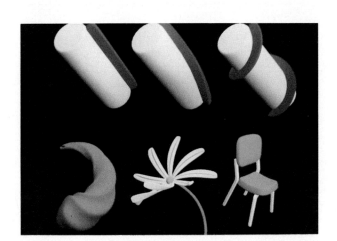

PANEL

COMPUTER-INTEGRATED MANUFACTURING IN JAPAN

CHAIR: Tosiyasu L. Kunii - University of Tokyo
PANEL: Naomasa Nakajima - University of Tokyo
         Takeaki Kubo - Hitachi, Ltd.
         Kazuo Nakagawa - Mitsui Engineering & Shipbuilding
                                   Co., Ltd.
         Hajime Inaba - GM Fanuc Robotics Co., Ltd.
         Ikuo Nishioka - Sharp Co., Ltd.

Recent progress in Japanese computer-integrated manufacturing (CIM) includes the integration of computer graphics, data base management systems, local area networks, robotics and software engineering technology. This panel will discuss advanced CAD, CAM CAT (computer-aided testing) and FMS (flexible manufacturing systems) available in Japan.

After the overview by the Chair Prof. Kunii, the basic CIM related researches to support industrial applications will be explained by Prof. Nakajima of the University of Tokyo. A wide spectrum of recent industrial advances and future trends in Japanese CIM are covered by four panelists from reputed manufacturers and users of CIM facilities and equipments. As one of the features of Japanese CIM, it will be noticed throughout the panel presentations and discussions that manufacturers always send out their products into the market after extensive internal use of them. Mr. Kubo of Hitachi Omika Work will present new networked CIM workstation. A typical example of very large CIM will be shown by Mr. Nakagawa of Mitsui Engineering and Shipbuilding. Very aggressive lines of products and plans are expected from Fanuc and will be presented by Mr. Inaba of GM Fanuc Robotics. Mr. Nishioka of Sharp will conclude the session explaining how he has developed and marketed very practical CIM successfully.

Interpolating Splines with Local Tension, Continuity, and Bias Control

Doris H. U. Kochanek

Computer Motion Graphics Centre
National Film Board of Canada
Box 6100, Station A, P-36
Montreal, Quebec, Canada, H3C 3H5
(514) 333-3434

Richard H. Bartels

Computer Graphics Laboratory
University of Waterloo
Waterloo, Ontario, Canada N2L 3G1
(519) 886-1351

Abstract

This paper presents a new method for using cubic interpolating splines in a key frame animation system. Three control parameters allow the animator to change the tension, continuity, and bias of the splines. Each of these three parameters can be used for either local or global control. Our technique produces a very general class of interpolating cubic splines which includes the cardinal splines as a proper subset.

CR Categories and Subject Descriptors: G.1.1 [**Numerical Analysis**]: Interpolation – *spline and piecewise polynomial interpolation*; I.3.5 [**Computer Graphics**]: Computational Geometry and Object Modeling – *curve, surface, solid and object representations*; I.3.7 [**Computer Graphics**]: Three-Dimensional Graphics and Realism – *animation*.

General Terms: algorithms

Additional Key Words and Phrases: key frames, inbetweening, bias, continuity, tension

Permission to copy without fee all or part of this material is granted provided that the copies are not made or distributed for direct commercial advantage, the ACM copyright notice and the title of the publication and its date appear, and notice is given that copying is by permission of the Association for Computing Machinery. To copy otherwise, or to republish, requires a fee and/or specific permission.

© 1984   ACM   0-89791-138-5/84/007/0033 $00.75

1. Introduction

One of the oldest techniques used in computer animation is the automatic generation of *inbetweens* (intermediate frames) based on a set of *key frames* supplied by the animator [5]. This same principle is frequently used in computer assisted 3-D animation where camera and object positions are defined only at key points in the animation, leaving the calculation of intermediate positions to the computer. The straightforward *linear interpolation* algorithm used in many systems produces some undesirable side effects which give the animation a mechanical look, often referred to as the "computer signature." The most objectionable characteristic of this type of animation is the lack of smoothness in the motion. The key frames may be clearly visible in the animation because of sudden changes in the direction of motion (Figure 1).

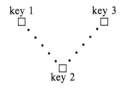

Figure 1. Discontinuity in direction with linear interpolation

Discontinuities in the speed of motion may also be visible with linear interpolation, for example when the animator requests a different number of frames between successive keys (Figure 2).

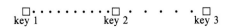

Figure 2. Discontinuity in speed with linear interpolation

A third common problem is distortion, which may occur whenever the movement has a rotational component (Figure 3).

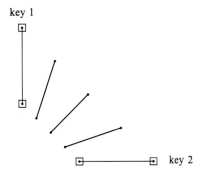

key 1

key 2

Figure 3. Distortion in length when rotation is simulated linearly.

In view of these serious drawbacks of linear interpolation, a number of different methods which produce smoother motion have been published. These techniques include *P-curves* [1], *skeletons* [6], *action overlap* [11], and *moving point constraints* [9]. All of these techniques require the animator to specify additional information other than just the key frames. A completely automatic system which uses only the key positions supplied by the animator was implemented by one of the authors [8]. The approach used there was based on fitting a set of interpolating splines through the key positions, resulting in much smoother animation than can be produced with linear interpolation.

2. Interpolating Splines

We assume that each of the objects in the ith key frame in a sequence can be described by a collection of *points*. (As an example, the two designated endpoints of the line segment in key 1 shown in Figure 3 completely define the segment.) We assume that to each point in one key frame there will be a corresponding point in all other key frames of a motion sequence. (For example, the same two endpoints reappear in key 2 of Figure 3 to specify a later position of the line segment.) These assumptions are not as restrictive as they may appear to be. Even quite complicated curved objects can be expressed in terms of small numbers of *control points* using the techniques described in, for example, [7]. For the purposes of the discussion, we will fix our attention on one such point, designated P_i and referred to as the *key position*, in the ith key frame:

$$P_i = (x_i, y_i, z_i)$$

(We will carry on the discussion in terms of 3-D animation.) Given a sequence of corresponding key positions,

$$\cdots, P_{i-1}, P_i, P_{i+1}, \cdots$$

we want to interpolate them using a simple smooth curve. For sufficient generality to handle the multi-valued case, all curves will be treated parametrically as

$$P(s) = (x(s), y(s), z(s))$$

where s varies from 0 to 1 between each two key frames. Thus, we want to find smooth functions $x(s)$, $y(s)$, and $z(s)$ so that, for example,

$$P(0) = (x(0), y(0), z(0)) = (x_i, y_i, z_i) = P_i$$

and

$$P(1) = (x(1), y(1), z(1)) = (x_{i+1}, y_{i+1}, z_{i+1}) = P_{i+1}$$

on the interval between the ith and $i+1^{st}$ key frames. The positions of the inbetween frames which will correspond to the key position in question, then, will be $P(s)$ for $s = \Delta, 2 \cdot \Delta, \cdots 1 - \Delta$ for

$$\Delta = \frac{1}{N_i} + 1$$

where N_i is the number of inbetweens to be generated between the key frame containing P_i and the key frame containing P_{i+1}. Polynomials are a natural choice for the smooth functions because of their simplicity, but using a single interpolating polynomial of high degree for the entire sequence could result in motion which oscillates about the path we expect the animation to follow. A more "natural" fit of the key positions can be obtained by interpolating them with a cubic spline, a curve consisting of a succession of different cubic polynomial segments which are joined together with certain continuity constraints.

Each cubic polynomial extends between two key positions and is uniquely defined by four coefficients which we can determine from four independent constraints. Two constraints are given directly by the interpolation conditions: the spline segment must pass through the key positions at the start and the end of the interval. This leaves two free constraints which we can choose. The choice which defines the most commonly used form of cubic spline imposes first and second derivative continuity at the keys, but this approach is computationally expensive and quite inflexible. Instead, we choose to specify tangent vectors at the two adjacent keys to define each spline segment. In our notation the tangent vector to the curve we wish to construct through key position P_i is given by

$$D_i = \left(\frac{dx}{ds}, \frac{dy}{ds}, \frac{dz}{ds} \right)$$

No conditions will be imposed on second derivatives.

By default, we determine appropriate tangent vectors from the geometry of the surrounding keys. This approach can be generalized to produce a very flexible class of cubic splines by the introduction of control parameters which modify the length and direction of the tangent vectors.

Any cubic polynomial can be expressed as a scaled sum of four basis functions. Frequently these functions are taken to be the monomials s^3, s^2, s, 1, however, for our purposes the *Hermite interpolation basis functions* shown in Figure 4 are more useful.

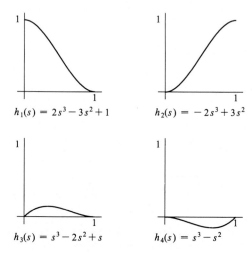

$$h_1(s) = 2s^3 - 3s^2 + 1 \qquad h_2(s) = -2s^3 + 3s^2$$

$$h_3(s) = s^3 - 2s^2 + s \qquad h_4(s) = s^3 - s^2$$

Figure 4. Basis functions for Hermite interpolation.

These functions have the following convenient properties:

	h_1	h_2	h_3	h_4
function value at $s=0$	1	0	0	0
function value at $s=1$	0	1	0	0
derivative at $s=0$	0	0	1	0
derivative at $s=1$	0	0	0	1

Note that h_1 alone determines the function value of the composite cubic at the start of the interval. Therefore, h_1 can be scaled with a coefficient of P_i to obtain the desired point P_i at $s=0$. Similarly, h_2 can be scaled with P_{i+1}. The derivative of the composite cubic is determined by h_3 at the start and by h_4 at the end of the interval, therefore D_i and D_{i+1}, the desired derivatives at the interval ends, can be used as scaling factors for h_3 and h_4. These observations lead to a triplet of cubic polynomials given by

$$P(s) = (x(s), y(s), z(s))$$
$$= P_i \cdot h_1(s) + P_{i+1} \cdot h_2(s) + D_i \cdot h_3(s) + D_{i+1} \cdot h_4(s)$$

Equation 1. Parametric cubic curve using the h basis.

In matrix form this expression reduces to

$$P(s) = \mathbf{s} \cdot \mathbf{h} \cdot \mathbf{C}$$

$$= \begin{bmatrix} s^3 & s^2 & s & 1 \end{bmatrix} \cdot \begin{bmatrix} 2 & -2 & 1 & 1 \\ -3 & 3 & -2 & -1 \\ 0 & 0 & 1 & 0 \\ 1 & 0 & 0 & 0 \end{bmatrix} \cdot \begin{bmatrix} P_i \\ P_{i+1} \\ D_i \\ D_{i+1} \end{bmatrix}$$

Equation 2. Matrix format for parametric cubics using the h basis.

Note that the vector $\mathbf{s}$ only changes from one frame in the animation to the next. Within a given frame it applies to the x, y, and z components of all key positions which are being interpolated. The matrix $\mathbf{h}$ contains the coefficients of the Hermite interpolation basis functions and is therefore constant for all frames and all key positions. In practice, $\mathbf{s} \cdot \mathbf{h}$ is calculated only once per frame. By contrast, each $\mathbf{C}$, which is a 4×3 matrix, corresponds to a single key position and is independent of the $\mathbf{C}$ associated with any of the other key positions being interpolated. It does not change from one frame to another (except at a key frame), and the independence implies that all key positions can be interpolated "in parallel".

3. A General Class of Interpolating Cubic Splines

Using this formulation as a framework, the remaining open question is how to find "appropriate" values for the components of D_i and D_{i+1}, the tangent vectors at the key positions, needed to fully specify $P(s)$. [10] describes the approach used for a class of cubic splines which are commonly called *cardinal splines*. Even though cardinal splines are not usually formulated in terms of the Hermite interpolation basis functions, the tangent vectors at the key positions are used to constrain the cubic segments. The tangent vector at P_i is calculated as $D_i = a \cdot (P_{i+1} - P_{i-1})$, where a is a constant which affects the tightness of the curve. A particular example of this class of splines is the Catmull-Rom spline for which $a = \frac{1}{2}$. Thus the tangent vector for the Catmull-Rom spline is

$$D_i = \frac{1}{2} \cdot (P_{i+1} - P_{i-1}) = \frac{1}{2} \cdot \left((P_{i+1} - P_i) + (P_i - P_{i-1}) \right)$$

Equation 3. The Catmull-Rom spline.

which is simply the average of the *source chord* $P_i - P_{i-1}$ and the *destination chord* $P_{i+1} - P_i$. The technique presented in this paper uses this average of adjacent chords as the default tangent vector. Thus our default spline, even though formulated differently, is exactly the Catmull-Rom spline (Figure 5).

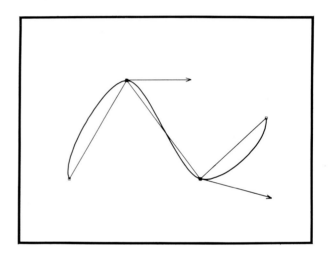

Figure 5. The Catmull-Rom spline.

At the beginning of a motion sequence some arbitrary choice for the source chord (e.g. (0,0,0)) must be made. Similarly, the destination chord must be specified arbitrarily at the end of the sequence. Alternatively a specification of the tangent beginning and ending vectors can be made without regard to any chords. Setting $D = (0,0,0)$ was tried with some success in [8].

A "standard" smooth motion through a given set of keys does not always produce the effect desired by the animator. In certain cases he may want the motion to follow a wider, more exaggerated curve, while in other cases he may want the motion path to be much tighter, maybe almost linear. Even continuity in the direction and speed of motion is not necessarily desirable at all times. Animating a bouncing ball, for example, actually requires the introduction of a discontinuity in the motion at the point of impact.

The research described in this paper replaces the standard interpolating spline used in [8] by a highly flexible class of cubic splines which interpolate the same key positions but vary in several control parameters. These three parameters, *tension, continuity* and *bias*, allow the animator to fine-tune the animated sequence by changing certain characteristics of the "standard" interpolating spline either locally (applying only in the vicinity of a specific key frame), or globally (applying to the entire motion sequence). The introduction of these three control parameters produces a highly flexible class of interpolating cubic splines which include the cardinal splines as a proper subset.

The concepts of tension and bias have been introduced before in connection with *approximating splines* in [2], [3], [4]. Our use of the term "bias" is similar to the concept being used by the authors of these references. The concept of "tension" which we are using is different, however. Their use of the word "tension" refers to an effect produced by adjusting the match between the second derivatives of adjoining polynomial segments, and we are exercising control only over first derivatives. We are able to produce visually similar effects, however, and so have chosen to borrow the use of their term. An excellent introduction to the theory of interpolating and approximating splines for computer animation can be found in [10].

The three control parameters tension, continuity, and bias are introduced by the convention of separating each tangent at the ith key position into an *incoming* and an *outgoing* part, respectively the *source derivative* DS_i and the *destination derivative* DD_i as indicated in Figure 6.

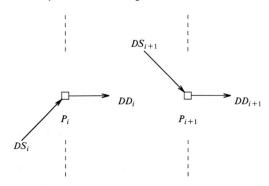

Figure 6. Incoming and outgoing tangents of two key positions.

These replace the single derivative D of the Catmull–Rom spline (Equation 3). Furthermore, the average $a = \frac{1}{2}$ of Equation 3 is relaxed in favor of a more selective average of the source and destination chord.

In the following three sections we will treat each of these three parameters independently of the other two. Then the three will be tied together in a fourth section.

3.1. Tension

The tension parameter t controls how sharply the curve bends at a key position (Figure 7).

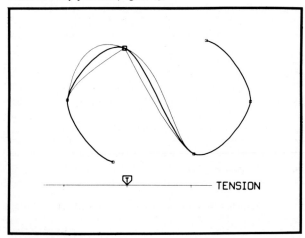

Figure 7. Bending of the curve under various tensions.

Tension is implemented as a scale factor which changes the length of both the incoming and outgoing parts of the tangent vector equally at a key position:

$$DS_i = DD_i = (1-t)\cdot\frac{1}{2}\cdot\left((P_{i+1}-P_i)+(P_i-P_{i-1})\right)$$

Equation 4. Tension equation.

For the default curve $t = 0$, and the tangent vector is the average of the two adjacent chords (Figure 8).

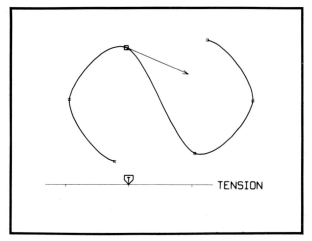

Figure 8. Default tension.

Increasing the tension to $t = 1$ reduces the length of the tangent vector to zero and thus tightens the curve (Figure 9).

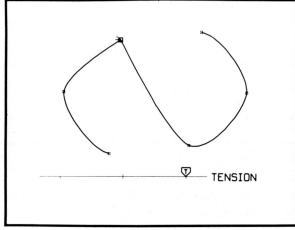

Figure 9. The effect of increasing the tension parameter.

Reducing the tension to $t = -1$ increases the tangent vector to twice its default length and produces more slack in the curve (Figure 10).

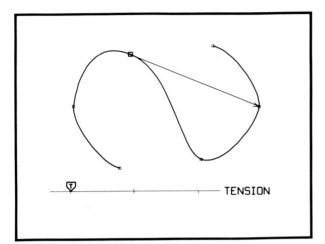

Figure 10. The effect of reducing the tension parameter.

If the same value of t is applied to all key positions in the sequence, varying t generates the entire class of cardinal splines with $a = \frac{1-t}{2}$ (Figure 11).

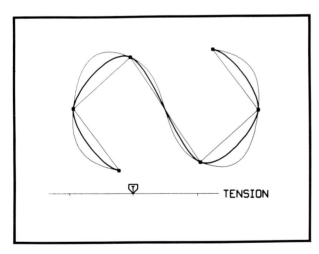

Figure 11. Several tension values applied uniformly to all keys.

The default case ($t = 0$) is equivalent to the Catmull-Rom spline, where $a = \frac{1}{2}$.

3.2. Continuity

The principal reason for using splines in key frame animation is to avoid discontinuities in the direction and speed of motion which are produced by linear interpolation. However, in animation discontinuities are sometimes necessary to create realistic effects such as punching, bouncing, etc. A common technique to introduce such a discontinuity into an otherwise continuous spline is to repeat a key position or to simply terminate the spline at a key and start an entirely independent spline to interpolate the next sequence of key frames.

Neither of these approaches is very satisfactory because the discontinuity cannot be controlled. While it is true that, mathematically speaking, a spline's derivative is either continuous or discontinuous, the artist's view is quite different. He would like to have more control over continuity than a simple on/off switch. In fact, from the animator's point of view two curve segments which have very different tangent vectors at their joint appear "more discontinuous" than two curve segments which have fairly similar tangent vectors. This concept is implemented in our system as a parameter which controls the continuity/discontinuity at a key position (Figure 12).

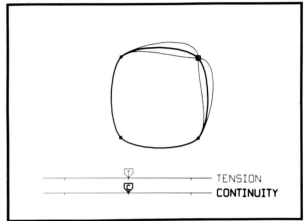

Figure 12. The effect of varying the continuity parameter.

Assuming default tension and using c to denote the continuity parameter, we allow the source and destination components of the tangent vector to differ from each other according to:

$$DS_i = \left(\frac{1-c}{2} \cdot (P_i - P_{i-1}) + \frac{1+c}{2} \cdot (P_{i+1} - P_i) \right)$$

Equation 5. The "incoming" continuity equation.

$$DD_i = \left(\frac{1+c}{2} \cdot (P_i - P_{i-1}) + \frac{1-c}{2} \cdot (P_{i+1} - P_i) \right)$$

Equation 6. The "outgoing" continuity equation.

Note that with $c = 0$ (which we use as a default) we obtain $DS_i = DD_i$, which produces a spline with tangent vector continuity at the keys (Figure 13).

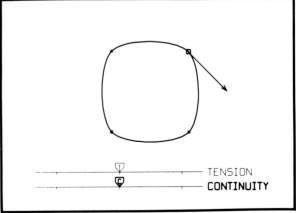

Figure 13. Default continuity.

As $|c|$ increases, the two tangent vectors become increasingly distinct. When $c=-1$, the source tangent vector DS_i reduces to the source chord, and the destination tangent vector DD_i is the destination chord, producing a pronounced corner in the curve (Figure 14).

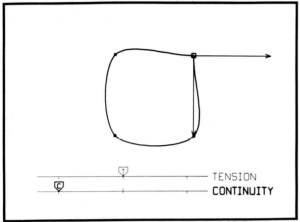

Figure 14. The effect of decreasing the continuity parameter.

Going in the opposite direction, at $c=1$, $DS_i = P_{i+1} - P_i$ and $DD_i = P_i - P_{i-1}$, produces a corner pointing in the opposite direction (Figure 15).

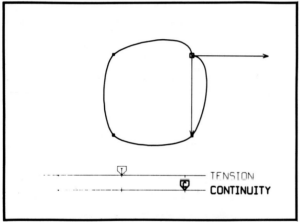

Figure 15. The effect of increasing the continuity parameter.

In Figure 16 some results of applying the same value of c to all key positions are depicted.

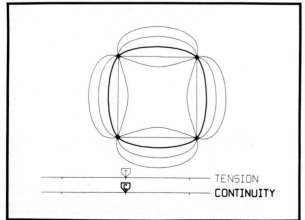

Figure 16. Several continuity values applied uniformly to all keys.

Looking only at the *path* of motion, the effects of increasing the tension or reducing the continuity seem to be rather similar (Figures 17 and 18).

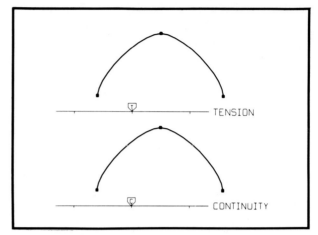

Figure 17. Default tension and continuity.

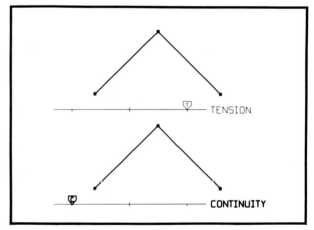

Figure 18. Increasing tension, reducing continuity.

However, the *motion dynamics* are quite different (Figure 19).

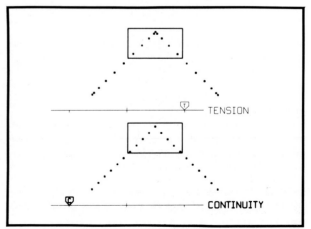

Figure 19. Differences in motion: tension vs. continuity.

Increasing the tension does *not* introduce discontinuities in the velocity. Instead the length of the tangent vector, and therefore the speed, is eventually reduced to zero. By contrast, reducing the continuity produces an abrupt change in the direction of motion at the key position while the speed remains constant. This effect is often necessary to create realistic animation. For example, to make the movement of a ball careening off a tree look convincing, the animator must introduce a sharp corner in the path as the ball hits the tree. Increasing the tension would produce a corner in the path, but the speed at this corner would be zero, resulting in a *deceleration* before the ball actually hits. Reducing the continuity would produce the desired abrupt change, with the ball altering its direction of motion at the point of impact without slowing down ahead of time.

Generating the appropriate motion dynamics is extremely important in animation. If we look only at the motion path, the use of maximum tension appears to generate a discontinuity. However, this effect is simply a *geometric* discontinuity. What is needed in the case of the ball's encounter with the tree is a *parametric* discontinuity, a sudden change in the magnitude and/or direction of the velocity. This effect cannot be achieved by changing the tension because the tangent vector will always remain continuous under such a change, thus guaranteeing parametric continuity.

3.3. Bias

The bias parameter b controls the direction of the path as it passes through a key position (Figure 20).

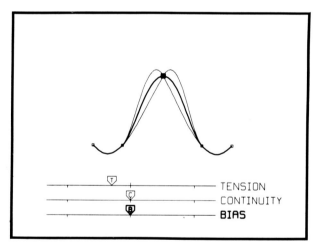

Figure 20. The behaviour of a curve under changing bias.

Both incoming and outgoing parts of the tangent are formed as an average of the incoming and outgoing chords, but the bias assigns different weights to the two chords when forming the average. Assuming default tension and continuity ($t = c = 0$), the tangent vector is given by:

$$DS_i = DD_i = \frac{1+b}{2}\cdot(P_i - P_{i-1}) + \frac{1-b}{2}\cdot(P_{i+1} - P_i)$$

Equation 7. The bias equation.

Note that with $b = 0$ the two chords are weighted equally, and we obtain the default spline shown in Figure 21. When $b = -1$, the tangent vector is completely determined by the destination chord (Figure 22),

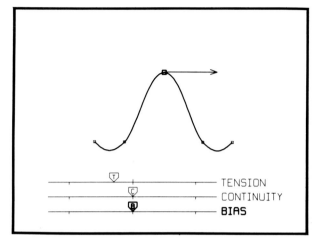

Figure 21. Default bias.

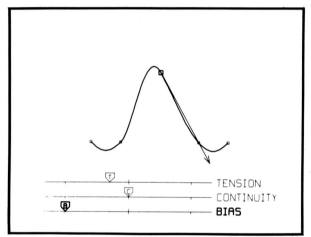

Figure 22. Bias set to -1.

whereas with $b = 1$ it is completely determined by the source chord (Figure 23).

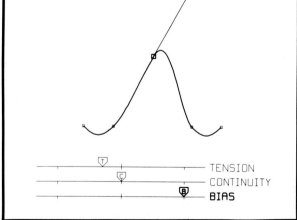

Figure 23. Bias set to +1.

The bias parameter easily simulates the traditional animation effect of following through after an action by "overshooting" the key position ($b = 1$), or exaggerating a movement by "undershooting" a key position ($b = -1$).

3.4. Composite Control

Combining the tension, continuity, and bias control parameters we obtain the following general equations for the source and destination tangent vectors at the key position P_i:

$$DS_i = \frac{(1-t)\cdot(1-c)\cdot(1+b)}{2} \cdot (P_i - P_{i-1})$$
$$+ \frac{(1-t)\cdot(1+c)\cdot(1-b)}{2} \cdot (P_{i+1} - P_i)$$

Equation 8. The "incoming" composite equation.

$$DD_i = \frac{(1-t)\cdot(1+c)\cdot(1+b)}{2} \cdot (P_i - P_{i-1})$$
$$+ \frac{(1-t)\cdot(1-c)\cdot(1-b)}{2} \cdot (P_{i+1} - P_i)$$

Equation 9. The "outgoing" composite equation.

The spline segment between P_i and P_{i+1} can now be defined in terms of P_i, P_{i+1}, DD_i, and DS_{i+1}. All inbetween positions within this interval can then be generated by using Equation 2, varying the interpolation parameter s from 0 to 1 over the interval.

4. Adjustments for Parameter Step Size

If we assume default continuity ($c = 0$) at key P_i, the spline segment between P_i and P_{i+1} should join smoothly with the segment used between P_{i-1} and P_i. While this is true when looking only at the path of the motion, it may not necessarily be true for the speed of motion. The formulas given in Equation 8 and Equation 9 assume an equal time spacing of key frames, implying an equal number of inbetweens within each key interval. A problem can exist if the animator requests a different number of inbetweens for adjacent intervals. Consider the case where 10 inbetweens are supposed to be generated in the interval from P_{i-1} to P_i, but only 5 inbetweens between P_i and P_{i+1} as was shown in Figure 2. In the first interval, the step size for the interpolation parameter s will be $\Delta_1 = \frac{1}{11}$ whereas for the second interval the step size will be $\Delta_2 = \frac{1}{6}$. If the same parametric derivative is used for both splines at P_i, these different step sizes will cause a discontinuity in the speed of motion. What is required, if this discontinuity is not intentional, is a means of making a local adjustment to the interval separating successive frames before and after the key frame so that the speed of entry matches the speed of exit. This can be accomplished by adjusting the specification of the tangent vector at the key frame based on the number of inbetweens in the adjacent intervals. In practice this turns out to be very simple, because we have already made provisions for two distinct tangent vectors at each key position in order to accommodate the continuity control parameter. Once the tangent vectors have been found for an equal number of inbetweens in the adjacent intervals, the adjustment required for different numbers of inbetweens (N_{i-1} frames between P_{i-1} and P_i followed by N_i frames between P_i and P_{i+1}) can be made by weighting the tangent vectors appropriately:

$$\text{adjusted } DD_i = DD_i \cdot \frac{2 \cdot N_{i-1}}{N_{i-1} + N_i}$$

$$\text{adjusted } DS_i = DS_i \cdot \frac{2 \cdot N_i}{N_{i-1} + N_i}$$

Equation 10. Adjustment for parameter stepsize.

5. Current Experience and Future Developments

The tension, continuity, and bias parameters were designed to correspond closely to traditional animation effects. These ideas were tested and refined using a simple interactive spline display package. In one test we asked the animators to interactively modify the three control parameters until a spline passing through a set of key positions looked "natural" to them. We found that most animators left the continuity and bias at their defaults (c=0, b=0) but reduced the tension parameter. The tension values which animators considered to produce a "natural" looking curve for a given set of keys ranged from -0.1 to -0.4. It was interesting to note that while there was some disagreement between animators about the "best" tension value, each animator was surprisingly consistent in his choice.

These individual preferences are most likely related to differences in personal style. For example, some animators tend to animate movements more tightly (larger tension value) than others. This indicates that the tension is especially useful as a global default parameter which the animator can define according to his style preference. The continuity and bias parameters are mostly used in a local context, i.e. to achieve a particular effect at a specific key position. In practice, a small number of parameter combinations will probably be sufficient for most sequences. Several animators noted that the system should **include but not be limited to** a small set of predefined effects (e.g. "overshoot": t=-0.3, c=0, b=1). They still wanted to have the full power and flexibility of the three independent parameters available for more advanced users.

The algorithm described in this paper is currently being implemented at the National Film Board of Canada (free-form drawn 2-D and 2 1/2-D multiplane key frames) and the University of Waterloo (3-D key positions with skeleton control). These implementations will be used to test various user interface strategies for both inexperienced and advanced users.

6. Summary

The introduction of tension, continuity, and bias control produces a very general class of interpolating cubic splines. The flexibility which these parameters provide is especially useful in key frame animation, because it allows the animator to adjust the movement of objects without having to adjust or redraw the key frames (Figure 24).

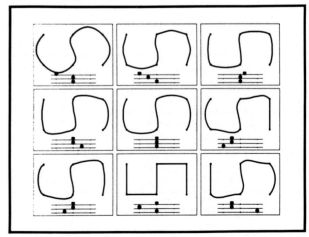

Figure 24. The effect of various parameter settings used together.

We have provided these control parameters by a simple technique of separating the tangent vector at each key frame into an incoming and an outgoing part and specifying these parts as a weighted average of the chords defined by the nearest neighbor key frames. Our system has the additional benefit that it can make adjustments to overcome speed discontinuities when the number of inbetweens is changed between key frames.

7. Acknowledgements

Feedback from animators is particularly important in a project such as this. We would especially like to thank Robert Forget, Rene Jodoin, Daniel Langlois, and Marc Aubry from the French Animation Studio of the National Film Board of Canada who as "test users" made many valuable suggestions which helped to clarify and refine our ideas.

Most of the illustrations in this paper are frames from the film "Interpolating Splines with Variable Tension, Continuity, and Bias" (National Film Board of Canada, 1984). We gratefully acknowledge the assistance of the Defence and Civil Institute of Environmental Medicine, Toronto, in the filming of this production.

This research was supported in part by the National Film Board of Canada, the National Sciences and Engineering Research Council of Canada, the Province of Ontario's BILD program, the University of Waterloo, and the Computer Graphics Laboratory.

8. Bibliography

[1]   R. Baecker, "Interactive Computer-Mediated Animation", PhD Thesis, MIT, Project MAC Technical Report MAC-TR-61, 1969.

[2]   B. Barsky, "The Beta-spline: A Local Representation Based on Shape Parameters and Fundamental Geometric Measures", Ph. D. dissertation, Department of Computer Science, University of Utah, December, 1981.

[3]   B. Barsky and J. Beatty, "Local Control of Bias and Tension in Beta-Splines", *Computer Graphics (SIGGRAPH '83)*, **17** (3), pp. 193-218, July, 1983.

[4]   R. Bartels, J. Beatty, and B. Barsky, "An Introduction to the Use of Splines in Computer Graphics", Department of Computer Science, University of Waterloo, TR CS-83-09, August 1983.

[5]   N. Burtnyk and M. Wein, "Computer Generated Key Frame Animation", *Journal of the SMPTE 80*, pp. 149-153, March, 1971.

[6]   N. Burtnyk and M. Wein, "Interactive Skeleton Techniques for Enhancing Motion Dynamics in Key Frame Animation", Communications of the ACM **19** (**10**) pp. 564-569, October, 1976.

[7]   D. Greenberg, S. Wu, and J. Abel, "An Interactive Computer Graphics Approach to Surface Representation", Communications of the ACM **20** (**10**) pp. 703-712, October, 1977.

[8]   D. Kochanek, "A Computer System for Smooth Keyframe Animation", MMath Thesis, Department of Computer Science, University of Waterloo, Technical Report CS-82-42, December, 1982.

[9]   W. Reeves, "Inbetweening for Computer Animation Utilizing Moving Point Constraints", *Computer Graphics (SIGGRAPH '81)*, **15** (3), pp. 263-269, August, 1981.

[10]   A. Smith, "Spline Tutorial Notes – Technical Memo No. 77", *SIGGRAPH '83 Tutorial Notes: Introduction to Computer Animation*, pp. 64-75, July, 1983.

[11]   M. Tuori, "Tools and Techniques for Computer-aided Animation", MSc Thesis, Department of Computer Science, University of Toronto, 1977.

Efficient Octree Conversion by Connectivity Labeling

Markku Tamminen
Laboratory of Information Processing Science
Helsinki University of Technology, 02150 Espoo 15, Finland

Hanan Samet
Computer Science Department
University of Maryland, College Park, MD 20742

ABSTRACT

We present an algorithm for converting from the boundary representation of a solid to the corresponding octree model. The algorithm utilizes an efficient new connected components labeling technique. A novelty of the method is the demonstration that all processing can be performed directly on linear quad- and octree encodings. We illustrate the use of the algorithm by an application to geometric mine modeling and verify its performance by analysis and practical experiments.

CR Categories and Subject Descriptors: I.3.5 [Computer Graphics]: Computational Geometry and Object Modeling -- Solid and Object Representations, Geometric Algorithms, Languages, and Systems

General Terms: Algorithms, Data Structures, Performance

Additional Key Words and Phrases: Image Processing, Octree, Conversion

1. Introduction

A solid modeler is a system for manipulating spatially complete data on the geometric form of three-dimensional solid objects. Each modeler uses one or more solid representation schemes and conversion algorithms between representations have become increasingly important (Requicha and Voelcker 1983).

The main representation of constructive solid geometry (CSG) modelers is a tree of set operations and rigid motions applied to primitive building blocks while boundary representation modelers define a solid by a collection of faces, edges and vertices. A radically different approach, receiving increasing atten-

Permission to copy without fee all or part of this material is granted provided that the copies are not made or distributed for direct commercial advantage, the ACM copyright notice and the title of the publication and its date appear, and notice is given that copying is by permission of the Association for Computing Machinery. To copy otherwise, or to republish, requires a fee and/or specific permission.

© 1984   ACM   0-89791-138-5/84/007/0043 $00.75

tion, is exemplified by the octree scheme (Meagher 1982a) of hierarchic spatial enumeration. It divides a region of space recursively into eight cubic parts until each one is simple (empty or solid) or a fixed maximal resolution is reached.

Relaxing some of the assumptions of the octree model we shall more generally consider block models or three-dimensional image trees. Figure 1-1 shows a polyhedron with 588 faces (a) and part of its block model formed at resolution 2^4 x 2^4 x 2^4 (b).

(a) Polyhedron   (b) Block Model

Figure 1-1
Polyhedron and Part of Corresponding Block Model

The methods used for analyzing the integral properties of solids and for converting between representations depend intimately on the underlying solid representation as discussed by Lee and Requicha (1982), whose algorithm converts efficiently from the CSG scheme into a block model. We shall present a technique for converting from a boundary representation into a block model. This topic has not been much treated in the literature: neither Meagher (1982b) nor Lee and Requicha (1982) nor Requicha and Voelcker (1983) report efficient solutions. Ourselves, we have heretofore used an algorithm reported in (Tamminen et al. 1984).

Block models, and octrees in special, are direct derivatives of the two-dimensional quadtree representation of images, originally introduced by Klinger (1971). See (Samet 1983) for a comprehensive survey. There exist many different encodings of quadtrees, octrees and similar hierarchical data structures. The explicit pointer based tree representation of a block model is not well suited for external storage and ordinarily requires 20 to 40 times as much space as the most compact linear tree representations (Kawaguchi and Endo 1980, Meagher 1982a, Gargantini 1982b, Yamaguchi et al. 1983, Tamminen 1984).

The space complexity of an octree corresponding to a general polyhedron is proportional to the surface area of the polyhedron measured at the chosen resolution (Meagher 1982b). Even at moderate resolution the block model may contain hundreds of thousands of nodes. Thus, it is not always sufficient to formulate a general conversion algorithm; it may be as important that it supports a linear tree representation.

In (Samet and Tamminen 1983) we have presented a new technique of determining geometric properties, such as the perimeter, of linear quadtree encodings and in (Samet and Tamminen 1984) the method has been applied to 3-dimensional connected components labeling. Now we show how the same approach can be used in the conversion problem. The demonstration that all phases of our algorithm can operate directly on linear tree representations without utilizing explicit neighbor finding techniques (Samet 1981) is one of its main interests.

The practical framework of our research is the Geometric Workbench (Mantyla and Sulonen 1982), an experimental solid modeler constructed at the Helsinki University of Technology. The conversion problem originates from applying GWB to geometric mine modeling (Karonen et al. 1983). Through the conversion program, GWB has been connected to the octree modeler OCTGRAS (Yamaguchi et al. 1984), made available to us through co-operation with the Kunii Laboratory of the University of Tokyo.

We first describe briefly the application and previous conversion efforts. Section 3 defines linear image tree representations. In Section 4 we formulate the new conversion algorithm. Its performance is analyzed in Section 5 and finally the claims verified by experimental results.

2. Background

2.1. Why Conversions

We first briefly discuss an example application, geometric mine modeling, to demonstrate why conversions are needed.

The methods of this article were first motivated by an experimental geometric mine modeling system implemented together with a Finnish mining company, Outokumpu Oy. The system operates on boundary models representing entities, such as ore bodies, tunnels, or planned excavations. Three dimensional solids describing ore bodies are constructed by connecting two-dimensional sections by a three-dimensional boundary (Figure 1-1a).

The principal analysis task of mine design consists of intersecting a planned excavation with an ore body and determining the amount of minerals and side material thus formed (Figure 2-1). This requires a volume integration of the type:

$$(I) \qquad \int_S f(x,y,z)dV,$$

where $f(x,y,z)$ is the (unknown) function describing mineral content at each point of space and S is the solid modeling the extracted part of the ore body.

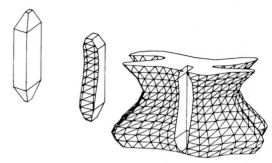

Figure 2-1
Modeling Excavation by a Boolean Set Operation

The function f is empirical, in that it must be estimated at each relevant point separately by geostatistical methods, or kriging (Journel and Huijbregts 1978). Therefore, discrete approximations (Lee and Requicha 1982) must be employed to evaluate (I). The determination of one value of $f(x,y,z)$ necessitates a spatial search among the hundreds or thousands of drill samples and is an expensive operation.

Geostatistics is applied to the boundary representation of an ore body by first converting into a block model. Each block is estimated separately and the results summed for a total value.

2.2. Existing Algorithms

There do not exist many publications on converting a boundary representation into an octree. However, such a component is used in some practical systems (Meagher 1983, Requicha and Voelcker 1983). The algorithms utilized can be divided into two groups: those based on connectivity (Meagher 1983) and those based on explicit block classification (Tamminen et al. 1984). A third approach would be to make M sections of the polyhedron, convert each one of them into a quadtree at resolution M^2 and combine the results into an octree at resolution M^3 by the algorithm of Yau and Srihari (1983).

Conversion algorithms based on connectivity reflect the structure of the quadtree algorithm of Samet (1980). They first determine the volume elements lying on the boundary of the solid. The partial tree thus formed is then traversed and each unclassified leaf is determined to be empty or full by inspecting its neighbors. This approach can also be implemented by using a connected components labeling algorithm. For efficiency, the method has required an explicit tree representation.

In the geometric mine modeling system we have utilized an algorithm where each leaf of the block model is explicitly classified by a point-in-polyhedron test. The main computational operations of this algorithm are to determine whether a block intersects the boundary of the solid and, if so, whether it is contained in it. These operations typically have to be performed tens of thousands of times with the boundary model containing hundreds of faces. The technique has been made efficient by using a spatial in-

dex based on the EXCELL method (Mantyla and Tamminen 1983). In practice computation time is almost
independent of the number of polygons defining the
polyhedron.

This method has not been a main bottleneck of the
mine modeling system. However, with the results of
Samet and Tamminen (1983), implementing the connectivity approach has become justified.

3. Binary Image Trees

Solid modeling by spatial enumeration is closely related to three-dimensional image processing, which will
be reflected in our terminology. This section per-
tains to both two- and three-dimensional images but,
for conciseness, we present mainly the three-
dimensional case.

3.1. Definitions

We shall consider two- (2D) and three dimensional
(3D) binary images (i.e., 2- or 3-dimensional matrices
of pixels, respectively voxels) and speak of the pixels
and voxels as image elements. We use the same
term also for the homogeneous blocks (leaves), which
are the basic elements of quadtrees and octrees. Let
$M = 2^n$ describe the resolution of the image so that
the total number of pixels (voxels) is M^2 (M^3).

An octree is defined as a recursive 8-ary partition of
a three-dimensional image into octants until homogeneous blocks (BLACK or WHITE) are reached
(Srihari 1981, Meagher 1982a, Jackins and Tanimoto
1980,1983). A three-dimensional binary image tree is
formed exactly analogously but by dividing only in
two parts at each level of recursion. We assume the
first partition to be in the x-direction with the y-,
z- and x-directions alternating thereafter. Figure
3-1 illustrates this concept. In the x-partition we
postulate the left subtree to correspond to the
western (W-) half of the image; in the y-partition it
corresponds to the S-half. Let us similarly speak of
the lower (L) and upper (U) halves of the z-partition.

A node in a 3D binary image tree has six sides (W,
E, S, N, L, U) and a neighbor node (of equal size), in
each of these directions. In the ordering of nodes
induced by a preorder traversal of the binary tree all
the nodes in a W- or S- or L-neighbor of a given
node come before that node. We utilize binary image trees mainly because tree traversal algorithms
become somewhat simpler than for octrees.

3.2. Representations

We use a linear tree representation that is based on
the preorder traversal of the binary image tree. The
traversal yields a string over the alphabet "(", "B",
"W" corresponding respectively to internal nodes
(GRAY), BLACK leaves, and WHITE leaves. We call
this string a DF-expression as Kawaguchi and Endo
(1980) do in the case of quadtrees. A different but
related representation is the linear octree of Gargantini (1982). For the image of Figure 3-1 the DF-
expression becomes (B(B(BW. Its most straightforward bit-encoding requires two bits per node both
for octrees and binary image trees. Explicit pointer

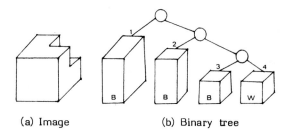

(a) Image   (b) Binary tree

Figure 3-1
Three-dimensional Binary Image Tree

based representations ordinarily require at least one
computer word per node (Meagher 1982b).

In (Tamminen 1984) we have reported methods of
compacting the DF-expression. First of all, encode
"(" by "1" and "B" and "W" by "01" and "00", respectively. Further, at the lowest level of a condensed
tree there may exist only two types of node pairs,
"BW" and "WB". Thus these pairs may be encoded by
"0" and "1", respectively. In practice the above
method has required about one bit per node of a
three-dimensional binary image tree.

A binary image tree always contains at most as many
leaves (but often more nodes) than the corresponding
octree. For instance, at resolution $M = 2^6$ the condensed binary tree of the surface of a unit sphere
contains 25600 leaves while the corresponding octree
has 43800 leaves.

4. Conversion Algorithm

4.1. General Outline

In Figure 4-1 we give the outline of an algorithm for
converting from a boundary representation to a 3D
image tree. The method supports multiple solids
without interior voids, but the 3D outside of the
solids must be connected.

First, in procedure COMBINE3(), each face is
separately converted into a linear image tree
representation. The trees are recursively
OVERLAY'ed in pairs to give the tree of the whole
boundary. In the second phase - FILL3() - the image tree is traversed and its WHITE components,
which are not connected to the outside of the image
are extracted and changed to BLACK as described in
the next section. As there is not enough space for
detailed algorithms of all the (simple) subroutines of
Figure 4-1 we only present their outlines.

OVERLAY() forms the boolean union of two (linear)
binary image trees by traversing them synchronously
according to the following rules:

(1) If either of the nodes is BLACK the resulting
    node is BLACK. The other subtree is skipped
    (by sequential traversal).

```
procedure BR_TO_BLOCKS3();
/* Convert boundary representation defined by face-
array FACES into binary image tree at resolution M
= 2ⁿ. */
begin
    global value integer M,NFACES;
    global pointer face array FACES[0:NFACES-1];
    global pointer nodelist DF; /* DF-expression */
    DF <- COMBINE3(0,NFACES-1);
    FILL3(); /* see Section 4.2 */
end;
```

```
pointer nodelist procedure COMBINE3(N1,N2);
/* Convert separately faces with indices between N1
and N2 to image trees and combine results into a
tree of the corresponding part of the boundary.  */
begin
    global value integer NFACES;
    global pointer face array FACES[0:NFACES-1];
    value integer N1,N2;
    if N2 - N1 > 1 then
        return(OVERLAY(COMBINE3(N1,(N1+N2)/2),
                       COMBINE3((N1+N2)/2+1,N2)));
    else if N2 - N1 = 1 then
        return(OVERLAY(CONVERT3(FACES[N1]),
                       CONVERT3(FACES[N2])));
    /* CONVERT3() converts one face */
    else return(CONVERT3(FACES[N1]));
end
```

Figure 4-1
Conversion Algorithm Outline

(2) If either of the nodes is WHITE the other subtree is copied to the result (by sequential traversal).

(3) If both nodes are GRAY the result is also GRAY.

(4) Replace recursively (BB by B and (WW by W.

CONVERT3() converts one face with plane equation

$$P(x,y,z) = ax + by + cz + d = 0$$

into a binary image tree as follows:

(1) Choose a projection plane, say xy, so that the remaining coefficient (c) has maximal absolute value.

(2) Form the 2D binary image tree TWODT of the projection of the face on the xy-plane by procedure BR_TO_BLOCKS2().

(3) The rest of the conversion is performed similarly to forming the image tree of the whole plane $P(x,y,z) = 0$, except that nodes, whose xy-projection is WHITE in TWODT, become WHITE in the result. The universe is halved recursively by planes alternatingly perpendicular to the x-, y-, and z-axes while keeping track of the minimum and maximum values of $P(x,y,z)$ in each block thus formed. To each block corresponds a node N2 of TWODT so that the block can be classified as WHITE, BLACK, or GRAY as follows:

    - if N2 is WHITE, the block is WHITE
    - if zero does not lie between the minimum and maximum of $P(x,y,z)$ in the block, the

    block is WHITE and N2 is skipped
    - if the block is at voxel level and N2 is BLACK then the block is BLACK (division continues to voxel level on a face)
    - otherwise the block is GRAY and is further subdivided.

(4) Replace recursively (BB by B and (WW by W.

The recursive halving directly produces the desired DF-expression.

BR_TO_BLOCKS2() forms the 2D image tree of a polygon. For simplicity we have implemented it completely analogously to BR_TO_BLOCKS3():

(1) Each edge of the face is converted into a 2D image tree by CONVERT2() similarly to the method applied in CONVERT3().

(2) The trees of the edges are recursively OVERLAY'ed in pairs by COMBINE2().

(3) The WHITE components of the 2D image not connected with the outside are changed to BLACK by FILL2(). (If necessary, holes within a face are treated by dividing the face into simply connected parts.)

The main virtue of CONVERT3() is that, to classify a block, we do not have to perform any point-in-polygon test. Also, the $P(x,y,z)$-range within each block can be efficiently computed during the recursive subdivision and no sorting is required to arrive at the correct DF-order of the blocks.

As a result of providing all xy-information in the 2D image tree, some spurious BLACK leaves may result when compared to the exact face/voxel -intersection tests. This is not serious considering the overall nature of the block model approximation. The choice of the projection plane minimizes the occurrencies of this event while guaranteeing that the inside of a solid is never connected with the outside.

The boundary conversion method described above has been satisfactory, even though we chose it mainly for its simplicity. We do not want to emphasize it because other, potentially more efficient, techniques can be imagined and combined with the core of our approach, described in the next section.

4.2. Connectivity Labeling

As discussed in Section 2.2 a variant of connected components labeling can be utilized in block model conversion. We show how it can be applied to linear tree representations.

Two elements of a 3D image are called (face-) connected to each other if they share a boundary (called adjacency) with non-zero area. Labeling the connected components of a binary image is ordinarily defined as transforming it into a symbolic image in which every maximally connected subset of BLACK elements is labeled by a distinct positive integer. However, in our case the image elements intersecting the boundary of the solid are BLACK and we want to extract and change to BLACK the WHITE components not connected to the outside of the image.

Connected components labeling can be performed by the union–find algorithm (Tarjan 1975). At the start each image element is assumed to form a separate component. The final components are determined by processing once each adjacency between image elements. For each relevant adjacency we must determine the putative components of the two elements (find). If they differ, they are combined (union).

The above algorithm, applied to a DF–expression, must be able to determine adjacencies as the tree is traversed in the fixed order. When processing a node we know that its W–, S–, and L–neighbors have been processed. Therefore there must exist data structures to record the information of respectively the E–, N–, and U–sides of the processed part. Let us call these data structures the active yz–, xz–, and xy–borders. They consist of active face elements. (In the rest of this section "face" means an active face of the above borders, not a face of the solid.)

The main change compared to the two–dimensional connected components algorithm reported in (Samet and Tamminen 1983) is that there are now three active borders, instead of two and that the size of a border element is defined as its area, not width. Further, the active borders can be represented as linked lists (instead of arrays), which is most important in the three–dimensional case. See (Samet and Tamminen 1984) for more details on connectivity labeling.

We give the filling algorithm in three parts. In the main program (Fig. 4–2) the three face element lists are first initialized so that each contains one WHITE face element of size M^2. The solid can be imagined as situated in the positive octant of coordinate space with all the other octants having been processed and WHITE. This mirrors the state of the active borders at the start of processing any node: its W–, S–, and L–neighbors have been processed and their color and component information is contained in the active border. Then procedure TRAVERSE() (Fig. 4–4) is called to traverse the DF–expression of the binary image tree. Finally PHASEII() traverses the tree once more. For each WHITE leaf it checks whether the leaf is in the component of the outside. If not, its color is changed to BLACK.

The main function of TRAVERSE() is to provide, at each call to its sub–procedures, a pointer to the parts of the active face element lists bordering that subtree. It calls itself twice recursively at each internal node. At each leaf node it calls procedure INCREMENT() three times to perform the actual updating of the active borders and the connected components. If a WHITE leaf is not identified with any existing component then a putative new component is formed. Labels of WHITE leaves are stored for processing by PHASEII(). After processing a leaf each list of active face elements is advanced to the element following it.

To illustrate the working of the algorithm we show, in Figure 4–3, the state of the active xy–border and the start of the sublist XYL when entering and leaving TRAVERSE() at each of its calls corresponding to leaf nodes of Figure 3–1.

```
procedure FILL3();
/* First compute connected WHITE components of a
binary tree of an M by M by M (M = 2^n) three-
dimensional image represented by preorder traversal
DF. Then change components not connected with out-
side of image to BLACK in PHASEII(). Each active
border surface xy, xz and yz is represented as a
linked list of records of type facelist, which contain
pointers to the active faces comprising the border.
Each active face is represented as a record of type
face with four fields SIZ, LAB, COL, and CRD,
which give respectively, the size (area), the com-
ponent label, the color, and the value of the third
coordinate (z for an xy border) of a face. A record
of type facelist has two fields, DATA and NEXT,
containing respectively, a pointer to a face and a
pointer to the next element in the list. */
begin
    global value integer M;
    global value pointer nodelist DF;
    pointer facelist XYL, XZL, YZL; /* borders */
    pointer face XY,XZ,YZ;
    XYL <- create(facelist); XZL <- create(facelist);
    YZL <- create(facelist);
    DATA(XYL) <- XY <- create(face);
    DATA(XZL) <- XZ <- create(face);
    DATA(YZL) <- YZ <- create(face);
    SIZ(XY) <- SIZ(XZ) <- SIZ(YZ) <- M*M;
    LAB(XY) <- LAB(XZ) <- LAB(YZ) <- outside;
    COL(XY) <- COL(XZ) <- COL(YZ) <- WHITE;
    CRD(XY) <- CRD(XZ) <- CRD(YZ) <- 0;
    if not empty(DF) then begin
        TRAVERSE(M,M,M,XYL,XZL,YZL);
        PHASEII() /* change inside to BLACK */
    end
end;
```

Figure 4–2
Main Procedure for Filling Inside

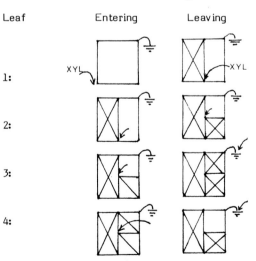

Figure 4–3
State of XYL at Each Call to TRAVERSE()

The purpose of procedure INCREMENT() (Figure 4–5) is to process all the active face elements bordering a face of a new leaf. Whenever an adjacency between WHITE faces is encountered, the connected components information is updated. Processing divides into three cases. In each of them INCREMENT() per-

```
procedure TRAVERSE(SX,SY,SZ,XYL,XZL,YZL);
/* Process SX by SY by SZ segment of image where
DF presents the preorder traversal of its binary tree.
XYL, XZL, and YZL are pointers to the lists of ac-
tive faces on the xy, xz-, and yz-borders of this
part of the image.  Once the three faces of a leaf
that are adjacent to the active borders have been
processed, XYL, XZL, and YZL are advanced to point .
to the portion of the active border that is adjacent
to the image element to be processed next.  The list
LL stores the putative labels of WHITE nodes for
PHASEII().  */
begin
  value integer SX,SY,SZ;
  reference pointer facelist XYL,XZL,YZL;
  global pointer nodelist DF;
  global pointer labellist LL;
  pointer facelist T; /* auxiliary */
  pointer node L;
  L <- create(node);
  COL(L) <- next_node(DF);
  if COL(L) = GRAY then begin
    if SX = SZ then begin /* partition on x */
      T <- YZL; /* save start of yz border */
      TRAVERSE(SX/2,SY,SZ,XYL,XZL,YZL);
      TRAVERSE(SX/2,SY,SZ,XYL,XZL,T)
    end
    else if SZ = SY then begin /* on y */
      T <- XZL; /* save start of xz border */
      TRAVERSE(SX,SY/2,SZ,XYL,XZL,YZL);
      TRAVERSE(SX,SY/2,SZ,XYL,T,YZL)
    end
    else begin /* partition on z */
      T <- XYL; /* save start of xy border */
      TRAVERSE(SX,SY,SZ/2,XYL,XZL,YZL);
      TRAVERSE(SX,SY,SZ/2,T,XZL,YZL)
    end
  end
  else begin /* A leaf node. */
    LAB(L) <- unknown;
    INCREMENT(L,XYL,SX*SY,SZ); /* xy- border */
    INCREMENT(L,XZL,SX*SZ,SY); /* xz- border */
    INCREMENT(L,YZL,SY*SZ,SX); /* yz- border */
    if COL(L) = WHITE then begin
      if LAB(L) = unknown then /* new label */
        LAB(L) <- create(label);
        /* update active borders with label: */
      LAB(DATA(XYL)) <- LAB(L);
      LAB(DATA(XZL)) <- LAB(L);
      LAB(DATA(YZL)) <- LAB(L);
      add_to_list(LL,LAB(L)) /* for PHASEII() */
    end
    XYL <- NEXT(XYL); /* advance lists */
    XZL <- NEXT(XZL); YZL <- NEXT(YZL)
  end
end;
```

Figure 4-4
Tree Traversal

forms the necessary union operations and updates the
active border as follows with the face of the new
leaf:

(1) The entering face is larger than the corresponding
first element of the active border. Neighboring
face elements are determined from the size
(area) of the new face. The new face replaces
the last neighboring element and all others are
disposed of.

(2) The entering face is equal in size with the first
border element, which it replaces.

(3) The entering face is smaller than the first border
element, which it replaces. A new active face
is created to account for the rest of the old
border element.

Finally the data of the border element corresponding
to the new face are updated. For simplicity we have
omitted the disposal of active face elements touching
the outside of the image.

```
procedure INCREMENT(L,FL,S,W);
/* Process a leaf L of area  S in the present direc-
tion (xy, xz, or yz) and width W in the perpendicular
direction.  The leaf is  adjacent to the first element
of the border represented by FL, pointer to a list of
active faces.  See (Sedgewick 1983) for the imple-
mentation of union(), a combined find and union
operation.  */
begin
 value pointer node L;
 value pointer facelist FL;
 value integer S,W;
 global value integer M;
 integer I; /* auxiliary */
 pointer facelist P,Q; /* auxiliary */
 if S > SIZ(DATA(FL)) then begin /* case 1 */
   I <- 0; P <- FL;
   while I < S do begin /* all bordering elements */
     if COL(L) = WHITE
       and COL(DATA(P)) = WHITE then
         LAB(L) <- union(LAB(L),LAB(DATA(P)));
     I <- I + SIZ(DATA(P));
     P <- NEXT(P)
   end;
   Q <- NEXT(FL); NEXT(FL) <- P; /* delete and */
   facelist_dispose(Q,P) /* reclaim storage for
   elements from Q up to but not including P */
 end
 else begin /* cases 2 and 3 */
   if COL(L) = WHITE
     and COL(DATA(FL)) = WHITE then
       LAB(L) <- union(LAB(L),LAB(DATA(FL)));
   if S < SIZ(DATA(FL)) then begin /* case 3 */
     P <- create(facelist); /* new element = */
     DATA(P) <- create(face); /* rest of old one */
     SIZ(DATA(P)) <- SIZ(DATA(FL)) - S;
     COL(DATA(P)) <- COL(DATA(FL));
     LAB(DATA(P)) <- LAB(DATA(FL));
     CRD(DATA(P)) <- CRD(DATA(FL));
     NEXT(P) <- NEXT(FL);
     NEXT(FL) <- P; /* insert into list */
   end
 end;
 SIZ(DATA(FL)) <- S; /* update first element */
 COL(DATA(FL)) <- COL(L);
 CRD(DATA(FL)) <- CRD(DATA(FL)) + W;
 if CRD(DATA(FL)) = M /* touches outside */
   and COL(L) = WHITE then
     LAB(L) <- union(LAB(L),outside)
end;
```

Figure 4-5
Processing one Side of a Leaf

5. Analysis

Let us analyze separately the procedures OVERLAY(), CONVERT2(), COMBINE2(), FILL2(), CONVERT3(), COMBINE3(), and FILL3() focusing on the effect of using linear tree representations.

With linear tree representations OVERLAY() clearly inspects once each node of both trees and its complexity is thus proportional to the total number of input nodes, which is also a bound on the number of output nodes. With explicit tree representations the complexity of OVERLAY() is at most proportional to the size of the smaller input tree.

CONVERT2() performs a fixed amount of computation for each node of the 2D image tree of an edge segment and directly outputs the DF-expression. The analysis of COMBINE2() and FILL2() for each face corresponds closely to that of COMBINE3() and FILL3() given below.

CONVERT3() also performs a fixed amount of computation for each node of the output tree, except for the case where an output leaf is WHITE and the corresponding portion of the 2D tree must be skipped. (In this case the brother of the leaf will not be WHITE.) Because of the choice of the projection plane, the amount of skipping can be at most proportional to the number of output nodes. With explicit tree representations the skipping could be performed more efficiently. However, its contribution to processing time is minor.

When there are N faces, COMBINE3() calls OVERLAY() N − 1 times. Each node resulting from CONVERT3() passes through OVERLAY() at most $\lceil \log(N) \rceil$ times (logarithms are to base 2). This follows from the remark above on the size of the output of OVERLAY(). Thus for a total of I input nodes in the image trees of the faces the complexity of all the OVERLAY's is at most $I \lceil \log(N) \rceil$. Of course, the elementary operations are very simple. COMBINE3() requires at most twice the amount of space needed for storing the image trees of the faces. Using techniques similar to external sorting, disk storage may be used for this purpose.

FILL3() performs a fixed amount of work for each node, except for the contribution of the union-find -algorithm. Tarjan (1975) has shown that this contribution is almost linear in the number of operations performed. Thus the complexity of FILL3() is very nearly linear in the number of nodes. The worst case complexity of FILL3() is better than that of the connected components algorithm of (Samet 1981). However, the boundary determination method of Jackins and Tanimoto (1983) could be applied to achieve equal performance with explicit tree structures.

The worst case space complexity of the connectivity labeling algorithm is about $3M^2$ face elements: It is easy to construct 3D checkerboard-like images, which would require the active borders to contain only face elements at voxel level. The union-find -algorithm requires a label array with size determined by the highest label used. In practice, central memory requirements are somewhat difficult to determine à priori. In the following section we report some experiences.

6. Experiences

We have programmed the conversion algorithm in C language and run it on a VAX 11/750 (without a floating point accelerator), under Unix to determine its practical efficiency. Even though processing costs depend heavily on implementation details we report below various cost components to give an indication of their relative magnitudes.

Detailed performance testing is based on the following solids:

(1) B(100) – ball approximated by 100 faces

(2) B(400) – ball approximated by 400 faces

(3) Ore – the ore body of Figure 1–1a (588 faces)

(4) Exc. – an excavation (Figure 6–1, 40 faces).

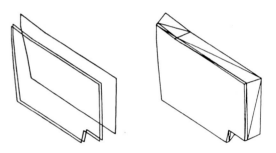

Figure 6–1
Test Solid, an Excavation

The effect of the theoretical non-linearity of the union-find -algorithm is so small that we can combine the experimental results into the following overall average costs per node.

(1) OVERLAY() requires about 17 microseconds per input node. Thus to COMBINE N trees containing a total of I nodes, the summed OVERLAY'ing time is at most $17 I \lceil \log(N) \rceil$ microseconds.

(2) CONVERT2() requires about 170 microseconds per output node.

(3) CONVERT3() requires about 130 microseconds per output node. (The subroutine has been optimized further than CONVERT2().)

(4) FILL3() requires about 380 microseconds per input node and the resource requirements for FILL2() are a bit smaller.

The implementations, save that of OVERLAY(), use recursion so that subroutine calls account for much of the above costs.

To help appreciate the unit costs we note that the condensed binary image tree of a unit sphere at resolution $M = 2^7$ contains 208000 nodes. (A corresponding condensed completely BLACK ball only contains 117000 nodes!)

Tables 1 and 2 compare the run times (in VAX 11/750 CPU seconds) of the new method and the old one reported in (Tamminen et al. 1984). Alas, we have not found other publications to compare to.

	B(100)	B(400)	Ore(588)	Exc.(40)
New method	165	237	245	22
Old method	1350	1400	1600	324

Table 1. Processing Time at Resolution 128

	B(100)	B(400)	Ore(588)	Exc.(40)
New method	53	100	100	8
Old method	380	400	410	79

Table 2. Processing Time at Resolution 64

Tables 3 and 4 help in a detailed evaluation of the choices made in constructing the algorithm. Table 3 shows the contribution of each phase (in CPU seconds) to total processing time. Table 4 gives summed sizes (number of nodes) of the various kinds of image trees: Output is the final result, Boundary (3D) is the boundary of the final result, Faces denotes the trees of all faces taken separately, Proj. faces the 2D projections of faces, Boundary (2D) the trees of polygon boundaries, Segments the trees of polygon edges taken separately, and Overlay the number of nodes passing through the various invocations of OVERLAY().

	B(100)	B(400)	Ore(588)	Exc.(40)
FILL3()	79.6	84.0	62.2	7.7
CONVERT3()	32.3	46.3	47.4	4.9
OVERLAY()	29.7	45.1	40.7	2.8
FILL2()	16.9	32.1	41.6	3.2
CONVERT2()	9.2	23.0	29.2	2.6

Table 3. Processing Costs at Resolution 128

	B(100)	B(400)	Ore(588)	Exc.(40)
Output	116711	122485	98947	12331
Boundary (3D)	201668	207794	169108	20880
Faces	259758	346778	360062	34403
Proj. faces	29022	68692	92664	7825
Boundary (2D)	41370	90350	117034	10299
Segments	54088	142552	179604	15090
Overlay	1650000	2580000	2390000	180000

Table 4. Summed Sizes of Trees at Resolution 128

From Table 3 we see that the main part of the time is taken by determining the image tree of the boundary of the polyhedron. Our approach to this task was chosen for its uniformity (2D and 3D phases are almost identical) and robustness. However, there is much room for improvement by using different techniques.

The only part of our algorithm, whose efficiency is seriously affected by the use of linear tree representations, is OVERLAY(). Its contribution to the total run time is generally less than 20%. Also, a more efficient (in the expected case) FILL3() is conceivably possible with an explicit tree structure. This is because we need not form exact connected components but only extract the part connected to the outside.

This can be performed using depth first search for leaves lying on the image border and recursive neighbor finding, starting from each unlabeled one of them.

The central memory requirements of FILL3() for B(400) at resolution 128 consist of about 3500 records for active faces. This compares favorably to the worst case of about 50000 records. Further, about 1500 tentative labels are formed. As resolution is increased by a factor of two the size of the output tree grows by a factor of four. The same holds for processing time of the connectivity labeling phase and for the number of putative labels. However, the number of active faces seems to grow only linearly with resolution.

The number of nodes in the two-dimensional image trees depends on the summed length of edges measured at the chosen resolution and to a lesser extent on the number of edges of the polyhedron. The length of edges grows linearly with resolution. Similarly, the summed size of the three-dimensional image trees depends on the surface area of the polyhedron and its number of faces. The surface area grows with the square of resolution. The processing time of the new algorithm is affected by both the above factors and thus grows somewhat more slowly than that of the old one, whose cost depends almost exclusively on the number of leaves output.

Our connected components labeling technique seems to outperform that of Lumia (1983), based on the voxel matrix representation, by orders of magnitude, in cases typical of the conversion problem (Samet and Tamminen 1984). This is mainly explained by the lesser amount of image elements in our representation.

The constituent parts of our algorithm can be connected in various ways. We recommend keeping the conversion of the boundary and the final connectivity labeling as separate programs communicating through a Unix pipe. With this structure the first phase can be easily replaced by another one, say, for processing curved surfaces.

7. Conclusions

We have presented an algorithm, efficient in practice, for converting a polyhedron into an octree-like block model. A characteristic of the algorithm is that all its phases operate directly on linear tree representations.

We believe that the method presented can be applied as a general conversion tool in boundary representation modelers. Up to the present conversion seems to have been possible in practice only for basic building block solids, which have then been combined on the octree side by using boolean set operations. The conversion program links our modeler (GWB) with that of (Yamaguchi et al. 1984). An interesting practical research problem is to find the optimal division of labor between boundary representations and octrees in similar combined systems.

Our experiences on applying the solid modeling techniques described here to mine modeling have been very encouraging but will be reported in more detail elsewhere.

ACKNOWLEDGEMENTS

The work has been supported by the Academy of Finland and by the National Science Foundation under grant MCS-83-02118. We thank Reijo Sulonen for his comments and Olli Karonen for help with the mine modeling data and figures.

REFERENCES

1. Gargantini, I., Linear octtrees for fast processing of three dimensional objects. CVGIP **20**(1982)4, pp. 363-374.

2. Jackins, C.L. and Tanimoto, S.L., Oct-trees and their use in representing three-dimensional objects. CGIP **14**(1980), pp. 249-270.

3. Jackins, C.L. and Tanimoto, S.L., Quad-trees, oct-trees and K-trees: a generalized approach to recursive decomposition of Euclidean space. IEEE **PAMI**-5(1983)5, pp. 533-539.

4. Journel, A.G. and Huijbregts, Ch, J., Mining Geostatistics. Academic Press, 1978.

5. Karonen, O., Tamminen, M., Kerola, P., Mitjonen, M., and Orivuori, E., A geometric mine modeling system. Proc. Autocarto Six Conference, Ottawa, 1983 pp. 374-383.

6. Kawaguchi, E. and Endo, T., On a method of binary picture representation and its application to data compression. IEEE PAMI 5(1980)1, pp. 27-35.

7. Klinger, A., Patterns and search statistics. In Optimizing Methods in Statistics, Rustagi, J.S. (Ed.), Academic Press, New York, 1971, pp. 303-337.

8. Lee, Y.T. and Requicha, A.A.G., Algorithms for computing the volume and other integral properties of solids. II. A family of algorithms based on representation conversion and cellular approximation. CACM **25**(1982)9, pp. 642-650.

9. Lumia, R., A new three-dimensional connected components algorithm. CVGIP **23**(1983), pp. 207-217.

10. Meagher, D., Geometric modeling using octree encoding. CGIP **19**(1982a), pp. 129-147.

11. Meagher, D., Octree generation, analysis and manipulation Report IPL-TR-027, Rensselaer Polytechnic Institute, Troy, New York, 1982b.

12. Meagher, D., Personal communication. 1983.

13. Mantyla, M. and Sulonen, R., GWB - A Solid Modeler With Euler Operators. IEEE Computer Graphics & Applications 2(1982)7, pp. 17-31

14. Mantyla, M. and Tamminen, M., Localized set operations for solid modeling. Computer Graphics**17**(1983)3, pp. 279-288.

15. Requicha, A.A.G. and Voelcker, H.B., Solid modeling: current status and research directions. IEEE Computer Graphics and Applications **3**(1983)7, pp. 25 - 37.

16. Requicha, A.A.G., Representations of rigid solids: theory, methods and systems. ACM Comp. Surv. **12**(1980), pp. 437-464.

17. Samet, H., Region representation: quadtrees from boundary codes. CACM **23**(1980)3, pp. 163-170.

18. Samet, H., Connected component labeling using quadtrees. JACM **28**(1981)3, pp. 487-501.

19. Samet, H., The quadtree and related hierarchical data structures. To appear in ACM Comp. Surv. Also TR-1329, Computer Science Department, University of Maryland, College Park, MD, 1983.

20. Samet, H. and Tamminen, M., Computing geometric properties of images represented by linear quadtrees. Report TR-1359, Computer Science Department, University of Maryland, College Park, MD, 1983.

21. Samet, H. and Tamminen, M., Efficient image component labeling. Report TR-1420, Computer Science Department, University of Maryland, College Park, MD, 1984.

22. Sedgewick, R., Algorithms. Addison-Wesley, Reading, 1983.

23. Srihari, S.N., Representation of three-dimensional digital images. ACM Comp. Surv. **13**(1981)4, pp. 399-423.

24. Tamminen, M., Encoding pixel trees. To be published in CVGIP, 1984.

25. Tamminen, M., Karonen, O., and Mantyla, M., Block model conversion using an efficient spatial index. To be published in CAD Journal, 1984.

26. Tarjan, R.E., On the efficiency of a good but not linear set union algorithm. JACM **22**(1975), pp. 215-225.

27. Yamaguchi, K., and Kunii, T.L., A layered string data structure for an octree model. Techn. Rep. 83-15, Dept. of Information Science, Univ. of Tokyo, 1983.

28. Yamaguchi, K., Kunii, T.L., Fujimura, K. and Toriya, H., Octree-related data structures and algorithms. IEEE Computer Graphics and Applications 4(1984)1, pp. 53-59.

29. Yau, M-M and Srihari, S.N., A hierarchical data structure for multidimensional images. CACM 26(1983)7, pp. 504-515.

Automatic Synthesis of Graphical Object Descriptions

Mark Friedell

Center for Research in Computing Technology
Harvard University

Abstract

A technique is presented for automatically synthesizing graphical object descriptions from high-level specifications. The technique includes mechanisms for describing, selecting, and combining primitive elements of object descriptions. Underlying these mechanisms are a referential framework for describing information used in the construction of object descriptions and a computational model of the object-synthesis process.

This technique has been implemented in two prototype systems to synthesize object descriptions in near-real time. One system creates graphical displays of information that resides in a conventional database. The other system is a computer graphicist's tool for creating backgrounds of complex, three-dimensional scenes.

1. Introduction

Algorithms for computing images from scene descriptions require that objects in the scene be described at a very fine level of graphical detail. Typical representation primitives are points, lines, polygons, and RGB color coordinates. While such representations are well suited to algorithms for image computation, they make the creation of object descriptions tedious and time-consuming. Techniques for expediting the production of object descriptions would substantially reduce the development cost of computer-graphics applications. In addition, fully automatic techniques would allow the use of computer graphics in situations for which predefined graphics could not be provided, e.g., advanced man-machine interfaces in which the system initiated dialogues with the user and decided what information to present.

Specifications of objects often are naturally articulated by giving the identity of the object type (e.g., aircraft) and the identities and values of its important descriptive attributes (e.g., style = ultralight). This paper describes a technique for automatically synthesizing detailed, graphical object descriptions from this type of high-level object specification. These high-level object specifications will be called quasi-descriptions.

2. Previous Work

Previous efforts to generate graphics automatically have been based on the instantiation of pre-defined, parametric descriptions. Two interesting examples are the BARAT system [GNANAMGARI], developed at the University of Pennsylvania, and the AIPS system [ZYDBEL et al.], developed at Bolt, Beranek, and Newman, Inc.

CR Categories and Subject Descriptors: I.2.1 [Artificial Intelligence]: Application and Expert Systems; I.3.5 [Computer Graphics]: Computational Geometry and Object Modelling.

Permission to copy without fee all or part of this material is granted provided that the copies are not made or distributed for direct commercial advantage, the ACM copyright notice and the title of the publication and its date appear, and notice is given that copying is by permission of the Association for Computing Machinery. To copy otherwise, or to republish, requires a fee and/or specific permission.

© 1984   ACM   0-89791-138-5/84/007/0053 $00.75

Author's address: Aiken Computation Laboratory 13, Harvard University, Cambridge, Massachusetts 02138 telephone: 617-495-5841   arpanet: friedell@harvard

BARAT uses procedures for making pie charts, bar graphs, and line graphs to create graphical displays of numeric, tabular data. A decision tree based on intrinsic properties of the table of data is used to select the most appropriate procedure.

AIPS generates displays of information that resides in a knowledge base described using the KL-ONE [BRACHMAN] knowledge-representation language. Graphical displays are generated from a repertoire of display formats. AIPS chooses appropriate formats by comparing their applicability patterns to the information to be presented.

Systems such as BARAT and AIPS succeed in narrow, well-defined domains for which it is practical to provide an adequate repertoire of predefined, parametric object descriptions. The approach to automatic object synthesis described in this paper differs from previous work in three ways:

1. Object descriptions are _synthesized_ by reasoning about how to select and combine widely applicable primitive elements of object descriptions. This allows a broader range of object descriptions to be created.

2. The approach described in this paper is directed at producing both two-dimensional objects for use in information displays and three-dimensional objects for use in realistic scenes. Previous work concerned only the former problem.

3. This new technique is designed for real-time performance.

3. Applications and Examples

The technique for object synthesis described here has been implemented as parts of two prototype systems. The first system is a graphical user interface to databases called the View System [FRIEDELL et al.]. With the View System, the database user poses a query using a graphical query menu and is presented with the query response in the form of a graphical display. Typically, these graphical displays are too large to fit on a single screen. To manage these oversized displays, two screens are used. One, a _data map_, presents the entire display in miniature (Figure 3.1). A highlighted rectangle on the data map indicates the extents of the information display that is presented in full detail on the main screen (Figure 3.2). Figure 3.3 shows a quasi-description used by the View

System's object synthesizer to create, in real time, the description for the object in the upper-left of Figure 3.2.

The viability of the View System depends on its ability to automatically synthesize object descriptions. For any non-trivial database, it is impossible to provide a complete repertoire of predefined object descriptions for every object that might exist within an information display.

The second prototype system is a computer-graphicist's tool for creating backgrounds of complex, three-dimensional scenes. With this tool, critical foreground objects are formulated manually by the computer graphicist, and less critical background objects are created automatically by the object synthesizer. Automatic synthesis of backgrounds can greatly reduce the cost of preparing descriptions of complex scenes. Figure 3.4 presents an automatically synthesized scene background. Figure 3.5 shows the computer graphicist's quasi-description for the background.

4. The Object Frame

Object synthesis proceeds incrementally. The focal point of this process is a data structure called the _object frame_. Each step in object synthesis is effected by the application of a _synthesis operator_ to the object frame. The choice of which synthesis operator to apply at a given point is based on a computational model of object synthesis called the _synthesis agenda_. _Synthesis control_ supervises the selection of synthesis operators based on the synthesis agenda and coordinates the overall object synthesis process.

The object frame is an extended object representation. It is suitable for describing an object at any point during object synthesis. This includes the starting point, at which the object is only very abstractly defined, and the end point, at which every graphic detail is specified.

The object frame includes primitive graphical descriptors similar to those of conventional object representations. In addition, it includes descriptors for describing structural interrelationships important to object synthesis.

The object frame is illustrated in Figures 4.1 and 4.2. Its major components are:

1. The _ELEMENT_ is the primitive object component manipulated during object

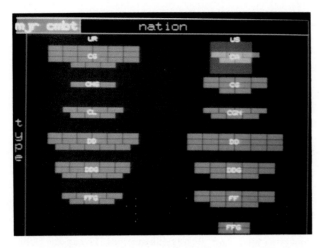

Figure 3.1   View System's Data Map

Figure 3.2   View System's Main Screen

synthesis. An ELEMENT can play a representational or compositional Role. If the ELEMENT is representational, it graphically realizes either

1. the common aspects of all objects of the type specified in the quasi-description, or

2. one of the attributes specified in the quasi-description.

If the ELEMENT is compositional, it provides part of the infrastructure required to combine the representational ELEMENTs into a valid, graphical object description.

2. FRAGMENTs are ordered sequences of ELEMENTs. The concatenation of the GRAPHICAL_DESCRIPTION_SEGMENTs of the ELEMENTs within a FRAGMENT compose a fragment of the graphical object description being generated. FRAGMENTs are incrementally merged during object synthesis. When object synthesis is complete, only one FRAGMENT remains in the object frame. The concatenation of the GRAPHICAL_DESCRIPTION_SEGMENTs of the ELEMENTs composing this FRAGMENT is the synthesized graphical description of the object. (See figure 4.2.)

3. A REGION represents a region of space that may be occupied by the object being synthesized. REGIONs help prevent the over-subscription of space by modelling its availability and consumption during object synthesis.

4.1 The Object Frame's Embedded Graphical-Description Language

GRAPHICAL_DESCRIPTION_SEGMENTs within the object frame are sequences of atomic

object type: ship
attributes: category = major combat
               nationality = US
               type = CA
               name = Canaberra

Figure 3.3   Quasi-Description for Object in Upper-Left of Figure 3.2

Figure 3.4   Background of Three-Dimensional Scene

object type: mountain background
attributes: terrain = snow
               sky = clear
               time of day = 0:00

Figure 3.5   Quasi-Description for Objects in Figure 3.4

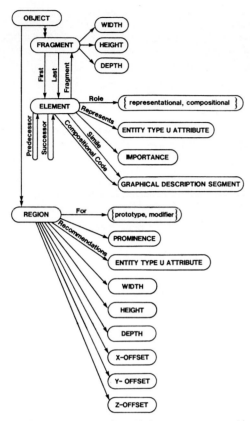

Figure 4.1   The Object Frame Schema

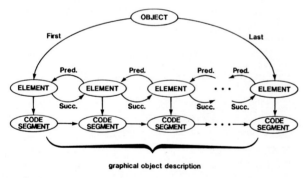

graphical object description

Figure 4.2   An Instantiated Object Frame

graphics descriptors and operators. The graphics descriptors are those of the target image computation (e.g., point, line, and surface patch). The graphics operators are geometric transformations and color transformations. The geometric transformations are the usual ones encounted in computer graphics: rotation, translation, and scaling. The color transformations change a source color into a target color. These atomic descriptors are the vocabulary of a graphical-description language embedded within the object frame.

This embedded language is interpreted as follows: The interpreter maintains a

current positioning transformation (CPT) and a current color map. Initially, the CPT is the identity transformation. As each geometric transformation is encountered, it is combined with the CPT, and the result becomes the new CPT. There are two operators for saving and restoring the CPT. One operator pushes a copy of the CPT onto a stack, the other operator pops the stack into the CPT.

The color map initially maps all colors to themselves. As each color transformation is encountered, it is applied to the color map, and the result becomes the new color map. As with the CPT, there are two operators for saving and restoring the current color map. One pushes a copy of the color map onto a stack, and the other restores it from the stack.

As graphical descriptors are encountered, they are treated as if they were transformed by the interpreter's CPT and color map.

The object frame's embedded graphical-description language is designed to facilitate manipulation of the object frame. Once object synthesis is complete, and the object's graphical description is assembled by concatenating GRAPHICAL_DESCRIPTION_SEGMENTs, the description can be translated easily from the embedded graphical-description language to the format of the target image-computation system.

5. Synthesis Operators

The collection of all synthesis operators is the graphics knowledge base. The graphics knowledge base is a formalized body of knowledge pertinent to object synthesis that has been encoded for automatic use by a computer.
It can be thought of as including:

1. A dictionary of object elements

2. A guide to structural relations within objects

3. A standards manual for graphic design

4. A reference manual for the target image-computation system

Creating the knowledge base is a sizable task. Technicians familiar with the synthesis-operator format and synthesis agenda (described in Section 6) conduct interviews with specialists in computer graphics, human factors, and graphic design. The technicians encode the advice provided by these specialists into synthesis operators, thus capturing the specialists' expertise in the knowledge base.

Since the knowledge base can be incrementally expanded, it may become very large over time. Since it is encoded in an unambiguous notation, it may be subjected to critical review. Hence, the knowledge base may become more complete and more correct than the knowledge of any single, human computer graphicist.

Each synthesis operator in the knowledge base comprises a predicate and an action. The predicate ranges over the object frame and specifies the logical preconditions for applying the action. The action affects the object frame in a way that contributes to object synthesis. The action may create new ELEMENTs, elaborate ELEMENTs by filling in their attributes, merge FRAGMENTs, or otherwise manipulate the object frame.

There are three types of synthesis operators in the knowledge base:

1. Simile inferences

2. Structural couplers

3. Object grids

5.1 Similes and Simile Inferences

Similes are the smallest segments of graphical description that are manipulated during object synthesis. Similes are defined using the primitives discussed above in Section 4.1. Unlike atomic primitives, like point and line, similes have a semantic association in the application domain. Simile inferences describe the conditions under which similes should be incorporated into the object frame.

There are two major classes of similes: prototypes and modifiers. Each object is constructed from one prototype and any number of modifiers. Prototypes are semantically linked to object types. Each prototype graphically defines the common components of all objects of its associated type. Modifiers are semantically linked to attributes. Modifiers define changes to the prototype that make it conform to the particular instance of the object type specified by the quasi-description.

There are two subclasses of modifier similes: transformative and structural. Transformative modifiers are uniform changes to objects. These include the common geometric transformations of scaling, rotation, and translation; color transformations; and changes in object shading. Structural modifiers define specialized alterations to object geometries. The alterations required to convert a generic ship to an aircraft carrier are an

example of a structural modifier.

Structural modifiers are further divided into intrinsic structural modifiers and extrinsic structural modifiers. Intrinsic structural modifiers affect the intrinsic nature of the object's geometry. Conversion of a generic ship into an aircraft carrier requires an intrinsic structural modifier. Extrinsic structural modifiers effect ancillary alterations to the object's geometry. Attachment of a flag to the mast of a ship is an example of an extrinsic structural modifier. Intrinsic structural modifiers are acted on by transformative modifiers; extrinsic structural modifiers are not.

5.2 Structural Couplers

Structural couplers describe how to apply structural modifier similes to prototype similes. Each structural coupler is defined with respect to a particular prototype and a particular structural modifier. All couplers referring to a particular modifier can be thought of as the embedded intelligence for using that modifier.

A structural modifier might not have an exhaustive set of associated couplers for all object synthesis situations. Whenever a structural coupler is unavailable, object synthesis must rely on more general advice for applying modifiers. This more general advice is embedded in object grids.

5.3 Object Grids

The object grid is a set of guidelines, or heuristics, for determining how structural modifiers may be appropriately combined with the prototype into a coherent, composite object. Conceptually, the object grid is an extension of the design grids used by graphic designers [VIGNELLI].

6. The Synthesis Agenda

Object synthesis proceeds according to a sequence of sequential tasks that are referred to collectively as the synthesis agenda. The synthesis agenda is:

1. Select similes

2. Apply intrinsic structural modifiers

3. Apply transformative modifiers

4. Apply extrinsic structural modifiers

5. Select an object grid (optional)

6. Position unassimilated structural modifiers (optional)

6.1 Task 1: Select Similes

To select similes, simile inferences are activated which fill in the Simile attributes of each ELEMENT in the object frame. A prototype simile is selected based on the type of object to be represented. Modifier similes are chosen to conform with the object's attributes.

6.2 Task 2: Apply Intrinsic Structural Modifiers

To accomplish this task, structural couplers designated for the combination of the prototype and the intrinsic structural modifiers chosen in task 1 are activated. The action of a structural coupler involves three steps:

1. Create new, compositional, First and Last ELEMENTs of the FRAGMENT containing the intrinsic modifier. Fill the Compositional_Code attribute of the First ELEMENT with code to push the current positioning transformation (CPT), and orient the modifier with respect to the prototype. Fill the Compositional_Code attribute of the Last ELEMENT with code to pop the CPT stack.

2. Append the list of ELEMENTs of the FRAGMENT containing the intrinsic modifier to the list of ELEMENTs of the FRAGMENT containing the prototype.

3. Delete the FRAGMENT initially containing the intrinsic modifier.

If there are no suitable structural couplers for any intrinsic modifier, optional agenda tasks 5 and 6 are added to the agenda for this object.

6.3 Task 3: Apply Transformative Modifiers

Transformative modifiers are applied using the following procedure:

1. For each transformative modifier:

   a. Insert the transformative modifier ELEMENT before the First ELEMENT of the FRAGMENT contain-

ing the prototype. (This creates a new First ELEMENT.)

   b. Delete the FRAGMENT that initially contained the transformative modifier.

2. Create new, compositional, First and Last ELEMENTS of the FRAGMENT containing the prototype. Fill the Compositional_Code attribute of the First ELEMENT with code to push the current color map. Fill the Compositional_Code attribute of the Last ELEMENT with code to pop the color map.

6.4 Task 4: Apply Extrinsic Structural Modifiers

This task is very similar to task 2. In this case, structural couplers designated for the combination of the prototype and the extrinsic structural modifiers are activated. The effects of these structural couplers on the object frame are the same as those of the structural couplers for intrinsic structural modifiers described under task 2.

6.5 Task 5: Select an Object Grid

This task and task 6 are included in the synthesis agenda if no suitable structural coupler is available for any intrinsic or extrinsic structural modifier. Detection of the lack of a suitable structural modifier and subsequent modification of the synthesis agenda may occur during task 2 or task 4.

If task 5 is included in the agenda, one object grid -- the most suitable one in the knowledge base -- is activated. Its effect is to divide the available REGION of space into smaller REGIONs for the FRAGMENTs containing the prototype and the unassimilated modifiers. Activation of the object grid results in deletion of the original REGION and creation of new, smaller REGIONs, one for each remaining FRAGMENT.

6.6 Task 6: Position Unassimilated Structural Modifiers

This task is accomplished procedurally. The ELEMENTs graphically realized by the unassimilated modifiers are examined in order of Importance. For each such ELEMENT, the available REGIONs are examined in order of Prominence. If

1. the modifier fits in the REGION, and

2. the object attribute represented by the ELEMENT is in the list of Recommendations for the region,
then the following steps are taken:

1. Create new, compositional First and Last ELEMENTs for the FRAGMENT containing the modifier. Fill the Compositional_Code attribute of the First ELEMENT with graphical-description code to push the CPT, and translate by the X-Offset, Y-Offset, and Z-Offset of the REGION. Fill the Compositional_Code attribute of the Last ELEMENT with code to pop the CPT.

2. Append the list of ELEMENTs of the FRAGMENT containing the unassimilated modifier to the list of ELEMENTs of the FRAGMENT containing the prototype.

3. Delete the FRAGMENT initially containing the unassimilated modifier.

4. Delete the selected REGION.

If this process fails to position any modifiers, it is repeated without the second clause of the predicate.

7. Synthesis Control

Synthesis control is responsible for directing the overall process of object synthesis. It does this by selecting, in order, the synthesis operators and procedures to be applied.

Synthesis control pursues the synthesis agenda described above. The synthesis agenda prescribes a hierarchic structuring for the object synthesis process. Synthesis proceeds by incremental refinement from the initial quasi-description to the completed, graphical object description. Each level of refinement results from elaborations to the object frame made to accomplish a single task in the synthesis agenda. This hierarchical approach results in better-informed selection of synthesis operators.

The selection of a synthesis operator often is dependent on many components of the object frame, not just the component being refined. Facts relevant to the selection of a synthesis operator often are asserted during previous stages of the hierarchic refinement. The more facts that are available, the better informed the synthesis operator choice will be.

Object synthesis control is based on a strategy that is itself hierarchic. The process that determines how to proceed in object synthesis first makes an abstract decision about what to do next, then refines that decision at two, more detailed levels of decision making until a specific synthesis operator is chosen. The three, hierarchic levels of control are:

1. Task selection
2. Component selection
3. Operator selection

In the final level, operator selection, a specific synthesis operator is chosen and passed to the operator processing subsystem. Figure 7.1 shows the relationships between the levels of control and operator processing.

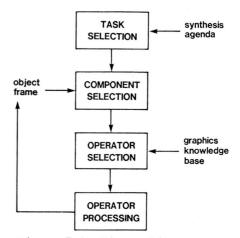

Figure 7.1 Hierarchic Structure of Synthesis Control

7.1 Task Selection

Task selection sequentially steps through the agenda of synthesis tasks. For each task, task selection instructs the next level of control, component selection, to choose from the synthesis state an ELEMENT, FRAGMENT, or REGION upon which to perform the selected task. If component selection reports that no such component exists, the current agenda task is considered complete, and task selection advances to the next agenda task. If there are no more tasks in the synthesis agenda, object synthesis is finished.

7.2 Component Selection

Component selection accepts the current synthesis task from task selection. It examines the object frame and selects the next component of the object frame -- an ELEMENT, FRAGMENT, or REGION -- to be processed in completing the task.

It instructs the next level of control, operator selection, to choose a synthesis operator that will transform the selected component in a way that contributes to the completion of the synthesis task.

The nature of the synthesis task specifies the type of component to be selected. Tasks 1, 2, 3, and 4 (select similes, apply intrinsic structural modifiers, apply transformative modifiers, and apply extrinsic structural modifiers) affect ELEMENTs. Task 5 refines the REGION of available space. Task 6 affects FRAGMENTs of the object.

The component selection process is straightforward: of those components that are yet to be affected in completing the current synthesis task, choose the one with the greatest importance as defined in the initial quasi-description. This simple, most-important-first heuristic ensures that as object synthesis proceeds and the number of constraints on future, synthesis-operator choices increases, the most important aspects of the object will be least susceptible to compromise.

7.3 Operator Selection

Operator selection is invoked by component selection to choose the best synthesis operator or procedure to apply next during object synthesis. Operator selection supplies the chosen synthesis operator to the operator processing system.

The challenge of operator selection is the avoidance of saturation, or knowledge inundation. Saturation refers to the phenomenon of decreased performance as the size of the system's knowledge base increases. It is symptomatic of the greater effort expended in searching a large set of knowledge sources and deciding which of the logically applicable knowledge sources is the best to apply. Saturation is a chronic problem in the construction of knowledge-based systems and is a current research topic in artificial intelligence (e.g., [DAVIS]).

Operator selection chooses the best synthesis operator by selecting the one that is:

1. logically applicable according to its predicate; and

2. recommended for the object synthesis situation that is most similar to, without being more restrictive than, the current situation.

Operator selection identifies the best synthesis operator through simple, best-first search of a directed-graph-like structure referred to as the situation space.

7.3.1 The Situation Space

The situation space is a performance oriented, knowledge-indexing scheme that is the basis of operator selection. The structure of the situation space facilitates efficient search for synthesis operators that are most relevant to the current object-synthesis situation.

The situation space takes the form of a directed graph. Each node or situation is defined by the 4-tuple:

1. Object type

2. List of object attributes

3. Viewer identity

4. Viewer's task

All possible situations in the application domain and viewer community are included in the situation space.

There is an edge in the situation space from situation A to situation B if exactly one of the following conditions is met:

1. Entity type A is a specialization of entity type B.

2. Attribute list A is a superset of B with exactly one additional attribute.

3. User identity A is not user identity B.

4. User task A is not user task B.

Each situation in the situation space indexes a set of synthesis operators. A synthesis operator is indexed by the most general situation for which it is recommended. If a synthesis operator is applicable in two or more disjoint situations, it will be indexed by multiple situations. Generality is determined principally by the position of the object type in the specialization-generalization taxonomy of object types in the application domain. A secondary factor is the cardinality of the attribute list, with fewer attributes implying greater generality.

Of all situations in the situation space, the situation that exactly matches the quasi-description is termed the home situation. The situations on all paths from the home situation collectively index the active knowledge set. The active knowledge set contains all potentially useful synthesis operators. All other synthesis operators are ignored. Thus, the situation space provides dynamic, quasi-description-sensitive partitioning of the knowledge base of synthesis operators. This partitioning guarantees that no resources will be expended considering completely unusable synthesis operators.

The search for a synthesis operator begins at the home situation and proceeds in a breadth-first fashion:

1. Put the home situation in the situation queue.

2. Consider the first situation in the queue. This situation is called the <u>active</u> <u>situation</u>.

3. Check the set of synthesis operators indexed by the active situation. If a logically applicable operator is found, it is the best synthesis operator as defined by the criteria described above, and the search is complete. If no logically applicable synthesis operator can be found, put all immediate successors of the active situation in the situation queue, and go to step 2.

8. Subobjects

Computer graphicists commonly build object descriptions by:

1. decomposing an object into simpler <u>subobjects</u>;

2. building descriptions of the subobjects; and

3. combining these subobject descriptions into a description of the aggregate object.

Consequently, it typically is easier for human computer graphicists to articulate advice for synthesizing subobjects than for complex aggregate objects.

To take advantage of this more-easily articulated advice directly, the object synthesis technique presented here must be extended to make use of subobjects. Such an extension entails two problems:

1. Decomposing an object into subobjects before synthesis takes place
2. Combining descriptions of subobjects into a description of the aggregate object after synthesis

Solutions to these problems can be provided by a structural-descriptions knowledge base and interpreter.

The knowledge base of structural descriptions defines objects in terms of an arrangement of subobjects. Each object is linked through the subobject relation to the subobjects that compose it. These subobjects are linked by structural relations that define how they are oriented with respect to each other. Figure 8.1 illustrates structural descriptions.

The interpreter of structural descriptions is responsible for accepting the quasi-description for the aggregate object, generating quasi-descriptions for the appropriate subobjects, and combining the resulting, subobject descriptions into an object description for the aggregate object. These tasks are accomplished by a recursive, stack-based processor. Two stacks are used, the <u>operator</u> <u>stack</u> and the <u>object</u> <u>stack</u>. The operator stack contains a list of instructions for the interpreter. The object stack is used to store intermediate object descriptions.

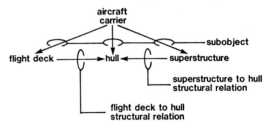

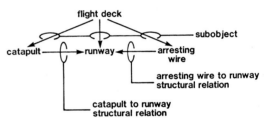

Figure 8.1 Structural Descriptions

Using the interpreter, object synthesis begins by pushing the quasi-description for the aggregate object on the operator stack. The algorithm used by the interpreter is:

1. If the operator stack is empty, return the object on the object stack.

2. Pop the first operator from the operator stack.

3. If the operator is a quasi-description, perform step 3A. Otherwise (the operator is a structural relation), perform step 3B.

   A. If the quasi-description is defined in the structural descriptions knowledge base, perform step 3Aa. Otherwise (the quasi-description is for a primitive object), perform step 3Ab.

a. Push quasi-descriptions followed by structural relations for the object's subobjects on the operator stack.

b. Invoke object synthesis and place the resulting object description on the object stack.

B. Use the structural relation to combine the first two subobjects on the object stack, and push the result on the object stack.

4. Go to step 1.

The interpreter uses the structural-descriptions knowledge base to recursively grow an object-reduction tree in depth-first fashion, as shown in Figure 8.2.

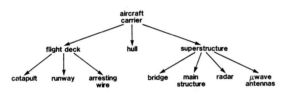

Figure 8.2 An Object Reduction Tree

9. Concluding Remarks

This paper describes a technique for automatically synthesizing object descriptions from high-level, entity-attribute specifications. While this technique has been used successfully in two experimental systems, much more research is required to develop a powerful and comprehensive theory of automatic graphics generation.

Special effort should be directed at two problems. First, better techniques are needed for acquiring graphics knowledge from people. It should be possible for people with relevant expertise -- computer graphics, graphic design, and ergonomics -- to "teach" the machine in a natural way. Second, all embedded graphics knowledge should be exploited as fully as possible. Mechanisms are needed to enable a graphics generator to apply its knowledge base in original ways as unanticipated graphics-generation tasks are encountered.

10. Acknowledgements

I would like to thank Fred Parke at New York Institute of Technology and Ronni Rosenberg and Diane Smith at Computer Corporation of America for their helpful comments on an earlier version of this text.

11. References

[BRACHMAN]
Brachman, R. J. "The Evolution of a Structural Paradigm for Representing Knowledge." Ph.D. Dissertation, Harvard University.

[DAVIS]
Davis, Randy. "Meta-rules: Reasoning about Control." Artificial Intelligence.

[FRIEDELL et al.]
Friedell, Mark, Barnett, Jane, and Kramlich, David. "Context-Sensitive Graphic Presentation of Information." SIGGRAPH '82 Proceedings. Also published as Computer Graphics, 16, 3 (July, 1982).

[GNANAMGARI]
Gnanamgari, Sakunthala. Information Presentation through Default Displays. Ph.D. dissertation and technical report 81-05-02, Computer and Information Sciences, University of Pennsylvania, Philadelphia, Pennsylvania 19104.

[VIGNELLI]
Vignelli, M. Grids: Their meaning and use for federal designers. Stock no. 036-000-00038-4, Superintendent of Documents, U.S. Government Printing Office, Washington, D.C. 20402.

[ZYDBEL et al.]
Zdybel, Frank; Greenfeld, Norton R.; Yonke, Martin D.; and Gibbons, Jeff. "An Information Presentation System." Proceedings of IJCAI '81.

PANEL

COMPUTING IN THE FAST LANE: SUPERSYSTEMS FOR COMPUTER GRAPHICS

CHAIR: Richard Weinberg - Fifth Generation Graphics, Inc.

PANEL: Mike Cosman - Evans and Sutherland Computer Co.
        Joe Cychosz - Control Data Corp.
        Gary Demos - Digital Productions
        Koichi Omura - Osaka University
        Rodney Stock - Lucasfilm Ltd.

The fast generation of complex synthetic
images by digital computing systems requires immense computational resources,
which can be provided by several means.

Supercomputers, flight simulators and
special purpose image synthesis architectures will be examined and compared by
the panel. Each of these systems represents the very high end of the computational spectrum, with performance measured
in hundreds of millions of operations per
second.

Supercomputers are the fastest general
purpose computers available. Today's
supercomputers feature a small number of
extremely fast general purpose vector
processors, and have been used primarily
for scientific and engineering calculations, until the recent interest in their
use for generating images.

Flight simulator graphics systems were one
of the earliest uses of real time computer
graphics. Current flight simulator systems can generate several complex images
simultaneously at television resolution,
in real time. The images generated are of
high enough quality that pilots can be
trained almost entirely through the use of
simulation. These systems consist of a
small number of special purpose processors
dedicated to different stages of image
synthesis.

Special purpose architectures are now
being developed for synthesizing images.
These architectures can provide large
scale parallelism, and hardware tailored
to graphics oriented calculations. They
hold the promise of low cost and high
speed by virtue of their special purpose
nature.

The panel will discuss the architectural
features, programming, price/performance,
complexity, utility, philosophy, numerical
accuracy, speed requirements and evolu-
tionary trends behind these systems.

PANEL

"A RETROSPECTIVE: SIX PERENNIAL ISSUES IN COMPUTER GRAPHICS"

CHAIR: Robert M. Dunn - R.M. Dunn & Associates, Inc.

PANEL: Alan Kay - Apple Computer
        Carl Machover - Machover Associates
        David Evans - Evans and Sutherland
        Robert Sproull - Sutherland, Sproull & Associates
        James Foley - George Washington University
        Robin Forrest - University of East Anglia
        Ed Catmul - Lucasfilm, Ltd.
        Steve Levine - Electronic Graphics Associates
        Gwenn Bell - Computer Museum
        Oliver Strimple - Computer Museum
        Dave Wilson - Technical Marketing Limited

Graphics has been an industry for more than 15 years. Some workers trace its origins almost 30 years. The dramatic gains in silicon technology along with more highly developed understanding of the mathematics of graphics have transformed the architecture of computer graphic systems and produced a bewildering array of products and services.

This retrospective panel will try to put several key things in perspective. Dr. Alan Kay, recently of Atari Computer and currently an Apple Fellow, will characterize the role of graphics in the overall world of computing and information processing. Carl Machover of Machover Associates will trace the development of display technology and its employment in computer graphics systems. Dr. David Evan, Chairman of the Board of Evans and Sutherland will create the retrospective on our ability to produce realism in imagery. In turn, Dr. Robert Sproull, Sutherland, Sutherland and Associates will trace the development of transformation that have found their way into silicon technology. Dr. James Foley, of George Washington University will track our progress in the technology of interaction, while Dr. Robin Forrest of the University of East Anglia will trace geometric modelling and Dr. Ed Catmul, Director of Development at Lucasfilm will put our progress in animation in perspective.

The session will conclude with a five minute A/V production created by Dr. Steve Levine of Electronic Graphics Associates and Mr. David Wilson of Technical Marketing Limited. This A/V summary not only will conclude the session, but will be made available to the Computer Museum in Boston, Massachusetts as part of its permanent 5,000 sq. ft. exhibit on computer graphics. The session will be chaired by Robert M. Dunn of R.M. Dunn & Associates, and the CADWARE Group, Ltd., and is co-sponsored by each of the Computer Museum, Computer Graphics Pioneers and Siggraph.

A Parallel Processor System for Three-Dimensional Color Graphics

Haruo Niimi
Dept. of Information Science
Kyoto University
Sakyo-ku, Kyoto, 606, Japan

Yoshirou Imai
Takuma Radio Technical College
Mitoyo-gun, Kagawa, 769-11, Japan

Masayoshi Murakami
Nippon Denshi Kagaku Co., Ltd.
Joyo-shi, Kyoto, 610-01, Japan

Shinji Tomita and *Hiroshi Hagiwara*
Dept. of Information Science
Kyoto University
Sakyo-ku, Kyoto, 606, Japan

Abstract

This paper describes the hardware architecture and the employed algorithm of a parallel processor system for three-dimensional color graphics. The design goal of the system is to generate realistic images of three-dimensional environments on a raster-scan video display in real-time. In order to achieve this goal, the system is constructed as a two-level hierarchical multi-processor system which is particularly suited to incorporate scan-line algorithm for hidden surface elimination. The system consists of several Scan-Line Processors (SLPs), each of which controls several slave PiXel Processors (PXPs). The SLP prepares the specific data structure relevant to each scan line, while the PXP manipulates every pixel data in its own territory. Internal hardware structures of the SLP and the PXP are quite different, being designed for their dedicated tasks.

This system architecture can easily execute scan-line algorithm in parallel by partitioning the entire image space and allotting one processor element to each partition. The specific partition scheme and some new data structures are introduced to exploit as much parallelism as possible. In addition, the scan-line algorithm is extended to include smooth-shading and anti-aliasing with the aim of rendering more realistic images. These two operations are performed on a per-scan-line basis so as to preserve scan-line and span coherence.

Performance estimation of the system shows that a typical system consisting of 8 SLPs and 8×8 PXPs can generate, in every 1/15th of a second, the shadowed image of a three-dimensional scene containing about 200 polygons.

CR Categories and Subject Descriptors: B.1.5 [Control Structures and Microprogramming]: Microcode Applications - Special-purpose; B.5.1 [Register-Transfer-Level Implementation]: Design - Data-path design; Memory design; C.1.2 [Processor Architectures]: Multiprocessors - Parallel processors; I.3.1 [Computer Graphics]: Hardware Architecture - Raster display devices; I.3.7 [Computer Graphics]: Three-Dimensional Graphics and Realism - Color, shading, and shadowing; Visible surface algorithm.

1. Introduction

Recent advances in LSI and video display technologies have brought remarkable changes in the computer graphics world. For instance, raster-scan graphic terminals have become widely used, with the display resolution growing higher and the graphical functions becoming richer and more powerful. At the same time, instead of the conventional wire-frame modeling, surface or solid modeling technique is more often adopted in various applications such as CAD/CAM or simulation of natural phenomena [8]. In these applications, especially in an interactive environment, rapid generation of a shaded image of the three-dimensional scene is essential for effective man-machine communication.

In order to make this feasible, it is necessary to reduce the time required for scan conversion. This speeding up can be attained by the use of a parallel and/or pipelined architecture as well as the proper adaptation of appropriate algorithm to the specific architecture.

Several multi-processor systems for high-speed image synthesis have been proposed [2][3][4][7]. Most of these proposals exploited parallelism offered by depth-buffer (z-buffer) algorithm. Since this algorithm is an integral collection of simple, granular processes performed on a per-pixel basis, it is fairly easy to adopt parallel processing. However, it is very difficult to embed in this algorithm, such calculations as anti-aliasing and shadowing, because these calculations require several values for pixels at a time and are history sensitive.

We are now designing an alternative to these systems: a high-speed parallel processor system for three-dimensional color graphics, called EXPERTS (an EXPandable Parallel processor Enhancing Real-Time Scan conversion). In the course of our design process, the following two major decisions were made.

First, scan-line algorithm is incorporated for the purpose of hidden surface removal, since
1) it is one of the most efficient hidden-surface algorithms over the domain of polyhedral models,
2) it can simply be extended to include techniques for achieving realism, such as smooth-shading or

Permission to copy without fee all or part of this material is granted provided that the copies are not made or distributed for direct commercial advantage, the ACM copyright notice and the title of the publication and its date appear, and notice is given that copying is by permission of the Association for Computing Machinery. To copy otherwise, or to republish, requires a fee and/or specific permission.

© 1984   ACM   0-89791-138-5/84/007/0067 $00.75

shadowing, and

3) it can be executed in parallel by partitioning the image space, so that the advantage of parallel processing can be exploited.

Second, the system is constructed as a two-level hierarchical multi-processor system. This is because scan-line algorithm can be divided into two distinct processing stages. The entire system is composed of several Scan-Line Processors (SLPs), each of which in turn controls several slave PiXel Processors (PXPs). The SLP prepares the specific data structure relevant to each scan-line, while the PXP manipulates every pixel data in its own territory. Internal hardware structures of the SLP and the PXP are quite different, being designed for their dedicated tasks. Hence, intra-level parallel processing as well as inter-level pipeline processing can be performed.

This system architecture is derived very naturally from deep investigation into scan-line algorithm and its parallel execution. The details of the system structure, the scan-line algorithm, and their relationship are described in chapter 2. Chapters 3 and 4 describe the processor architecture of the SLPs and the PXPs in detail, introducing their microinstruction formats and specific features.

The other hardware elements equipped to exploit parallelism are summarized in chapter 5. Chapter 6 suggests the strategy for dynamic load balancing among the processor elements, which is essential to make the best use of parallelism. System performance in the hypothetically typical cases is shown in chapter 7, using the number of relevant polygons and the depth complexity of the scene as parameters.

2. Scan-line Algorithm and the Processor Hierarchy of the EXPERTS

In generating images of three-dimensional environments, two kinds of processings must be executed:

(1) *Calculations executed prior to hidden-surface removal, e.g., coordinate transformations, polygon clipping, etc.* These processes take a substantial amount of time. However, since most of these operations are simple arithmetic loops, conventional hardware techniques such as pipelined array processors or matrix multipliers could work well. We have already developed a

dynamically microprogrammable computer with low-level parallelism, called QA-2[10]. Since the QA-2 employs four powerful ALUs which work in parallel, these geometrical calculations can be performed very efficiently.

(2) *Hidden-surface removal using scan-line algorithm (SLA).* This process requires sorting several list-structured data. Since sorting a list involves sequentially traversing the data-structure, it is hard to execute it in parallel. In addition, its computational complexity might grow according to a square-law. Thus, high-speed execution of SLA would require sophisticated techniques to make the best use of parallel and/or pipeline processing capability.

As a result of these considerations, we designed the EXPERTS to serve as a post-processor to the host machine. After geometrical computations, the host machine calculates a list of polygon data in the entire scene and transmits it to the EXPERTS. The EXPERTS receives the data and performs high-speed hidden-surface elimination (HSE) and some succeeding processes for enhancing realism.

In order to make the most use of parallel and pipeline processing capability of the hardware, we tried to divide the SLA into the following sub-tasks.

(I) Since SLA computes visible surfaces in a single scan line at a time and proceeds from the top scan line to the bottom, the entire image space can be divided into some bundles of scan lines where the algorithm is applicable independently of each other. This division means that, for each region, the display size is diminished in the vertical direction. Hence, no modification of the algorithm is required, and parallelism can be incorporated simply by allocating each bundle of scan lines to one of the processor elements.

(II) A process within one scan line can also be divided clearly into the following two successive processing stages, maintaining a data structure called Active Segment List (ASL) as the interfacing data between the two. The ASL is a linked list of active segments (intersections of polygons with a scan line – see Figure 1) which are sorted by the position of a segment's left edge.

[Stage-1]: This stage sets up an initial ASL for the first scan line at the top of the screen by reading a polygon list (PL) sent from the host machine. For each scan line in the rest of the display, this stage updates the previous ASL to make up the new ASL. Updating ASL involves deleting and appending segment data blocks from/to the list, calculating new positions of

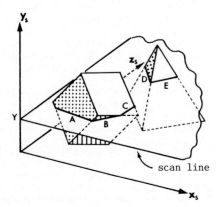

Figure 1(a). Polygons and a scan line in the screen coordinate system

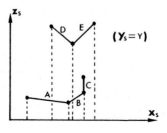

Figure 1(b). Active segments

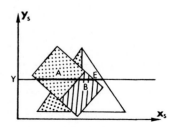

Figure 1(c). Segments: A, B, and E are visible.

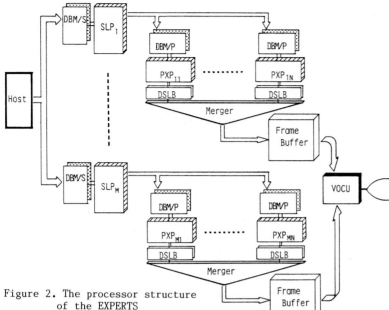

Figure 2. The processor structure
of the EXPERTS

DBM/S : Dual Buffer Memory for the SLP
DBM/P : Dual Buffer Memory for the PXP
DSLB : Dual Scan-Line Buffer
VOCU : Video Output Control Unit

all segments in the list, and reordering the data blocks so as to keep the ASL correctly sorted. These computations may seem to be a serious burden. However, due to scan-line coherence [6], most of the computations are simple comparisons or additions using pre-computed edge slope values stored in each segment data block.

[Stage-2]: This stage, in turn, determines the set of visible segments in one scan line by exploring (or consuming) the ASL from the left to the right and identifying sample spans. Within each span, depth comparisons of segments are made to decide which segment is really visible, and then ultimate values of the pixels for the visible segments are calculated. If the identified visible segment is of a shadow polygon, it is treated as a transparent segment and the intensity of the next visible segment in the span is degraded. Techniques for rendering more realistic images such as smooth-shading or anti-aliasing are also applied to the calculation. To reduce these workloads, the algorithm also makes use of span coherence.

There is neither feed-back of data nor that of control from Stage-2 to Stage-1. Therefore, execution of Stage-2 might be completely overlapped in a pipelining manner with that of Stage-1, which is then processing the next scan line. Further, Stage-2 must be executed in parallel. This is because the computational amount involved in this stage is considerably larger than that in Stage-1. To keep a data stream in the pipeline smooth and regular, processing time taken by both stages must be balanced, or at least comparable.

These considerations are reflected in the processor structure of the EXPERTS, as shown in Figure 2; a multi-processor system having two levels of hierarchy. For convenience, the first (or higher) level processor element is called SLP (Scan Line Processor) and the second (or lower) level processor element is called PXP (PiXel Processor). The SLPs are prepared for Stage-1; performing initialization and updating of the

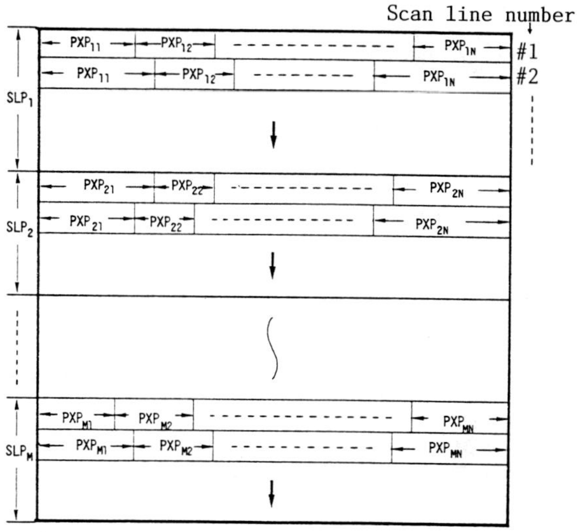

Figure 3.   Image space partitioning scheme

Active Segment List. The PXPs serve to execute hidden-surface elimination and anti-aliasing or smooth-shading in Stage-2. The resulting scheme of image space partitioning is depicted in Figure 3. The SLP and the PXP are designed to meet the requirements for high-speed processing of each dedicated task. The numbers of the SLPs ("M") and the PXPs ("N") need not be fixed, rather they can be so selected as to satisfy the performance requirement of the system. In our preliminary design, both are limited to 16 by hardware implementation constraints, but the value 16 is never crucial to the system design.

The Scan-Line Algorithm employed here is a novel one in that it introduces some new data structures to reduce the overhead which might appear in parallel processing. It should also be noted that the algorithm is extended to execute smooth-shading and anti-aliasing on a per-scan-line basis so as to preserve scan-line coherence and span coherence of the algorithm.

3. Processor Element: SLP (Scan Line Processor)

An SLP was particularly designed to enhance processing speed of ASL-initialization and ASL-updating processes, and transfers the results to its slave PXPs.

3.1 Hardware for ASL-initialization

ASL-initialization is only performed at the first of the scan lines allocated to the SLP. Suppose that a triangle *ABC* intersects the first scan line and will be registered in the ASL. Each vertex of the triangle is defined by a four-dimensional vector (three for screen coordinates and one for intensity), such that

$A(X_a,Y_a,Z_a,I_a)$, $B(X_b,Y_b,Z_b,I_b)$, and $C(X_c,Y_c,Z_c,I_c)$.

Using these vertex vectors, the ASL-initialization process calculates such coefficients as dx/dy, dz/dy, dz/dx, di/dx, etc. These coefficients will be maintained in the triangle *ABC*'s segment data block of the ASL and will be used in ASL-updating process as long as this triangle intersects the successive scan lines. A typical time-consuming computation appears in calculating dz/dx:

$$\frac{dz}{dx}=\frac{(Y_b-Y_c)(Z_a-Z_c)-(Y_a-Y_c)(Z_b-Z_c)}{(Y_b-Y_c)(X_a-X_c)-(Y_a-Y_c)(X_b-X_c)}.$$

Since every calculation is performed in the screen-coordinate system, 16-bit-wide data can offer sufficient precision. Only in division is floating-point arithmetic necessary to guarantee ample precision. To perform these computations at a high speed, the SLP employs a powerful functional unit (FU) as shown in Figure 4. It consists of
a) a 16-bit ALU (Arithmetic Logic Unit), using four AMD Am2903As,
b) a 16×16-bit multiplier, using an AMD Am29516,
c) a full adder attached to b) for calculating exponent parts of floating-point data,
d) an inverse approximation table for high-speed division,
e) data format converters between fixed-point and floating-point numbers, and
f) abundant register files.
In addition, interconnection buses among these components are designed to make their concurrent operations work efficiently.

3.2 Hardware for ASL-updating

ASL-updating is repeated until the allocated scan lines are exhausted. The total amount of computation will become large, but the inner computation is not so complicated as that of ASL-initialization. This is due to scan-line coherence. The problem here is rather how to access data blocks in an ASL efficiently and how to sort an ASL quickly.

Because access to a linked list is inherently sequential, the only way to speed up the process is to overlap the three operations: reading, modifying, and writing data. The SLP, therefore, is equipped with Scratch Pad Memory (SPM) for this purpose.

The SPM is composed of five logical banks of a high-speed, 32-word register file with autonomous memory access capability. As illustrated in Figure 4, the SPM is connected to five data buses; two memory buses (read and write buses) and three

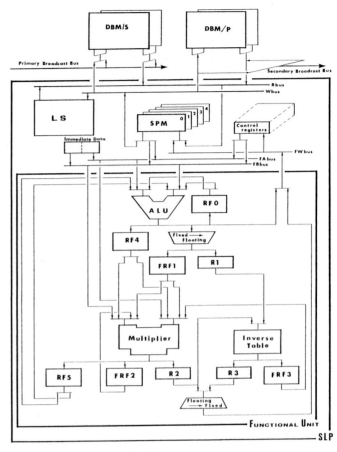

LS (Local Storage): 16bits × 64Kwords
SPM(Scratch Pad Memory): 16bits × 32words × 5
RF (Register File):
 RF0: 16bits × 16words
 RF4: 16bits × 16words
 RF5: 32bits × 16words
FRF(Floating point Register File):
 FRF1: 24bits × 16words
 FRF2: 24bits × 8words
 FRF3: 24bits × 8words
R-bus, W-bus: 16bits
FA-bus, FB-bus, FW-bus: 16bits

Figure 4. Hardware structure of the SLP

Functional-Unit buses (right source, left source and destination buses). All of the five banks can work simultaneously, and arbitrary one-to-one interconnection between banks and buses is possible. Data transfer between SPM and memory is carried out by hardware, so a program only signals its invocation specifying a transfer word count. The following operation, for instance, can be executed simultaneously:

While a completed data block in the bank-0 SPM (SPM0) is being stored into the memory, calculation using operands fetched from the SPM1 and SPM2 can proceed with its result being written to the SPM3, and at the same time, the next data block is being loaded into the SPM4.

Each access to the SPM is to be done through its logical bank number. For the programmers' convenience, the correspondence between the logical bank numbers and the physical bank numbers can be instantly changed under program control.

Therefore, by successively exchanging the role of each bank of the SPM, sequential processing of list structured data, such as ASL-updating, can be executed effectively on the SLP. In fact, since memory accesses are performed autonomously by hardware and asynchronously with Functional-Unit operations, the time required for loading and storing data blocks can be thoroughly overlapped by the time for data modification process.

There are other facilities equipped for list processing: auxiliary MARs (Memory Address Registers) and a trap mechanism for illegal memory access. The auxiliary MAR is located at address 0 of each SPM bank (thus there are five, in total), and its contents are modified whenever the data is transferred from memory to that SPM bank. They are functionally equivalent to other ordinary MARs, but can be forced to hold a pointer value to the next data block in the list as long as data blocks are so designed. If a certain MAR contains "nil" and memory access using this MAR is signaled, the trap mechanism will be invoked. Through this hardware mechanism, successive traversal of a list structure can be initiated by a program without worrying about illegal memory access.

The SLP also contains various control registers, which are used for residual control, for saving system conditions or constants, and for other specific purposes. These include MARs and interrupt vector registers. The control registers are allocated in the address space of the SPM, hence they can be equally accessed from the Functional-Unit.

The SLP is designed as a microprogrammable computer. As shown in Figure 5, various hardware components are concurrently controlled by the different fields of a 101-bit wide microinstruction. The cycle time of the microinstruction is 200 nano seconds, using an AMD Am2910 for controlling the execution sequence of microinstructions.

4. Processor Element: PXP (PiXel Processor)

A PXP takes an Active Segment List (ASL) as input from its master SLP, and performs hidden-surface elimination (HSE). When a visible segment is identified, the span is determined in which pixels are filled with some values. Then the PXP calculates color and intensity value of each pixel in the span. Smooth-shading technique and anti-aliasing technique are applied to each pixel within the span and at the boundaries of the span, respectively. Finally the PXP transfers resulting color and intensity values to an image memory.

4.1 Hardware for Accessing List-structured Data

As in the case of SLP, the PXP needs to make frequent accesses to list-structured data. So, many features of the PXP hardware organization are the same as those of the SLP (see Figure 6). The SPM (Scratch Pad Memory) is analogous to that of the SLP, composed of high-speed, 32-word register files. But the number of logical banks is reduced to 4, as that is sufficient in this case. On the other hand, two words of auxiliary MARs are prepared in each bank of the SPM, because there is a substantial amount of processing performed over doubly-linked list structered data. The trap mechanism for nil-pointer access is also incorporated.

4.2 Hardware for Clipping

As already mentioned, each PXP is responsible for only a part of the entire scan line. As an ASL transferred from the SLP contains all active segments, the PXP must first perform clipping of the ASL. Notice here, that this clipping is done only at the left boundary of the allotted range of pixels. The end of the process can be recognized when the calculation of pixel values has reached the right most pixel, hence there is no need for a priori clipping for the right boundary. Since this clipping involves many multiplications, the PXP has a fixed-point hardware multiplier. The PXP does not support floating-point arithmetic, because every calculation is carried out in a screen coordinate system with at most 12-bits precision, and no division other than those by 2 is required.

4.3 Hardware for Smooth-shading

A smooth-shading technique employed here is based on the technique proposed by Gouraud [5]:

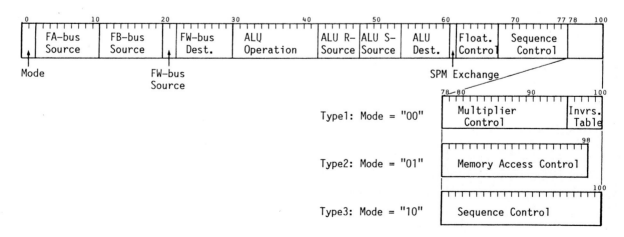

Figure 5. The microinstruction format of the SLP

linear interpolation of intensity values. Suppose that a segment PQ is identified as being visible, and hence, the intensities at every pixel between the left edge P and the right edge Q must be computed. Let the intensity at P be Ip and the intensity at Q be Iq. Then intensity of every pixel between P and Q can be expressed by a linear combination of Ip and Iq, with the sum of their coefficients equal to 1. Notice that the differential coefficient of intensity, di/dx, has already been computed by the SLP, and is held in the segment block with the intensity Ip. Therefore, the calculation of smooth-shading is simplified to an incremental addition of the constant di/dx. Because this computation is trivial, it would be too wasteful for the ALU to be engaged in it.

As shown in Figure 6, S.S.Special is prepared for this computation. It is composed of a full-adder, a counter and some registers, and is able to operate concurrently with the ALU. Each of the registers plays a unique role in the course of computation. After values of the initial intensity "Ip", the constant "di/dx", and the length of the segment "PQ" are set to these registers and the counter, the S.S.Special can start calculating. The computation proceeds one pixel after another autonomously with the counter value being decremented. When the counter value gets equal to 0, the S.S.Special stops and a flag is set to indicate termination of smooth-shading.

4.4 Hardware for Anti-aliasing

An anti-aliasing technique employed here is unique among those proposed in many systems [1]. Since the PXP performs Hidden-Surface Elimination (HSE) scan-line by scan-line, computation for anti-aliasing must also be completed within the extent of one scan line. Aliases may occur only at the boundaries of polygons (i.e., at the edge), where visible segments are changing from the left to the right in the course of HSE. And if the pixel value at the boundary is determined from these values of left and right visible segments alternatively, alias will inevitably appear. Instead of selecting only one of the two pixel values of neighboring visible segments, a technique used here calculates a new value from the two by using the following formula;

Let Cl and Cr be pixel-values of the left segment and the right segment respectively. Then the pixel value of the boundary pixel can be calculated as:

$$C = \alpha \cdot Cl + (1-\alpha) \cdot Cr,$$

where the coefficient α takes a value between 0 and 1.

Since both Cl and Cr are calculated by the Scan-Line Algorithm and the succeeding smooth-shading process, the only problem is how to decide the value of α. Ideally, using the value of the area occupied by the left segment in the boundary pixel is supposed to be the most exact solution (see Figure 7a:"A"). However, it requires a considerable amount of computation. Our solution is to use the fractional part of a coordinate value of the boundary edge position, as illustrated in Figure 7b:"d". Note that, the calculation must be

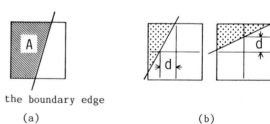

the boundary edge

(a)   (b)

Figure 7. Calculation of the anti-aliasing coefficient: α

Figure 6. Hardware structure of the PXP

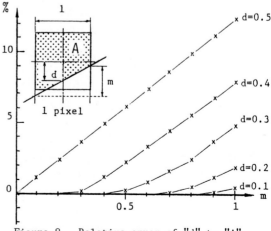

Figure 8. Relative error of "d" to "A"

altered according to whether the gradient of the boundary edge is larger than 45° or not.

This solution is fairly simple, because all of the necessary values have already been obtained in the segment data blocks and used by the Scan-Line Algorithm. Figure 8 shows that this is not a bad approximation. The problem is to minimize computational overhead in executing the above formula. Since each pixel value of $C1$ and Cr is expressed as a 4 dimensional vector (Red, Green, Blue, and Intensity), the calculation must be carried out four times.

A.A.Special in Figure 6 is specially designed for these computations. This component is in fact a set of look-up tables. Let's see the case of calculating a value for Red, for instance. After the values $C1:(R1,G1,B1,I1)$, $Cr:(Rr,Gr,Br,Ir)$, and α are all set to the specific registers, the A.A.Special concatenates $R1$, Rr, and α together (3, 3, 6 bits for each, and altogether 12 bits), and feeds it into the look-up table as an address. Then the result R will be put out from the table. The same process is also applied to the cases of Green and Blue. Only for the case of Intensity, is computation carried out through the ALU, because the number of bits assigned for the Intensity is too large (7 bits) to construct a look-up table (7, 7, 6 bits for each, hence altogether 20 bits!).

The PXP is also a microprogrammable processor controlled by a microinstruction of 88-bit wide. The cycle time for a microinstruction is 200 nsec. The microinstruction format of the PXP is presented in Figure 9.

5. Hardware Facilities for Inter-processor Communication

As already mentioned, the EXPERTS employs a two-level hierarchical multi-processor architecture, incorporating pipeline processing and parallel processing. In order to make these processor elements co-operate smoothly, the following hardware components are installed around the processor elements (see Figure 2,4,6):

5.1 The Dual Buffer Memory for the SLP (DBM/S) and for the PXP (DBM/P).

The DBM/S is installed in each SLP and is used as a data buffer of the Polygon List (PL) transmitted from the host machine to the SLP. In order to overlap the PL generation process of the host machine with the PL reading process of the SLP, the DBM/S is composed of two identical memory planes (we call these as plane-A and plane-B). While the host machine is putting out the PL to the plane-A(-B), the SLP can simultaneously make read-accesses to the plane-B(-A). Thus, the DBM/S is working as a FIFO queue of length 2. Although there are several DBM/Ss against a single host machine, all the DBM/Ss are allocated in the same position in the memory address space of the host machine. This is because the transmission of the PL is done in a broadcasting manner. From the SLP's view, in turn, the DBM/S is merely a local storage that can be freely read from or written to.

The DBM/P is identical to the DBM/S in its construction as well as in its function, except that the DBM/P is installed in each PXP and that it is used for the broadcasting of the Active Segment List (ASL) from the master SLP to the PXPs.

5.2 The Dual Scan-Line Buffer (DSLB) and the Merger.

Remember that several PXPs are connected to a single master SLP, and that they calculate pixel values in a certain scan-line simultaneously. Therefore, an access conflict problem of the image memory will arise among the PXPs. To solve this problem, the DSLB and the Merger were introduced.

The DSLB is a high-speed, pixel data cache for one scan-line which is equipped in each PXP, and is composed of two identical memories (the DSLB-A and the DSLB-B), one to be read from by the Merger and the other to be written to by the PXP.

The Merger is equipped in each SLP, and is directly connected to all the DSLBs of the slave PXPs.

Each PXP outputs the allotted extent of pixel values to its own DSLB. After all the PXPs finish their computations in a scan line, the roles of the DSLB-A and the DSLB-B are interchanged by the direction of the master SLP. Then, the Merger collects the latest output data scattered among the DSLBs, merges them correctly into an entire scan-line, and finally transfers them to the Frame Buffer.

The combination of the DSLBs and the Merger unit enables the PXP-level parallel processing to work more efficiently, since the memory access speed is enhanced through the high-speed memories in the DSLB and there will be no overhead caused due to memory contention.

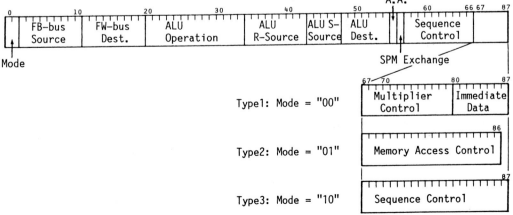

Figure 9. The microinstruction format of the PXP

5.3 Distributed Frame Buffers (FBs) and the Video
    Output Control Unit (VOCU).

As in the case of the PXP-level parallel
processing, there will be an access conflict
problem of the Frame Buffer among the SLPs, more
precisely among the Mergers. However, note that
the FB need not be constructed as a single,
contiguous plane of memory, since only one scan-
line of pixels should be prepared at a time for the
raster-scan display. Here, we can bring in the
remedy which is analogous to the DSLB and the
Merger, i.e., distributed data placement and their
regulated collection by hardware.

The entire screen of the FB is divided into
some bundles of scan-lines and these bundles are
distributed to each of the SLPs. At the same time,
the autonomous hardware unit, the Video Output
Control Unit (VOCU), is prepared for the data
collection. Each distributed FB is a dual-plane
memory, which enables the simultaneous operation of
the Merger's data storing and the VOCU's data
reading. Since each FB is accessed only by one SLP
or by the VOCU, there will be no FB memory
contention. Due to these hardware facilities, the
SLP-level parallel processing is also enhanced.

6. Load Balancing Problem

In a parallel processing environment on a
multi-processor system, it is ideal to distribute
the total system workload equally among all the
processor elements. However, in the case of the
EXPERTS, it is very difficult or almost impossible
to do such an ideal scheduling prior to the actual
execution. This is because the total processing
workload in the system does not simply depend on
the number of input polygons, but deeply depends on
the complexity of the geometrical relations between
the polygons. Hence, some kind of feed-back
control must be employed in controlling the load
balance in order to tune the system activity and to
attain higher performance.

Similarly, in a pipeline processing
environment, the maximum pipeline processing effect
is gained when every processing stage in the pipe
completes its computation in an identical time. In
the case of the EXPERTS, the processing time should
be balanced among these three stages: i.e., the
host machine, the SLPs, and the PXPs. However, if
the number of the SLPs and the PXPs are not
appropriately selected for the problem size of the
application, this balancing cannot be controlled
effectively by the processor elements themselves.

Therefore, it might be reasonable for the
programs of the processor elements to assume that
the system is appropriately configured for the
given application.

Then, for example, if none of the slave PXPs
has finished their computation when the master SLP
terminates, any attempt of the SLP to balance the
PXPs' workloads would have no effect upon the
performance improvement of the entire system. On
the contrary, if all the slave PXPs have finished
their computations before their master SLP
terminates its own computation, the SLP would not
need to invoke the process to control the load
balance among the PXPs.

Consequently, the following strategy for
dynamic load balancing is planned to be applied to
the EXPERTS. Here, we only present the case which

will be executed on the SLP in order to manage the
workload distribution among its slave PXPs. The
analogous procedure will be executed on the host
machine in turn, to manage the SLPs.

Step-1) Until the SLP completes its own process,
    the SLP only receives the completion signals
    from the PXPs;
Step-2) When the SLP terminates, it counts the
    number of completed PXPs [Ncp];
Step-3) If the Ncp is less than $N/2$ (where N is the
    number of the PXPs connected to the master SLP)
    then the SLP waits idly until $N/2$ of the PXPs
    terminate;
Step-4) The SLP identifies the PXPs which have not
    yet terminated, and squeezes their allotted
    extent by a constant number of pixels, the sum
    of which, in turn, are distributed to the rest
    of the PXPs.

7. System Performance Estimation

The two types of processor elements of the
EXPERTS: the Scan-Line Processor (SLP) and the
PiXel Processor (PXP), are both microprogrammable
processors, and all the programs are directly
written in microcode.

Table 1 summarizes the size of the
microprograms coded for various processing stages
in the SLP and in the PXP. Due to the powerful
hardware facilities and the optimal design of the
microinstruction formats, the program sizes are
small enough and the effective usage ratios of the
various control fields of the microinstruction
indicate high values.

The performance estimation of the EXPERTS has
been carried out based on the results of the flow
analysis applied to these microprograms. Each
microprogram was analyzed into such components as
straight paths, loops, and branches. Then, the
number of microinstruction steps for every path and
loop was calculated. And the success probabilities
of the branch conditions were approximated. These
data were collected and used in the calculation of
the executed microinstruction steps.

We chose the parameters of performance
estimation similar to those used in [9]; namely the
number of relevant polygons:"Nr", the number of
shadow polygons:"Ns", the depth complexity of
polygons:"DCr", and the depth complexity of the
shadow polygons:"DCs". For the accurate and
precise definitions of these, see [9].

In addition, we assumed that the average number
of the edges of a polygon is 4, and that the
resolution of the display is 512×512.

As a result, we have obtained the following
expressions which calculate necessary micro-steps
executed. Note that they are the values obtained
for the best case when the workload is completely
balanced among all the processor elements.

1a) Initialization of the Active Segment List on
    the SLP:

$$(15+30 \cdot Nr+28 \cdot Ns) + (73 \cdot Nr+61 \cdot Ns)/M$$
$$[\text{micro-steps}],$$

where "M" is the number of the SLPs in the
system.

1b) Updating the ASL on the SLP:

$$((1044 \cdot N+18065) \cdot S + 11.3 \cdot (Nr+Ns) + 22528)/M$$
$$[\text{micro-steps}],$$

where "N" is the number of the PXPs

Table 1. The size of the microprograms

(a) Initialization of the ASL on the SLP

	Size [micro-steps]				Type1: Field usage [micro-steps]				
	Type1	Type2	Type3	Total	ALU	MPY	INV	Fixed → Float	Float → Fixed
Initialization	11	4	0	15	11	0	0	0	0
Generation of Real Polygon Blocks	27	5	4	36	28	13	2	5	3
Generation of Real Edge Blocks	171	54	28	253	195	81	12	21	21
Generation of Shadow Polygon Blocks	14	5	2	21	16	5	1	2	1
Generation of Shadow Edge Blocks	52	8	16	76	60	26	4	6	6
Total	275 (68.5%)	76 (19.0%)	50 (12.5%)	401	310 (77.3%)	125 (45.5%)	19 (6.9%)	34 (12.4%)	31 (11.3%)

(b) Updating of the ASL on the SLP

	Size [micro-steps]				Type1: Field usage [micro-steps]				
	Type1	Type2	Type3	Total	ALU	MPY	INV	Fixed → Float	Float → Fixed
Deletion of Out-going Edges	1	3	5	9	4	0	0	0	0
Handling of In-coming Edges	44	40	40	124	89	0	0	0	0
Updating of Segment Lists	52	35	35	122	73	2	0	0	0
Dynamic Load Balancing	84	2	110	196	114	32	0	0	0
Total	181 (40.1%)	80 (17.7%)	190 (42.1%)	451	280 (62.1%)	34 (18.8%)	0 (0.0%)	0 (0.0%)	0 (0.0%)

(c) Calculation of pixel data on the PXP

	Size [micro-steps]				Type1: Field usage		
	Type1	Type2	Type3	Total	ALU	MPY	A.A.
Initial Clipping	42	26	27	95	59	0	0
Determination of Visible Segment	35	30	57	122	86	1	0
Handling of Penetrating Segments	75	42	70	187	136	3	0
Handling of Non-penetrating Segments	98	89	75	262	205	12	0
Anti-aliasing	41	2	18	61	51	8	2
Total	291 (40.1%)	189 (17.7%)	247 (42.1%)	727	537 (73.9%)	24 (8.2%)	2 (0.3%)

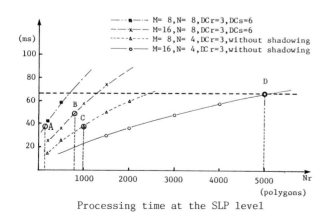

Processing time at the SLP level

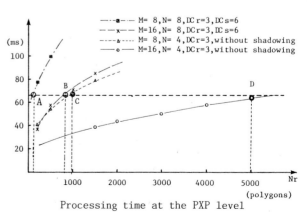

Processing time at the PXP level

Figure 10. Estimated processing time

connected to one SLP, and "S" is the number of relevant segments in a scan-line, such that

$$S = SQRT(DCr \cdot Nr) + SQRT(DCs \cdot Ns).$$

2) Typical case of the processing on the PXP:

$$(512/M) \cdot (80 + (2944 + S \cdot (100+21.6 \cdot DCt$$
$$+\log_2(256/S) \cdot (6.5+6 \cdot DCt)))/N)$$
$$[\text{micro-steps}],$$

where "DCt" is the average number of the total depth complexity at the sample point, defined as

$$DCt = 2 \cdot (DCr+DCs).$$

The fraction coefficients appeared above are derived from the probability estimations attributed to the branch alternatives.

Using the expressions above, the system performance is estimated in various system configurations. Each graph in Figure 10 represents the respective cases when the relations between the parameters are varied or when some specific values of the parameters are used.

Figure 10 shows that, for example, the system configured with 8 SLPs and 8×8 PXPs will be able to generate the shadowed image of the three-dimensional scene which contains about 200 polygons, every 1/15th of a second (point "A" in the graph).

8. Concluding Remarks

We have described the design of a parallel processor system for three-dimensional color graphics, called EXPERTS. The EXPERTS employs a two-level hierarchical multi-processor architecture, which is suited to perform scan-line algorithm in high-speed. Two types of processor elements, called the SLP and the PXP, are newly designed. These processor elements are powerful, microprogrammable element equipped with many special facilities optimized to graphic applications, and supporting anti-aliasing and smooth-shading.

We are currently constructing a prototype of the EXPERTS, installing two SLPs and four PXPs, with two PXPs connected to one SLP. Although this is the minimum configuration capable of parallel and pipeline processing, every hardware function will be successfully tested on this prototype.

Each SLP is made of about 2,000 pieces of MSI and SSI ICs, and each PXP is made of about 1,100 pieces of MSI and SSI ICs.

The design of the EXPERTS enables 16 SLPs to be connected to each other and 16 PXPs to be connected to each SLP. So, the maximum configuration contains 16 SLPs plus 256 PXPs, in total 272 processor elements, constituting a huge multi-processor system.

Any intermediate scale of configuration is possible, that is, any SLP-PXP ratio will do. Hence, the system user will be able to choose the most cost-effective configuration. In addition, if any processor element gets out of order, the entire system can be restored to work well simply by disconnecting that processor element and with no serious influence on other components. So, the MTTR (Mean Time To Repair) of the EXPERTS is very short, and the system reliability as well as availability is greatly enhanced.

Acknowledgements

The authors wish to thank Yasuko Sakamoto for proposing the parallel scan-line algorithm employed in the EXPERTS, Takashi Fukunishi for writing microprograms of the SLP and the PXP, and Kouji Ohtani for designing the logic circuits of the SLP. We also thank Takayasu Obata, Kouichi Takeuchi and Yukihiro Kawaguchi for their enthusiastic cooperation to this project. Toshiyuki Nakata gave us a number of valuable comments on the earlier version of this paper.

This work is supported mainly by the Ministry of Education in Japan, Grant in Aid for Scientific Research (58850069), and in part by Wireless Research Laboratory of Matsushita Electric Industrial Co., Ltd.

References

[1] Crow, F.C.: "A Comparison of Anti-Aliasing Techniques," IEEE Computer Graphics and applications, Vol.1, No.1 (Jan. 1981), pp.40-48.

[2] Kaplan, M., and Greenberg, D.P.: "Parallel Processing Technique for Hidden Surface Removal," ACM Computer Graphics, Vol.13, No.2 (Aug. 1979), pp.300-307.

[3] Fiume, E., Fournier, A., and Rudolph, L.: "A Parallel Scan Conversion Algorithm with Anti-Aliasing for a General-Purpose Ultracomputer," ACM Computer Graphics, Vol.17, No.3 (Jul. 1983), pp.141-150.

[4] Fuchs, H., and Johnson, B.W.: "An Expandable Multiprocessor Architecture for Video Graphics(Preliminary Report)," IEEE 6th Conf. on Computer Architecture (1979), pp.58-67.

[5] Gouraud, H.: "Continuous Shading of Curved Surfaces," IEEE Trans. on Computers, Vol.C-20, No.6 (Jun. 1971), pp.623-629.

[6] Newmann, W.M., and Sproull, R.F.: "Principles of Interactive Computer Graphics," 2nd Ed. McGraw-Hill, 1979.

[7] Parke, F.I.: "Simulation and Expected Performance Analysis of Multiple Processor Z-Buffer Systems," ACM Computer Graphics (Jul. 1980), pp.48-56.

[8] Schachter, B.J. (Ed.): "Computer Image Generation," Wiley-Interscience, New York, 1983.

[9] Sutherland, I. E., Sproull, R. F., and Schumacker, R.A.: "A Characterization of Ten Hidden-Surface Algorithms," ACM Computing Surveys (Mar. 1974), pp.1-55.

[10] Tomita, S., Shibayama, K., Kitamura, T., Nakata, T., and Hagiwara, H.: "A User-microprogrammable, Local Host Computer with Low-level Parallelism," Proc. 10th Annu. Int'l Symp. on Computer Architecture (Jun. 1983), pp.151-157.

Chap - A SIMD Graphics Processor

Adam Levinthal
Thomas Porter

Computer Graphics Project
Lucasfilm Ltd.

ABSTRACT

Special purpose processing systems designed for specific applications can provide extremely high performance at moderate cost. One such processor is presented for executing graphics and image processing algorithms as the basis of a digital film printer. Pixels in the system contain four parallel components: RGB for full color and an alpha channel for retaining transparency information. The data path of the processor contains four arithmetic elements connected through a crossbar network to a tessellated scratchpad memory. The single instruction, multiple data stream (SIMD) processor executes instructions on four pixel components in parallel. The instruction control unit (ICU) maintains an activity stack for tracking block-structured code, using data-dependent activity flags for conditional disabling subsets of the ALUs. Nested loops and if-then-else constructs can be programmed directly, with the ICU disabling and reenabling ALUs on the basis of their individual status bits.

CR Categories and Subject Descriptors: B.2.1 [**Arithmetic and logic structures**]: design styles — parallel; B.3.2 [**memory structures**]: design styles — interleaved memories; C.1.2 [**processor architectures**]: Multiple data stream architectures — SIMD. I.3.1 [**computer graphics**]: Hardware architectures — Raster display devices. I.4.0 [**Image Processing**]: General — Image displays.

General Terms: Design

Additional Key Words and Phrases: digital film printers, compositing, computer graphics, parallel processing, SIMD architecture, tesselation.

Permission to copy without fee all or part of this material is granted provided that the copies are not made or distributed for direct commercial advantage, the ACM copyright notice and the title of the publication and its date appear, and notice is given that copying is by permission of the Association for Computing Machinery. To copy otherwise, or to republish, requires a fee and/or specific permission.

© 1984   ACM   0-89791-138-5/84/007/0077 $00.75

1. Introduction

The Lucasfilm Pixar project is producing high-performance machines for film-quality image creation. The first machine to be completed is a digital film printer that provides digital processing capabilities for special-effects film production. The system, called the Lucasfilm *Compositor*, is a digital realization of a conventional optical film printer under computer control [2].

A laser printing/scanning system replaces the projectors and process camera of an optical printer. A high-speed digital processor brings digital signal processing techniques to bear on each frame, extending the range of capabilities of a conventional optical film printer. These include:

- Merging multiple images to form a single image, handling partially transparent objects and edges;

- Creation of mattes for live-action blue screen shots;

- Hand touchups and simple creation of *garbage mattes;*

- Filtering to provide for diffusion, tinting, highlighting, defocusing, and edge enhancement;

- Color correction to account for non-linearities and crosstalk between the dye layers of color film;

- Rotation and perspective transformation of frames to correct for original camera misalignment or to simulate complex camera moves.

The Compositor is designed to execute a number of key algorithms at an average rate of one microsecond per pixel. This performance allows for interactive use on limited resolution images, as well as acceptable performance for production work on high resolution, movie-quality images.

The heart of the system is the Channel Processor (Chap), a programmable pixel processor for performing all the computation and controlling the flow of pixels in the Compositor. The Chap is based on a four operand vector data pipeline operating with a single instruction sequencer. This design was adopted to take advantage of the four component data structure used to represent digital images in the Compositor.

2. 4-Channel Pictures

Pixels contain four components. Frame buffers and disk files contain red, green, and blue color channels as well as an *alpha* or *matte* channel. The matte channel is used to specify transparency so that elements which do not cover an entire frame can be stored separately for later compositing. An alpha of 0 is interpreted to mean full transparency; an alpha of 1 indicates full coverage.

As presented in [7], the color channels are stored *premultiplied* by the alpha channel in the sense that half coverage of a pixel by a yellow object is stored as (.5,.5,0,.5), not (1,1,0,.5). This choice puts each channel on equal footing: so that most algorithms that process RGBA pictures can treat the alpha channel with precisely the same instructions as the color channels.

The SIMD architecture was originally considered based on the fact that many algorithms execute identical operations on all four components of each pixel. This is true of many key algorithms in the digital film printing process, including color correction of images, scaling and translation to align images, and merging of images during the compositing operation. Some algorithms however do not perform identical operations on each component. In particular, the matte algorithm [6] computes a final alpha value based on the initial values of the RGB component at each pixel.

The crossbar connection between memory and processors in the Chap architecture was introduced to support different possible approaches to pixel processing. Using the crossbar mechanism, Chap programs can be structured to access the *four components* of a *single pixel*, or the *same component* of *four consecutive pixels*.

2.1. 12-bit Channels

For film applications, 8-bit linear intensity values are insufficient. Consequently, in the prototype system, the frame buffer memory banks are configured with 12 bits per channel. The Chap internal scratchpad memory and registers are 16 bits wide to maintain extra precision for intermediate products. The frame buffer memory will support up to 16 bits per channel, and it is anticipated that this precision will be required in future applications.

The 12-bit values stored in frame buffer memory are skewed slightly upon access as shown in table 1.

12 Bit Value	Sign extended Value	Range
10xxxxxxxxxx	000010xxxxxxxxxx	(1.5, 1.0]
01xxxxxxxxxx	000001xxxxxxxxxx	(1.0, 0.5]
00xxxxxxxxxx	000000xxxxxxxxxx	(0.5, 0.0]
11xxxxxxxxxx	111111xxxxxxxxxx	(0.0, -0.5]

Table 1

This skewing means that sign extension is performed based on the uppermost two bits of the 12 bit components, instead of simply copying the most significant bit directly. This format was chosen in order to represent values in the range (1.5,-.5], providing 11 bits of fraction and sufficient range for underflow and overflow. As

importantly, this representation assures an accurate representation of unity.

All of the algorithms critical to compositor operation can be handled with integer arithmetic; in fact, 16-bit integers are sufficient for most general image processing work, though 32 bits are needed for the accumulation of intermediate products in digital filtering.

3. Compositor Overview

Figure 1 shows the communication channels inside the Compositor.

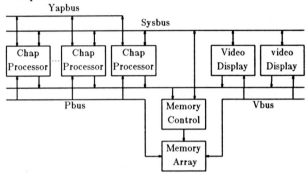

Figure 1: Compositor Communications Channels

The Chap communicates through three separate data paths:

- The *Pbus,* or Processor Access Bus, is the common data bus between the processors and framebuffer memory. The extremely high data rates on the Pbus (240 Mbytes/sec) allow multiple processors to operate in parallel on common framebuffer data. The Chap hardware DMA controller allows data to be transferred between processor memory and framebuffer memory with minimal processor overhead.

- The *Yapbus* (Yet Another Pixar Bus) is a high bandwidth (80 Mbytes/sec) data channel operating as a local area network between compositor system components. In particular, the Yapbus provides the data channel to the laser printer/scanner system.

- The *Sysbus,* or System bus, is a low bandwidth (2 Mbytes/sec) control interface between the host computer and compositor subsystems. Operating parameters, microcode instructions, and diagnostic commands are transferred to the Chap through the system bus interface.

The high bandwidth I/O channels of the compositor system contribute to the Chap processor's ability to operate as a high performance, general purpose, image processor.

4. Processor Architecture

The Chap is a microcoded four operand parallel vector processor. It operates as a single instruction, multiple data stream (SIMD) processor, executing each instruction on four operands at the same time. The processor performs arithmetic operations, operand addressing, I/O operations, and program sequencing in parallel with a highly horizontal instruction word. This parallelism, along with extensive pipelining, allows the Chap to achieve performance approaching 64 MIPS.†

The Chap processor block diagram is shown in Figure 2.

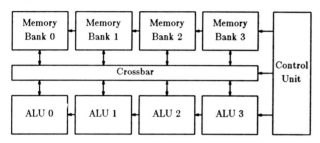

Figure 2: Chap Block Diagram

Four arithmetic elements (processors) are connected through a crossbar network to four Scratchpad memories. The processor data path is optimized for 16 bit integer arithmetic. All processor and memory operations are controlled by a single microcoded control unit. During each micro-cycle, all four processors receive the same instruction. Special condition code and memory control logic allows individual processor and memory operations to be conditionally inhibited during certain program segments.

The instruction control unit is designed to support common program control constructs such as $while(loopvariable)$, $if(condition)$, $if(condition)/else$, etc. Scalar (uniprocessor) support is provided in the data path to allow any of the processors to access non-vector parts of the machine.

4.1. Processor Elements

Each processor element is of the form shown in Figure 3, with a 16-bit arithmetic unit and 16-bit multiplier.

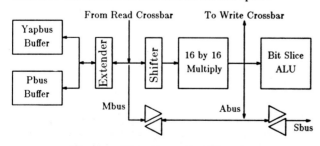

Figure 3: Chap Processing Element

The multiplier and ALU can operate in parallel for certain operations such as multiply/accumulate. Data is

loaded into the multiplier over the Mbus, and data is loaded into the ALU over the Abus. Each arithmetic element can read and write the scalar (control) parts of the machine over the Sbus.

The arithmetic-logic units are bipolar 'bit slice' devices with 32 working registers, an accumulator, and a status register. Although a single multiplexed I/O port is used to load and store from the ALUs, internal latches allow reading external operands and writing results to external destinations (memory to memory, for example) in the same ALU instruction.

The multipliers are designed to multiply component values by alpha values and components by coefficients, producing component values as the product. In order to produce properly aligned and rounded component values in the top 16 bits of the product, multiplicands must be shifted up to three places. This is accomplished by shifter circuitry external to the multiplier inputs. The multiplier product is a full 32 bit number; However, the bus structure allows access to only 16 bits of the product in any instruction.

4.2. Scratchpad Memory

Four scratchpad memories provide 64K 16 bit words of general purpose memory for program data storage. The address calculation unit uses a register file containing pointer values to specify data elements in Scratchpad memory. Programs use these pointer to reference four operands (pixel data) or one operand (e.g., filter coefficients) during each access to Scratchpad. An arbitrary offset can be added to a pointer value at each instruction to allow sequential access of memory.

A single pointer value can be used to access four operands by ordering data in memory using a special processor-memory connection network. This network, called the memory *crossbar* allows *tessellated* access to the Scratchpad memory [8]. A number of tessellated access formats appropriate for graphics processing support are built into the crossbar network. The access format is specified in the Chap instruction word as in Table 2.

n	format
00	pixel
01	component
10	broadcast
11	indexed

Table 2

Pixel access is the normal access mode to scratchpad pixel data. Each access references a full pixel in parallel, with the red component going to the red processor, green to the green processor, etc.

Component access, where each processor works on a separate pixel, references a single component from four consecutive pixels in parallel. This format is provided to support vector processing in algorithms that do not operate on all components of a single pixel in parallel.

---

† This figure represents the peak rate for data moves in the Chap, where four operands are transfered every 62ns. The chap can perform multipies or ALU operations, as well as multiply accumulates, at a sustained 32 MIPS.

SIGGRAPH'84

Broadcast access allows each of four processors to receive a single memory element. This is useful for operations where one scratchpad coefficient is sent to all four multipliers.

Indexed access uses a computed value from each processor as an index into a scratchpad table. indexed access is useful for color mapping applications, where each component is mapped from a different table.

Table 3 shows the tessellated nature of the scratchpad memory. The memory is actually four memory banks (S_0, S_1, S_2, S_3) partitioned in such a fashion as to optimize either Pixel (R_p, G_p, B_p, A_p) or Component $(C_p, C_{p+1}, C_{p+2}, C_{p+3})$ access, where p is the effective pixel address and C is some particular component. Notice that neither case causes contention by attempting multiple accesses to a single bank of memory.

	S_0	S_1	S_2	S_3
0	R_0	G_0	B_0	A_0
1	A_1	R_1	G_1	B_1
2	B_2	A_2	R_2	G_2
3	G_3	B_3	A_3	R_3
4	R_4	G_4	B_4	A_4
...	...	...	...	...

Table 3

5. SIMD Control

The Chap performs single-instruction, four-component processing. This type of architecture has been used succesfully in previous arithmetic processors [1][5]. We have found that many image processing problems can be solved with identical code for each of the RGBA components of every pixel.

There are occasions, however, where the ability to suspend some subset of processors over a range of instructions is desired. For example, some programs might switch to single processor operation to find a coefficient in a table and then switch back to four processor operation to multiply that coefficient by each component. Clamping is a another example; when clamping, we wish to set each processor's accumulator to unity only for those accumulators which exceed unity. We make the comparison to unity, suspend if less, set to unity, and resume each processor.

To support this conditional processing, the Instruction Control Unit (ICU) includes not only the standard *sequencer* functions for finding the next instruction, but also *runner* functions for determining which processors execute each instruction. Let us review the capabilities of the ICU, to illustrate its operation.

The Chap executes instructions stored in writable instruction memory. The first job of the ICU is to decide where the next instruction lies. Along with the standard sequencer opcode and condition select information, Chap ICU instructions specify a *Source Processor* qualifier. Thus, instructions like "jump (opcode) if alpha (processor) is zero (condition code)" are possible. The jump address may be computed, or included as a literal in the instruction word.

The ICU must also direct the flow of execution for individual processors based on conditions involving their own execution. It becomes necessary to suspend some processors while others execute a particular program segment. Note that this is somewhat complex when we consider nested if-then-else constructions and procedures.

To provide a mechanism for controlling individual processor activity, The ICU maintains a *runflag* register and a *stack* that contains runflag vectors at each program level. The current runflag indicates which processors are running and which are suspended.

At conditional test instructions, a four-bit condition vector is created, one bit for each processor, corresponding to that processor's condition with regard to the ICU condition select field. The logic of the ICU determines the current runflag and maintains the runflag stack based on this condition vector and immediate runflag bits in the instruction word.

Standard if-then, if-then-else, and while-do programming constructs are translated into runner instructions as shown in table 4.

action	C construct	assembler
push	{	push
pop.	}	done, fi
push; R &= C	if () {	if *e* then
R = (!R) & S0	} else {	else
R &= C	while () {	while *e* do

Table 4

R refers to the current runflag register; S0 is at the top of the runflag stack; C is the new condition runflag.

The complete set of 16 conditional ICU instructions expands on these five runner instructions. The complete set controls three concurrent stacks: the runflags, return addresses, and loop counters.

Let us consider the C program fragment:

```
if (c1) {
        if (c2) {
                do0;
        } else {
                do1;
        }
} else {
        do2;
}
```

Assume that condition c1 generates a runflag of 1110, suspending processor 3, and condition c2 generates a runflag of 1100. Table 5 shows the state of the current runflag R and the top two runflag stack locations after each ICU instruction.

80

ICU instruction	R	S0	S1
calculate c1	1111	....	....
push; R &= c1	1110	1111	....
calculate c2	1110	1111	....
push; P &= c2	1100	1110	1111
do0	1100	1110	1111
R = (!R) & S0	0010	1110	1111
do1	0010	1110	1111
pop	1110	1111	....
R = (!R) & S0	0001	1111	....
do2	0001	1111	....
pop	1111	....	....

Sequencer conditions are specified with an *any/all* qualifier as well as the normal true/false qualifier of typical instruction sequencers.

This allows a while loop which runs until all four processors are satisfied, suspending individual processors as it goes, to be simply stated:

```
while any (c1) do
        statement;
done
```

and translates into:

```
        push
loop: calculate c1
        R &= c1; jump out if all disabled
        statement
        jump loop
out:  pop
```

The previous example, that of clamping accumulator values that exceed unity, takes the form:

```
if any alu positive then
        acc = 1;
fi
```

and translates to:
```
        temp = acc - 1 ;
        push; r &= positive;
        acc = 1;
        pop
```

The appendix contains code fragments from actual Chap programs. Code fragment (1) illustrates the inner loop for a scanline linear interpolate of the form:

$$Target_0 = Source_0 + (1 - \alpha_0)Source_1$$

6. Chap Programming

The wide Chap instruction word can be split into six parts, offering control over the ALUs, multipliers, data paths, scratchpad address calculation unit, crossbar tessellation, and instruction control unit. The assembler [4] provides a powerful syntax for maintaining control. The runtime monitor [5] provides linking and loading facilities to promote modular program development. Pipeline delays built into the hardware modules complicate programming, but become a distinct advantage (over unpipelined designs) when writing optimized standard modules. Features of the machine and the assembler allow the programmer to stretch out the instruction timing and overlook the pipeline delays when developing code for the first time.

6.1. Chap/Host Interface

A number of features allow the Chap to support host interaction during program execution.

- 16 words of shared memory are used for parameter passing.
- 4096 'virtual register' locations are decoded in the Sysbus interface which allow the host to initiate Chap processes by reading and writing memory-mapped function registers.
- Interrupt logic allows the Chap to interrupt the host under program control.

7. Conclusion

We have described a digital processor specifically designed to support digital pixel processing, providing parallel vector arithmetic with convenient programming language support. Tne SIMD architecture appears well suited to the particular algorithms used in the digital film printing process.

8. Acknowledgments

Particular credit should go to Loren Carpenter, who originally suggested the basic four channel SIMD architecture, and contributed to elements of the design throughout the project.

Special thanks is also due to Mark Leather, who shared in the final design stages and debugged the prototype design, writing much diagnostic software in the process to verify the design.

Rodney Stock should be credited for his role as hardware manager, as well as logic designer, on the Pixar system, and should be identified as one of the principal architects of the Pixar system.

In addition, the processor working group of Bill Reeves, Tom Duff, and Sam Leffler, provided many important criticisms and suggestions during the design and review phases.

Sam Leffler should also be credited for his work in providing the assembler and monitor that we use to develop Chap code.

Thanks to Andy Moorer and Curtis Abbott, who stressed the importance of complete diagnostic support for program debugging, resulting in important improvements to the host interface section.

Thanks also to Tom Noggle for his contribution to the design of the Yapbus network.

APPENDIX

This section is included to provide a little detail about specific issues in generating code for the Chap.

(1) This code fragment is an example of chas assembly code to lerp (linearly interpolate) between two scan lines:

$$Target_0 = Source_0 + (1 - alpha_0)Source_1$$

$Source_0$, $Source_1$ and $Target_0$ are all stored in scratchpad memory. This is an example of assembly code where no instruction overlap is attempted. Comments are delimited by the C styles /* and */ constructs.

```
Lerp: loop Xcount do
        multx = unity - @s0ptr; round
        { multy = (comp)(s1ptr); round;
            s1ptr = s1ptr + p_inc }
        { acc = (s0ptr);
            s0ptr = s0ptr + p_inc }
        { (tptr) = acc + msp;
            tptr = tptr + p_inc }
        done
```

The inner loop can be translated as follows:

/* the "loop e do" construct pushes the current address + 1 onto the return stack, and loads the loop counter with the value e, in this case a literal value of Xcount from the immediate field */

```
        loop Xcount do
```

/* Read from scratchpad in broadcast mode (specified by the @ sign) using pointer s0ptr, and subtract it from unity (a predefined ALU register) and load the results into the multiplier X inputs with the rounding bit set. */

```
        multx = unity - @s0ptr; round   /* 3 ticks */
```

/* Read from scratchpad in pixel mode (specified by the () around s1ptr) using pointer s1ptr, and then load that pixel into the multiplier Y inputs shifted up by 2 places (specified by the qualifier (comp)) with the rounding bit set. Furthemore, increment s1ptr by the value defined by p_inc (in this case 4). */

```
        { multy = (comp)(s1ptr); round;
            s1ptr = s1ptr + p_inc }   /* 3 ticks */
```

/* Read from scratchpad in pixel mode using pointer s0ptr and load them into the ALU accumulators, and increment s0ptr by p_inc. */

```
        { acc = (s0ptr);
            s0ptr = s0ptr + p_inc }   /* 4 ticks */
```

/* Add the values in the multiplier most significant result register (top 16 bits) to the current accumulator, and store the results as a pixel in scratchpad at the location pointed to by tptr, and then increment tptr by p_inc. */

```
        { (tptr) = acc + msp;
            tptr = tptr + p_inc }   /* 2 ticks */
```

/* The next statement terminates the loop and causes the PC to be loaded from the top of the stack without popping it. The test for termination is done at the top, and if it fails, execution continues at the point after the done statement. */

```
        done
```

(2) The code can be rewritten to take advantage of pipelined operation, with an increase in performance of 50% as shown below. The code takes advantage of the machine pipelining the details of which are beyond the scope of this paper. Suffice to say that the duration of each instruction can be specified in clock ticks, overriding the default assembler durations, and that the first scratchpad read is repeated at the bottom of the loop to maintain the pipelining around the loop. Also note that whereas the previous loop required 16 clock cycles to execute, the following loop executes in 8 clock cycles.

```
        xbar = @s0ptr; push
loop:   { unity = unity - xbar; special;
            spad = (comp)(s1ptr); 1tick }
        { multx = unity - latch; round;
            spad = (s0ptr); 1tick }
        { multy = xbar; round;
            s1ptr = s1ptr + p_inc; 1 tick }
        { acc = xbar; special;
            s0ptr = s0ptr + p_inc; 1 tick }
        acc = xbar; 1 tick
        acc = acc + msp; special; 1 tick
        { dowhile !lc zero;
            spad = @s0ptr; tptr = tptr + p_inc;
            acc = acc + msp; special; 1tick }
        { (tptr) = acc + latch;
            tptr = tptr + p_inc; 1 tick }
```

References

[1] Barnes, G., et all, The ILLIAC IV Computer. *IEEE Transactions on Computers* Vol C-17, No 8 (August 1968), pp 746-757.

[2] Fielding, R., *The Technique of Special Effects Cinematography.* Hastings House, New York, 1977.

[3] Kubo, M., Taguchi, Y., Agusa, K., Ohno, Y., A multi-microprocessor system for three dimensional color graphics. *Proc of IFIP 80, 1980.*

[4] Leffler, S., Chap Assembler Reference Manual. Technical Memo 98, Computer Division, Lucasfilm Ltd, December, 1983.

[5] Leffler, S., Chap Runtime Monitor Reference Manual. Technical Memo 102, Computer Division, Lucasfilm Ltd, December, 1983.

[6] Porter, T., Matte Box Design. Technical Memo 63, Computer Division, Lucasfilm Ltd, August 1983.

[7] Porter, T., Duff, T., Compositing Digital Images. *Computer Graphics* Vol 18, No 3, 1984, To be published

[8] Shapiro, H. D. Theoretical Limitations on the Efficient Use of Parallel Memories. *IEEE Transactions on Computers*, Vol C-27, No. 5 (May 1978), .

A Hardware Stochastic Interpolator
for Raster Displays

Timothy S. Piper†

CAE Electronics Ltd
PO Box 1800
Ville St Laurent, Quebec Canada
H4L 4X4

Alain Fournier

Department of Computer Science
University of Toronto
Toronto, Ontario, Canada
M5S 1A4

ABSTRACT

Stochastic modeling has found uses so far mainly for expensive very realistic graphics display. The cost of rendering is not intrinsic to the technique, but mainly due to the high resolution and the sophisticated display techniques which accompany it. We describe here a basic tool for a less expensive approach to stochastic modeling which is designed for a more "down to earth" type of application, and brings the display of stochastic models nearer to real-time.

A special purpose board for stochastic interpolation has been built, which can generate an array of up to 129x129 12 bit stochastic values to be used by the rest of the display system as a texture source, or for more elaborate algorithms. The board functions as a coprocessor in a traditional frame buffer system, and includes a micro-coded bit-slice processor, a multiplier, special hardware to generate uniformly distributed random numbers, memory to store a look-up table for random numbers with the required distribution, and two buffers for the resulting arrays.

†Current Address: Vertigo Computer Imagery Inc.
221-119 West Pender St., Vancouver, B.C. Canada,
V6B 1S5

Permission to copy without fee all or part of this material is granted provided that the copies are not made or distributed for direct commercial advantage, the ACM copyright notice and the title of the publication and its date appear, and notice is given that copying is by permission of the Association for Computing Machinery. To copy otherwise, or to republish, requires a fee and/or specific permission.

© 1984   ACM   0-89791-138-5/84/007/0083 $00.75

The current implementation generates values at less than 4 microseconds per point, and in conjunction with a standard graphics processor can display nearly 10000 stochastic points in real-time, or can update a full screen of stochastic values in less than one second. Illustrations are given of the output of the board and of pictures and animations generated with it.

CR Categories and Subject Descriptors: B.1.5 [**Control Structures and Microprogramming**]: Microcode Applications - *Special-Purpose*; G.3 [**Probability and Statistics**]: Random Number Generation; I.3.1 [**Computer Graphics**]: Hardware Architecture - *Raster display devices*; I.3.3 [**Computer Graphics**]: Picture/Image Generation - *Display algorithms*; I.3.7 [**Computer Graphics**]: Three-Dimensional Graphics and Realism.

Additional Key Words and Phrases: Stochastic modelling

1. Introduction

In Computer Graphics one builds complex objects from fairly regular collections of simple primitives. The modeling primitives used in computer graphics: points, lines, polygons, parametric surfaces, are such that they can be represented by a small number of 3-D points, and transformations for these primitives have only to be on these points. The modeling of natural objects (or more generally of visually complex objects) has been often accomplished by using large numbers of simple primitives. This obviously exacts a heavy price on storage and time necessary to process and display such objects.

The first, and still the most powerful approach to model complex objects without increasing the number of primitives used is texture mapping, as used originally by Catmull [Catm75], and refined and improved by Blinn [Blin78] and others [Will83]. Textures are generally predefined (digitized "real" pictures, procedure generated textures, hand drawn etc.) and stored in arrays, often to be mapped repetitively.

A second approach, a functional one, is to define the object as a procedure. Well chosen procedures can generate complex objects such as the surface of the sea [Nort82, Max81]. This approach allows for a better mapping between image space and texture space, and specific solution to the aliasing problem. It is also more expensive to compute in general.

A third approach, which in some sense includes the previous two, is to use stochastic modeling. The strategy here is to include stochastic processes in the functions used for the object generation. Random elements in texture generation has been used for quite some time [Fu80], but the main challenge is to develop the techniques to incorporate the stochastic elements with the traditional primitives, and to incorporate the whole into existing display systems [Four82, Reev83].

So far, most of these techniques have been used to produce high quality, high resolution pictures, taking hours of CPU time. An improvement in speed of several orders of magnitude is necessary if stochastic modeling is to be applied to real-time systems, both the expensive kind (flight simulators) or the medium to low cost kind (displays for Solid Object Modeling and video-games). There has been recently a proposal for a parallel architecture for generation of fractal surfaces [Step83], but it is specialized to triangular subdivision, and is still only a preliminary study.

This paper describes a prototype hardware solution to generate and use stochastic data in near real-time.

2. Stochastic interpolation

Stochastic interpolation consists of using an interpolation formula that includes a stochastic function. It is generally used along with a recursive subdivision technique with midpoint interpolation (midpoint in object space, or in parametric space). In one dimension:

$$Value\ (P) = D_{interp}\ (P_1, P_2) + ST_{interp}\ (P_1, P_2)$$

where P is a point interpolated from P_1 and P_2.

$D_{interp}\ ()$ is the result of the deterministic interpolation, and $ST_{interp}\ ()$ a sample value of the stochastic process. As stressed in [Four82], stochastic is to be read as pseudo-stochastic, since we want consistency from frame to frame and primitive to primitive. The speed of the computation depends of course on the cost of computing $D_{interp}\ ()$ and $ST_{interp}\ ()$. Midpoint interpolation is usually chosen because it is simple for most ordinary functions (for linear functions, only an add and a shift are necessary). The stochastic interpolation can be costly so a lookup table method is often used. Instead of computing $ST_{interp}\ ()$, an index $INDEX_{interp}\ ()$ is computed and the corresponding entry in a table filled with random values having the distribution of $ST_{interp}\ ()$ is used. Of course $INDEX_{interp}\ ()$ should be uniformly distributed over the range of table indices. This has the additional advantage that a different stochastic process can be used simply by loading a different set of values in the table.

In two dimensions, a 2-D array of values has to be generated. The stochastic process used has to be a random function of two parameters. In general, the interpolation formula can be different for each parameter. The stochastic interpolation used in the hardware implementation described in this paper is the one used in [Four82], that is, an approximation of fractional Brownian motion [Mand68, Mand82]. Here the additional problem is that fractional Brownian motion (fBm) is not Markovian, and a straightforward recursive subdivision is not appropriate. The scheme given in [Four82] to interlace the evaluations of the interpolated points (see Fig. 1) has been used. This of course means that if four corners are used to reenter into the algorithm the correlation across the boundary required by fractional Brownian motion cannot be achieved. In this case, not only the four corners but the values obtained for the next few levels of subdivisions have to be reentered. This ensures a sufficient amount of continuity at all levels. Again we had to sacrifice mathematical purity to other desirable properties, like speed, continuity across common boundaries and reentrant subdivision. It should be noted this is not a problem if the process is Markovian.

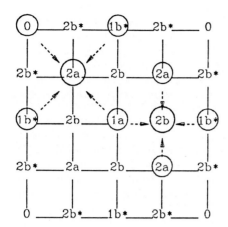

Order of Computation is 0, 1a, 1b, 2a, 2b....
Figure 1

3. Functional requirements

The University of Toronto Computer Systems Research Group uses an Adage 3000 (commonly known as IKONAS) raster display system in its computer graphics lab. It is a modular frame buffer system on its own synchronous bus and is interfaced to a VAX 11/780 which acts as a host. Figure 2 shows the overall IKONAS system architecture.

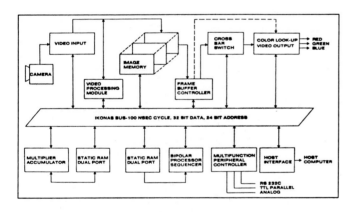

The Ikonas Graphics System Architecture
Figure 2

As with many contemporary graphics systems it gains high performance with the addition of modular processors acting in parallel. The Display Controller handles screen refreshing from the 512x512x24 frame buffer, routing the data at video rates through a crossbar switch and colour lookup tables. The IKONAS gains much of its performance through the use of a 200ns cycle, 32-bit, bit-slice processor,

referred to as the BPS, which draws into the frame buffer. Optional processors include the Peripheral Microprocessor (MPC), a matrix multiplier and video input module.

It was in this graphics system environment that a stochastic interpolation processor (henceforth referred to as STINT) was proposed. At the time the project began the BPS was not yet up and running. Thus the design was based on estimates of the performance requirements of a fully functioning graphics system in which rapid 2D stochastic interpolation was desirable. Building a piece of hardware was therefore an experiment to investigate its utility rather than based on a demonstrated need.

One of the most time consuming steps in image formation is that of scan conversion, which is usually a linear interpolation of position and colour based on the vertices of a polygon. Generating a stochastically interpolated array to replace the linear interpolation would be the function of a STINT processor that should give the most significant improvement in performance. It was assumed that for each of three coordinates (say RGB) the STINT array value would be multiplied by a scaling factor and added to a previously calculated deterministic value. Counting microcode steps gave an estimate of $5\mu s$ per point for this function if performed by the BPS.

The next obvious concern is whether there is an advantage to be gained by having a separate STINT processor rather than simply microcoding a STINT subroutine on the IKONAS BPS. It was estimated that it would require $15\mu s$ per STINT array value in a subroutine, where about half that time is needed to obtain a normally distributed random value, as required in the algorithm. It was concluded that an increase in throughput of four times ($20\mu s$ vs. $5\mu s$) could be obtained with a separate STINT processor that could operate in parallel with the BPS at faster than $5\mu s$ per point. A double buffer to store the final array would be essential to allow parallel operation.

4. Implementation

The STINT algorithm was first implemented in the high level language Concurrent Euclid [Holt83]. This software was designed to simulate the proposed hardware, so that there would be a basis for comparing results after the hardware was built. Table 1 gives the time required to execute the STINT algorithm on a

PDP 11/45 and VAX minicomputer using this software.

After an actual implementation on the IKO-NAS BPS, it was found that the time required to calculate a STINT value in firmware was almost twice (28 μs vs. 15 μs) the estimate used to specify the functional requirements. The result is shown in Table 1 along with the final performance obtained by the custom STINT processor.

Machine	CPU time (129x129 array)	CPU time (one point)
PDP 11/45	12s.	680 μs.
VAX 11/780	6s.	370 μs.
BPS	0.5s.	28 μs.
STINT	0.06s.	4 μs.

Time to compute a 129x129 stochastic
array on various processors
Table 1

4.1. Architecture

Based on the above considerations, the STINT processor was designed to operate in the following manner. The BPS hands the STINT processor the parameters necessary to generate a particular array. The array of values calculated using the STINT algorithm is the returned result. While the STINT processor is calculating an array in one buffer, the BPS is reading the previously calculated array from the other buffer.

In more detail, the parameters passed to the STINT processor are:

- a seed for each corner

- an initial value for each corner

- the initial standard deviation

- the ratio by which to multiply the standard deviation between levels

- an indication of the maximum level to do the calculations.

In the particular case of the approximation to fBm, the ratio is 2^{-H}, where H is the self similarity parameter. For a first time calculation of an array, the initial corner values are set to 0 and the standard deviation to 1. This ensures that the resulting array will be in a sense normalized to preserve accuracy and avoid overflow in the integer calculations. A reentrant

version of the algorithm is accommodated by setting the corner values and standard deviation to other than 0 and 1 respectively. To avoid problems with continuity, the reentrant computation should be started at a higher level of subdivision by setting the first few values obtained previously in addition to the corners.

The interface to the IKONAS bus was simplified to save hardware and because the IKONAS was not initially available for testing. To the rest of the system only a single result array buffer is visible as well as some handshaking flags in a command and status register as illustrated in Fig. 3.

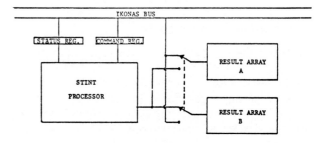

The STINT processor as a slave memory device
Figure 3

The parameters are passed by loading them into predetermined locations in the result memory buffer available to the IKONAS bus.

The handshaking protocol is summarized in Fig. 4. The flags used are *GO*, results ready, (*RRA*, *RRB*) and buffer available to IKONAS (*BA*).

Most of the implementation of the STINT processor is quite straightforward. The data paths are shown in Fig. 5. It is basically a two bus structure bridged by a bit-slice ALU, a multiplier, a result array and a random value generator which will be described later. Cost, space and time constraints limited the data path widths and memory size to the minimum judged adequate. Generally, eight bits are used with twelve bits necessary to accumulate the interpolated values. Each result memory buffer handles up to a 129 by 129 array at 12 bits precision, that is, to a recursion level of 7.

The microprogram control architecture is also a standard one with a single level of pipelining, as shown in Fig. 6. The sequencer is very simple, supporting only the four instructions:

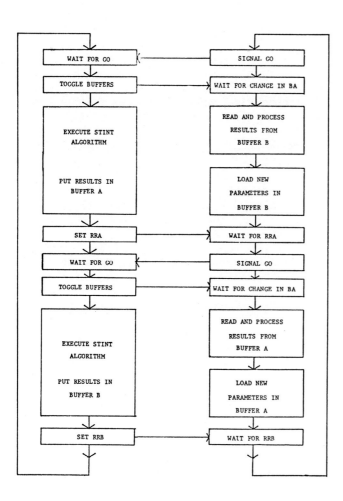

Handshaking between the Ikonas
and the STINT processor
Figure 4

continue ,   *jump* ,   *jump* if *go flag not set* ,   and
jump if *not zero* . The cycle time is 200ns.

4.2. Random number generation

Designing a simple and fast hardware
method for obtaining the required random
sample proved to be one of the most interesting aspects of the design. As with the STINT
algorithm itself, the motivation was not to
maintain mathematical rigor but to obtain a
visually acceptable result in a short time.

Recall that in the case of approximation to
a fBm the STINT algorithm requires a random
sample from a normal distribution whose mean
is the average of the four neighbouring points
and whose standard deviation is multiplied by a

ratio (2^{-H}) after each level. The STINT processor uses a pre-computed look-up table with
4096 eight-bit entries that approximate a continuous normal distribution by rectangles of
constant width as shown in Figure 7.

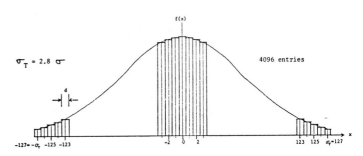

Discrete approximation to a
continuous normal distribution
Figure 7

By imposing the constraint of a single entry at
the truncated tail, σ_T , of the discrete distribution, the value $\sigma_T = \pm 2.8$ and the corresponding
width of the rectangle is determined.

The problem is now reduced to obtaining a
uniformly distributed number to use as an
address into the table with the required consistency properties and in a short time. This
will be referred to as obtaining a *seed* with the
seed function.

For internal consistency the seed used in
the calculation of the random perturbation of
each point must depend on the initial seeds
given for the whole array and also on the position within the array. The dependence on the
position or index implies a dependence on the
current level of the point being calculated.
Internal consistency guarantees that if the
array is recalculated, the same values will
result, and if the calculation is carried to a
deeper level, then the coarser values obtained
will be the same as if the calculation was to a
lesser level.

The external consistency requirement
allows adjacent arrays to be continuous at their
shared edge. It is to satisfy this requirement
that there are four seeds given as parameters,
(the *cornerseeds*), one corresponding to each
corner point.

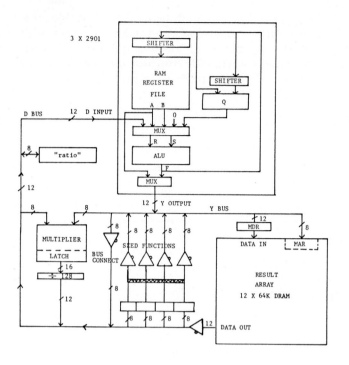

Architecture of STINT with data paths
Figure 5

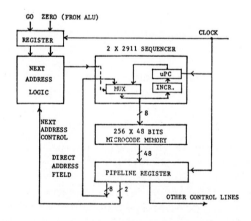

Microcode memory,
pipeline register and sequencer
Figure 6

For the calculation of the boundary, the values have to depend solely on edge information. Ultimately the whole edge must depend just on the two cornerseeds for that edge since they are the only information shared with an adjacent array.

A simple hardware implementation of the

seed function that solves the problem is presented here. The basic idea is to have the seed depend on the *value*, and thus indirectly on the index, of the four neighbours used to calculate a point. The seed is obtained by taking three bits from each neighbour and combining them together such that the resulting 12-bit address has a nearly uniform distribution. Since the neighbours' values come from a normal distribution the probability of obtaining any of eight consecutive values (corresponding to the three LSB) is almost uniform. In other words, over a small range of x, the normal density function $f(x)$ does not vary much because it is continuous and smooth. This approximation is better the larger the word size since eight consecutive x in the table will then cover a smaller range in x.

The bit-mapping scheme used in the STINT processor is shown in Fig. 8. Note that the most random bits, the LSBs of the neighbours, are mapped to the MSBs of the address.

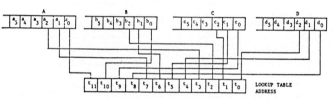

The *seed4* function
Figure 8

This is done because it is assumed that there may be some correlation between the address and the value from the table.

Edges of the array and corners as neighbours are handled as special cases. For external consistency edge values are based on two edge neighbours and the *seed2* function shown in Fig. 9.

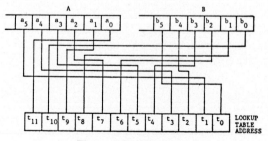

The *seed2* function
Figure 9

Since corners are usually initialized to zero

their value is not random and so are not a suitable input to the seed functions. Instead the seeds passed as parameters for each corner are used.

Since the seed function is only an approximation, the ordering of entries in the lookup table can be used to advantage so that the overall result is more nearly normal. For instance if the addresses xxxxxxxx00 are more likely than random to occur, then the 1024 entry subtable corresponding to this address pattern can be arranged so that it approximates a normal distribution. This process can be carried out recursively so that all subtables are approximately normal.

The results obtained using this hardware seed function have passed visual tests despite the obvious approximations. The addresses generated for the lookup table were also submitted to several empirical tests (the frequency test, the pair test, the serial correlation test and the run test. For a description of these tests, see [Knut69]). Except for the run test, they were applied to high, low and middle bits as well. Most of the tests give results consistent with a random hypothesis, except for the serial correlation, which is positive and around 0.2, and the pair tests when the top four bits and the bottom four bits are used. Those anomalies, however, are not sufficient to cause visible problems in the array generated. An address is generated within 200ns to apply to the lookup table stored in the result memory array.

5. Testing and Performance

The STINT processor includes hardware added primarily to ease debugging. The clock can be stopped or single stepped and the internal buses can be read from the host. The STINT processor was initially interfaced to a single board 6809 microcomputer. This allowed debugging of the hardware at less than full speed.

Testing software was written in the high-level language Concurrent Euclid, compiled on the VAX and run in the 6809. It allows setting control bits, reading status information, setting breakpoints, loading parameters and reading results.

The STINT processor executes the STINT algorithm in about 170 lines of microcode. An assembler was written using the pattern matching language **awk** under UNIX†. It

---

†UNIX is a trademark of AT&T

translates mnemonics, label names, and does some primitive syntax checking. For instance, a typical line is

data_out seedDin D + accum /2-> accum jmpnz c_continue

A software memory refresh is provided by the line.

refresh_counter + 1 -> Y,refresh_counter ras

Readers familiar with microcode will recognize these lines as relatively "high level". The microcode was debugged fully with the 6809 host so that the results matched the software simulation of the hardware.

The testing software was used to count the clock cycles required by the hardware by quickly single-stepping and incrementing a software counter. The results of this test are given in Table 2.

Size	#points	#cycles	#cycles/pts
3x3	9	125	13.9
5x5	25	430	17.2
9x9	81	1477	18.2
17x17	289	5376	18.6
33x33	1089	20451	18.8
65x65	4225	79766	18.9

Measured performance of the STINT processor
Table 2

The table suggests that the average number of cycles needed to calculate a point asymptotically approaches 19 as the array size increases. This is expected since the inner loops that calculate an interior point are exactly 19 cycles long. At 200ns per cycles in the IKONAS system, points are calculated in $3.8\mu s$, faster than the goal speed of $5\mu s$. With hindsight, a microcoded 8 by 8 bit multiply probably would have sufficed, instead of the hardware multiplier. A comparison of running time with a BPS microcoded implementation, and software implementations was given in Table 1.

The goal for the STINT processor was to match or better the speed at which the graphics system can use the data it generates. With an estimated $5\mu s$ per point for a typical microcoded application, that goal was reached. Since the STINT works strictly in parallel with the rest of the system, there is little advantage in trying to speed it up further in the current setting. It is still interesting, however, to speculate on possible improvements to match potential increases in speed of the graphics processor. We estimated that a combination of microcode optimization, use of static RAMs and faster ALU and multipliers could speed up the STINT by a factor of five. Further improvements could be achieved only by a radical redesign of the architecture.

For further details on the circuits, programs and specifications, see [Pipe83].

6. Examples of applications

The goal of the design and implementation of STINT is to demonstrate "cheap" and fast techniques for stochastic modeling. The full range of application for the values generated is still being explored. The following examples will merely suggest some applications.

Figure 10 is a display of a 129x129 array generated by STINT, and simply written into the frame buffer, with a pseudo-colour colour map. The picture shows no obvious anisotropy or periodic pattern that could be caused by deficient pseudo-random numbers. In figure 11 the same array of values has been used to map to a quadrilateral (chosen to look like a rectangle in perspective) with each point offset from the corresponding quadrilateral pixel by a quantity proportional to its value. A shading computation is done by computing a normal vector from the neighbours' values. The hidden surfaces are removed by writing the pixels front to back. The lakes are obtained by thresholding the values in the array. The whole computation and display take about 4 seconds of the bit-slice processor time.

Figure 12 shows the result when a quadrilateral covering most of the screen is subdivided until each part is small enough to be filled by the STINT processor data. The reentrant property of the STINT algorithm is used in this case to generate the subdivision. The values from an initial array are used to ensure continuity across subdivisions. The whole process took about 40 seconds of the BPS time. In Figure 13, two 129x129 arrays are mapped to a circle using an approximation of an inverse Mercator projection. The colours of the "sea" and "land" are obtained through a colour map. The mapping is fast enough so that the planet can be made to "rotate" in real time. The terrain can change either by colour map manipulation or by recomputing the stochastic arrays (which would take about four frames). Figure 14 shows the same picture with a grey colour map. This again can be made to "rotate" in real

time.

7. Conclusion

Our goal was to show that stochastic modeling can be used within a medium to low cost graphics system, and at speed near or at real time. For this purpose we built dedicated hardware to generate arrays of stochastic values, based on a bit-slice processor and a hardware random number generator. The performance met the design goal, which was to match it in speed to the graphics system to which it is interfaced. The STINT proved to be about 7 times the speed of a firmware implementation, and almost 100 times the speed of a software implementation. The first examples of its use are shown here, and they prove that stochastic modelling can be brought very close to the frame buffer, and made close to real time without sacrificing much of its power to generate visually complex images.

Acknowledgements

This research has been partially funded by NSERC Grant No A-5057, a NSERC post-graduate scholarship, and other NSERC grants. We wish to acknowledge the assistance of Safwat Zaky, who co-supervised the development of the hardware, and of Tom Milligan, who brought STINT to life on the Ikonas system, and implemented all its applications.

References

[Blin78] Blinn, J. F. "Simulation of wrinkled surfaces", in *Proceedings of SIGGRAPH '78*, also published as Comput. Graphics, *12*, 3, (Aug 1978), 286-292.

[Catm75] Catmull, E., "Computer display of curved surfaces", in *Proc. IEEE Conference on Computer Graphics, Pattern Recognition and Data Structure*. (May 1975).

[Four82] Fournier, A., Fussell, D. and Carpenter, L. "Computer Rendering of Stochastic Models", Communications of the ACM, *25*, 6, (June 1982), 371-384.

[Fu80] Fu, K. S. "Syntactic Image Modeling using Stochastic Tree Grammars", Computer Graphics and Image

Processing, *12*, (1980), 136-152.

[Holt83] Holt, R.C., *Concurrent Euclid, The UNIX Operating System, and TUNIS*, Addison-Wesley, (1983).

[Knut69] Knuth, D. E., *The Art of Computer Programming*, Volume 2: "Seminumerical Algorithms", Addison-Wesley, (1969).

[Mand68] Mandelbrot, B. B. and Van Ness, J. W. "Fractional Brownian motions, fractional noises and applications", SIAM Review, *10*, 4, (Oct 1968), 422-437.

[Mand82] Mandelbrot, B. B. *The Fractal Geometry of Nature*. Freeman, (1982).

[Max81] Max, N. "Vectorized Procedural Models for Natural Terrains: Waves and Islands in the Sunset", in *Proceedings of SIGGRAPH 81*, also published as Comput. Graphics, *15*, 3, (Aug 81), 317-324.

[Nort82] Norton, A., Rockwood, A. P. and Skolmoski, P. T. "Clamping, A Method of Antialiasing Textured surfaces by Bandwidth Limiting in Object Space", in *Proceedings of SIGGRAPH 82*, also published as Comput. Graphics,, *16*, 3, (July 82), 1-8.

[Pipe83] Piper, T. S. *A Hardware Stochastic Interpolator for Three Dimensional Computer Graphics*, Master Thesis, Department of Electrical Engineering, University of Toronto, (1983).

[Reev83] Reeves, W. T., "Particle Systems-A Technique for Modeling a Class of Fuzzy Objects", Transactions on Graphics, *2*, 2, (April 83), 91-108.

[Step83] Stepoway,S. L., Wells, D. L. and Kane, G. R., "An Architecture for Efficient Generation of Fractal Surfaces", *Proceedings of the 1983 International Conference on Parallel Processing*, (August 83), 261-268.

[Will83] Williams, L. "Pyramidal Parametrics", in *Proceedings of SIGGRAPH 83*, also published as Comput. Graphics,, *17*, 3, (July 83), 1-11.

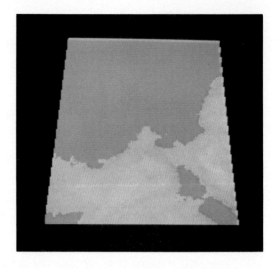

Figure 11. Patch mapped with texture of Fig. 10

Figure 10. 129x129 texture array

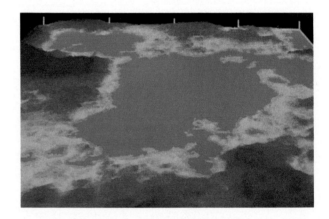

Figure 12. Landscape filled with 24 arrays

Figure 13. Array mapped on a circle

Figure 14. Array mapped on a circle with grey colour map.

PANEL

INTERNATIONAL TECHNOLOGY TRANSFER

CHAIR: Carl Machover - Machover Associates Corporation
PANEL: John Watts - GMW Computers Ltd.
        Richard Guedj - Thomson-CSF
        Tsuneo Ikedo - Seillac
        Ulrich Rethfeld - Siemens AG
        J.G. Scott - Ferranti Cetec Graphics Ltd.
        David Skok - Skok Systems

For the past two and one half decades, USA
suppliers have generally dominated the
computer graphics marketplace, providing
an estimated 90 percent of computer graphics shipments worldwide. In the past few
years, however, a number of non-USA
sources have begun to develop products
which not only have captured a growing
percentage of their domestic markets, but
also have begun to be competitive worldwide. USA companies have increasingly
turned to non-USA sources for licenses and
products. This panel brings together ex-
ecutives from European, Asian and South
African companies to discuss the growing
exchange of computer graphics technology
among USA and non-USA suppliers.

INVISIBILITY COHERENCE FOR FASTER
SCAN-LINE HIDDEN SURFACE ALGORITHMS

Gary A. Crocker

General Electric Company
Corporate Research and Development
Schenectady, New York 12345

Abstract

Invisibility coherence is a new technique developed to decrease the time necessary to render shaded images by existing scan-line hidden surface algorithms. Invisibility coherence is a technique for removing portions of a scene that are not likely to be visible. If a large portion of the scene is invisible, as is often the case in three-dimensional computer graphics, the processing time eliminated may be substantial. Invisibility coherence takes advantage of the observation that a minimal amount of processing needs to be done on objects (polygons, patches, or surfaces) that will be hidden by other objects closer to the viewer. This fact can be used to increase the efficiency of current scan-line algorithms, including both polygon-based and parametrically curved surface-based algorithms.

Invisibility coherence was implemented and tested with the polygon hidden surface algorithm for constructive solid geometry developed by Peter Atherton [1]. The use of invisibility coherence substantially increases the efficiency of this scan-line algorithm. Invisibility coherence should work as well or even better with other scan-line hidden surface algorithms, such as the Lane-Carpenter, Whitted, and Blinn algorithms for parametrically curved surfaces [2], or the Watkins, Romney, and Bouknight algorithms for polygons [3, 4, 5].

CR Categories: I3.7 [Computer Graphics]: Three-dimensional Graphics and Realism — Visible Line/Surface Algorithms; **I3.5** [Computer Graphics]: Computational Geometry and Object Modeling — Curve, surface, solid and object representations; **I3.3** [Computer Graphics]: Picture/Image Generation — Display Algorithms.

Key Words and Phrases: computer graphics, hidden surface removal, coherence, constructive solid geometry, scan-line algorithms.

Permission to copy without fee all or part of this material is granted provided that the copies are not made or distributed for direct commercial advantage, the ACM copyright notice and the title of the publication and its date appear, and notice is given that copying is by permission of the Association for Computing Machinery. To copy otherwise, or to republish, requires a fee and/or specific permission.

© 1984   ACM   0-89791-138-5/84/007/0095 $00.75

1. INTRODUCTION

A major topic in computer graphics has been one of determining the visible portions of computer representations of objects and their environments. Much work has been dedicated to this area of graphics. Currently, there are many algorithms that generate these images. They fall into two major classifications: object space algorithms and image space algorithms [6]. Object space algorithms are usually more precise and yield results that are as accurate as corresponding representations of the objects. Image space algorithms, on the other hand, calculate a picture to the accuracy of the viewing device. In cases where the modeled environment contains many surfaces, image space algorithms tend to render images more quickly.

There are presently many techniques for object space hidden line-surface removal. The first being the L.G. Roberts algorithm (1963), which tests each relevent edge to see if it is obstructed by the volume of some other object [6]. The edge-to-edge and edge-to-vertex comparison algorithms of A. Appel (1967), P.P. Loutrel (1967), and R. Galimberti & U. Montarari (1969) were developed in the latter 1960s [6]. More recent advances include: the Weiler-Atherton algorithm (1977) [7], which is based on a two-dimensional polygon clipper; the Hamlin-Gear algorithms (1967) [8], which use a recursive list processing on each span, the W.R. Franklin linear time algorithm (1980) [9], which uses grids and blocking faces to eliminate unused portions of the picture; and the visible polygon reconstruction algorithm by Sechrest and Greenberg (1981) [10], which works something like a scan-line algorithm, but at object resolution. The four more recent algorithms are significant because that can use information about the front faces to eliminate some of the processing required on invisible faces.

Image space algorithms are of three basic types: Z-buffer, area sorting, and scan-line. Z-buffer algorithms paint a picture polygon-by-polygon, testing the depth at each pixel to see if the new polygon will be visible at that pixel. These algorithms are often preprocessed to enable the determination of depth quickly enough for real-time movement, such as in flight simulators. Area sorting algorithms use area subdivision to determine visible portions of the picture. Scan-line algorithms calculate pictures by determining the foremost surface at each pixel.

This paper focuses on a method developed that makes scan-line algorithms more efficient in cases where the modeled environment is complex in depth. The sorting order of scan-line algorithms is Y,X,Z, where Y is up and down, X is across, and Z is the depth [6]. In this paper the left-handed coordinate system will be used with the greater Z values going away from the viewer. The Z sort at each pixel will determine the surface with the minimum Z depth. If many faces exist at each pixel, this sort will consume a lot of computational time. One method for improving the Z sort in scan-line algorithms was mentioned by Sutherland et al. [6]. This method consists of doing a partial Z (Zp) sort before the Y,X,Z algorithm. The result is a Zp,Y,X,Z method of sorting.

Invisibility coherence uses a sorting order of Y,Zp,X,Z. Surfaces are first sorted by Y values. The Y sort is usually a bucket sort into K buckets (where K is the screen Y resolution). As each surface is removed from its Y bucket, it is compared to the Z depth of the visible surfaces of the previous scan-line. If the surface has greater Z depth (away from the viewer) than the visible surfaces of the previous scan-line, it is likely to be invisible. The visible surfaces are processed as usual by the scan-line hidden surface removal algorithm, while the invisible surfaces are put into an invisible list and eliminated from the bulk of the hidden surface processing. The elimination of some of the surfaces by their Z depth constitutes a partial Z-sort. The X and Z sorts then proceed as usual in the scan-line algorithm. At each pixel the minimum Z (nearest) of the invisible list is compared to the Z value of the visible surface to make sure the visible surface is correctly chosen. In cases where this check fails, the closest surface of the invisible list is removed from the invisible list and processed as a surface that could be visible. The removed surface may or may not actually be seen but will be processed by the host hidden surface algorithm.

2. INVISIBILITY COHERENCE DEFINITION

INVISIBILITY COHERENCE eliminates surfaces from the active list that are not likely to be visible prior to the processing of the active list for each scan-line in the hidden surface removal process. To eliminate these surfaces it is necessary to retain information about the Z depth of the pixels of the previous scan-line. The Z depth at the pixels where no surface is visible is a value greater than the Z depth of any surface in the scene. The rest of the Z_BUFFER will contain the Z depth of the visible surface at each pixel. This single scan-line Z_BUFFER is used as the criterion for determining which surfaces are likely to be invisible. As surfaces are removed from the Y_BUCKET, they are compared to the Z_BUFFER to see if they lie behind the visible surfaces of the previous scan-line; if a surface's minimum Z depth is behind the Z_BUFFER at the surface's minimum and maximum X positions, it will be put into an invisible list rather than into the usual active list, and will be processed by the scan-line hidden surface algorithm in the usual manner. Thus, surfaces that are likely to be invisible are eliminated from the bulk of the processing done in the hidden surface removal procedure.

The word "likely" has been used because a surface that is chosen as invisible will not necessarily be invisible. There are many cases in which this will happen, the simplest being a set of surfaces that are completely in front of another surface, but having a hole through which the back surface can be seen (see Figure 4). In order to take into account the fact that incorrect decisions will occasionally be made, at each pixel the Z depth of the visible surface is compared with the minimum Z depth of the CURRENT_INVIS list. The CURRENT_INVIS list is also checked when there are no visible surfaces at a pixel. These final checks will ensure that the correct surface is always chosen to be visible.

A simple example of the criteria used to determine if a surface is likely to be invisible is shown in Figures 1 through 4. Figure 1

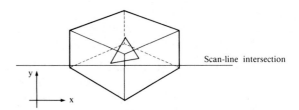

Figure 1. Sample case of triangle within a cube.

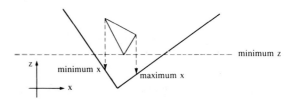

Figure 2. Top view of Figure 1 with Z-buffer of scan-line and triangle projected into x, z plane. Triangle in this figure will be eliminated by invisibility coherence.

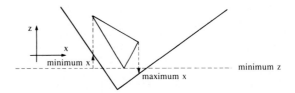

Figure 3. Same top view as Figure 2. Triangle not eliminated by invisibility coherence.

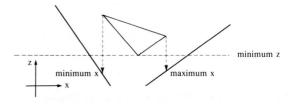

Figure 4. Same top view as Figure 2. Triangle incorrectly eliminated by invisibility coherence. This is a two-dimensional error.

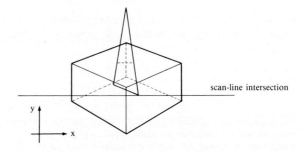

Figure 5. Triangle incorrectly eliminated by invisibility coherence. This is a three-dimensional error because the triangle goes through the top of the cube.

shows a triangle within a cube and the scan-line intersection. At this scan-line the triangle will be removed from the Y_BUCKET and checked to see if it is likely to be invisible. Figures 2 through 4 show the view of the X, Z plane at that scan-line. Also shown is the Z buffer generated by the previous scan-line, the projection of the triangle into the X, Z plane, and the triangle's minimum Z, minimum X, and maximum X. In Figure 2 the triangle will be put into the invisible list because the minimum Z at both the triangle's minimum X and maximum X is behind the Z buffer of the previous scan-line. In Figure 3 the triangle will not be put into the invisible list because the minimum Z of the triangle is not behind the Z buffer at its maximum X. Figure 4 shows a two-dimensional case where the triangle would be incorrectly determined to be invisible. Figure 5 shows a three-dimensional case where the triangle would be incorrectly determined to be invisible.

The elimination of invisible surfaces by INVISIBILITY COHERENCE is possible partially because of SCAN-LINE COHERENCE, partially because of DEPTH COHERENCE, and partially because of SPAN COHERENCE. Scan-line coherence states that there are relatively few changes from one scan-line to the next. Therefore, the next scan-line is likely to have approximately the same faces. Depth coherence states that the relative Z ordering of surfaces is likely to remain the same; thus, if a surface is behind other surfaces, it is likely to remain behind those surfaces. Span coherence states that the visible portion of each surface across a scan-line is likely to remain the same. Invisibility coherence utilizes all of these ideas and states that if the nearest Z depth of a surface is behind the Z buffer of the previous scan-line at its minimum and maximum X, it is likely to be invisible. If the surface is actually invisible, it will remain behind the Z buffer across its entire width (minimum X to maximum X) and also remain behind the Z buffer of following scan-lines across its entire vertical extent (min Y to max Y).

3. GENERIC SCAN-LINE HIDDEN SURFACE DEFINITION

Invisibility coherence works in the context of scan-line hidden surface algorithms. There are several known scan-line algorithms. They fall into two major categories: polygon-based and parametric surface-based. The paper by Sutherland et al. [6] describes and classifies three polygon-based hidden surface removal algorithms. The paper by Lane et al. [2] describes three methods for displaying curved surfaces. From these six descriptions a generic scan-line hidden surface removal procedure can be produced. This generic algorithm does not replicate any one of these algorithms. Instead, it creates a conceptual model through which all of the algorithms can be understood. The generic algorithm is used as the context for the invisibility coherence description. In the generic description a SURFACE is either a polygon or a curved patch. It should be noted that algorithms for curved surface display do present some problems that are not discussed here. All references X, Y, and Z correspond to the left-handed screen coordinate system, Typically, the following four variables and five phases will exist in scan-line hidden surface algorithms:

Y_BUCKET	: object of bucket sort of surfaces by min Y value
ACTIVE_LIST	: list of surfaces that intersect current scan-line
CURRENT	: list if surfaces that intersect current pixel
VISIBLE	: surface that is visible at a given pixel

1. sort surfaces into Y_BUCKETS by minimum Y
    FOR each scan-line do the following:
2.   remove surfaces from Y_BUCKET of the current scan-line
        put these surfaces on ACTIVE_LIST
3.   sort ACTIVE_LIST by minimum X
        FOR each pixel do the following:
4.   determine CURRENT surfaces from sorted ACTIVE_LIST
            sort the CURRENT surfaces by Z
            choose surface with minimum Z (nearest) from CURRENT to be VISIBLE at this pixel
5.   calculate shade and display pixel

Steps three, four and five above are very general because scan-line algorithms vary greatly in how they perform these steps. See the papers mentioned above by Sutherland et al. and Lane et al. for a more detailed description of these scan-line hidden surface algorithms. For the purpose of describing the use of invisibility coherence, this generic description is sufficient.

4. INVISIBILITY COHERENCE ALGORITHM

In some cases many surfaces could be eliminated by using invisibility coherence, but unless it can be implemented efficiently, invisibility coherence is of little use. Invisibility coherence has been implemented and tested. The implementation developed requires little computational cost. The exact computational costs will be given in the section that analyzes the results of the test implementation of invisibility coherence. First, a few key variables and important functions need to be defined to assist in the explanation of the algorithm.

VARIABLES:

CURRENT_INVISIBLE : a list of invisible surfaces that are likely to intersect the current pixel.

INVIS_X_BUCKETS : two X_BUCKETS that contain pointers to surfaces. These buckets will determine when surfaces are entering and leaving the CURRENT_INVISIBLE list. The surfaces will be indexed into the X_BUCKETS using their minimum and maximum X values.

INVIS_Z_MIN : minimum Z value for closest surface in the CURRENT_INVISIBLE list.

CLOSEST_SURF : surface that is closest in the invisible list for a given pixel.

Z_BUFFER : a single scan-line Z buffer that will hold the Z values of each pixel of the previous scan-line.

FUNCTIONS:

RESET_INVIS_Z_MIN (current_invisible, invis_z_min, closest_surf): will search the CURRENT_INVISIBLE list and find the CLOSEST_SURF and its Z min. The INVIS_Z_MIN will be reset to the CLOSEST_SURF's Z minimum.

SURFACE_LIKELY_TOBE_INVISIBLE (asurface, answer): will compare the Z minimum (closest) of a

surface at the surfaces X minimum and X maximum to
the Z_BUFFER. If the surface is behind the
Z_BUFFER at both points, then answer will be
TRUE., else the answer will be .FALSE.

INTO_INVIS (asurface,invis_x_buckets):
will put a surface into the INVIS_X_BUCKETS.

OUTOF_INVIS (asurface,invis_x_buckets):
will remove a surface from the INVIS_X_BUCKETS.

INTO_ACTIVE_LIST (asurface, active_list):
will put a surface in the ACTIVE_LIST of the generic
scan-line algorithm.

OUTOF_ACTIVE_LIST (asurface,active_list):
will remove a surface from the ACTIVE_LIST of the
generic scan-line algorithm.

UPDATE_CURRENT (current_invis,invis_x_buckets,
invis_z_min): will add and delete invisible surfaces from
the CURRENT_INVIS using the INVIS_X_BUCKETS.
When surfaces are added, their Z min is compared to
the INVIS_Z_MIN. If the surface Z min is smaller, the
INVIS_Z_MIN is changed to the surface's Z minimum.

The following is a pseudo code description of the implementation of invisibility coherence in the context of the generic scan-
line algorithm:

```
      determine Z min, X min and X max of each surface
      initialize invisible data structures
1.    sort surfaces into Y_BUCKETs by minimum Y
      FOR each scan-line do the following:
2.       remove surfaces from Y_BUCKET of the scan-line
             IF SURFACE_LIKELY_TOBE_INVISIBLE
               THEN INTO_INVIS structure
               ELSE INTO_ACTIVE_LIST
         determine which surfaces no longer intersect
             scan-line
         IF the surface is in the invisible structure
             THEN OUTOF_INVIS structure
             ELSE OUTOF_ACTIVE_LIST
         remove old surfaces from INVIS_X_BUCKETS
3.       sort ACTIVE_LIST by minimum X
         FOR each pixel do the following:
             UPDATE_CURRENT invisible list
4.           determine CURRENT surfaces using
                 ACTIVE_LIST
             sort the CURRENT surfaces by Z
             choose surface with minimum Z (nearest) from
                 CURRENT to be VISIBLE at this pixel
4. a         IF Z of VISIBLE less than INVIS_Z_MIN
                 THEN RESET_INVIS_Z_MIN
             IF Z of VISIBLE still less than
                 INVIS_Z_MIN
               THEN OUTOF_INVIS (CLOSEST_SURF)
               INTO_ACTIVE_LIST
                                    (CLOSEST_SURF)
             put surface into CURRENT list of
                 algorithm
             resort CURRENT and choose visible
                 surface
             go to 4. a and check again to make sure
5.           calculate shade and display pixel
             put Z value of pixel into Z_BUFFER
```

There are four additional inner loop computational costs in the
generic algorithm that uses invisibility coherence. The first extra
cost is the updating of the CURRENT invisible list. This calculation is proportional to the number of invisible surfaces. On each
scan-line the surface will have to be added to the CURRENT_IN-
VIS list once and deleted once. If the average surface height in Y
is 20 scan-lines, each invisible surface will be added and deleted
about 20 times. Even if there are a great number of surfaces in the
invisible list, the cost of this calculation is not an added burden.
If the surfaces remained visible instead of becoming invisible, a
similar calculation would have to be done to each surface by the
host scan-line algorithm. This calculation is similar to the portion
of the X sort required to determine which surfaces are visible at a
given pixel in the hidden surface algorithm. Therefore, the first
invisibility coherence computational cost is offset by a corresponding decrease in the cost of determining the visible surface at each
pixel within the host hidden surface algorithm.

The second major computational cost is that of RESET_IN-
VIS_Z_MIN. This function looks at each surface in the CUR-
RENT_INVIS list to determine which surface is closest. If the
average size of the surface is 20 by 20 pixels, up to 400 searches
may be done for each surface. This calculation is at worst proportional to the square of the size of the number of polygons. The
frequency of this calculation has been reduced greatly in the
algorithm. Depth coherence states that the depth ordering of surfaces is likely to remain about the same. Therefore, this calculation is done only when the INVIS_Z_MIN is less than the VISI-
BLE surface's Z value. INVIS_Z_MIN is always less than or
equal to the smallest Z depth of the CURRENT_INVIS. When
comparing the VISIBLE surface Z value at each pixel to IN-
VIS_Z_MIN, it is not necessary to RESET_INVIS_Z_MIN. IF
AND ONLY IF the Z value of the VISIBLE surface is greater
than INVIS_Z_MIN is the function RESET_INVIS_Z_MIN invoked. Even in complex intersecting scenes with many holes, the
cost of RESET_INVIS_Z_MIN should be more than offset by
the corresponding decrease in the cost of determining the VISI-
BLE surface from the CURRENT surfaces at each pixel.

The third inner loop computational cost is that of setting the
Z_BUFFER for each scan-line. The cost of this computation is
linear with respect to the number of pixels displayed. The actual
cost should be quite small with respect to the cost of the entire
algorithm.

The fourth inner loop computational cost is that of removing a
surface from the invisible surface list and putting it into the
ACTIVE_LIST and CURRENT list. This calculation will have
to be done when the invisibility coherence removes a surface incorrectly. In the boolean views of the two complex cases (Figs.
6d, 6f), each of which have many holes, at most 15 percent of the
polygons were incorrectly classified as 'INVISIBLE' by invisibility coherence.

Another major cost required in the implementation of invisibility coherence is that of calculating the minimum Z,
minimum X, and maximum X for each surface. In the polygon-
based algorithms this calculation can be done by choosing the
minimum Z, minimum X, and maximum X from the vertices of
each polygon. In the BEZIER surface algorithms the same can be
done for the points that define a surface, because the surface will
lie completely within its defining points. When using other
curved surface forms, the cost of calculating the minimum Z,
minimum X, and maximum X may be more substantial. Before
implementing invisibility coherence with other curved surface
forms, the requirements of this calculation should be weighed

against the possible savings.

In most algorithms, the cost of using invisibility coherence should be relatively small compared to the overall computational cost of the algorithm. The first major reduction in cost is that of sorting by Z at each pixel. If a scene has an average of 8 surfaces in depth, and 200 by 200 pixels, there will be 40,000 sorts of 8 surfaces each. Assuming invisibility coherence is used and that these sorts are linear, there would be 320,000 comparisons. If on the average of 4 surfaces can be eliminated, the result for the Z sort time would be 160,000 comparisons. The second major reduction in computational cost is that of determining the intersection of a surface with a scan-line and with the individual pixels on the scan-line. In the polygon-based algorithms this cost has already been substantially reduced by scan-line coherence. In the surface-based algorithms the cost of determining the intersections is much greater, and thus, the possibility of savings by using invisibility coherence is greater. In modeled environments which are complex in depth, the time savings possible with invisibility coherence should be substantial.

5. TEST IMPLEMENTATION OF INVISIBILITY COHERENCE

Invisibility coherence is designed to make scan-line hidden surface algorithms operate more efficiently in cases where the depth of the modeled environment is greater than one surface. Because invisibility coherence is designed to increase the speed of scan-line algorithms, the ideal test case to prove that invisibility coherence works would be a STATE of the ART scan-line algorithm designed to determine visible surfaces quickly. An obvious choice is that of the Atherton Constructive Solid Geometry Display algorithm [1]. This algorithm already makes use of the following coherences: span, scan-line, and depth. This algorithm is more complex than most scan-line algorithms because the criterion for determining visible surfaces is a boolean combination, rather than simply choosing the closest point at each pixel.

Four test cases were chosen. They vary in complexity from simple to very intricate. For the first three cases, different screen sizes and polygon counts were used. The first three test cases were as follows: a single sphere; a box with a rounded box and three cylinders; and a cube with nine cylinders through it in each of three directions. The fourth test case was a model of an electric motor. The original code by Atherton was modified to use invisibility coherence. Two copies were made of the software. One copy was used for invisibility coherence implementation. The other copy was used in its original form in order to compare it to the modified version.

Two different types of views were used. First, the simple hidden surface view was tested. This view also was tested with backfacing polygons removed, because many algorithms remove backfacing surfaces of enclosed objects to increase efficiency. Second, the boolean combination of primitives approximated by polygons was performed on the last three models. It should be noted that the algorithm with invisibility coherence produced the exact same picture as the original algorithm. I believe that it is possible to produce a slightly different picture in tangency cases where the Z depth of two surfaces is exactly the same and the order in which that occurs is altered by invisibility coherence.

All tests were done on a VAX 11/780 using FORTRAN 77. The tests of each model are numbered from 1 to 6 as follows:

Test #1 — Low resolution polygons

Test #2 — Mid resolution polygons
Test #3 — High resolution polygons
Test #4 — Small screen size
Test #5 — Large screen size
Test #6 — Backfacing polygons removed

The constant parameters used were:

Screen resolution 512 × 512
View orthogonal
Rotations of 30 about the X axis and 30 about the Y axis

The test models used were:

Model 1 — A single sphere approximated by 3 and 4 sided polygons

Model 2 — A box with a rounded box and three cylinders. In the boolean view the rounded box and cylinders will be subtracted from the box. All geometry approximated with 3 and 4 sided polygons.

Model 3 — A box with 27 cylinders completely through it, 9 cylinders in each direction and perpendicular to the faces they intersect. In the boolean view the cylinders will be subtracted from the box. All geometry approximated with 3 and 4 sided polygons.

Model 4 — A motor modeled with cylinders, boxes, slabs, a torus, surfaces of revolutions, and boxes. All geometry approximated with 3 and 4 sided polygons.

Timing test results are shown in Table 1. Raster images of the test models are shown in Figure 6.

6. ANALYSIS OF TEST RESULTS

The timing tests show that in the complex models (Figs. 6c-6f) the time savings were substantial (up to 51 percent of the original). It can also be seen that in the simple case of the sphere, the overhead was at only 11 percent (actual time difference 2.9 seconds). As the modeled scenes became more complicated, the time savings resulting from the use of invisibility coherence increased substantially (largest savings of 100 seconds). The substantial savings on the high end of the scale should more than outweigh the slight overhead in very simple models. Invisibility coherence would be a worthwile addition to this algorithm, unless only the simplest models were expected.

Table 2 gives information pertaining to the number of polygons removed by invisibility coherence. The first column gives the total number of polygons processed in the scene. The second column gives the number of polygons removed by invisibility coherence. The third column gives the number of polygons that were processed only by the hidden surface algorithm. The fourth column contains the number of polygons that remained invisible throughout the process. The number of polygons invisibility coherence incorrectly processed can be obtained by subtracting column 4 from 2. The percentage of polygons incorrectly determined to be invisible by invisibility coherence is found in column 5. Column 6 shows the percentage of polygons that were eliminated by invisibility coherence and remained eliminated throughout the hidden surface process. The models with the BPR are models whose back planes were removed prior to processing.

Table 1

TIMING TEST RESULTS

Model	View	Test	# Pixels	# Polygons	CPU Original	CPU with IC	% Decrease
1	—	1	71 K	128	25.6	28.5	− 11
1	—	2	71 K	512	27.3	29.9	− 10
1	—	3	71 K	2312	32.8	33.1	− 01
1	—	4	23 K	128	13.1	13.5	− 03
1	—	5	146 K	128	44.5	48.0	− 10
1	—	6	71 K	512	24.0	27.1	− 13
2	Solid	1	77 K	1088	36.2	34.2	06
2	Solid	2	77 K	4352	46.0	39.7	14
2	Solid	3	77 K	9792	52.6	46.5	12
2	Solid	4	19 K	4352	19.1	17.6	08
2	Solid	5	120 K	4352	59.6	52.8	12
2	Solid	6	77 K	4352	32.2	34.4	− 07
2	Boolean	1	75 K	128	45.5	43.2	05
2	Boolean	2	75 K	512	55.3	56.8	− 03
2	Boolean	3	75 K	2312	65.1	62.9	12
2	Boolean	4	18 K	128	23.3	24.5	− 04
2	Boolean	5	115 K	128	73.7	70.8	04
3	Solid	1	67 K	2970	55.1	44.1	20
3	Solid	2	67 K	8250	71.1	55.2	22
3	Solid	3	67 K	16170	89.2	73.3	18
3	Solid	4	22 K	8250	50.3	29.5	41
3	Solid	5	137 K	8250	111.5	82.7	26
3	Solid	6	67 K	8250	50.9	46.5	09
3	Boolean	1	65 K	2970	100.4	57.5	43
3	Boolean	2	65 K	8250	123.6	68.1	45
3	Boolean	3	65 K	16170	144.5	86.1	40
3	Boolean	4	21 K	8250	68.1	35.2	48
3	Boolean	5	133 K	8250	203.5	103.5	49
4	Solid	1	77 K	8950	87.3	64.0	27
4	Solid	6	77 K	14005	59.2	53.7	09
4	Boolean	1	73 K	8950	179.0	120.0	33

Table 2

FACES REMOVED WITH INVISIBILITY COHERENCE

Model	View	Total # Polygons	Initial Invisible	Final Visible	Final Invisible	% Incorrect Invisible	% Correct Invisible
Sphere	Solid	288	120	184	105	05	36
	Solid BPR	157	3	157	0	02	00
Box, Rounded	Solid	612	406	219	393	02	64
Box, 3 Cylinders	Solid BPR	306	148	167	139	03	45
	Boolean	612	184	482	130	10	21
Box and 27	Solid	15146	9418	5760	9386	00	62
Cylinders	Solid BPR	7437	2364	2211	5326	02	30
	Boolean	15146	9113	6511	8635	03	57
Motor	Solid	8012	6143	2161	5851	04	73
	Solid BPR	4005	2805	1479	2526	07	63
	Boolean	8012	5714	3487	4525	15	56

6a: Box, rounded box, 3 cylinders — solid view

6b: Box, rounded box, 3 cylinders — boolean view

6c: Box, 27 cylinders — solid view

6d: Box, 27 cylinders — boolean view

6e: Motor — solid view

6f: Motor — boolean view

Figure 6. Raster images of test models used in invisibility coherence implementation.

The figures in Table 2 can be used to estimate the effect invisibility coherence would have on other scan-line hidden surface algorithms. It should be noted that although fewer polygons were eliminated in the boolean tests, the boolean tests were generally better. The reason for the improvement in the boolean case results lies in the fact that at each pixel the faces have to be sorted by Z into ascending order to allow for the boolean operation to be done. This sorting takes longer than in the solid case, where only the polygon with the largest Z value is chosen. Also shown in the table is the fact that the larger the number of polygons eliminated by invisibility coherence, the greater the increase in time savings (see Table 1). The conclusion can be drawn that the more surfaces involved in a model, the larger the possible savings from invisibility coherence.

It should be noted that some of the polygons were eliminated because they were either too small or parallel to the line of sight. These figures give a rough estimate of the percentage of faces that can be eliminated completely from the normal processing of a scan-line hidden surface removal procedure.

7. CONCLUSION

Invisibility coherence eliminates many surfaces from the processing required in the scan-line hidden surface removal process. In complex modeled environments the efficiency of a scan-line algorithm should be greatly improved, while at the same time only a minor amount of performance is lost in the simplest cases. Most scan-line hidden surface algorithms should benefit from the use of invisibility coherence. It has been shown that in a very fast polygon algorithm the time savings are substantial. In algorithms such as the Lane-Carpenter subdivision algorithm, time savings should be much greater because of the high cost of Bezier surface subdivision associated with this algorithm [2]. The invisibility coherence technique should be almost directly transportable to the Romney [4], Bouknight [5], and Watkins [3] polygon algorithms, as well as derivatives of each. With some modifications, invisibility coherence should improve the Blinn and Whitted algorithms for curved surfaces [2].

8. ACKNOWLEDGEMENTS

I would like to express my appreciation to the General Electric Company for the use of their resources to complete this project. Karen Crocker, my wife, and Kevin Weiler, a co-worker, contributed greatly in the editing process. Virgil Lucke, my manager, answered many questions I had. Thanks go to Rensselaer Polytechnic Institute and Professor W. Franklin for encouraging research projects to fulfill course requirements.

9. REFERENCES

[1] Atherton, P.R., "A Scan-Line Hidden Surface Removal Procedure for Constructive Solid Geometry," *Computer Graphics,* Vol. 17, No. 3, July 1983, pp. 73-82.

[2] Lane, J.M., Carpenter, L.C., Whitted, T., Blinn, J.F., "Scan Line Methods for Displaying Parametrically Defined Surfaces," *Comm. ACM,* Vol. 23, No. 1, January 1980, pp. 23-34.

[3] Watkins, G.S., *A Real-Time Visible Surface Algorithm,* Computer Science Department, University of Utah, UTECH-CSC-70-101, June 1970.

[4] Romney, G.W., *Computer Assisted Assembly and Rendering of Solids,* Computer Science Department, University of Utah, TR-4-20, 1970.

[5] Bouknight, W.J., "A Procedure for Generation of Three-Dimensional Half-Toned Computer Graphics Representations," *Comm. ACM,* Vol. 13, No. 9, September 1970.

[6] Sutherland, I.E., Sproull, R.F., and Schumacher, R.A., "A Characterization of Ten Hidden-Surface Algorithms," *ACM Computing Surveys,* Vol. 6, No. 1, March 1974, pp. 1-55.

[7] Weiler, K. and Atherton, P., "Hidden Surface Removal Using Polygon Area Sorting," *Computer Graphics,* Vol. 11, No. 2, Summer 1977, pp. 214-222

[8] Hamlin, G. Jr and Gear, C.W., "Raster-Scan Hidden Surface Algorithm Techniques," *Computer Graphics,* Vol. 11, No. 2, Summer 1977, pp. 206-213.

[9] Franklin, W.R., "A Linear Time Exact Hidden Surface Algorithm," *Computer Graphics,* Vol. 14, No. 3, July 1980, pp. 117-123

[10] Sechrest, S., and Greenberg, D.P., "A Visible Polygon Reconstriction Algorithm," *Computer Graphics,* Vol. 15, No. 3, August 1981, pp. 17-27.

The A-buffer, an Antialiased Hidden Surface Method

Loren Carpenter

Computer Graphics Project
Computer Division
Lucasfilm Ltd

Abstract

The A-buffer (anti-aliased, area-averaged, accumulation buffer) is a general hidden surface mechanism suited to medium scale virtual memory computers. It resolves visibility among an arbitrary collection of opaque, transparent, and intersecting objects. Using an easy to compute Fourier window (box filter), it increases the effective image resolution many times over the Z-buffer, with a moderate increase in cost. The A-buffer is incorporated into the REYES 3-D rendering system at Lucasfilm and was used successfully in the "Genesis Demo" sequence in Star Trek II.

CR CATEGORIES AND SUBJECT DESCRIPTORS: I.3.3 [**Computer Graphics**]: Picture/Image Generation - Display algorithms; I.3.7 [**Computer Graphics**]: Three-Dimensional Graphics and Realism - Visible line/surface elimination.

GENERAL TERMS: Algorithms, Experimentation.

ADDITIONAL KEY WORDS AND PHRASES: hidden surface, image synthesis, z-buffer, a-buffer, antialiasing, transparency, supersampling, computer imagery.

1. Introduction

There are many hidden surface techniques known to computer graphics. A designer of a 3-D image synthesis system must balance the desire for quality with the cost of computation. The A-buffer method, a descendant of the well-known Z-buffer, has proven to deliver moderate to good quality images at moderate cost. At each pixel, sufficient information is available to increase the effective

Permission to copy without fee all or part of this material is granted provided that the copies are not made or distributed for direct commercial advantage, the ACM copyright notice and the title of the publication and its date appear, and notice is given that copying is by permission of the Association for Computing Machinery. To copy otherwise, or to republish, requires a fee and/or specific permission.

© 1984   ACM   0-89791-138-5/84/007/0103 $00.75

resolution of the image several times over that of a simple Z-buffer.

2. Historical Perspective

The A-buffer belongs to the class of hidden surface algorithms called "scanline". The REYES (Renders Everything You Ever Saw) system, of which the A-buffer is a part, is a scanline renderer, but scanline order is not required by the A-buffer.

The first scanline algorithms[7] did perspective, clipping, sorting, visibility determination, and "filtering" all at the same time. They resolved visibility at one point per pixel, and aliased terribly, although our standards were different then. In 1974, E. Catmull described the Z-buffer method[2]. A Z-buffer is a screen-sized array of pixels and Z's. Objects, in no particular order, are examined to determine which pixels they cover. At each covered pixel, the perspective Z depth of the object is determined and compared with the Z in the array. If the new Z is closer, then the new Z, and the object's shade at this point, replaces the array's Z and pixel. This development started the trend toward modularizing the rendering process, as a Z-buffer could comprise the visibility section of almost any kind of renderer. Although extremely fast and simple, the Z-buffer aliases too much and cannot render transparent objects correctly.

The aliasing problems of the Z-buffer can be softened somewhat by modifying it from a point sampler to a line sampler so that visibility is determined over horizontal segments of scanlines[1]. In this way the line Z-buffer is very similar to the classical polygon algorithms of Watkins and others[7]. Polygons are sliced horizontally as in Watkins, but no X sorting is done. Instead, polygon segments conditionally overwrite others based on Z depth. The segment boundaries do not have to be coincident with pixel boundaries. This added information clears up aliasing of nearly vertical edges. However, nearly horizontal edges still alias and dropouts of small objects still occur.

In 1978, E. Catmull introduced the "ultimate" visibility method[3], a full polygon hidden surface process, based on Weiler-Atherton[8], at each pixel. Dropouts are precluded, as every sliver is accounted for. The color of the resulting pixel is simply the weighted average of all the visible polygon fragments. This can be extremely expensive. It is so expensive that it's primary use is in 2-D animation of a few fairly large polygons. In that application, most pixels are completely covered by some polygon, where the hidden surface process has a trivial solution. Pixels needing the full power of the visibility resolver are rare, and so the total cost per frame is acceptable.

3. Goals and Constraints

The visibility techniques described above span a wide range of computational expense and image quality. What is needed is a method that combines the simplicity and speed of the Z-buffer with the two dimensional anti-aliasing benefits of Catmull's full polygon process at each pixel.

The method must support all conceivable geometric modeling primitives: polygons, patches, quadrics, fractals, and so forth. It must handle transparency and intersecting surfaces (and transparent intersecting surfaces). It must do all this while being fast enough for limited production using a DEC VAX 11/780.

4. Strategy

The rendering system (REYES) in which the visibility processor was to reside began to take shape in mid 1981. Adaptive subdivision[5] (splitting geometric primitives until "flat" *on the screen*) would produce a common intermediate form: polygons. Everything would be converted to polygons in approximately scanline order, as the picture developed. The polygons would be thrown away after the visibility resolver had finished with them and their memory space would be used for polygons to be created later. To reduce the scope and complexity of the visibility resolver, polygons would be clipped to pixel boundaries. The visibility resolver would only have to deal with one pixel at a time.

In a virtual memory computer, like the VAX, code space is not a serious limitation, so it was decided to optimize the algorithm for the common cases and write potentially voluminous code for the unusual situations.

5. Geometry inside the pixel

The geometric information inside a complex pixel is vital to the correct display of the pixel. Pictures produced by REYES had to be free of aliasing artifacts. The aliasing deficiencies of the simple Z-buffer precluded its use. More resolution inside the pixel was called for, but a full polygon intersector/clipper was too expensive. After some experimentation, a 4x8 bit mask (figure 1) was selected to represent the subpixel polygons. Clipping one

polygon against another becomes a simple boolean operation. The mask is similar in several ways to the mask of Fiume, Fournier and Rudolph[4], although both were developed independently.

Silhouettes of objects still exhibited coarse intensity quantization effects, so the actual screen area of subpixel-sized polygons was kept with the mask. Whenever possible, the actual area is used instead of the bit count in the mask.

6. The A-buffer Algorithm

The A-buffer works with two different data types: "pixelstructs" (distinct from pixels) and "fragments". A pixelstruct is two 32-bit words (figure 2), one containing a Z depth and the other either a color or a pointer. A fragment (figure 3) is for the most part a polygon clipped to a pixel boundary. Pixelstructs occur in an array the size and shape of the final image (like the Z-buffer). In REYES, the array is paged in software to save virtual memory space. If a pixel is simple, i.e. completely covered, the Z value is positive and the pixelstruct contains a color. Otherwise, the Z value is negative and the pointer points to a list of fragments sorted front-to-back by frontmost Z.

Figure 1. Pixel bit mask.

float	z;	/* negative Z */
fragment_ptr	flist;	/* never null */
	(or)	
float	z;	/* positive Z */
byte	r, g, b;	/* color */
byte	a;	/* coverage */

Figure 2. Pixelstruct definition.

fragment_ptr	next;	
short_int	r, g, b;	/* color, 12 bit */
short_int	opacity;	/* 1 - transparency */
short_int	area;	/* 12 bit precision */
short_int	object_tag;	/* from parent surface */
pixelmask	m;	/* 4x8 bits */
float	zmax, zmin;	/* positive */

Figure 3. Fragment definition.

The following discussion contains several symbols which we define here:

M   4x8 bit mask
A   area (0..1)
C   color (r, g, b)
Opacity 1 - transmission fraction
α coverage, usually area times opacity[6]

Sorting in Z is necessary for two reasons. Proper calculation of transparency requires all visible transparent surfaces to be sorted in Z. The other benefit of a Z-sort is that fragments from the same geometric primitive tend to cluster together in the list and so can be merged. For example, a bicubic patch may be turned into several polygons. These polygons are all from the same continuous parent surface, but they may be chopped into fragments in an unpredictable order (depending on screen orientation, etc.) (figure 4). Merging two or more fragments simplifies the data structure and reclaims the space used by the merged-in fragments. If the result is opaque and completely covers the pixel we cannot with certainty reclaim hidden fragments, as they may be part of an incomplete intersecting surface.

The process of merging fragments is fairly straightforward. Fragments are merged if and only if they have the same object tag and they overlap in Z. This test is performed whenever a new fragment is added to a pixel-struct list. Object tags are integers assigned to continuous non-self-intersecting geometric primitive objects, like spheres and patches. The tag is augmented by a bit indicating whether the surface faces forward or backward, so as to prevent improper merging on silhouettes. If the fragments do not overlap on the screen ($M_1 \cap M_2 = \emptyset$) then the bitmasks are or'ed, the colors blended

$$C = C_1 \times A_1 + C_2 \times A_2$$

and the areas added. If they overlap (which is highly abnormal), they are split into three parts.

$$M_{front-only} = M_{front} \cap \sim M_{back}$$

$$M_{back-only} = M_{back} \cap \sim M_{front}$$

$$M_{overlap} = M_{front} \cap M_{back}$$

The contribution of the front fragment is computed,

$$\alpha_{front} = A_{front-only} + Opacity_{front} \times A_{overlap}$$

the colors blended,

$$C = \alpha_{front} \times C_{front} + (1 - \alpha_{front}) \times C_{back}$$

and the area computed.

$$A = A_{front} + A_{back} \times \frac{A_{back-only}}{A_{back-only} + A_{overlap}}$$

When no more fragments are to be sent to a pixelstruct, the pixelstruct's color is determined and written into the picture. Generally, the pixel will be fully covered by some object and a few pixel-sized fragments will remain. If any fragments are present, a recursive packing process is invoked.

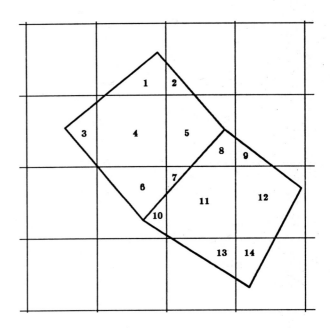

Figure 4. Typical fragment arrival order.

7. Packing fragments

Area-averaging means the color of a pixel is computed by the area-weighted average of the colors of the visible surfaces contained in the pixel. The problem is, then, how to determine the visible fragments and visible parts of fragments.

To understand the method used in the A-buffer, consider the following simplified example. Assume, for the moment, no transparency and no intersecting surfaces. If the fragment at the front of the list covers the pixel, we are done; otherwise, it covers part of the pixel. We divide the pixel into two parts, inside and outside, using the fragment's mask. The contribution of the inside part is the color of the fragment weighted by its area. The contribution of the outside part is some yet to be discovered color weighted by the complement of the fragment's area.

$$C = C_{in} \times A_{in} + C_{out} \times (1 - A_{in})$$

The yet to be discovered color is found by recursively calling the packing routine with the outside mask to represent the rest of the pixel and a pointer to the next item in the fragment list.

We can now describe the method in more detail. We start the packing process with a full 32 bit search mask to represent the entire pixel. Fragments are considered only if they overlap the search mask. When all or part of a fragment is found within the search mask, the search mask part of the pixel is partitioned using the fragment mask.

$$M_{in} = M_{search} \cap M_f$$

$$M_{out} = M_{search} \cap \sim M_f$$

If $M_{out} \neq 0$ we use a recursive call with M_{out} as the search mask to find the color of the rest of the searched area. If the fragment is transparent, a recursive call using M_{in} as a search mask is used to find the color of the surfaces behind the fragment to be filtered by the color of the fragment.

$$C_{in} = Opacity_f \times C_f + (1 - Opacity_f) \times C_{behind}$$

The composite coverage is computed similarly.

$$\alpha_{in} = Opacity_f \times \alpha_f + (1 - Opacity_f) \times \alpha_{behind}$$

Otherwise, the color of the fragment suffices for C_{in}. When we have the colors of the inside and outside regions we blend them weighted by their coverage.

$$C_{returned} = \frac{\alpha_{in} \times C_{in} + \alpha_{out} \times C_{out}}{\alpha_{in} + \alpha_{out}}$$

For all but the first fragment on the list, we use the number of one bits in a mask to estimate area.

Now for intersections.

Pixels where intersecting surfaces are visible usually number in the dozens or hundreds in a typical 512x512 resolution picture. Also, the antialiasing along the line of intersection is not quite as critical as that on a silhouette, for example, because the contrast is often lower. These observations suggest we can get by with simple approximations.

Since no orientation information (vertices or plane equations) is kept in a fragment, we define an intersection to occur when the object tags differ and the fragments overlap in Z. This works satisfactorily in all but a few cases. Since we don't know exactly how much of the frontmost fragment is visible, we estimate it from the minimum and maximum Z values (figure 5).

$$Vis_{front} = \frac{Zmax_{next} - Zmin_{front}}{(Zmax - Zmin)_{front} + (Zmax - Zmin)_{next}}$$

Since part of the front fragment obscures the next fragment and vice versa, we need to estimate the weighting factor to be used to blend the two fragment's colors.

$$\alpha_{in} = Vis_{front} \times Opacity_{front}$$
$$+ (1 - Vis_{front}) \times (1 - \alpha_{next})$$

Figure 5. Visible fraction of front fragment.

```
Pack_under_mask (fragment_ptr, mask, r, g, b, a)

if this is the last fragment on the list
        return fragment's color and coverage
else
            find inside and outside masks
            if outside mask not empty
                find color and coverage of outside area
                    (recursive call with outside mask)
            if fragment is transparent or overlaps in Z with next on list
                    find color and coverage of what's behind
                    (recursive call with inside mask)
            if nothing hidden behind the fragment affects its appearance
                    return a blend of the fragment and the outside area
            else
                    if Z's overlap with next fragment (maybe transparent)
                        estimate visibility ratio
                        estimate coverage of fragment
                        blend fragment with what's behind it
                        return blend of inside and outside
                    else (just transparent)
                        blend fragment with what's behind it
                        return blend of inside and outside
        end
```

Figure 6. Fragment packing procedure.

This is the sum of the unobscured part of the front fragment and the part of the front fragment filtered through the other fragment. Given these factors, we blend the front fragment with the other fragment within the inside mask.

$$C_{in} = \alpha_{in} \times C_{front} + (1 - \alpha_{in}) \times C_{next}$$

Then we blend the inside and outside part.

$$C_{returned} = \frac{\alpha_{in} \times C_{in} + \alpha_{out} \times C_{out}}{\alpha_{in} + \alpha_{out}}$$

A high level pseudocode description of the packer is given in figure 6.

8. Implementation details

The A-buffer is implemented in approximately 800 lines of C, including a substantial amount of debugging code. All arithmetic is done in fixed point (except for Z). There are two heavily used procedures inside the system that ought to be described in more detail.

The first is the bitmask constructor, which is designed to work correctly given arbitrary polygons. It begins with a polygon that has been clipped to a pixel boundary. The polygon bitmask is built up by exclusive or'ing together masks derived from the polygon's edges. Each polygon edge defines a trapezoid, bounded by the edge, the right side of the pixel, and the projection of the ends of the edge toward the right side of the pixel. (figure 7) The edge mask is constructed by or'ing together row masks taken from a table indexed by the quantized locations of the intercepts of the edge. The exclusive or of all these masks leaves one bits in the interior and zero bits elsewhere. All this sounds complicated, but it rarely involves more than eight boolean operations.

Figure 7. Polygon edge mask.

The other process computes the coverage ("area") of a polygon mask. Since the VAX has no bit counting instructions, the method is to strip off four bits at a time and look up the bit count in a table. The whole procedure can be put into a single C expression which generates efficient machine code.

9. Results

The REYES system, incorporating the A-buffer, has been used to make thousands of pictures. Figure 8 shows a magnified silhouette of the top of a teapot. Note the softness of the edge, even though the box filtering limits the edge intensity ramp to one pixel width. The Utah teapot, which appears in figures 8 and 9, is constructed so that its handle and spout penetrate its body. This is a common geometric modelling technique which avoids the explicit (and nearly intractable) calculation of the intersection curve. Figure 9 is a closeup of the upper part of the handle. The color of pixels through which the intersection curve passes is clearly a blend of the handle and body colors. Figure 10 is the "Genesis device". It is a collection of spheres, patches and polygons inside a partially transparent cylinder with quadrically modelled engines on the outside. Stars can be seen through the cylinder. All of figure 11, with the exception of the particle system grass plants, was rendered by REYES. The background of the picture was computed at 1024 lines and the foreground at 2048 lines resolution.

We have described a successful, relatively uncomplicated, anti-aliasing hidden surface mechanism. Like all visibility resolving methods, the A-buffer has its strengths, weaknesses, and limitations. It was designed to process the vast majority of pixels with minimum effort and maximum precision, spending compute time only on exceptional cases. On the other hand, the approximations used in the fragment intersection code can go astray if several surfaces intersect in the same pixel, and, of course, one cannot expect polygons smaller than the bitmask spacing to be sampled faithfully. Recognizing these limitations, we have found the A-buffer to be a practical, reliable means of producing synthetic images of high complexity.

References

1. CARPENTER, L., "A New Hidden Surface Algorithm," *Proceedings of NW76*, ACM, Seattle, WA, 1976.

2. CATMULL, E., *A Subdivision Algorithm for Computer Display of Curved Surfaces*, University of Utah, Salt Lake City, December 1974.

3. CATMULL, E., "A Hidden-Surface Algorithm with Anti-Aliasing," *Computer Graphics*, vol. 12, no. 3, pp. 6-11, ACM, 1978.

4. FIUME, E., A. FOURNIER, AND L. RUDOLPH, "A Parallel Scan Conversion Algorithm with Anti-Aliasing for a General-Purpose Ultracomputer," *Computer Graphics*, vol. 17, no. 3, pp. 141-150, ACM, July 1983.

5. LANE, J. M., L. C. CARPENTER, T. WHITTED, AND J. BLINN, "Scan-line methods for displaying parametrically defined surfaces," *Communications of the ACM*, vol. 25, no. 1, pp. 23-34, ACM, Jan. 1980.

6. PORTER, T. AND T. DUFF, "Compositing Digital Images," *Computer Graphics*, vol. 18, no. 3, ACM, 1984.

7. SUTHERLAND, I. E., R. F. SPROULL, AND R. A. SCHUMACKER, "A characterization of ten hidden-surface algorithms," *Computing Surveys*, vol. 6, no. 1, pp. 1-55, ACM, March 1974.

8. WEILER, K. AND P. ATHERTON, "Hidden Surface Removal Using Polygon Area Sorting," *Computer Graphics*, vol. 11, no. 3, pp. 214-222, ACM, 1977.

Figure 8. Detail of teapot silhouette. (4×)

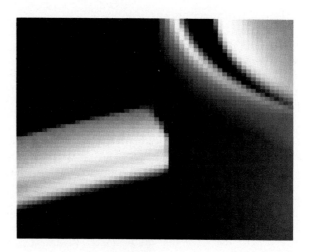

Figure 9. Detail of teapot handle intersection. (8×)

Figure 10. Genesis device. (4×)

Figure 11. Road to Point Reyes.

An Analytic Visible Surface Algorithm for Independent Pixel Processing

Edwin Catmull

Computer Division
Lucasfilm Ltd

Abstract

An algorithm is presented that solves the visible surface problem at each pixel independently. This allows motion blur and depth of field blurring to be integrated into the algorithm. It also allows parallel processing. The algorithm works on large numbers of polygons. An analytic Gaussian filter is used. The filter can be elongated or scaled differently for each polygon to adjust for its speed or distance from the focal plane. This is achieved by shrinking or scaling the polygon prior to solving the hidden surface problem so that blurring is correctly presented when objects obscure each other.

CR CATEGORIES AND SUBJECT DESCRIPTORS:
*I.3.7 [**Computer Graphics**]:* Three-Dimensional Graphics and Realism;

ADDITIONAL KEY WORDS AND PHRASES: anti-aliasing, motion blur, visible surface

1. Introduction

In 1982 the Image Synthesis Working Group was formed in the Lucasfilm Computer Division to do research into image synthesis algorithms that would be appropriate for vector computers, parallel computers or special purpose hardware. It was important that any solution include anti-aliasing, motion blur, shadows, and the capability of dealing with a very large number of polygons (on the order of 80 million). The group consisted of Loren Carpenter, Rob Cook, and the author. The research evolved into a friendly competition between two different approaches with successes in one approach being used to

Permission to copy without fee all or part of this material is granted provided that the copies are not made or distributed for direct commercial advantage, the ACM copyright notice and the title of the publication and its date appear, and notice is given that copying is by permission of the Association for Computing Machinery. To copy otherwise, or to republish, requires a fee and/or specific permission.

© 1984   ACM   0-89791-138-5/84/007/0109 $00.75

spur the other on. To our surprise both approaches yielded solutions to the motion blur problem. One approach is presented here. The other is published in these same proceedings[1].

Work continues on both because the tradeoffs between cost, capability, and the ability to take advantage of hardware architectures are still being worked out. It would seem for now that extremely complex environments require a combination of techniques.

Part of the synthesis work was to put together a testbed for tying all of the pieces together. This testbed is called Reyes and was originally conceived by Loren Carpenter. In it the generation of primitives, shading, and visible surface calculation are modules with common interfaces to allow for substituting different modules. The decision was made to do the shading before visible surface calculation instead of after as is usually done. This means that some shading will be calculated for surfaces that end up being obscured. An advantage of this approach is that we can take advantage of coherence in the textures. This appears to be more important than coherence for visible surface calculation. A second advantage is that the visible surface algorithm has a much looser coupling with the shader and can be thought of as a later stage in a pipeline. For this paper we assume that the shade of all polygons has been calculated and we are only concerned with visibility and filtering.

2. General Overview

We wish to render very complex scenes. One way of describing objects in such an environment is to represent objects with a large number of very small polygons. For example a curved surface can be represented with a mesh of small polygons.

As is usual with those who present new visible surface algorithms, we wish to take advantage of the coherence available in our data and present new techniques for sorting the polygons[5]. This algorithm is tuned to take advantage of the likely distribution of polygons in a scene. In general the following is true:

- Most edges of polygons are shared with other polygons.

- In most pixels, all polygons that are visible come from the same object.

- When there is a contour edge, the polygons in the pixel behind the contour usually come from one object. (A contour edge is one that is on the silhouette. This is in contrast with a shared edge where both polygons are visible.)

- Typically the polygons in a pixel can be thought of as groups of adjoining polygons with spatial separation in z between the groups. (The number of groups then would be the depth complexity.)

- The number of pixels with either visible intersections or more than two visible objects is comparatively small.

2.1. Data Preparation

The algorithm benefits if polygons are labeled with an object tag. This helps us group meshes of polygons with shared edges. This algorithm still works if object tags are not used correctly but at the cost of greater execution time. It would be more efficient to consider complex objects as being made of simpler objects, each with different tags. The low order bit of the object tag is used to indicate whether or not a polygon is front or back facing.

In addition it is desirable that edges be labeled as to whether or not they are contour edges. The ease with which this may be accomplished is dependent on the data structure used for the objects. There is a modification to the algorithm that makes this requirement unnecessary at little added time penalty. Discussion of that modification would take too much space and is not germane to the general algorithm.

2.2. Distributing Polygons to the Pixels

Polygons are first sorted on y and x using conventional bucket sorting techniques. At each pixel a list of polygons is created. Each list contains every polygon that overlaps the filter of the corresponding pixel. Thus when a polygon overlaps many pixels each one is given a copy of that polygon. The area of a pixel is defined to be that of its filter even if that filter may overlap other pixels.

From this point on, every pixel is considered to be independent from its neighbors. Pixel to pixel coherence is not used for two reasons: first, it allows us to consider parallel processing on pixels, and second, the technique used to introduce motion blur disrupts the coherence. The remainder of this paper addresses the visible surface question at the pixel.

2.3. Finding Visible Surfaces at the Pixel

The algorithm operates on the unsorted list of polygons to produce another list, all of which are visible. The steps are:

1. The closest set of overlapping polygons are extracted from the list with a technique we call the *head sort*. This new list of close polygons is called the *head list*. The next step is to determine if the polygons of the head list completely cover the pixel. If there are no contour edges in the head and if the center of the pixel is covered at least once then the pixel is entirely covered. If the pixel is not completely covered then skip to step 3.

2. The head list is sent to the filter routine. It is assumed that the head list covers all parts of the filter once and only once. When the filter routine calculates the contribution of each piece it can determine if that assumption was true. If it is true (and it usually is) then the calculations for this pixel are over. Otherwise go to step 3.

3. If the simple case didn't happen then a routine called the *resolver* must be called. This does the clipping necessary at contour edges and intersections. After obscured pieces are culled, the results are sent to the filter.

The head sort, filter, and resolver will each be explained in turn.

3. The Head Sort

A complete z sort of all n polygons at a pixel is an $O(n^2)$ problem. We want to consider very large numbers of polygons in a picture and estimate that the number overlapping any given pixel could average around 80. However a complete sort is not necessary since only the visible polygons need to be extracted. The sort can be simplified by taking advantage of the object tags and the gaps in z between groups of polygons. To do this we use the concept of the *head sort*. The *head* of a list is all of those polygons that are nearest the eye and overlap each other in z but do not overlap any of the rest of the polygons in the list (the *tail*) in z. Thus there is a z gap between the polygons in the head and the rest of the list. (See figure 1.) There is no z gap in the head.

Clearly if the polygons of the head completely cover the pixel then there is no need to sort the remaining polygons any further. The head sort is performed as follows:

- Find the polygon with the nearest z.

- Extract all polygons with the same object tag and put in the head list.

- Make sure that all polygons extracted so far overlap in z. If not, put those behind the gap back in the tail.

- Make sure that the furthest z so far in the head does not overlap the nearest z in the tail list. If so, repeat the process on the tail.

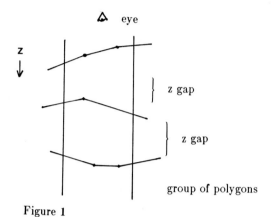

Figure 1

Thus if there are 80 polygons in the original list and 6 in the head then the number of comparisons would typically be 80+79+5+4+3+2+1+76, considerably better than 80 squared.

4. Filtering

Every pixel has a filter associated with it. The filter is circularly symmetric and the overlap with neighboring pixels is dependent on the size of the filter. The cross section of the filter is arbitrary but was chosen to have roughly a Gaussian shape. See figure 2.

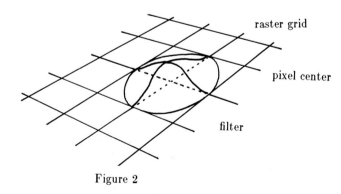

Figure 2

Rob Cook has published an algorithm for the analytic filtering of polygons[2]. With this approach we can convolve a polygon with a circularly symmetric filter that has an arbitrary cross section. The basic idea is that a polygon can be decomposed into a series of triangles each of which has one vertex at the center of the filter and an opposite edge that is an edge of the polygon. See figure 3.

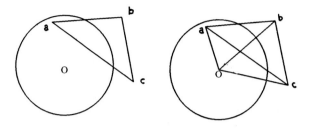

Figure 3

If we are consistent about labeling, then oab and obc will make positive contributions and oca will make a negative contribution leaving us with the contribution of the original polygon.

The next step is that each triangle may be decomposed into two right triangles. Each new triangle may be characterized by the distance d of point m from the origin (with d set to the radius of the filter if $d > radius$) and the angle ϕ. See figure 4.

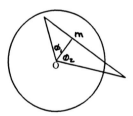

Figure 4

We can use these two values d and ϕ as indices into a table where the entries of the table have been determined previously by the shape of the filter. Thus by accumulating these values as we march around the edges of the polygon we end up with the polygon convolved with the filter.

This algorithm can with some difficulty be extended to include smooth shaded polygons. The extended filter is used in the hidden surface algorithm presented here. The presentation of that extension is beyond the scope of this paper.

While filtering, any pieces of polygons that lie outside of the circular boundary of the filter do not matter since the filter is zero in that region. Hence, the algorithm need not guarantee that all pieces lie inside the circle nor that their visibility be solved correctly if they are outside.

The process of filtering not only determines the contribution of each polygon but also its area under the filter. If the sum of the areas is not exactly one then the original assumption about covering the pixel was false and the resolver must be called to calculate visibility the hard way. This failure would occur if two surfaces intersected.

Note that even if the filter test fails, the polygons that were filtered may still be visible. So if they are not clipped in the resolver then it is not necessary to recalculate the filtered value for each polygon still visible.

5. The Resolver

When a polygon contains contour edges or intersections then the list of polygons must be ordered using a different method. The technique of polygon clipping is used. A polygon may be clipped against the edges and/or plane of a second polygon to remove any obscured pieces. The methods for doing this have been published elsewhere[6, 7].

First, a head sort on the tail is repeatedly done until the pixel is covered or the list is exhausted. The polygons extracted each time are added to the existing head. In the typical case only one head sort is required to fill in the pixel behind a contour.

Next, all of the potentially visible polygons are put into a list called the *unsafe list* and sorted in z increasing order. A new list will be formed containing only polygons that are visible - the *safe list*. The first element from the unsafe list (which is the closest) is compared with each polygon in the safe list. If they overlap in x and y then a polygon clip is necessary. Any pieces found to be obscured in this process can be discarded. It is not necessary to clip against shared edges that are not contour edges since they do not change the visibility of anything.

After the new polygon is compared with the polygons in the safe list then if anything is left it can be added to the safe list. Note that the new polygon can obscure polygons already in the safe list. The only guarantee is that polygons in the safe list do not obscure each other. When the unsafe list is empty, the safe list may be sent to the filter.

6. Motion Blur

The presentation of animation through a movie projector gives rise to a phenomenon knows as 'strobing.' A vertical edge moving horizontally appears to double up. This is because a projector actually projects each frame twice on the screen before advancing to the next frame. This is done by blocking the beam of light once without advancing the film. The reason for this is to get the flicker frequency of the image above what the eye objects to. Unfortunately when the eye tracks an edge across the screen the edge appears to double up because the edge appears in two different places on the retina. The problem is greatly alleviated in live action photography because the objects of interest move while the shutter is open thus causing blurring in the direction of motion.

Since the edge that doubles up is blurred, the doubling is not nearly as noticeable. In addition, still pictures of objects in motion look better when the objects are blurred because they convey better the desired scene.

Most computer graphics images have objects that are perfectly sharp. There have been some recent attempts to solve the blurring problem[3, 4]. Each has problems[1]. Either the blurring is applied after the hidden surface calculations have been formed or the different vertices of a polygon cannot move at different rates. This presents difficulties with complex motions in 3-space. There is also a problem with the solution presented here (discussed later) but it is an advance in that blurring is simply integrated into the hidden surface algorithm.

6.1. Adding Blur

One way to think about blur is to consider that the filter gets stretched out in the direction of motion. Moving the polygons under the filter as in figure 5:

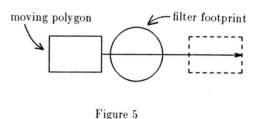

Figure 5

has the same quantitative effect as shown in figure 6:

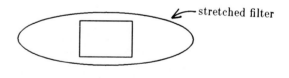

Figure 6

where the results of filtering are normalized to the amount of stretch.

However, there is a qualitative difference since we have converted a time contribution into a spatial one. Fortunately this difference does not prevent us from still doing visible surface calculations. In particular, objects can be blurred as they pass in front or in back of each other and appear correct. This is a weakness of previous blur algorithms. There is still a problem if a blurred polygon moves in such a way that it intersects a nonmoving polygon. For most uses this is not a serious restriction.

The stretching of the filter is equivalent to shrinking the polygon relative to the pixel. Thus our case above reduces to that of figure 7:

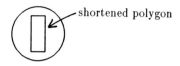

Figure 7

where the moving square is shortened in the direction of motion. This transformation is relative to the pixel. Each vertex may have its own velocity or more generally, its own path. Thus polygons moving in perspective do not develop cracks when the vertices move at different rates.

For the simple case where each vertex has a simple velocity the following calculations are used. Each vertex is scaled by the amount s.

$$s = \frac{d}{l+d}$$

where l is the length of the xy projection of the motion vector and d is the diameter of the filter. The scaling is in the direction of motion and is relative to the pixel center (p_x, p_y). The coordinates of the vertex are (c_x, c_y) and its velocity is (v_x, v_y). The polygon is scaled separately for each pixel that it overlaps as it moves.

First the point is put into the coordinate system of the pixel offset by half of the velocity vector to center it.

$$x = c_x - p_x + \frac{v_x}{2}$$

$$y = c_y - p_y + \frac{v_y}{2} .$$

It can be shown that the transformed vertex (x',y') is

$$[x' \ y'] = \frac{1}{l^2}[x \ y]\begin{bmatrix} sv_x^2+v_y^2 & sv_xv_y-v_xv_y \\ sv_xv_y-v_xv_y & v_x^2+v_y^2 \end{bmatrix}$$

It is this transformation relative to the center of the pixel that makes a polygon appear different to neighboring pixels. Similarly an object out of focus can be thought of as having a larger filter, or equivalently as being scaled down in size relative to the center of the pixel. This scaling is dependent on the distance to the eye. So there may be scaled and unscaled objects visible in the same pixel.

The key point is that if polygons are transformed relative to the pixel center as a result of motion and depth of field then the visible surface algorithm described above works without any modification. We have thus correctly determined visibility of blurred objects whether they are in front of or in back of other objects.

7. Other Things

We have ignored so far some important issues. Transparency has not been brought up although it fits well into this framework. Shading and textures are part of the preprocess of Reyes and are not applicable here. A key question is whether or not shadows are facilitated. The answer would seem to be no for the large number of polygons that we are discussing.

8. Pictures

Picture one has 4 by 4 pixels with many polygons per pixel. In this picture none of the hidden polygons are removed. The pixel that has three concentric sphere sections has about 120 polygons. The horizontal and vertical lines represent the pixel boundaries.

See picture 2 for the results after the algorithm is used. Lines that are generated by clipping are not displayed. Hence the intersection lines are not seen although they are calculated correctly.

Picture 3 has a few simple test polygons without motion blur. The bottom polygon demonstrates that the filtering method does handle smooth shading. In picture 4 some of the test polygons are put in motion. Note that there is and example of the motion blur being obscured and obscuring. On the upper right the white polygon is closer than the green one. In each case the appearance is what you would expect.

In picture 5 some more complex objects are displayed. These objects are part of an experiment to create the appearance of rocks. The surfaces are represented by fine meshes of polygons.

Acknowledgement

Loren Carpenter and Rob Cook helped make an exciting environment for developing new ideas. I had many deep conversations with Rob about filtering and blurring and he helped with the preparation of this paper.

References

1. COOK, ROB, THOMAS PORTER, AND LOREN CAR-PENTER, "Distributed Ray Tracing," *Computer Graphics*, vol. 18, no. 3, July 1984.

2. FEIBUSH, ELIOT, MARC LEVOY, AND ROB COOK, "Synthetic Texturing Using Digital Filtering," *Computer Graphics*, vol. 14, no. 3, pp. 294-301, July 1980.

3. KOREIN, JONATHAN AND NORMAN BADLER, "Temporal Anti-Aliasing in Computer Generated Animation," *Computer Graphics*, vol. 17, no. 3, pp. 377-388, July 1983.

4. POTMESIL, MICHAEL AND INDRANIL CHAKRAVARTY, "Modeling Motion Blur in Computer-Generated Images," *Computer Graphics*, vol. 17, no. 3, pp. 389-399, July 1983.

5. SUTHERLAND, IVAN, ROBERT SPROULL, AND ROBERT SCHUMACKER, "A Characterization of Ten Hidden-surface Algorithms," *ACM Computing Surveys*, March 1974.

6. SUTHERLAND, IVAN AND G. W. HODGMAN, "Reentrant Polygon Clipping," *CACM*, January 1974.

7. WEILER, KEVIN AND PETER ATHERTON, "Hidden-surface Removal Using Polygon Area Sorting," *Computer Graphics Proceedings*, 1977.

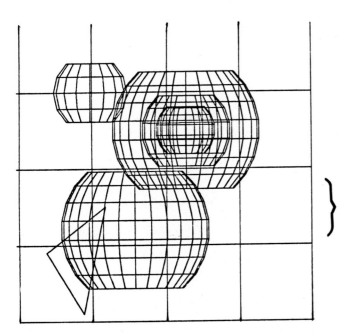

Picture 1

Scanline

Picture 2

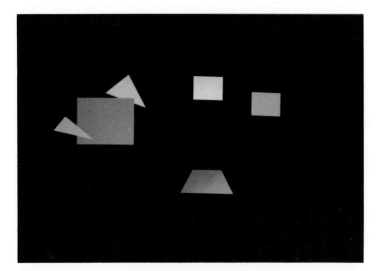

Picture 3

Picture 4

Picture 5

PANEL

INTERNATIONAL MARKET OPPORTUNITIES

CHAIR: Philip G. Husby - Peat Marwick Mitchell & Company
PANEL: Michael Prichard - Dorsey & Whitney
       Scott B. Hill - Arthur Young & Company
       Ronald E. Kramer - U.S. Department of Commerce
       Edward J. Hayward - Oppenheimer, Wolff, Forster, Shepard
        & Donnelly

The Panel will discuss the subject of entering foreign markets with the objective of increasing company revenues. The first panelist will discuss the general benefits of international trade and the potential for the computer graphics industry. Foreign markets which hold the greatest promise for penetration will be identified and an overview of the regulations governing the exports of the industry will be presented. The discussion will conclude with the identification of select services offered to U.S. firms by the U.S. Department of Commerce for the purpose of assisting companies in reaching foreign markets.

The Panel will then discuss alternative methods which can be used by companies to enter foreign markets. The use of foreign distributors will be analyzed by the second panelist. Distributor agreements will be reviewed with emphasis on the applicable law; territory and exclusivity; obligations of both the distributor and manufacturer; use of trademarks; terms and conditions of sale; and termination of the distributor agreement.

Attention will then turn to the use of licensing arrangements. The panelist will deal with the special considerations of hardware and software licensing in the international context. This presentation will cover questions such as software protection, royalty payments and governmental approvals -- with reference to both U.S. export controls and to import or exchange control authorizations required in some foreign countries.

The last panelist will address the business and tax considerations of direct investment abroad. Beginning with the structural decision of branch vs. subsidiary, the Panel will review issues including debt vs. equity financing of overseas operation; the concept of U.S. tax deferral on the earnings of a foreign subsidiary, using joint ventures and specific U.S. and foreign tax incentives.

The Panel will respond to questions from the audience and discuss the pros and cons of the various method of selling abroad.

BEAM TRACING POLYGONAL OBJECTS

Paul S. Heckbert
Pat Hanrahan

Computer Graphics Laboratory
New York Institute of Technology
Old Westbury, NY 11568

Abstract

Ray tracing has produced some of the most realistic computer generated pictures to date. They contain surface texturing, local shading, shadows, reflections and refractions. The major disadvantage of ray tracing results from its point-sampling approach. Because calculation proceeds *ab initio* at each pixel it is very CPU intensive and may contain noticeable aliasing artifacts. It is difficult to take advantage of spatial coherence because the shapes of reflections and refractions from curved surfaces are so complex.

In this paper we describe an algorithm that utilizes the spatial coherence of polygonal environments by combining features of both image and object space hidden surface algorithms. Instead of tracing infinitesimally thin rays of light, we sweep areas through a scene to form "beams." This technique works particularly well for polygonal models since for this case the reflections are linear transformations, and refractions are often approximately so.

The recursive beam tracer begins by sweeping the projection plane through the scene. Beam-surface intersections are computed using two-dimensional polygonal set operations and an occlusion algorithm similar to the Weiler-Atherton hidden surface algorithm. For each beam-polygon intersection the beam is fragmented and new beams created for the reflected and transmitted swaths of light. These sub-beams are redirected with a 4x4 matrix transformation and recursively traced. This beam tree is an object space representation of the entire picture.

Permission to copy without fee all or part of this material is granted provided that the copies are not made or distributed for direct commercial advantage, the ACM copyright notice and the title of the publication and its date appear, and notice is given that copying is by permission of the Association for Computing Machinery. To copy otherwise, or to republish, requires a fee and/or specific permission.

© 1984   ACM   0-89791-138-5/84/007/0119 $00.75

Since the priority of polygons is pre-determined, the final picture with reflections, refractions, shadows, and hidden surface removal is easily drawn. The coherence information enables very fast scan conversion and high resolution output. Image space edge and texture antialiasing methods can be applied.

CR Categories: I.3.3 [**Computer Graphics**]: Picture/Image Generation - *display algorithms;* I.3.7 [**Computer Graphics**]: Three-Dimensional Graphics and Realism - *visible line/surface algorithms.*

General Terms: algorithms.

Additional Key Words and Phrases: ray tracing, refraction, polygon, object space, coherence.

1. Introduction

Two of the most popular methods used to create frame buffer images of three-dimensional environments are ray tracing and scan line algorithms. Ray tracing generates a picture by casting a ray of light from the eye point through each pixel of the image and into the scene. Visible surfaces are determined by testing for line-surface intersections between the ray and each object in the scene. By recursively tracing reflected and refracted rays, considerable realism can be added to the final image. In contrast, a scan line rendering program generally takes advantage of coherence to draw surfaces incrementally. Comparing the two approaches we find:

Advantages of ray trace:
    Uses a global lighting model that calculates
        reflections, refractions, shadows.
    Can handle a variety of geometric primitives.
Disadvantages of ray trace:
    Often slow since the intersection calculations
        are floating point intensive.
    Point sampling the environment causes aliasing.

Advantages of scan line algorithms:
    Incremental calculation of geometry
        is very efficient.
Disadvantages of scan line:
    Local lighting model not as realistic.

Scan conversion of polygons is particularly popular, especially in computer animation, where many images must be produced and image generation time must be kept to a minimum [Crow, 1978]. Ray tracing has generated some very realistic still images, but generally has been impractical for animation. The only extensive ray traced animation made to date was done with the aid of special-purpose hardware [Kawaguchi, 1983; Nishimura et. al., 1983].

The differences between many hidden surface algorithms depends on the techniques used to exploit coherence in the scene. Most attempts at exploiting coherence in ray tracing have concentrated on techniques to limit the number of ray-surface intersections that are to be tested. This can be done by hierarchically decomposing the scene into a tree of enclosing volumes [Clark 1976; Rubin and Whitted, 1980; Dadoun, Kirkpatrick and Walsh, 1982]. The ray-surface intersection calculation proceeds by testing the outermost enclosing volume first and searches the subvolumes only if the ray pierces that volume. Another approach is to form a cellular decomposition of the scene, keeping track of which surfaces are within or border a given cell. If the ray is assumed to be in a particular cell then only the surfaces inside that cell need be tested for intersections [see for example Jones, 1971]. If no intersections are found the ray passes through that cell, enters a neighboring cell and the search continues. Another technique, applicable if rays are only traced to one level, is to enclose each surface with a bounding box in image space [Roth, 1982]. As the image is scanned, surfaces become active or inactive depending on whether the current raster location is within the surface's bounding box.

A different type of coherence results from the observation that in many scenes, groups of rays follow virtually the same path from the eye to the light source and thus can be bundled into coherent beams of light (see Figure 1) [Hanrahan and Heckbert, 1984]. This observation can be exploited by attempting to trace a beam of

rays in parallel rather than an individual ray. Exploiting this coherence is advantageous since it reduces the number of intersection. Also, once such coherence is identified it allows incremental techniques to be used for drawing a homogeneous region (a region over which the ray tree is constant). This would increase the speed of the rendering algorithm, especially at high resolutions. Finally, it is just this lack of coherence which causes many of the aliasing artifacts in ray traced images. It is possible to use the coherence to antialias textures and shading calculations within a homogeneous region and potentially, by identifying the boundaries between regions, to antialias their edges.

We propose an algorithm for tracing beams through scenes described by planar polygonal models. Beam tracing polygons is much simpler because of the large body of knowledge regarding both object space hidden surface calculations and image space display algorithms. Also, unlike the general case of a beam reflecting from a curved surface, beams formed at planar boundaries can be approximated by pyramidal cones. The algorithm we describe is similar in principle to a technique developed by Dadoun, Kirkpatrick and Walsh [1982] to trace sound beams from audio sources to a receiver. They noted that this problem is equivalent to the hidden surface problem and proposed computationally efficient algorithms for performing rapid hidden surface removal in static scenes. Our algorithm differs in that it is patterned closely after the classic ray trace and creates output that can directly drive image space rendering programs.

2. Beam Tracing

The beam tracer is a recursive polygon hidden surface algorithm. The hidden surface algorithm is designed to find all visible polygons within an arbitrary two dimensional region. The procedure begins with the viewing pyramid as the initial beam. The beam tracer builds an intermediate data structure, the *beam tree*, which is very similar to the ray tree [Whitted, 1980]. Like the ray tree whose links represent rays of light and whose nodes represent the surfaces those rays intersect, the beam tree has links which represent cones of light and nodes which represent the surfaces intersected by those cones. But unlike a link in a ray tree which always terminates on a single surface, the beam link may intersect many surfaces. Each node under the beam represents a visible surface element as seen along the beam axis. This is illustrated abstractly in figure 2 and a simple example is shown in figure 3. The beam tree is computed in object space and then passed to a polygon renderer for scan conversion to form the final shaded image.

2.1. Object Space Beam Tracing

The beam tree could be formed using any of several object space hidden surface algorithms. The pictures generated for this paper used an algorithm modeled along the lines of the classic ray tracing program. We now outline the procedure:

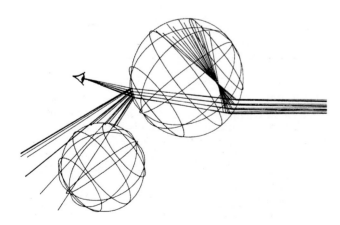

Figure 1. A bundle of rays passing through two spheres.

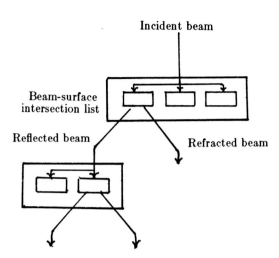

Figure 2. A schematic representation of the beam tree. Notice that the incident beam is fragmented into several pieces each of which may give rise to a reflected and refracted beam.

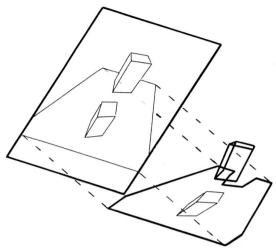

Figure 3. A beam tree corresponding to a cube on a mirrored surface. The bold lines indicate the beam fragments at that level in the tree.

```
function Beam-Trace( Beam : Polygon; Ctm : Matrix ) : PolygonList;
begin
   {Transform scene into the beam coordinate system
    using the current transformation matrix (Ctm)}
   {Priority sort all polygons in the scene (ScenePolygonList)}
   For each Polygon in the ScenePolygonList do begin
      P = Intersection( Beam, Polygon );
      if P ≠ nil then begin
        if RecurseFurthur( Depth, P, ... ) then begin
           if reflective(Polygon) then begin
              NewCtm = Ctm * ReflectionMatrix( Polygon );
              P.ReflectiveTree = Beam-Trace( P, NewCtm );
           end
           if refractive(Polygon) then begin
              NewCtm = Ctm * RefractionMatrix( Polygon );
              P.RefractiveTree = Beam-Trace( P, NewCtm );
           end
        end
        {Add P to the Beam polygon intersection list (FragmentList)}
        Beam = Difference( Beam, Polygon );
      end
   Beam-Trace = FragmentList;
end
```

Most ray tracers perform all their calculations in the world coordinate system. The beam tracer performs all calculations in a transformed coordinate system, initially the viewing coordinate system, called the beam coordinate system. In the beam coordinate system, beams are defined as the volume swept out as a two-dimensional polygon in the x-y plane is translated along the z-axis. Since the transformation into world space may contain perspective, the most general beam is a polygonal cone in world space. In a ray tracer, the ray is redirected after a reflection or refraction whereas in the beam tracer the scene is transformed into the beam coordinate system.

This technique is analogous to forming the virtual image of an optical system.

The closest beam-surface intersection is determined by searching a depth-sorted list of polygons using two dimensional set operators. The depth ordered list is formed by priority sorting the polygons [Newell, Newell, and Sancha, 1972]. In our implementation, intersecting polygons and cyclic dependencies are not allowed although this is not a theoretical limitation of the approach. Such sorting is not required during a ray trace but is characteristic of object space hidden surface algorithms [Sutherland, Sproull, and Schumacker, 1974] and implies that the worst case running time could be $O(n^2)$, which is worse than a ray trace which is $O(n)$. Since we must depth-sort the polygons after every beam intersection, algorithms that preprocess the scene so that priority ordering can be quickly determined from any viewpoint could be used here [Sutherland, Sproull, and Schumacker, 1972; Fuchs, Kedem, and Naylor, 1980].

To find the first visible polygon, we intersect the beam with the first polygon in the list. If the result is *nil* then the polygon is outside the beam, otherwise it is visible and is added to the list of visible surface elements within this beam. To ensure that no other polygon is classified as visible within the area of this visible polygon, we subtract it from the beam before continuing through the depth ordered list. The set operators used in this algorithm must be able to handle concave polygons containing holes. Different methods for performing polygonal spatial set operations (union, intersection, and difference) are discussed in [Eastman and Yessios, 1972; Weiler and Atherton, 1977].

To simulate reflection and refraction we call the beam tracer recursively by generating new beams whose cross-sections are the intersection polygon. The transformations for reflection and refraction are discussed further in the next section and the appendix.

Recursion of the beam tracer can be terminated by several criteria:

(1) Maximum tree depth: 5 levels is common.

(2) Threshold of insignificance: determine if the intensity contributed by this branch of the tree will make a perceptible difference (called "adaptive tree depth control" in [Hall and Greenberg, 1983]).

(3) Polygon size: terminate when polygon area is below some threshold, such as one pixel.

2.2. Reflection and Refraction Transformations

Reflection in a plane, which maps each point to its mirror image, is a linear transformation, and can be represented by a 4x4 homogeneous matrix. Refraction by a plane, however, is not a linear transformation in general. Figures 4 and 5, which were made with a standard ray tracer, show the distortion of an underwater checkerboard viewed from above, and an above-water checkerboard viewed from underwater, respectively. The second shows the effect of the *critical angle* which occurs when a ray is refracted from the denser material into the sparser one. Rays incident at the critical angle are refracted parallel to the surface (toward the horizon in our "fisheye" view). Outside the circle, when the incident angle is greater than the critical angle, there is no refraction, and one has *total internal reflection*. (Humans do not see this phenomenon when swimming because our eyes are not adapted to focus underwater [Walker, 1984]).

Since refraction bends lines, it cannot always be expressed as a linear transformation. There are two situations under which it is linear, however. For orthographic projections the incident angle is constant, and refraction is equivalent to a skew or shear. The other situation is for rays at near-perpendicular incidence, known as *paraxial rays* in geometrical optics. The latter corresponds to the centers of figures 4 and 5, where lines are approximately linear. Derivations of the matrix formulas for these transformations are given in the appendix.

Since beam tracing, as outlined here, is limited to linear transformations, we must choose one of these approximations in order to simulate refraction. The consequences are that beam traced perspective pictures exhibiting refraction will not be optically correct. There will be no critical angle, and lines will never become bent. Beam traced approximations to figures 4 and 5 would look like normal checkerboards. The error of the approximation is highest for refraction from dense materials to sparse ones, but fortunately for beam tracing, humans are normally on the sparser side (e.g. in air, looking into water). This explains why refraction's curvature of lines is not widely known.

2.3. Image Space Rendering

Associated with each screen-space polygon is the tree of face fragments which are projected onto that polygon by the reflection and refraction transformations. Final intensities can be computed by scan converting all of the faces covering a given area in parallel, and applying the recursive intensity formula

$$I = c_d I_d + c_s I_s + c_r I_r + c_t I_t$$

to the tree of faces. This blends the diffuse, specular, reflected, and transmitted intensities according to the coefficients c_d, c_s, c_r, and c_t to compute a color for each pixel.

Faceted or Gouraud shading of beam traced scenes can be done using a modified painter's algorithm. This was the technique used to produce the beam traced pictures in this paper (figures 6-9). Polygons are drawn into a frame buffer one-by-one as the beam tree is traversed. For each face or vertex, the diffuse and specular intensities I_d and I_s are computed using the Phong lighting model [Newman and Sproull, 1979]. Since the polygons in the fragment lists of the beam tree are defined in the beam coordinate system, they must be transformed back

Figure 4. View of an underwater checkerboard from air.

Figure 5. View of an above-water checkerboard from underwater.

Figure 6. A diffusely shaded cube resting on a mirror.

Figure 8. A reflective cube in the interior of a texture mapped, reflective cube.

Figure 7. A translucent dodecahedra within a cube of mirrors.

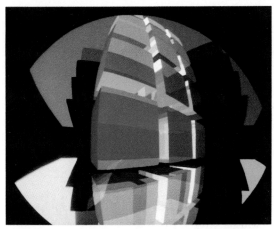

Figure 9. An example of post-processing a beam tree to simulate an Omnimax projection system.

to "world space" for all shading calculations; shading should not be done in a virtual or perspective space. If the coefficients c_d, c_e, c_r, c_t, and the material transparency are constant over each polygon, rendering can be done by simply adding the intensities into a frame buffer as each polygon is drawn. Since addition is commutative, the beam tree can be traversed in any order. This method requires a fairly robust polygon tiler, since the polygons are potentially concave with holes, and a single-pixel gap or overlap between polygons will result in an edge which is too dark or too light [Heckbert, 1983]. If the polygon tiler is limited to convex polygons, concavities and holes can be eliminated by polygon subdivision. Note that the pixel to pixel coherence allows antialiased texture mapping (figure 9).

3. Discussion

A useful measure of any ray traced image is average ray tree size. This statistic is similar to the notion of depth complexity used in analyzing polygon display algorithms. With the beam tree this is easily calculated since

average ray tree size =

$$\frac{total\ area\ (in\ screen\ space)\ of\ the\ beam\ tree\ polygons}{screen\ area}$$

The total time spent ray tracing an image is equal to the average ray tree size, multiplied by the time needed to determine the nearest ray-polygon intersection, times the resolution of the image. In contrast, the beam tracer is resolution independent and therefore the relative efficiency of beam tracing versus ray tracing increases linearly with resolution.

Beam tracing, however, is more complicated then ray tracing and may not always be worth the extra expense. The expected improvement depends more on the intrinsic coherence of the imaged scene rather than resolution. We can define coherence as

$$coherence = \frac{average\ ray\ tree\ size}{total\ beam\ tree\ size}$$

This measure indicates to what degree the beam is fragmented–the more it is fragmented the lower the scene's coherence. If the coherence is very high then many rays are being traced in parallel and therefore a beam tracer will be faster than a ray tracer. In summary, beam tracing is most efficient when there are large homogeneous regions in the picture.

Figures 6 and 7 took 30 seconds and 5 minutes, respectively, to generate. We estimate a standard ray tracer would take 20-100 times longer.

One nice feature of the beam tracer is that it generates a reasonably compact object space representation of the image. Because it produces object space coordinates, precise line drawings like figure 3 can be made. These are difficult to make with a ray tracer [Roth, 1982]. The intermediate representation can also be further manipulated. For example, the same tree can be rendered at different resolutions or a series of images can be produced which differ in their coloring and lighting parameters. Since the output of the beam tracer is in object space, fisheye projections such as Omnimax can be made by beam tracing in perspective with a very wide camera angle and distorting the result (figure 9). Methods for mapping and subdividing lines for the Omnimax projection are given in [Max, 1983].

There are, however, some rather severe limitations to the technique as we've developed it here. We exploit coherence by assuming that reflections and refractions form virtual images within a polygonal window and that these virtual images can be formed by linear transformations. As we've shown, refraction under perspective is not a linear transformation thus the pictures are not physically correct. In practice it is very difficult for "non-experts" to detect the discrepancy in the pictures we've generated. This linearity assumption is also not correct for curved surfaces since their normals vary from point to point.

We now discuss several possibilities for future extensions of beam tracing.

3.1. Light Beam Tracing

In standard ray tracing, diffuse shading of surface points is done by aiming rays toward each point light source and determining if any objects are blocking the path of direct illumination. Blocked lights create shadows; unblocked lights contribute to the reflected intensity using Lambert's law. Since rays are aimed only at the lights, and not in all directions, this does not realistically model indirect illumination. It is also intellectually unappealing because it creates an asymmetry between the light source and the eye point, contrary to the laws of physics.

Diffuse shading and shadows for a beam-traced model can be computed as a pre-process to the polygon database. We propose a recursive extension of the Atherton-Weiler shadow algorithm [1978]. Beams are traced from each light source just as they are from the viewpoint ("light beam" tracing as opposed to "eye beam" tracing). The first order intersections are the directly illuminated surfaces, (not shadowed) and higher order intersections are illuminated surfaces resulting from the reflected and refracted light sources, an effect difficult to achieve with a standard ray tracer. The illuminated polygons thus formed can be built into the model database as "surface detail", that is, polygons which do not affect the shape of the objects, but only their shading. If the light sources are infinitely distant, each face will have a constant diffuse intensity, which can be compactly saved in the database on this pre-process pass, for use during the rendering pass.

This algorithm has several other advantages over diffuse shading during rendering. Light sources can be directional and have a polygonal cross-section. They need not be point sources. The depth of the eye beam tree can also be reduced, since light beam tracing propagates shading information through several bounces (one could say that the light beams meet the eye beams half-way). Finally, if the model and lights are stationary during an animation, light beam pre-processing need be done only once.

3.2. Antialiasing

In classical ray tracing, antialiasing is usually done by adaptive subdivision of pixels near large intensity changes or small objects [Whitted, 1980; Roth, 1982]. The method attempts to use heuristic criteria to probe the image frequently enough that small details will not be overlooked. Depending on the criteria, it will sometimes subdivide too little, resulting in aliasing, or too much, in which case processing time is wasted.

Before rendering, it is possible to subdivide the beam tree into non-overlapping polygonal regions and form an adjacency graph which indicates which regions are neighbors. Given this information, antialiasing edges is straightforward. Since the beam tracer resolves all hidden-surface questions, all that is needed is a polygon scan converter with a pixel integrator. Pixel integration can be done by sub-sampling or with analytic methods [Catmull, 1978]. This same information might be useful when light beam tracing. The symmetry between eye and light allows us to relate partially-covered pixels to partially-obscured lights: the former suggests antialiasing, the latter suggests soft shadows. Consequently, if a region adjacency graph is made during light beam tracing, this can assist in the creation of soft-edged shadows.

3.3. Rendering Options

There are many other interesting variations to rendering the beam tree. If, as mentioned in the previous section, the output is divided into non-overlapping regions and we are doing faceted shading, the recursive shading formula can be calculated once for the entire region and a single polygon rendered. At the other extreme, it might be worth modifying the polygon renderer so that it simultaneously tiles all the polygons in a region. This would allow the simulation of light scattering through translucent materials, since in this case the intensity is an exponential function of material thickness [Kay and Greenberg, 1979] which varies over the polygons. As we've mentioned, because of the additive nature of the shading formula, the polygons can be rendered in any order but the overall intensity is modulated depending on the shading coefficients and the depth in the tree. If, on the other hand, we always render the scene in back-to-front order, one can accommodate spatially varying reflection and refraction coefficients. For example, cut glass could be simulated by modulating these parameters with a texture map. Finally, the coherence in the beam tree often allows certain aspects of the shading calculation to be done once per region which allows a more complicated shading model to be used. For example, we have used constant values for the four intensity coefficients, but more realistic results could be obtained using Fresnel's equations [Longhurst, 1967].

4. Acknowledgements

We would like to thank to Kevin Hunter and Jules Bloomenthal for proofreading and Jane Nisselson for assistance with the writing.

5. Appendix: Reflection and Refraction Transformations

We derive the homogeneous 4x4 matrix form for the reflection and refraction transformations.

Figure 10 shows the geometry of an incident ray I hitting a plane and generating a reflected ray R and refracted (transmitted) ray T. The three rays and the surface normal N all lie in a plane. The index of refraction changes

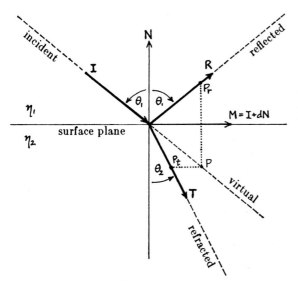

Figure 10. Geometry of reflection and refraction in the plane of incidence.

from η_1 to η_2 at the boundary. The angle of incidence is θ_1 and the angle of refraction is θ_2. We wish to find the transformations which map the real reflected and refracted points P_r and P_t to their virtual image P.

Notation:

$$I = incident\ ray\ direction,\ |I| = 1$$
$$N = (A\ B\ C\ 0)^T = normal\ to\ plane$$
$$|N| = \sqrt{A^2 + B^2 + C^2} = 1$$
$$L = (A\ B\ C\ D) = coefficients\ of\ plane\ equation:$$
$$LP = Ax + By + Cz + D = 0$$
$$P = (x\ y\ z\ 1)^T = any\ point$$

The direction of the reflected ray is given by:

$$R = I - 2(N \cdot I)N = I + 2dN \quad (a\ unit\ vector)$$
$$where:\ d = \cos\theta_1 = -N \cdot I > 0$$

The reflected point can be found by noting that LP_r gives the distance of a point P_r from the plane. The point formula has a form similar to the direction formula:

$$P = P_r - 2(LP_r)N = P_r - 2NLP_r = \mathbf{M}_r P_r$$

where $\mathbf{M}_r$ is the homogeneous 4x4 matrix for the reflection transformation:

$$\mathbf{M}_r = I - 2NL = \begin{pmatrix} 1-2A^2 & -2AB & -2AC & -2AD \\ -2AB & 1-2B^2 & -2BC & -2BD \\ -2AC & -2BC & 1-2C^2 & -2CD \\ 0 & 0 & 0 & 1 \end{pmatrix}$$

and I is a 4x4 identity matrix.

Snell's law relates the incident and refracted angles:

$$\eta_1 \sin\theta_1 = \eta_2 \sin\theta_2$$

The direction of the refracted ray is:

$$T = \eta I - (c - \eta d)N \quad (a\ unit\ vector)$$
$$where:\ \eta = \eta_1/\eta_2 = relative\ index\ of\ refraction$$
$$and \quad c = \cos\theta_2 = \sqrt{1 - \eta^2(1 - d^2)}$$

There is no refracted ray (total internal reflection) if $1 - \eta^2(1 - d^2) < 0$. Our formula for T is equivalent to, but simpler than, the one in [Whitted, 1980].

For orthographic projections, the incident direction I is independent of object position, and refraction is a skew transformation parallel to the plane which maps a point P_t as follows:

$$P = P_t + (\tan\theta_1 - \tan\theta_2)\hat{M}LP_t$$
$$where:\ M = N \times (I \times N) = I - (N \cdot I)N = I + dN,$$
$$M = vector\ tangent\ to\ plane, \quad |M| = \sin\theta_1$$

and $P = \mathbf{M}_t P_t$, where $\mathbf{M}_t$ is a 4x4 matrix:

$$\mathbf{M}_t = I + \alpha(I + dN)L$$

$$where:\ \alpha = \frac{\tan\theta_1 - \tan\theta_2}{\sin\theta_1} = \sec\theta_1 - \eta\sec\theta_2 = \frac{1}{d} - \frac{\eta}{c}$$

If viewing along the Z axis, then $I = (0\ 0\ 1\ 0)^T$, $d = -C$, and

$$\mathbf{M}_t = \begin{pmatrix} 1-\alpha A^2C & -\alpha ABC & -\alpha AC^2 & -\alpha ACD \\ -\alpha ABC & 1-\alpha B^2C & -\alpha BC^2 & -\alpha BCD \\ \alpha A(1-C^2) & \alpha B(1-C^2) & 1+\alpha C(1-C^2) & \alpha D(1-C^2) \\ 0 & 0 & 0 & 1 \end{pmatrix}$$

This formula is exact for orthographic projections. If the eye is local, however, I and d vary from point to point on the surface, and there is no linear transformation from P_t to P.

Observing figure 11, however, we see that rays with small incidence angles (paraxial rays) produce virtual refracted rays which nearly come to a focus. Thus, for paraxial rays,

$$\frac{D_1}{D_2} = \frac{\tan\theta_2}{\tan\theta_1} = \frac{\tan\phi_2}{\tan\phi_1} = constant$$

If we take the constant to be η_1/η_2, then

$$\eta_1\tan\theta_1 = \eta_2\tan\theta_2$$

We call this the *tangent law*. For paraxial rays, $\sin\theta \approx \tan\theta \approx \theta$, so Snell's law is in agreement with the tangent law. A graphical comparison of the two laws is shown in figure 12.

The virtual focus can be interpreted as follows: When looking across a boundary with relative index of refraction η, objects appear to be at η times their actual distance [Feynman, 1963]. Recall that light travels slower in denser materials by precisely this factor η. Within the paraxial approximation, then, refraction is equivalent to a scaling transformation perpendicular to the plane:

$$P = P_t + (\eta-1)(LP_t)N = \mathbf{M}_tP_t$$

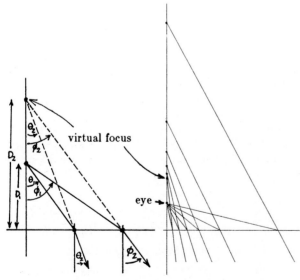

Figure 11. Refracted paraxial rays come to a virtual focus in the first medium at a distance $D_2 = \frac{1}{\eta}D_1$ from the plane. Left diagram illustrates tangent law, right illustrates Snell's law.

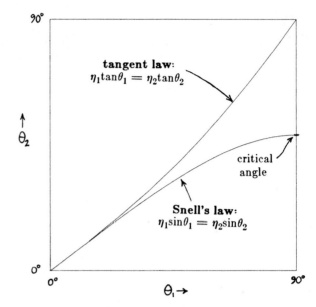

Figure 12. Refraction angle as a function of incidence angle using Snell's law and tangent law. For this graph, $\eta_2/\eta_1 = 1.33$.

$$\mathbf{M}_t = \mathbf{I}+\lambda NL = \begin{pmatrix} 1+\lambda A^2 & \lambda AB & \lambda AC & \lambda AD \\ \lambda AB & 1+\lambda B^2 & \lambda BC & \lambda BD \\ \lambda AC & \lambda BC & 1+\lambda C^2 & \lambda CD \\ 0 & 0 & 0 & 1 \end{pmatrix}$$

where: $\lambda = \eta-1$

Note the similarity between this and the reflection formula. Reflection is simply paraxial refraction with $\eta = -1$.

6. References

Atherton, Peter K., Kevin Weiler, and Donald Greenberg, "Polygon Shadow Generation." *Computer Graphics (SIGGRAPH '78 Proceedings)*, vol. 12, no. 3, Aug. 1978, pp. 275-281.

Catmull, Edwin, "A Hidden-Surface Algorithm with Anti-Aliasing." *Computer Graphics (SIGGRAPH '78 Proceedings)*, vol. 12, no. 3, Aug. 1978, pp. 6-11.

Clark, James, "Hierarchical Geometric Models for Visible Surface Algorithms." *C.A.C.M.* vol. 19, no. 10, 1976, pp. 547-554.

Crow, Franklin C., "Shaded Computer Graphics in the Entertainment industry." *Computer*, vol. 11, no. 3, March 1978, p. 11.

Dadoun, Norm, David G. Kirkpatrick, and John P. Walsh, "Hierarchical Approaches to Hidden Surface Intersection Testing." *Proceedings of Graphics Interface '82*, May 1982, pp. 49-56.

Eastman, C. M., and C. I. Yessios, "An Efficient Algorithm for Finding the Union, Intersection and Differences of Spatial Domains." Technical Report 31, Institute of

Physical Planning, Carnegie-Mellon University, Sept. 1972.

Feynman, Richard P., Robert B. Leighton, and Matthew Sands, *The Feynman Lectures on Physics.* Addison-Wesley, Reading, Mass., 1963, vol. I, pp. 27-3, 27-4.

Fuchs, Henry, Zvi M. Kedem, and Bruce F. Naylor, "On Visible Surface Generation by A Priori Tree Structures." *Computer Graphics (SIGGRAPH '80 Proceedings),* vol. 14, no. 3, July 1980, pp. 124-133.

Hall, Roy A., and Donald P. Greenberg, "A Testbed for Realistic Image Synthesis." *IEEE Computer Graphics and Applications,* vol. 3, no. 8, Nov. 1983, pp. 10-20.

Hanrahan, Pat, and Paul S. Heckbert, "Introduction to Beam Tracing." *Proc. Intl. Conf. on Engineering and Computer Graphics,* Beijing, China, Aug. 1984.

Heckbert, Paul, *PMAT and POLY User's Manual.* New York Inst. of Tech. internal document, Feb. 1983.

Jones, C. B., "A New Approach to the 'Hidden Line' Problem." *The Computer Journal,* vol. 14, no. 3, Aug. 1971, pp. 232-237.

Kawaguchi, Yoichiro, "Growth: Mysterious Galaxy." *SIGGRAPH '83 Film & Video Shows,* p. 5.

Kay, Douglas S., and Donald Greenberg, "Transparency for Computer Synthesized Images." *Computer Graphics (SIGGRAPH '79 Proceedings),* vol. 13, no. 2, Aug. 1979, pp. 158-164.

Longhurst, R. S., *Geometrical and Physical Optics.* Longman, London, 1967.

Max, Nelson, "Computer Graphics Distortion for IMAX and OMNIMAX Projection." *Nicograph '83 Proceedings,* Dec. 1983, pp. 137-159.

Newell, M. E., R. G. Newell, and T. L. Sancha, "A New Approach to the Shaded Picture Problem." *Proc. ACM Nat. Conf.,* 1972, p. 443.

Newman, William M., and Robert F. Sproull, *Principles of Interactive Computer Graphics, 2nd ed.* McGraw-Hill, New York, 1979.

Nishimura, Hitoshi, Hiroshi Ohno, Toru Kawata, Isao Shirakawa, and Koichi Omura, "Links-1: A Parallel Pipelined Multimicrocomputer System for Image Creation." *IEEE 1983 Conf. Proc. of the 10th Annual Intl. Symp. on Computer Architecture.*

Roth, Scott D., "Ray Casting for Modeling Solids." *Computer Graphics and Image Processing,* vol. 18, no. 2, Feb. 1982, pp. 109-144.

Rubin, S.W., and Turner Whitted, "A 3-dimensional Representation for Fast Rendering of Complex Scenes." *Computer Graphics (SIGGRAPH '80 Proceedings),* vol. 14, no. 3, July 1980, pp. 110-116.

Sutherland, Ivan E., Robert F. Sproull, and Robert A. Schumacker, "A Characterization of Ten Hidden-Surface Algorithms." *Computing Surveys,* vol. 6, no. 1, March 1974, p. 1.

Walker, Jearl, "The Amateur Scientist: What is a fish's view of a fisherman and the fly he has cast on the water?" *Scientific American,* vol. 250, no. 3, March 1984, pp. 138-143.

Walsh, John P., and Norm Dadoun, "What Are We Waiting for? The Development of Godot, II." presented at the 103rd meeting of the Acoustical Society of America, Chicago, April 1982.

Weiler, Kevin, and Peter Atherton, "Hidden Surface Removal Using Polygon Area Sorting." *Computer Graphics (SIGGRAPH '77 Proceedings),* vol. 11, no. 2, Summer 1977, pp. 214-222.

Whitted, Turner, "An Improved Illumination Model for Shaded Display." *C.A.C.M.* vol. 23, no. 6, June 1980, pp. 343-349.

Ray Tracing with Cones

John Amanatides

Department of Computer Science
University of Toronto
Toronto, Canada M5S 1A4

Abstract

A new approach to ray tracing is introduced. The definition of a "ray" is extended into a cone by including information on the spread angle and the virtual origin. The advantages of this approach, which tries to model light propagation with more fidelity, include a better method of anti-aliasing, a way of calculating fuzzy shadows and dull reflections, a method of calculating the correct level of detail in a procedural model and texture map, and finally, a procedure for faster intersection calculation.

CR Categories and Subject Descriptions: I.3.3 [**Computer Graphics**]: Picture/Image Generation - display algorithms; I.3.7 [**Computer Graphics**]: Three-dimensional Graphics and Realism - Shading, Shadowing, Texture, Visible Line/Surface Algorithms;

General Terms: Algorithms

Additional Keywords and Phrases: Ray Tracing, Anti-Aliasing

Introduction

Ray tracing is a very powerful yet simple approach to image synthesis. Though expensive computationally, it has generated some of

Permission to copy without fee all or part of this material is granted provided that the copies are not made or distributed for direct commercial advantage, the ACM copyright notice and the title of the publication and its date appear, and notice is given that copying is by permission of the Association for Computing Machinery. To copy otherwise, or to republish, requires a fee and/or specific permission.

© 1984   ACM   0-89791-138-5/84/007/0129 $00.75

the most realistic scenes to date [10, 13, 17]. It is also used for entertainment and computer aided design [9, 15]. However, apart from the computationally expensive method of supersampling, no general method exists to remove artifacts created by aliasing. Furthermore, at present, there is no general procedure to decide what level of detail is sufficient in a texture map or in a procedural or hierarchical model of an object when ray tracing. This is primarily because individual rays are infinitesimally thick and thus we cannot exploit area-sampling techniques to avoid aliasing artifacts. This paper goes beyond some of these limitations by redefining the concept of "ray".

The Problem

In ray tracing, rays are shot from the eye into the world. They are constrained so that they pass through the center of the pixels in the virtual screen. Once they have left, any relationship between the ray and the pixel on which the results will be displayed is severed. This is because a ray is defined as a starting point and a direction which together form a line. This simple definition allows for straightforward and fast intersection calculations with various objects [11, 13, 14]. Unfortunately, it also has drawbacks.

The main drawback with the above standard approach is that there is not enough information associated with the ray to perform anti-aliasing [5]. Rays allow us only to sample at the one point in the center of a pixel. There is no way of knowing or calculating what else is visible in the neighborhood surrounding the sample point.

The only way to anti-alias within standard ray tracing is to go to higher resolution. Whitted proposed adaptive supersampling and it is now almost universally used [17]. There are a couple of problems associated with this approach, however. First, the amount of computation can go up drastically in pixels where large variances of intensity occur. Small polygons with a texture mapped on them are a case in point. The second problem is that small details may "fall through the cracks" of the sample points. This is especially true of objects that are reflected or refracted by other objects.

One way of attacking the sampling problem outlined above is to modify the definition of "ray". The pixel should represent not a point but an area of the screen. This fact can be encorporated if the ray becomes a pyramid with the apex at the eye and the base defined by the four planes that cut the borders of the pixel. Intersection calculations between this extended ray and an object can decide not only if there is an intersection but also what fraction of the ray intersects the object. This fractional coverage information is sufficient to perform simple area anti-aliasing. Also, nothing can "fall through the cracks" as the ray covers the whole pixel. Now, only one ray per pixel is sufficient regardless of scene complexity.

The penalty of traveling this route, however, is that intersection calculations can become quite involved.[1] If a ray is reflected or refracted by a curved surface the resulting ray can be very distorted, furthering the complexity of the intersection calculations. Also, consider an object, A, that intersects only a portion of the ray. To correctly render objects behind A, the ray should be modified to indicate the portion that is blocked by A. The proposed new definition of a ray must be further extended to handle this. Approximations, such as coverage masks [7], may be used but these calculations quickly become prohibitive.

An Approximation: Cones

The above extended definition of a ray is too complex to be easily implemented so a simplifying approximation is proposed: Let the new definition of a ray be a circular pyramid or cone. This will be made possible by including the angle of spread and virtual origin of the ray in the definition which originally included only the origin and direction of the ray. The spread

---

1. In fact, Whitted started work in this direction but abandoned it due to the complexity of the intersection calculations [17].

angle is defined as the angle between the center line of the cone and the cone boundary as measured at the apex of the cone. This angle is chosen such that when the ray is sent from the eye the radius of the cone at the distance of the virtual screen is the width of the pixel. The virtual origin is the distance from the apex of the cone to the origin. This will not be zero for reflected or refracted cones. Reflected and refracted rays continue to keep this symmetric shape, modifying the spread angle and distance to the virtual origin so that a good approximation of the cone is constantly maintained.

Calculating the intersection between a cone and an object is still rather complex. This will be described in the next section. The result from the intersection calculations should indicate not only if there is an intersection but also the fraction of the cone that is blocked by the object. A sorted list is maintained of the eight closest objects that intersect the ray. This list is used for anti-aliasing. If the closest object does not completely fill the ray then the next object in the list contributes to the pixel value. Since at present only the fractional coverage value is used in mixing the contributions from the various objects, overlapping surfaces will be calculated correctly but abutting surfaces will not. Additional information in the sorted intersection list can be used to rectify this shortcoming.

Reflection and refraction calculations must take into account that the ray is now a cone. The new direction of the ray is calculated in the same manner as standard ray tracing and uses the center line of the cone. To calculate the new virtual origin and spread angle the surface curvature is required. A constant curvature is assumed throughout the area of intersection and the optical laws of spherical mirrors and lenses are used [12]. Unfortunately, we cannot use the simple lens equations that depend on the "paraxial" approximation (the incident angle of the incoming ray is close to zero). The more general equations are required.

Intersection Calculations

We now describe the intersection calculations between a cone and various objects. These objects include spheres, planes and polygons. In general, each intersection calculation should consist of two parts: a fast in/out test and then a more complicated area intersection approximation. The quick first test is desirable since most objects will intersect relatively few rays.

The intersection calculation between a sphere and a cone consists of two parts. The first part tests if an intersection will occur and the second part calculates the fractional coverage.

This test begins by finding the point on the cone's center line (CP) that is closest to the center of the sphere and the distance between the two points (SEP). In standard ray tracing this must also be performed with the test being negative if SEP is greater than the radius of the sphere. The above comparison must be modified to take into account that the ray is a cone. Let the distance between CP and the virtual origin of the ray be T, the spread angle A and the radius of the sphere R. We calculate the following:

$$D = T*tan(A) + R/cos(A)$$

If D is less than SEP, then there is no intersection between the ray and the sphere (see fig. 1). The above calculation requires the evaluation of two trigonometric functions. Notice, however, that these functions only depend on the spread angle and need be evaluated once, before any intersection calculations begin. This results in a test that is only a few floating point operations more expensive that regular ray tracing.

The second part of the intersection calculation evaluates the fractional coverage of the sphere within the ray. This is equivalent to finding the area of intersection of two circles, the outline of the sphere and the outline of the cone where it is closest to the sphere. To calculate this quickly an approximate solution involving a simple polynomial evaluation is performed.

The intersection calculation between a ray and a plane is now described. The calculation begins with a quick test to make sure that the plane is not behind the origin of the ray by calculating the intersection between the center line of the ray and the plane. If the intersection is behind the origin of the ray then the plane is discarded. Otherwise, the angle between the centerline of the ray and the plane normal is computed. This angle and the spread angle of the ray are compared and it is a simple matter to test for intersection.

The next part of the intersection calculation computes the fractional coverage. The problem can be reduced to two dimensions and involves finding the area of intersection between a circle (the cross section of the cone) and a half plane (the horizon). The spread angle and the angle between the ray and plane computed above together indicate how the distance between the center of the circle and the edge of the half plane. Given this distance, the area of intersection is computed using a polynomial approximation. This completes the intersection calculation for planes.

The intersection calculation between a cone and a polygon is now outlined. There are two reasonable strategies we can use. The first requires we intersect the cone with the plane defined by the polygon and perform an intersection test between the polygon and the cross section obtained. The cross section of a conic can be either a circle, ellipse, hyperbola or a parabola. This makes intersection calculations more complicated. The second strategy requires that we project the vertices of the polygon onto a plane perpendicular to the direction vector of the cone. Now the cross section of the cone with that plane is always a circle. We then must calculate the intersection between the projected polygon and a circle. This can be accomplished by calculating the distance from the center of the circle to each of the edges and then using the circle - half plane intersection estimation mentioned earlier.

Choosing a Representative

Most anti-aliasing schemes make some assumptions within a pixel to simplify the algorithm. Two common assumptions are that the depth (z value) and intensity of any individual object are constant within the pixel [5, 7]. But the choice of the representative, the sample point on the object within the pixel at which the intersection calculations will be performed, must be made with care or the attempt at anti-aliasing will falter.

There are two variables that can be altered when making this decision. The first is which point on the object should be chosen? The center of the pixel is universally used. Problems arise when the object does not occupy this point. Solutions that only pick the point on the object that is closest to the center (as seen from the eye) can lead one astray. For example, consider the case in which a cone partially intersects an infinite plane but the center of the cone does not intersect. The point closest to the center would be on the horizon. If we model the attenuation of light with distance this will result in an intensity of zero for this point since the distance to the horizon is infinite.

The second variable one has when choosing the representative is what surface properties should the sample point be given? They do not have to be exactly the same as the values found at the sample point. Why you may want to change these values is illustrated below:

Specular highlights can be a problem when the surface normal varies greatly within a pixel [6, 18]. By reducing the directional dependence of the specular highlight in these trouble spots the problem is diminished. For example, if we are using Phong shading, we can clamp the value of n, the power to which the specular dot product is raised, to a value that will subdue this form of aliasing.

Levels of Detail

A recurring problem with procedural and hierarchical models of objects is the level of detail to which they should be generated [3]. In classical ray tracing there is no good answer as there is no way of knowing how much of the screen an object will fill. Stochastic surfaces are a good example [8, 13]. If we do not subdivide the surface enough we will see the resulting polygons. If we subdivide too far, however, we will encounter two problems: First, we will waste computing resources and second, we will be forced to undersample. This is because further subdivision will introduce higher frequency components into the stochastic surface, frequencies that cannot be reproduced faithfully. We can use cones to advantage here. By calculating the size of the intersection, we can decide what level of detail is sufficient. Thus two different views of the same object, one direct and one reflecting off another surface, can both be rendered at the correct level of detail. Kajiya has performed ray tracing with prisms and surfaces of revolution [13]. His implementation of these objects require the use of strip trees, a hierarchical structure which represents a curve at various resolutions. We can speed up the intersection calculation with these objects by only subdividing the strip tree to a level sufficient for display.

Cones can also be used to anti-alias texture. At each intersection an estimate of the size and shape of the intersection can be

calculated. This information can be used to generate the filter to average the texture map.

Fuzzy Shadows

Virtually all graphics systems model light as either a point source or as a direction from which parallel light beams emanate [4]. Consequently, shadows cast by these light sources exhibit sharp boundaries. Cones allow us to extend our repertoire of light sources to include ones that cast fuzzy boundaries at almost no extra cost. For example, we can add spheres of varying radii as light sources. At each intersection, when a ray is sent to the light source to calculate the shadow, we broaden the ray to the size of the light source. By calculating how much of the light source is blocked by intervening objects, we have enough information to generate fuzzy shadows. Note that this does not produce completely correct shadows. The shadows of transparent objects will still be wrong. The concentration of light by these refracting surfaces cannot be generated using this simple approach.

Dull Reflections

In his classic paper [17], Turner Whitted raised the issue of generating specular highlights using ray tracing techniques. His approach, however, suffered from aliasing and fired off many rays at each intersection point. This is very expensive computationally and was thus abandoned. We produce similar results by simply broadening the reflected ray. In this manner, only one ray is required. When rays are broadened, reflecting surfaces become less glossy. This results in reflections that are less detailed. In a similar manner, translucency can be modeled by broadening the transmitted ray.

The above remarks suggest that the amount of ambient lighting can be estimated by firing very broad rays from each surface and using simple lighting models to prevent an infinite regress of rays.

Reducing Intersection Calculations

The cone approach provides a basis for reducing the number of intersection calculations required for ray tracing. By recursively firing cones of various sizes at the screen, we can perform a Warnock style culling process [16]. This can significantly reduce the number of intersection calculations required at each pixel by capitalizing on image coherence. A test case of six spheres (without reflection, refraction or shadows) resulted in an order of magnitude reduction in intersection calculations. This result can be immediately applied to ray casting [1], and with some modifications, to ray tracing in general.

Results

Figures 2 - 5 are examples of images generated using some of the above improvements to ray tracing. They all took approximately 50 minutes each to compute on a VAX 780. Figure 2 illustrates anti-aliasing and fuzzy shadows. The light source is a sphere of radius 20 units (each checkerboard is one unit wide) and approximately 300 units away from the scene. The checkerboard is modeled as a procedural texture map.

Figure 3 illustrates dull reflections. The balls become progressively less glossy from left to right. This is evidenced by the reflected checkerboard that varies in detail form ball to ball. The extra angular spread of the reflected rays for each of the balls in left to right order is 0., .2 and .4 radians.

Figures 4 and 5 illustrate ray tracing textures. The method of pyramidal parametrics [18] was used to filter the texture.

Conclusions

We have introduced a new approach to ray tracing: cones. With cones, only one ray per pixel is now required to perform anti-aliasing. The cone approach can also easily be used to decide the correct level of detail, generate fuzzy shadows and dull reflections and reduce intersection calculations. Work is still required to find efficient intersection algorithms for more complicated objects.

Acknowledgements

I wish to thank Alain Fournier for his support and valuable comments. I also wish to thank Eugene Fiume, Ralph Hill, Michael Hollosi and Delfin Montuno who were a sounding board for many ideas and contributed numerous suggestions.

References

1.   Amanatides, J., and Fournier, A., "Ray Casting using Divide and Conquer in Screen Space", *Proc. Intl. Conf. of Engineering and Computer Graphics*, Beijing, China, Aug. 27 - Sept. 1 1984.

2.   Blinn, J.F., and Newell, M.E., "Texture and Reflection in Computer Generated Images", *Comm. ACM*, Vol. 19(10), October 1976, pp. 542-547.

3.   Clark, J.H., "Hierarchical Geometric Models for Visible Surface Algorithms", *Comm. ACM*, Vol. 19(10), October 1976, pp.547-554.

4.   Crow, F.C., "Shadow Algorithms for Computer Graphics", *Computer Graphics*, Vol. 11(3), July 1977, pp. 242-248.

5.   Crow, F.C., "The Aliasing Problem in Computer-Generated Shaded Images", *Comm. ACM*, Vol. 20(11), November 1977, pp. 799-805.

6.   Crow, F.C., "A Comparison of Antialiasing Techniques", *IEEE Computer Graphics and Applications*, Vol. 1(1), January 1981, pp. 40-48.

7.   Fiume, E., Fournier, A., and Rudolph, L., "A Parallel Scan Conversion Algorithm with Anti-Aliasing for a General Purpose Ultracomputer", *Computer Graphics*, Vol. 17(3), July 1983, pp. 141-150.

8.   Fournier, A., Fussell, D., and Carpenter, L., "Computer Rendering of Stochastic Models", *Comm. ACM*, Vol. 25(6), June 1982, pp. 371-384.

9.   Goldstein, R.A., and Nagel, R., "3-D Visual Simulation", *Simulation*, January 1971, pp. 25-31.

10. Hall, R.A., and Greenberg, D.P., "A Testbed for Realistic Image Synthesis", *IEEE Computer Graphics and Applications*, Vol. 3(8), November 1983, pp. 10-20.

11. Hanrahan, P., "Ray Tracing Algebraic Surfaces", *Computer Graphics*, Vol. 17(3), July 1983, pp.83-90.

12. Hect, E., and Zajac, A., **OPTICS**, Addison Wesley Publishing Company, Reading Massachusetts, 1974.

13. Kajiya, J.T., "New Techniques For Ray Tracing Procedurally Defined Objects", *Computer Graphics*, Vol. 17(3), July 1983, pp. 91-102.

14. Rubin, S.M., and Whitted, T., "A 3-Dimensional Representation for Fast Rendering of Complex Scenes", *Computer Graphics*, Vol. 14(3), July 1980, pp. 110-116.

15. Roth, S.D., "Ray Casting for Modeling Solids", *Computer Graphics and Image Processing*, Vol. 18, 1982, pp. 109-144.

16. Warnock, J., *A Hidden-Surface Algorithm for Computer Generated Half-Tone Pictures*, Univ. Utah Computer Sci. Dept., TR 4-15, 1969, NTIS AD-733 671.

17. Whitted, T., "An Improved Illumination Model for Shaded Display", *Comm. ACM*, Vol. 23(6), June 1980, pp. 343-349.

18. Williams, L., "Pyramidal Parametrics", *Computer Graphics*, Vol. 17(3), July 1983, pp. 1-11.

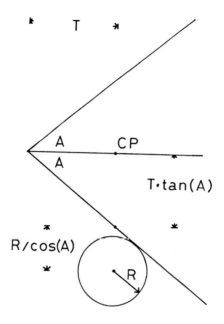

Figure 1

Figure 2

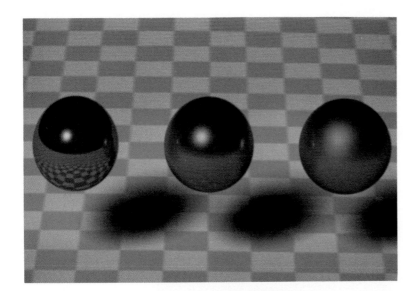

Figure 3

Figure 4

Figure 5

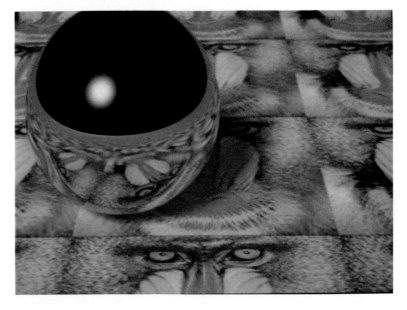

Distributed Ray Tracing

Robert L. Cook
Thomas Porter
Loren Carpenter

Computer Division
Lucasfilm Ltd.

Abstract

Ray tracing is one of the most elegant techniques in computer graphics. Many phenomena that are difficult or impossible with other techniques are simple with ray tracing, including shadows, reflections, and refracted light. Ray directions, however, have been determined precisely, and this has limited the capabilities of ray tracing. By distributing the directions of the rays according to the analytic function they sample, ray tracing can incorporate fuzzy phenomena. This provides correct and easy solutions to some previously unsolved or partially solved problems, including motion blur, depth of field, penumbras, translucency, and fuzzy reflections. Motion blur and depth of field calculations can be integrated with the visible surface calculations, avoiding the problems found in previous methods.

CR CATEGORIES AND SUBJECT DESCRIPTORS:
I.3.7 [**Computer Graphics**]: Three-Dimensional Graphics and Realism;

ADDITIONAL KEY WORDS AND PHRASES: camera, constructive solid geometry, depth of field, focus, gloss, motion blur, penumbras, ray tracing, shadows, translucency, transparency

1. Introduction

Ray tracing algorithms are elegant, simple, and powerful. They can render shadows, reflections, and refracted light, phenomena that are difficult or impossible with other techniques[11]. But ray tracing is currently limited to sharp shadows, sharp reflections, and sharp refraction.

Permission to copy without fee all or part of this material is granted provided that the copies are not made or distributed for direct commercial advantage, the ACM copyright notice and the title of the publication and its date appear, and notice is given that copying is by permission of the Association for Computing Machinery. To copy otherwise, or to republish, requires a fee and/or specific permission.

© 1984   ACM   0-89791-138-5/84/007/0137 $00.75

Ray traced images are sharp because ray directions are determined precisely from geometry. Fuzzy phenomenon would seem to require large numbers of additional samples per ray. By distributing the rays rather than adding more of them, however, fuzzy phenomena can be rendered with no additional rays beyond those required for spatially oversampled ray tracing. This approach provides correct and easy solutions to some previously unsolved problems.

This approach has not been possible before because of aliasing. Ray tracing is a form of point sampling and, as such, has been subject to aliasing artifacts. This aliasing is not inherent, however, and ray tracing can be filtered as effectively as any analytic method[4]. The filtering does incur the expense of additional rays, but it is not merely oversampling or adaptive oversampling, which in themselves cannot solve the aliasing problem. This antialiasing is based on an approach proposed by Rodney Stock. It is the subject of a forthcoming paper.

Antialiasing opens up new possibilities for ray tracing. Ray tracing need not be restricted to spatial sampling. If done with proper antialiasing, the rays can sample motion, the camera lens, and the entire shading function. This is called *distributed ray tracing*.

Distributed ray tracing is a new approach to image synthesis. The key is that no extra rays are needed beyond those used for oversampling in space. For example, rather than taking multiple time samples at every spatial location, the rays are distributed in time so that rays at different spatial locations are traced at different instants of time. Once we accept the expense of oversampling in space, distributing the rays offers substantial benefits at little additional cost.

- Sampling the reflected ray according to the specular distribution function produces gloss (blurred reflection).
- Sampling the transmitted ray produces translucency (blurred transparency).
- Sampling the solid angle of the light sources produces penumbras.

- Sampling the camera lens area produces depth of field.
- Sampling in time produces motion blur.

2. Shading

The intensity I of the reflected light at a point on a surface is an integral over the hemisphere above the surface of an illumination function L and a reflection function R[1].

$$I(\phi_r,\theta_r) = \int_{\phi_i} \int_{\theta_i} L(\phi_i,\theta_i)R(\phi_i,\theta_i,\phi_r,\theta_r)\,d\phi_i\,d\theta_i$$

where

(ϕ_i,θ_i) is the angle of incidence, and

(ϕ_r,θ_r) is the angle of reflection.

The complexity of performing this integration has been avoided by making some simplifying assumptions. The following are some of these simplifications:

- Assume that L is a δ function, i.e., that L is zero except for light source directions and that the light sources can be treated as points. The integral is now replaced by a sum over certain discrete directions. This assumption causes sharp shadows.
- Assume that all of the directions that are not light source directions can be grouped together into an ambient light source. This ambient light is the same in all directions, so that L is independent of ϕ_i and θ_i and may be removed from the integral. The integral of R may then be replaced by an average, or ambient, reflectance.
- Assume that the reflectance function R is a δ function, i.e., that the surface is a mirror and reflects light only from the mirror direction. This assumption causes sharp reflections. A corresponding assumption for transmitted light causes sharp refraction.

The shading function may be too complex to compute analytically, but we can point sample its value by distributing the rays, thus avoiding these simplifying assumptions. Illumination rays are not traced toward a single light direction, but are distributed according to the illumination function L. Reflected rays are not traced in a single mirror direction but are distributed according to the reflectance function R.

2.1. Gloss

Reflections are mirror-like in computer graphics, but in real life reflections are often blurred or hazy. The distinctness with which a surface reflects its environment is called *gloss*[5]. Blurred reflections have been discussed by Whitted[11] and by Cook[2]. Any analytic simulation of these reflections must be based on the integral of the reflectance over some solid angle.

Mirror reflections are determined by tracing rays from the surface in the mirror direction. Gloss can be calculated by distributing these secondary rays about the mirror direction. The distribution is weighted according to the same distribution function that determines the highlights.

This method was originally suggested by Whitted[11], and it replaces the usual specular component. Rays that reflect light sources produce highlights.

2.2. Translucency

Light transmitted through an object is described by an equation similar to that for reflected light, except that the reflectance function R is replaced by a transmittance function T and the integral is performed over the hemisphere behind the surface. The transmitted light can have ambient, diffuse, and specular components[5].

Computer graphics has included transparency, in which T is assumed to be a δ function and the images seen through transparent objects are sharp. Translucency differs from transparency in that the images seen through translucent objects are not distinct. The problem of translucency is analogous to the problem of gloss. Gloss requires an integral of the reflected light, and translucency requires a corresponding integral of the transmitted light.

Translucency is calculated by distributing the secondary rays about the main direction of the transmitted light. Just as the distribution of the reflected rays is defined by the specular reflectance function, the distribution of the transmitted rays is defined by a specular transmittance function.

2.3. Penumbras

Penumbras occur where a light source is partially obscured. The reflected intensity due to such a light is proportional to the solid angle of the visible portion of the light. The solid angle has been explicitly included in a shading model[3], but no algorithms have been suggested for determining this solid angle because of the complexity of the computation involved. The only attempt at penumbras known to the authors seems to solve only a very special case[7].

Shadows can be calculated by tracing rays from the surface to the light sources, and penumbras can be calculated by distributing these secondary rays. The shadow ray can be traced to any point on the light source, not just not to a single light source location. The distribution of the shadow rays must be weighted according the projected area and brightness of different parts of the light source. The number of rays traced to each region should be proportional to the amount of the light's energy that would come from that region if the light was

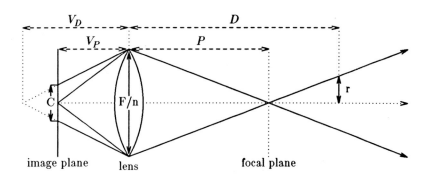

Figure 1. Circle of Confusion.

completely unobscured. The proportion of lighted sample points in a region of the surface is then equal to the proportion of that light's intensity that is visible in that region.

3. Depth of Field

Cameras and the eye have a finite lens aperture, and hence their images have a finite depth of field. Each point in the scene appears as a circle on the image plane. This circle is called the circle of confusion, and its size depends on the distance to the point and on the lens optics. Depth of field can be an unwanted artifact, but it can also be a desirable effect.

Most computer graphics has been based on a pinhole camera model with every object in sharp focus. Potmesil simulated depth of field with a postprocessing technique. Each object is first rendered in sharp focus (i.e., with a pinhole camera model), and later each sharply rendered object is convolved with a filter the size of the circle of confusion[8]. The program spends most of its time in the focus postprocessor, and this time increases dramatically as the aperture decreases.

Such a postprocessing approach can never be completely correct. This is because visibility is calculated from a single point, the center of the lens. The view of the environment is different from different parts of the lens, and the differences include changes in visibility and shading that cannot be accounted for by a postprocessing approach.

For example, consider an object that is extremely out of focus in front of an object that is in focus. Visible surface calculations done with the pinhole model determine the visibility from the center of the lens. Because the front object is not in focus, parts of the focused object that are not visible from the center of the lens will be visible from other parts of the lens. Information about those parts will not available for the postprocessor, so the postprocessor cannot possibly get the correct result.

There is another way to approach the depth of field problem. Depth of field occurs because the lens is a finite size. Each point on the lens "looks" at the same point on the focal plane. The visible surfaces and the shading may be different as seen from different parts of the lens. The depth of field calculations should account for this and be an integral part of the visible surface and shading calculations.

Depth of field can be calculated by starting with the traditional ray from the center of the lens through point p on the focal plane. A point on the surface of the lens is selected and the ray from that point to p is traced. The camera specifications required for this calculation are the focal distance and the diameter of the lens $\frac{F}{n}$, where F is the focal length of the lens and n is the aperture number.

This gives exactly the same circle of confusion as presented by Potmesil[8]. Because it integrates the depth of field calculations with the shading and visible surface calculations, this method gives a more accurate solution to the depth of field problem, with the exception that it does not account for diffraction effects.

Figure 1 shows why this method gives the correct circle of confusion. The lens has a diameter of $\frac{F}{n}$ and is focused at a distance P so that the image plane is at a distance V_P, where

$$V_P = \frac{FP}{P-F} \text{ for } P > F .$$

Points on the plane that is a distance D from the lens will focus at

$$V_D = \frac{FD}{D-F} \text{ for } D > F$$

and have a circle of confusion with diameter C of[8]

$$C = |V_D - V_P| \frac{F}{n V_D}$$

For a point I on the image plane, the rays we trace lie inside the cone whose radius at D is

$$r = \frac{1}{2} \frac{F}{n} \frac{|D-P|}{P}$$

The image plane distance from a point on this cone to a point on the axis of the cone is r multiplied by the magnification of the lens.

$$R = r\left(-\frac{V_P}{D}\right).$$

It is easily shown that

$$R = \frac{C}{2}.$$

Hence any points on the cone have a circle of confusion that just touches the image point I. Points outside the cone do not affect the image point and points inside the cone do.

4. Motion Blur

Distributing the rays or sample points in time solves the motion blur problem. Before we discuss this method and how it works, let us first look in more detail at the motion blur problem and at previous attempts to solve it.

The motion blur method described by Potmesil[9] is not only expensive, it also separates the visible surface calculation from the motion blur calculation. This is acceptable in some situations, but in most cases we cannot just calculate a still frame and blur the result. Some object entirely hidden in the still frame might be uncovered for part of the the time sampled by the blur. If we are to blur an object across a background, we have to know what the background is.

Even if we know what the background is, there are problems. For example, consider a biplane viewed from above, so that the lower wing is completely obscured by the upper wing. Because the upper wing is moving, the scenery below it would be seen through its blur, but unfortunately the lower wing would show through too. The lower wing should be hidden completely because it moves with the the upper wing and is obscured by it over the entire time interval.

This particular problem can be solved by rendering the plane and background as separate elements, but not all pictures can easily be separated into elements. This solution also does not allow for changes in visibility within a single object. This is particularly important for rotating objects.

The situation is further complicated by the change in shading within a frame time. Consider a textured top spinning on a table. If we calculate only one shade per frame, the texture would be blurred properly, but unfortunately the highlights and shadows would be blurred too. On a real top, the highlights and shadows

are not blurred at all by the spinning. They are blurred, of course, by any lateral motion of the top along the table or by the motion of a light source or the camera. The highlights should be blurred by the motion of the light and the camera, by the travel of the top along the table, and by the precession of the top, but not by the rotation of the top.

Motion blurred shadows are also important and are not rendered correctly if we calculate only one shade per frame. Otherwise, for example, the blades of a fan could be motion blurred, but the shadows of those blades would strobe.

All of this is simply to emphasize the tremendous complexity of the motion blur problem. The prospects for an analytic solution are dim. Such a solution would require solving the visible surface problem as a function of time as well as space. It would also involve integrating the texture and shading function of the visible surfaces over time. Point sampling seems to be the only approach that offers any promise of solving the motion blur problem.

One point sampling solution was proposed by Korein and Badler[6]. Their method, however, point samples only in space, not in time. Changes in shading are not motion blurred. The method involves keeping a list of all objects that cross each sample point during the frame time, a list that could be quite long for a fast moving complex scene. They also impose the unfortunate restriction that both vertices of an edge must move at the same velocity. This creates holes in objects that change perspective severely during one frame, because the vertices move at drastically different rates. Polygons with edges that share these vertices cannot remain adjoining. The algorithm is also limited to linear motion. If the motion is curved or if the vertices are allowed to move independently, the linear intersection equation becomes a higher order equation. The resulting equation is expensive to solve and has multiple roots.

Distributing the sample points in time solves the motion blur problem. The path of motion can be arbitrarily complex. The only requirement is the ability to calculate the position of the object at a specific time. Changes in visibility and shading are correctly accounted for. Shadows (umbras and penumbras), depth of field, reflections and intersections are all correctly motion blurred. By using different distributions of rays, the motion can be blurred with a box filter or a weighted filter or can be strobed.

This distribution of the sample points in time does not involve adding any more sample points. Updating the object positions for each time is the only extra calculation needed for motion blur. Proper antialiasing is required or the picture will look strobed or have holes[4].

5. Other Implications of the Algorithm

Visible surface calculation is straightforward. Since each ray occurs at a single instant of time, the first step is to update the positions of the objects for that instant of time. The next is to construct a ray from the lens to the sample point and find the closest object that the ray intersects. Care must be taken in bounding moving objects. The bound should depend on time so that the number of potentially visible objects does not grow unacceptably with their speed.

Intersecting surfaces are handled trivially because we never have to calculate the line of intersection; we merely have to determine which is in front at a given location and time. At each sample point only one of the surfaces is visible. The intersections can even be motion blurred, a problem that would be terrifying with an analytic method.

The union, intersection, difference problem is easily solved with ray tracing or point sampling[10]. These calculations are also correctly motion blurred.

Transparency is easy even if the transparency is textured or varies with time. Let τ be the transparency of a surface at the time and location it is pierced by the ray, and let R be the reflectance. R and τ are wavelength dependent, and the color of the transparency is not necessarily the same as the color of the reflected light; for example, a red transparent plastic object may have a white highlight. If there are $n-1$ transparent surfaces in front of the opaque surface, the light reaching the viewer is

$$R_n \prod_{i=1}^{n-1} \tau_i + R_{n-1} \prod_{i=1}^{n-2} \tau_1 + \cdots + R_2 \tau_1 + R_1 = \sum_{i=1}^{n} R_i \prod_{j=1}^{i-1} \tau_j.$$

If the surfaces form solid volumes, then each object has a τ, and that τ is scaled by the distance that the transmitted ray travels through that object. The motion blur and depth of field calculations work correctly for these transparency calculations.

The distributed approach can be adapted to a scanline algorithm as well as to ray tracing. The general motion blur and depth of field calculations have been incorporated into a scanline algorithm using distributed sampling for the visible surface calculations. Special cases of penumbras, fuzzy reflections, and translucency have been successfully incorporated for flat surfaces.

6. Summary of the Algorithm

The intensity of a pixel on the screen is an analytic function that involves several nested integrals: integrals over time, over the pixel region, and over the lens area, as well as an integral of reflectance times illumination over the reflected hemisphere and an integral of transmittance times illumination over the transmitted hemisphere. This integral can be tremendously complicated, but we can point sample the function regardless of how complicated it is. If the function depends on n parameters, the function is sampled in the n dimensions defined by those parameters. Rather than adding more rays for each dimension, the existing rays are distributed in each dimension according to the values of the corresponding parameter.

This summary of the distributed ray tracing algorithm is illustrated in Figure 2 for a single ray.

- Choose a time for the ray and move the objects accordingly. The number of rays at a certain time is proportional to the value of the desired temporal filter at that time.

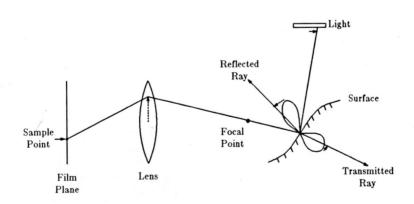

Figure 2. Typical Distributed Ray Path

- Construct a ray from the eye point (center of the lens) to a point on the screen. Choose a location on the lens, and trace a ray from that location to the focal point of the original ray. Determine which object is visible.

- Calculate the shadows. For each light source, choose a location on the light and trace a ray from the visible point to that location. The number of rays traced to a location on the light should be proportional to the intensity and projected area of that location as seen from the surface.

- For reflections, choose a direction around the mirror direction and trace a ray in that direction from the visible point. The number of rays traced in a specific direction should be proportional to the amount of light from that direction that is reflected toward the viewer. This can replace the specular component.

- For transmitted light, choose a direction around the direction of the transmitted light and trace a ray in that direction from the visible point. The number of rays traced in a specific direction should be proportional to the amount of light from that direction that is transmitted toward the viewer.

7. Examples

Figure 3 illustrates motion blurred intersections. The blue beveled cube is stationary, and the green beveled cube is moving in a straight line, perpendicular to one of its faces. Notice that the intersection of the faces is blurred except in in the plane of motion, where it is sharp.

Figures 4 and 5 illustrate depth of field. In figure 4, the camera has a 35 mm lens at f2.8. Notice that the rear sphere, which is out of focus, does not blur over the spheres in front. In figure 5, the camera is focused on the center of the three wooden spheres.

Figure 6 shows a number of moving spheres, with motion blurred shadows and reflections.

Figure 7 illustrates fuzzy shadows and reflections. The paper clip is illuminated by two local light sources which cast shadows with penumbras on the table. Each light is an extended light source (i.e., not a point light source) with a finite solid angle, and the intensity of its shadow at any point on the table is proportional to the amount of light obscured by the paper clip. The table reflects the paper clip, and the reflection blurs according to the specular distribution function of the table top. Note that both the shadows and the reflection blur with distance and are sharper close to the paper clip.

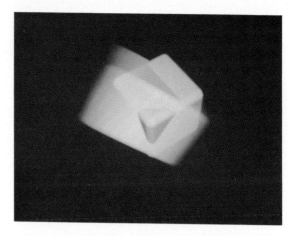

Figure 3. Motion Blurred Intersection.

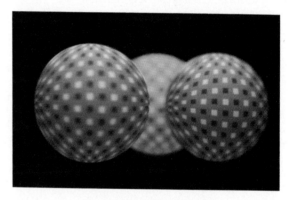

Figure 4. Depth of Field.

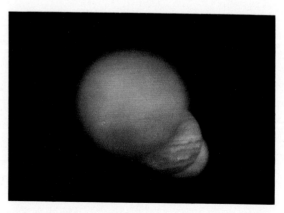

Figure 5. Depth of Field.

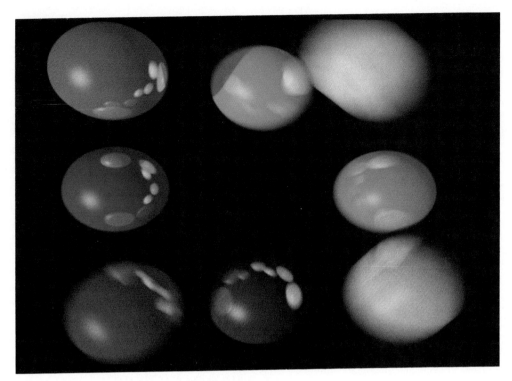

Figure 6. Balls in Motion.

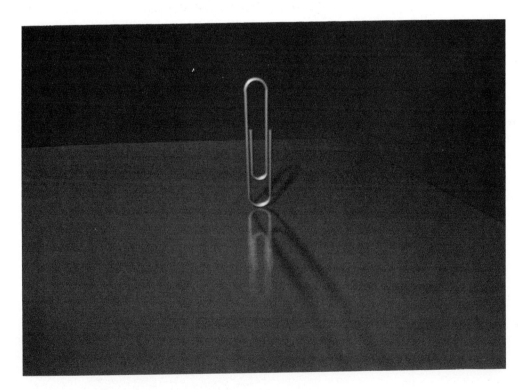

Figure 7. Paper Clip.

Figure 8 shows 5 billiard balls with motion blur and penumbras. Notice that the motion is not linear: the 9 ball changes direction abruptly in the middle of the frame, the 8 ball moves only during the middle of the frame, and the 4 ball only starts to move near the end of the frame. The shadows on the table are sharper where the balls are closer to the table; this most apparent in the stationary 1 ball. The reflections of the billiard balls and the room are motion blurred, as are the penumbras.

Figures 3, 5, and 7 were rendered with a scanline adaptation of this algorithm. Figures 4, 6, and 8 were rendered with ray tracing.

8. Conclusions

Distributed ray tracing a new paradigm for computer graphics which solves a number of hitherto unsolved or partially solved problems. The approach has also been successfully adapted to a scanline algorithm. It incorporates depth of field calculations into the visible surface calculations, eliminating problems in previous methods. It makes possible blurred phenomena such as penumbras, gloss, and translucency. All of the above can be motion blurred by distributing the rays in time.

These are not isolated solutions to isolated problems. This approach to image synthesis is practically no more expensive than standard ray tracing and solves all of these problems at once. The problems could not really be solved separately because they are all interrelated. Differences in shading, in penumbras, and in visibility are accounted for in the depth of field calculations. Changes in the depth of field and in visibility are motion blurred. The penumbra and shading calculations are motion blurred. All of these phenomena are related, and the new approach solves them all together by sampling the multidimensional space they define. The key to this is the ability to antialias point sampling.

9. Acknowledgements

Rodney Stock proposed the approach to antialiased point sampling that formed the basis of the paradigm explored in this paper. John Lasseter drew the environment map of the pool hall for "1984". Ed Catmull worked with us in the image synthesis working group and helped develop and refine these ideas. He and Alvy Ray Smith provided invaluable suggestions along the way. Tom Duff wrote the ray tracing program that we adapted to distributed ray tracing.

References

1. COOK, ROBERT L., TURNER WHITTED, AND DONALD P. GREENBERG, *A Comprehensive Model for Image Synthesis.* unpublished report

2. COOK, ROBERT L., "A Reflection Model for Realistic Image Synthesis," Master's thesis, Cornell University, Ithaca, NY, December 1981.

3. COOK, ROBERT L. AND KENNETH E. TORRANCE, "A Reflection Model for Computer Graphics," *ACM Transactions on Graphics*, vol. 1, no. 1, pp. 7-24, January 1982.

4. COOK, ROBERT L., "Antialiased Point Sampling," Technical Memo #94, Lucasfilm Ltd, San Rafael, CA, October 3, 1983.

5. HUNTER, RICHARD S., *The Measurement of Appearance,* John Wiley & Sons, New York, 1975.

6. KOREIN, JONATHAN AND NORMAN BADLER, "Temporal Anti-Aliasing in Computer Generated Animation," *Computer Graphics*, vol. 17, no. 3, pp. 377-388, July 1983.

7. NISHITA, TOMOYUKI, ISAO OKAMURA, AND EIHACHIRO NAKAMAE, *Siggraph Art Show*, 1982.

8. POTMESIL, MICHAEL AND INDRANIL CHAKRAVARTY, "Synthetic Image Generation with a Lens and Aperture Camera Model," *ACM Transactions on Graphics*, vol. 1, no. 2, pp. 85-108, April 1982.

9. POTMESIL, MICHAEL AND INDRANIL CHAKRAVARTY, "Modeling Motion Blur in Computer-Generated Images," *Computer Graphics*, vol. 17, no. 3, pp. 389-399, July 1983.

10. ROTH, S. D., "Ray Casting for Modeling Solids," *Computer Graphics and Image Processing*, no. 18, pp. 109-144, 1982.

11. WHITTED, TURNER, "An Improved Illumination Model for Shaded Display," *Communications of the ACM*, vol. 23, pp. 343-349, 1980.

Figure 8. 1984.

PANEL

TRENDS IN SEMICONDUCTOR HARDWARE FOR GRAPHICS SYSTEMS

CHAIR: Henry Fuchs - University of North Carolina

PANEL: John Atwood - Silicon Compilers
         Robert Bruce - Metheus Corporation
         James Clark - Silicon Graphics
         Karl Guttag - Texas Instruments
         Edmund Sun - Weitek

During the next 5 - 10 years, text and
graphic systems will tend to merge because
of the demand for a more productive man/
machine interface, falling memory costs
and the availability of higher performance
VLSI controllers. This panel will discuss
video controllers, memory components and
their architectures, graphic systems configurations and the evolution of enhanced
system performance versus reduced system
cost.

An Adaptive Subdivision Algorithm and Parallel Architecture for Realistic Image Synthesis

Mark Dippé
Berkeley Computer Graphics Laboratory

John Swensen
Computer Science Division

Department of Electrical Engineering
and Computer Sciences
University of California
Berkeley, California 94720
U.S.A.

Abstract

An algorithm for computing ray traced pictures is presented, which adaptively subdivides scenes into S subregions, each with roughly uniform load. It can yield speedups of $O(S^{2/3})$ over the standard algorithm.

This algorithm can be mapped onto a parallel architecture consisting of a three dimensional array of computers which operate autonomously. The algorithm and architecture are well matched, so that communication overhead is small with respect to the computation, for sufficiently complex scenes. This allows close to linear improvements in performance, even with thousands of computers, in addition to the improvement due to subdivision.

The algorithm and architecture provide mechanisms to gracefully degrade in response to excessive load. The architecture also tolerates failures of computers without errors in the computation.

CR Categories and Subject Descriptors: C.1.2 [**Processor Architectures**]: Multiple Data Stream Architectures (Multiprocessors) - *Multiple-instruction-stream, multiple-data-stream processors (MIMD)* I.3.3 [**Computer Graphics**]: Picture/Image Generation - *display algorithms*; I.3.7 [**Computer Graphics**]: Three-dimensional Graphics and Realism - *animation; color, shading, shadowing, and texture; visible line/surface algorithm;*

General Terms: Algorithms

Additional Key Words and Phrases: adaptive, parallel, ray tracing, subdivision

Permission to copy without fee all or part of this material is granted provided that the copies are not made or distributed for direct commercial advantage, the ACM copyright notice and the title of the publication and its date appear, and notice is given that copying is by permission of the Association for Computing Machinery. To copy otherwise, or to republish, requires a fee and/or specific permission.

© 1984   ACM   0-89791-138-5/84/007/0149 $00.75

1. Introduction

Realistic three dimensional image synthesis is computationally very expensive. Rather than becoming less expensive, the use of more realistic techniques with highly complex scenes has increased the cost per image.[12] We are interested in efficient realistic rendering of scenes that change over time, using algorithmic and architectural strategies.

The most viable rendering algorithm to date for creating realistic images is ray tracing, because it models the complex effects of light in an environment more effectively than other existing synthesis techniques.

In the ray tracing model, rays are sent from the eye through each pixel of the picture plane and traced as they are reflected and transmitted by objects in space. When a ray hits an object, new rays may be generated, due to reflection, transmission, and/or relevant light sources. These new rays are in turn traced. The ray tracing process thus forms a tree with the eye at the root and rays as the branches. The initial branch is the ray piercing the picture plane. Internal nodes represent objects intersecting the ray, and leaves represent light sources or rays leaving the picture space. The reader is referred to Turner Whitted's excellent introduction[22] for a more detailed description of ray tracing.

Our approach is to adaptively subdivide the ray tracing process, and to implement this subdivision on parallel hardware.

The three dimensional space of a scene to be rendered is divided into several subregions. Initially the space is divided to assign volume more or less uniformly, and object descriptions are loaded into the appropriate subregions. As computational loads are determined, the space is redistributed among the subregions to maintain uniformity of load.

The rendering process begins when the subregion containing the eye or camera casts rays at the desired image resolution. Associated with each ray is its home pixel, so that the pixel can be appropriately colored after the ray tracing operations are complete. When a ray enters a subregion, it is intersected with the object descriptions contained within the subregion. Rays that exit a subregion are passed to the appropriate neighbor.

Each ray resulting from a ray-object interaction contains the fraction of the ray's contribution to its pixel. This fraction is the product of the fractional value of the impinging ray and the value resulting from the object intersection. Color information associated with the spectral properties of the ray/object interaction is also included.

When a ray terminates, becoming a leaf of the ray tracing tree, the rendered value is added to a frame buffer.

Subregion loads are monitored to determine the need for redistributions of space. When a subregion's load becomes too large relative to its neighbors' loads, a change in subregion definition is initiated.

A parallel architecture implementing this algorithm uses a three dimensional array of computers, each with its own independent memory. Each of the computers is assigned one or more subregions. Neighboring computers contain adjacent subregions, and communicate via a variety of messages. Messages not directed toward an immediate neighbor are passed on in the appropriate direction.

Image quality can be traded off with performance, and to this end, the algorithm and architecture provide various means of degrading to achieve a desired rate of image generation.

2. Adaptive Subdivision Algorithm

The synthesis problem is primarily concerned with the visibility of objects with respect to a viewpoint and with the interaction of light in the environment with these visible objects. Visibility is determined by a two dimensional projection of three dimensional space. Lighting interaction is much more complex in that its effect spans three dimensional space in a non-projective manner.

Previous synthesis techniques can be categorized by their generality of lighting model, and by their use of projective qualities of images.[18]

1) projective: z-buffer, painter, Watkins, priority, Warnock, Franklin[8]

These algorithms render and determine surface visibility primarily in image space, using projective transformations. They effectively model those aspects of the scene that are naturally projective with respect to the viewpoint. However, phenomena that are not directly projective with respect to viewpoint, such as shadows or inter-object reflections, introduce many complications.

2) quasi-projective: shadow polygons,[5] cluster planes, three dimensional cookie cutter[1]

These algorithms operate to a greater degree in three dimensional space. They do this by adding information that is non-projective, such as shadow polygons, and/or by attempting to sort three dimensional space, either by separating planes or by the faces of polygonal objects. However, complexity is increased when shadow polygons are incorporated in the rendering process. In addition, objects are often split, because three dimensional space cannot be easily sorted on the basis of visibility. These algorithms generally prepare the information for an efficient projective solution of the visibility problem.

3) non-projective: ray tracing, hierarchical bounding volumes,[17] wave based algorithms[14]

Algorithms in this group perform image synthesis in three dimensions. Modeling of a general class of lighting effects is facilitated. Hierarchical bounding volumes can be thought of as a modeling operation rather than a rendering one, but it is intimately related to rendering. It is a type of three dimensional subdivision which does not sort but uses containment information to aid in visibility determination. Ray tracing is the primary example of algorithms that inherently operate in three dimensional space, i.e. no projection with respect to viewpoint is necessary. The main disadvantage is that, in general, all of three dimensional space must be considered to arrive at a solution.

The complexity of ray tracing is associated with the testing of rays for intersection with the objects of the scene. The distribution of complexity in space is determined by the distribution of objects, and by the distribution or flow of rays among the objects. A region of space with many objects but with no rays has low complexity, as does a region with many rays but no objects. On the other hand, a region in which many rays are interacting with many objects has very high complexity.

Up to now, most algorithms have subdivided the two dimensional projection of three dimensional space when rendering. Our algorithm is completely non-projective in nature, and subdivides three dimensional space itself. The essential characteristics of the algorithm are:

1) Three dimensional space is divided into several subregions. Object and light source descriptions are distributed among the subregions according to their position. Each of the subregions is processed independently.

2) Rays are cast into three dimensional space and processed in the subregions along their paths. The rays within a particular subregion are tested for intersection with only those objects within that subregion. Rays that exit the subregion are passed to neighboring subregions. The rays are processed until they terminate and become leaves of the ray tracing tree.

3) The shapes of the subregions are adaptively controlled to maintain a roughly uniform distribution of load.

For any given ray, we only consider subregions along the path of the ray, and ignore all others. Thus, the problem is reduced from considering all objects, to considering only those objects along the one dimensional ray.

The three dimensional method for subdividing the ray tracing problem can be applied to the general image synthesis problem. The parameters can be thought of as:

1) objects, and

2) distribution of light through space.

The problem is to find the visual stimulus from such a world.

2.1. Subregions

There are several issues concerning the shape of the subregions that subdivide space:

1) the complexity of subdividing the problem, e.g. intersecting objects or rays with the boundaries,

2) the ability to subdivide space without splitting objects, and

3) the uniformity of the distributed loads attainable with the shape.

The complexity of scenes is certainly not uniform, but varies according to the characteristics of the components of the scene. Our subregions do not divide space uniformly, but allow arbitrary subdivisions of space within the topological and geometrical constraints of the subregions. This provides us with a very powerful technique with which to subdivide the space to accommodate non-uniform complexity. The ability to dedicate processing power where complexity is concentrated and not waste it where it is unneeded is one of the fundamental aspects of the system.

Among the polyhedral shapes which could bound the subregions, the three most promising candidates are orthogonal parallelepipeds, "general cubes", and tetrahedra. More general shapes such as quadric surfaces are under investigation and may be useful in the future, but are not considered in this paper.

The most intuitively simple polyhedra are orthogonal parallelepipeds, which are constrained to have all boundaries parallel or perpendicular to the major axes. Figure 1a shows a two dimensional analog of orthogonal parallelepipeds. As subregions grow and shrink to redistribute the complexity of the scene, the boundaries remain orthogonal, and the subregions remain convex.

Boundary-intersection testing for orthogonal parallelepipeds is not a significant overhead. However, the orthogonality constraint does not allow local adjustments to a subregion to be made without affecting many other subregions, and in general, a scene's computational complexity will be less uniformly distributed than with more general boundaries. Unless either very few basic objects are contained in each subregion, or the scene has a uniform distribution of complexity over space, the low overhead of orthogonal parallelepipeds is unlikely to offset their greater non-uniformity of load.

General cubes resemble the familiar cube, except they have relaxed constraints on planarity of faces and on convexity. 2-D analogs of general cubes are shown in figure 1b.

With these relaxed constraints, the complexity of boundary testing is increased over that for the orthogonal polyhedra, and hence the overhead for each subregion is increased. However, general cubes allow much more local control of subregion shape, with the consequence that more uniform distributions of load can be achieved than with orthogonal subregions. Furthermore, the redistributions can be performed locally.

Tetrahedra are the simplest shapes, and are inherently convex. A space-filling collection of tetrahedra can be constructed with groups of six tetrahedra forming a cube, which are then arranged to fill space. The boundary of each subregion is defined by its four corners, and the interface with two neighboring subregions is defined by three of these corners. Figure 1c shows an analog of

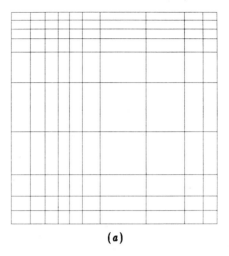

(a)

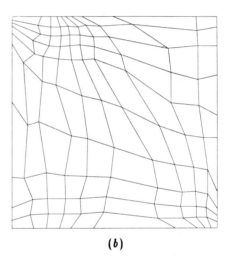

(b)

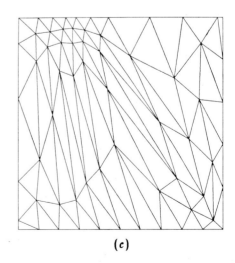

(c)

Figure 1. 2-D analogs of orthogonal parallelepipeds, general cubes, and tetrahedra, simulated with the same load.

tetrahedral subregions.

Tetrahedra have fewer boundaries than cubes, so the overhead of boundary testing is lower for them than for general cubes. They allow local control of subregion shape, but because vertices are shared among more subregions with tetrahedra than with general cubes, the control cannot be as local. Because tetrahedra have fewer vertices than cubes, they may not contain subregion-sized objects as well.

Simple, fixed connectivities have been assumed throughout the discussion. We have also considered arbitrary topologies for the subregions. However, fixed connectivities allow simpler calculations for the determination of how rays move among subregions, and the tradeoffs between more general topologies and shapes have yet to be fully determined. For these reasons, we only discuss arrays of general cubes for the remainder of the paper.

Given the basic scenario of how the subdivision algorithm operates and how space is subdivided, how do we carry out an actual subdivision to yield a uniform distribution of the problem? A direct optimal solution requires global knowledge, and is quite difficult. We would like to avoid these problems if possible.

Our solution is to allow neighboring subregions to share each others' load information, and to allow relatively more loaded subregions to adjust their boundaries to reduce load. This mechanism is a feedback scheme. It also provides a mechanism for adapting to the changing complexity of a scene in a distributed manner.

2.2. Adaptive Redistribution

It is difficult to calculate the distribution of load without actually simulating the ray tracing process. The algorithm redistributes the load among the subregions to adapt to changing conditions induced by the movement of objects, lights, the eye or camera, and other time varying behavior.

Load is redistributed by moving the points defining subregions and passing the object information as needed. The load of each subregion is compared to that of its neighbors. When a subregion's load is higher than its neighbors, some load should be transferred to them. More general relative load measures can also be used.

The load metric is determined primarily by the product of

1) number of objects and their complexity, and

2) number of rays.

Load is transferred by moving corners of a subregion. To simplify matters we only move one corner at a time. The corner's new position is chosen such that enough volume is transferred to equalize loads.

Once the new position for a corner of a subregion has been determined, object descriptions and other information are redistributed to reflect the new subdivision.

If the scene being rendered is too complex, then redistribution cannot entirely alleviate the problem. In such a case, degradation techniques must be applied. These techniques are discussed later.

This is a simplified scenario of the redistribution process, some of the more difficult points of which we discuss in the following section.

2.2.1. More Sophisticated Approaches

Subregions with elongated shapes, or those which are very concave, may cause rays to pass through more subregions than would be necessary with fatter, convex subregions. The load metric reflects the undesirability of elongated or concave subregions. When a subregion becomes too undesirable in shape, its load can be increased by a factor indicating its desire to become shapely. This more general framework will allow subregions to become unshapely when it is advantageous, while maintaining shapely subregions in general.

When selecting a corner of a subregion to move, we must take into account the difficulty involved in shifting the load; it may be easier to transfer load from one corner than another. We also wish to transfer the load differently to each of the affected neighbors, with more of the load going to those that are least loaded. Another important constraint on redistribution is to minimize the splitting of objects among neighboring subregions. This can be done relatively easily, because the overloaded subregion which is exporting objects can choose the new position of a corner to avoid splitting. In addition, by subdividing the subregions into smaller regions, within which statistics are kept about object distribution and ray flow, more precise decisions about object splitting and load movement can be made.

Our mechanisms for redistribution will not necessarily produce exactly uniform load distributions; this is tolerable, as long as the differences in load are small percentages of the average.

We would like to avoid oscillations in the redistribution process. Small oscillations can be damped by adding hysteresis so that load disparities of a certain size are required before a redistribution is allowed. Instability due to the shuffling of large objects across boundaries can also be detected and limited.

Global information about the distribution of loads is maintained, and is used to direct effective redistribution. When loads are highly disparate, large transfers of load are used. As the disparity decreases, smaller loads are transferred.

There are many subtle issues involved with the redistribution process, and further analyses and experiments must be performed to determine the best choices for this application. We hope to complete these studies in the near future.

3. Parallel Architecture

Our parallel implementation of the algorithm uses independent computers, each communicating with a few neighbors. Computers are responsible for one or more subregions and communicate with neighboring computers using messages. To simplify the discussion, we assume one subregion per computer.

Computers handle all rays and redistributions affecting their subregions. They have several other tasks as well. Messages may be sent to non-neighboring computers by passing them through intervening computers. Thus, computers must route messages.

Computers at the boundary of the array handle infinite extents of space. They also have fewer neighbors than those in the center, and so they are logical candidates to manage auxiliary storage devices and network interfaces. Computers in the center would access these devices via requests through messages. Because we do not want a direct connection to a frame buffer for each computer, the frame buffer will be connected to boundary computers and accessed via messages.

Besides the special role of disk and frame buffer connections for boundary computers, there are other special roles that certain other computers have:

1) The computer containing the eye or camera must cast the initial rays for each frame.

2) Interface and monitoring tasks, assigned to some computers, are used for dealing with user controlled system parameters as well as any other global tasks, such as initially distributing the image description or watching the system load as a whole and changing certain parameters automatically in response to load changes.

The parallelization of the image synthesis problem is based on subdivision of three dimensional space into adjacent polyhedral regions. The computers responsible for the subregions operate independently, adaptively redistributing the space as loads are determined, and gracefully degrading if their load is too large.

3.1. Architectural Perspective

A number of special purpose graphics engines and systems have been proposed and/or built. We briefly describe some of this work in the context of our architecture.

3.1.1. Multicomputers

The LINKS-1[15] multicomputer has been built to generate ray traced pictures. It consists of 64 unit computers, each of which is connected to two neighbor computers, a root computer, and a result collection computer. The root computer controls the system and facilitates non-neighbor communication among computers.

This topology allows work to be distributed by the root computer so that it can be performed independently in parallel, or pipelined from neighbor to neighbor, or some combination of both. Unfortunately, if scene descriptions are too complex to be duplicated in each computer's memory, then substantial communication among the computers is required, but this is hindered by the restricted connection topology. Furthermore, expansion of the system will be limited by the use of the global root and collection computers.

Recent work by other researchers[4,20] has also addressed the application of parallelism to ray tracing. They consider geometrically uniform, orthogonal subdivisions of space. Both efforts favor two dimensional arrays of computers over three dimensional arrays.

However, they do not address the issues of achieving uniform load distribution over the subregions. The ability to adaptively redistribute over time is crucial to the success of this approach, not only because of temporal changes in the scene, but because load distributions are extremely difficult to calculate without actually simulating the ray tracing process.

3.1.2. Graphics Engines and Sub-processors

Clark uses twelve of his specialized VLSI processors, Geometry Engines,[11] to perform the floating point calculations necessary for geometric calculations prior to the rendering process. These types of operations are also useful for ray tracing operations, and similar hardware should be eventually be included in our system. However, we feel that because of the experimental nature of our system, hardware complexity should initially be applied to support general purpose processing, at the expense of special purpose operations.

Fiume and Fournier[7] describe a multiprocessor architecture which processes spans of scanlines using parallel processors, allowing some degree of anti-aliasing to be performed in each processor. The Pixel Planes system developed by Fuchs[9] uses a 1-bit processor per small number of pixels to perform scan-conversion and hidden-surface elimination on a per-polygon basis, using a z-buffer technique. In Pixel Planes, polygons are broadcast to the array of processors, one at a time, and are processed in parallel. The applicable algorithms for both of these architectures are by nature restricted to projected image space, and are not appropriate for our application.

A number of processor per polygon architectures have been proposed.[10,21] These determine surface visibility at the pixel level using a number of depth comparators. As these have all worked in projected image space, they are also not appropriate for our approach.

3.2. The Nature of the Parallelization

A ray crossing the three-dimensional array of computers can pass over many computers, so global information about the system may be old. In particular, knowledge that all computers have completed their ray tracing operations may be out of date.

Rather than wait for messages to propagate, we adjust the computation so that all computers complete at approximately the same time. This has the consequence that new frames might be started before older frames have finished. This is not a problem, because minor variations can be absorbed by allowing computations on old frames to continue after newer frames begin. Ray tracing and frame buffer updating can overlap if several image frames are stored. In this way, late updates to frames can be made before displaying them.

3.3. Parallel Redistribution

Messages are used to initiate a redistribution. Each computer has 26 neighboring computers, even though it is only directly connected to 6, and each corner is shared among 8 computers. Thus, the load and redistribution messages must be routed through neighbors to allow complete determination of redistribution parameters for each computer (see figure 2). Load and redistribution messages will contain routing information to speed up the process.

In addition to object information and ray flow within a computer, other factors are related to load in the parallel architecture:

1) the number of messages dealt with,

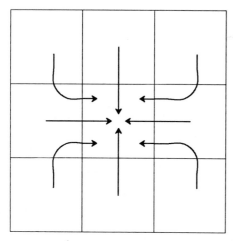

Figure 2. Load message routing.

2) the size of message queues (this measures how far behind a computer is, relative to its neighbors), and

3) idle time.

There other possible factors which are under investigation.

Once the computer has determined the new position for a corner, it sends out redistribution messages and begins passing objects and other information. To handle ties between two computers which decide to move the same corner at the same time, each computer is assigned a priority according to its position in the array.

If an overloaded computer's neighbors are also overloaded, so that no load transfers can take place, the computer must reduce its load using the degradation techniques discussed later.

To ensure that redistributions are carried out as quickly as possible, computers check their message queues periodically. If a redistribution message is found, it is acted upon immediately.

Note that the redistribution process is carried out in a local manner without a complex protocol.

3.4. Messages

We list some of the different messages and their fields:

1) ray: pixel, point of origin, direction, percentage of contribution to the pixel of this ray, color parameters of the ray

2) pixel: address, value

3) global parameter: name, value; for instance there is a message that tells the computer containing the eye or camera whether or not to send out the initial rays and perform rendering

4) object information: description; general objects such as splines,[2] fractals,[13] or blobby models[3] will be handled

5) disk i/o: request type, associated data

6) load value: computer ID, value, and possibly volume information for redistribution purposes; these messages are copied to a monitoring computer for global load statistics tracking

7) redistribution notification: corner to move, new location, routing information

By monitoring the messages being passed as well as examining load messages, the performance of the system can be easily measured. Thus, messages form a direct basis for evaluating the system.

4. Performance Degradation

If our algorithm/architecture is to be successful in an interactive environment, it must allow performance to degrade gracefully. Since any machine constructed must be finite, some problems will exceed its resources, and degradation will be unavoidable. If a computer is unable to reduce its load by moving boundaries, it can decrease its load by more drastic means.

One possible load-reducing action is to delete ray messages in a controlled manner, until a computer can keep up with the desired frame rate. This amounts to a local reduction in the height of the ray tracing tree. Messages significantly older than the youngest received message would be logical candidates for deletion. Some messages, such as disk requests, should not be deleted.

At a more global level, the image resolution or the depth of the ray tracing tree can be reduced, creating fewer rays, at the expense of less realistic simulation. In addition, the level of detail for rendering of objects can be reduced; for example, splines or fractals might be subdivided into fewer polygons.

Generally, the small errors in pixel intensity these degradation measures introduce will be visually tolerable. If they are not acceptable, the total workload must be decreased by reducing the rate of image generation.

By allowing a user to trade image quality for speed, an extremely effective tool for practical image synthesis is provided.

These adaptivity parameters may be controlled by the user, or by a computer which has been gathering statistics. They are used to tune the performance of the system.

5. Analysis

Symbol	Meaning
B	number of objects
C	number of parallel computers
D	depth of ray tracing tree
L	number of lights
N	number of rays from an object interaction
R	number of rays
S	number of subregions
β	boundary-intersection cost
κ	co-resident object overhead
ν	non-uniform distribution cost
π	ray passing overhead
σ	pixel energy summation cost
τ	subregion traversal overhead

We analyze the standard ray tracing algorithm, the adaptive subdivision algorithm, and the parallel architecture. Our coupled parallel implementation is also compared with a frame-parallel implementation.

The cycle counts for data transfers and floating point operations assume the computers are implemented using microprocessors augmented with floating point chips. Computers with faster floating point speeds will also tend to have wider data paths, so the relative speeds of arithmetic operations and data transfers will be similar.

5.1. Standard Algorithm

To perform ray tracing, rays are cast into a scene, and are tested for intersection with each object in the scene. As a result of an intersection, each ray may produce 0, 1, or more offspring, depending on the reflective and refractive properties of the objects, as well as the number of light sources. In a highly reflective environment, several levels of interaction testing - new ray generation must be performed for a realistic rendering.

We assume the ray tracing tree generated by recursive reflection/refraction rays is a complete tree of depth D. It has R_i nodes at each level, where $R_{i+1} = R_i N$ and N corresponds to the average number of rays produced by a ray-object interaction. The total number of arcs in this tree is given by

$$R_0 \sum_{i=0}^{D-1} N^i = R_0 \left(\frac{N^D - 1}{N-1} \right),$$

where R_0 is the number of pixels, typically 512^2 to 1024^2. In addition to recursive rays, rays to light sources are cast at each node, so the total number of rays is

$$R \approx R_0 \left(\frac{N^D - 1}{N-1} \right) (1 + L),$$

where L is the number of light sources. We assume 10% of the intersections transmit rays, as well as reflect them. In addition, we consider two light sources and 500×500 pixels, and a ray tracing tree of depth 5 (a depth of 4 has been used to produce reasonable pictures). Thus, $N = 1.1$, $L = 2$, $R_0 = 250000$, and $D = 5$, so that the total number of rays is

$$R = 2.5 \times 10^5 \frac{(1.1^5 - 1)}{(1.1 - 1)} (1 + 2) \approx 4.6 \times 10^6.$$

The number of ray tracing operations for the standard algorithm is RB, for B objects, and if $B = 1000$, 4.6×10^9 ray tracing operations must be performed.

The cost of each ray tracing operation depends on the complexity of the objects; while a sphere is almost trivial to intersect with rays, a fractal object can be extremely costly. We assume a basic object which has roughly the same complexity as 250 triangles represented using a Rubin-Whitted[17] style model. This is a reasonable unit of object complexity, but is still simpler than many object models used today. When a ray is tested against one of our basic objects, we assume it will almost always be rejected after one bounding volume intersection test, at a cost of the equivalent of 25 floating point multiplications, which each require 100 cycles to execute. Thus a basic object requires about 2500 machine cycles to test for intersection with a ray, on the average.

5.2. Subdivision Algorithm

Testing each ray against each object can be avoided by adaptively subdividing the scene into a number of subregions, each with approximately the same load, and checking only the objects within the subregions along the ray's path. The algorithm for computing the image performs the ray tracing operations within the restricted domain of the subregions.

Subdividing space distributes load so that it is roughly uniform, but has accompanying overhead. We discuss the sources of the overhead before continuing with the analysis.

Breaking space up into subregions forces rays to pass through several subregions in order to cross the entire space; this traversal cost is τ. If the subregions are well-shaped, τ is bounded by $3S^{1/3}$. Each ray may be processed up to τ times, but this has no effect on the total number of rays.

Each ray must be tested for intersection not only with each object in the subregion, but with the boundaries as well, because a ray may intersect an object at a point outside the subregion, even though the object is partially inside the subregion. This adds a cost of β for each subregion, which is about the same as testing 4 basic objects.

Although our redistribution algorithm tries to avoid splitting objects across subregion boundaries, some splitting will be unavoidable, so some testing will be duplicated. If κ is the co-residency cost, this is as if there were κ times as many non-co-resident basic objects. For a scene consisting of a single sphere, κ could be S, but this type of scene is inappropriate for our algorithm. If instead we assume complex objects, such as spline surfaces, the amount of testing duplication may be small. Such object models are usually expanded into more primitive representations (e.g. triangles), and these expanded representations are distributed among the subregions. Determination of realistic values for κ require further investigation.

The number of ray tracing operations required to compute an image using the improved algorithm is the sum, over all subregions, of the traversal cost for each ray, times the number of rays in the subregion, times the sum of the objects in the subregions (including co-residency) and the boundary testing cost:

$$\sum_S \tau R_S (\kappa B_S + \beta).$$

If the distribution of load is uniform over all the subregions, then $R_S B_S$ is the same for all subregions. Using the arithmetic-geometric mean inequality,[16] it can be shown that

$$R_S B_S \leq RB / S^2.$$

Therefore, the number of ray tracing operations is bounded by

$$\sum_S \frac{\tau R (\kappa B + \beta S)}{S^2} = \frac{\tau R (\kappa B + \beta S)}{S}.$$

Assuming β is 4, τ is $S^{1/3}$, $S = 125$, and ignoring κ, we have

$$\frac{5 \times 4.6 \times 10^6 (10^3 + 4 \times 125)}{125} \approx 2.8 \times 10^8.$$

This is an order of magnitude improvement over the standard algorithm. As long as κ is less than 10, this algorithm is faster than the standard algorithm. Note that B must be greater than S if the speedup is to be large; otherwise the overhead of boundary testing will become significant.

Assuming complex scenes, boundary testing overhead is small relative to object intersection calculations. Under these conditions, the cost reduces to

$$\frac{\kappa \tau RB}{S} \approx \frac{\kappa S^{1/3}RB}{S} = \kappa RBS^{-2/3}.$$

Thus we obtain an $O(S^{2/3})$ speedup over the standard algorithm.

5.3. Parallel Architecture

In a parallel implementation of the algorithm, each computer is responsible for one or more subregions. We consider the limiting case of one subregion per computer.

Each ray may in the worst case be passed across a subregion boundary after each iteration. The cost, π, of passing a ray is less than 1/5 the cost of one basic object intersection, assuming a 100-byte ray message can be copied in 400 cycles or less.

When ray tracing is carried out in parallel, the pixel energies are distributed among all the computers, and must be collected before they can be sent to a frame buffer. In the worst case, one half of all rays will contribute to pixel intensities, and if the ten-byte energy messages are sent across at most $C^{1/3}$ computers, at a cost of 50 cycles per message per computer, the energy summation cost, σ, is $25RC^{1/3}$ cycles for all computers, or roughly $25RC^{-5/3}$ for each computer. The ratio of σ to the ray tracing cost per computer is less than 1%, and therefore σ can be ignored.

Unlike σ, the ray passing overhead must be included in the cost of a parallel implementation. The worst case number of ray tracing operations performed by each computer is bounded by

$$\max_{C} \{ \tau R_C (\kappa B_C + \beta + \pi) \}.$$

If a uniform distribution of load can be achieved, then the worst case number of ray tracing operations per computer is

$$\frac{\tau R (\kappa B + \beta C + \pi C)}{C^2}.$$

When we substitute the same values as before (again ignoring κ), with $C = 125$ and $\pi = 1/5$, we get

$$\frac{5 \times 4.6 \times 10^6 (10^3 + 4 \times 125 + .2 \times 125)}{125^2} \approx 2.3 \times 10^6.$$

This is three orders of magnitude faster than the standard algorithm, due to both the $C^{2/3}$ factor from the subdivision, and the linear speedup from the C computers.

In general, loads will not be completely uniform. The cost, ν, of this non-uniformity is proportional to the ratio of the maximum load for any computer to the average load over all computers. This changes the number of ray tracing operations to

$$\frac{\nu \tau R (\kappa B + \beta C + \pi C)}{C^2}.$$

Accurate estimates of ν will require more extensive analysis, although preliminary studies indicate that values below 2 can be achieved for some scenes.

We have demonstrated speedups of $S^{2/3}$ due to subdivision, and C due to parallelism, with some loss due to ν, κ, β, and π. These improvements will increase with scene complexity.

5.4. Comparison of Coupled and Frame-Parallel Implementations

In justifying a specialized architecture, we must show that the performance of the coupled parallel architecture will exceed that of an equivalent number of independent computers assigned to the problem. In particular, when producing films of computer-generated images, an obvious exploitation of parallelism is to assign to each computer the task of generating a single frame, and let them compute independently, using a serial implementation of our new algorithm, or the standard algorithm. We compare this alternate parallel strategy to our parallelization.

5.4.1. Storage Requirements

The new algorithm implemented on the parallel architecture requires considerably more storage than a standard implementation. With the frame-parallel implementation, each pixel's tree of rays may be traced separately, and by traversing each tree of rays in depth-first order, very few rays need to be maintained in storage. With our parallel implementation, the entire ray tracing tree is traced concurrently, and is traversed in breadth-first order.

All objects must generally be maintained in local storage for a frame-parallel implementation, as each ray must be tested against all objects. When the new algorithm is implemented on our coupled parallel architecture, all objects must be held in some local memory, but they are distributed among all computers; each computer has on the order of B/C objects in its memory, on the average.

Each computer of the coupled parallel architecture need only be configured with on the order of $1/C$ times the data memory of a single computer, with consequent savings in addressing and decoding hardware, and memory management tables. However, if frame-parallelism is used, the C independent computers would each require separate image stores and access to a full memory complement, so that C times as much total memory could be required. Were a memory hierarchy using disk backing store used, the additional cost of many disk units, as well as the time penalty of remote access would be incurred.

Therefore, the coupled parallel architecture can use less total storage than as many frame-parallel computers running serial algorithms.

5.4.2. Storage Structures

For independent computers, it is assumed that memory is implemented in the standard hierarchy of paging disk / main memory / (possibly) cache memory. As always, performance will be severely degraded if the program's working sets do not fit in the appropriate memory.

A dense interconnection of the coupled parallel architecture does not allow convenient communication between computers and disk memory. Assuming only computers at the boundaries of the architecture are connected to backing-store devices, most disk accesses must pass through several other computers. This of course increases the cost of paging, and in order for coupled parallel computers to achieve memory performance similar to that of the independent parallel computers, a relatively higher ratio of local memory to problem size is necessary; sufficient local memory is crucial to this architecture.

6. System Considerations

An initial implementation of a parallel system would consist of eight computers, each managing one or more subregions. With so few computers, each would communicate with only three others, instead of six, as discussed earlier. One computer would communicate with a host computer, which would provide interactive control and access to disk storage. Another computer would communicate either with a frame buffer, or with a host connected to the frame buffer.

Each computer would consist of a commercial microprocessor with floating point support, 1/4 to 1/2 megabytes of RAM, and six unidirectional byte-parallel ports (possibly with DMA access to memory). Those computers communicating with a host or frame buffer would have additional ports. Each computer would run with its own clock, independent of the others.

After performing studies with the initial implementation to verify costs of communication, redistribution, etc., a larger system could be constructed. With larger systems, each computer would communicate with six neighbors or peripheral devices, and dedicated frame buffers and disks would be used.

An obvious physical topology for such a system would be an array of cubical modules, appropriately interconnected. However, this topology would not allow convenient access to central computers for debugging during operation.

An alternate topology resembles the layout of the CDC 6600,[19] with a number of panels fanning out from a central core. Each panel would house several subregion computers and their cooling. Inter-panel communication would be routed through the core, and because the topology is relatively compact, inter-computer communication times should be small. If panels were attached to the core with hinges, they could be spread apart to allow a technician to access all computers during operation.

As an alternative to many medium-speed computers, a few very fast computers could be used, such as the multiprocessor Cray X/MP. A two-processor version of the algorithm would have multiple subregions managed by each processor. Inter-processor communication would make use of the high speed inter-CPU data paths available on the Cray X/MP. The extreme speed of the CPUs would allow studies to be performed in a reasonable period of time, including efficient simulations of different topologies.

6.1. Hardware Issues

The parallel architecture for this algorithm allows high bandwidth, inexpensive communication among the computers, tolerance of computer failures, and great flexibility in the choice of CPU.

Messages are sent between neighboring computers via dedicated links, which allows each communication to be independent of all other computers. Because links are not shared, all communication can run in parallel, and very simple hardware and protocols can be used for them.

This lack of sharing also allows failed or uncooperating computers to be ignored by other computers, so failures are localized at the computer, and do not propagate into the system. Furthermore, there are simple extensions to the adaptive subdivision algorithm which allow subregions lost to failed computers to be adopted by healthy neighbors.

The algorithms executed in each computer are general purpose, and require no special-purpose hardware. Consequently, any processor with a large address space and support for floating point computations can be used. This would allow development of a prototype using commercial microprocessors, while leaving the option of later upgrading to more sophisticated microprocessors, other CPUs, or special purpose ray tracing hardware, as appropriate, with virtually no impact on software.

7. Conclusions

We have presented an adaptive subdivision algorithm and a parallel architecture for the image synthesis problem. The algorithm provides a roughly uniform distribution of load among the computers. Degradation in response to overloading is also part of the system, ensuring that cost/quality tradeoffs in image generation can easily be made. The architecture has a fixed polyhedral connectivity, with communication between computers via messages. Failures of computers are tolerated by the system without loss of accuracy, and without severe degradation of performance.

The algorithm can yield performance improvements on the order of $S^{2/3}$, and the parallelization itself will provide linear gains in the number of computers used (i.e. C computers can reduce actual compute time by a factor of C). Since messages are directly correlated with load,

Figure 3. Image generated by a preliminary simulator.

simulation and performance analysis of the system is simplified. We are carrying out such simulations at the current time (figure 3).

The adaptive nature of the system is a very important property, and we are examining other techniques for adaptive control of the synthesis problem. In addition, the synchronic nature of the parallelization may provide additional improvements.

It is interesting to note that a two dimensional analog of our algorithm/architecture can be applied to the projective style of image synthesis. While subdivision of projective solutions has been studied to a great extent, the adaptability of our algorithm and the high degree of parallelism in the architecture will provide new performance gains.

There are many issues left to be resolved, but some, such as antialiasing of the subdivision algorithm,[6] have already been addressed. The algorithm is also applicable to the general image synthesis problem, and we are investigating new methods for increased realism within this framework.

Acknowledgments

We would like to thank the anonymous referees, as well as Brain Barsky, Rick Speer, Steve Upstill, Helena Winkler, and Princess Minnie for their careful readings and helpful criticisms and comments on this paper. A special thanks to E.B. for the *Lemma in Eb minor*, and a host of others, for wagging the appropriate tails.

This work was supported in part by the National Science Foundation, under grant number ECS–8204381, the Semiconductor Research Corporation under grant number 82–11–008, and Lawrence Livermore National Laboratories under grant number LLL–4695505.

References

1. Peter R. Atherton, Kevin J. Weiler, and Donald P. Greenberg, "Polygon Shadow Generation," pp. 275-281 in *SIGGRAPH '78 Conference Proceedings*, ACM,(August, 1978).

2. Richard H. Bartels, John C. Beatty, and Brian A. Barsky, *An Introduction to the Use of Splines in Computer Graphics*, Technical Report No. UCB/CSD 83/136, Computer Science Division, Electrical Engineering and Computer Sciences Department, University of California, Berkeley, California, USA. (August, 1983). Also Tech. Report No. CS-83-9, Department of Computer Science, University of Waterloo, Waterloo, Ontario, Canada.

3. James F. Blinn, "A Generalization of Algebraic Surface Drawing," *ACM Transactions on Graphics*, Vol. 1, No. 3, July, 1982, pp. 235-256. Also published in *SIGGRAPH '82 Conference Proceedings* (Vol. 16, No. 3),

4. John G. Cleary, Brian Wyvill, Graham M. Birtwistle, and Reddy Vatti, *Multiprocessor Ray Tracing*, Technical Report No. 83/128/17, Department of Computer Science, The University of Calgary (October, 1983).

5. Franklin C. Crow, "Shadow Algorithms for Computer Graphics," pp. 242-248 in *SIGGRAPH '77 Conference Proceedings*, ACM,(July, 1977).

6. Mark E. Dippé, *Spatiotemporal Functional Prefiltering*, Ph.D. Thesis, University of California, Berkeley, California (1984).

7. Eugene Fiume, Alain Fournier, and Larry Rudolph, "A Parallel Scan Conversion Algorithm with Anti-Aliasing for a General-Purpose Ultracomputer: Preliminary Report," pp. 11-21 in *Proceedings Graphics Interface '83*, (May, 1983).

8. W. Randolph Franklin, "A Linear Time Exact Hidden Surface Algorithm," pp. 117-123 in *SIGGRAPH '80 Conference Proceedings*, ACM,(July, 1980).

9. Fuchs, H. and Poulton, J., "Pixel-Planes: A VLSI-Oriented Design for a Raster Graphics Engine," *VLSI Design*. No. 3, 1981, pp. 20-28.

10. Fussell, D. and Rathi, B., "A VLSI-Oriented Architecture for Real-Time Display of Shaded Polygons," pp. 373-380 in *Graphics Interface '82*, (1982).

11. Clark, James H., "The Geometry Engine: A VLSI System for Graphics," pp. 127-133 in *SIGGRAPH '82 Conference Proceedings*, (July, 1982).

12. Roy A. Hall and Donald P. Greenberg, "A Testbed for Realistic Image Synthesis," *IEEE Computer Graphics and Applications*, Vol. 3, No. 8, November, 1983, pp. 10-19.

13. James T. Kajiya, "New Techniques for Raytracing Procedurally Defined Objects," *ACM Transactions on Graphics*, Vol. 2, No. 3, July, 1983, pp. 161-181.

14. Hans P. Moravec, "3D Graphics and the Wave Theory," pp. 289-296 in *SIGGRAPH '81 Conference Proceedings*, (August, 1981).

15. H. Nishimura, H. Ohno, T. Kawata, I. Shirakawa, and K. Omura, "LINKS-1: A Parallel Pipelined Multimicrocomputer System for Image Creation," pp. 387-394 in *Proceedings of the 10th Symposium on Computer Architecture*, SIGARCH,(1983).

16. George Pólya and Gabor Szegö, *Problems and Theorems in Analysis I*, Springer-Verlag, New York (1972).

17. Steven M. Rubin and J. Turner Whitted, "A 3-Dimensional Representation for Fast Rendering of Complex Scenes," pp. 110-116 in *SIGGRAPH '80 Conference Proceedings*, ACM,(July, 1980).

18. Ivan E. Sutherland, Robert F. Sproull, and Robert A. Schumacker, "A Characterization of Ten Hidden Surface Algorithms," *ACM Computing Surveys*, Vol. 6, No. 1, March, 1974, pp. 1-55.

19. J. E. Thornton, *Design of a Computer: The Control Data 6600*, Scott, Foresman and Company, Glenview, Illinois (1970).

20. Michael Ullner, *Parallel Machines for Computer Graphics*, Ph.D. Thesis, California Institute of Technology, Pasadena, California (1983).

21. Weinberg, Richard, "Parallel Processing Image Synthesis and Anti-Aliasing," pp. 55-62 in *SIGGRAPH '81 Conference Proceedings*, (August, 1981).

22. J. Turner Whitted, "An Improved Illumination Model for Shaded Display," *Communications of the ACM*, Vol. 23, No. 6, June, 1980, pp. 343-349.

RAY TRACING OF STEINER PATCHES

Thomas W. Sederberg
Department of Civil Engineering
Brigham Young University
Provo, Utah 84602

David C. Anderson
School of Mechanical Engineering
Purdue University
West Lafayette, Indiana 47907

ABSTRACT

Steiner patches are triangular surface patches for which the Cartesian coordinates of points on the patch are defined parametrically by quadratic polynomial functions of two variables. It has recently been shown that it is possible to express a Steiner patch in an implicit equation which is a degree four polynomial in x,y,z. Furthermore, the parameters of a point known to be on the surface can be computed as rational polynomial functions of x,y,z. These findings lead to a straightforward algorithm for ray tracing Steiner patches in which the ray intersection equation is a degree four polynomial in the parameter of the ray. The algorithm presented represents a major simplification over existing techniques for ray tracing free-form surface patches.

CR Categories and Subject Descriptions: I3.5 [Computer Graphics]: Computational Geometry and Object Modeling - Surface Representations;

Additional Keywords and Phrases: Display Algorithms, Algebraic Geometry.

This research was supported in part by Control Data Corporation Grant No. 81PO4.

Permission to copy without fee all or part of this material is granted provided that the copies are not made or distributed for direct commercial advantage, the ACM copyright notice and the title of the publication and its date appear, and notice is given that copying is by permission of the Association for Computing Machinery. To copy otherwise, or to republish, requires a fee and/or specific permission.

© 1984   ACM   0-89791-138-5/84/007/0159 $00.75

1. INTRODUCTION

Ray tracing is a technique for generating images of three dimensional data with a computer. Programs using ray tracing can simulate the effects of reflection, refraction and shadows to produce computer images that possess a strikingly high degree of realism. In addition, ray tracing algorithms are simple to program compared to most other rendering schemes.

Most of the execution time in a ray tracing program involves the computation of the intersection of a ray with a surface of an object. Consequently, the time required to ray trace an image is proportional to the time required to compute the intersection of each of the surfaces in the scene with a ray. This generally means that the feasibility of using a given surface in a ray traced scene depends on how quickly and reliably the surface can be intersected with a ray.

The class of surfaces simplest to ray trace are those defined implicitly by a function $f(x,y,z)=0$. In this case, the ray intersection equation can be obtained easily by expressing the ray as $x=x_0+x_1\alpha$, $y=y_0+y_1\alpha$ and $z=z_0+z_1\alpha$ which when substituted into the implicit surface equation results in a function $g(\alpha)=0$. The variable α is the ray parameter which is proportional to distance from the eye (or from a point of reflection, etc.). Consequently, only the positive real roots of $g(\alpha)$ have any significance. Those roots can be found using standard numerical techniques. It may be impossible in the case of some non-polynomial functions $g(\alpha)=0$ to be certain that all roots have been found. For algebraic surfaces, however, $f(x,y,z)$ and $g(\alpha)$ are polynomials and the roots of $g(\alpha)=0$ are particularly easy to compute [4]. References [1] and [2] discuss ray tracing of certain useful surfaces for which the defining function $f(x,y,z)$ is not a polynomial.

Free-form surface patches are not ray traced as easily as algebraic surfaces. Free-form surface patches are defined by $x=x(s,t)$, $y=y(s,t)$ and $z=z(s,t)$ where $x(s,t)$, $y(s,t)$ and $z(s,t)$ are polynomials in the parameters s and t. The intersection of a free-form surface with a ray can be performed using numerical root-finding and optimization techniques, such as minimizing the angle between the ray and a line from the ray origin to a point on the surface [3]. Kajiya [6] pioneered the application of algebraic methods to ray tracing free-form surface patches. His approach was to define the ray as the intersection of two planes. Each plane intersects the surface in a curve in parameter space, and the two intersection curves intersect in a set of points in parameter space which map to the points of intersection of the ray with the surface.

This paper discusses an algorithm for ray tracing the simplest free-form surface patch: the Steiner patch. The Steiner patch is defined by functions $x(s,t)$, $y(s,t)$, $z(s,t)$ which are quadratic polynomials in the parameters s and t. It has recently been shown that any free-form surface patch can be expressed in an implicit algebraic equation $f(x,y,z)=0$ [8] and that Steiner patches are particularly simple to convert to that form [9]. Furthermore, the parameter of a point known to lie on the Steiner surface can be computed using closed form rational polynomial equations in x, y and z. These capabilities make it possible to ray trace a Steiner parametric free-form surface as easily as an algebraic surface.

The paper begins by reviewing the theory from [9] regarding parametric to implicit conversion of Steiner patches. Then it is shown that an intermediate form which is produced during the implicitization process is well suited to generating the ray intersection equation. Numerical considerations are also discussed.

2. STEINER PATCHES

Steiner patches can be defined by a Bezier control net consisting of six control points on a "warped" triangle - one control point on each corner and one along each edge (see Figure 1). A weight w_{ij} is assigned to each control point and the surface is defined:

$$\vec{X}(s,t,u) = \frac{\sum_{i+j\leq 2} \binom{2}{i\ j} s^i t^j (u-s-t)^{2-i-j} w_{ij} \vec{P}_{ij}}{\sum_{i+j\leq 2} \binom{2}{i\ j} s^i t^j (u-s-t)^{2-i-j} w_{ij}}$$

where the multinomial coefficient $\binom{2}{i\ j} = \frac{2!}{i!j!(2-i-j)!}$. In our case, the multinomial coefficient equals two if i=1 or

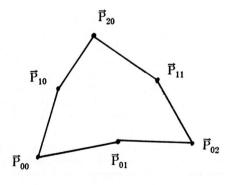

$$\vec{P}_{20}$$
$$\vec{P}_{10} \qquad \vec{P}_{11}$$
$$\vec{P}_{00} \qquad \vec{P}_{01} \qquad \vec{P}_{02}$$

Figure 1
Bezier Control Net for a Steiner Patch

if j=1, and it equals one otherwise. The variables s,t,u are called homogeneous parameters. To each pair of ratios $(\frac{s}{u},\frac{t}{u})$ there corresponds a unique point on the surface. Thus the parameters $(s,t,u) = (.5,.4,1)$ and $(s,t,u) = (1,.8,2)$ correspond to the same point. It is common practice in computer graphics applications to simply set u=1 and deal with the two non-homogeneous parameters s,t. However, it is advantageous in the present case to work with the homogeneous parameters s,t,u.

As the values s,t,u vary over the range $\frac{s}{u} \geq 0$, $\frac{t}{u} \geq 0$, $\frac{s}{u} + \frac{t}{u} \leq 1$, a triangular patch is swept out which is bounded by the curves s=0, t=0, s+t=u. As $\frac{s}{u}$ and $\frac{t}{u}$ vary outside these limits, a surface is swept out that can extend infinitely. The name "Steiner surface" generally refers to the unbounded surface, whereas "patch" always refers to the bounded surface.

From this definition, it is noted that the corner control points $\vec{P}_{00}, \vec{P}_{02}, \vec{P}_{20}$ lie on the surface whereas the interior control points generally do not. Also, the plane defined by a corner control point and its two neighboring interior control points is tangent to the surface at the corner point. If all the weights w_{ij} are identical, the denominator reduces to a constant after expanding and simplifying the expression, and the surface is said to be integral. Otherwise, the surface is said to be rational.

The Bezier control point equation can be expanded into the following rational parametric polynomial equations:

$$x = a_{20}s^2 + a_{11}st + a_{02}t^2 + a_{10}su + a_{01}tu + a_{00}u^2 \qquad 1a$$

$$y = b_{20}s^2 + b_{11}st + b_{02}t^2 + b_{10}su + b_{01}tu + b_{00}u^2 \qquad 1b$$

$$z = c_{20}s^2 + c_{11}st + c_{02}t^2 + c_{10}su + c_{01}tu + c_{00}u^2 \qquad 1c$$

$$w = d_{20}s^2 + d_{11}st + d_{02}t^2 + d_{10}su + d_{01}tu + d_{00}u^2 \qquad 1d$$

It is easy to see that the a_{ij}, b_{ij}, c_{ij}, d_{ij} are simple linear functions of the Bezier control points.

The Steiner surface is mentioned in most classical works on algebraic surfaces beyond quadrics [7],[5],[10]. A crucial characteristic of a Steiner surface is that it is a degree four surface containing a triple point at the intersection of three double lines [10]. The fact that it is degree four means that its implicit equation $f(x,y,z)=0$ is a degree four polynomial in x, y and z. According to Bezout's theorem [6], any line will intersect a degree four surface in at most four points, or lie completely in the surface. However, any line through a triple point will have three coincident intersections at that point, and therefore can intersect the Steiner surface at only one other point. For a Steiner surface defined in homogeneous, parametric equations in s, t and u, to each ratio s/u and t/u there corresponds exactly one point on the surface, and one line that connects that point with the triple point. This geometric insight engenders a technique for determining the implicit equation $f(x,y,z)=0$ of a Steiner patch from its parametric equations 1a-d. The strategy is to define such a line as the intersection of two planes P and Q whose orientations vary with s, t and u. If (x_{tp}, y_{tp}, z_{tp}) is the triple point, the equations of P and Q can be written:

$$P = (P_{xs}s + P_{xt}t + P_{xu}u)(\frac{x}{w} - x_{tp}) + \qquad 2$$

$$(P_{ys}s + P_{yt}t + P_{yu}u)(\frac{y}{w} - y_{tp}) +$$

$$(P_{zs}s + P_{zt}t + P_{zu}u)(\frac{z}{w} - z_{tp}) = 0$$

$$Q = (Q_{xs}s + Q_{xt}t + Q_{xu}u)(\frac{x}{w} - x_{tp}) + \qquad 3$$

$$(Q_{ys}s + Q_{yt}t + Q_{yu}u)(\frac{y}{w} - y_{tp}) +$$

$$(Q_{zs}s + Q_{zt}t + Q_{zu}u)(\frac{z}{w} - z_{tp}) = 0.$$

Let

$$P_{ws} = -P_{xs}x_{tp} - P_{ys}y_{tp} - P_{zs}z_{tp}$$

$$P_{wt} = -P_{xt}x_{tp} - P_{yt}y_{tp} - P_{zt}z_{tp} \qquad 4$$

$$P_{wu} = -P_{xu}x_{tp} - P_{yu}y_{tp} - P_{zu}z_{tp}.$$

After multiplying through by w, substituting equations 4 into equations 2 and collecting factors of x, y, z and w,

$$P=(P_{xs}s + P_{xt}t + P_{xu}u)x + (P_{ys}s + P_{yt}t + P_{yu}u)y \qquad 5$$

$$(P_{zs}s + P_{zt}t + P_{zu}u)z + (P_{ws}s + P_{wt}t + P_{wu}u)w = 0$$

and likewise for Q.

The immediate goal is to find the triple point, x_{tp}, y_{tp}, z_{tp}, and the 18 coefficients P_{ij} and Q_{ij}. If x, y, z and w in equation 5 are replaced with their

parametric expressions in s, t and u from equations 1a-d, the result is a degree three polynomial in s, t and u with coefficients which are linear in P_{ij}:

$$s^3 (P_{xs}a_{20} + P_{ys}b_{20} + P_{zs}c_{20} + P_{ws}d_{20}) + \qquad 6$$

$$t^3 (P_{xt}a_{02} + P_{yt}b_{02} + P_{zt}c_{02} + P_{wt}d_{02}) +$$

$$s^2t (P_{xs}a_{11} + P_{xt}a_{20} + P_{ys}b_{11} + P_{yt}b_{20} +$$

$$P_{zs}c_{11} + P_{zt}c_{20} + P_{ws}d_{11} + P_{wt}d_{20}) +$$

$$st^2 (P_{xs}a_{02} + P_{xt}a_{11} + P_{ys}b_{02} + P_{yt}b_{11} +$$

$$P_{zs}c_{02} + P_{zt}c_{11} + P_{ws}d_{02} + P_{wt}d_{11}) +$$

$$s^2u (P_{xs}a_{10} + P_{xu}a_{20} + P_{ys}b_{10} + P_{yu}b_{20} +$$

$$P_{zs}c_{10} + P_{zu}c_{20} + P_{ws}d_{10} + P_{wu}d_{20}) +$$

$$stu (P_{xs}a_{01} + P_{xt}a_{10} + P_{xu}a_{11} + P_{ys}b_{01} +$$

$$P_{yt}b_{10} + P_{yu}b_{11} + P_{zs}c_{01} + P_{zt}c_{10} +$$

$$P_{zu}c_{11} + P_{ws}d_{01} + P_{wt}d_{10} + P_{wu}d_{11}) +$$

$$t^2u (P_{xt}a_{01} + P_{xu}a_{02} + P_{yt}b_{01} + P_{yu}b_{02} +$$

$$P_{zt}c_{01} + P_{zu}c_{02} + P_{wt}d_{01} + P_{wu}d_{02}) +$$

$$su^2 (P_{xs}a_{00} + P_{xu}a_{10} + P_{ys}b_{00} + P_{yu}b_{10} +$$

$$P_{zs}c_{00} + P_{zu}c_{10} + P_{ws}d_{00} + P_{wu}d_{10}) +$$

$$tu^2 (P_{xt}a_{00} + P_{xu}a_{01} + P_{yt}b_{00} + P_{yu}b_{01} +$$

$$P_{zt}c_{00} + P_{zu}c_{01} + P_{wt}d_{00} + P_{wu}d_{01}) +$$

$$u^3 (P_{xu}a_{00} + P_{yu}b_{00} + P_{zu}c_{00} + P_{wu}d_{00}) = 0$$

This equation defines a family of planes which contain the triple point and which vary with s, t and u in such a manner that they always contain the point on

$$
\begin{bmatrix}
a_{20} & 0 & 0 & b_{20} & 0 & 0 & c_{20} & 0 & 0 & d_{20} \\
0 & a_{02} & 0 & 0 & b_{02} & 0 & 0 & c_{02} & 0 & 0 \\
a_{11} & a_{20} & 0 & b_{11} & b_{20} & 0 & c_{11} & c_{20} & 0 & d_{11} \\
a_{02} & a_{11} & 0 & b_{02} & b_{11} & 0 & c_{02} & c_{11} & 0 & d_{02} \\
a_{10} & 0 & a_{20} & b_{10} & 0 & b_{20} & c_{10} & 0 & c_{20} & d_{10} \\
a_{01} & a_{10} & a_{11} & b_{01} & b_{10} & b_{11} & c_{01} & c_{10} & c_{11} & d_{01} \\
0 & a_{01} & a_{02} & 0 & b_{01} & b_{02} & 0 & c_{01} & c_{02} & 0 \\
a_{00} & 0 & a_{10} & b_{00} & 0 & b_{10} & c_{00} & 0 & c_{10} & d_{00} \\
0 & a_{00} & a_{01} & 0 & b_{00} & b_{01} & 0 & c_{00} & c_{01} & 0 \\
0 & 0 & a_{00} & 0 & 0 & b_{00} & 0 & 0 & c_{00} & 0
\end{bmatrix}
\begin{Bmatrix}
P_{xs} \\ P_{xt} \\ P_{xu} \\ P_{ys} \\ P_{yt} \\ P_{yu} \\ P_{zs} \\ P_{zt} \\ P_{zu} \\ P_{ws}
\end{Bmatrix}
=
\begin{Bmatrix}
0 \\ -d_{02} \\ -d_{20} \\ -d_{11} \\ 0 \\ -d_{10} \\ -d_{01} \\ 0 \\ -d_{00} \\ 0
\end{Bmatrix} P_{wt}
+
\begin{Bmatrix}
0 \\ 0 \\ 0 \\ 0 \\ -d_{20} \\ -d_{11} \\ -d_{02} \\ -d_{10} \\ -d_{01} \\ -d_{00}
\end{Bmatrix} P_{wu}
$$

Figure 2
Matrix Equation for Computing the P_{ij}

the surface which corresponds to s, t and u. Any two planes of this family can be designated P and Q. P and Q are determined by noting that the only way equation 6 will vanish for any s, t and u is for each of the ten coefficients to vanish. This defines a set of ten homogeneous equations in the twelve unknowns P_{ij}, and another set in Q_{ij}. But because this linear system of equations is underconstrained, two linearly independent solutions can be found. One of those solutions can be selected as the definition of plane P and any other as the definition of plane Q.

In practice, this can be accomplished by forming the matrix equation in Figure 2. That equation can be written in more compact notation as:

$$[A]\vec{P} = \vec{V}_1 P_{wt} + \vec{V}_2 P_{wu} \qquad 7$$

A similar set of equations can be written to solve for the Q_{ij}:

$$[A]\vec{Q} = \vec{V}_1 Q_{wt} + \vec{V}_2 Q_{wu}. \qquad 8$$

If $\vec{V}_1$ and $\vec{V}_2$ are not linearly independent, i.e. $\vec{V}_1 = k\vec{V}_2$ where k is any scalar, the linear equations in Figure 2 must be rearranged to select two other independent variables so that the two vectors on the right hand side of the equation are not parallel, and are not null. One can arbitrarily set $P_{wt} = 1$ and $P_{wu} = 0$ and solve 7 for the remaining P_{ij}. Likewise, one can set $Q_{wt} = 0$ and $Q_{wu} = 1$ and solve 8 for the remaining Q_{ij}. Using either of these solution sets, equations 4 can be solved for the triple point.

It should be noted that for certain degenerate forms of the Steiner patch such as planes, quadrics and cubics, this algorithm can not be applied. For example, for a planar Steiner patch the triple point is undefined. These degenerate cases are easily detected and handled with simpler intersection algorithms, as discussed in [9].

2.1. Inversion

The developments in the preceding section lead directly to a simple, closed form inversion equation for computing the parameters of a point on the surface as a function of the Cartesian coordinates of the point. Making the substitution,

$$x' = \frac{x}{w} - x_{tp}$$

$$y' = \frac{y}{w} - y_{tp} \qquad 9$$

$$z' = \frac{z}{w} - z_{tp}$$

one can rewrite equations 2 and 3 as

$$P_s s + P_t t + P_u u = 0$$

$$Q_s s + Q_t t + Q_u u = 0$$

where $P_s = P_{xs}x' + P_{ys}y' + P_{zs}z'$, etc. Solving this pair of linear equations for the parameters s, t and u yields the inversion equations:

$$S = s(x',y',z') = P_t Q_u - P_u Q_t$$

$$T = t(x',y',z') = P_u Q_s - P_s Q_u \qquad 10$$

$$U = u(x',y',z') = P_s Q_t - P_t Q_s$$

These inversion equations are quadratic polynomials in x', y' and z' because the P_i and Q_j are linear in x', y' and z'. Inversion equations are useful for the ray tracing problem in determining whether a point at which a ray intersects a Steiner surface lies within the patch boundaries.

2.2. Implicitization

The implicit equation of the Steiner surface involves only x, y and z and is satisfied by any point (x,y,z) on the surface. Equations 1a-d, 9 and 10 can be combined in any of several ways to obtain such an equation. For example, selecting the first of equations 9:

$$x' = \frac{x(S,T,U)}{w(S,T,U)} - x_{tp}$$

or rearranged:

$$w(S,T,U)x' = x(S,T,U) - x_{tp}w(S,T,U) \qquad 11$$

where S, T and U are the quadratic polynomials in x', y' and z' defined in equations 10. Note that $w(S,T,U)$, $x(S,T,U)$, $y(S,T,U)$ and $z(S,T,U)$ are all homogeneous degree four polynomials in x', y' and z' because equations 10 are homogeneous degree two polynomials in x', y' and z'. Therefore, the left hand side of equation 11 is a homogeneous polynomial of degree five in x', y' and z' whereas the right hand side is a degree four homogeneous polynomial. It is known, however, that a Steiner surface whose triple point is at the origin contains only terms of degree four and three. Therefore it must be possible to factor an x' from the right hand expression in equation 11. Thus, the implicit equation is

$$w(S,T,U) - \frac{x(S,T,U) - x_{tp}w(S,T,U)}{x'} = 0 \qquad 12$$

whose degree four terms are (from equation 1d)

$$w(S,T,U) =$$

$$d_{20}S^2 + d_{11}ST + d_{02}T^2 + d_{10}SU + d_{01}TU + d_{00}U^2$$

and whose degree three terms are

$$-\frac{x(S,T,U) - x_{tp}w(S,T,U)}{x'}$$

or,

$$-[\, S^2\,(\,a_{20} - x_{tp}d_{20}\,) + ST\,(\,a_{11} - x_{tp}d_{11}\,) +$$

$$T^2\,(\,a_{02} - x_{tp}d_{02}\,) + SU\,(\,a_{10} - x_{tp}d_{10}\,) +$$

$$TU\,(\,a_{01} - x_{tp}d_{01}\,) + U^2\,(\,a_{00} - x_{tp}d_{00}\,)\,]\, /\, x'$$

3. RAY INTERSECTION EQUATION

With the implicit surface and directed ray equations in hand, it is now possible to express the intersection equation for a Steiner patch in the manner conventionally used for algebraic surfaces. Consider the ray:

$$x(\alpha) = x_0 + x_1\alpha \qquad \text{13a}$$

$$y(\alpha) = y_0 + y_1\alpha \qquad \text{13b}$$

$$z(\alpha) = z_0 + z_1\alpha \qquad \text{13c}$$

Finding the intersections of this ray with the surface whose implicit equation is $f(x,y,z)=0$ is equivalent to finding the roots of the equation $g(\alpha) = f(x(\alpha),y(\alpha),z(\alpha)) = 0$, which is a degree four polynomial in α.

There are several ways in which $g(\alpha)$ can be formed. One way is to work directly from the implicit equation $f(x,y,z)=0$. The polynomial $f(x,y,z)$ is degree four, and consequently has 35 terms. Each of the 35 terms would have to be symbolically expanded, and the resulting 35 polynomials in α would have to be added together to form $g(\alpha)$. For example, one of these terms is $cx^2yz=c(x_0+x_1\alpha)^2(y_0+y_1\alpha)(z_0+z_1\alpha)$, which expands into a degree four polynomial in α which would be added to the 34 polynomials generated by the other terms to create $g(\alpha)$.

A more practical way to produce $g(\alpha)$ is to substitute the ray equations 13a-c upstream in the implicitization process, replacing $\frac{x}{w}$ by $x(\alpha)$ and so on in equations 9. Carrying this substitution through to equations 10 produces inversion equations $S(\alpha)$, $T(\alpha)$ and $U(\alpha)$, which are quadratic polynomials in α. These inversion equations can be used in equations 12 to produce the ray intersection equation, $g(\alpha)$:

$$w(S(\alpha),T(\alpha),U(\alpha)) - \qquad \text{14a}$$

$$\frac{x(S(\alpha),T(\alpha),U(\alpha)) - x_{tp}w(S(\alpha),T(\alpha),U(\alpha))}{x'(\alpha)} = 0.$$

As noted earlier implicit equations 12 can also be expressed as,

$$w(S,T,U) - \frac{y(S,T,U) - y_{tp}w(S,T,U)}{y'} = 0 \qquad \text{14b}$$

or as,

$$w(S,T,U) - \frac{z(S,T,U) - z_{tp}w(S,T,U)}{z'} = 0. \qquad \text{14c}$$

Using exact arithmetic all three implicit equations would produce identical values for α. In practice, however, they are not exactly equal due to floating point round-off errors during the computations. In fact, the round-off perpetuated by these polynomials can seriously limit the accuracy of the ray intersection equation. It has been observed that round-off error is minimized by selecting the implicit equation, either 14a, 14b or 14c, corresponding to the largest direction component of the ray vector x_1,y_1,z_1. Thus, equation 14a should be used if x_1 is largest, equation 14b if y_1 is largest, and equation 14c if z_1 is largest.

For the integral Steiner, equations 14a-c simplify considerably. The d_{ij} coefficients are zero, except for $d_{00} = w_{00}$, which can be assigned the value 1. In this case, $w(S,T,U)$ reduces to $U^2(\alpha)$, and equation 14a becomes:

$$U^2(\alpha) - \frac{x(S(\alpha),T(\alpha),U(\alpha)) - x_{tp}U^2(\alpha)}{x_0 + x_1\alpha - x_{tp}} = 0 \qquad \text{15}$$

and likewise for equations 14b and 14c. In practice, the coefficients of the quartic implicit equation $g(\alpha)$ corresponding to equation 15 are most conveniently found by first finding the coefficients of the quartic polynomial in α for the numerator of the quotient term. Based on the expected Steiner form discussed in section 2.2, synthetic division is used to reduce this quotient to coefficients of a cubic polynomial in α, and a remainder. This remainder is insignificant, provided the procedure given above for selecting the proper form of $g(\alpha)$ is used. Finally, summing like coefficients from the quotient and the $U^2(\alpha)$ term yields the coefficients of the quartic ray intersection equation $g(\alpha) = 0$.

The algorithm was coded in FORTRAN IV in two subprograms, an initialization routine which computed the P_{ij}, Q_{ij} and triple point for a Steiner patch given the Bezier control points, and an intersection routine which computed the coefficients and roots of $g(\alpha)$ for a given ray and patch. The initialization routine consisted of about 60 lines of code excluding the linear matrix solver. The intersection routine was about 80 statements in length. The Modified Regula Falsi root finding method [11] was used to find the roots of the quartic equation $g(\alpha)$.

Figure 3 shows six Steiner surfaces rendered using this algorithm. The figure contains shadows, but no reflection or refraction. The execution time on a CYBER 170-720 computer for the intersection and lighting calculations for this 1000 by 1000 pixel figure was 8436 CPU seconds. The ray intersection computations alone have been measured at approximately 700 solutions per second. It is noteworthy that this algorithm has been implemented on a vector processor, the CYBER 205. On the vector processor the image in Figure 3 required only 186 CPU seconds.

4. SUMMARY

A new algorithm for ray tracing Steiner surface patches has been discussed. The algorithm combines new methods for representing parametric surfaces in implicit form with geometric insight resulting in a major simplification over existing techniques.

The steps in ray tracing a Steiner patch may be summarized as follows:

1. Preprocesses to be performed once only.

    a. Compute the coefficients of a pair of two parameter (three homogeneous parameter) families of planes which contain the triple point of the Steiner surface, as well as the variable point on the surface which corresponds to the patch parameters (see equations 7 and 8).

b. Determine the inversion equations (equations 10) which compute the parameter values of a point which lies on the surface.

2. Steps to be performed once for each ray.

a. Express the inversion equations as quartic polynomials in the ray parameter.

b. Set up the quartic polynomial whose roots are the ray parameter values which correspond to points of intersection (equation 14a,b, or c). This step requires approximately 100 floating point operations.

c. Find the positive roots (in ascending order) of the quartic polynomial from step 2b.

d. As each root is found, compute the patch parameters of the point of intersection using the equations from step 2a to see if the intersection point lies within the patch bounds.

e. The surface normal, needed for shading computation, is obtained by taking the cross product of two directional derivatives:

$$\vec{N} = \frac{\partial \vec{X}(s,t)}{\partial s} \times \frac{\partial \vec{X}(s,t)}{\partial t}$$

5. ACKNOWLEDGEMENTS

The authors express their appreciation to Joe Cychosz for coding and testing the Modified Regula Falsi root solver and for producing Figure 3. Thanks also go to Warren Waggenspack for his diligent proofreading of the equations and manuscript, and to David Plunkett for including the Steiner surface in his BIA ray tracing code for testing. The reviewers were very thorough and provided several constructive comments. The authors also wish to acknowledge the support of Control Data Corporation Grant No. 81PO4.

6. REFERENCES

[1] J. F. Blinn, "A Generalization of Algebraic Surface Drawing," *ACM Transactions on Graphics,* Vol. 1, No. 3, pp. 235-256, 1982.

[2] B. E. Edwards, "Implementation of a Ray-Tracing Algorithm for Rendering Superquadric Solids," Master Thesis, Rensselaer Polytechnic Institute, 1982.

[3] I. D. Faux and M. J. Pratt, *Computational Geometry for Design and Manufacture,* Ellis Harwood, Chichester, 1981.

[4] P. Hanrahan, "Ray Tracing Algebraic Surfaces", *Computer Graphics,* Vol. 17, no. 3, pp.83-90, 1983.

[5] C. M. Jessop, *Quartic Surfaces,* Cambridge University Press, 1916.

[6] J. Kajiya, "Ray Tracing Parametric Patches," *Computer Graphics,* Vol. 16, No. 3, pp. 245-254, 1982.

[7] G. Salmon, *Analytic Geometry of Three Dimensions, Volume II,* Longmans, Green and Co., London, 1912.

[8] T. W. Sederberg, "Implicit and Parametric Curves and Surfaces for Computer Aided Geometric Design", Ph.D. Thesis, Purdue University, 1983.

[9] T. W. Sederberg and D. C. Anderson, "Steiner Surface Patches," (submitted for publication).

[10] D. M. Y. Sommerville, *Analytical Geometry of Three Dimensions,* Cambridge University Press, 1951.

[11] J. R. Rice, *Numerical Methods, Software, and Analysis: IMSL Reference Edition,* McGraw Hill Book Company, New York, New York, pp. 222-223 (1983).

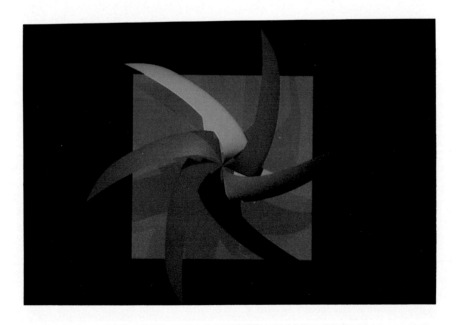

Figure 3
Six Steiner Patches

RAY TRACING VOLUME DENSITIES

James T. Kajiya
Brian P. Von Herzen

California Institute of Technology
Pasadena, Calif

ABSTRACT   This paper presents new algorithms to trace objects represented by densities within a volume grid, e.g. clouds, fog, flames, dust, particle systems. We develop the light scattering equations, discuss previous methods of solution, and present a new approximate solution to the full three-dimensional radiative scattering problem suitable for use in computer graphics. Additionally we review dynamical models for clouds used to make an animated movie.

KEYWORDS: computer graphics, raster graphics, ray tracing, stochastic modelling, simulation of natural phenomena, radiative transport, light scattering, clouds, particle systems.

CR CATEGORIES: I.3.3, I.3.5, I.3.7

§1 Introduction

A large class of natural phenomena is described by partial differential equations. In almost all cases, the description of these phenomena is given by a set of vector or scalar fields defined on a uniform mesh in 3–space. This paper will render objects defined in this way via the ray tracing method (Whitted 1980, Appel 1968, Goldstein 1971, Kajiya 1982, 1983).

Recently, the synthesis of images with clouds and, more generally, of objects defined as volume densities has been pursued by a number of investigators (Blinn 1982, Max 1983, Voss 1983). This paper is a continuation of that work in the context of ray tracing.

Blinn introduced the use of density models in computer graphics in Blinn (1982), where he considers plane parallel atmospheres. Other researchers have adapted

his models to more general shapes. Max defines clouds as densities with boundaries defined by analytic functions. Voss has fractally generated densities with a series of plane parallel models, yielding images of striking realism.

The work presented here extends previous efforts in two ways: first, we present an alternative to the Blinn scattering model which models multiple radiative scattering against particles with high albedo. Second, we show how to ray trace these models.

We emphasize that the rendering techniqes presented here are general. We are able to view the models from any angle, with multiple arbitrarily placed light sources (even within the densities). The density model may intersect other procedural models. The viewing point may lie inside the density function. With these techniques we are able to render clouds that cast shadows on their environment as well as on themselves. We may have scenes in which mountain peaks disappear into a cloud interior. We may fly through the clouds. And, of course, the clouds appear reflected and refracted in other objects in the scene. There is one situation, however, which we do not handle correctly: other procedural objects, while they may be shadowed accurately by clouds, do not themselves cast shadows upon the clouds.

While clouds are the most obvious application of this representation, other phenomena also lend themselves well to this representation. For example, it is possible to model media which do not simply scatter, but also absorb and emit light. In this way we can model flames. Additionally, it is possible to generate models of very high geometric complexity which are treated simply as volume densities. In this way these techniques allow the application of ray tracing to Reeves' particle systems (Reeves 1983).

Permission to copy without fee all or part of this material is granted provided that the copies are not made or distributed for direct commercial advantage, the ACM copyright notice and the title of the publication and its date appear, and notice is given that copying is by permission of the Association for Computing Machinery. To copy otherwise, or to republish, requires a fee and/or specific permission.

© 1984   ACM   0-89791-138-5/84/007/0165 $00.75

§2 The scattering equation

In this section we discuss the relevant physical parameters and set up an equation which describes the scattering of radiation in volume densities. This section loosely follows the derivation in Chandrasekhar(1950).

The quantity to be calculated in a scattering problem is the energy per unit solid angle per unit area:

$$dE = I(x, \omega) \sin \vartheta \, d\omega \, d\sigma$$

This quantity is called the *intensity* of radiation at a point x in the direction of the solid angle $d\omega$.

The scattering equation can be derived by considering a differential cylindrical volume $dV = d\sigma ds$, where $d\sigma$ is the cross section of the cylinder and ds is the length (figure 1). If we follow a pencil of radiation along the length of the cylinder, we find that the difference in intensity between the two ends is given by

$$dI = -\text{absorbed} + \text{emitted}$$
$$= -\kappa \rho \, ds \, d\sigma \, d\omega + \jmath \rho \, ds \, d\sigma \, d\omega \qquad (2.1)$$

where ρ is the density of matter in the volume element; κ is the absorbption coefficient, viz. optical depth per unit density; and $\jmath$ is the emission coefficient.

The emission coefficient can be broken into two terms

$$\jmath = \jmath^{(e)} + \jmath^{(s)}$$

where $\jmath^{(e)}$ is the emission coefficient due to pure emission of the medium, for example a black body term for flames or stellar interiors; and $\jmath^{(s)}$ is the emission term due to pure scattering of incident radiation into the direction of interest. The form of this term is usually written as

$$\jmath^{(s)} = \kappa \frac{1}{4\pi} \int_{\|\bar{s}\|=1} p(s, \bar{s}) I(x, \bar{s}) \, d\bar{s}.$$

This expression says that the light scattered in direction s is a linear operator of the light incident upon the volume element from all angles. The function $p(s, \bar{s})$ is called the *phase function* and gives the amount of light scattered from direction s to direction $\bar{s}$. In many situations the medium is *isotropic*, in the case the phase function depends only on the *phase angle* Θ, the angle between s and $\bar{s}$. Although there are many interesting phenomena in which the emission coefficient $\jmath^{(e)}$ is nonzero, let us for simplicity assume it is zero in the remainder of this paper.

The phase function embodies all the information about the scattering behavior of the medium. From it we may derive all the other lighting parameters popular in computer graphics. For example, Lambert and Phong surfaces are simply phase functions with particular shape parameters. In these cases anisotropy prevails: there are preferred angles—for example, the normal of the surface element. Thus the phase function varies with more than just the phase angle. When the medium is composed of a large number of particles, no preferred orientations occur and isotropy obtains. In this case the phase angle completely determines the phase function value. Blinn (1982) discusses a number of important phase functions. For the work on clouds, two will be of particular interest: 1) perfectly diffuse scattering: $p(\cos \Theta) = \varpi_0$ where ϖ_0 is an arbitrary constant, and 2) Rayleigh scattering: $p(\cos \Theta) = \varpi_0 \frac{3}{4}(1 + \cos^2 \Theta)$.

The scattering equation can be brought into general form by dividing both sides of equation (2.1) by $-\kappa \rho ds$. But the derivative along the cylinder is simply a directional derivative along s

$$\frac{dI}{ds} = s \cdot \nabla_x I.$$

This gives us the scattering equation:

$$\frac{-1}{\kappa \rho} s \cdot \nabla_x I(x, s) - I(x, s)$$
$$+ \frac{1}{4\pi} \int_{\|s\|=1} p(s, \bar{s}) I(x, \bar{s}) \, d\bar{s} = 0.$$

§3 Solving the scattering equation

The scattering equation is solvable analytically only in a few very special cases: indeed, it is very difficult to solve even numerically without assumptions which reduce the dimensionality of the intensity field $I(x, s)$, a function of six real variables.

Various assumptions are customarily made to reduce the difficulty of the problem. Here are some common assumptions: 1) the medium is *isotropic*—the phase function is only dependent on the phase angle; 2) the medium is uniform—its density does not change from point to point in space; 3) the geometry is simple—the medium may vary in space but only along, say, the z-axis (this is the *plane parallel* or scattering in a slab problem); 4) the phase function is of a very simple type, viz. isotropic; 5) the albedo is very small or very large.

Various combinations of these assumptions have been treated extensively in the literature. The slab scattering problem has been the most common assumption (Chandrasekhar 1950).

The method of Wick-Chandrasekhar or *discrete ordinates* is a numerical method for plane parallel atmospheres. It sets up a coupled array of PDEs each of which represents one scattering angle. A finite Euler approximation is made for the phase integral which is the coupling mechanism of the individual equations. Convergence results for such approximations have appeared in Keller (1960ab) and more recently Anselone and Gibbs (1974).

Unfortunately, the discrete ordinates method is relatively unsuitable for computer graphics: we need to most often finely sample a given portion of the solid angle sphere, rather than have a uniform sampling across the whole sphere.

It may well be that a finite element approach would be a promising alternative to Wick-Chandrasekhar, but we have found that simpler schemes are effective for image synthesis.

3.1 Blinn's Low Albedo approximation

Blinn (1982) was the first to introduce a volume density scattering model to computer graphics. In this paper he made a number of approximations well suited to the problem he was studying: the rings of Saturn. Blinn chose to model a uniform medium of relatively low albedo with a single illuminating light source. (Although his method generalizes easily to multiple light sources.)

Assuming the above and, in addition, only a *single scattering* of the radiation from the light source to the eye, he was able to solve the problem analytically. Of course, multiple scattering is a second order effect for a medium with low albedo. The Blinn model is thus valid for a wide variety of phenomena.

Voss (1983) has adapted Blinn's procedure to more general geometries, by essentially modelling a sandwich of several Blinn models. With it, he has made some exceptional images of clouds. Both the Blinn and Voss methods place restrictions on the lighting and viewing geometry of the scene.

Unfortunately, clouds have a very high albedo—the single scattering approximation does not hold. A number of visible defects appear when rendering by the new technique. This is because the older method imposed viewing geometry restrictions which hid the defects.

It is one finding of this paper that realistic rendering of clouds demands more accuracy in the scattering model.

3.2 A ray tracing algorithm for the low albedo case

In this section we will describe a new technique which allows one to ray trace volume densities without any viewing or lighting restrictions. But for one slight twist, this method is essentially a brute force development of the Blinn single scattering model for ray tracing.

The key to the new method is that it separates the rendering procedure into two steps. The first step drives the radiation from light source i through a density array $\rho(x, y, z)$ into an array $I_i(x, y, z)$ which holds the contribution of each light source to the brightness of each point in space. This is done simply by calculating in parallel the following line integrals for each path $\Gamma_{x,y,z} = (x(t), y(t), z(t))$ from the light source through $\rho(x, y, z)$.

$$I_i(x, y, z) = \exp\left(-\tau \int_{\Gamma_{x,y,z}} \rho(\gamma)\, d\gamma\right)$$

where $\kappa = \tau\rho$. The principal observation is that this computation need only be done from at most once per frame to at least once per scene.

The second step occurs once per ray trace. Each ray is first culled against a bounding rectangular prism as an extent. The brightness of a ray sums the contribution of each volume element. It is given by:

$$B = \int_{\lambda_1}^{\lambda_2} e^{-\tau \int_{\lambda_1}^{t} \rho(x(\mu), y(\mu), z(\mu))\, d\mu}$$
$$\times \left[\sum_i I_i(x(t), y(t), z(t)) p(\cos \Theta_i)\right]$$
$$\times \rho(x(t), y(t), z(t))\, dt$$

In this expression, λ_1, λ_2 are the beginning and ending of the path between the eye and furthest visible volume element. It is set by

$$\lambda_1 = \max(0, d_1)$$
$$\lambda_2 = \min(d_{\text{global}}, d_2)$$

Where d_1 is the distance to the nearest intersection point with the bounding extent, d_{global} is the distance to the nearest intersection point with the rest of the world database, and d_2 is the distance to the farthest intersection point with the bounding extent.

The first exponential in the brightness integral gives the amount of attenuation due to absorption and scattering of the material visible to the eye. The sum term gives the brightness contribution of each light source to the brightness of the particular point.

According to the integral there are two remaining steps which must be done. The first is to compute the integrated optical path length along a particular ray.

This is done by simply bilinearly sampling and summing the density array along the ray. The second step is to compute and sum the actual brightness integral. Note that each of the integral terms has been precomputed so that a point sampling is all that is needed to compute the brightness term. We have used the Romberg integration method to actually compute the integral (Dahlquist and Bjork 1974).

§4 High Albedo approximation.

The low albedo approximation suffers from a number of defects when used to model clouds, a scattering medium of very high albedo. This can be seen in the results section. There are portions of the clouds which are abnormally dark due to shadowing of one part of a cloud upon another. In the actual physical situation these dark portions are illuminated by the second and higher order scattering centers within the cloud.

If one observes these clouds from above, the shadowing problem is not observable, since the eye and the light source are on the same side of the cloud. When looking from the underside of the cloud on the opposite side of the light source, one cannot determine what the actual thickness of the cloud is, so again the eye cannot discern an artificial darkening. However, clouds observed to shadow themselves viewed from the side show this problem quite clearly (see the figures).

Blinn (1982) has suggested treating the multiple scattering problem by a Neumann expansion involving the phase integral. This method is likely to work well only with lower albedo media, since the series is geometric in the albedo ϖ_0. If the albedo ϖ_0 is close to one, many terms will be needed to converge to a solution.

4.1 A Perturbation solution, conservative systems

In order to approximate the high albedo solution, we perform a perturbation expansion on $\beta = (1 - \varpi_0)$. We normalize the phase function to

$$p(\Theta) = \varpi_0 \, \overline{p}(\Theta)$$
$$= (1 - \beta) \, \overline{p}(\Theta)$$

For compactness, we write the scattering equation

$$\frac{-1}{\kappa \rho} s \cdot \nabla_x I(x, s) - I(x, s)$$
$$+ \frac{1}{4\pi}(1 - \beta) \int_{\|s\|=1} \overline{p}(s, \overline{s}) I(x, \overline{s}) \, d\overline{s} = 0$$

as the sum of two linear operators

$$LI + (1 - \beta) MI = 0$$

where

$$LI = \frac{-1}{\kappa \rho} s \cdot \nabla_x I(x, s) - I(x, s)$$
$$MI = \frac{1}{4\pi} \int_{\|s\|=1} \overline{p}(s, \overline{s}) I(x, \overline{s}) \, d\overline{s}.$$

Expanding I into a power series in β gives

$$I = \sum_{k=0}^{\infty} \beta^k I_k.$$

Substituting into the original equation for I and equating like powers of β gives a set of equations

$$LI_k + MI_k = -MI_{k-1}.$$

Thus the perturbation solution presents us with a series of forced conservative ($\varpi_0 = 1$) scattering equations. We now develop techniques which allow us to approximate the solutions for the conservative case.

4.2 The Scattering equation expressed in Spherical Harmonics

We expand $I(x, s)$ into spherical harmonics in s to obtain

$$I(x, s) = \sum_{l=0}^{\infty} \sum_{m=-l}^{l} I^{lm}(x) Y_{lm}(s).$$

The functions Y_{lm} are the customary normalized spherical harmonics of degree l and order m

$$Y_{lm}(\vartheta, \phi) = P_{lm}(\vartheta, \phi) e^{im\phi}$$

where the P_{lm} are the associated Legendre polynomials of degree l and order m (Courant and Hilbert 1953).

Substituting the spherical harmonic expansion into the scattering equation we obtain

$$\sum_{l,m} -\frac{1}{\kappa \rho} s \cdot [\nabla I^{lm}(x)] Y^{lm}(s) - I^{lm}(x) Y_{lm}(s)$$
$$+ I^{lm} \int p(s \cdot \overline{s}) Y_{lm}(\overline{s}) \, d\overline{s} = 0.$$

Multiplying this equation by $Y^{*}_{l'm'}(s)$ and integrating we get

$$\sum_{l,m} \frac{1}{\kappa\rho} \nabla I^{lm}(x) \cdot \int Y^{*}_{l'm'}(s) s Y_{lm}(s)\, ds$$
$$- I^{lm}(x)\delta_{ll'}\delta_{mm'}$$
$$+ \int\int Y^{*}_{l'm'}(s) p(s\cdot\bar{s}) Y_{lm}(\bar{s})\, d\bar{s}\, ds = 0$$

or, writing it in Dirac "bra–ket" notation

$$\sum_{l,m} \frac{1}{\kappa\rho} \nabla I^{lm}(x) \cdot \langle Y_{l'm'}(s)|s|Y_{lm}(s)\rangle$$
$$- I^{lm}(x)\delta_{ll'}\delta_{mm'}$$
$$+ I^{lm}(x)\langle Y_{l'm'}(s)|p|Y_{lm}(s)\rangle = 0;$$

where we write $\langle X|O|Y\rangle$ for the integral

$$\int_{0}^{\pi}\int_{-\pi}^{\pi} X^{*}OY \sin\vartheta\, d\phi\, d\vartheta.$$

This gives us a coupled set of first order PDEs for $I^{lm}(r)$. If we know the coupling coefficients given by the matrix elements

$$\langle Y_{l'm'}(s)|p|Y_{lm}(s)\rangle$$

and

$$\langle Y_{l'm'}(s)|s|Y_{lm}(s)\rangle$$

then we can solve this system by relaxation. For graphics applications, only the first few spherical harmonics are necessary for a convincing image. We truncate the so-called "p–wave", viz. after the $l = 1$ term. The next order of business is then to calculate the matrix coupling coefficients.

4.3 Matrix elements for the position

To calculate the matrix element $\langle Y_{l'm'}(s)|s|Y_{lm}(s)\rangle$ for the direction operator s, we calculate the matrix element for each component of s,

$$\langle Y_{l'm'}(s)|x|Y_{lm}(s)\rangle = \langle Y_{l'm'}(s)|\sin\vartheta\cos\phi|Y_{lm}(s)\rangle$$
$$\langle Y_{l'm'}(s)|y|Y_{lm}(s)\rangle = \langle Y_{l'm'}(s)|\sin\vartheta\sin\phi|Y_{lm}(s)\rangle$$
$$\langle Y_{l'm'}(s)|z|Y_{lm}(s)\rangle = \langle Y_{l'm'}(s)|\cos\vartheta|Y_{lm}(s)\rangle.$$

Now we may save a bit of work by setting

$$u = x + iy$$
$$= \sin\vartheta e^{i\phi}.$$

Now,

$$\langle Y_{l'm'}(s)|u|Y_{lm}(s)\rangle$$
$$= \int \left[P_{lm}(\cos\vartheta)e^{im\phi}\right]^{*}\left[P_{l'm'}(\cos\vartheta)e^{im\phi}\right]$$
$$\times\, e^{i\phi}\sin^{2}\phi\, d\vartheta\, d\phi$$
$$= \left[\int_{0}^{\pi} P_{lm}(\cos\vartheta)P_{l'm'}(\cos\vartheta)\sin^{2}\vartheta\, d\vartheta\right]$$
$$\times\left[\int_{-\pi}^{\pi} e^{i(m-m'+1)\phi}\, d\phi\right]$$
$$= \left[\int_{0}^{\pi} P_{lm}(\cos\vartheta)P_{l'm'}(\cos\vartheta)\sin^{2}\vartheta\, d\vartheta\right]\delta_{m+1,m'}2\pi.$$

Letting $\mu = \cos\vartheta$ and taking into account the Kronecker δ, the matrix element becomes:

$$\langle Y_{l'm'}(s)|u|Y_{lm}(s)\rangle = \int_{-1}^{1} P_{lm}(\mu)P_{l'm+1}(\mu)(1-\mu^2)^{1/2}\, d\mu$$
$$(4.1)$$

But from a recursion relation for the Legendre polynomial we have

$$P_{l,m+1}(\mu)(1-\mu^2)^{1/2} = k_0 P_{l+1,m} - k_1 P_{l-1,m},$$

where

$$k_0 = \frac{(l-m+1)(l-m+2)}{2l+1}$$
$$k_1 = \frac{(l+m-1)(l+m)}{2l+1}.$$

Using this relation in equation (4.1) we obtain

$$\langle Y_{l'm'}(s)|u|Y_{lm}(s)\rangle$$
$$= \int_{-1}^{1} P_{l'm}(\mu)[k_0 P_{l+1,m}(\mu) - k_1 P_{l-1,m}(\mu)]\, d\mu$$
$$= k_0\delta_{l',l+1} - k_1\delta_{l',l-1}.$$

The last equality follows from the orthogonality for the Legendre polynomials. Since

$$x = \mathrm{Re}(u)$$
$$y = \mathrm{Im}(u)$$

we have

$$\langle Y_{l'm'}(s)|x|Y_{lm}(s)\rangle = \langle Y_{l'm'}(s)|u|Y_{lm}(s)\rangle$$
$$\langle Y_{l'm'}(s)|y|Y_{lm}(s)\rangle = 0.$$

Now to compute the z matrix element we get

$$
\begin{aligned}
&\langle Y_{l'm'}(s)|z|Y_{lm}(s)\rangle \\
&= \left[\int_0^\pi P_{l'm'}(cos\vartheta)P_{lm}(cos\vartheta)\cos\vartheta\sin\vartheta\,d\vartheta\right] \\
&\quad \times \left[\int_{-\pi}^\pi e^{i(m-m')\phi}\,d\phi\right] \\
&= \left[\int_0^\pi P_{l'm'}(cos\vartheta)P_{lm}(cos\vartheta)\cos\vartheta\sin\vartheta\,d\vartheta\right] \\
&\qquad\qquad \delta_{mm'}2\pi \\
&= \left[\int_{-1}^1 P_{l'm}(\mu)P_{lm}(\mu)\mu\,d\mu\right]\delta_{mm'}2\pi.
\end{aligned}
\tag{4.2}
$$

Now from a recursion relation for the Legendre polynomial P_{lm} we have

$$
\mu P_{lm}(\mu) = k_2 P_{l+1,m}(\mu) - k_3 P_{l-1,m}(\mu)
$$

where

$$
k_2 = \frac{l+m}{2l+1}
$$
$$
k_3 = \frac{l-m+1}{2l+1}.
$$

Substituting into (4.2) we obtain

$$
\begin{aligned}
&\langle Y_{l'm'}(s)|z|Y_{lm}(s)\rangle \\
&= \int_{-1}^1 P_{l'm}(\mu)[k_2 P_{l+1,m}(\mu) - k_3 P_{l-1,m}(\mu)]\,d\mu \\
&= [k_2\delta_{l',l+1} - k_3\delta_{l',l-1}]\delta_{mm'}2\pi,
\end{aligned}
$$

where the last equality follows from the orthogonality of the P_{lm}.

4.4 Matrix elements for the phase integral

We assume the phase function to vary with the phase angle only. In this case we may expand the phase function into Legendre polynomials

$$
p(\cos\Theta) = \sum_{k=0}^\infty \varpi_k P_k(cos\Theta)
$$

and substitute into the matrix expression

$$
\begin{aligned}
&\langle Y_{l'm'}(s)|p|Y_{lm}(s)\rangle \\
&= \int_{\|s\|=1}\int_{\|\bar{s}\|=1} Y_{l'm'}^*(\bar{s})\left[\sum_k \varpi_k P_k(s\cdot\bar{s})\right] \\
&\qquad \times Y_{lm}(s)\,ds\,d\bar{s} \\
&= \sum_k \varpi_k \int\int Y_{l'm'}^*(\bar{s})P_k(s\cdot\bar{s})Y_{lm}(s)\,ds\,d\bar{s}.
\end{aligned}
\tag{4.3}
$$

Now, $s\cdot\bar{s}$ in polar coordinates is

$$
\begin{aligned}
s\cdot\bar{s} &= \cos\gamma \\
&= \cos\vartheta\cos\overline{\vartheta} + \sin\vartheta\sin\overline{\vartheta}\cos(\phi-\overline{\phi}).
\end{aligned}
$$

This allows us to apply Laplace's formula,

$$
P_l(\cos\gamma) = \frac{4\pi}{2l+1}\sum_{m=-l}^l Y_{lm}(\vartheta,\phi)Y_{lm}^*(\overline{\vartheta},\overline{\phi}).
$$

Using this identity in (4.3) we obtain

$$
\begin{aligned}
&\langle Y_{l'm'}(s)|p|Y_{lm}(s)\rangle \\
&= \sum_k \varpi_k \frac{4\pi}{2k+1} \\
&\quad \times \sum_{p=-k}^k \left[\int Y_{l'm'}(\bar{s})Y_{kp}^*(\bar{s})\,d\bar{s}\right]\left[\int Y_{lm}^*(s)Y_{kp}(s)\,ds\right] \\
&= \sum_k \varpi_k \frac{4\pi}{2k+1}\sum_{p=-k}^k \delta_{l'k}\delta_{m'p}\delta_{lk}\delta_{mp}. \\
&= \sum_k \varpi_k \frac{4\pi}{2k+1}\delta_{l'k}\delta_{lk}\delta_{mm'} \\
&= \frac{4\pi}{2l+1}\varpi_l\delta_{ll'}\delta_{m'm}.
\end{aligned}
$$

So the phase function matrix is diagonal with respect to spherical harmonics: no scattering occurs between different spherical harmonics. Each diagonal element is given by the Legendre expansion coefficients ϖ_k.

§5 Generating density models

There are many ways to generate volume density models for the above procedure. Voss (1983) has used fractal densities with great success. We show a number of images based on these. In our images we follow Voss in setting the densities with $1/f$ noise generated by a 3 dimensional FFT. They make convincing clouds. Unfortunately, it is unlikely that this method will elicit realistic dynamical behavior.

A second set of models which appears promising is Reeves' particle systems (Reeves 1983). We can use his techniques to fill the density array by interpolation. Ray tracing can then be used to render the array. Flows of ODEs and PDEs can be used to model the action of flowing water and to model hair and fuzzy surfaces, as well as trees. These methods are obvious generalizations of Reeves' method.

Finally we mention actual physical models of the atmosphere to generate motion studies of clouds.

5.1 A Cloud Model for Generating Density Functions

A numerical model for cumulus convection is used to generate three-dimensional optical density functions. The model incorporates the equations of motion, continuity, condensation, and evaporation. It models the convective motions of the atmosphere, the latent heat of vaporization of water, and frictional effects. Coriolis effects due to the rotation of the Earth are ignored.

The cloud simulation commences in a convectively unstable atmosphere with high relative humidity. A constant heat source is applied at the base of the model, representing sunlight heating the earth. In the model, a warm layer of air forms close to the ground, and starts to rise. The cloud starts forming as soon as moist air rises enough to become supersaturated. The output of the model is the mixing ratio of liquid water in the atmosphere at each 3D grid point. The liquid water mixing ratio is directly interpreted as the optical density of the cloud. An image is then generated from these optical densities using the diffuse rendering algorithm.

The following symbols are used to represent atmospheric quantities:

u, v, w wind velocities in the x, y, and z directions, respectively

V the velocity vector consisting of the components (u, v, w)

F the friction vector consisting of the components (F_x, F_y, F_z)

θ potential temperature

q total water mixing ratio

q_l liquid water mixing ratio

Nine equations define the model. The first three equations define the acceleration of an air parcel. Acceleration is determined from the momentum of the airflow, frictional effects, and from buoyancy.

$$\frac{\partial u}{\partial t} = -V \cdot \nabla u - F_x$$

$$\frac{\partial v}{\partial t} = -V \cdot \nabla v - F_y$$

$$\frac{\partial w}{\partial t} = -V \cdot \nabla w - F_z + \theta$$

The buoyancy term is proportional to the potential temperature of the air parcel, θ. Potential temperature is defined as the temperature an air parcel would have if it were brought down to sea level. It is more convenient to use in the model instead of absolute temperature for the following reason: as an air parcel ascends, its temperature will decrease due to the decreasing pressure, and must be recalculated at each altitude

of the air parcel. However, the potential temperature of the air parcel will remain constant. Therefore, it is computationally more efficient to use potential temperature instead of absolute temperature in the model. Potential temperature effectively measures the amount of heat energy contained in an air parcel.

The change in potential temperature is determined by the advection of temperature into the local region and the heat released by condensing cloud vapor. The term "advection" is used to describe the change of a parameter at a fixed location due to transportation by the winds. Thus an increase in potential temperature due to transportation of warm air into the local region is called advective warming. An external heat source such as sunlight is represented by the variable Q:

$$\frac{\partial \theta}{\partial t} = -V \cdot \nabla \theta + \frac{L_{vw}}{c_p} \frac{\partial q_l}{\partial t} + Q.$$

L_{vw} is the latent heat of vaporization of water. c_p is the specific heat of air at constant pressure.

Frictional effects are approximated by a simple relation yielding an exponential decay of wind velocities with time:

$$F = \frac{1}{t_f} V$$

where t_f is the friction timescale.

The equation of continuity constrains the motions of the air parcels. The requirement is that air is neither created nor destroyed at any given location, which implies that

$$\nabla \cdot V = 0.$$

The density of air is assumed to be constant over the scale of the model. A corollary of this requirement is that the upward velocity over any horizontal plane in the model must average to zero.

The change in water mixing ratios is determined by the advection of water and the amount of evaporation and condensation which takes place. Evaporation is assumed to take place until the air is saturated or all the liquid water is evaporated. Condensation takes place whenever the air is supersaturated. The change in total water content is simply determined by the advection of water:

$$\frac{\partial q}{\partial t} = -V \cdot \nabla q$$

The saturation mixing ratio at any given level is an exponential function of altitude:

$$q_s = A \exp^{-\alpha z}$$

where A and α are exponential scaling constants. q_s is interpreted to be the mass ratio of water to air at saturation for a given volume of air. The constants are determined by the boundary conditions that $q_s = 0.02$ at the bottom level of the model, and $q_s = 0.002$ at the top of the model. The liquid water mixing ratio is determined by the amount of water present in the air parcel in excess of the saturation mixing ratio:

$$q_l = \max(q - q_s, 0).$$

An important advantage of using a physical model for clouds is that the cloud evolves realistically with time. This approach lends itself to realistic cloud animation whereas other modelling approaches do not automatically produce realistic cloud behavior. An animation of an evolving cumulus cloud is discussed in the next section.

§6 Computer Results

Figures 1 through 4 show the low albedo rendering technique with fractal volume densities. Figure 1 is defined on a $16 \times 16 \times 16$ grid, while 2 and 3 show a cloud fractally generated on a $128 \times 128 \times 16 grid$. These frames were computed at 512×512 resolution on an IBM4341 processor. CPU times ranged from 1 to 4 hours. Figure 4 shows a fractal cloud in combination with a fractally generated mountain at 256×256 resolution, on the same machine this frame consumed 6 hours of CPU time.

Figures 5 through 10 show a cumulus cloud at various stages of development. The optical densities were calculated using the above model on a VAX 11/780 using a three dimensional grid of (10 by 10 by 20) grid elements. A simple forward-differencing scheme was used to integrate the above differential equations in time. Each time step took around 10 cpu seconds to compute, representing roughly one second of cloud evolution. The cloud was allowed to evolve for several minutes to generate the images shown. Rendering was done on an IBM4341 at 512×512 resolution, with CPU times of 2 hours each.

§7 Summary

This paper has presented new methods for the synthesis of images which contain volume densities. We have found that single scattering is a poor approximation for clouds when more general viewing geometries are used. We have offered a new method for solving the scattering equations in an approximate manner suitable for computer graphics. We have also presented

equations which will model the dynamic behavior of clouds.

§8 References

Anselone, P.M., and Gibbs, A.G., 1974: Convergence of the discrete ordinates method for the transport equation, *Constructive and Computational methods for differential and integral equations*, Springer Verlag Lecture notes in math 430.

Appel, A., 1968: Some techniques for shading machine renderings of solids, 1968 SJCC, 37-45.

Blinn, J.F., 1982: Light reflection functions for simulation of clouds and dusty surfaces. Proc. SIGGRAPH82. In *Comput. Gr.* 16,3, 21-29.

Chandrasekhar, S., 1950: *Radiative Transfer*, Oxford University Press.

Clark, T.L., 1979: Numerical Simulations with a three-dimensional cloud model: lateral boundary condition experiments and multicellular severe storm simulations. *J. of the Atmospheric Sciences*, 36, 2191.

Courant, R. and Hilbert, D., 1953: *Methods of Mathematical Physics* v.1, Interscience, New York.

Dahlquist, G., and Bjork, A., 1974: *Numerical Methods*, Prentice Hall, New York.

Goldstein, E. and Nagle, R. 1971: 3D visual simulation, *Simulation* 16, 25-31.

Kajiya, J.T., 1983: Ray tracing procedurally defined objects, SIGGRAPH83, *Comput. Gr.* 17,3, 91-102.

Kajiya, J.T., 1982: Ray tracing parametric patches, SIGGRAPH82, *Comput. Gr.* 16,3, 245-254.

Keller, H.B., 1960a: Approximate solutions of transport problems, *SIAM J. Appl. Math.* 8, 43-73.

Keller, H.B., 1960b: On the pointwise convergence of the discrete ordinates method, *SIAM J. Appl. Math.* 8, 560-567.

Max, N., 1983: Panel on the simulation of natural phenomena, Proc. SIGGRAPH83, In *Comput. Gr.* 17,3, 137-139.

Schlesinger, R.E., 1975: A three-dimensional numerical model of an isolated deep convective cloud: Preliminary results. *J. of the Atmospheric Sciences*, 32, 934-957.

Schlesinger, R.E., 1978: A three-dimensional numerical model of an isolated thunderstorm, part I: comparative experiments for variable ambient wind shear. *J. of the Atmospheric Sciences*, 35, 690-713.

Schlesinger, R.E., 1980: A three-dimensional numerical model of an isolated thunderstorm, part II: dynamics of updraft splitting and mesovortex couplet evolution. *J of the Atmospheric Sciences*, 37, 395.

Simpson, J., Van Helvoirt, G., McCumber, M., 1982: Three-dimensional simulations of cumulus congestus clouds on GATE day 261. *J. of the Atmospheric Sciences*, 39, 126.

Reeves, W.T., 1983: Particle systems—a technique for modeling a class of fuzzy objects, *ACM Trans. on Graphics*, 2,2.

Voss, R., 1983: Fourier synthesis of gaussian fractals: $1/f$ noises, landscapes, and flakes, *Tutorial on State of the Art Image Synthesis* v.10, SIGGRAPH83.

Wallace, J. M., and Hobbs, P. V., 1977: *Atmospheric Science*, Academic Press, pp.359-407.

Whitted, T., 1980: An improved illumination model for shaded display, *Comm. ACM* 23, 343-349.

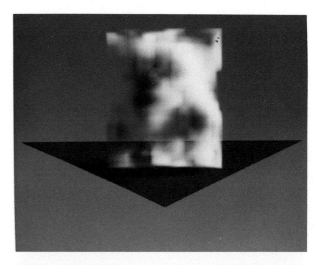

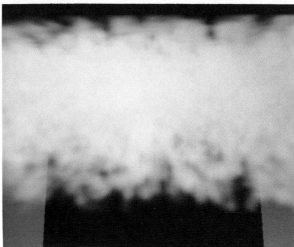

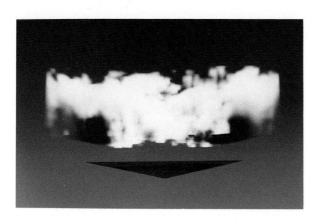

Fig. 3

Fig. 1&2

Fig. 4

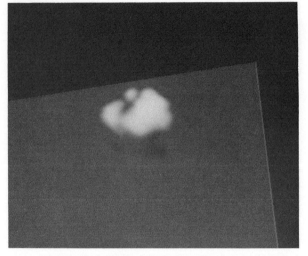

Fig. 5

Fig. 8

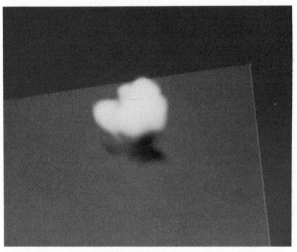

Fig. 6

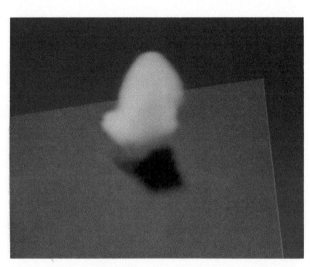

Fig. 9

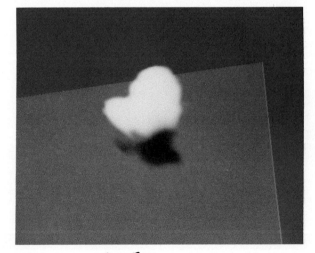

Fig. 7

Fig. 10

PANEL

MICROCOMPUTER GRAPHICS

CHAIR: Howard Pearlmutter - Knoware Institute of Technology

PANEL: Bill Atkinson - Apple Computer
          Susan Kare - Apple Computer
          Charles Moore - Novix
          Doug Clapp - InfoWorld
          Gabrielle Savage - Tom Snyder Productions
          R.J. Mical - Amiga Computer
          Scott Kim - Stanford University

Ranging from home computers for entertainment and education to personal workstations for design and presentation,
microprocessor hardware spans the entire
spectrum of graphic applications. Through
live demonstrations of the latest and most
popular hardware and software offerings,
we hope to give you a feeling for the
rapidly growing field of personal, "human
scale" computing. The session will
include a visual tour of the MacPaint
package and the Quickdraw firmware on
Apple's Macintosh personal computer, as
well as brief demos of software for
educational videogrames, low resolution
typography and interactive, real-time
animation.

Depending on audience questions, we might
also take a look at issues and trends
involved in mass marketing of software,
personalization of technology and owner-
ship of knowledge...and what the ramifica-
tions might be for the future of computer
graphics and the human(-)computer
dialogue.

A System for Algorithm Animation[†]

Marc H. Brown
Robert Sedgewick

Dept. of Computer Science
Brown University
Providence, RI 02912

Abstract: A software environment is described which provides facilities at a variety of levels for "animating" algorithms: exposing properties of programs by displaying multiple dynamic views of the program and associated data structures. The system is operational on a network of graphics-based, personal workstations and has been used successfully in several applications for teaching and research in computer science and mathematics. In this paper, we outline the conceptual framework that we have developed for animating algorithms, describe the system that we have implemented, and give several examples drawn from the host of algorithms that we have animated.

Introduction

Computer programs in execution are complex objects whose properties can be difficult to fathom. Our central thesis is that it is possible to expose the fundamental characteristics of a broad variety of programs through the use of dynamic (real-time) graphic displays and that such algorithm animation has the potential to be quite useful in several contexts. In this paper, we describe a system which we have built based on this thesis and detail some of our experiences in using it over the past year.

One obvious application is computer science education. At Brown University, we have a laboratory/lecture hall containing 60 high-performance scientific workstations (Apollos) with bitmap graphic displays, connected together on a high-bandwidth resource-sharing local area network. Courses in introductory programming, algorithms and data structures, differential equations, and assembly language have been taught in the lab using the software environment described in this paper as the principal medium of communication. Rather than explain a concept using a blackboard or a viewgraph projector, instructors in these courses have been able to use dynamic graphic presentations.

A second application is in research in the design and analysis of algorithms. The courseware that we have developed for teaching the algorithms and data structures course provides a firm basis to allow our software environment to be used for advanced research in a variety of areas. The ready availability of dynamic graphic displays exhibiting various properties of algorithms in execution has the poten-

[†]Support for this research was provided by the Exxon Education Foundation, and by the ONR and DARPA under Contract N00014-83-K-0146 and ARPA Order No. 4786. Equipment support was provided by NSF Grant SER80-04974 and by Apollo Computer, Inc. Support for the second author was provided in part by NSF Grant MCS-83-08806.

Permission to copy without fee all or part of this material is granted provided that the copies are not made or distributed for direct commercial advantage, the ACM copyright notice and the title of the publication and its date appear, and notice is given that copying is by permission of the Association for Computing Machinery. To copy otherwise, or to republish, requires a fee and/or specific permission.

© 1984   ACM   0-89791-138-5/84/007/0177 $00.75

Figure 1. An iconic table of contents for some BALSA animations. This may be thought of as an "index" to a "dynamic book." Selecting an icon with a mouse causes a 10–15 minute dynamic simulation of the corresponding topic to be run, with pauses at key images, after which the "reader" can interact with the algorithms and images. These particular icons represent animations on mathematical algorithms (top row, left to right: Euclid's GCD Algorithm, 3/4 Recursion, Random Numbers, Curve Fitting), sorting (Insertion Sort, Quicksort, Radix Sort, Priority Queues, Mergesort, External Sorting), and searching (bottom row: Sequential Search, Balanced Trees, Hashing, Radix Searching). Several are described in more detail in following figures. The reader must bear in mind that these figures are static "snapshots" from real-time simulations, the essence of many is in their dynamic character.

One of the primary applications of the BALSA environment has been for instruction in an "Electronic Classroom" in the Dept. of Computer Science at Brown (see Fig. 10). Two exemplary courses which integrated the dynamic simulations into lectures were the first semester introductory Pascal programming course (see Fig. 3) and the third semester algorithms and data structures course (see Fig. 4).

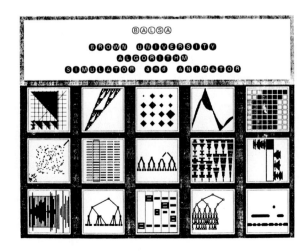

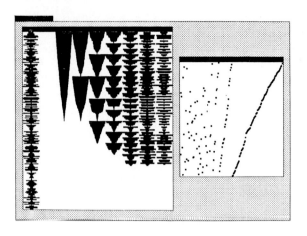

Figure 2. The image above shows top-down recursive
mergesort; the image below shows bottom-up
non-recursive mergesort. The large window in both
images is a "horizontal bars with history" view: the
array being processed is at the leftmost column (bottom
to top) with lengths of bars corresponding to values
of elements. The contents of the array during various
stages in the algorithms are displayed in successive
columns. The small window in both images is a "dots"
view: each element of the array is portrayed as a dot
whose x coordinate corresponds to its position in
the array, and y coordinate corresponds to its value.

In the algorithms and data structures course, a typical
lecture would consist of each student's workstation
displaying a previously created animation script of the
material from the corresponding chapter of the textbook.
Rather than using a viewgraph or blackboard, diagrams
such as those shown here would be presented through
BALSA. Moreover, the BALSA diagrams are dynamic,
which better models the true nature of the material and
thus allows fuller explanations of more complex material
than is available using other modes of communication.
The facilities were available to students during non-class
hours for completing programming assignments,
replaying classroom scripts, and experimenting.

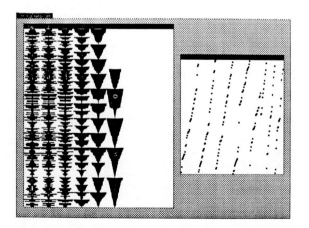

tial to significantly impact advanced research in this area.

A third application is in advanced debugging and systems programming. To date, we have done little specific work in this area, but we believe our work on techniques for visualizing properties of fundamental data structures to be of central importance in such applications. We plan to explore interfaces to performance monitors, debuggers, program development environments and other software systems in future research.

These applications illustrate that "algorithm animation" can involve a variety of different types of users and thus requires support on a variety of different levels. In this paper, we describe the technical aspects of BALSA (Brown ALgorithm Simulator and Animator), the software system we have developed to support these activities, and give examples illustrating various modes of utilization.

Certainly it is a fundamental axiom of computer graphics that visualization of abstract concepts is invaluable, and many researchers have considered the natural question of applying this principle to better understand tools of their own trade (algorithms and data structures). Some previous examples may be found in [1], [2], [3], [5], [7], [9], and [10]. Discussion of some work relating to monitoring programs in execution and to visualizing the operation of large systems programs may be found in [11] and [8], respectively. Also relevant (though not directly related) is the excellent treatment of visual displays in [14]. Many of these efforts involved considerable expense of time and money (for the use of expensive real-time systems or for the production of movies), but they do demonstrate the potential of the concept, especially [2].

The availability of high-performance scientific workstations has made it possible for us to more fully realize that potential. We have developed a software environment which makes real-time simulations of programs (as opposed to movies) using high-resolution graphics readily available to students and researchers. The BALSA system has been in production use by over 450 students and a dozen researchers since September 1983. We have gained extensive experience in actually using the system to animate scores of algorithms. Moreover, it has allowed a dynamic graphic interface to become a natural mode of interaction for a large number of students, teachers, and researchers.

The next section describes our general conceptual framework for animating algorithms. Following that, we describe in more detail what is involved in the implementations. The final section offers concluding comments and outlines some future plans. Illustrations of images from animations that we have implemented are included throughout the paper, with detailed commentary and discussion of some of the applications included in the figure captions.

User Perspective

Many of the facilities provided by BALSA are present in state-of-the-art graphics-based object-oriented programming systems such as Smalltalk [6]. The main reason that we chose to build a tailored special-purpose system is that the real-time dynamics of the programs in operation is of fundamental importance: we were not prepared to pay the performance penalties inherent in the use of a general-purpose system. Essentially, BALSA may be thought of as a laboratory for experimentation with dynamic real-time representations of algorithms. As will become apparant below, our experience with the system has uncovered a variety of fundamental issues concerning processing such objects, which we hope will be of relevance in considering the possibility of supporting BALSA-type operations with acceptable performance in general-purpose systems of the future.

The figures in this paper are only representative of the scores of algorithms that we have animated. In principle, we could make any of these animations available for any type of user at any time. A major goal of our research is to continue development of high-level facilities which might allow this as well as to integrate and assimilate generally useful views and algorithms into BALSA. We fully expect our various system "users" to be using higher level graphic and dynamic primitives as the system matures. Several different types of people can make effective use of the BALSA system, and we have found it convenient to use specific descriptive terms for each mode of use.

Users

We use the term *user* to describe a person who is interested in watching algorithms in execution, using BALSA's interactive facilities. This person does not write code; rather he invokes code written by others. He might be thought of as a "reader" of a dynamic book.

A *scriptwriter* is a person who prepares material for users, using BALSA's high level facilities. This person does not write code in the ordinary sense either, but he may make sophisticated use of interactive facilities and store away material for users. He might be thought of as an "author" of a dynamic book, using raw material developed by others.

An *algorithm designer* in BALSA jargon is a programmer who is interested in using BALSA's facilities to get a dynamic graphical display of his program in execution, so that it might be more easily understood. If the domain of operation of his program is close to something that has already been animated, he may use a previous implementation, and therefore not have to worry about low-level graphics. We have animated algorithms from a variety of domains, so we expect this case to be typical.

An *animator* is a person who designs and implements programs which actually display programs in execution, using BALSA's low-level facilities. This involves two types of programs: those implementing algorithms, which often come from some other source, and those involving the actual

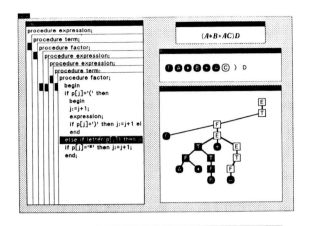

Figure 3. These two images illustrate how a generalized regular expression pattern matcher (*grep*) works. The image above is a recursive descent compiler. In the code view at the left, the current line is highlighted and each procedure is displayed in its own overlapping subwindow. The views on the right show the regular expression, the scanning of the expression, and the parse tree. Note the correspondence between the recursive procedure invocations and the parse tree. The image below shows the workings of the non-deterministic finite state automaton built from the compiler above as it determines whether a text string can be generated by a regular expression. The views at the right show the primary data structure – a "deque." Each element in the deque is a state of the FSA, which can be identified by the tabs. The letter inside the state indicates what input character (if any) must be scanned to advance to that state.

In the introductory Pascal programming course, the principal mode of communication was for each student's machine to mimic what the instructor was doing in the BALSA environment on his machine. Students could also run programs on their own and supply data and answers in response to prompts. (Note that there are no CAI-like facilities for "response judging" in BALSA.) The animations in this course emphasized single-stepping of source code, often simultaneously with multiple levels of pseudo-code, and watching the corresponding effect on the variables and data structures. The style of overlapping subwindows for procedure invocation illustrated above proved to be a very effective method for teaching recursion.

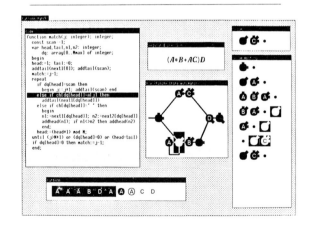

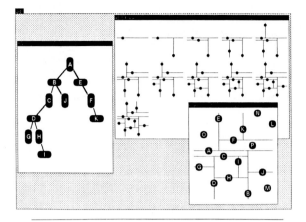

Figure 4. The image above shows the construction of a 2D tree used for range searching. The views are of the tree, the planar subdivisions induced by the tree, and a "history" of the planar subdivisions after each point is inserted. The image below shows a much larger data set (about 75 points). The dark rectangle in the planar view indicates the query range (i.e., the algorithm returns all points which fall in that area). The state of each node indicates the result of the search algorithm: circular nodes have not been accessed; hollow square nodes have been searched and found not to be in the range; filled squares are those points searched and found in the range. The view above the planar view is a 1D representation of the points: each point is drawn with a vertical bar above it corresponding to its x coordinate and the vertical bar below it corresponding to its y coordinate.

BALSA provides facilities for displaying multiple views of a data structure, all of which are updated simultaneously during program execution to give a motion picture of the program in action. Note that the representation of nodes in all views is consistent; this serves to unite the views and make a more effective total picture. Note also how the nodes are drawn in different sizes and with various levels of detail depending on both the size of the data set and the size of window in which the view is displayed. The user is able to "zoom" in or out of any view to any level of detail, as well as "scroll" the image in the window both horizontally and vertically. For studying small cases (and introducing material to students), a "history" view proved to be very useful as did using examples directly from the textbook – with textual data. For large cases, the dynamics of the algorithm in action with abstract graphical representations of the data was the most important aspect.

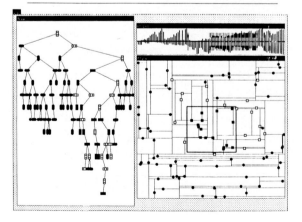

graphic orders to draw pictures.

Facilities

As stated above, our general system philosophy is to provide dynamic *views* of *algorithms* in execution. To support this, the "user" of the BALSA system has three different types of capabilities: *interpretive*, for controlling the execution of the algorithms; *display*, for manipulating the presentation of the views; and *shell*, for higher-level control of BALSA primitives.

The *display* primitives of BALSA allow the user to create, size and position "algorithm windows" which contain "view windows." For example, the screen images in Fig. 4 each show one algorithm window containing three different view windows, while the second image in Fig. 8 shows two algorithm windows each containing three view windows. One possible view is a "code" view which shows the code being executed (see Fig. 3). The user has full flexibility in building his screen environment, subject only to the choice of algorithms and views left to him by the algorithm designer and animator. Commands are invoked by using a mouse on popup menus, and include create, delete, size, move, and other standard window operations. Zooming, panning, and overlapping windows are also supported.

The *interpretive* primitives of BALSA allow the user to start, stop, slow down, or even run an algorithm backwards. Breakpoints and stepping are supported, in units meaningful to the algorithm. It is possible to disable algorithms and views or to run several simultaneously. After an algorithm has run once, an entire history of that run is saved by the system, so it can be rerun (perhaps for comparison with another algorithm) efficiently and easily. In no sense is this part of the system intended to be a general-purpose interpreter: rather it is a set of facilities to allow control of execution of algorithms, tailored to facilitate animation.

The *shell* primitives of BALSA allow the user to save or restore window configurations and to save or invoke *scripts* consisting of sequences of BALSA primitive operations, which are typically quite long. For example, Fig. 8 shows snapshots from two scripts on the same algorithms and views: one that was developed for use in the classroom in an introductory lecture on graph algorithms, the other that was developed for use in research on graph algorithms. Both scripts use the same algorithms and views. Normally, the algorithm designer or the animator will leave a set of window configurations for the user and the scriptwriter will leave a script which loads these configurations and invokes the interpretive facilities of BALSA so as to tell the story of the algorithms. Or, the user may build and save his own window configurations and scripts for later use. Additional utilities such as screen hardcopy and communications with other BALSA users are also supported.

Animating an Algorithm

The following sequence of events would typically be involved to animate a "new" algorithm (unlike any that has ever been done before) in BALSA. First, the algorithm designer implements a "clean" version of the algorithms to be animated (for most of the examples in this paper, we started with the Pascal implementations in [13]), along with programs which provide various types of input to the algorithm. Next, the animator and algorithm designer agree on a general plan for various visualizations of the algorithms, mainly for the purpose of identifying the *interesting events* in the algorithm which should lead to changes in the image being displayed. Then the animator writes the software which maintains the image (changing it in response to interesting events) and the designer adds interesting event signals to the algorithm to pass requisite information to the graphics software. This results in a set of *algorithms* and *views* which are accessible to the user and to the scriptwriter. Then either the user could invoke the BALSA interpreter and window manager directly to create dynamic images of the type described below, or he could invoke *scripts* consisting of sequences of BALSA primitive operations previously created by the scriptwriter. More details on the creation of algorithms, views and scripts are given below, and in Figs. 6 and 7.

The Algorithm

The primary role of the *algorithm designer* is to take an algorithm and to prepare it for animation. If a similar algorithm has already been prepared for BALSA animation, he need only augment the algorithm with interesting event "signals" and inform BALSA which views and inputs are valid for the particular algorithm, using a *configuration* file. The views and inputs can be from the BALSA library, or tailored to the particular algorithm or the particular genre of algorithm (e.g., graph algorithms, or sorting algorithms, or convex hull algorithms, etc.).

At the conceptual level, the *view* paradigm is that of a "monitor" during the execution of an algorithm. As the algorithm executes and data structures are modified, the views update their graphical displays appropriately, based on information from interesting event signals. As mentioned above, we prefer this to the alternative of having the view react to general monitors on the algorithm data structures, because the needs of the view may or may not correspond directly to specific changes in the algorithm's data structures. The interesting event signals are implemented simply as procedure calls to the BALSA *IE-manager*; the parameters are the name of the interesting event followed by algorithm-specific entities. When the user causes BALSA to start normal execution of the algorithm, the algorithm will call the BALSA IE-manager for each interesting event. The IE-manager will then call all of the "active" views (i. e., those views that the user has opened on the screen). The view updates itself graphically, based on the interesting events.

Another modification that must be made to the al-

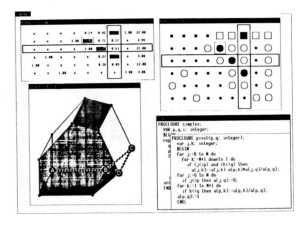

Figure 5. These images illustrate the Simplex method for solving linear programming. The image above shows the tableaux in the upper left view, an iconic version of the tableaux, the code, and the 3D object formed by plotting the system of linear equations. The algorithm is currently in the "pivot" phase, and the effect of previous pivots can be seen by tracing the object edges along the labelled vertices. The image below shows four different wire frame pictures of an object corresponding to a different set of linear constraints. The views (from left to right) are the object from the front, top, side, and finally, with some perspective (actually, it uses a "shearing" transformation). The dotted row in the iconic tableaux indicates a probe to find an appropriate row for the pivot operation, and the solid row is the current choice.

BALSA has been used in a number of non-computer disciplines to model physical experiments, as well as abstract material such as differential equations and differential geometry. These images, for example, are well-suited for a course in operations research or linear algebra. These images also illustrate a use of icons: what is important in the tableaux is not the value of the elements, but whether the element is zero (a bullet), negative (dark dot), or positive (hollow dot). Note also that the top row (which represents the condition we are solving) is displayed differently from the others (each of which represents a given constraint).

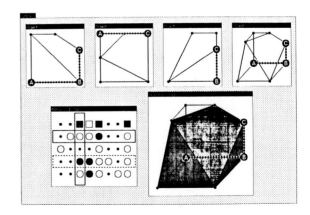

```
now:=0;
for k:=1 to V do
   begin val[k]:=unseen; dad[k]:=0 end;
pqconstruct;
repeat
   k:=pqremove;
   if val[k]=unseen then
      begin
      IE(IEaddfringe,dad[k],k,val[k]);
      val[k]:=0;
      now:=now+1;
      end
   IE(IEaddtree,dad[k],k,val[k]);
   t:=adj[k];
   while t<>z do
      begin
      if val[t↑.v]=unseen then now:=now+1;
      if onpq(t↑.v) and (val[t↑.v]>now) then
         begin
         IE(IEaddfringe,k,t↑.v,now);
         pqchange(t↑.v,now);
         dad[t↑.v]:=k
         end;
      t:=t↑.next
      end
until pqempty;
```

Figure 6. Shown above is a fragment from a typical algorithm after it has been augmented with interesting event markers (shown in italics). This algorithm was used to generate the breadth-first graph traversal images in Figs. 8 and 10, and is taken directly from the textbook.

Shown below is an excerpt from the configuration file that the algorithm designer uses to inform BALSA which views and inputs are valid for a given algorithm. The algorithm in this example is a routine called BreadthFirst (see excerpt above). When the user is prompted with a popup menu of possible algorithms, BALSA will use the label BFS. The algorithm designer has specified that this algorithm has two possible input routines and three different views.

```
ALGORITHMS =>
   BreadthFirst "BFS"
      INPUTS: GRAPHinputFile GRAPHinputRandom
      VIEWS: GRAPHviewPlane GRAPHviewFringe
```

gorithm is the I/O routines. Calls to conventional input routines (e.g., `readln` in Pascal and `scanf` in C) must be replaced by calls to a BALSA *input-manager*, which in turn calls the input module which the user has selected. Tools from the window manager/user interface package are available for the implementation of input modules, so that interaction can be arranged. However, the identity of the input module which is actually in use is transparent to the algorithm. The effect of calls to output routines (e.g., `writeln` and `printf`) are not visible in the BALSA environment per se; however, the user can see conventional, textual output by linking an "output-view" using interesting events with parameters analogous to output statements. For teaching introductory programming, this type of view (and also a view of the input stream) has proven very helpful.

BALSA can take this modified algorithm and generate a *code view*, a "pretty-printed" version (with uniform indentation, interesting event calls removed, and I/O statements restored) with special interesting event calls inserted at each line of code (see Fig. 3). These interesting events are fielded by the BALSA library code view routine, so that the user can see each line of his program highlighted as it is exectued, etc.

Views

The primary role of the *animator* is to implement the graphics commands that actually produce images, in response to interesting events signals.

Our experience has been that sophisticated views can require costly computations to update the graphics on the screen. Since many views (including multiple instantiations of the same view) frequently use the results of the costly computation, we have developed the concept of *view data structure managers* (VDSMs). A VDSM is a set of routines, frequently shared among views, that performs various computations required by the views. Thus, at each interesting event, the BALSA IE-manager calls all VDSMs associated with active views and then calls all active views. Note that computation done in one view cannot be used by another view, since the other view will only be called when the user has opened a window of the view. The shared work must be done by the VDSM.

If an algorithm is executing when the user first opens an instantiation of the view on the screen, the view must display itself corresponding to the current state of the algorithm. This could be done in one of two ways. First, BALSA could replay its saved history of interesting events and the view would update itself incrementally as if the program were executing. This method has the problem that one might not be interested in what happened in the algorithm over history; rather the current state is of interest. The second option, which is more difficult for the animator to implement, is for the view to refresh itself from the current VDSMs. (In this mode, the VDSM —if it was not already active because of another dependent view— would be called incrementally with the history of interesting events so that it would be current.)

VDSMs and views must also be able to reverse execution. Our current BALSA interpreter, when told by the user to run in reverse, will go through the history of interesting events in reverse order and call the VDSMs and views with a flag indicating that the direction is reverse. The VDSMs and views must undo the graphics associated with the interesting events. This is also another reason for VDSMs: while conventional compilers and interpreters do not run code backwards, the VDSM data structures need to be undone to some extent. Undoing the graphics for some views is simple. For example, to undo the effects of exchanging the contents of two elements from an array is usually identical to exchanging them in the first place. In contrast, undoing the insertion of a node in a balanced 2-3-4 tree is non-trivial.

The final responsibility of views is that of "inquiry." For example, if an animator writes an input module for a binary tree deletion algorithm, the user might want to specify which node to delete by pointing at it with a mouse. The view must be able to map a point on the screen into a coordinate system meaningful to the view, VDSM, and input modules.

In summary, a view can be called in one of five "modes": forward, backward, rerun (usually the same as forward), refresh, or inquiry. The VDSMs can be called in either the forward or backward mode. Most successful animators take the approach of designing for all modes, but only implementing the forward and (if the input module requires) inquiry modes to start. As the view matures, the other modes are gradually implemented. For example, animators will often not invest the time needed to make a view reverse itself until the view has become more versatile, at which time it would probably also be added the BALSA library.

Scripts

The primary job of the *scriptwriter* is to assemble algorithms and views into a coherent dynamic entity to tell a story. The mechanism currently provided in BALSA to allow this is quite rudimentary: the scriptwriter simply uses the interactive facilities of BALSA in a mode where everything that he does is saved in a file to be later played back. Some features are provided to allow different things to happen on playback: the most commonly used is the *future freeze* which is a no-op during interaction, but a "pause" (wait for the user to press a button) during playback. Also, it is possible to save complex window configurations (*scenes*) to be loaded later. Typically, the scriptwriter will create scenes or sequences of scenes consisting of several algorithms and views, then create a script to run the algorithms on a variety of inputs, with future freezes inserted at particularly interesting points.

It is possible, albeit difficult, to edit scripts: this is an area in which we plan to significantly extend the capabilities of BALSA. Also, we expect to allow various types of conditional execution of scripts (extensions to future freeze) in future versions of the system.

```
IES=>
  IEinit "Initialize" "%d %d %d %d"
    -- xmin, ymin, xmax, ymax
  IEinitvertex "Init Vertex" "%d %d %d"
    -- vertex id, xcoord, ycoord
  IEinitedge "Init Edge" "%d %d %d"
    -- vertex1, vertex2, weight
  IEaddtree "Add Vertex to Tree" "%d %d %d"
    -- father vertex, vertex, value
  IEaddfringe "Add Vertex to Fringe" "%d %d %d"
    -- father vertex, vertex, value

INPUTS=>
  GRAPHinputFile "File"
  GRAPHinputRandom "Random"

VIEWS=>
  GRAPHviewPlane "Points in Plane"
    IES: IEinit IEinitvertex IEinitedge
         IEaddtree IEaddfringe
    VDSMS: GRAPHvdsm
```

Figure 7. Shown above is an excerpt from the configuration file that the animator uses to provide BALSA with detailed information about interesting events, inputs, and views. Each interesting event registers with BALSA a control string specifying the data types of the algorithm-specific parameters, and each view lists its associated VDSMs and the interesting events to which it will respond.

Shown below is pseudo-code for the VDSM and view that displays the graph. With the VDSM as shown below, the view could not refresh itself from the current state of the data structures, nor could it execute in the "backward" direction (because the old mark-state of each node is not known). Thus, a more sophisticated VDSM would be needed, but the view would not be any more complicated than above. Note carefully that the view data structure does *not* include graph edges (they are just drawn on the screen). This view and VDSM are very versatile, and can be used for many very different graph algorithms, including those for dense graphs which are based on an adjacency matrix rather than an adjacency list.

```
GRAPHvdsm:
  switch (type of interesting event)
    case IEinitedge:
      save x and y coords of vertex
      mark all vertices as "unseen"
    case IEaddtree:
      mark vertex as "tree"
    case IEaddfringe:
      mark vertex as "fringe"
  endcase

GRAPHviewPlane:
  switch (type of interesting event)
    case IEinit:
      initialize graphics window to parms
    case IEinitvertex:
      draw vertex node in its mark-state
    case IEinitedge:
    case IEaddtree:
    case IEaddfringe:
      if both vertices are "unseen" =>
        style=THIN
      else if either vertex is "fringe" =>
        style=DASHED;
      else style=THICK
      draw edge from v1 to v2 in style
      draw v1 node in its mark-state
      draw v2 node in its mark-state
  endcase
```

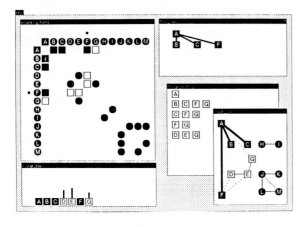

Figure 8. The image above illustrates a breadth-first traversal of a small undirected graph. The display style of each node and edge indicates its state: dark circular nodes with thin edges have not yet been visited; hollow square nodes with dotted edges are nodes on the priority queue data structure ready to be visited in the near future; and dark square nodes with thick edges are nodes which have already been visited. The large view at the left shows the adjacency matrix; the view below that shows the current contents of the priority queue (the height of the stick above each node indicates its priority); the view at the upper right shows the connected components; the view below that shows a "history" of the fringe; and finally, the view in the lower right corner shows the graph itself. The image below is a comparison of depth-first (top) and breadth-first (bottom) traversal algorithms.

BALSA has been used for research in the design of algorithms. It is especially useful when designing new variants of old algorithms, or new algorithms which operate within standard contexts. The image below illustrates the BALSA feature of executing multiple algorithms in parallel. This has proven to be a very effective means for comparing and contrasting different methods. (BALSA synchronizes the algorithms by allowing each to execute a fixed number of *interesting events*.)

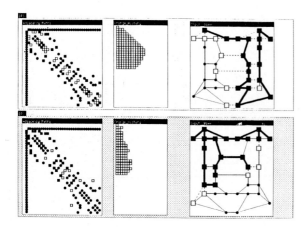

Conclusion

One thing that we have learned from our experience in animating algorithms is that algorithms in execution are even more complex and intricate objects than we had anticipated, and we can make good use of further improvements in hardware technology. For example, preliminary experiments show that color is likely to play a prominent role in future animations (see Figs. 9–10). We have several plans for extending animations that we have done in black-and-white to make full use of color.

By contrast, a second thing that we have learned from our experience is that many of the animations that we finally settled on could be done on much more modest hardware. Accordingly, we are investigating the development of a BALSA that could be made widely available, say on Apple Macintoshes or IBM PCs. This does not imply that it would have been prudent to use such hardware from the beginning: most of our animations are the product of a significant amount of experimentation and development, which would not have been feasible on less powerful machines.

Our highest priority is to evaluate and assess the views that we have implemented, with a general goal of assimilating and integrating them into the system, so that more complicated animations can be easily built from them. This is likely to be quite difficult, for example, we have over a dozen animations involving trees, but each has slightly different characteristics (see, for example, Figs. 3 and 4).

Also under study is the addition of more general-purpose capabilities to the system (e.g., a syntax-directed editor), automation of some of the stages of animation (e.g., the addition of interesting events), and the implementation of BALSA-like animations on general-purpose systems (e.g., those which support monitors, such as PECAN [12]). Of prime concern here is the balance between performance (as stressed in BALSA) and functionality (as stressed in PECAN).

Another area of interest is to provide more powerful facilities for the scriptwriter. Certainly, he should be able to edit scripts, perhaps using a generalized undo-redo facility such as [15], though the extensive amount of context in BALSA makes this challenging. Yet another possibility is to consider nonlinear or conditional scripts, as in traditional computer-aided-instruction systems. Also, we have plans for providing graphical aids to the scriptwriter, allowing him to manipulate iconic representations of window configurations, algorithms, views, input modules, and scripts.

Finally, we are continually interested in extending the applicability of BALSA by animating more programs from more domains. In particular, we would like to address the problem of animating very large programs, so that BALSA could be of use in systems programming applications. For these and other applications, it is our hope that the tools that we have built to date will convince teachers and researchers that there is the potential to make a quantum step forward in the way in which they interact with computer systems.

References

[1]   Baecker, Ronald, "Two System Which Produce Animated Representations of the Execution of Computer Programs," *ACM SIGCSE Bulletin* **7**, 1 (February 1975), 158-167.

[2]   Baecker, Ronald, "Sorting out Sorting," 16mm color sound file, 25 minutes, 1981. (SIGGRAPH 1981, Dallas, Texas)

[3]   Booth, Kellogg, "PQ Trees," 16mm color silent file, 12 minutes, 1975.

[4]   Brown, Marc H. and Sedgewick, Robert, "Progress Report: Brown University Instuctional Computing Laboratory," *ACM SIGCSE Bulletin* **16**, 1 (February 1984).

[5]   Dionne, Mark S. and Mackworth, Alan K., "ANTICS – A System for Animating LISP Programs," *Computer Graphics and Image Processing* **7** (1978), 105-119.

[6]   Goldberg, Adele, *Smalltalk*, Addison-Wesley, Reading, MA, 1983.

[7]   Guibas, Leo and Sedgewick, Robert, "A Dichromatic Framework for Balanced Trees," in *Proc. 19th Annual Symp. on Foundations of Computer Science*, October 1978, pp.8-21.

[8]   Herot, Christopher F., et. al., "An Integrated Environment for Program Visualization," in *Automated Tools for Information Systems Design*, H.J. Schneider and A.I. Wasserman, Ed., North Holland Publishing Co., 1982, pp. 237-259.

[9]   Knowlton, Kenneth C., "L6: Bell Telephone Laboratories Low-Level Linked List Language," two black and white sound films, 1966.

[10]   Myers, Brad A., "Displaying Data Structures for Interactive Debugging," CSL-80-7, Xerox PARC, Palo Alto, CA, 1980. (Summary in SIGGRAPH 1983)

[11]   Plattner, Bernhard and Nievergelt, Jurg, "Monitoring Program Execution: A Survey," *Computer* **14** (November 1981), 76-93.

[12]   Reiss, Steven P., "PECAN: A Program Development System that Supports Multiple Views," , Orlando, FL, March, 1984.

[13]   Sedgewick, Robert, *Algorithms*, Addison-Wesley, Reading, MA, 1983.

[14]   Tufte, Edward R., *The Visual Display of Quantitative Information*, Graphics Press, Cheshire, CT, 1983.

[15]   Vitter, Jeffrey S., "USeR: Undo, Skip, et Redo," , Pittsburg, PA, April, 1984.

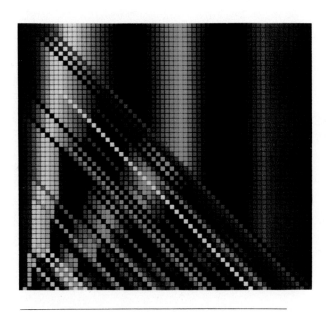

Figure 9. These two images are "chips" views of Bubble Sort (above) and Quicksort (below). The contents of the array are displayed as a row of paint chips (from left to right), with color corresponding to value. Each row (from bottom to top) shows the the array at various stages of the algorithm. It is instructive to note that the number of "stages" does not determine a fast or slow algorithm; rather, it is the amount of work that must be done during each stage. In the Quicksort image, the dot at the center of each chip indicates this "work": a white dot indicates that the element was moved, and a black dot indicates that the element was accessed but not modified. Thus, it is the sum of these dots that gives a realistic first-approximation of the algorithm running times. In a "dots" image of Bubblesort, about half of the total chips would contain dots. Note how color is used to illustrate the time dimension.

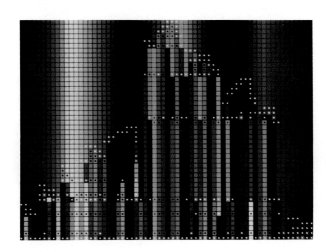

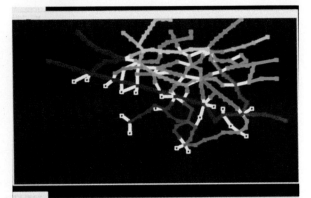

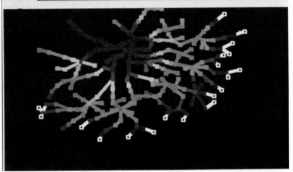

Acknowledgements

To date, the primary use of BALSA has been in the instructional computing laboratory at Brown. Although many people have helped to make the project successful, Andy van Dam's tireless efforts to ensure an impressive physical environment certainly must be singled out for acknowledgement. He has also contributed to the project as the instructor of the introductory programming course.

Much of the current version of BALSA was implemented by Mike Strickman. Steve Reiss, Joe Pato, and Dave Nanian wrote significant pieces of the underlying software. Tom Freeman did preliminary work for some of the color images.

As usual, Janet Incerpi's TEXpertise has been invaluable, and thanks are due to Steve Feiner for advice and support in producing the images. These two also provided detailed comments and suggestions on earlier drafts of the paper.

A prototype on which some of the graph traversal views are based was developed by the second author with Leo Guibas at Xerox PARC, using the Cedar environment on the Dorado.

Figure 10. The image above illustrates a depth-first (top) and a breadth-first (bottom) traversal of the graph representing the Paris Metro system. Colors spanning the spectrum from red to blue are used to indicate when in time a particular node has been visited. The nodes in white are on the data structure ready to be visited; those in black have not yet been visited (see Fig. 8).

The picture below (reprinted courtesy of Bryce Flynn — Picture Group Inc.) shows the "Electronic Classroom" at Brown, a specially built auditorium/lecture hall housing 60 powerful graphics-based workstations. This picture was taken during a lecture on elementary sorting (see Fig. 9).

Priority Windows: A Device Independent, Vector Oriented Approach

Richard J. Littlefield
Battelle, Pacific Northwest Laboratories

Abstract

Priority windows are a basic tool for interactive graphics, underlying such techniques as pop-up menus and single screen viewing and control of multiple contexts. Most implementations of priority windows are raster oriented, frequently relying on special hardware capabilities such as high speed rasterops. This paper discusses an alternative approach, based on vector clipping, that works with any display device capable of drawing and erasing vectors. It has been used to implement a general purpose windowing package that supports application programs using a vector graphics model. It is device independent, running without change on a desktop computer with integral graphics and on a timesharing system with a peripheral display. In purely device independent form, windowing performance depends on host processing speed and communications bandwidth. Techniques are described for improving responsiveness by overlapping some windowing computations with the user's think time. Performance improvements based on extended device capabilities such as rectangular fill, hardware characters, and local display lists with clipping are also suggested.

Presentation of this paper included a videotape showing the dynamics of one application on an HP-9000 desktop computer and on a VAX 11/780 plus Ramtek Marquis configuration.

Keywords: CR Categories and Subject Descriptors: D.2.2 [Software Engineering]: Tools and Techniques - user interfaces; I.3.3 [Computer Graphics]: Picture/Image Generation - display algorithms; I.3.4 [Computer Graphics] Graphics Utilities - graphics packages; software support; I.3.6 [Computer Graphics] Methodology and Techniques - device independence

General Terms: Algorithms, Design, Experimentation

Permission to copy without fee all or part of this material is granted provided that the copies are not made or distributed for direct commercial advantage, the ACM copyright notice and the title of the publication and its date appear, and notice is given that copying is by permission of the Association for Computing Machinery. To copy otherwise, or to republish, requires a fee and/or specific permission.

© 1984   ACM   0-89791-138-5/84/007/0187 $00.75

1. INTRODUCTION

Priority windows provide a basic tool for implementing certain graphical interaction techniques, such as pop-up menus and single screen control of simultaneous processes. These techniques provide a very powerful and natural user interface. They are becoming common in vendor-specific products, and support for priority windows is now an integral part of several computer systems, including the Apple Lisa [1], Apollo Domain [2], Symbolics Lisp machine [3], Xerox Star [4], and Bell Labs Blit [5], among others.

Unfortunately, all this has been of little use to developers of portable application programs. The commercial implementations listed above are all tied to a particular hardware/software combination. Their priority windows are supported only on a few specific displays that are very tightly coupled to the operating system and processor. Frequently special hardware capabilities are required, such as high speed block transfer rasterops. This provides optimum performance, but is extremely inflexible. For example, one cannot add a foreign graphics display and expect the priority windows to work with it. This has hindered more widespread use of pop-up menus and similar techniques, because program developers are understandably reluctant to spend much effort making their programs less portable.

This paper describes a different approach to priority windowing. It assumes that the display device can draw and selectively erase vectors, nothing more. Because of these minimal requirements, the approach works with virtually any current generation display. We have used it to create a device-independent priority windowing package to support interactive graphics programs. Aside from the advantages of portability, the package has also proved to have surprisingly high performance in a highly interactive application. In part, this is because the package is structured to allow overlapping of some computations with the user's think time.

The paper is organized as follows. Section 2 describes functional specifications of the windowing package, while Section 3 discusses the implementation of these functions. Section 4 describes extensions that allow overlapping computations and think time. Statistics on package performance are in Section 5, and potential improvements are outlined in Section 6. Finally, Section 7 summarizes the major points and conclusions.

2. FUNCTIONAL SPECIFICATIONS

Figure 1 shows several typical screens produced by an application program using the windowing scheme. In Figure 1a, three windows are active. The lowest priority window, in the background, covers the entire display area and has no frame. It contains a complex graphics display incorporating several thousand vectors and a little text. This window is used by the application for all of its graphics output. Two other windows overlay this. One of them contains the current menu and prompt/input line. This window was opened by the application's input module. The highest priority window, in the foreground, contains help text. It too was opened by the input module, in response to the user requesting assistance.

In this application, all windows except the background are transient. The help window will disappear, as shown in Figure 1b, when the user indicates he is done reading it. Similarly, the menu window will disappear when the user provides the requested input, as shown in Figure 1c. A new menu window, probably a different size, will appear when the application is ready for more input. In the event that the menu window should overlay important graphics, it can be relocated or temporarily removed, upon user request.

The functional specifications of the windowing package are designed for convenient use by an application program. In a multiple process environment, the windowing package could be used by a screen driver at the operating system level, supporting many application programs simultaneously. In that context, this paper's use of the term "application program" should be translated to "the caller of the windowing package".) Routines are provided for opening, closing, and moving windows, and changing their priorities. Routines are also provided for temporarily removing a window from the display and subsequently restoring it with contents intact. The package maintains a display list for each window and assumes all responsibility for updating the

a)

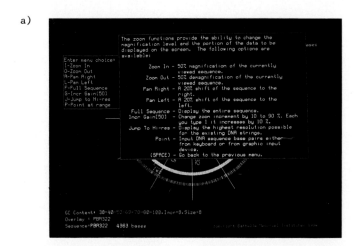

b)

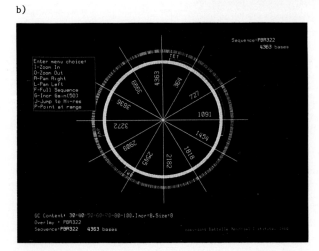

c)

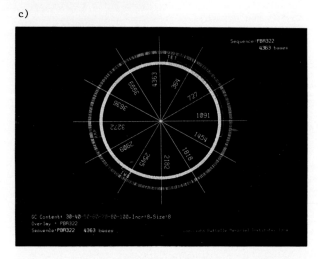

Figure 1. These application program displays show several active windows. A large background window containing most of the graphics is continuously active. Menu and help windows are dynamically opened and closed as required.

screen as windows come and go. However, the windowing package is responsible only for maintaining the graphics. User interface issues, such as when and where to open new windows, are left to the application program or its other helpers.

Each window has its own local coordinate system, which is initially specified by the application program and can be changed at any time. By adjusting the local coordinate system and/or the screen location and size, windows can be zoomed and panned, as well as just being moved on the screen. Routines are provided for performing forward and inverse coordinate transformations. These are particularly useful for processing graphic input that may be directed to any of several windows. They allow the input to be accepted in screen coordinates, with local coordinates being determined by which window the input appears to be directed to.

A concept of "current window" simplifies interfacing to the windowing package. At any instant, one window is declared to be current, and all drawing primitives are directed to it. To draw in a different window, the application program must first declare it to be the current window. This shortens the calling sequences. It also allows primitive drawing routines in the windowing package to have the same arguments as older, nonwindowing graphics packages. This facilitates adding windows to existing applications programs.

The windowing package can be envisioned as a graphics filter. Its input consists of vectors and window specifications, and its output consists of transformed and clipped vectors. Input to the windowing package can come directly from an application program. It could also come from another graphics support package such as CORE, GKS, or one of the many higher level special purpose packages. In that case, the windowing package would ordinarily be far along in the pipeline, after all other device independent operations. Output from the windowing package is directed to lower level device dependent routines for actually driving the display.

3. IMPLEMENTATION

The whole idea of priority windows is to display only what is inside each window and outside all windows of higher priority. Other implementations commonly accomplish this by converting graphics and text to raster form, then transferring the highest priority pixels to the display. The techniques presented in this paper work directly on vectors.

Figure 2 illustrates the organization of the windowing package. For the most part, the algorithms and data structures are straightforward. The windowing package maintains tables that describe the position, size, and priority of each window. Each window has a display list containing vectors drawn in that window. Incoming vectors are saved in the display list. Then they are clipped inside their own window, and outside all windows of higher priority. Any surviving fragments are drawn. When a

window is opened, its screen area is erased. When a window is closed or moved, affected areas of the screen are erased, then redrawn by extracting vectors from the display lists and clipping them again.

Conventional algorithms are used for clipping vectors and maintaining the display lists. They can be found in any computer graphics text and will not be discussed here. Some subtle problems do arise, however, in attempting to optimize the erase/redraw operation.

In general, display devices support selective erase in three ways:

1. not at all (pen plotters, direct view storage tubes);
2. removing a vector from a local display list (refresh stroke writers); or
3. writing over graphics using background color (raster displays).

Most new devices being introduced fall in the third category, and the techniques discussed here apply primarily to them. These devices combine a raster display with a vector oriented communications protocol. Selected areas can be erased by filling them with closely spaced vectors in background color. The exact spacing is not critical as long as it corresponds to no more than one pixel. However, finite display resolution can produce two undesirable effects if one does not take special care to avoid them.

The first effect is intermittent thickening of lines that are drawn clipped and then redrawn unclipped. This could happen, for example, if a line were partially hidden by a foreground window when first drawn, and then the foreground window were closed. Figure 3 illustrates the effect.

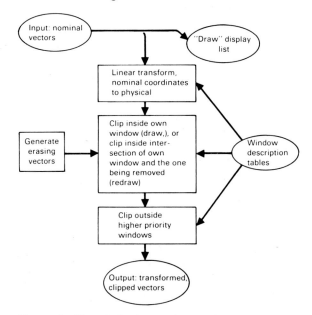

Figure 2. The windowing package acts as a filter. Vectors and window descriptions go in; transformed, clipped vectors come out.

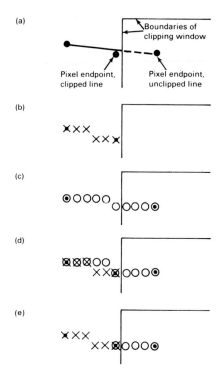

(a)

Boundaries of clipping window

Pixel endpoint, clipped line

Pixel endpoint, unclipped line

(b)

(c)

(d)

(e)

Figure 3. Only newly visible segments of lines should be redrawn. Suppose a line is clipped as shown in (a). After rasterizing, the clipped and unclipped versions may not line up perfectly (b, c). Drawing the entire unclipped line on top of the clipped can cause intermittent thickening because of the misalignment (d). Better results are obtained by drawing only the newly visible part (e).

Because rasterizing is done by the display device, based on pixel coordinate endpoints, the rasterized versions of clipped and unclipped vectors generally will not line up perfectly. This problem is addressed in [5], where it is solved by using a restartable rasterizing algorithm (DDA) on the individual fragments. Unfortunately, this approach cannot be used on most devices because their DDA parameters cannot be specified. To avoid the effect completely, one could erase the entire affected vector before redrawing its unclipped version. Unfortunately, this causes other problems if different colored lines cross each other. A more workable solution is to redraw only the newly visible portion of each vector when it is uncovered (see "clip inside", Figure 2). This approach restricts potential perturbations to the pixel or two at the boundary of the window. In practice, they are not noticeable.

The second effect is an incorrect display caused by erasing slightly too much or too little. The tricky part is erasing a low priority window without also erasing any part of a higher priority window that overlaps it. If one ignores the finite display resolution, and clips exactly at the nominal window boundaries, then some pixels may be contained in both windows. When the low priority

window is erased, lines on the edge of the high priority window may disappear also.

One possible solution is to allow the erase to occur, and then redraw the boundary region of the high priority window. Unfortunately, this produces unpleasant flickering effects. A better approach is illustrated in Figure 4. A "safety margin" is provided around each window. Vectors inside a window are clipped to the inner margin, while vectors in lower priority windows are clipped to the outer margin. Filling vectors to erase both windows are clipped half-way through the margin. Thus, any pixels belonging to both windows may simply be erased more frequently. The safety margin width is not critical, as long as it corresponds to at least two pixels.

It might seem more reasonable to deal directly in pixel coordinates for both erasing and vector clipping, because then the operations are straightforward. However, there are good reasons to avoid this approach. Device driver support software often does not allow one to specify or obtain pixel coordinates. Even if nominal pixel coordinates are available, they cannot always be trusted. For example, if the same protocol is used to drive several devices, the actual resolution may well be different from the nominal resolution assumed by the support software. For these reasons, software is more portable and reliable if it does not require exact pixel coordinates. The techniques described above produce quite good results with only a very rough estimate of display resolution.

The simple scheme described above works very well with applications that update windows primarily by adding to them, with complete erases occurring periodically. Providing selective erase is somewhat more complicated, at least in the general case. One classic method that application programs use to erase something is to just draw it again, in background color. Although this method often works with windows, it can have unfortunate

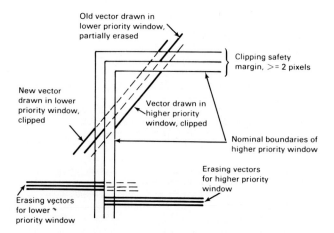

Old vector drawn in lower priority window, partially erased

Clipping safety margin, >= 2 pixels

New vector drawn in lower priority window, clipped

Vector drawn in higher priority window, clipped

Nominal boundaries of higher priority window

Erasing vectors for higher priority window

Erasing vectors for lower priority window

Figure 4. A "clipping safety margin" around each window guarantees correct results, without requiring exact pixel coordinate calculations.

side effects. All the vectors ever drawn will accumulate in the display lists, increasing the memory and processor time required for window operations. Another problem arises if window visibility is changed between drawing and erasing a vector. As Figure 2 illustrates, a line drawn in two or more pieces often is not quite the same as a one piece line between the same endpoints. If one is supposed to erase the other, chances are good that a ghost will be left. A final problem is that when part of a window is made visible, its entire history will be replayed. Although this effect is occasionally amusing, it would not be appreciated for long.

The best solution to these problems would be to identify selective erase as a desired function, and provide application program interface routines specifically for that purpose. The approach seems straightforward. The existing drawing routines would be changed to keep track of the various pieces of any lines that are drawn clipped. New erase routines would use this information to update the graphics display, and would also delete the indicated entries from the display lists. It should be noted, however, that we have not yet needed to do this.

The windowing package is currently implemented as a set of Fortran subroutines, whose calling sequences are outlined in Table 1. Most of the routines and functions have been described in the preceding discussion. PREPARE_REMOVE_WINDOW is discussed in the next section. One routine, FRAME_WINDOW_USER, requires some explanation. The issue is how to draw a frame around a window. Since the package is general purpose, it is not appropriate to mandate any particular frame style. It might seem that the application program could frame its own windows as they are opened, using the standard drawing primitives. However, the frame requires special treatment, since it must be adjusted if the window changes size. This would not be possible if the frame were subjected to normal display list processing.

FRAME_WINDOW_USER is the solution to this quandary. It is supplied by the application program,

being known to the windowing package by its special name. Whenever a window is opened or redrawn, the windowing package turns off display list processing and calls FRAME_WINDOW_USER, which uses the standard primitives to draw the frame. A flag is set during this time so that the frame graphics are not entered into the display list. The window identifier and associated parameters are passed in so that the frame style can be adjusted appropriately.

4. OVERLAPPING COMPUTATIONS WITH USER THINK TIME

In the vector oriented approach, the most expensive operation is removing a window from the display. This requires scanning the display lists of all windows that are overlapped by the one being removed, clipping them against the removed window, and redrawing the results. If the display is complicated, this can require a significant amount of processor time. In our applications, the processor time per se is of no concern, but the associated delay is perceived by the user as degraded response.

This problem can be avoided in some cases by overlapping the time-consuming calculations with the user's think time. This is done by introducing a new application interface routine, called PREPARE_REMOVE_WINDOW in Table 1. This routine is called after all prompts are issued, but before waiting for input. It goes through all the internal processing to remove the window from the display, but does not produce any graphics output. Instead, its results are stored as physical plotting coordinates in another display list associated with the window, as shown in Figure 5. When the window is subsequently removed, this list is simply dumped to the display. Thus, the removal starts instantly and goes as fast as the device driver, communications line, and display device will allow. The total computation time is not affected, but the user sees greatly improved response.

This technique is excellent for pop-up menus and help windows, for which it is certain that the windows will be opened and closed in stack order.

Table 1. Calling sequences for windowing package subroutines.

```
INITIALIZE_WINDOWING_PACKAGE
OPEN_INDOW (user_id,screen_limits,plot_limits,window_id)
SET_CURRENT_WINDOW (window_id)
CLOSE_WINDOW
POP_WINDOW
PREPARE_REMOVE_WINDOW
REMOVE_WINDOW
RESTORE_WINDOW
SET_WINDOW_LIMITS_AND_REDRAW (screen_limits,plot_limits)
PLOT_IN_WINDOW (x,y,ipen)
WHERE_IN_WINDOW (x,y)
NEWPEN_IN_WINDOW (npen)
NEWPAGE_IN_WINDOW
CONVERT_SCREEN_TO_PLOT (window_id,x_screen,y_screen,x_plot,y_plot)
CONVERT_PLOT_TO_SCREEN (window_id,x_plot,y_plot,x_screen,y_screen)
FRAME_WINDOW_USER (user_id,screen_limits,plot_limits,window_id)
```

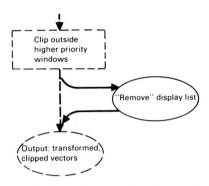

Figure 5. The addition of a "remove" display list improves response time by allowing time consuming calculations to be overlapped with the user's think time.

It cannot be used in all cases, however. The window's visibility must not be changed between calling PREPARE_REMOVE_WINDOW and actually removing it. Also, graphics must not be drawn behind a window for which PREPARE_REMOVE_WINDOW has been called. Both cases invalidate the remove display list and can cause improper results.

5. PERFORMANCE

The windowing package as currently implemented is extremely device independent. It assumes that the display device can just draw vectors. Overall high performance relies on host processing power and fast transmission of vectors. As described in the next section, significant performance improvements could be made by taking advantage of more powerful display capabilities.

Priority windows for graphics are usually implemented on a bitmap display equipped with high speed rasterops [5]. These represent the obvious standard for comparison. To be blunt, vector oriented windowing cannot hope to be as fast as the rasterop approach. After all, just erasing part of a window will generally take at least half as long as a rasterop that completely updates the same pixels. (The erase only stores every pixel, while the rasterop must also fetch them.) The vector redrawing time is usually much longer. However, this is a specious comparison. We do not claim that vector clipping should be used instead of rasterops, but merely that it is a good substitute when a rasterop display is not available. This is an important point for anyone trying to produce a portable application, since rasterop displays are still much more the exception than the rule.

It is more appropriate to consider some absolute measure of performance, such as responsiveness. The application shown in Figure 1 runs on an HP 9000, a desktop computer with integral graphics. The time to open menu and help windows is negligible, a small fraction of a second. The plotting time to remove a window depends on the amount of graphics behind it. Removing the menu window in Figure 1b requires a fraction of a second; the help window in Figure 1a takes two seconds. The time to prepare for removing a window depends on

the total amount of graphics in lower priority windows. Figure 1 requires about 4 seconds per window. However, since this is overlapped with the user's think time, the average user normally is not aware of it.

The same application also runs on a VAX 11/780 using a Ramtek Marquis display system. This configuration is approximately twice as fast as the HP-9000.

The overhead introduced by passing graphics through the windowing package is small. In the application shown in Figures 1-3, the decrease in plotting speed caused by introducing windowing was about 30%. This application directs all output to the highest priority window, so the extra time is used mainly for subroutine calls, coordinate transformations, and display list management. If output were directed to lower priority windows, the extra clipping would require some additional time.

6. SUGGESTIONS FOR IMPROVING PERFORMANCE

The most likely bottlenecks in vector-oriented windowing are transmission time and host computing resources. Performance in both areas could be significantly improved by taking advantage of commonly available extended device capabilities. Many devices support filled rectangles as a primitive. The windowing package could take advantage of this by decomposing areas to be erased into rectangles that the display could fill by itself. This would avoid generating, clipping, and transmitting the closely spaced erasing vectors. Many devices also have hardware characters. Using these would greatly reduce the transmission time for pop-up menus and help windows. This would require modifying the clipping algorithms to treat character cells as indivisible units, as well as extending the display list formats. Finally, some newer devices support local display lists and clipping. The windowing package could use these by decomposing an area to be repainted into rectangular areas showing only a single window. Then each rectangle could be repainted by setting the device's clipping window and having it rerun the local display list. This would greatly reduce both transmission time and host processing, since the host would no longer have to traverse and clip potentially long display lists. These modifications could be applied to many newer displays, such as the Tektronix 41xx series color displays.

If the device does not support local display list management and clipping, then these operations must be done on the host. In this case, nothing can be done about the transmission time for redrawing. However, the host computational requirements could be greatly reduced by using more highly organized display lists. The performance described in the previous section comes from treating the display lists as strictly linear. The entire display list for each background window is scanned whenever a foreground window is opened, closed, or moved. Since the foreground window is typically rather small, the package spends much of its redraw computation time determining that vectors do not in fact intersect the affected area. Most of this time could be avoided by indexing the display lists on vector endpoint position, so that vectors far away from the affected area would not even be considered. As our applications become more complicated, we will probably have to do this.

7. SUMMARY AND CONCLUSIONS

This paper has described a device independent approach to priority windowing. The method is based on vector clipping operations, and assumes only that the display can draw and erase lines. Special hardware capabilities, such as high speed rasterops, are not required. The approach can thus be used with a wide variety of devices, including virtually all raster displays and terminals. Extended device capabilities such as rectangular fill, hardware characters, and local display lists and clipping can be used to improve the performance, without changing the basic ideas or the application program interface.

Even in its device independent form, the approach works surprisingly well. In one highly interactive application, it supports background displays containing several thousand vectors, with pop-up menus and help windows in the foreground. Responsiveness is enhanced by overlapping computations with the user's think time. In most cases, the user perceives no delay when windows are opened and closed.

This vector oriented approach to priority windowing provides an interesting alternative to more conventional raster oriented methods. By providing both device independence and good performance, it allows program developers to take advantage of powerful interaction techniques while still supporting a wide variety of devices.

ACKNOWLEDGMENTS

Thanks are due to Jim Thomas, whose enthusiasm for pop-up menus and their ilk encouraged me to stick with this problem, and to Dan Rosier, who used the result so convincingly in a real application. This work was funded by Battelle Corporate Technical Development for Battelle Memorial Institute.

REFERENCES

[1] Williams, G., "The Lisa Computer System", BYTE Magazine, February 1983, pp.33-50.

[2] Apollo Computer, Inc., 1982, Apollo System User's Guide, Release 4.0., Chelmsford, MA.

[3] Weinreb, D., and Moon, D., Introduction to Using the Window System, Symbolics, Inc., 1981.

[4] Xerox Corporation, 1982, 8010 Star Information System Reference Guide, Dallas, TX.

[5] Pike, R., "Graphics in Overlapping Bitmap Layers", Computer Graphics, Vol.17, No.3, July 1983, pp.331-356.

Manipulating Simulated Objects with Real-world Gestures using a Force and Position Sensitive Screen

Margaret R. Minsky
Atari Cambridge Research
Cambridge, Massachusetts

Author's present address:
Media Laboratory
Massachusetts Institute of Technology
Cambridge, Massachusetts

Abstract

A flexible interface to computing environments can be provided by gestural input. We describe a prototype system that recognizes some types of single-finger gestures and uses these gestures to manipulate displayed objects. An experimental gesture input device yields information about single finger gestures in terms of position, pressure, and shear forces on a screen. The gestures are classified by a "gesture parser" and used to control actions in a fingerpainting program, an interactive computing system designed for young children, and an interactive digital logic simulation.

CR Categories and Subject Descriptors: I.3.6 [Computer Graphics] Methodology and Techniques - interaction techniques; H.1.2 [Models and Principles]: User/Machine Systems - human information processing; D.2.2 [Software Engineering] Tools and Techniques - user interfaces; I.3.1 [Computer Graphics] Hardware Architecture - input devices

General Terms: Design, Experimentation, Languages

Additional Key Words and Phrases: gesture, touch-sensitive screen, visual programming, computers and education, paint programs

1. Introduction

We want to create worlds within the computer that can be manipulated in a concrete natural way using gesture as the mode of interaction. The effect is intended to have a quality of "telepresence" in the sense that, to the user, the distinction between real and simulated physical objects displayed on a screen can be blurred by letting the user touch, poke, and move the objects around with finger motions.

Permission to copy without fee all or part of this material is granted provided that the copies are not made or distributed for direct commercial advantage, the ACM copyright notice and the title of the publication and its date appear, and notice is given that copying is by permission of the Association for Computing Machinery. To copy otherwise, or to republish, requires a fee and/or specific permission.

© 1984   ACM   0-89791-138-5/84/007/0195 $00.75

One goal of this research is to make a natural general purpose interface which feels physical. Another goal is to extend some ideas from the Logo pedagogical culture - where young children learn to program and control computing environments [5] - to gestural and dynamic visual representations of programming-like activities.

How could we introduce programming ideas to very young children? They already know how to accomplish goals by using motions and gestures. So we speculate, it would be easier for them to learn new things if we can give them the effect of *handling* somewhat abstract objects in our displayed worlds. For this we need to find simple languages of gesture that can be learned mostly by exploration, and to find visual representations that can be manipulated and programmed by these "gesture languages".

The "Put-That-There" project at the MIT Architecture Machine Group [2] has some goals and techniques in common with this research. We also share some goals with the "visual programming" research community.

We wanted multiple sources of gesture information including position and configuration of the hand, velocity, and acceleration to experiment with hand gestures. Our first step was to build an experimental input device by mounting a transparent touch-sensitive screen in a force-sensing frame. This yields information about single finger gestures in terms of position, pressure and shear forces on the screen. Thus our system can measure the position of a touch, and the direction and intensity of the force being applied.

Sections 2, 3 and 4 of this paper describe environments that we have built that are controlled through this kind of gesture input, and our gesture classification. Section 5 decribes the hardware and signal processing we use to recognize these gestures. Section 6 discusses the future directions of this work.

2. Fingerpaint: A First Gesture Environment

To explore the issues involved in this kind of gestural input, we first built a fingerpaint program. The program tracks the motion of a finger (or stylus) on the screen and paints wherever the finger moves. This application makes essential use of the finger's pressure as well as its location. It also uses the shear-force information to smooth the interpretation of the gesture information.

The user's finger squooshes a blob of paint onto the screen (Fig. 1).

Figure 1: Fingerpaint

If the user presses harder, he gets a bigger blob of paint (Fig. 2).

Figure 1: Fingerpaint with Varying Pressure

The user can choose from several paint colors, and can also paint with simulated spray paint (Fig. 3).

In one version of this program, brush "pictures" can be picked up and stamped in other places on the screen.

Directions for a Gesture Paint Program

We would like to improve fingerpaint in the direction of making a painting system that allows more artistic control and remains sensually satisfying. At the same time we want to avoid making the system too complex for young beginners. We plan to implement a "blend" gesture, a set of paint pots out of which to choose colors with the fingers, and some brushstrokes which depend on the force contour of the painting gesture.

The idea of magnification proportional to pressure used in the paint program suggests use of pressure to scale objects in other environments.

3. Parsing Gestures for Manipulating Simulated Objects

The paint program follows the finger and implicitly interprets gestures to spread paint on the screen. For applications in which discrete, previously defined objects are to be manipulated using gestures, we need more complex gesture recognition. We want the user to be able to indicate, by gestures, different actions to perform on objects. The process of recognizing these gestures can be though of as parsing the gestures of a "gesture language".

Our gesture parser recognizes the initiation of a new gesture (just touching the screen after lifting off), then dynamically assigns to it a gesture type. It can recognize three gesture types: the "selection" gesture, the "move" gesture that consists of motion along an approximate line, and the "path" gesture that moves along a path with inflections. We are planning to introduce recognition of a gesture that selects an area of the screen. These gesture types, along with details of their state (particular trajectory, nearest object, pressure, pressure-time contour, shear direction, and so forth) are used by the system to respond to the user's motions.

4. Soft Implementations of Some Existing Visually Oriented Systems

To support our experimentation, we built a fairly general system to display the 2-D objects that are manipulated by gestures.

The following sections describe environments built from these components (gesture parser and 2-D object system), and some anecdotal findings.

4.1 Button Box

The gesture system Button Box was inspired by some experiments by Radia Perlman with special terminals (called Button Box and Slot Machine) built for preliterate children [6,7]. The Slot Machine is a plexiglass bar with

Figure 3: Fingerpaintings

Figure 4: Forward

Figure 5: Arranging Buttons

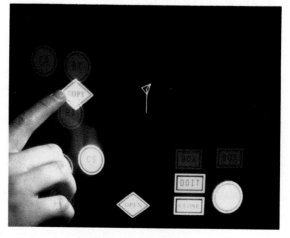

Figure 6: A Button being Copied

slots to put cards in. Each card represents a program command, for example, a Logo turtle command. A child writes a program by putting the cards in the slots in the order they want, then pushing a big red button at the end of the bar. Each card in sequence is selected by the progam counter (a light bulb lights up at the selected card) and that card's command is run. This provides a concrete model of computation and procedure. With various kinds of jump and iteration cards, kids use this physical equipment to learn about control structures and debugging.

The gesture system Button Box is even more flexible than the original specially constructed hardware devices; since it is software it can be modified and reconfigured. The current implementation makes use of some force and gesture information. It can be viewed as work in progress toward making models of computation that are particularly suited to having their pieces picked up, tapped upon, tossed about, and smudged by finger gestures.

Pictures of buttons that control various actions appear on the screen. In our example domain, the buttons are commands to a Logo-style turtle [1]. For example, one button is the FD (FORWARD) command, another is the RT (RIGHT TURN) command. If the user taps a button rather hard (think of hitting or pressing a mechanical button), the button "does its thing". Whatever action the button represents happens. If the FD button is tapped, the display turtle moves forward (Fig. 4).

If the user selects a button by applying fairly constant pressure to it for a longer time than a "tap" gesture, the gesture is interpreted as a desire to move the selected button on the screen. The button follows the finger until the finger lifts off the screen, and the button remains in its new position.

This allows the user to organize the buttons in any way that makes sense to him, for example, the user may place buttons in a line in the order in which they should be tapped to make the turtle draw something (Fig. 5).

Some of these buttons control rather concrete actions such as moving the turtle or producing a beep sound. Other buttons represent more abstract concepts, for example, the PU/PD button represents the state of the turtle's drawing pen. When the PU/PD button is tapped it changes the state of the turtle's pen, and it also changes its own label.

There are also buttons which operate on the other buttons. The COPY button can be moved to overlap any other button, and then tapped to produce a copy of the overlapped button (Fig. 6).

Some concepts in programming are available in the button box world. The environment lends itself to thinking about the visual organization of actions. In our anecdotal studies of non-programmers using the button box, most of our subjects produced a library of copies of turtle commands and arranged them systematically on the screen. They then chose from the library the buttons that allowed them to control the turtle in a desired way and arranged them at some favored spot on the screen.

There are mechanisms for explicitly creating simple procedures. At this time, only unconditionally ordered sequences of action represented by sequences of button pushes are available; we are working on representations of conditionals and variables. The user can specify a sequence of buttons to be grouped into a procedure.

We have experimented with two ways of gathering buttons into procedures: boxes and magic paint.

The first method uses boxes. The BOX button, when tapped, turns into a box. The box is stretchy and its corners can be moved, so it can be expanded to any size, and placed around a group of buttons (or the user can move buttons into the box). There are buttons which, when tapped, make the system "tap" every button in the box in sequence (Fig. 7).

The second method uses "magic paint". Magic paint is a genie button. As the user moves it, it paints. The user uses it to paint over a sequence of buttons. The path created shows the sequence in which buttons should be pushed. When the end of the paint path is tapped, the system "goes along" the path, tapping each button in sequence (Fig. 8).

The user can group buttons with either method and have the system "push its own buttons". The user can also tell the system to create a new button from this grouping. The CLOSE button closes up a box and makes a new button. The new button becomes part of the button box world with a status equal to any other button. The new button appears on the screen and can be moved and can be tapped like any other. Thus it becomes a subroutine (Fig. 9).

Most of our experiments so far have used the box metaphor. We plan to develop gesture semantics for magic paint, which seems more promising because the paint path makes the order of button pushes more explicit than the box grouping. It feels more "gestural" to program by drawing a swooping path.

4.2 Logic Design - Rocky's Boots

We have applied the same set of gestures to make a smooth interface to another environment: a graphic logic-design system based on Warren Robinett's program, Rocky's Boots [Robinett 82].

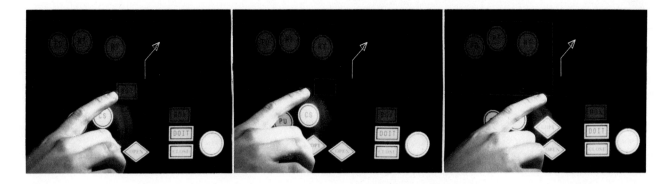

Figure 7: Making a Box and Using it to Group Buttons

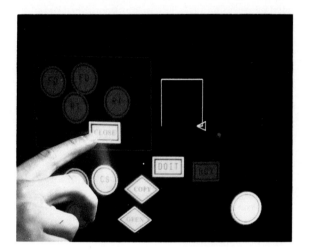

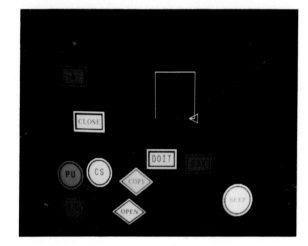

Figure 9: Creating a New Button by Closing a Box

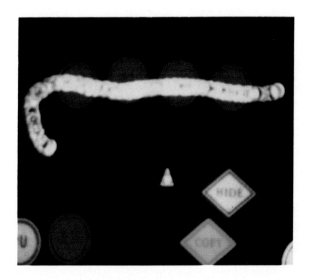

Figure 8: Using Magic Paint to Group Buttons

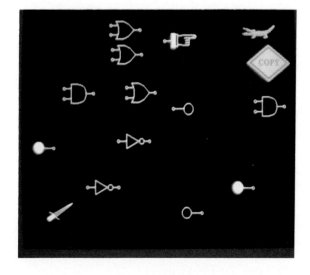

Figure 10: Logic objects:
Gates, HI input, clock input (blurred), output light

Gates, wires, logic inputs, and outputs are the objects in this environment. The user moves them around in the same way as buttons. They are always "doing their thing" They connect to each other when an input is brought close to an output. The user can cut them apart by making a gesture while holding a knife (Figs. 10, 11, 12).

Since these logic components are objects, like buttons, we can operate on them the same ways we can with buttons (e.g. copying with the COPY button) (Fig. 13).

There are actions we plan to implement in the logic world, by creating buttons to perform new actions on the objects or in some cases by recognizing new gestures. For example, we could get rid of the need for the knife object by recognizing a "cutting" gesture. We haven't yet defined mechanisms for creating new logic elements from combinations of existing ones but these are the kinds of extensions that can be made with the current gesture repertoire.

4.3 Rooms

All of the gesture-controlled environments: button box programming, interactive logic simulation, and a rudimentary Colorforms[tm]-like environment, have been combined in an information environment we call Rooms.

Rooms is an extension of a visual representation for adventure game maps and other visual information designed by Warren Robinett [8,9]. There are rooms which contain objects. The rooms connect to each other through doorways. In our implementation, each room takes up the whole screen, doors are at the edge of the screen. As the user's finger moves through a doorway, the adjacent room appears on the screen, filled with whatever objects it contains. The user can drag any object (button, logic gate, etc) through a doorway.

Our environment starts with a room containing the button box environment, a room containing the logic objects, a room containing colorforms, and an extra room with a few miscellaneous buttons in it.

Colorforms is a more free-form environment consisting of colorform-like shapes that can be moved around and stamped with finger gestures to create pictures. Our shapes are a face, eyes, mouth, and so forth, that can be grabbed and moved around (Fig. 14).

4.4 Combining Environments

One of the tenets of developing good gesture interfaces is that the objects being manipulated by gestures should act like possible physical objects in their reactions to the user's gestures. When the objects are brought near each other they

should interact in plausible ways. We have seen that the COPY button can copy logic elements. We introduced logic elements that can act on buttons. A special output, the HAND, taps a button when it is clocked (Fig. 15).

The circuit in the figure is an example of parallel processing invented by a user who was experimenting with the interface between the Button World and the Logic World (Fig. 16).

Amazing! Or is it? Nobody is amazed when a real object, like a teapot, can be stacked on top of another kind of real object, for example, a table. However, programs can hardly ever fit together meaningfully, much less smoothly. The object nature of these programming-like environments, and their necessary analogy to physical objects deriving from the gesture interface, has allowed this smooth combination to happen.

Reflecting on our box and magic paint programming metaphors, we can see that in these worlds, *procedures* are *things* which embody processes in their behavior. Here, the processes are represented by the paths of the user's gestures as he constructs a configuration of objects on the screen.

5. Gesture System Hardware and Software

Hardware Configuration

We mounted a commercially available transparent, resistive-film, touch-sensitive screen on the face of a color display monitor. The touch screen is supported by four force-measuring strain gauges ("load-cells") at the four corners of the screens. The mechanical arrangement is shown (Fig. 17).

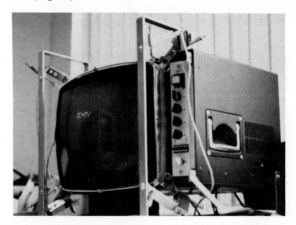

Figure 17: Mounted Force Sensors and Position Sensitive Screen

We note that a touch screen that used a different arrangement to obtain some force information from strain gauges was built in the 1970's at the MIT Architecture Machine Group.

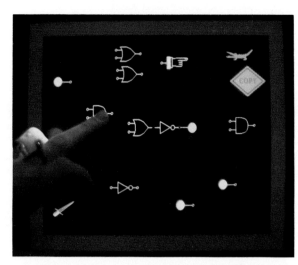

Figure 11: A Circuit with a Connection being Put In

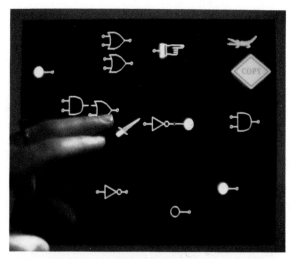

Figure 12: The Knife being used to Remove a Component

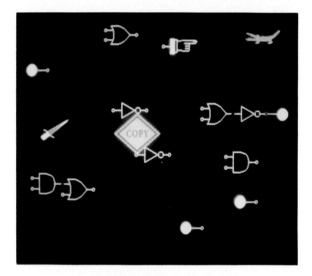

Figure 13: Copying a Logic Object

Figure 14: Colorforms Room

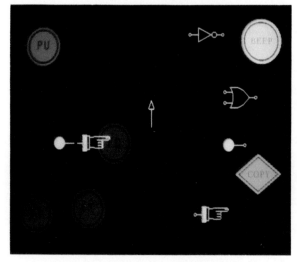

Figure 15: HAND Tapping the FD Button

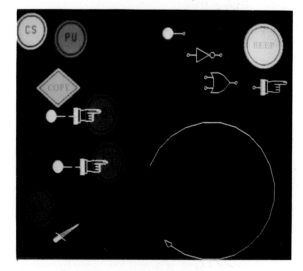

Figure 16: A "Program" that Draws a Circle

The load cells are mounted so that they supply useful force information through a 0-10 lb. range for finger gestures, and are protected from damage due to overloading. To make the user feel that they are actually "touching" objects on the screen, the surface touched by the user must be as close as possible to the monitor face to prevent parallax problems. In this arrangement, the position sensitive panel floats about 1/8" above the display surface.

This is a block diagram of mechanical connections and information flow in our system (Fig. 18).

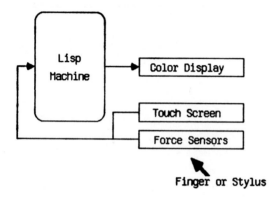

Figure 18: Block Diagram

Our gesture system software is written in LISP and runs on a LISP Machine. Raw position and load information is processed by the gesture software into recognized motions or gestures. The effects of the gestures on one of our gesture-interfaced environments is computed, and the LISP Machine color system creates the display seen through the transparent gesture sensing screen.

Signal Processing

A variety of smoothing and calibration strategies are necessary.

The position screen reports a finger position with a nominal resolution of 4K x 4K. The force sensor hardware reports twelve bits of force data from each of the four load cells.

To get the display and touch screens into good registration, the system performs an initial calibration when it is turned on. This includes finding linear scaling factors and offsets for the x and y position components. The x and y force offsets are also calculated.

During operation, an asynchronous process interprets the position and the four force sensor inputs in terms of finger gestures. This process looks for .the initiation of a touch, waits until it has computed a trustworthy, filtered initial position, and then signals that a new gesture has begun.

This process tracks the trajectory of the finger during a gesture. The tracking of touched positions is aided by a three-point median smoothing algorithm applied to the position data and by using continuity constraints derived from the force data.

The gesture process uses local continuity of the shear force magnitude and direction to ignore sudden changes in sensed position which may be due to position screen noise. Most position readings that are associated with these sudden changes must be ignored, since finger trajectories on the screen are mechanically constrained (over short time scales) to have shear forces parallel to the direction of motion, and smooth rotation of shear at inflection points.

Another asynchronous process recalibrates the force sensors every few seconds.

The load cells are arranged at the corners of the screen:

If the loads (corrected for zero force offset) on the load cells are $S1$, $S2$, $S3$, and $S4$, the z-force (pressure) is:

```
PRESSURE = S1 + S2 + S3 + S4
```

We compute force components in the plane of the screen from:

```
X-FORCE (horizontal)
    = (S1 + S3) - (S2 + S4)
             - zero calibration offset

Y-FORCE (vertical)
    = (S1 + S2) - (S3 + S4)
             - zero calibration offset
```

During calibration and for these calculations we assume that the screen is flat, the load cells are at the corners, the load cells' data is not noisy, and the touch position from the position sensing screen (after smoothing) is correct.

There are no corrections for nonlinearity over the screen. There is noticeable nonlinearity, but it does not seem to affect gesture recognition and tracking. Thus the user has to "get the feel" of the screen, since tracking in the corners feels slightly different than in the center. We plan to correct for this. It may become more important if the system is trying to recognize more complex gestures than we have worked with so far.

We have gained an advantage in this setup from multiple

sources of gesture information, e.g. the use of local continuity of forces to help track positions. We could theoretically derive position from the force sensors, but the touch-sensitive screen gives us higher position resolution and perhaps more reliability. We do not cross-check because this system worked well enough for our purposes.

6. Future Directions

Directions for Gesture Programming

There are several force controlled gestures with which we have experimented briefly and on which we plan to do more work.

An example is "flicking". The user can send an object to another part of the screen by flicking it with the finger, as in tiddlywinks. Shear is used to determine the direction of motion and the force determines the initial velocity of the object, which slows down by "friction".

We intend to create more application worlds to put into the Rooms. For example, we plan extensions to the Button Box, a gesture controlled kit for making treasure maps, and a button environment in which the buttons represent musical notes and phrases.

We would like to study classes of gestures that are useful in systems intended for expert use, in other words, systems where the gestures may be useful once learned but are not as easy or obvious as the ones in our current repertoire.

We see the need to do more careful motion studies, and to record more data about people's ability to use the gestures we recognize. There is already extensive literature in related areas, for example [4]. We have several ideas for gestures we would like to recognize that make more use of force and force-time contours to express analog quantities. We also plan to build a multiple finger touch version of our current hardware to allow gestures that use more of the hand.

We also intend to explore vision based gesture input, which allows the user much more freedom. There is ongoing research in this laboratory on real-time visual interpretation of whole body gesture as input to a motion and animation display [3]. We may also explore recognition of hand gestures through vision of hand silhouettes.

Directions for Information Layout

This research has prompted the beginning of a project to use gestural input in "Information Spaces". A prototype of an information organization system has been created that displays representations of file systems and large programs. There are objects displayed in these representations that are analogous to our logic gates and buttons. This system uses a

modified mouse and recognizes more "iconic" gestures than the systems described in this paper.

Acknowledgements

I would like to thank Danny Hillis for providing the initial leadership for this project, and for continuing ideas, inventions, and support. Ed Hardebeck has done a large amount of the design and much of the implementation of the systems described in this paper. Others who worked on this project are Dan Huttenlocher, Gregor Kiczales, Warren Robinett, and Fred Thornburgh. David Wallace and David Chapman partipated in early design of the gesture environments.

Special thanks go to Cynthia Solomon, Director of Atari Cambridge Research, for reading many drafts of this paper; thanks for help with the paper also go to Ed Hardebeck, Danny Hillis, Dan Huttenlocher, and Marvin Minsky.

References

1. Abelson, Harold, and Andrea DiSessa. *Turtle Geometry*. MIT Press, 1981.

2. Schmandt, C. and Hulteen, E. "The Intelligent Voice-Interactive Interface". *Proc. Human Factors in Computer Systems*, Gaithersburg, MD, 1982

3. Hardebeck, Edward F. "Gestural Input to Computers through Visual Recognition of Body Silhouettes". Atari Cambridge Research Internal Memo 3, Atari Cambridge Research, January 1984.

4. Loomis, Jeffrey, Poizner, Howard, Bellugi, Ursula, Blakemore, Alynn, and John Hollerbach. "Computer Graphic Modeling of American Sign Language". Proc. Siggraph '83, *Computer Graphics* 17, no. 3, July 1983.

5. Papert, Seymour A. *Mindstorms*. Basic Books, New York, 1980.

6. Perlman, Radia. "Tortis: Toddler's Own Recursive Turtle Interpreter System", Logo Memo 9, Logo Laboratory, Massachusetts Institute of Technology, Cambridge, July 1974.

7. Perlman, Radia. "How to Use the Slot Machine", Logo Working Paper 43, Logo Laboratory, Massachusetts Institute of Technology, Cambridge, January 1976.

8. Atari VCS Adventure. Software product of Atari, Inc., Sunnyvale, CA, 1979.

9. Rocky's Boots. Software Product of The Learning Co., Portola Valley, CA, 1982.

Colorforms is a trademark of Colorforms, Inc.

PANEL

COMPUTER GRAPHICS IN COMMERCIAL AND BROADCAST PRODUCTION

CHAIR: Carl Rosendahl - Pacific Data Images, Inc.

PANEL: Charles Csuri - Cranston/Csuri Productions
         Larry Elin - MAGI
         Lance Williams - New York Institute of Technology

The goal of this panel is to acquaint the
listener with what is perhaps the most
visible area of computer graphics - the
use of animation in television and motion
pictures.

Creating animation for commercial use is
subject to many factors outside of the
animator's control. Pieces are constrained by deadlines and budgets and yet
must be "new, fresh and different" in
order to satisfy the client. The speakers
on the panel represent four of the leading
computer animation production houses and
are well acquainted with having to work
with these constraints while still de-
livering work of the highest possible
quality. In addition to showing some of
their work, the participants will discuss
methods for creating animation for
commercial use.

Possible topics to be addressed are:

Production flow: where jobs come from and
what the procedure is for producing them.
Design methods for modelling, motion and
lighting.
Future trends for hardware and software,
including more advanced rendering techniques and better tools for the designer,
modeller and animator.
Technology and art: discussion appeal of
computer animation to television networks,
stations and advertising agencies and what
new freedoms and limitations there are for
the designer.

These topics will be highlighted with
examples out of familiar productions.

Summed-Area Tables for Texture Mapping

Franklin C. Crow
Computer Sciences Laboratory
Xerox Palo Alto Research Center

Abstract

Texture-map computations can be made tractable through use of precalculated tables which allow computational costs independent of the texture density. The first example of this technique, the "mip" map, uses a set of tables containing successively lower-resolution representations filtered down from the discrete texture function. An alternative method using a single table of values representing the integral over the texture function rather than the function itself may yield superior results at similar cost. The necessary algorithms to support the new technique are explained. Finally, the cost and performance of the new technique is compared to previous techniques.

CR Categories and Subject Headings: I.3.3 [Computer Graphics]: Picture/Image Generation — display algorithms; I.3.7 [Computer Graphics]: Three-Dimensional Graphics and Realism — color, shading, shadowing and texture.
General Terms: Algorithms, Performance
Additional Keywords and Phrases: antialiasing, texture mapping, shading algorithms, table lookup algorithms

1.0 Introduction

A frequent criticism of early attempts at realism in computer-synthesized images was that the surfaces lacked interest. At first all surfaces had a dull matte finish. Later surfaces acquired shininess and transparency. However, much of the attraction of real surfaces lies in the incredibly complex local surface variations known as texture. These variations are much too complicated to be modeled by conventional means which require enough vertices or control points to accurately reproduce the surface.

In 1974, Catmull [3] conceived and implemented the first system to use images of texture applied to surfaces to give the affect of actual texture. Blinn and Newell [1] generalized Catmull's work and extended it to include environmental reflections. Blinn [2] then further extended the notion (rather spectacularly!) to achieve the appearance of undulations on the surface (the earlier efforts achieved only flat texture, such as the fake wood texturing found on many plastic desk tops). Carrying things a bit farther, researchers at Ohio State [7] experimented with various expansions of polygonal surfaces to achieve "real" texture. Although some very interesting

Permission to copy without fee all or part of this material is granted provided that the copies are not made or distributed for direct commercial advantage, the ACM copyright notice and the title of the publication and its date appear, and notice is given that copying is by permission of the Association for Computing Machinery. To copy otherwise, or to republish, requires a fee and/or specific permission.

© 1984   ACM   0-89791-138-5/84/007/0207 $00.75

images resulted, the technique would be too cumbersome for anything very complex.

When texture is mapped onto a surface it must be stretched here and compressed there in order to fit the shape of the surface. 3-D perspective views further distort texture mapped onto a curving surface. As a digital image is synthesized, a pair of texture coordinates must be calculated for each pixel representing a textured surface. The most straightforward implementation of texture mapping simply chooses the pixel from the texture image which lies closest to the computed texture coordinates (the "nearest pixel" algorithm). This works well for a certain class of textures and surfaces.

A frequent example of texture mapping uses a rectangular texture image mapped onto a sphere. Here the compression that each part of the texture image will undergo when mapped is known in advance. The texture can be designed in such a way that it is "pre-stretched" along the top and bottom where it will be mapped near the poles of the sphere. However, unless the texture image is very smooth, with no sharp detail, aliasing becomes an immediate problem. Sharp details will become jagged and the texture will break up where it is highly compressed. Where the mapping is not known in advance, aliasing cannot be controlled just by judiciously designing the texture.

Blinn [2] and later Feibush et al [5] discuss this problem in detail and implemented good, but very expensive solutions. If the pixel being computed is considered a small area, texture coordinates may be computed for the corners of each such area. The pixel intensity is then the average of all texture elements bounded by the corners, weighted by a filter function. In places where the texture is highly compressed (e.g., at the poles of a sphere), this operation may require a weighted sum of hundreds of texture values.

Catmull and Smith [4] show a way of simplifying the calculation of the texture intensity by separating the convolution into two passes. The method was initially applied just to represent transformed images on a raster. A horizontal pass over the texture is followed by a vertical pass, producing texture values as they should appear in the image. The simplicity of the process makes it amenable to hardware implementation; a similar technique is currently very much in vogue for special-effects in television. However, where the texture is highly compressed, many texture pixels must still be processed to yield a single image pixel.

Norton, Rockwood and Skomolski [9] report a method for limiting texture detail to the appropriate level by expressing

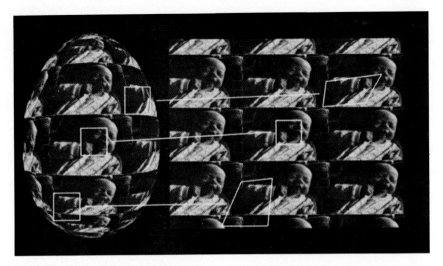

Figure 1: Texture distortion under mapping.

texture as a sum of band-limited terms of increasing frequencies. Where the frequency of a term (i.e., its level of detail) exceeds the pixel frequency, that term is "clamped" (forced to the local average value for the term). The method has been applied, in a very restricted way, but with excellent effect, in a real-time visual system for flight simulators. In order to use this method the texture must be divided into terms using Fourier analysis or similar techniques. Alternatively, the texture may be synthesized from Fourier terms.

In a remotely similar vein, Haruyama and Barsky [8] describe implementation of a fractal texture synthesis technique as suggested by Fournier, Fussell, and Carpenter [6]. Fractal synthesis has the advantage that the level of detail is controlled very naturally. This makes antialiasing easier as the texture is compressed on the surface. However, we are still left with no way to handle sharp detail in a texture.

Williams [10], some time ago, conceived and directed the implementation of a very clever algorithm which extends practical texture mapping to a much, much larger class of textures. Instead of using a single texture image, many images at varying resolution are derived from the original by averaging down to lower resolutions. Thus, in a lower resolution version of the texture, each pixel represents the average of some number of pixels in the higher resolution version. Since only

a limited number of tables may be stored, values from two adjacent tables must be blended to avoid obvious differences between areas of texture represented at different resolutions. Now where highly compressed texture must be dealt with, computation need only determine which tables to address. Texture computation can be more or less constant over all pixels.

Williams calls his technique "mip" mapping (for "multum in parvo", Latin for "many things in a small place"). Mip mapping achieves speed at the expense of some accuracy by assuming that texture intensity at any pixel can be adequately represented by the average over a square region of texture. Square regions assume that texture compression is symmetric. However, where a surface curves away from the viewer, texture may be compressed along only one dimension (figure 1). Since table addressing must be based on the axis of maximum compression, mip mapped texture may appear fuzzier than would otherwise be necessary.

A generalization of Williams' technique can provide a better approximation to the proper texture intensity by allowing rectangular regions of texture to be used. A single table of much larger numbers is used, from which a virtually continuous range of texture densities may be drawn.

2.0 Using A Table Of Summed Areas For Texture Mapping

2.1 The Basic Technique

Mip mapping can be done using a single table in which each texture intensity is replaced by a value representing the sum of the intensities of all pixels contained in the rectangle defined by the pixel of interest and the lower left corner of the texture image. The sum of all intensities in any rectangular area of the texture may easily be recovered from such a table. Dividing the sum by the area of the rectangle gives the average intensity over the rectangle.

To find the sum of intensities over an arbitrary rectangle, it is sufficient to take a sum and two differences of values from the table. As an example assume that we want the sum over an area bounded by xl on the left, xr on the right, yb on the bottom, and yt on the top (figure 2). The sum is given by:

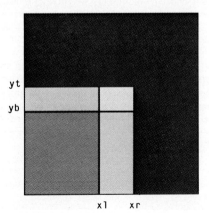

Figure 2: Calculation of summed area from table.

T[xr,yt] - T[xr,yb] - T[xl,yt] + T[xl,yb]
where T[x,y] is the value in the table addressed by the coordinate pair (x,y).

In other words, starting with the table entry at the upper right corner of the area, subtract first the table entry at the lower right then the entry at the upper left. This removes all area below the rectangle of interest then all area to the left. Note that the area lying below *and* to the left of the rectangle has been subtracted twice. This area must be restored by adding back in the table entry at the lower left of the rectangle.

The best approximation to the proper texture intensity would be calculated by multiplying by a filter function superposed over the texture rectangle before summing the intensities. Unfortunately, since the sums must be precomputed, only a constant filter function is possible. However, very convincingly antialiased images are routinely made under this restriction.

As with the multiple table mip map described above, it is necessary to interpolate between table entries to smoothly represent sharp edges when the texture is not greatly compressed (or when the texture is expanded). Furthermore, if texture values are taken only at pixel locations, the resulting discretized mapping will sometimes cause jittering as the surface moves. More accurate mapping may be obtained by allowing the corners of a rectangular region to lie between texture pixels. Therefore, the summed area at each corner of the rectangle must be calculated by interpolating from four values in the table. Once the corner values are found, the computation proceeds as above.

2.2 Comparisons with the Multiple Table Mip Map

To get a rough idea of the relative expense of the summed area table mip map versus the multiple table mip map, let us count the necessary arithmetic operations and texture accesses. This will give us an approximation of the processing power and bandwidth to the texture memory required. Texture memory bandwidth is important when the texture is stored in a frame buffer, where access may be slow, or in virtual memory, where many accesses may substantially increase the short-term working set size, causing excess page swapping.

For both methods, most of the cost goes into linear interpolations. A linear interpolation costs two multiplicative operations and two additive operations if done as:
      b * (1 - alpha) + c * alpha
 or, better, two additive operations and one multiplicative operation if done as:
      b + (c - b) * alpha,
where alpha is used to interpolate between b and c. A bilinear interpolation, interpolating to a value lying within a region defined by four adjacent pixels, requires three simple interpolations.

The multiple map method requires two bilinear interpolations to get a value from each of two adjacent tables, plus an additional interpolation between the two values. This requires a total of 8 texture accesses, 7 multiplicative operations, and 14 additive operations. The summed area table method requires four bilinear interpolations to get the four corners of a rectangle, then three additive operations to get the sum over the rectangle, then a multiply to get the area and a divide to find the average. That adds up to a total of 16 texture accesses, 14 multiplicative operations and 27 additive operations.

There is an optimization for the summed area method where the texture is highly compressed. In such cases the large size of the rectangular region from the summed area table makes the effect of interpolation at the corners negligible. Without interpolation, the cost of the summed area method reduces to 4 texture accesses, two multiplicative operations and 3 additive operations.

Of course, the above is concerned only with finding the value for the texture intensity once the texture coordinates and the size of the texture area are known. For the multiple table approach, the two tables must be selected and the value of "d" (used to interpolate between the tables) calculated [10]. For the summed area table method, increments giving the texture coordinates at the adjacent pixels may be used to define the corners of the rectangular area. In both cases, the necessary computation appears small next to the texture intensity calculation.

2.3 Calculating Texture Coordinates

To be more specific, the summed area table code which produced figures herein calculates the texture rectangle as follows: A given scan segment is generated by linear interpolation of the state at its endpoints. The endpoints of a set of scan segments representing a portion of surface are generated by linear interpolation between the endpoints of the top and bottom segments. Since the texture coordinates are included in the endpoint information, they are linearly interpolated along with everything else.

The texture coordinate at a pixel is calculated by an incremental bilinear interpolation; at each pixel, the texture coordinates are found by adding increments to the coordinates from the previous pixel. Those increments, which are constant over a scan segment, are used to partially determine the texture rectangle. Let's call them the horizontal increments.

The other necessary information is the pair of increments needed to get the texture coordinates at the corresponding pixel on the next scanline. Increments are kept which allow incremental interpolation of the texture coordinates of the endpoints of one scan segment from those of the previous one. Using those increments at each end of a scan segment, a pair of vertical texture coordinate increments can be computed by incremental interpolation between the vertical increments at the scan segment ends.

Given both horizontal and vertical texture increments at a pixel the texture rectangle is determined by taking the maximum of the absolute values of both x-coordinates and similarly for the y-coordinates. This gives a sort of bounding box on the true texture area which works quite well. Since a rough approximation to the true texture area is all that can be achieved using the summed area table, a more efficient determination of the rectangle may be possible. However this computation is only a small part of the total; any improvements will only marginally effect total running time.

2.4 Handling Texture Image Boundaries

Since a texture map may be replicated many times over a surface, or may cover only part of a surface, it is important to properly handle the case where a pixel contains a texture image boundary. In the case where a surface is only partially covered by texture, it is sufficient to truncate texture image coordinates while calculating the area from the unmodified coordinates.

Where a texture is replicated many times over a surface, values lying to the right or above a boundary must be increased by the value at the boundary. In extreme cases, a pixel may contain several boundaries, implying that several whole texture images are mapped into one pixel. This case would require several additions to arrive at the proper values for the right and upper corners of the rectangle.

3.0 Building And Storing A Summed Area Table

Computing the values to be stored in a summed area table is quite simple. A table can be generated at an arithmetic cost of two adds per entry. The most straightforward method would be to invert the method used for taking summed areas from the table. To get a table entry: Add the pixel intensity to the sum at the pixel below plus the sum at the pixel to the left. Doing this counts the sum at the pixel below and to the left twice. Therefore, that sum must then be subtracted. The arithmetic cost is three additive operations.

The table can be built with only two additive operations per entry by maintaining a sum of intensities along a scanline. Using this method, a table entry is calculated by adding the pixel intensity to the sum for the scanline then adding that to the sum at the pixel below. Generating the table is inexpensive enough (for reasonably-sized texture images) that it should not be an important consideration in deciding whether to use a mip map technique or the more accurate (and expensive) techniques of Blinn [2] and then Feibush et al. [5].

A potential disadvantage for the summed area table is that it requires many more bits per entry than there are bits per texture intensity. If the texture intensity is stored in 8 bits, then a 1024 by 1024 entry table could require entries as long as 28 bits. A table could be built with as little as 24 bits per entry by restricting texture images to 256 by 256 pixels. However, most machines handle 32-bit words more gracefully than 24-bit words, so why restrict ourselves?

Various bit-saving techniques may be concocted to reduce the number of bits per entry to 16 or less. For example, the texture image may be divided into regions of 16 pixels square to limit the sum within such a region to 16 bits (256 entries of 8 bits each). A 32-bit quantity would be stored for each region giving the sum at its lower left corner. To recover a value from the table would require adding the appropriate 32-bit quantity to the table entry. Trying to reduce the number of bits per entry to 12 yields diminishing returns. Storing a 32-bit quantity for each group of 16 entries involves an overhead of 2 bits per entry, for an effective 14 bits per entry.

It must be noted that the multiple table mip map method does considerably better in terms of required storage. The number of bits per texture pixel is increased by only one-third in preparing the table, as opposed to a factor of from two to four for the summed area table.

4.0 Conclusions

As can be seen from figures 3-7, the summed area table works well for antialiasing mapped texture. The egg-shaped surfaces are polygonal approximations, which causes the apparent creases in the texture patterns. The examples used here were deliberately chosen to try to show any inadequacies in the texturing techniques. Ideally the texture should roll off smoothly into a uniform grey at the ends of the striped eggs in figure 3. The more accurate renditions afforded by more expensive means [2, 5] may do better in such situations. However, nearly all images are more forgiving than the examples used here. Such differences are most often not visible.

A trial implementation of the multiple table mip map method has yielded inconclusive results. Both the summed table and multiple table methods roughly doubled the time needed to compute an image. My decidedly non-optimized implementation of the multiple table method runs about ten percent slower than my implementation of the summed area method, which would appear to contradict the implications of section 2.2 above. Since neither implementation has been subjected to careful scrutiny for bottlenecks, however, speed comparisons must be considered inconclusive.

The images in figures 3-6 appear to show that the summed area method offers some superiority in image quality over the multiple table method. However, I would prefer independent confirmation of that result. Both methods offer ample opportunities for tuning. Furthermore, the multiple table method has not really reached its potential as yet. Both Williams' and my implementations use tables which are generated using unweighted averages. Tables generated using proper filtering techniques could well yield better results. On the other hand, the summed area approach may well have extensions allowing the use of better filters.

It should be pointed out that the general notion of recovering the integral over a rectangular region of a function of two variables undoubtedly has broader application than shown here. I know of no other applications as yet, but I believe that they must exist.

This work was made possible and pleasurable by the incomparable facilities of the Xerox Palo Alto Research Center and my colleagues there in imaging. All text, figures and code development were done on a Dorado personal workstation using the Cedar programming environment.

References

1. Blinn, J. and Newell, M., "Texture and Reflection on Computer Generated Images", *Communications of the ACM*, Vol. 19, #10, Oct. 1976.
2. Blinn, J., "Computer Display of Curved Surfaces", PhD. Dissertation, Department of Computer Science, University of Utah, December 1978.
3. Catmull, E., "A Subdivision Algorithm for Computer Display of Curved Surfaces", PhD. Dissertation, Department of Computer Science, University of Utah, Tech. Report UTEC-CSc-74-133, December 1974.
4. Catmull, E. and Smith A. R., "3-D Transformation of Images in Scanline Order", *Computer Graphics* (Proc. Siggraph '80), Vol. 14, July 1980.

5. Feibush, E. A., Levoy, M., and Cook, R. L., "Synthetic Texturing Using Digital Filters", *Computer Graphics* (Proc. Siggraph '80), Vol. 14, July 1980.

6. Fournier, A., Fussell, D., and Carpenter, L., "Computer Rendering of Stochastic Models", *Communications of the ACM*, Vol. 25, #6, June 1982.

7. Hackathorn, R. and Parent, R., Private Communication, 1980.

8. Haruyama, S, and Barsky, B. A., "Using Stochastic Modeling for Texture Generation", IEEE *Computer Graphics and Applications*, Vol. 4, # 3, March 1984.

9. Norton, A., Rockwood, A. P., and Skomolski, P. S., "Clamping: A Method of Antialiasing Textured Surfaces by Bandwidth Limiting in Object Space", *Computer Graphics* (Proc. Siggraph '82), Vol. 16, #3, July 1982.

10. Williams, L., "Pyramidal Parametrics", *Computer Graphics*, Vol. 17, #3, July 1983.

Figure 3: Left: nearest pixel (1 min. CPU time), middle: multiple table (2 1/4 min.), right: summed table (2 min.).

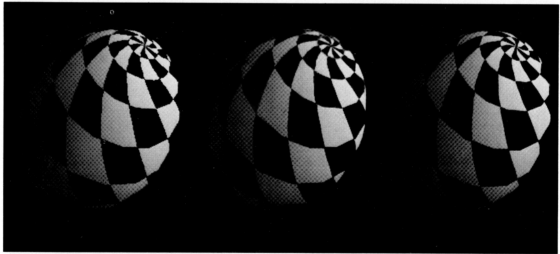

Figure 4: Left: nearest pixel, middle: multiple table, right: summed table.

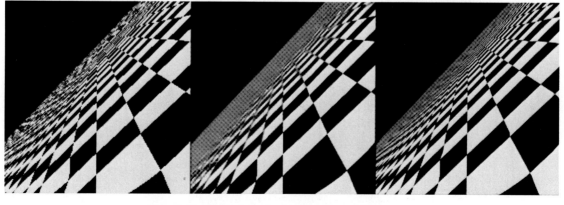

Figure 6: CheckerBoards showing laterally compressed texture.

Figure 5: CheckerBoards mapped onto a square showing vertically compressed texture.

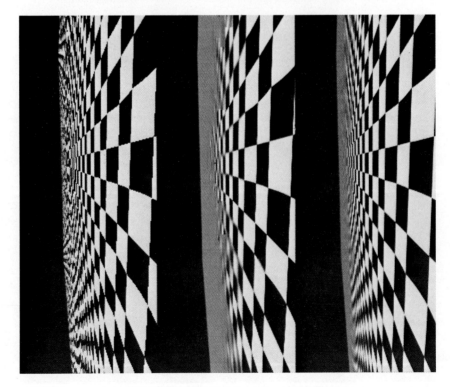

Figure 7: CheckerBoards showing horizontally compressed texture.

Modeling the Interaction of Light Between Diffuse Surfaces

Cindy M. Goral, Kenneth E. Torrance, Donald P. Greenberg and Bennett Battaile
Cornell University
Ithaca, New York 14853

ABSTRACT

A method is described which models the interaction of light between diffusely reflecting surfaces. Current light reflection models used in computer graphics do not account for the object-to-object reflection between diffuse surfaces, and thus incorrectly compute the global illumination effects. The new procedure, based on methods used in thermal engineering, includes the effects of diffuse light sources of finite area, as well as the "color-bleeding" effects which are caused by the diffuse reflections. A simple environment is used to illustrate these simulated effects and is presented with photographs of a physical model. The procedure is applicable to environments composed of ideal diffuse reflectors and can account for direct illumination from a variety of light sources. The resultant surface intensities are independent of observer position, and thus environments can be preprocessed for dynamic sequences.

CR Categories and Subject Descriptors: I.3.7 [Computer Graphics]: Three-Dimensional Graphics and Realism; I.3.3 [Computer Graphics]: Picture/Image Generation

General Terms: Algorithms

Additional Key Words and Phrases: Diffuse reflections, light reflection models, radiosity, shading, form factors

Permission to copy without fee all or part of this material is granted provided that the copies are not made or distributed for direct commercial advantage, the ACM copyright notice and the title of the publication and its date appear, and notice is given that copying is by permission of the Association for Computing Machinery. To copy otherwise, or to republish, requires a fee and/or specific permission.

© 1984   ACM   0-89791-138-5/84/007/0213 $00.75

1 Introduction

Most real environments consist primarily of surfaces which reflect light diffusely. In such environments, direct illumination and the object-to-object reflections between diffuse surfaces may account for the overwhelming proportion of the total light energy in an environment. Current light reflection models used in computer graphics do not account for the interaction between diffuse surfaces, and thus incorrectly compute the global illumination effects.

In order to generate images which realistically simulate an actual scene, the physical behavior of visible light as it is propagated through an environment must be modeled. Since the intensity and distribution of light in a scene are governed by energy transport and conservation principles, these must be considered if one wishes to accurately simulate different light sources and materials in the same scene.

This paper describes a method which can be used to determine the intensity of light diffusely reflected within an environment. The method is based on energy principles and may be applied monochromatically or to finite wavelength intervals. The key assumption is that all surfaces are ideal diffuse (Lambertian) reflectors. The procedure is applicable to arbitrary environments composed of such surfaces, and it can account for direct illumination from a variety of light sources and all multiple reflections within the environment. A major advantage of the method is that the resultant surface intensities are independent of observer position. Thus, environmental intensity information can be preprocessed for dynamic sequences. Furthermore, since small specular areas may contribute little to the total light energy, such surface reflections can later be added to the diffuse reflection solutions with minimal error.

The initial realistic image synthesis approaches for raster displays were concerned primarily with the visible surface determination of polygonal environments. Early algorithms assumed diffuse (Lambertian) reflections to determine the color of the displayed polygons. In 1973, Phong [7] proposed a reflection model for the determination of the color of each pixel as a function of the direction of the surface normal. The Phong reflection model has been significant in the evolution of realistic image synthesis methods and is still widely in use. The formulation includes ambient and diffuse terms that provide surface color and shading, and a specular term that provides realistic highlights from direct light source reflections. Based upon the Torrance-Sparrow reflection model [11], Blinn [2] suggested improvements which recognized that the magnitude of the specular component is related to the intensity that reaches the surface from the mirror direction.

Cook and Torrance [3] proposed a reflection model that describes the behavior of light in terms of energy equilibrium and electromagnetic wave theory. Application of this model results in a very realistic appearance when rendering a wide variety of materials with varied surface finishes. Unfortunately, the model requires spatial integration of the global illumination information to provide the incident energy on a surface. None of the present methodologies for image synthesis are able to generate the information required for application of this model to situations other than an isolated object suspended in space.

In an attempt to solve the global illumination problem, the ray tracing methodology was introduced by Whitted [13]. Ray tracing is used as a method of determining the global illumination information that is relevant to the image plane [6]. This method traces a ray from the eye through each pixel into the environment and generates new reflected and/or refracted rays at each surface a ray strikes. The reflection models employed to date in ray tracing approaches are empirical in nature and do not account for the required energy conservation conditions. Furthermore, the ray tracing methodology, which inherently provides only point-sampled information, is not sufficient for the application of energy equilibrium models to light behavior. Lastly, due to the "tree of rays" approach, only the intra-environment specular effects are considered.

Many existing reflection models require the addition of an ambient or background illumination term. The magnitude of this ambient term is usually specified arbitrarily. The procedure described in this paper correctly accounts for

not only the "global ambient" term [7, 13, 6], but also the object-to-object reflection between diffuse surfaces. In section 2, the theory and mathematical formulations are presented. Section 3 describes the program implementation. Resultant images are shown in section 4 and photographic results of a physical model appear in section 5.

2 Theory And Mathematical Formulation

This section describes a method for determining the magnitude and color composition of light reflected within an environment. The major assumption is that all surfaces are ideal diffuse (i.e., Lambertian) reflectors. Illumination sources and surface reflective properties can be arbitrary within this constraint. The analysis, which is explained below, is similar to that used in thermal engineering for the calculation of radiative heat exchange in enclosures [8, 10, 14].

The analytical procedure is built up by first introducing the concept of radiant intensity. Radiant energy in the form of visible light is presumed to emanate in all directions from a differential element of area, dA (Figure 1). The radiant intensity in a particular viewing direction is:

$$i = dP/(\cos\phi\,d\omega) \qquad (1)$$

where,

i = intensity of radiation in a particular viewing direction, expressed as the radiant energy leaving a surface per unit time per unit projected area (projected in the viewing direction) per unit solid angle (watts/meter**2 steradians)

dP = the radiant energy leaving the surface in the direction ϕ within a solid angle $d\omega$ expressed per unit time and per unit surface area (unprojected) (watts/meter**2)

ϕ = polar angle measured from the surface normal to the viewing direction (degrees)

$d\omega$ = differential solid angle of the pencil of rays (steradians)

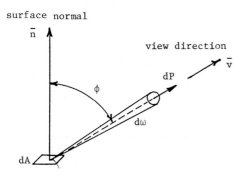

Figure 1. Geometry of Radiation Leaving a Surface.

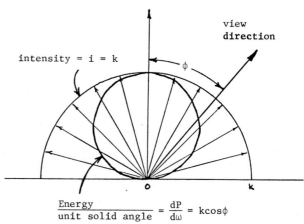

$$\frac{Energy}{unit\ solid\ angle} = \frac{dP}{d\omega} = k\cos\phi$$

Figure 2. Ideal Diffuse Reflection from a Surface.

The human eye senses intensity; it perceives projected areas, and receives energy within a solid angle $d\omega$ defined by the pupil size. Intensity is thus an appropriate quantity for use in the construction of computer-generated images.

Next consider the properties of ideal diffuse or Lambertian reflection. For ideal diffuse reflection, the distribution of the reflected light energy is expressed by $dP/d\omega = k\cos\phi$, where k is a constant. Since intensity is a function of the projected area, and the projected area varies with $\cos\phi$, the corresponding intensity i of the reflected light is:

$$i = \frac{dP/d\omega}{\cos\phi} = \frac{k\cos\phi}{\cos\phi} = k \qquad (2)$$

Thus, the intensity of the diffusely reflected light is constant and of uniform visual intensity from all viewing directions. Angular distributions of intensity and $dP/d\omega$ for an ideal diffuse reflector are shown in Figure 2.

The total energy leaving the surface is found by integrating (1) over the hemisphere (solid angle 2π) above the surface:

$$P = \int_{2\pi} dP = \int_{2\pi} i\,\cos\phi\,d\omega \qquad (3)$$

P = total energy leaving the given surface and passing into the hemispherical space above the surface per unit time and area (watts/meter**2)

For an ideal diffuse (Lambertian) surface, the total energy and intensity are related by:

$$P = i \int_{2\pi} \cos\phi\,d\omega = i\pi \qquad (3a)$$

Now consider the general problem of diffuse light reflection within an environment. Two concepts necessary for modeling the reflection of light are enclosures and form factors. A calculation of the light energy at any surface must include all of the radiation arriving at that surface from all directions in space. To account for the arriving radiation, a hypothetical enclosure is constructed. The enclosure is a set of surfaces that completely define the illuminating environment. The illumination and reflection properties of each surface of the enclosure must be specified. The walls of the enclosure consist of light sources and reflecting walls, and one or more of the surfaces of the enclosure may be fictitious (e.g., an open window). An N-surface enclosure is sketched in Figure 3. The light arriving at a surface j, denoted by H(j), is found by summing the contributions from the other N-1 surfaces, and from surface j if it sees itself. The light emerging from the surface j is denoted by B(j).

All surfaces of the enclosure are assumed to be ideal diffuse reflectors, ideal diffuse light emitters, or a combination of the two. Each surface is assumed to be of uniform composition, with uniform illumination, reflection, and emission intensities over the surface. This assumption can generally be satisfied by subdividing the original surfaces of the enclosure. If diffuse light sources are used, such sources are treated as surfaces of the enclosure with specified illuminating intensities. If an arbitrary directional light source is used, the surfaces illuminated by the source are identified. The light directly reflected by these surfaces can be treated as diffuse light sources. For example, a spotlight which provides illumination over a finite area can be replaced by an equivalent diffuse illuminating panel. Isolux contours [12] can be computed for the panel, and each constant intensity region can be modeled as a separate diffuse light source. As a consequence, all reflected and illuminating light in the enclosure is diffuse, and can be combined for purposes of analysis.

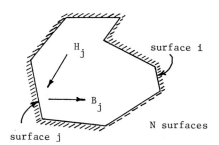

Figure 3. Enclosure Consisting of N Surfaces. H(j) and E(j) Denote Incident and Emergent Fluxes for the jth Surface.

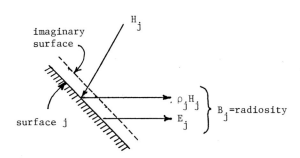

Figure 4. Details at a Particular Surface j.

The second concept to be introduced is the <u>form factor</u>, F. It is defined as the fraction of the radiant light energy leaving one particular surface which strikes a second surface. The radiant light may have an arbitrary angular distribution of intensity. However, the most useful form factors are those for ideal diffuse emission or reflection. In this case, the form factor is purely geometrical in nature and is dependent only on the shape, size, position and orientation of the participating surfaces.

With the foregoing introduction, it is now possible to formulate expressions for the intensity of all the surfaces in an enclosure. Consider the surface j in Figure 4. An imaginary surface is stretched above the actual surface, as shown by the dashed line. The radiosity B(j) is the hemispherical integral of the energy leaving the surface. To an observer, the surface j appears to be emitting a flux, B(j), from the imaginary surface. This flux consists of two parts given by:

$$B_j = E_j + \rho_j H_j \qquad (4)$$

where,

B_j = radiosity of surface j and is the total rate at which radiant energy leaves the surface in terms of energy per unit time and per unit area   (watts/meter**2)

E_j = rate of direct energy emission from surface j per unit time and per unit area (watts/meter**2)

ρ_j = reflectivity of surface j and represents the fraction of incident light which is reflected back into the hemispherical space

H_j = incident radiant energy arriving at surface j per unit time and per unit area (watts/meter**2)

However, the observer sees a total flux B(j), and is unable to distinguish between the two components on the right side of equation (4) because they both have the same directional distribution in space (i.e., diffuse). Thus, there is no need to treat the emitted and reflected radiation separately. The analysis is simplified by considering only one quantity, B(j). There is a radiosity B(j) for each surface in the enclosure.

Consider next the incident flux H(j) on surface j in Figure 3. This is the sum of fluxes from all surfaces in the enclosure that "see" j. The fraction of the flux leaving surface i, B(i), and reaching surface j is specified by the form factor, F(ij). Since all surfaces contribute to the irradiation onto j, the incident flux is found by summing the contributions from all surfaces:

$$H_j = \sum_{i=1}^{N} B_i F_{ij} \qquad (5)$$

B = radiosity of surface i (watts/meter**2)

F = form factor and represents the fraction of radiant energy leaving surface i and impinging on surface j

The summation includes surface j because surface j might see itself (i.e., F(ii) need not be zero if, for example, the surface is concave). Combining equations (4) and (5) results in:

$$B_j = E_j + \rho_j \sum_{i=1}^{N} B_i F_{ij} \quad \text{for } j=1,N \qquad (6)$$

Such an equation exists for every surface in the enclosure. Since the procedure is based on computing radiosities, within this paper it is referred to as the "radiosity method". The radiosity formulation accounts for all light leaving and incident upon a surface. The incident light is simply expressed in terms of the incident radiosity; no further ray tracing is needed to account for all interchanges (including multiple reflections) in an enclosure.

In general, equation (6) yields a set of N linear equations with N unknown B(j) values, containing parameters E(j), ρ(j), and F(ij) which must be known or calculated for each surface. The emission terms, E(j), represent the illumination sources for the system. If all the E(j)'s are zero, there is no illumination and all the B(j)'s are zero. The E(j)'s are nonzero only at surfaces that provide illumination to the enclosure. Such surfaces could represent a diffuse illumination panel, or the first reflection of a directional light source from a diffuse surface. The E(j)'s are thus determined by the conditions of illumination, and represent the external source terms.

A system of equations of the form of equation (6) may be applied monochromatically, for any finite bandwidth of radiation, or over the entire visible spectrum (provided that the wavelength-dependent quantities E(j) and ρ(j) are appropriately-defined average values). This result follows because none of the visible light in the enclosure, defined by the B(j)'s, is absorbed by the walls and reradiated back into the enclosure. As a result, the E(j)'s and B(j)'s are effectively uncoupled, and the E(j)'s may be specified independently.

For synthetic image generation, radiant intensity rather than radiant energy is computed since the eye senses intensity. Since all the radiant energy terms in equation (6) are diffuse in character, they may be converted to radiant intensities by simply dividing by π (see equation (3a)). Dividing by π, and denoting the radiant intensities corresponding to B(j) and E(j) by b(j) and e(j), respectively, yields:

$$b_j = e_j + \rho_j \sum_{i=1}^{N} b_j F_{ij} \quad \text{for } j=1,N \qquad (7)$$

2.1 Form Factors

In order to determine the form factors for radiative exchange between two finite surfaces with areas A(i) and A(j), first consider the form factors for exchange between two infinitesimal surfaces with differential areas dA(i) and dA(j)

(Figure 5). Consistent with the assumptions made earlier, all the reflected and emitted light leaving a surface is assumed to be diffusely distributed. As seen from dA(i), the solid angle subtended by dA(j) is:

$$d\omega = \frac{\cos \phi_j \, dA_j}{r^2} \qquad (8)$$

Using equations (1) and (3a), the radiant energy leaving dA(i) directly incident on dA(j) is:

$$dP_i dA_i = i_i \cos\phi_i d\omega \, dA_i = \frac{P_i \cos\phi_i \cos\phi_j \, dA_i \, dA_j}{\pi r^2} \qquad (9)$$

The total energy leaving surface dA(i) into the hemisphere is P(i)dA(i). Noting that the form factor represents the fraction of the total energy emanating from dA(i) which is directly incident on surface dA(j), one obtains:

$$F_{dA_i - dA_j} = \frac{P_i \cos\phi_i \cos\phi_j \, dA_i \, dA_j / \pi r^2}{P_i \, dA_i}$$

$$= \frac{\cos\phi_i \cos\phi_j \, dA_j}{\pi r^2} \qquad (10)$$

It is evident that the value of the form factor is proportional to the infinitesimal area dA(j). To compute the fraction of radiation leaving dA(i) and reaching the finite area A(j),

$$F_{dA_i - A_j} = \int_{A_j} \frac{\cos\phi_i \cos\phi_j \, dA_j}{\pi r^2} \qquad (11)$$

The form factor between the finite surfaces, A(i) and A(j), is defined as the area average of equation (11):

$$F_{A_i - A_j} = F_{ij} = \frac{1}{A_i} \int_{A_i} \int_{A_j} \frac{\cos\phi_i \cos\phi_j \, dA_i \, dA_j}{\pi r^2} \qquad (12)$$

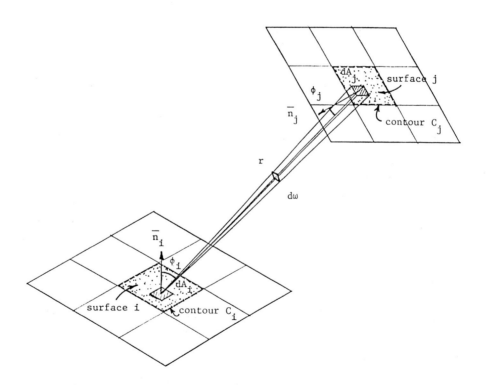

dA(i) = elemental area on surface i
A(i) = area of surface i
C(i) = contour of surface i
r   = distance between dA(i) and dA(j)
dω = solid angle subtended by dA(j) as seen from dA(i)
ϕ(i) = angle between surface normal of i, $\bar{n}$(i), and the line r
ϕ(j) = angle between surface normal of j, $\bar{n}$(j), and the line r

dA(j) = elemental area on surface j
A(j) = area of surface j
C(j) = contour of surface j

Figure 5. Geometry for Form Factor Derivation

In equation (12), the form factor is expressed as a double area integral. There are more efficient methods of computing form factors. One method is the contour integral representation which is obtained by transforming the area integrals into contour integrals using Stokes' theorem [9, 10].

$$F_{ij} = \frac{1}{2\pi A_i} \oint_{C_j} \oint_{C_i} \left[\ln(r)dx_i dx_j + \ln(r)dy_i dy_j \right.$$

$$\left. + \ln(r)dz_i dz_j \right] \quad (13)$$

Equation (13) above was used in our implementation.

From the formulation of the form factors, some simple identities which also serve as checks or shortcuts for calculations can be derived:

1. A reciprocity relationship can be derived from (12) for radiosity distributions which are diffuse and uniform over each surface:

$$A_i F_{ij} = A_j F_{ji} \quad (14)$$

A knowledge of $F(ij)$, $A(i)$ and $A(j)$ thus allows $F(ji)$ to be determined.

2. In order to achieve conservation of energy in a closed environment of N surfaces, all of the energy leaving a surface must be accounted for. Thus, the form factors for each surface must sum to unity:

$$\sum_{j=1}^{N} F_{ij} = 1 \quad \text{for } i=1,N \quad (15)$$

3. For a plane or convex surface (one that does not see itself),

$$F_{ii} = 0 \quad (16)$$

For an enclosure with N surfaces, the matrix containing the form factors $F(ij)$ has N**2 elements, but many of the elements can often be found by using equations (14), (15), and (16).

3 Program Implementation

A program has been implemented which demonstrates the radiosity approach described above. The program reads an environment description, subdivides the polygons of the environment into subpolygon elements, computes the form factors between the elements, and forms and solves the matrix version of equation (7) to obtain element intensities. It then performs intensity smoothing between elements and displays the resultant image.

The program is limited to convex, polygonal surfaces. The present implementation is restricted to quadrilaterals and did not account for hidden surfaces.

The first module reads a description of a polygonal environment. This information consists of vertex coordinates, and the reflectivity and emitted energy terms for each color band for each polygon (equation 7). Three constant spectral energy bands, which approximated the red, green, and blue primary colors of the display device were used.

The second module subdivides the polygonal surfaces of the environment into subpolygons called "elements". This procedure is similar to mesh generation in finite element analysis [5]. A subdivision routine has been implemented where the number of elements for each polygonal surface is an input parameter to the program.

Form factors are then computed between all pairs of elements. The smaller the elements, the more accurate the results, but the longer the computation time. For the evaluation of form factors, the contour integration method (equation 13) was used. To discretize the contour integral, each edge of each element is divided into an equal number of segments. The approximate contour integral between elements i and j can then be expressed as a summation by the following pseudo-program:

```
/* FF is used to accumulate the form factor value */
    FF := 0.
    for each segment of the perimeter of element i:
    {
      for each segment of the perimeter of element j:
      {
        evaluate the distance between the segments;
        take the natural log of the distance;
        evaluate the lengths of the segments along
          each axis (dx_i, dx_j, dy_i, dy_j, dz_i, dz_j);

        multiply the natural log by
              (dx_i dx_j + dy_i dy_j + dz_i dz_j);

        add the result to FF;
      }
    };
    divide FF by 2π  times the area of element i;
/* FF is now an approximation to the form factor */
/*     from element i to element j                */
```

The actual program makes two extensions to the above algorithm. First, the approximate integral over each segment is evaluated with a quadratic (three-point) open formula. The double contour integration leads to a nine-point two dimensional quadrature formula [1, p. 892]. Second, when segments lie on the same line, the integral is evaluated analytically both to improve the accuracy of the integration of $\ln(r)$ and to avoid the singularity when r goes to zero.

After the form factors have been computed, the matrix which determines intensity is formed and solved. To solve the radiosity equations of (7) for N surfaces, the matrix is:

$$
\begin{bmatrix}
1-\rho_1 F_{1,1} & -\rho_1 F_{1,2} & \cdots & -\rho_1 F_{i,N} \\
-\rho_2 F_{2,1} & 1-\rho_2 F_{2,2} & \cdots & -\rho_2 F_{2,N} \\
\vdots & & \vdots & \\
-\rho_N F_{N,1} & -\rho_N F_{N,2} & \cdots & 1-\rho_N F_{N,N}
\end{bmatrix}
\begin{bmatrix}
b_1 \\ b_2 \\ \vdots \\ b_N
\end{bmatrix}
=
\begin{bmatrix}
e_1 \\ e_2 \\ \vdots \\ e_N
\end{bmatrix}
$$

The unknowns are the intensities, $b(i)$'s. The matrix system must be set up each time the reflectivities (ρ's) change. Since the form factors are a function of geometry only, they remain the same for each wavelength and need only be computed once. Note that if only the emitted intensities are changed (i.e., e's), the matrix remains the same.

Once the matrix has been established, any standard matrix solver can be used to derive the resulting radiosities. A Gaussian elimination scheme with partial pivoting was used.

Because the polygons are subdivided into elements of constant color larger than pixel resolution, a smoothing routine can enhance the quality of the image. Initially, a linear smoothing of the elements across the screen projection of each original polygon was implemented [4].

The final step is the display of the image. The images are displayed on a 3-channel, 27-bit, 512X480 resolution Grinnell frame buffer. The program was written in C on a VAX 11/780 under VMS.

4 Results

A simulated environment consisting of the interior of a cube was used to illustrate the radiosity method. One wall was modeled as a diffuse light source and the other five were modeled as diffuse reflectors. One wall was red, one wall was blue, and the top, bottom, and wall facing the light source were gray. The reflectivity (ρ) and intensity of emission(e) of each surface were specified in three RGB wavelength bands as shown in Figure 9a.

The six surfaces of the cube were each divided into n elements and the associated form factors were computed. Using the nomenclature of the previous section, the walls were treated as polygons, and the polygons were subdivided into equal area square elements. The pictures in Figure 6 show the effect of subdividing the walls (polygons) into 1, 4, 9, 16, 25, and 49 elements. The figures illustrate that the more subdivisions, the more realistic the simulation. The graphs of the red, green, and blue intensities on a given scanline show the correct

interaction and "color bleeding" of the red and blue walls on the gray walls. This effect can not be simulated using previous reflection models. It is instructive to compare the radiosity method to conventional diffuse shading models. Current light reflection models compute the intensities of diffuse surfaces usually by assuming point light sources located at an infinite distance. This assumption results in a constant intensity per polygon. If the light source is positioned at a finite distance, the computed intensity varies across the polygonal surface. None of the current models consider the effect caused by a light source of finite area, i.e., an "area source" as contrasted to a point source [12].

Figure 7 depicts a series of pictures, with each wall subdivided into twenty-five elements. The pictures show a progression of images computed by another program. In this progression, the number of multiple reflections is successively increased. The first picture depicts an image in which each element is illuminated only by the diffuse "area light source" on the front wall. There are no red or blue contributions from the side walls onto the other surfaces. This is equivalent to using Lambert's law for an area light source and not allowing object-to-object reflections. Figures 7b,c,d,e depict the results of adding one, two, four, and eight intermediate reflections, respectively. Figure 7e is visually identical to the result obtained using the radiosity approach (Figure 7f), where all possible illumination paths have been included. The RGB scanline intensity plots show not only the interaction of the walls and the "color bleeding", but also the fact that the overall picture brightness increases with the number of internal reflections.

Figures 8a and 8b use the same constant element intensities as in Figures 6c and 6f, respectively, but linear interpolation [4] was used to smooth the spatial variation of intensities prior to display generation. Linear interpolation, as contrasted to further element subdivision, is a reasonable choice for improving the representation of the true diffuse reflection behavior.

5 Comparison With Physical Model

To qualitatively verify the theoretical results by comparison with a real environment, a physical model of a simple environment was constructed and photographed. Fiber board panels, painted with flat latex paints to minimize specular reflections, were used to construct a test cube (Figure 9b). This cube consisted of one red, one blue, and three white panels. One side was left open for viewing and photographic purposes.

In order to verify the reflective properties of the physical model, separate tests were conducted in which individual wall panels were illuminated with a parallel beam of incident light. The intensity of the reflected light was measured as a function of reflection angle and angle of incidence. For near normal illumination ($\phi < 60$), essentially ideal diffuse behavior was observed. Equipment was not available for measuring the RGB reflectivities of the paints for comparison with the values used for the simulation (see Figure 9a). This precludes

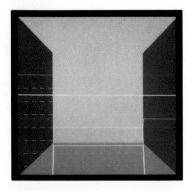

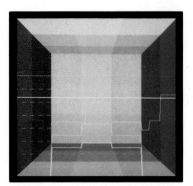

(a) 1 patch per side   **(b) 4 patches per side**   **(c) 9 patches per side**

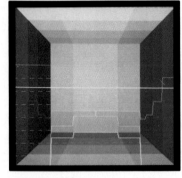

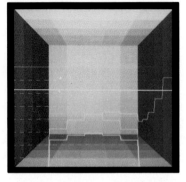

(d) 16 patches per side   **(e) 25 patches per side**   **(f) 49 patches per side**

**Figure 6. Simulated Cube with Varying Wall Subdivisions and Constant Element Intensity.
RGB Intensity Distributions at Mid-height Scanline are Shown.**

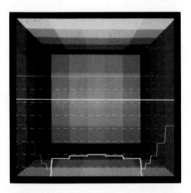

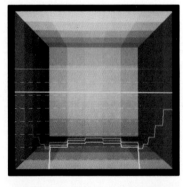

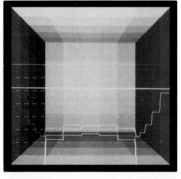

(a) 0 internal reflections   **(b) 1 internal reflection**   **(c) 2 internal reflections**

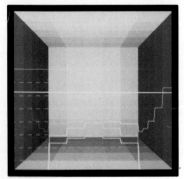

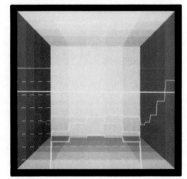

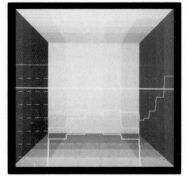

(d) 4 internal reflections   **(e) 8 internal reflections**   **(f) Using Radiosity**

**Figure 7. Simulated Cube Showing the Effect of Increasing the Number of Reflections,
25 patches per side.**

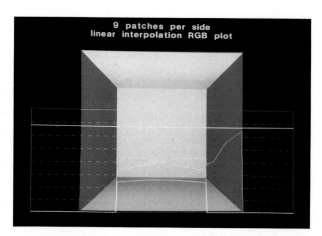

(a)

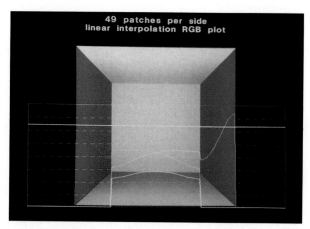

(b)

Figure 8.   Simulated Cube with Two Wall Subdivisions and Linear
Interpolation Over each Element (Patch).

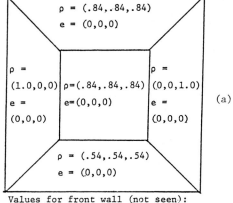

(a)

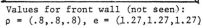

Values for front wall (not seen):
ρ = (.8,.8,.8), e = (1.27,1.27,1.27)

(b)

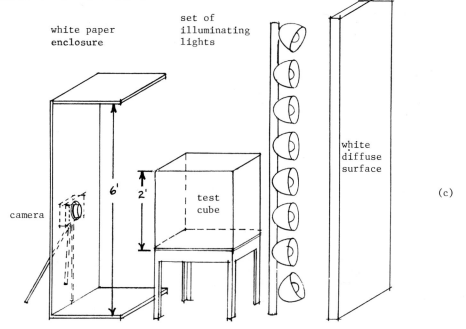

(c)

Figure 9.   Diagram of Experimental Test.   Reflectivity and Emissivity Values of Simulated Model
are Shown in (a).   Photograph of Real Model (b).   Schematic of Environment (c).

quantitative comparison between simulated and real models.

For the physical model, the open face of the test cube was illuminated with diffuse white light. A second larger enclosure with white inside walls and an open side faced the cube. The diffuse white light was obtained by illuminating this second enclosure with white lights (Fig. 9c). Through a small hole cut in the second enclosure, photographs of the cube's interior were taken. This allowed the pictures to be taken without interfering with the diffuse lighting requirements for the experiment. The illuminating wall was isotropic and uniform to approximately ten percent.

A photograph of the real model is shown in Figure 9b. The most significant observation is the color-bleeding on the top, bottom, and back walls. This color-bleeding is apparent in the simulated images using the radiosity approach (Figures 6 and 8), but not in Figure 7a, which displays the effect of neglecting object-to-object multiple reflections.

6 Conclusions

A method has been described which models the correct interaction and object-to-object reflections between diffusely reflecting surfaces. Current light reflection models used in computer graphics do not account for this interaction, and thus incorrectly compute the global illumination effects. The procedure explicitly contains the effects of diffuse light sources of finite area, as well as the "color-bleeding" effects which are caused by the diffuse reflections.

Although computationally expensive, the procedure has a major advantage in that the results are independent of the observer position. Once the intensities have been computed for a static environment, the scene can be displayed from any position without recomputing intensity values. Thus, environmental intensities can be preprocessed for dynamic sequences. Furthermore, since small specularly reflecting objects may contribute little to the total light energy, the effects of such specular reflections can be superimposed on the diffuse solutions with minimal error.

Future work should include creating a smarter subdivision algorithm to obtain finer meshes in regions of high intensity gradients and considering occluded surfaces and non-polygonal objects.

7 Acknowledgements

This research was performed at the Program of Computer Graphics at Cornell University and supported by the National Science Foundation under grant number MCS8203979. Thanks go to Michael Cohen, Kevin Koestner, and Tim McCorry for their assistance in the model building, to Dottie Harrelson for typing, to Phil Brock for drawings, and to Emil Ghinger for photography. Thanks also go to an anonymous reviewer for providing many helpful comments.

8 References

[1] Abramowitz, Milton and Stegun, Irene (Ed.). Handbook of Mathematical Functions with Formulas, Graphs, and Mathematical Tables. US Dept of Commerce National Bureau of Standards, Applied Mathematics Series 55, June 1964.

[2] Blinn, James F. Models of light reflection for computer synthesized pictures. ACM Computer Graphics (Siggraph Proc '77) 11, 2, (Summer 1977), 192-198.

[3] Cook, Robert L. and Torrance, Kenneth E. A reflectance model for computer graphics. ACM Computer Graphics (Siggraph Proc '81) 15, 3, (August 1982), 307-316.

[4] Gouraud, Henri. Computer display of curved surfaces. PhD dissertation, University of Utah, Salt Lake City, 1971.

[5] Haber, Robert, Shepard, Mark, Abel, John, Gallagher, Richard and Greenberg, Donald. A generalized graphic preprocessor for two-dimensional finite element analysis. ACM Computer Graphics (Siggraph Proc '78) 12, 3, (August 1978), 323-329.

[6] Hall, Roy and Greenberg, Donald P. A testbed for realistic image synthesis. IEEE Computer Graphics and Applications 3, 8, (November 1983), 10-20.

[7] Phong, Bui Tuong. Illumination for computer-generated images. PhD dissertation, University of Utah, Salt Lake City, 1973.

[8] Siegel, Robert and Howell, John R. Thermal Radiation Heat Transfer. Hemisphere Publishing Corporation, Washington, 1981.

[9] Sparrow, E.M. A new and simpler formulation for radiative angle factors. Transactions of the ASME, Journal of Heat Transfer 85, 2, (1963), 81-88.

[10] Sparrow, E.M. and Cess, R.D. Radiation Heat Transfer. Hemisphere Publishing Corporation, Washington, 1978.

[11] Torrance, Kenneth E. and Sparrow, Ephraim M. Theory for off-specular reflection from roughened surfaces. Journal Optical Society of America 57, 9, (September 1967), 1105-1114.

[12] Verbeck, Channing P. and Greenberg, Donald P. A comprehensive light source description for computer graphics. submitted for publication, 1984.

[13] Whitted, Turner. An improved illumination model for shaded display. Communications of the ACM 6, 23, (June 1980), 343-349.

[14] Wiebelt, John A. Engineering Radiation Heat Transfer. Holt, Rinehart and Winston, Inc., New York, 1966.

Shade Trees

Robert L. Cook

Computer Division
Lucasfilm Ltd.

Shading is an important part of computer imagery, but shaders have been based on fixed models to which all surfaces must conform. As computer imagery becomes more sophisticated, surfaces have more complex shading characteristics and thus require a less rigid shading model. This paper presents a flexible tree-structured shading model that can represent a wide range of shading characteristics. The model provides an easy means for specifying complex shading characteristics. It is also efficient because it can tailor the shading calculations to each type of surface.

CR CATEGORIES AND SUBJECT DESCRIPTORS: I.3.7 [**Computer Graphics**]: Three-Dimensional Graphics and Realism; E.1 [**Data Structures**]: *Graphs, Trees.*

ADDITIONAL KEY WORDS AND PHRASES: color, computer graphics, illumination, lighting, reflection, shading, shadows, texture

1. Introduction

Making synthetic images look realistic is an important goal in computer imagery for two reasons. First, some applications require a high degree of realism as an end in itself. Second and more generally, realism acts as a measure of our techniques and understanding. To the degree that we lack the ability to make pictures look realistic, we also lack some artistic control.

Making a realistic image involves solving a number of different problems. This paper addresses the problem of shading, or selecting colors for points on each surface, and more specifically the problem of controlling and directing the shading calculations. Other problems, such as constructing a model and animating it, are equally important to realistic image synthesis but are not addressed in this paper.

At the heart of the shading calculations is the simulation of the way light interacts with objects. Early work in reflection models was done by Henri Gouraud[10] and by Phong[16], with more accurate models being developed by Jim Blinn[2] and by the author[7], who applied the shading model to the simulation of specific materials. Blinn has developed a separate shading model for clouds[5]. Turner Whitted included reflection and refraction[18].

Textures allow us to map shading properties onto a surface mathematically, greatly increasing the visual complexity and richness of an image without the overhead of explicitly modeling those properties. Texturing was first used in computer graphics by Ed Catmull[6]. Jim Blinn later extended the use of texturing to surface bumps, roughness, and reflections[1, 4, 3]. Geoff Gardner included texturing of transparency[9].

The trend in shaders has been toward more flexibility and generality, as evidenced by Blinn's generalization of texturing[1] and Whitted's shader dispatcher[19]. What has been lacking is an overall system that integrates the various shading and texturing techniques. This paper introduces such a system, one that is based on a more general approach to shading. The new approach provides a language for describing surfaces and allows traditional shading techniques to be combined in novel ways.

Previous shaders have been limited by the use of fixed models of light reflection into which all surfaces must be fit. The new approach is modular and assumes that no single shading model is appropriate for all surfaces. In some cases utter simplicity is desired, while in others we may require a complexity that would normally be a burden. Because of its modular nature, the new shader can handle both of these extremes in the same image; it performs only the calculations needed for the simple cases while allowing arbitrarily complex calculations where they are required.

Permission to copy without fee all or part of this material is granted provided that the copies are not made or distributed for direct commercial advantage, the ACM copyright notice and the title of the publication and its date appear, and notice is given that copying is by permission of the Association for Computing Machinery. To copy otherwise, or to republish, requires a fee and/or specific permission.

© 1984   ACM   0-89791-138-5/84/007/0223 $00.75

2. Appearance Parameters

A number of different geometric, material, and environmental properties together determine the color of a surface. Any value that is used in the shading calculation is called an *appearance parameter*. Appearance parameters include the surface normal, the color of the light source, the shininess of the surface, bump maps, etc.

The traditional approach to shading is to divide the calculations into two stages:

1. Determining the values of the appearance parameters.
2. Using those values to evaluate the fixed shading equation.

This approach can offer a great deal of generality in the first stage but is inflexible in the second. Appearance parameters may be determined in a number of ways, including texture mapping and normal interpolation. The shading equation itself, however, is fixed. All surfaces must be fit into it, no matter how complex and no matter how simple. Little allowance is made for the extremely diverse ways in which objects interact with light.

3. Shade Trees

A more general approach is to eliminate the fixed shading equation and the entire two stage approach. Rather than attempt to describe all possible surfaces with a single equation, the shader orchestrates a set of basic operations, such as dot products and vector normalization. The shader organizes these operations in a tree.

Each operation is a node of the tree. Each node produces one or more appearance parameters as output, and can use zero or more appearance parameters as input. For example, the inputs to a "diffuse" node are a surface normal and a light vector, and the output is an intensity value. The normal might come from the geometric normal, a bump map, or a procedural texture. The output might be the input to a "multiply" node, which would multiply the intensity by its other input, a color.

The shader performs the calculations at the nodes by traversing the tree in postorder. The output of the root of the tree is the final color. Basic geometric information, such as the surface normal and the location of the object, are leaves of the tree. (In general, the nodes actually form a directed acyclic graph, because a single appearance parameter can be used as input to more than one node.)

Even an appearance parameter that is usually thought of as the final shade can itself be treated as an intermediate step. This is particularly useful in rendering a surface that consists of different materials. The final shade can be a combination of the shades of the various materials, with the amount of the various materials based perhaps on a texture map.

Shade trees can describe a wide range of shading situations from simplest to the most complex. Different types of shading calculations can coexist in a single image, with each surface using as many or as few operations as it requires.

4. Light Trees

The appearance parameters used in the shading calculations include the light source direction and color. These appearance parameters are described by their own tree. Light trees are separate from shade trees so that each light tree can be grafted onto several different shade trees.

Different types of lights require different calculations[17, 11]. The intensity of a local light source changes as the square of the distance from the light. Spotlights have a goniometric curve that describes their intensity as a function of direction. Some lights have flaps that abruptly restrict their illumination. All of these lights are easily described by light trees. For example, the inputs to the "spotlight" tree are the direction of the central axis of the light beam and the rate at which the intensity of the beam decreases with angle, in addition to the position of the light and the location of the point being illuminated. It uses the relevant formulas to calculate the intensity of the light at that location. These calculations, which are so specific to this one particular type of light source, are isolated from the rest of the shading, communicating only through the appearance parameters.

5. Atmosphere Trees

The final output of a shade tree is the *exitance*, the color and intensity of the light leaving the surface. But this is not necessarily the same color and intensity as the light that reaches the eye. Atmospheric effects are described by a tree that has the exitance as one of its inputs and the light actually reaching the eye as its output.

Atmospheric effects are often described by procedural models. For example, haze is an exponential function of distance[14, 13] and can vary with direction. Loren Carpenter simulated sky and haze in his film *Vol Libre* and developed a general atmosphere model for the Genesis sequence in *Star Trek II*. These models are easily incorporated into atmosphere trees.

Rainbows can also be described by an atmosphere tree, with light being added in the primary and secondary bows and subtracted in Alexander's dark band[15, 12]. The color and intensity are a function of the angle between the light direction and the viewing direction.

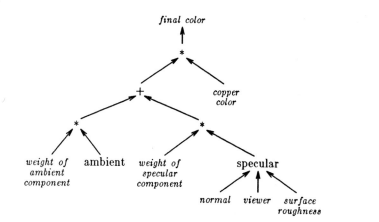

Figure 1a. Shade tree for copper.

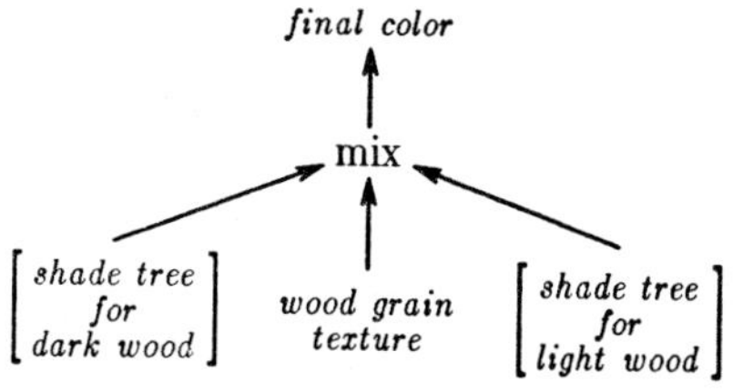

Figure 1b. The mix node in a shade tree for wood.

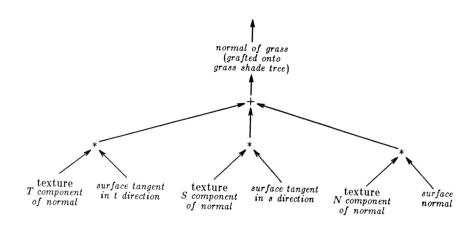

Figure 1c. Textured grass normal.

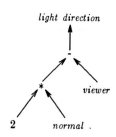

Figure 1d. "Highlight at" branch of a light tree.

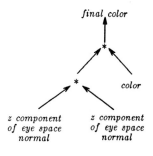

Figure 1e. Simple shade tree.

6. Implementation

To facilitate describing shade trees and building up a library of surfaces, we have developed a special shade tree language. A program written in this language is compiled into an internal representation of a shade tree. Programs in this language are also used to describe light trees and atmosphere trees.

A number of keywords, such as *normal* and *location*, refer to the basic geometric information provided as input to the shader. The final results are referred to by the keywords *final_color* and *final_opacity*.

Several types of nodes are built into the language, including mathematical functions such as *square root* and *normalize* and shading functions such as *diffuse* and *specular*. Other more specialized nodes can be added dynamically; when such a node is declared in the language, the shader searches for a file by that name and loads it. This provides enough flexibility to add new and exotic shading functions easily.

Variables in the language represent appearance parameters, and statements describe how to connect the nodes with appearance parameters. For example, the following program describes metallic shading and defines the shade tree shown in Figure 1a. Note that the ambient and specular nodes are built into the language, and that the output of the light trees is available to all nodes.

```
float a=.5, s=.5 ;
float roughness=.1 ;
float intensity ;
color metal_color=(1,1,1) ;
intensity = a*ambient() +
        s*specular(normal,viewer,roughness);
final_color = intensity * metal_color ;
```

Point variables can be specified in eye space or in world space, whichever is more convenient. World space coordinates are indicated by preceding them with the keyword "world_space".

This language works in conjunction with a modeling language to associate surfaces and light sources with objects. A light can be assigned to the group of objects because some lights affect only part of the environment. Its light tree calculations are performed only for the objects it affects.

The *surface* command in the modeling language designates a shade tree for an object. The values of variables in the surface language can be overridden here. For example, for the above "metal" surface, the statement

```
surface "metal",
    "metal_color", material bronze,
    "roughness", .15
```

in the modeling language initializes the variable "roughness" to be .15 instead of the default .1 and "metal_color" to be the color of bronze instead of white.

7. Experience with Shade Trees

This section presents several specific examples of shade trees and discusses the benefits of this new way of thinking about shading. Since we first started using shade trees, we have discovered many more uses for them than originally expected.

One surprise was the new uses of textures. For example, we rendered some leaves of grass generated by Bill Reeves by creating a texture map of transparency that could be mapped onto a polygon. Instead of using the texture to store the color of the blades for a particular orientation relative to the light source, the surface normal can be encoded in the texture and used in a shade tree as shown in figure 1c. The shading uses the correct normal and changes appropriately as the lights move.

Shadows, including penumbras, can be calculated or painted ahead of time and stored as textures that are accessed by the light tree. The ambient light is a separate light source; it is usually a constant, but it can also be textured to account for the dimming of the ambient light in corners.

Perhaps the most useful shade tree node has been the "mix" node, which uses one of its inputs to interpolate between the other two. This can be used to select between two types of materials, so that a pattern of one material can be inlaid into another. The mix node can also be used for a single material that is not homogeneous, such as wood. Many types of wood have a grain pattern of a light and dark wood. The light and dark wood are really separate materials, with separate sets of appearance parameters such as color and shininess. The grain is a single channel of texture that selects between these two materials. We compute the color of light oak and the color of the dark oak and then mix the two based on the grain texture. Figure 1b shows how the mix node is used in a shade tree for wood.

Metal fleck paint has flecks are oriented in random directions about the surface normal. A special node generates the location of each fleck on the surface and the orientation of each fleck relative to the surface normal. We add this relative normal to the surface normal and renormalize to get the true fleck normal, which is used to shade the fleck. The final color of the surface is a mixture of the color of the base paint and the color of the flecks, based on the procedural texture for the location of the flecks. Because the reflection from the flecks is highly directional, the "mix" node is essential. We can not simply shade a blend the appearance parameters (including the normals) of the flecks and the paint.

The input to the "texture" node is a set of texture coordinates. Texture coordinates are traditionally the same as the object's natural coordinates u and v. But once we regard the texture coordinates as an appearance parameter, we see that they do not need to be identical to u and v. We call the texture coordinates s and t to distinguish them from patch coordinates u and v. If we choose s and t properly, a single texture can extend over several patches without seams.

One of the more exotic uses of shade trees is an extension to bump maps called *displacement maps*. Since the location is an appearance parameter, we can actually move the location as well as perturbing the surface normal. Displacement maps began as a solution to the silhouette problems that arise when bump maps are used to make beveled edges. They are useful in many situations and can almost be considered a type of modeling. This use of shade trees, however, depends on performing the shading calculations (or at least the displacement map part of them) before the visible surface calculations.

In many cases, we are interested not in the actual location of a light source, but in the position of its highlight on a particular surface. The position of the desired highlight can be an input to the light tree, which calculates the light direction that would make a highlight appear at that given location. The tree for this calculation is shown in Figure 1d. It has proved useful in setting up the lighting for a scene.

Unusual shading functions can added to the library of shades easily. "Cat's eye" reflectors on highways reflect light back toward the light source. They are essentially a specular reflection with the normal pointed toward the light source. Marble has a textured diffuse component and a mirror-like specular component. The glowing shock wave in the Genesis sequence in *Star Trek II* was rendered by Loren Carpenter using a special purpose shading function he developed. This function was later easily described as a shade tree.

Other shade trees are used just for debugging. For example, a shade tree that assigns each patch a different random color can be useful in detecting bugs in the patch splitting code. The surface normal can be encoded in the color to look for discontinuities. It is easy to use a simple shading model, such as the one shown in Figure 1e, for trial images and to switch to more elaborate calculations for the final image.

Intermediate results can be computed by one shade tree and stored in a texture for later use by another shade tree. This is useful in calculating shading information that does not change from frame to frame within the scene.

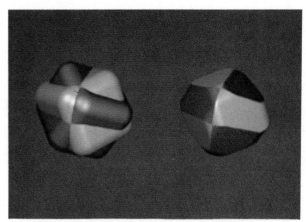

Figure 2. Union and Intersection of Two Cubes Beveled With Displacement Maps.

Figure 3a. Grass Normal Texture Map.

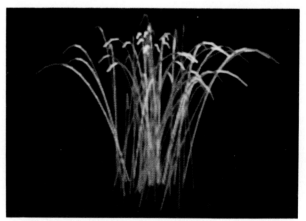

Figure 3b. Grass Rendered with Textured Normals.

8. Examples

Figure 2 shows the union and intersection of a plastic and a copper beveled cube. Each cube is described by 6 polygons that are beveled in the shader according to a procedural texture. The beveling is a displacement map that moves the locations as well as the normals.

Figure 3a is a grass texture map generated Bill Reeves. This texture was used to generate Figure 3b, which consists of a single polygon with texture mapped transparency. In addition, the red, green, and blue components of the texture are used to encode the three components of the normal relative to the normal of the surface. The resulting picture has highlights that are appropriate to the local lighting environment.

Figure 4 is *Road to Point Reyes* [8] The road lines, asphalt, and oil spots are each described by shade trees; the outputs of these trees are grafted to a "mix" node and mixed according to a texture map. The wooden fence posts and bronze chain links are described with shade trees. The hills are rendered with a three channel color texture map generated procedurally by Tom Porter. The rainbow is described by an atmosphere tree. During the early stages of design, texture maps were used to render the grass, the bushes, and the puddles quickly; these were later replaced by more exact models.

Figure 5c, *Bee Box,* illustrates light trees, displacement maps, and the "mix" node. The light is a spotlight, and its shadow (including penumbra) is produced by a texture map in a light tree. The regions of wood, ivory, copper, and bronze are selected by three channels of the texture map shown in figure 5a. Another channel controls the surface roughness in the copper and bronze regions. By contrast, figure 5b shows the same box rendered with diffuse blue shading and no displacement maps or shadows.

9. Efficiency

The overhead involved in using shade trees is small since the tree construction and traversal is done ahead of time by the shade tree compiler. At run time there is just a list of routines to call for each surface and a list of arguments (i.e., appearance parameters) for each routine.

Some of the surfaces described by shade trees are complex, and the shading time increases with the complexity of the shade tree. Shade trees are very useful in optimizing the shading calculations, however, because it is easy to adjust surface descriptions to the appropriate level of computation. If a surface is perfectly diffuse, the specular shading calculations are never used. If the geometrical attenuation of the Torrance-Sparrow[2] shading model is not necessary for a particular surface, it can easily be avoided. Reflections can be calculated with a "trace a ray" node or with an an environment map, as appropriate. Color maps, bump maps, or displacement maps can be used depending on the distance to the object.

Notice that in *Bee Box*, the wood uses only one channel of texture (the amount of grain) instead of the three one would expect (red, green, and blue). This one channel controls an entire set of appearance parameters, including color and roughness. Since wood is a mixture of surfaces, based on a texture map, only one branch of the shade tree need be descended in places where the texture calls for only one of surfaces.

10. Conclusions

Shade trees offer a way to specify and change shading properties quickly and easily. They are flexible because they are not based on a fixed shading formula; instead they provide a general way to connect basic shading operations. They are efficient because they customize the shading calculations for each type of surface.

11. Acknowledgements

Many of the ideas in this paper came out of discussions with Loren Carpenter. In some cases it is hard to say exactly who thought of what, because many of the ideas came out in the course of brainstorming sessions. Our discussions included displacement maps and shadow textures, which led to the extension of shade trees to light trees.

Tom Duff provided the nugget of code (a run time loader) that inspired a flexible implementation of shade trees. The modeling language that provides all of the hooks for lights and surfaces was written by Bill Reeves and Tom Duff. John Lasseter painted the texture of the bee. Discussions with Dan Silva were helpful in the early stages. This work began as a continuation of work done at the Program of Computer Graphics at Cornell University.

Figure 4. Road to Point Reyes.

References

1. BLINN, JAMES F. AND MARTIN E. NEWELL, "Texture and Reflection in Computer Generated Images," *Communications of the ACM*, vol. 19, pp. 542-547, 1976.

2. BLINN, JAMES F., "Models of Light Reflection for Computer Synthesized Pictures," *Computer Graphics*, vol. 11, no. 2, pp. 192-198, 1977.

3. BLINN, JAMES F., "Simulation of Wrinkled Surfaces," *Computer Graphics*, vol. 12, no. 3, pp. 286-292, August 1978.

4. BLINN, JAMES F., "Computer Display of Curved Surfaces," PhD dissertation, University of Utah, Salt Lake City, 1978.

5. BLINN, JAMES F., "Light Reflection Functions for Simulation of Clouds and Dusty Surfaces," *Computer Graphics*, vol. 16, no. 3, pp. 21-29, July 1982.

6. CATMULL, EDWIN, "A Subdivision Algorithm for Computer Display of Curved Surfaces," Phd dissertation, University of Utah, Salt Lake City, 1974.

7. COOK, ROBERT L. AND KENNETH E. TORRANCE, "A Reflection Model for Computer Graphics," *ACM Transactions on Graphics*, vol. 1, no. 1, pp. 7-24, 1982.

8. COOK, ROBERT L., LOREN CARPENTER, THOMAS PORTER, WILLIAM REEVES, DAVID SALESIN, AND ALVY RAY SMITH, "Road to Point Reyes," *Computer Graphics*, vol. 17, no. 3, July 1983. title page picture

9. GARDNER, GEOFFREY Y., EDWIN P. BERLIN JR., AND BOB GELMAN, "A Real-Time Computer Image Generation System Using Textured Curved Surfaces," *The 1981 Image Generation/Display Conference II*, pp. 60-76, June 1981.

10. GOURAUD, HENRI, "Computer Display of Curved Surfaces," PhD dissertation, University of Utah, Salt Lake City, 1971.

11. HALL, ROY A. AND DONALD P. GREENBERG, "A Testbed for Realistic Image Synthesis," *IEEE Computer Graphics and Applications*, vol. 3, no. 8, pp. 10-20, November 1983.

12. HULST, H. C. VAN DE, *Light Scattering by Small Particles*, pp. 228-266, Dover, New York, 1957.

13. MCCARTNEY, EARL J., *Optics of the Atmosphere*, pp. 1-49, John Wiley & Sons, New York, 1976.

14. MINNAERT, M., *The Nature of Light and Color in the Open Air*, Dover, New York, 1954.

15. NUSSENZVEIG, H. MOYSES, "The Theory of the Rainbow," *Scientific American*, vol. 236, no. 4, pp. 116-127, April 1977.

16. PHONG, BUI TUONG, "Illumination for Computer Generated Pictures," *Communications of the ACM*, vol. 18, pp. 311-317, 1975.

17. WARN, DAVID R., "Lighting Controls for Synthetic Images," *Computer Graphics*, vol. 17, no. 3, pp. 13-21, July 1983.

18. WHITTED, TURNER, "An Improved Illumination Model for Shaded Display," *Communications of the ACM*, vol. 23, pp. 343-349, 1980.

19. WHITTED, TURNER AND DAVID M. WEIMER, "A Software Testbed for the Development of 3D Raster Graphics Systems," *ACM Transactions on Graphics*, vol. 1, no. 1, pp. 44-58, January 1982.

Figure 6a. Plain Box.

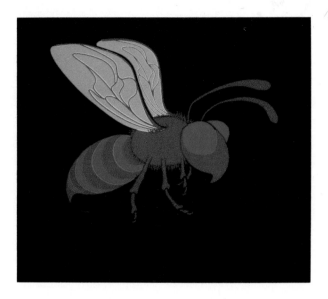

Figure 6b. Bee Texture.

Figure 6c. Bee Box

PANEL

THE ROLE AND REALITY OF GRAPHICS STANDARDS

CHAIR: James R. Warner - Precision Visuals
PANEL: Mark Skall - National Bureau of Standards
        Jose Encarnacao - TH Darmstadt--FB Informatik
        Fred Langhorst - Digital Research

ABSTRACT

Graphics standards are formally sanctioned
guidelines for graphics programming. Just
as ANSI standards provide FORTRAN programmers with a common ground among compilers,
the role of graphics standards is to
define a set of common procedures or subroutines for developing graphics applications. The primary objectives underlying
graphics standards are program portability
and a common methodology for application
program development.

Graphic standards are clearly desirable
and efforts to bring them about are well
underway. Nevertheless, the role of
graphics standards must be matched with
the reality of software development environments.

A common problem faced by all standards
committees is the very long lead time required to arrive at consensus. Most
standards groups are staffed by volun-
teers, chartered to develop standards
models around generally-accepted current
professional practices. Often, this is a
time-consuming process relying on compromise and diplomacy and hampered by long
intervals between meetings.

As a result, standards inevitably lag
behind the industry, where competitive
hardware vendors play leapfrog with one
another, pushing the state of the art.
Much of the concern surrounding standards
implementations stems from the low level
of standards literacy in the graphics user
community. Beyond a vague understanding
of functionality, most graphics software
shoppers have little understanding on the
different levels of standards, how to
measure a good implementation, and methods
of programming efficiently using a graphics standards methodology. As a result,
standards-based packages face the difficult challenge of balancing the theoretical world of standards with the down-
to-earth needs of application developers
working against deadlines.

This session will measure the several
standards proposals now in the ANSI pipeline against the requirements and literacy
level of the buying public. The evolution
of a standard through ANSI and the implications of certification procedures will
be presented and discussed. The problems
of implementing a graphics standard will
also be discussed, along with the general
buying criteria to follow when shopping
for standards-based graphics software.

A Family of New Algorithms for Soft Filling

Kenneth P. Fishkin

Brian A. Barsky

Berkeley Computer Graphics Laboratory
Computer Science Division
Department of Electrical Engineering and Computer Sciences
University of California
Berkeley, California 94720
U.S.A.

Abstract

Soft filling algorithms change the color of an anti-aliased region, maintaining the anti-aliasing of the region. The two published algorithms for soft filling work only if the foreground region is anti-aliased against a black background. This paper presents three new algorithms. The first fills against a region consisting of any *two* distinct colors, and is faster than the published algorithms on a pixel-by-pixel basis for an RGB frame buffer; the second fills against a region composed of *three* distinct colors; and the third fills against a region composed of *four* distinct colors. As the power of the algorithms increases, so do the number of assumptions they make, and the computational cost.

CR Categories and Subject Descriptors: **I.3.4** [**Computer Graphics**]: Graphics Utilities; **I.4.6** [**Image Processing**]: Segmentation

General Terms: Algorithms, Color

Additional Key Words and Phrases: Convex hull, Linear algebra

1. Introduction

A *region* is a group of connected pixels in a frame buffer. This region possesses a certain color, which may have been created by direct user "painting", or by a rendering algorithm. The problem of changing the displayed color of this region is known as *filling*. The filling algorithm has no world knowledge of how the region "came to be"; it is given only the old color of the region, the new color desired for it, and one *seed point* known to be inside. The algorithm then traverses the region, changing the old region color to the new.

If the region is anti-aliased, or was painted with a non-opaque brush, the process is known as *soft filling*, and the region is termed *soft-edged*. If the region is defined by a boundary, its color is changed by *boundary-filling* algorithms; if the region is defined by its interior values, its color is changed by *flood-filling* algorithms. In this paper, we focus on flood filling although our algorithms work equally well in either case.

The region whose color is to be changed is the *foreground*, and its color is the *foreground color*. For every region, there is a set of underlying colors, combinations of which form the region; these are termed *basis colors*. The foreground color is a particular basis color. Using this terminology, the region is defined as the set of connected pixels with any portion of foreground color present in their composition. Under this definition, blurred pixels on the boundary of the region are considered inside the region; therefore, even a single colored region is actually composed of *two* colors (the foreground and background). A *background* color is a basis color that corresponds to a physical region found on the boundary of the filled region.

A filling algorithm can be decomposed into four components:

- The *propagation method*: decides where to search for the borders of the region.
- The *START procedure*: initializes the fill.
- The *INSIDE procedure*: decides whether a pixel is to be filled. (Smith's[11] GET procedure is contained in this).
- The *SET procedure*: changes the color of a given pixel.

The two published algorithms for soft filling[5,11] work (for an RGB frame buffer) only if the foreground region is rendered against a black background. In this paper, a family of new algorithms is presented. The published algorithms are shown to be computationally less efficient special cases of the first new algorithm, which fills against an *arbitrary* single-colored background (*two* basis colors; the foreground and the background). The second fills a region with *three* basis colors, and the third a region with *four* basis colors. As the power of the algorithms increases, so does the cost of computation, and the assumptions they make.

Permission to copy without fee all or part of this material is granted provided that the copies are not made or distributed for direct commercial advantage, the ACM copyright notice and the title of the publication and its date appear, and notice is given that copying is by permission of the Association for Computing Machinery. To copy otherwise, or to republish, requires a fee and/or specific permission.

© 1984   ACM   0-89791-138-5/84/007/0235 $00.75

2. Existing Algorithms

2.1. Interior Fill

When the region is not anti-aliased, a simple, quick algorithm known as *interior fill*[11] can be used. This algorithm successfully fills against any set of background colors.

The START, INSIDE, and SET procedures are simple. START is a null procedure, INSIDE will return true if and only if the pixel read is the same color as the old foreground color, and SET simply writes a pixel. The details of the propagation algorithm are unimportant for this presentation.

2.2. Tint Fill

For a soft-edged region, the problem is much harder. The edge of the region (or even the interior, if the region has shadows or specular reflection) fades into other colors. Deciding whether a pixel is INSIDE and, if so, determining which basis colors comprise it, is very difficult, and sometimes impossible.

The most popular algorithm for soft filling is Smith's *tint fill.*[11] In a later paper, Smith[12] presented an improvement on the propagation algorithm; a more substantial revamping of the propagation algorithm is discussed by Levoy.[5]

All three papers use the same INSIDE and SET procedures. Since those are the focus of this presentation, only the INSIDE and SET procedures will be discussed. For a treatment of the remainder of the algorithm, see Smith.[11, 12]

Briefly, in tint fill, each pixel is read in terms of its *tint* and its *value*. The tint contains the hue and saturation of the pixel, and the value contains the intensity. In the HSV system, tint = (H, S), and value = V. To avoid confusion, we will use V exclusively to represent value.

In the INSIDE procedure (for an RGB frame buffer), "tint and value are algorithmically computed from the RGB primary components"[11] by an RGB to HSV transformation. The present V is then compared to the V at the preceding inside pixel. If the new V is less than or equal to the old V, and the tint is equal to the old foreground tint, then the new pixel is considered inside. As the foreground color blurs into black, V will gradually decrease, down to the minimum possible V of zero at black.

The SET procedure sets the pixel tint to the tint of the foreground color. The old V of the pixel is retained. An HSV to RGB conversion is then done, and the pixel is written.

The START procedure is null for tint fill.

2.2.1. Disadvantages of tint fill

Tint fill is a significant improvement over interior fill for many soft-edged regions. However, it has two disadvantages:

(1) "To fill a pixel with tint fill means to change the ... tint of the pixel color only, not its [V], or blackness".[11] This is only appropriate when the V of the new foreground is the same as that of the old foreground. For most renderings, this is not the case.

(2) The algorithm only works against a black background. Consider filling a green foreground rendered against a red background. Being of the same V, tint fill would be unable to detect any coherent flow from red to green. Tint fill will stop at any blurring of the two and declare that blurring outside the region, since it would detect a change in tint. The degree of change, a valuable piece of information, is not examined. Similarly, consider a black foreground against a white background; V would gradually increase, not decrease.

These disadvantages apply only for RGB frame buffers; tint fill was "tuned" for a color-mapped environment, and within that environment can be modified to work for any single background color. Advances in technology have made full RGB frame buffers more commonplace, prompting our attempt to develop filling algorithms for the RGB environment.

At the end of his article, Smith[11] briefly presents several speculations about his algorithm which, as we understand them, could mitigate both of these disadvantages by using a number of special cases. Smith has since stated[14] that these speculations were not implemented; therefore, we will restrict discussion of tint fill to ignore these alternatives. Smith later solved the problem of filling against a single-colored background,[12] but has not published or discussed the algorithm and therefore it cannot be evaluated here.

2.3. Alpha fill

Levoy's *alpha fill*[4] algorithm solves the soft filling problem in a quite different manner. Tint fill, given the background color, finds the proportion of foreground in each pixel. Alpha fill solves the *inverse* problem; given the proportion of foreground in each pixel, it finds the background color. Associated with each pixel is a number α, created through prior user interaction, which is precisely the percentage of the foreground in each pixel. The filling algorithm "[knows] the proportion at each pixel without the necessity of performing any computations at all".[6]

The background color(s), by contrast, are "computed on the fly during the filling process without recourse to either global information or user intervention".[6] Since the background color is computed for each pixel, alpha fill allows any number of background colors; however, at most one may be present *in any given pixel*.

The INSIDE procedure for alpha fill is

read α value from extra buffer
if $\alpha > 0$, then the pixel is INSIDE

The SET procedure performs "extrapolation based on the color at this pixel and the color at the seed position to compute the color of the background".[6]

Alpha fill solves a related, but different problem; while it is more powerful than tint fill, it requires more information.

3. The Family of New Algorithms

We present a family of three new filling algorithms, each of which makes three assumptions:

(1) The basis color(s), whatever they may be, are known. Although this is much less restrictive than assuming a black background, it may not hold for all applications. Furthermore, we stress that a basis color is any color that contributes to the color of pixels within the region. It is possible that no pixel purely consists of the basis color, or that the basis color does not correspond to a *physical* background region. For example, if a region is partially in shadow, black will be one of the basis colors, even though there may be no black pixel, and no black "region" per se. Regions painted with fuzzy brushes and regions with specular highlights are similar examples. In section 6, we discuss a technique that sometimes removes this assumption.

(2) Anti-aliasing operates in the linear space between colors; an anti-aliased pixel lying between β basis colors will have a color that is a convex combination of those colors in color space. It is not assumed that the anti-aliasing *process* is linear, that is that the interpolation of color points between two colors proceeds in equally-spaced linear increments. The assumption is that the set of points *resulting* from this process lies within a geometric simplex. This assumption is the key to all the algorithms; it holds for all additive color spaces (XYZ, RGB, YIQ, etc.) due to the additive nature of light.

(3) No pixel is considered INSIDE twice. When a pixel is SET, which occurs whenever it is considered INSIDE, its color is altered; if this altered color were read back, the INSIDE test on this new color could yield unpredictable results. While this assumption does not hold for Smith's original propagation algorithm,[11] it does for his latter,[12] and also for Levoy's.[5]

The new algorithms are independent of propagation method; they can be implemented using either Smith's[11, 12] or Levoy's[5] propagation methods.

The three new algorithms solve a system of three equations in one, two, and three unknowns, respectively. As the number of unknowns increases, so does the power of the algorithm, as well as the computational expense. The algorithms approach the problem uniformly; they differ only in their generality and speed. Each basis color is a basis vector in color space; the algorithms determine the combination of basis vectors that reproduce the color in each pixel.

A color will be represented as the vector triple $\mathbf{C}$. The components will be referred to as $C^{[0]}, C^{[1]}$, and $C^{[2]}$. In the case of a color in the RGB system, $C^{[0]}$, $C^{[1]}$, and $C^{[2]}$ refer to the red, green, and blue components, respectively. In general, we use the notation of Table 3.1.

3.1. Linear Fill

This section presents a simple, fast algorithm to soft fill against any single-colored background, termed *linear fill*.

Table 3.1: Notation and Symbols	
Symbol	**Meaning**
$\mathbf{B}$	color of the background
$B^{[j]}$	j'th component of the background color
$\mathbf{B}_i$	i'th basis color
	$\mathbf{B}_0$ refers to the foreground color
$B_i^{[j]}$	j'th component of the i'th basis color
β	number of basis colors
$\hat{\mathbf{B}}$	$\{ \mathbf{B}_0, \mathbf{B}_1 \cdots \mathbf{B}_{\beta-1} \}$
d	denominator/determinant
$\mathbf{F}$	old foreground color, also denoted $\mathbf{B}_0$
$\mathbf{G}$	new foreground color
n	number of bits in each color component
N	2^n
$\mathbf{P}$	color of an arbitrary pixel
t	an interpolation factor
$\mathbf{T}$	vector of interpolation factors
v_X	value (V) of the color X

Given the assumptions of the previous section, the algorithm is almost embarrassingly simple. Let the color of the old foreground be $\mathbf{F}$ (known by user specification), the background be $\mathbf{B}$ (known by assumption (1)), and the present pixel be $\mathbf{P}$. Then, by assumption (2), $\mathbf{P}$ is a linear interpolation between $\mathbf{F}$ and $\mathbf{B}$:

$$\mathbf{P} = t\,\mathbf{F} + (1-t)\,\mathbf{B}$$

where $0 \leq t \leq 1$ is the proportion of foreground color in the present pixel color.

The value of t is the same for all components of the vector, and can be found from any component i in which $F^{[i]} \neq B^{[i]}$. Choosing i to maximize $|F^{[i]} - B^{[i]}|$ minimizes discretization error, a problem discussed in the Appendix. If $\mathbf{F} = \mathbf{B}$, the algorithm will fail. This pathological case can be trivially detected in advance, and it is usually assumed that it will not occur.

The START procedure is

  find i which maximizes $|F^{[i]} - B^{[i]}|$
  set $d = F^{[i]} - B^{[i]}$

The INSIDE procedure is

  set t to $(P^{[i]} - B^{[i]})/d$
  if $t > 0$, the pixel is inside the region *

And the SET procedure is

  $\mathbf{P} = t\,\mathbf{G} + (1-t)\,\mathbf{B}$
  where $\mathbf{G}$ is the new foreground color.

3.1.1. Tint Fill is a special case

Tint fill is a special case of linear fill. If the region was rendered in some color $\mathbf{F}$, each pixel colored $\mathbf{P}$ can be expressed, from above, as

$$\mathbf{P} = t\,\mathbf{F} + (1-t)\,\mathbf{B} \quad where \quad 0 \leq t \leq 1 \qquad (3.1)$$

When the background color is black, $\mathbf{B} = 0$,

---

* Some thresholding is necessary; we threshold at $t \geq 0.5N$.

$$P = t\,\mathbf{F}, \quad 0 \le t \le 1.$$

The V of a color $\mathbf{C}$ is defined in RGB space as $\max(C^{[0]}, C^{[1]}, C^{[2]})$.[3] Let the value of F be denoted as $v_{\mathbf{F}}$. Then the value $v_{\mathbf{P}}$ at a pixel colored $\mathbf{P}$ is

$$
\begin{aligned}
v_{\mathbf{P}} &= \max(\,P^{[0]}, P^{[1]}, P^{[2]}) \\
&= \max(\,tF^{[0]}, tF^{[1]}, tF^{[2]}) \\
&= t\,\max(\,F^{[0]}, F^{[1]}, F^{[2]}) \\
v_{\mathbf{P}} &= t\,v_{\mathbf{F}}
\end{aligned}
$$

Therefore, decreasing t is exactly equivalent to decreasing $v_{\mathbf{P}}$, in this special case of a black background.

3.1.2. Time comparison of the two algorithms

As linear fill is independent (within the third assumption of section 3) of the propagation algorithm, the two algorithms can be compared solely on the work done by INSIDE and SET. Three assumptions are made about the comparison:

(1) An RGB frame buffer is used, which severely handicaps the performance of tint fill due to the expense of color system conversion. If that is not the case, tint fill is much quicker than linear fill.

(2) Performance is based on a region with an interior of i pixels, and a boundary of b pixels; this causes i calls to SET, and $i + b$ calls to INSIDE.

(3) Smith's RGB to HSV conversion[13] is used. The HSV to RGB conversion is from the same source, with a minor optimization that replaces 5 multiplications and 4 subtractions by 2 multiplications, 1 addition, and 1 subtraction.[2]

	SET (i)		INSIDE (i+ b)		Total	
op	linear	tint	linear	tint	linear	tint
test	0	1	1	8.5	i+ b	9.5i+ 8.5b
:=	3	11	1	9	4i+ b	20i+ 9b
+	3	1	0	0.5	3i	1.5i+ 0.5b
-	3	4	1	4.5	4i+ b	8.5i+ 4.5b
*	6	3	0	0	6i	3i
/	0	0	1	5	i+ b	5i+ 5b
floor	0	0	0	1	0	i+ b

Table 3.2: linear fill versus tint fill

Assuming that subtraction is equivalent to addition in time, and that division is equivalent to multiplication (both assumptions aiding the comparison in favor of tint fill), Table 3.2 shows that linear fill is faster than tint fill for all regions.

3.1.3. Disadvantages of Linear Fill

Linear fill fails in the pathological case when the foreground and background are the same color, but it has a more significant limitation; although it can fill against an arbitrary *single-colored* background, it is not applicable if the region is formed by more than two colors, as is common in a complex shaded scene.

Formally, let the basis colors be denoted by the set $\hat{B} = \{\,\mathbf{B}_0, \mathbf{B}_1, \ldots, \mathbf{B}_{\beta-1}\,\}$. The foreground color $\mathbf{F} \equiv \mathbf{B}_0$. Linear fill works only if $\beta = 2$. The most general filling algorithm would work for arbitrary β.

3.1.4. Increasing β

Writing the components of equation (3.1) yields

$$
\begin{aligned}
P^{[0]} &= t F^{[0]} + (1-t)B^{[0]} \\
P^{[1]} &= t F^{[1]} + (1-t)B^{[1]} \\
P^{[2]} &= t F^{[2]} + (1-t)B^{[2]} \\
&\text{where } 0 \le t \le 1
\end{aligned}
$$

This is a system of three equations in one unknown. The next two algorithms, *triangle fill* and *tetrahedron fill*, will replace this system of equations by similar systems in two and three unknowns. A fill algorithm in β unknowns works for a set of basis colors $\hat{B} = \{\,\mathbf{B}_0, \mathbf{B}_2, \cdots \mathbf{B}_{\beta-1}\,\}$. Unlike alpha fill,[4] we allow a pixel to be formed by any or all β basis colors. This is often the case at pixels that lie at the intersection of regions or are in shadow, for pixels with specular reflection, etc.

3.2. Triangle Fill

Linear fill assumed a background composed of exactly one underlying color, not equal to the foreground color. Every pixel in the region was composed of two colors, and lay on the line between them. Triangle fill solves a slightly more difficult case, a region formed by three colors. In color space, the basis colors now form the vertices of a triangle; by assumption (2) of section 3, all pixels found will lie inside this triangle. Extending assumption (2) of linear fill to this problem,

$$\mathbf{P} = T^{[0]}\mathbf{B}_0 + T^{[1]}\mathbf{B}_1 + T^{[2]}\mathbf{B}_2.$$

This can be written as an equation in two variables, since $T^{[0]} + T^{[1]} + T^{[2]} = 1$.

$$\mathbf{P} = T^{[0]}\mathbf{B}_0 + T^{[1]}\mathbf{B}_1 + (1 - T^{[0]} - T^{[1]})\mathbf{B}_2$$

In terms of the unknowns,

$$\mathbf{P} - \mathbf{B}_2 = T^{[0]}(\mathbf{B}_0 - \mathbf{B}_2) + T^{[1]}(\mathbf{B}_1 - \mathbf{B}_2)$$

Writing in component form,

$$P^{[j]} - B_2^{[j]} = T^{[0]}(B_0^{[j]} - B_2^{[j]}) + T^{[1]}(B_1^{[j]} - B_2^{[j]}), \\ \text{for } j = 0,1,2$$

This is an over-constrained system of three equations in two unknowns, and can be solved by using Cramer's rule on some two of the three equations:

$$T^{[0]} = \frac{\begin{vmatrix} P^{[i]} - B_2^{[i]} & B_1^{[i]} - B_2^{[i]} \\ P^{[j]} - B_2^{[j]} & B_1^{[j]} - B_2^{[j]} \end{vmatrix}}{d} \tag{3.2}$$

$$T^{[1]} = \frac{\begin{vmatrix} B_0^{[i]} - B_2^{[i]} & P^{[i]} - B_2^{[i]} \\ B_0^{[j]} - B_2^{[j]} & P^{[j]} - B_2^{[j]} \end{vmatrix}}{d}$$

$$\text{where } i \ne j \in \{\,0,1,2\,\}$$

$$\text{and } d = \begin{vmatrix} B_0^{[i]} - B_2^{[i]} & B_1^{[i]} - B_2^{[i]} \\ B_0^{[j]} - B_2^{[j]} & B_1^{[j]} - B_2^{[j]} \end{vmatrix}$$

3.2.1. Implementation

For triangle fill, the START procedure is:
find i,j such   that d is   maximized*,
$i \neq j \in \{ 0,1,2 \}$
The INSIDE procedure is:

Compute $T^{[0]}, T^{[1]}$ by equation (3.2).
If $T^{[0]} > 0$, the pixel is inside the region.
($T^{[0]}$ is in [0..1] by assumption (2) of section (3))

The SET procedure replaces the percentage of the old foreground with an equal percentage of the new, as in linear fill:

$$\mathbf{P} = T^{[0]}\mathbf{G} + T^{[1]}\mathbf{B}_1 + (1 - T^{[0]} - T^{[1]})\mathbf{B}_2$$

3.2.2. Limitations

Triangle fill will fail when the denominator of equation (3.2) is equal to zero for all choices of i and j, $i \neq j$. To determine when this condition holds, assume the denominator is zero. Then

$$0 = (B_0^{[j]} - B_2^{[j]})(B_1^{[j]} - B_2^{[j]}) - (B_0^{[j]} - B_2^{[j]})(B_1^{[j]} - B_2^{[j]}) ,$$
$$\forall \; i,j \in \{ 0,1,2 \}, i \neq j$$

This set of scalar equations is exactly equivalent to the vector equation:

$$\mathbf{0} = (\mathbf{B}_0 - \mathbf{B}_2) \times (\mathbf{B}_1 - \mathbf{B}_2),$$

This equation holds if and only if $\mathbf{B}_0$, $\mathbf{B}_1$, and $\mathbf{B}_2$ are colinear. If one of the colors is black, this condition arises if and only if the remaining two colors possess the same chromaticity (hue and saturation).

A sufficient (but not necessary) condition for degeneracy is equality of any two of the three vectors. This implies that triangle fill is more likely than linear fill to fail, as its failure condition is a superset of linear fill's. This is expanded upon in section 4.

When the three colors are colinear, the filling problem is inherently ambiguous. Consider a white foreground with additional basis colors of grey and black. When a pixel colored grey is encountered, it is equally valid to consider it 100% grey, or 50% white mixed with 50% black.

It is far worse to make the wrong decision than to make no decision. Suppose that the foreground was filled to red, and a heuristic was employed that led the algorithm to consider grey as 50% white mixed with 50% black. In this case, it is possible that solid grey shapes unfortunate enough to abut the foreground would be changed incorrectly to burnt orange.

3.2.3. Triangle fill summary

Triangle fill fills a region formed by three colors. It is more expensive computationally than linear fill. The start-up cost of computing the 2-by-2 determinant of equation (3.2) is added, and the per-pixel processing is also increased. Unlike linear fill, which works whenever

---

* as in linear fill, choosing the maximum denominator minimizes discretization error

the basis colors are not coincident, triangle fill requires a slightly stronger condition; they must not be colinear.

3.3. Tetrahedron fill

Tetrahedron fill solves a system of three equations in three unknowns to fill against four basis colors ($\beta = 4$).

We wish to find $T^{[0]}, T^{[1]}, T^{[2]}, T^{[3]}$ such that

$$\mathbf{P} = T^{[0]}\mathbf{B}_0 + T^{[1]}\mathbf{B}_1 + T^{[2]}\mathbf{B}_2 + T^{[3]}\mathbf{B}_3. \quad (3.3)$$

Tetrahedron fill finds a unique linear combination of four vectors in a three-dimensional space by adding the knowledge that the weights sum to unity. Using this observation, equation (3.3) becomes an equation in three variables,

$$\mathbf{P} = T^{[0]}\mathbf{B}_0 + T^{[1]}\mathbf{B}_1 + T^{[2]}\mathbf{B}_2$$
$$+ (1 - T^{[0]} - T^{[1]} - T^{[2]})\mathbf{B}_3$$

In terms of the unknowns $T^{[0]}, T^{[1]}$, and $T^{[2]}$:

$$\mathbf{P} - \mathbf{B}_3 = T^{[0]}(\mathbf{B}_0 - \mathbf{B}_3) + T^{[1]}(\mathbf{B}_1 - \mathbf{B}_3) + T^{[2]}(\mathbf{B}_2 - \mathbf{B}_3).$$

Let the row vector $\mathbf{T}$ be $[T^{[0]}, T^{[1]}, T^{[2]}]$. Then this can be rewritten as

$$\mathbf{P} - \mathbf{B}_3 = \mathbf{T} * \begin{bmatrix} \mathbf{B}_0 - \mathbf{B}_3 \\ \mathbf{B}_1 - \mathbf{B}_3 \\ \mathbf{B}_2 - \mathbf{B}_3 \end{bmatrix}$$

This is one vector-valued equation in one vector-valued unknown ($\mathbf{T}$):

$$\begin{bmatrix} \mathbf{P} - \mathbf{B}_3 \end{bmatrix} = \mathbf{T}\overline{\mathbf{M}}, \; where$$

$$\overline{\mathbf{M}} = \begin{bmatrix} \mathbf{B}_0 - \mathbf{B}_3 \\ \mathbf{B}_1 - \mathbf{B}_3 \\ \mathbf{B}_2 - \mathbf{B}_3 \end{bmatrix} \quad (3.4)$$

The unknown $\mathbf{T}$ can be found by two different approaches: matrix inversion and Gaussian reduction.

3.3.1. Matrix inversion

By computing the inverse of $\overline{\mathbf{M}}$, the unknown $\mathbf{T}$ can be found by

$$\mathbf{T} = [\mathbf{P} - \mathbf{B}_3]\overline{\mathbf{M}}^{-1}$$

This multiplication of a matrix by a row vector requires (for a three-by-three matrix) nine multiplications and six additions.

The matrix $\overline{\mathbf{M}}^{-1}$ is independent of $\mathbf{P}$ and can be computed in the START procedure.

3.3.2. The reduction approach

Using Gaussian reduction of $\overline{\mathbf{M}}$ into an upper-triangular matrix $\overline{\mathbf{U}}$,

$$\begin{bmatrix} \mathbf{P} - \mathbf{B}_3 \end{bmatrix} = \mathbf{T}\overline{\mathbf{U}}$$

For each pixel, $\mathbf{T}$ is then found by back-substitution which (for a three-by-three matrix) requires three multiplications, three subtractions, and three divisions.

3.3.3. Which approach to use

The two approaches differ in their INSIDE and START expense. The START expense is incurred exactly once in the fill, while the INSIDE expense is incurred at each pixel. Therefore, we consider the START expense of negligible importance compared to the INSIDE expense. The reduction approach requires three more divisions and three more subtractions than the inversion approach for the INSIDE test, but uses six fewer multiplications and six fewer additions.

The particular target machine dictates the approach. At Berkeley, a floating-point accelerator is used that makes a division much more than twice as slow as a multiplication; accordingly, we focus on the inversion approach in the remainder of this paper.

3.3.4. Tetrahedron fill procedures

The START procedure for tetrahedron fill computes $\overline{\mathbf{M}}^{-1}$ for the inversion approach and computes $\overline{\mathbf{U}}$ for the reduction approach.

The INSIDE procedure for tetrahedron fill is

$$\mathbf{T} = [\mathbf{P}{-}\mathbf{B}_3]\overline{\mathbf{M}}^{-1} \text{ for inversion}$$
$$\mathbf{T}\overline{\mathbf{U}} = [\mathbf{P}{-}\mathbf{B}_3] \text{ for reduction}$$

If $T^{(0)}>0$, the pixel is inside the region

The SET procedure is a trilinear interpolation:

$$\mathbf{P}{=}T^{(0)}\mathbf{G} + T^{(1)}\mathbf{B}_1 + T^{(2)}\mathbf{B}_2 + (1{-}T^{(0)}{-}T^{(1)}{-}T^{(2)})\mathbf{B}_3$$

3.3.5. Summary of tetrahedron fill

Tetrahedron fill will fill a region with four basis colors. It is more expensive computationally than triangle fill; a start-up cost of computing a matrix inverse is added, and the per-pixel processing is also increased. Tetrahedron fill is also not perfectly robust, requiring the invertibility of a matrix, as shown in equation (3.4).

4. A comparison of failure probabilities

Each of the fill algorithms fails under certain conditions. Linear fill fails if and only if

$$\mathbf{0} = \mathbf{B}_0 - \mathbf{B}_1$$

Triangle fill fails if and only if

$$\mathbf{0} = (\mathbf{B}_0{-}\mathbf{B}_2){\times}(\mathbf{B}_1{-}\mathbf{B}_2),$$

while tetrahedron fill fails if and only if

$$0 = \left|\overline{\mathbf{M}}\right|$$

If a fill against β basis colors fails, could the fill succeed by adding a dummy $(\beta+1)$'st basis color, and using a different algorithm? Theorems 1 and 2 show that this cannot be done.

Theorem 1: *Linear failure implies triangle failure*
Proof: We are interested in the cross product

$$(\mathbf{B}_0{-}\mathbf{B}_2){\times}(\mathbf{B}_1{-}\mathbf{B}_2)$$

Linear failure implies that

$$\mathbf{B}_0 = \mathbf{B}_1 \ ,$$

$$(\mathbf{B}_0{-}\mathbf{B}_2){\times}(\mathbf{B}_1{-}\mathbf{B}_2) \ = \ (\mathbf{B}_0{-}\mathbf{B}_2){\times}(\mathbf{B}_0{-}\mathbf{B}_2)$$

But the cross product of any vector with itself is $\mathbf{0}$: thus

$$(\mathbf{B}_0{-}\mathbf{B}_2){\times}(\mathbf{B}_1{-}\mathbf{B}_2) \ = \ \mathbf{0}$$

This is exactly the failure condition for triangle fill.

Theorem 2: *Triangle failure implies tetrahedron failure*

Proof: Triangle failure implies that

$$\mathbf{0} \ = \ (\mathbf{B}_0{-}\mathbf{B}_2){\times}(\mathbf{B}_1{-}\mathbf{B}_2)$$

It must be shown that tetrahedron fill will fail on these basis colors, for all possible new $\mathbf{B}_3$. Since $\mathbf{B}_0{-}\mathbf{B}_2$ is a linear multiple of $\mathbf{B}_1{-}\mathbf{B}_2$, the above equation can be rewritten (assuming $\mathbf{B}_1{-}\mathbf{B}_2{\neq}0$) as

$$\mathbf{B}_0{-}\mathbf{B}_2{=}k(\mathbf{B}_1{-}\mathbf{B}_2) \ , \ \text{for some} \ k \qquad (3.5)$$

Recall that adding a linear multiple of any row of a matrix to another does not change its invertibility. From equation (3.4), we wish to invert

$$\overline{\mathbf{M}} \ = \ \begin{bmatrix} \mathbf{B}_0{-}\mathbf{B}_3 \\ \mathbf{B}_1{-}\mathbf{B}_3 \\ \mathbf{B}_2{-}\mathbf{B}_3 \end{bmatrix}$$

Subtracting the third row from the first and second rows,

$$= \begin{bmatrix} \mathbf{B}_0{-}\mathbf{B}_2 \\ \mathbf{B}_1{-}\mathbf{B}_2 \\ \mathbf{B}_2{-}\mathbf{B}_3 \end{bmatrix}$$

By equation (3.5), subtracting k times the second row from the first yields

$$= \begin{bmatrix} \mathbf{0} \\ \mathbf{B}_1{-}\mathbf{B}_2 \\ \mathbf{B}_2{-}\mathbf{B}_3 \end{bmatrix}$$

which is not invertible, guaranteeing failure of tetrahedron fill regardless of the choice of $\mathbf{B}_3$.

These two theorems above prove it is impossible to "step around" a degenerate fill by adding another color.

The converse is easily shown; if $\hat{\mathbf{B}}$ can be successfully filled, then for all $\hat{\mathbf{C}}$ such that $\hat{\mathbf{C}} \subset \hat{\mathbf{B}}$ and $|\hat{\mathbf{C}}|{\geq}2$, $\hat{\mathbf{C}}$ can be filled.

5. Summary of the three fills

A brief summary of the algorithms' characteristics is shown in Table 5.1.

Procedure	Algorithm		
	linear	triangle	tetrahedron [*]
START	minimal	find 2-by-2 determinant	invert 3-by-3 matrix
INSIDE	multiply	compute 2-by-2 determinant	multiply row vector by 3-by-3 matrix
SET interpolation	linear	bilinear	trilinear
fails when basis colors	coincident	colinear	coplanar

Table 5.1: Summary of fill algorithm expense

[*] using the inversion approach for tetrahedron fill.

A performance count has been done for the INSIDE and SET procedures. The START expense is considered negligible. One minor optimization has been employed for the INSIDE procedures of triangle and tetrahedron fill; if $T^{[0]} = 0$, the procedure will not compute the other elements of T.

Again making the two assumptions that addition and subtraction, and multiplication and division, are each approximately equivalent in time, Table 5.2 shows that the computational expense monotonically increases among algorithms.

op	Algorithm		
	Linear	Triangle	Tetrahedron [*]
tests	$i + b$	$i + b$	$i + b$
:=	$4i + b$	$5i + b$	$6i + b$
+	$3i$	$6i$	$15i + 2b$
-	$4i + b$	$16i + 5b$	$12i + 3b$
*	$6i$	$13i + 2b$	$21i + 3b$
/	$i + b$	$2i + b$	0

Table 5.2: Performance comparison

[*] using the inversion approach for tetrahedron fill.

6. Finding the basis colors

We have assumed that the basis colors are known to the filling algorithm. This can be supplied either by explicit world knowledge, or by user interaction. What if, for some reason, this assumption is unreasonable; can the basis colors be determined by the filling algorithm? This section describes our current efforts to solve this problem.

Note that we seek more than just the geometric edge of the region; this tells us only when to stop examining the colors in the frame buffer. It is the set of examined colors that is truly crucial; from it we seek to determine $\hat{B}$ for the region. There are, therefore, two related but separate problems: finding the edge of the region, and finding the basis colors comprising the region.

We are presently experimenting with the use of Sobel edge detection[9] to determine the edge of the region; in the rest of this section, we focus on finding $\hat{B}$, given the area of interest.

Assume that some procedure, then, finds the set of pixels in the region. Each point in this set is a convex combination of two (linear fill), three (triangle fill), or four (tetrahedron fill) colors.

In general, the points found will lie in the geometric simplex formed by $\hat{B}$. (note that a line, a triangle, and a tetrahedron are the simplices with 2, 3, and 4 points respectively). Therefore, $\hat{B}$ can be found by applying existing convex hull algorithms[8, 10] to this set of points; the vertices returned will be exactly $\hat{B}$. We heuristically choose F from this set by computing T for the seed pixel; whichever vector has the highest weight is F.

If the convex hull algorithm returns more than four points, the present algorithms are not applicable without some coherence analysis.

We are presently implementing this technique, with mixed success. As stated in section 3, there may be no pixel which contains "pure" basis color; in this case, the filling algorithm must extrapolate to "deduce" it.

7. Conclusion

This paper presents a family of new algorithms for soft filling. The computational expense and power increase monotonically among the algorithms. The specific algorithm that is "best" is determined solely by the particular rendering: linear fill for two basis colors, triangle fill for three basis colors, and tetrahedron fill for four.

The algorithms presented are an intermediate step, a foundation upon which more powerful algorithms can be built.

There are two classes of problems remaining; (1) automatically finding the basis colors, and (2) increasing the number of basis colors which can be handled.

No algorithmic distinction was made between basis colors that represented background colors, and those that did not. Using this distinction, we further split class 2 into three problem classes: (2.1) filling regions where the basis colors are exclusively foreground and background colors, (2.2) filling regions where there is exactly one background color, and (2.3) filling regions which are too complex to fit in either of the first two categories.

We are currently finishing two much more powerful filling algorithms, one applicable to classes (2.1, 1), and one applicable to situations (2.2, 1). The former uses image processing edge-detection algorithms in conjunction with coherence, and the latter uses the convex hull algorithms mentioned in section 6. These algorithms have yielded promising results to date; more concrete explanation will have to await further study.

Acknowledgements

The authors wish to thank Marc S. Levoy of Hanna-Barbera Productions, who provided many comments and suggestions regarding this paper, the filling problem, and existing algorithms. We also thank Pauline Y. J. Ts'o of the Berkeley Computer Graphics Laboratory, who painted Figures 1 and 2.

This work was supported in part by the Semiconductor Research Corporation under grant number 82-11-008, and by the National Science Foundation under grant number ECS-8204381.

Appendix: Perturbation analysis.

The filling algorithms assume an "ideal frame buffer", where all color triples can be represented precisely. In practice, the color triples are integers; some perturbation occurs when the fractional values are rounded for pixel storage.[†]

This perturbation causes an information loss. When a pixel P is read, there is no longer a unique value of T that will recreate it, but rather a set of such Ts, a set of weights that all map to P when rounded. The infinitely-fine "grain" of pixel values of the ideal frame buffer has been quantized into a larger grain.

Therefore, for each filling algorithm, we create an *error metric*, which maps from the set of fills to $[1, \infty]$; the larger the error metric, the greater the error possible in the fill.

Happily, these error metrics tend to have very low values for much of their input, increasing very sharply as the fills degenerate. Before filling begins, the algorithms compute the error metric. If the error metric exceeds a user-defined maximum,[*] a warning message is printed and the fill is not performed.

A.1 Linear Fill

In linear fill, the line segment between the two colors is divided into grains, each grain representing an area of the line segment that maps (when rounded) to the same pixel. For example, when $B_0 = 0$ and $B_1 = (10,10,10)$, then all points on the line on the segment $[(4.5, 4.5, 4.5),(5.5, 5.5, 5.5))$ will map to $(5,5,5)$. The coarseness of this granularity depends on the maximum of the three component distances between the foreground and background color vectors; the greater this distance, the less the error.

Let the vector Λ represent this distance. For example, with foreground $(23,97,3)$ and background $(53,17,31)$, $\Lambda = (30, 76, 28)$. Let $\lambda = \max(\Lambda^{[0]}, \Lambda^{[1]}, \Lambda^{[2]})$. The greater the λ, the finer the grain, and the less the error. In the worst case, when the foreground and background colors are coincident, $\lambda = 0$. In the best case, when the two colors are maximally separated, $\lambda = N$, where N is the maximal value for a color component. In order to normalize the linear error metric E_1 to lie on $[1, \infty]$, we define

$$E_1 = \frac{N}{\lambda}$$

This error metric does not necessarily decrease with the Euclidean distance between the two colors, as λ depends only on the component-wise distances. Rather, the linear error metric varies inversely with component-wise distance. Practically speaking, many fills have very small E_1, and a few fills have very large E_1. This property makes it easy to decide what value(s) of E_1 are permissible for the fill.

It can be shown[1] that the expected value of E_1 when all possible $\hat{B}$ are equally likely is

$$2.3 + \frac{12\ln(N)-37}{6N^2} + \frac{4}{N^3} - \frac{2}{15N^4}$$

Since the first term predominates,

$$\lim_{N \to \infty} E(E_1) = 2.3$$

A.2 Planar Fill

Planar fill recreates the barycentric coordinates of a point in the interior of a triangle, the triangle formed by the $\hat{B}$ colors. The triangle is now *tesselated* into a set of (topological) hexagons; each hexagonal tile encloses the set of colors that, when rounded, map to the same three-dimensional point.

Planar fill error comes from two sources. First, the fewer the number of tiles, the coarser the reconstruction, and the greater the information loss. The number of tiles is a function of the area of the triangle.

Secondly, the *shape* of the triangle influences the error. Intuitively, long, skinny triangles cause more error than equilateral triangles of the same area. When the triangles are sufficiently skinny, colors on two *different* edges of the triangle may round to the same point, a great error. The more equilateral the triangle, the more infrequent this error.

Therefore, planar error is a function of both the area of the triangle and the shape of the triangle. We use the following heuristic metric:

$$E_2 = k\frac{P}{A},$$

where $P =$ Perimeter of the triangle, A the area.

$E_2 = \infty$ in the worst case, when the triangle has degenerated to a line. The value of k is chosen such that the range of E_2 is $[1, \infty]$. The best case triangle is an equilateral triangle of maximum area. The endpoints of this triangle all must lie within a cube of side N, the cube of all possible values for colors in $\hat{B}$. The largest equilateral triangle that fits in such a cube has sides of length $\sqrt{2}N$. In this case, $P = 3\sqrt{2}N$, $A = (\sqrt{3}N^2)/2$, $k = N/(2\sqrt{6})$. Therefore, the general formula is

$$E_2 = \frac{NP}{2\sqrt{6}A} \qquad (A.1)$$

Just as in E_1, E_2 is very small for most values; when the triangle becomes very close to a line, the error metric increases drastically.

A.3 Tetrahedron Fill

Tetrahedron fill extends the error of planar fill into another dimension. Instead of hexagonal tessellations of the plane, we now have hexahedral tessellations of the tetrahedron.

[†] we assume rounding for the remainder of this section; we consider pixel truncation a less typical case.

[*] we use 10

Similarly, the error is a function of the number of tiles (a function of the volume of the tetrahedron), and the shape of the tetrahedron (the error metric increases as the tetrahedron collapses into a triangle). The error metric, therefore, is a one-dimensional extrapolation of equation (A.1),

$$E_3 = \frac{kA}{V} ,$$

where V is the volume of the tetrahedron.

The value of k is found by considering the best case tetrahedron. In the best case, the tetrahedron is a regular tetrahedron, with all sides of length $\sqrt{2}N$. In this case, the area of the tetrahedron is $2\sqrt{3}N^2$, and the volume is $\frac{1}{3}N^3$. In this best case,

$$E_3 = \frac{kA}{V} = \frac{k2\sqrt{3}N^2}{\frac{1}{3}N^3} = \frac{6\sqrt{3}k}{N}$$

Therefore, $k = N/6\sqrt{3}$,

$$E_3 = \frac{NA}{6\sqrt{3}V}$$

E_3, then, varies inversely with the distance from the base of the tetrahedron to its altitude.

References

1. Kenneth P. Fishkin and Brian A. Barsky, *Linear Fill Perturbation Analysis*, University of California, Berkeley, California (1983). Berkeley Computer Graphics Laboratory internal document.

2. Kenneth P. Fishkin, *Applying Color Science to Computer Graphics*, Master's Thesis, University of California, Berkeley, California (December, 1983).

3. Graphics Standards Planning Committee, "Status Report of the Graphics Standards Committee," *Computer Graphics*, Vol. 13, No. 3, August, 1979.

4. Marc S. Levoy, *Computer-Assisted Cartoon Animation*, Master's Thesis, Cornell University, Ithaca, N.Y. (August, 1978).

5. Marc S. Levoy, *Area Flooding Algorithms*, Report, Hanna-Barbera Productions (June, 1981).

6. Marc S. Levoy, private communication. December, 1983.

7. Henry Lieberman, "How To Color in a Coloring Book," pp. 111-116 in *SIGGRAPH '78 Conference Proceedings*, ACM,(1978).

8. F. P. Perparata and S. J. Hong, "Convex Hulls of Finite Sets of Points in Two and Three Dimensions," *Communications of the ACM*, Vol. 20, No. 2, February, 1977, pp. 87 - 93.

9. William K. Pratt, *Digital Image Processing*, John Wiley & Sons, New York (1978).

10. Michael I. Shamos, *Computational Geometry*, Ph.D. Thesis, Yale University, New Haven, Connecticut (May, 1978). Book of same title to be published by Springer-Verlag.

11. Alvy Ray Smith, "Tint Fill," pp. 276-283 in *SIGGRAPH '79 Conference Proceedings*, ACM,(August, 1979). Also Technical Memo No. 6, New York Institute of Technology.

12. Alvy Ray Smith, *Fill Tutorial Notes*, Report No. 40, LucasFilm (1981).

13. Alvy Ray Smith, *Color Tutorial Notes*, Report No. 37, LucasFilm (1981).

14. Alvy Ray Smith, private communication. September, 1982.

Figures

Figures marked with an asterisk (*) were filled using the convex hull technique of section 6. Otherwise, the basis colors were supplied by the user.

Figure 1.
* Linear fill: green dragon and bottle changed to purple and red. $\mathbf{B}_0 = (1,32,1)$, $\mathbf{B}_1 = (179,152,35)$, $\mathbf{G} = (50,0,50),(200,0,0)$, $E_1 = 1.43$.

Figure 2.
* Triangle fill: brown cat changed to green. $\mathbf{B}_0 = (1,0,0)$, $\mathbf{B}_1 = (0,159,254)$, $\mathbf{B}_2 = (255,229,153)$. $\mathbf{G} = (0,50,0)$, $E_2 = 1.19$.

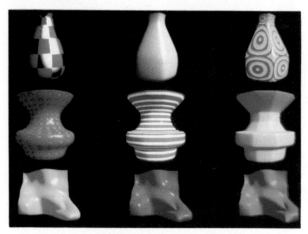

Figure 3.

A sample set of regions; an array of three different Beta-spline objects with tension increasing from left to right and bias fixed.

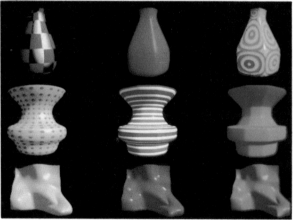

Figure 4.

Nine applications of the filling algorithms to Figure 3 (two linear, five triangle, two tetrahedron).

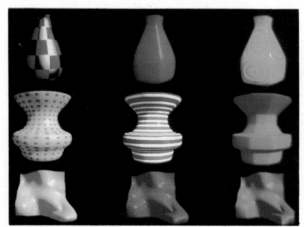

Figure 5.

* Using the convex hull technique for the same regions (five linear, two triangle, two tetrahedron). Note the significant error by this technique in the upper right fill, and the smaller error in the bottom row.

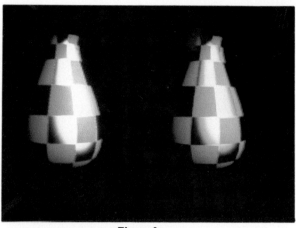

Figure 6.

* Triangle fill: closeup of the top left region in figure 3. $B_0 = (255, 255, 255)$, $B_1 = (148, 29, 29)$, $B_2 = (0,0,0)$. $G = (0,255,0)$, $E_2 = 2.26$.

Figure 7.

* Tetrahedron fill: closeup of the middle left region in Figure 3. $B_0 = (255,0,0)$, $B_1 = (255,255,255)$, $B_2 = (0,0,0)$, $B_3 = (0,0,255)$. $G = (0,255,0)$, $E_3 = 1.61$

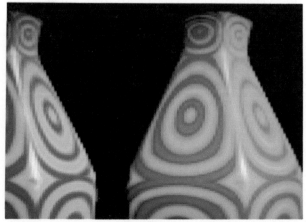

Figure 8.

Tetrahedron fill: extreme closeup of top right region in Figure 3. $B_0 = (255,0,0)$, $B_1 = (255,255,255)$, $B_2 = (0,0,0)$, $B_3 = (0,255,0)$. $G = (0,0,255)$, $E_3 = 1.61$.

Texture Synthesis for Digital Painting

John-Peter Lewis

Massachusetts Institute of Technology

Abstract

The problem of digital painting is considered from a signal processing viewpoint, and is reconsidered as a problem of directed texture synthesis. It is an important characteristic of natural texture that detail may be evident at many scales, and the detail at each scale may have distinct characteristics. A "sparse convolution" procedure for generating random textures with arbitrary spectral content is described. The capability of specifying the texture spectrum (and thus the amount of detail at each scale) is an improvement over stochastic texture synthesis processes which are scalebound or which have a prescribed $1/f$ spectrum. This spectral texture synthesis procedure provides the basis for a digital paint system which rivals the textural sophistication of traditional artistic media. Applications in terrain synthesis and texturing computer-rendered objects are also shown.

CR Categories and Subject Descriptors: I.3.3 [Computer Graphics]: Picture/Image generation; I.3.7 [Computer Graphics]: Three Dimensional Graphics and Realism - color, shading, shadowing, and texture.

Additional Key Words and Phrases: texture synthesis, painting, terrain models, fractals.

1. Introduction

The motivation for texture synthesis lies in the observation that the absence of texture is often responsible for the characteristic stark or geometric appearance of computer

Permission to copy without fee all or part of this material is granted provided that the copies are not made or distributed for direct commercial advantage, the ACM copyright notice and the title of the publication and its date appear, and notice is given that copying is by permission of the Association for Computing Machinery. To copy otherwise, or to republish, requires a fee and/or specific permission.

© 1984   ACM   0-89791-138-5/84/007/0245 $00.75

generated images, and, more generally, in the recognition that current image synthesis techniques are inappropriate for rendering many natural phenomena [Reeves, 1983].

The lack of texture is felt particularly in digital painting. While it appears initially that a "put-that-color-there" paint program (in which any region of the display screen may be shaded with any desired color) is a comprehensive definition of painting, its limitations are severe, as can be seen by the following argument: The number of distinct color regions in a digitized (non-computer) image is generally found to be a significant fraction of the total number of pixels. In a typical medium resolution (250,000 pixel) digitized image there are on the order of 10^5 distinct color regions, depending on the color resolution of the digitizer and image buffer. This can be visually demonstrated by applying a unique mapping of the pixel values of a digitized image onto relatively incoherent or random values [Figure 1]. Thus, on the order of 10^5 manual operations would be required to digitally paint a medium resolution image of comparable complexity using a put-that-color-there procedure. As a result many digital paintings incorporate digitized images or use geometrical patterns to achieve visual complexity, while in other cases the 'jaggie', low resolution appearance resulting from the put-that-color-there procedure provides the "digital" character of the painting.

In contrast much of the detail in traditional media is generated as a desired effect of the painting process. Paints, brushes, and painting surfaces are carefully selected for their characteristic effects. It may be said that, whereas the paint program *ignores* the nuances of the artist's gesture to produce a uniform, analytical mark, an expressive (physical) painting medium *amplifies* the artist's gesture. Figure 2 is presented to emphasize that digital painting is far from a "solved problem", as a single brushstroke in an traditional (and ostensibly primitive) medium produces a quantity and character of textural information which would be difficult to digitally generate.

Computer artists make the point that digital simulation of traditional artistic media is not an appropriate goal. While

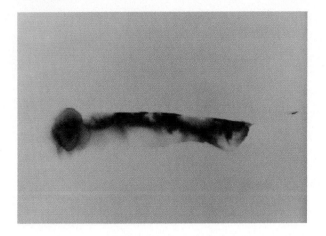

Figure 2. A watercolor brushstroke.

this is agreed, it is also inappropriate to identify the intrinsic character of computer images with hardware and software primitives which were originally developed to accomodate information display rather than image synthesis. Since this medium is essentially defined in software, organic effects are no less intrinsic than geometrical effects though the former will require new techniques.

The ultimate form of computer-assisted image creation will certainly depart from the painting metaphor. The immediate potential of a programmable painting medium is nevertheless attractive, remembering that a good illustrator can render an arbitrary scene in the time sometimes required to ray trace relatively simple scenes. As an initial approximation the problem of developing an expressive digital painting medium will be viewed as a problem of texture synthesis.

Texture is defined here as object detail which we do not care to explicitly specify though some of its aggregate characteristics may be known. This definition encompasses many natural phenomena as well as the small-scale detail usually associated with the term. The size and location of a geographic feature may be of interest, for example, but it is not desirable to design or measure its surface beyond a certain scale. The *textural threshold* is the scale beyond which image detail may be replaced by other, similar detail without affecting the viewer's perception of subject.

While this is a broad definition of texture, the consideration of texture as an essentially planar phenomenon is restrictive. It will be seen that texture fields may be interpreted as height fields for terrain synthesis, and the development of three-dimensional generalizations of planar texture synthesis methods is conceivable.

2. Texture Models

Texture models trade depth for generality in attempting to reproduce the appearance of a texture without considering its underlying structure. Natural textures exhibit local variations which are modelled as a random process although the responsible phenomena are not random from other viewpoints. A number of stochastic texture models have been proposed and are discussed in the references. A brief description of several important models follows.

Time-series modelling considers periodicities in the row scan of an image; this approach is fundamentally limited in that it cannot easily describe the structure of the texture in the dimension(s) perpendicular to the scan.

Planar random point processes generate a texture consisting of a distribution of points on a planar background. Bombing processes generalize the planar point process by replacing the point primitive with a shape possesing orientation, color, and other characteristics [Schachter & Ahuja, 1979].

Cell growth processes partition the plane into cells. The Voronoi tesselation is an exemplary cell growth process which distributes cell nuclei by a point process; a cell is defined as the boundary of the collection of points which are closest to a particular nucleus. The resulting texture resembles natural cellular structures [Mezei, Puzin, and Conroy].

Syntactic texture models equate tokens of a formal grammar with structural primitives of the texture. A highly structured but nondeterministic texture may be generated if probabilities are assigned to the rewrite or expansion rules of the grammar [Lu and Fu, 1978].

Two-dimensional Markov random field models consider the conditional probability of color values over a sample region of the texture [Hassner and Sklansky, 1980; Cross and Jain, 1983]. The Markovian property is modified by defining the transition probabilities on a neighborhood of adjacent or non-adjacent pixels, so the term describes a finite memory process rather than a planar Markov chain. This method has achieved good results in simulating prototype textures. Unfortunately it is not practical for textures sampled at high resolution since the number of conditional probablities is G^S if G is the number of quantized color levels and S is the number of adjacent pixels to be considered.

Several authors have used Brownian sheets to model rugged terrain [Fournier, Fussell, and Carpenter, 1983; Mandelbrot, 1982]. Though not originally conceived of as a texture model, the height values of the Brownian sheet may be reinterpreted as color values of a planar texture.

Figure 3. A field of pebbles (taken from [Brodatz, 1966]).

3. Texture & Scale

An important characteristic of natural texture is that textural detail may occur at more·than one scale. Detail may be noticable at all scales from the textural threshold to the limit of visual acuity. For example a field of pebbles has an overall shape; closer inspection shows the contour of individual pebbles, each of which has its own surface texture [Figure 3]. With the exception of the Brownian model of terrain, the texture models mentioned above describe textures with detail at only one scale (this is true of Markov textures because of practical limitations on the size of the region determining the transition probabilities). An overview of these textures affirms that the generating process is stationary and devoid of global character while close examination can reveal only the constituent pixels of the texture.

The Brownian model of terrain does have the property that closer observation yields more detail. This application of Brownian motion resulted from Mandelbrot's interest in fractals, a collection of mathematical objects united by the criterion of recursive self-similarity: the objects are defined as analytic or probabilistic functions of scale [Mandelbrot, 1982]. Brownian motion can be considered self-similar since the statistical moments of any sample are similar to any other sample, when adjusted by a scaling factor.

In fact unmodified Brownian motion generates a very rugged terrain. Mandelbrot has proposed a revised model in which B(t) is filtered to adjust its amplitude spectrum to f^{-q} (the unfiltered B(t) has the parameter $q=1$). The filtering is conceived as a Riemann-Liouville integral of B'(t) [Oldham and Spanier, 1974]:

$$RL_{q,s}(B(t)) = 1/\Gamma(q)\int_s^t (t-x)^{q-1} dB(x)$$

(The dB(x) form of the integral is used to sidestep the problems of formally defining the derivative of B(t) or the integral thereof using the limit calculus). This is seen to be a convolution of the derivative of B(t) (white noise) with a

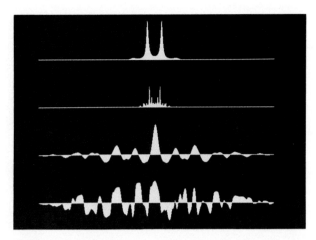

Figure 4. Windowed plot of the grey levels in one row of Figure 3 (bottom), autocorrelation, power spectrum, and ten pole autoregressive spectrum estimate obtained by linear prediction (top).

filter $h(t)=t^{q-1}$. The $1/\Gamma(q)$ scaling factor cancels the numerator in the transform of h(t),

$$L(t^n) = n! / s^{n+1}$$

(for integer values n). When q is an integer RL(B(t)) reduces to q-fold repeated integration of B(t) with the consequent smoothing effect of multiplying the spectrum of B(t) by $1/f^q$. Fractional values of q produce an intermediate amount of smoothing. (In practice the filtering is carried out by multiplying the spectrum of a Gaussian white noise by the desired exponent and inverse transforming [Voss, 1983]).

4. Frequency Domain Interpretation of Texture

What is important here is that the preceeding discussion should suggest the frequency domain interpretation of texture. Consider again the pebbles in Figure 3. The dominant structure defined by the repetition of similarly sized pebbles is reflected by peaks in the power spectrum centered at the frequency which is the inverse of the typical pebble size [Figure 4]. The attenuated high-frequency portion of the spectrum reflects the relatively smooth surface texture of the pebbles.

This example illustrates the wide bandwidth and varied spectra of natural textures, reflecting the variety of natural structures. Although the fractal 1/f spectra are analytically tractable and have resulted in very attractive computational methods [Fournier, Fussell, and Carpenter, 1982] they are not universal. The following procedure generates random textures with arbitrary spectra.

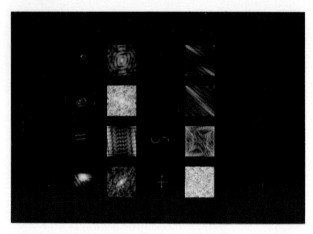

Figure 5. Painted patterns (left) and textures realized by Fourier transformation (right). The lower texture on the right is the phase of the transform while the remaining textures are transform magnitudes.

5. Texture Synthesis Procedure

5.1. Spectrum Painting
The spectral interpretation of texture suggests the direct specification of the spectrum as input to the texture synthesis procedure, with the texture generated by inverse Fourier transformation. For "organic" textures the spectrum may be as difficult to analytically define as the texture itself. Instead, the desired spectrum is painted using a digital paint program [Figure 5]. (This is a "bootstrap" procedure since the paint program incorporates the textures which it creates).

Two quadrants of the amplitude spectrum are painted and the remaining two quadrants are generated by symmetry. The phase spectrum is painted or set to random values. Inverse transformation generates a complex texture, with the real and imaginary components having a similar visual character. The magnitude, log magnitude, or phase of the inverse transform may also serve as textures.

Using the near duality between forward and inverse Fourier transforms, it is also effective to implement the spectrum painting procedure by the forward transform from a real, asymmetric pattern. The resulting texture exhibits the quadrant symmetry of a spectrum,

$$F(u,v) = F^*(-u,-v)$$

which may be undesirable.

Experience with the spectrum painting method shows that it is possible to acquire an intuitive feel for the relation between characteristics of a painted spectrum or pattern and its transform, and the author can reliably paint amplitude spectra to simulate some simple textures including canvas and wood grain. Painting phase spectra is more difficult because the histogram display method produces an apparent discontinuity between two π and zero radians. The method is fairly robust, however, and variations such as setting the phase to zero or at random have produced useful textures.

When the spectrum painting method is not intuitive it nevertheless produces rich and organic textures which would be difficult to paint in the spatial domain using current techniques. One is tempted to suggest an 'inverse symmetry of visual complexity', by which perceptually simple figures in one domain possess visually sophisticated transforms. This is in part a visual application of the uncertainty principle, which states that a signal and its transform cannot both be "of short duration". Thus, a pattern consisting of a few non-zero points transforms to a texture which extends over the transform area [Figure 5].

5.2. Sparse Convolution
The texture sample realized by spectrum painting has several undesirable properties, however:

1. It is periodic.

2. If standard fast Fourier transform software is used then the texture is contained in a square area whose pixel resolution is a power of two.

3. The texture has well-defined edges which are not characteristic of natural textures.

In the second stage of the texture synthesis procedure a random texture field is produced from the texture sample. The sample is windowed to remove edge discontinuities by multiplying the sample by the radial Gaussian

$$e^{-(x^2+y^2)^{0.5}}$$

The texture field is initialized to a constant value and developed by weighted additions of the displaced sample. The weights and displacements are given by a white random number generator.

This procedure is equivalent to an out-of-order convolution of the windowed texture sample with a white noise. Thus, the texture sample assumes the role of the filter impulse response or point spread funcion, and the expected spectrum of the texture field is that of the sample.

In practice excellent results are obtained when the white noise is replaced by a "sparse" (white) noise or point process containing approximately ten non-zero values per point spread area. The out-of-order convolution with a sparse noise results in a significant computational advantage relative to direct convolution. Further savings may be realized if the noise is quantized to integer values.

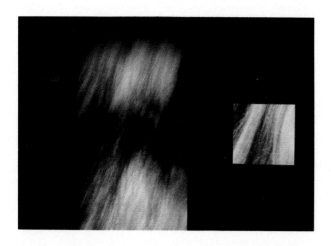

Figure 6. Sampled impulse response (right, from [Bryant, 1978]) and resulting synthetic texture (left).

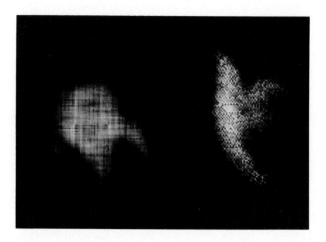

Figure 9. Painting on a virtual surface. Illustration board (left) and sandpaper (right) surfaces are shown.

5.3. Sampled Impulse Response Filtering

When it is desired to generate a random texture field which emulates a prototype texture and a sample of that texture is available, we use the result that, if a stochastic process is modelled as a finite impulse response filter excited by white noise, then a properly windowed sample of the process is expected to resemble the impulse response of the filter. The transform of the window should be a narrowband approximation to the delta function since the windowing multiplication (modulation) is equivalent to the convolution of the sample spectrum with the window spectrum. Modest spectral averaging is appropriate since it reduces the local variance of the sample spectrum with respect to "true" (prototype) spectrum; see the discussion of modified periodogram spectrum estimation in a text such as [Beauchamp and Yuen, 1979]. The transform of a Gaussian window is also Gaussian and the bandwidth of the transform is inversely proportional to the size of the window.

Considered in the spatial domain, the window should be large enough to include one or more periods of the lowest frequency components which characterize the texture. For the purposes of painting or image synthesis the window size can be determined by inspection and adjusted if necessary. "As big as possible" is not a good size because spatial convolution is an $O(size^2)$ procedure; the unused source texture is put to a better use by averaging several samples in the frequency domain and inverse transforming, thereby reducing the variance of the sample as an estimate of the prototype impulse response.

The sparse convolution procedure is used to produce a random texture field from the windowed sample. While the resulting textures roughly resemble their prototypes (Figure 6), the sampled impulse response procedure is attractive in that it does not require estimation of texture

parameters. As such it should be noted that sampled impulse response filtering is a synthesis procedure rather than a texture model.

6. Applications

6.1. Digital painting

Several variations on these texture synthesis procedures form the basis of a digital paint program [Figures 7,8].

Sparse convolution allows large, textured areas to be generated rapidly. The painter designs a texture sample using one of the methods described above and specifies the extent, mean, spread, and "sparseness" of the sparse noise. Noise points lying outside the designated extent are discarded. In the current implementation on a nine-bit frame buffer with a twenty-four-bit color lookup table, the resulting texture field is copied into the frame buffer and the lookup table is adjusted to contain a color wash in the portion of the table indexed by the texture field. The texture field merges smoothly with its surroundings because the edges of the texture field inherit the window applied to the texture sample.

Many variations on the copying operation are possible, ranging from the linear interpolation

$$pic[x,y] \leftarrow pic[x,y] + d*(tex[row,col] - pic[x,y])$$

[Whitted, 1983; Smith, 1982] to a "dry-brush" in which a second texture modulates the density of application of the principal texture. The effect of the texture application then depends on where it is applied (in relation to the second texture) so a *virtual surface* results. The virtual surface can serve analogously to the textured surfaces of traditional media. The periodic textures resulting from the spectrum painting procedure may be repeated in a mosaic to form an extended, virtual surface. This is implemented simply by indexing the virtual surface texture with the current screen address, modulo the size of the texture.

In the most versatile texture application configurations the texture is used as a weight to interpolate between the background and some other color source, rather than interpolating between the texture and the background. These configurations are described in the "painter's raster-op":

$$pic[x,y] \leftarrow pic[x,y] + d*tex[row,col] * f(pic[x,y],...)$$

(the ellipses indicate the presence of additional parameters). For example, if **f** is set to **c · pic[x,y]** where **c** is a scalar color mixed by the painter, then the texture describes the density or spread function of a "textured airbrush". In an eight-bit or nine-bit frame buffer it is practical to precompute the function **f** and store it in a table indexed by **pic[x,y]**. The table is recomputed when the auxiliary parameters change (this does not happen more than once per texture application). The effect of the painter's raster-op depends on the contents of the target area as well as on the applied texture, so each texture application builds upon the existing texture rather than replacing it.

In addition it is often useful to reference the texture through a shaping table **v[t]**. The default value of the table is **v[t]=t**, making the table invisible. By altering the slope of the table function as **v[t] = a*t + b** linear compression and negation are achieved. Rectification, clipping, power modification, and non-linear filtering are obtained without additional programming by using appropriate shaping functions.

This is a cheap and powerful filtering method. It is similar to color lookup table techniques but it may be applied locally and its effect depends on the current texture application configuration. The spectral shaping effects and design procedures for this method are developed in [LeBrun, 1979]. In keeping with the intuitive approach used in the texture synthesis procedure, the user draws the shaping function using a digitizing tablet and evaluates it interactively.

A painting is created by using the texture synthesis procedure as a brush with a definable shape and textural properties. The size of the synthesis region is reduced in order to paint details. If the specified size is smaller than the size of the texture sample then the texture sample is applied in place of the synthesized texture. In this case the "brushstroke" (applied texture) is no longer random and the repeated application of the texture sample may be evident.

This is usually not a serious problem, since in most painting styles the semantic detail (detail explicitly specified by the artist) occurs at a much larger scale than the process

texture. Several approaches to the problem of creating small, random textures (on the order of ten square pixels) have been attempted, however.

One approach is to synthesize the texture with an all-pole filter driven by noise. The all-pole filter can 'predict' a small area of texture provided than an adjacent area of 'support' or filter memory has been obtained. In our application the filter memory is set to the neighboring areas of the painting (if not zero) or to the texture prototype or sample. The filter is designed by a linear prediction fit to the sample. The linear prediction method is very attractive in that it can monitor the filter stability (a common problem in the design of all-pole filters) and in that it accomplishes the filter design task [Makhoul]. This would be an ideal method if the filter were implemented in hardware, but it is rather slow for interactive painting when implemented in software.

A second approach is to precompute some of the desired texture and obtain a "brushfull" of it by positioning a window corresponding to the size of the brush. If the window is moved with each texture application then each "brushstroke" is distinct but characteristic of the desired texture.

The success of texture synthesis in painting is in part indicated by the statistic that Figures 7,8 were created using between 2000 and 10,000 points entered from a digitizing tablet, while each picture contains approximately 100,000 separate color regions. The input streams from the digitizing tablet and keyboard may be recorded to produce a relatively compact representation of a painting. A more controversial indication of success is that these paintings do not suggest their computer origin, and they have been mistaken for digitized images.

6.2. Terrain synthesis and texture mapping

Synthetic textures may be interpreted as height fields to create a variety of terrain types. Figure 10 is reminiscent of a terrain shaped by erosion, while Figure 11 resembles a filtered fractal surface with the qualification that it has a modest directional trend.

It is interesting to note that if the texture sample is a step function then the out-of-order convolution procedure reduces to a variant of the Levy faulting process which was used to implement the first Brownian terrain simulations [Mandelbrot, 1977]. The preservation of the sample spectrum in the texture field is evident as both have a 1/f (amplitude) spectrum.[1] Recently Haruyama and Barsky have similarly considered the fractal 1/f type spectra as an instance of a more general spectral approach to texture [Haruyama & Barsky, 1984]. Their paper adapts the attractive recursive-subdivision fractal construction to produce non-fractal textures with a variety of possible spectra.

The periodic textures resulting from inverse Fourier transformation are useful in texture mapping computer-rendered objects since they may be repeated to cover large areas without producing the border discontinuities which are visible in the non-periodic texture map used in Figure 8.

7. Conclusions

The frequency domain interpretation of texture motivates the development of a spectral texture synthesis method which can generate synthetic textures having the broad bandwidth and irregular spectra characteristic of natural textures. An interactive procedure for generating textures with arbitrary spectra was presented. This procedure has been used to realize some of the potential of digital painting as a software medium possessing few inherent limitations or characteristics. The textural complexity of the resulting images approaches that obtainable in traditional artistic media.

Acknowledgements.

The author would like to mention Patrick Purcell, Alyce Kaprow, David Backer, and Lynn Fulkerson, and to acknowledge the inspiration provided by the pioneering work of Loren Carpenter, Alain Fournier, Don Fussell, Benoit Mandelbrot, and William Reeves in the computer modelling of natural phenomena.

References

1. Beauchamp, K. and Yuen, C. *Digital Methods for Signal Analysis.* Allen and Unwin, London, 1979.

2. Brodatz, P. *Texture.* Dover, New York, 1966.

3. Bryant, P. in *Playboy* **25**, 4 (April 1978), 118-127.

4. Cross, G. and Jain, A. Markov random field texture models. *IEEE Transactions on Pattern Analysis and Machine Intelligence* **5**, 1 (1983), 25-38.

5. Fournier, A., Fussell, D., and Carpenter, L. Computer rendering of stochastic models. *Communications of the ACM* **25**, 6 (1982), 371-384.

6. Haruyama, S. and Barsky, B. Using stochastic modelling for texture generation. *IEEE Computer Graphics and Applications* March, 1984 7-19.

7. Hassner, M. and Sklansky, J. The use of Markov random fields as models of texture. *Computer Graphics and Image Processing* **12**, 4 (1980) 357-370.

8. LeBrun, M. Digital waveshaping synthesis. *J. Audio Engineering Society* **27**, 4 (April 1979), 250-265.

9. Lu, S. and Fu, K. Computer generation of texture using a syntactic approach. *Computer Graphics* **12**, 13 (1978), 147-152.

10. Makhoul, J. Linear prediction: a tutorial review. *Proc. IEEE* **63**, (1975) 561-580.

11. Mandelbrot, B. *Fractals-Form, Chance, and Dimension.* Freeman, San Francisco, 1977.

12. Mandelbrot, B. *The Fractal Geometry of Nature.* Freeman, San Francisco, 1982.

13. Mezei, L., Puzin, M., and Conroy, P. Simulation of patterns of nature by computer graphics. *Information Processing* **74**, 52-56.

14. Oldham, K. and Spanier, J. *The Fractional Calculus.* Academic Press, New York, 1974.

15. Reeves, W. Particle systems-a technique for modelling a class of fuzzy objects. *Computer Graphics* **17**, 3 (July 1983), 359-376.

16. Schachter, B. and Ahuja, N. Random pattern generation processes. *Computer Graphics and Image Processing* **10**, 2 (1979), 95-114.

17. Smith, A. Paint, in *Tutorial: Computer Graphics*, J.C.Beatty and K.S.Booth eds. (IEEE 1982), 501-515.

18. Voss, R., Fourier synthesis of Gaussian fractals: 1/f noises, landscapes, and flakes. Presented at ACM Siggraph Conference, 1983.

19. Whitted, T. Anti-aliased line drawing using brush extrusion. *Computer Graphics* **17**, 3 (July 1983), 151-156.

---

[1] In the two-dimensional case the step is randomly rotated before each weighted addition to create an isotropic 1/f texture. In general the rotation of the texture sample is avoided in order to achieve textures with directional characteristics.

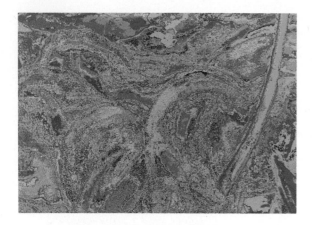

Figure 1. Random false-coloration of a digitized painting. The number of distinct color regions is a large fraction of the total number of pixels.

Figure 7. A digital painting incorporating synthetic textures.

Figure 8. The background in this picture is painted while the stone figures are a texture-mapped computer rendered object. The edge of the (non-periodic) texture map is visible as a horizontal seam on the left figure; this was retained for an esthetic reason.

Figure 10. A synthetic terrain generated from a lumpy texture sample.

Figure 11. A synthetic terrain resembling a fractal surface. A directional characteristic ("north-south ridges") is evident.

Compositing Digital Images

Thomas Porter
Tom Duff †

Computer Graphics Project
Lucasfilm Ltd.

ABSTRACT

Most computer graphics pictures have been computed all at once, so that the rendering program takes care of all computations relating to the overlap of objects. There are several applications. however, where elements must be rendered separately, relying on compositing techniques for the anti-aliased accumulation of the full image. This paper presents the case for four-channel pictures, demonstrating that a matte component can be computed similarly to the color channels. The paper discusses guidelines for the generation of elements and the arithmetic for their arbitrary compositing.

CR Categories and Subject Descriptors: I.3.3 [**Computer Graphics**]: Picture/Image Generations — Display algorithms; I.3.4 [**Computer Graphics**]: Graphics Utilities — Software support; I.4.1 [**Image Processing**]: Digitization — Sampling.

General Terms: Algorithms

Additional Key Words and Phrases: compositing, matte channel, matte algebra, visible surface algorithms, graphics systems

---

† Author's current address: AT&T Bell Laboratories, Murray Hill, NJ 07974, Room 2C465

Permission to copy without fee all or part of this material is granted provided that the copies are not made or distributed for direct commercial advantage, the ACM copyright notice and the title of the publication and its date appear, and notice is given that copying is by permission of the Association for Computing Machinery. To copy otherwise, or to republish, requires a fee and/or specific permission.

© 1984   ACM   0-89791-138-5/84/007/0253 $00.75

1. Introduction

Increasingly, we find that a complex three dimensional scene cannot be fully rendered by a single program. The wealth of literature on rendering polygons and curved surfaces, handling the special cases of fractals and spheres and quadrics and triangles, implementing refinements for texture mapping and bump mapping, noting speed-ups on the basis of coherence or depth complexity in the scene, suggests that multiple programs are necessary.

In fact, reliance on a single program for rendering an entire scene is a poor strategy for minimizing the cost of small modeling errors. Experience has taught us to break down large bodies of source code into separate modules in order to save compilation time. An error in one routine forces only the recompilation of its module and the relatively quick reloading of the entire program. Similarly, small errors in coloration or design in one object should not force the "recompilation" of an entire image.

Separating the image into *elements* which can be independently rendered saves enormous time. Each element has an associated *matte,* coverage information which designates the shape of the element. The *compositing* of those elements makes use of the mattes to accumulate the final image.

The compositing methodology must not induce aliasing in the image; soft edges of the elements must be honored in computing the final image. Features should be provided to exploit the full associativity of the compositing process; this affords flexibility, for example, for the accumulation of several foreground elements into an aggregate foreground which can be examined over different backgrounds. The compositor should provide facilities for arbitrary dissolves and fades of elements during an animated sequence.

Several highly successful rendering algorithms have worked by reducing their environments to pieces that can be combined in a 2 1/2 dimensional manner, and then overlaying them either front-to-back or back-to-front [3]. Whitted and Weimar's graphics test-bed [6] and Crow's image generation environment [2] are both designed to deal with heterogenously rendered elements. Whitted and Weimar's system reduces all objects to horizontal spans which are composited using a Warnock-like algorithm. In Crow's system a supervisory process decides the order in which to combine images created by independent special-purpose rendering processes. The imaging system of Warnock and Wyatt [5] incorporates 1-bit mattes. The Hanna-Barbera cartoon animation system [4] incorporates soft-edge mattes, representing the opacity information in a less convenient manner than that proposed here. The present paper presents guidelines for rendering elements and introduces the algebra for compositing.

2. The Alpha Channel

A separate component is needed to retain the matte information, the extent of coverage of an element at a pixel. In a full color rendering of an element, the RGB components retain only the color. In order to place the element over an arbitrary background, a mixing factor is required at every pixel to control the linear interpolation of foreground and background colors. In general, there is no way to encode this component as part of the color information. For anti-aliasing purposes, this mixing factor needs to be of comparable resolution to the color channels. Let us call this an *alpha* channel, and let us treat an alpha of 0 to indicate no coverage, 1 to mean full coverage, with fractions corresponding to partial coverage.

In an environment where the compositing of elements is required, we see the need for an alpha channel as an integral part of all pictures. Because mattes are naturally computed along with the picture, a separate alpha component in the frame buffer is appropriate. Off-line storage of alpha information along with color works conveniently into run-length encoding schemes because the alpha information tends to abide by the same runs.

What is the meaning of the quadruple (r,g,b,α) at a pixel? How do we express that a pixel is half covered by a full red object? One obvious suggestion is to assign $(1,0,0,.5)$ to that pixel: the .5 indicates the coverage and the $(1,0,0)$ is the color. There are a few reasons to dismiss this proposal, the most severe being that all compositing operations will involve multiplying the 1 in the red channel by the .5 in the alpha channel to compute the red contribution of this object at this pixel. The desire to avoid this multiplication points up a better solution, storing the *pre-multiplied* value in the color component, so that $(.5,0,0,.5)$ will indicate a full red object half covering a pixel.

The quadruple (r,g,b,α) indicates that the pixel is α covered by the color $(r/\alpha, g/\alpha, b/\alpha)$. A quadruple where the alpha component is less than a color component indicates a color outside the $[0,1]$ interval, which is somewhat unusual. We will see later that luminescent objects can be usefully represented in this way. For the representation of normal objects, an alpha of 0 at a pixel generally forces the color components to be 0. Thus the RGB channels record the true colors where alpha is 1, linearly

darkened colors for fractional alphas along edges, and black where alpha is 0. Silhouette edges of RGBA elements thus exhibit their anti-aliased nature when viewed on an RGB monitor.

It is important to distinguish between two key pixel representations:
$$black = (0,0,0,1);$$
$$clear = (0,0,0,0).$$
The former pixel is an opaque black; the latter pixel is transparent.

3. RGBA Pictures

If we survey the variety of elements which contribute to a complex animation, we find many complete background images which have an alpha of 1 everywhere. Among foreground elements, we find that the color components roll off in step with the alpha channel, leaving large areas of transparency. Mattes, colorless stencils used for controlling the compositing of other elements, have 0 in their RGB components. Off-line storage of RGBA pictures should therefore provide the natural data compression for handling the RGB pixels of backgrounds, RGBA pixels of foregrounds, and A pixels of mattes.

There are some objections to computing with these RGBA pictures. Storage of the color components pre-multiplied by the alpha would seem to unduly quantize the color resolution, especially as alpha approaches 0. However, because any compositing of the picture will require that multiplication anyway, storage of the product forces only a very minor loss of precision in this regard. Color extraction, to compute in a different color space for example, becomes more difficult. We must recover $(r/\alpha, g/\alpha, b/\alpha)$, and once again, as alpha approaches 0, the precision falls off sharply. For our applications, this has yet to affect us.

4. The Algebra of Compositing

Given this standard of RGBA pictures, let us examine how compositing works. We shall do this by enumerating the complete set of binary compositing operations. For each of these, we shall present a formula for computing the contribution of each of two input pictures to the output composite at each pixel. We shall pay particular attention to the output pixels, to see that they remain pre-multiplied by their alpha.

4.1. Assumptions

When blending pictures together, we do not have information about overlap of coverage information within a pixel; all we have is an alpha value. When we consider the mixing of two pictures at a pixel, we must make some assumption about the interplay of the two alpha values. In order to examine that interplay, let us first consider the overlap of two semi-transparent elements like haze, then consider the overlap of two opaque, hard-edged elements.

If α_A and α_B represent the opaqueness of semi-transparent objects which fully cover the pixel, the computation is well known. Each object lets $(1-\alpha)$ of the background through, so that the background shows through only $(1-\alpha_A)(1-\alpha_B)$ of the pixel. $\alpha_A(1-\alpha_B)$ of the background is blocked by object A and passed by object B; $(1-\alpha_A)\alpha_B$ of the background is passed by A and blocked by B. This leaves $\alpha_A\alpha_B$ of the pixel which we can consider to be blocked by both.

If α_A and α_B represent subpixel areas covered by opaque geometric objects, the overlap of objects within the pixel is quite arbitrary. We know that object A divides the pixel into two subpixel areas of ratio $\alpha_A{:}1-\alpha_A$. We know that object B divides the pixel into two subpixel areas of ratio $\alpha_B{:}1-\alpha_B$. Lacking further information, we make the following assumption: *there is nothing special about the shape of the pixel; we expect that object B will divide each of the subpixel areas inside and outside of object A into the same ratio* $\alpha_B{:}1-\alpha_B$. The result of the assumption is the same arithmetic as with semi-transparent objects and is summarized in the following table:

description	area
$\bar{A}\cap\bar{B}$	$(1-\alpha_A)(1-\alpha_B)$
$A\cap\bar{B}$	$\alpha_A(1-\alpha_B)$
$\bar{A}\cap B$	$(1-\alpha_A)\alpha_B$
$A\cap B$	$\alpha_A\alpha_B$

The assumption is quite good for most mattes, though it can be improved if we know that the coverage seldom overlaps (adjacent segments of a continuous line) or always overlaps (repeated application of a picture). For ease in presentation throughout this paper, let us make this assumption and consider the alpha values as representing subpixel coverage of opaque objects.

4.2. Compositing Operators

Consider two pictures A and B. They divide each pixel into the 4 subpixel areas

B	A	name	description	choices
0	0	0	$\bar{A}\cap\bar{B}$	0
0	1	A	$A\cap\bar{B}$	0, A
1	0	B	$\bar{A}\cap B$	0, B
1	1	AB	$A\cap B$	0, A, B

listed in this table along with the choices in each area for contributing to the composite. In the last area, for example, because both input pictures exist there, either could survive to the composite. Alternatively, the composite could be clear in that area.

A particular binary compositing operation can be identified as a quadruple indicating the input picture which contributes to the composite in each of the four subpixel areas 0, A, B, AB of the table above. With three choices where the pictures intersect, two where only one picture exists and one outside the two pictures, there are $3\times2\times2\times1=12$ distinct compositing operations listed

in the table below. Note that pictures A and B are diagrammed as covering the pixel with triangular wedges whose overlap conforms to the assumption above.

operation	quadruple	diagram	F_A	F_B
clear	(0,0,0,0)		0	0
A	(0,A,0,A)		1	0
B	(0,0,B,B)		0	1
A **over** B	(0,A,B,A)		1	$1-\alpha_A$
B **over** A	(0,A,B,B)		$1-\alpha_B$	1
A **in** B	(0,0,0,A)		α_B	0
B **in** A	(0,0,0,B)		0	α_A
A **out** B	(0,A,0,0)		$1-\alpha_B$	0
B **out** A	(0,0,B,0)		0	$1-\alpha_A$
A **atop** B	(0,0,B,A)		α_B	$1-\alpha_A$
B **atop** A	(0,A,0,B)		$1-\alpha_B$	α_A
A **xor** B	(0,A,B,0)		$1-\alpha_B$	$1-\alpha_A$

Useful operators include *A* **over** *B*, *A* **in** *B*, and *A* **held out by** *B*. *A* **over** *B* is the placement of foreground A in front of background B. *A* **in** *B* refers only to that part of A inside picture B. *A* **held out by** *B*, normally shortened to *A* **out** *B*, refers only to that part of A outside picture B. For completeness, we include the less useful operators *A* **atop** *B* and *A* **xor** *B*. *A* **atop** *B* is the union of *A* **in** *B* and *B* **out** *A*. Thus, *paper* **atop** *table* includes *paper* where it is on top of *table*, and *table* otherwise; area beyond the edge of the table is out of the picture. *A* **xor** *B* is the union of *A* **out** *B* and *B* **out** *A*.

4.3. Compositing Arithmetic

For each of the compositing operations, we would like to compute the contribution of each input picture at each pixel. This is quite easily solved by recognizing that each input picture survives in the composite pixel only within its own matte. For each input picture, we are looking for that fraction of its own matte which prevails in the output. By definition then, the alpha value of the composite, the total area of the pixel covered, can be computed by adding α_A times its fraction F_A to α_B times its fraction F_B.

The color of the composite can be computed on a component basis by adding the color of the picture A times its fraction to the color of picture B times its fraction. To see this, let c_A, c_B, and c_O be some color component of pictures A, B and the composite, and let C_A, C_B, and C_O be the true color component before pre-multiplication by alpha. Then we have

$$c_O = \alpha_O C_O$$

Now C_O can be computed by averaging contributions made by C_A and C_B, so

$$c_O = \alpha_O \frac{\alpha_A F_A C_A + \alpha_B F_B C_B}{\alpha_A F_A + \alpha_B F_B}$$

but the denominator is just α_O, so

$$c_O = \alpha_A F_A C_A + \alpha_B F_B C_B$$
$$= \alpha_A F_A \frac{c_A}{\alpha_A} + \alpha_B F_B \frac{c_B}{\alpha_B}$$
$$= c_A F_A + c_B F_B \qquad (1)$$

Because each of the input colors is pre-multiplied by its alpha, and we are adding contributions from non-overlapping areas, the sum will be effectively pre-multiplied by the alpha value of the composite just computed. The pleasant result that the color channels are handled with the same computation as alpha can be traced back to our decision to store pre-multiplied RGBA quadruples. Thus the problem is reduced to finding a table of fractions F_A and F_B which indicate the extent of contribution of A and B, plugging these values into equation 1 for both the color and the alpha components.

By our assumptions above, the fractions are quickly determined by examining the pixel diagram included in the table of operations. Those fractions are listed in the F_A and F_B columns of the table. For example, in the A **over** B case, picture A survives everywhere while picture B survives only outside picture A, so the corresponding fractions are 1 and $(1-\alpha_A)$. Substituting into equation 1, we find

$$c_O = c_A \times 1 + c_B \times (1-\alpha_A).$$

This is almost the well used linear interpolation of foreground F with background B

$$B' = F \times \alpha + B \times (1-\alpha),$$

except that our foreground is pre-multiplied by alpha.

4.4. Unary operators

To assist us in dissolving and in balancing color brightness of elements contributing to a composite, it is useful to introduce a darken factor ϕ and a dissolve factor δ:

darken$(A,\phi) \equiv (\phi r_A, \phi g_A, \phi b_A, \alpha_A)$
dissolve$(A,\delta) \equiv (\delta r_A, \delta g_A, \delta b_A, \delta \alpha_A)$.

Normally, $0 \le \phi, \delta \le 1$ although none of the theory requires it.

As ϕ varies from 1 to 0, the element will change from normal to complete blackness. If $\phi > 1$ the element will be brightened. As δ goes from 1 to 0 the element will gradually fade from view.

Luminescent objects, which add color information without obscuring the background, can be handled with the introduction of a opaqueness factor ω, $0 \le \omega \le 1$:

opaque$(A,\omega) \equiv (r_A, g_A, b_A, \omega \alpha_A)$.

As ω varies from 1 to 0, the element will change from normal coverage over the background to no obscuration. This scaling of the alpha channel alone will cause pixel quadruples where α is less than a color component, indicating a representation of a color outside of the normal range. This possibility forces us to clip the output composite to the [0,1] range.

An ω of 0 will produce quadruples $(r,g,b,0)$ which do have meaning. The color channels, pre-multiplied by the original alpha, can be plugged into equation 1 as always. The alpha channel of 0 indicates that this pixel will obscure nothing. In terms of our methodology for examining subpixel areas, we should understand that using the **opaque** operator corresponds to shrinking the matte coverage with regard to the color coverage.

4.5. The PLUS operator

We find it useful to include one further binary compositing operator **plus** . The expression A **plus** B holds no notion of precedence in any area covered by both pictures; the components are simply added. This allows us to dissolve from one picture to another by specifying

dissolve(A,α) **plus dissolve**$(B,1-\alpha)$.

In terms of the binary operators above, **plus** allows both pictures to survive in the subpixel area AB. The operator table above should be appended:

operation	diagram	F_A	F_B
(0,A,B,AB) A plus B		1	1

5. Examples

The operations on one and two pictures are presented as a basis for handling compositing expressions involving several pictures. A normal case involving three pictures is the compositing of a foreground picture A over a background picture B, with regard to an independent matte C. The expression for this compositing operation is

$$(A \text{ in } C) \text{ over } B.$$

Using equation 1 twice, we find that the composite in this case is computed at each pixel by

$$c_O = c_A \alpha_C + c_B(1 - \alpha_A \alpha_C).$$

As an example of a complex compositing expression, let us consider a subwindow of Rob Cook's picture *Road to*

Point Reyes [1]. This still frame was assembled from many elements according to the following rules:

$$Foreground = FrgdGrass \text{ over } Rock \text{ over } Fence$$
$$\text{over } Shadow \text{ over } BkgdGrass;$$

$$GlossyRoad = Puddle \text{ over } (PostReflection \text{ atop }$$
$$(PlantReflection \text{ atop } Road));$$
$$Hillside = Plant \text{ over } GlossyRoad \text{ over } Hill;$$

$$Background = Rainbow \text{ plus } Darkbow \text{ over }$$
$$Mountains \text{ over } Sky;$$

$$Pt.Reyes = Foreground \text{ over } Hillside \text{ over } Background.$$

Figure 1 shows three intermediate composites and the final picture.

Foreground = FrgdGrass **over** *Rock* **over** *Fence*
over *Shadow* **over** *BkgdGrass;*

Hillside = Plant **over** *GlossyRoad* **over** *Hill;*

Background = Rainbow **plus** *Darkbow* **over**
Mountains **over** *Sky;*

Pt.Reyes = Foreground **over** *Hillside* **over** *Background.*

Figure 1

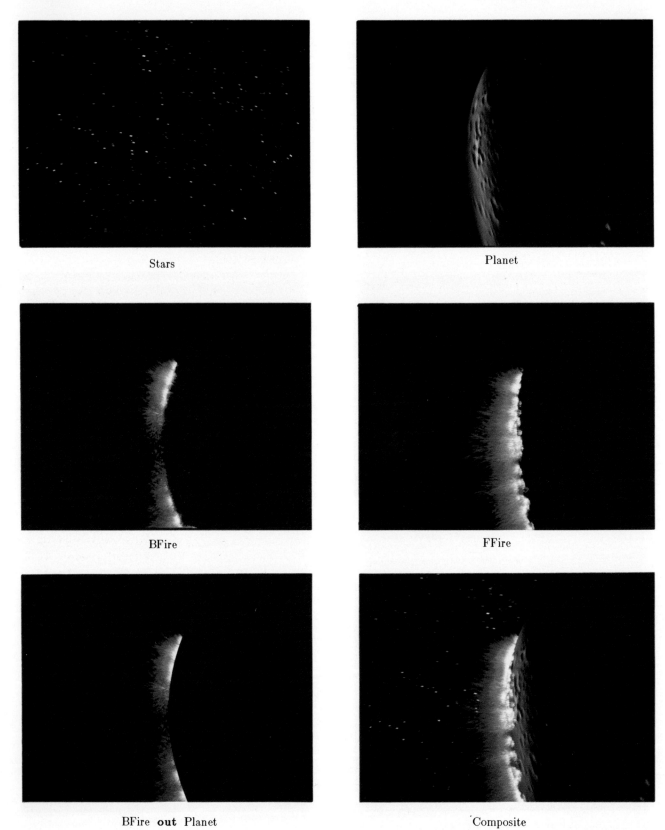

Stars

Planet

BFire

FFire

BFire **out** Planet

Composite

Figure 2

A further example demonstrates the problem of *correlated mattes*. In Figure 2, we have a star field background, a planet element, fiery particles behind the planet, and fiery particles in front of the planet. We wish to add the luminous fires, obscure the planet, darkened for proper balance, with the aggregate fire matte, and place that over the star field. An expression for this compositing is

(*FFire* **plus** (*BFire* **out** *Planet*))
    over darken(*Planet*,.8) **over** *Stars* .

We must remember that our basic assumption about the division of subpixel areas by geometric objects breaks down in the face of input pictures with correlated mattes. When one picture appears twice in a compositing expression, we must take care with our computations of F_A and F_B. Those listed in the table are correct only for uncorrelated pictures.

To solve the problem of correlated mattes, we must extend our methodology to handle n pictures: we must examine all 2^n subareas of the pixel, deciding which of the pictures survives in each area, and adding up all contributions. Multiple instances of a single picture or pictures with correlated mattes are resolved by aligning their pixel coverage. Example 2 can be computed by building a table of survivors (shown below) to accumulate the extent to which each input picture survives in the composite.

FFire	BFire	Planet	Stars	Survivor
			•	Stars
		•		Planet
		•	•	Planet
	•			BFire
	•		•	BFire
	•	•		Planet
	•	•	•	Planet
•				FFire
•			•	FFire
•		•		FFire
•		•	•	FFire
•	•			FFire,BFire
•	•		•	FFire,BFire
•	•	•		FFire
•	•	•	•	FFire

6. Conclusion

We have pointed out the need for matte channels in synthetic pictures, suggesting that frame buffer hardware should offer this facility. We have seen the convenience of the RGBA scheme for integrating the matte channel. A language of operators has been presented for conveying a full range of compositing expressions. We have discussed a methodology for deciding compositing questions at the subpixel level, deriving a simple equation for handling all composites of two pictures. The methodology is extended to multiple pictures, and the language is embellished to handle darkening, attenuation, and opaqueness.

There are several problems to be resolved in related areas, which are open for future research. We are interested in methods for breaking arbitrary three dimensional scenes into elements separated in depth. Such elements are equivalent to clusters, which have been a subject of discussion since the earliest attempts at hidden surface elimination. We are interested in applying the compositing notions to Z-buffer algorithms, where depth information is retained at each pixel.

7. References

1. Cook, R. Road to Point Reyes. *Computer Graphics* Vol 17, No. 3 (1983), Title Page Picture.

2. Crow, F. C. A More Flexible Image Generation Environment. *Computer Graphics* Vol. 16, No. 3 (1982), pp. 9-18.

3. Newell, M. G., Newell, R. G., and Sancha, T. L.. A Solution to the Hidden Surface Problem, pp. 443-448. *Proceedings of the 1972 ACM National Conference*.

4. Wallace, Bruce. Merging and Transformation of Raster Images for Cartoon Animation. *Computer Graphics* Vol. 15, No. 3 (1981), pp. 253-262.

5. Warnock, John, and Wyatt, Douglas. A Device Independent Graphics Imaging Model for Use with Raster Devices. *Computer Graphics* Vol. 16, No. 3 (1982), pp. 313-319.

6. Whitted, Turner, and Weimer, David. A Software Test-Bed for the Development of 3-D Raster Graphics Systems. *Computer Graphics* Vol. 15, No. 3 (1981), pp. 271-277.

8. Acknowledgments

The use of mattes to control the compositing of pictures is not new. The graphics group at the New York Institute of Technology has been using this for years. NYIT color maps were designed to encode both color and matte information; that idea was extended in the Ampex AVA system for storing mattes with pictures. Credit should be given to Ed Catmull, Alvy Ray Smith, and Ikonas Graphics Systems for the existence of an alpha channel as an integral part of a frame buffer, which has paved the way for the developments presented in this paper.

The graphics group at Lucasfilm should be credited with providing a fine test bed for working out these ideas. Furthermore, certain ideas incorporated as part of this work have their origins as idle comments within this group. Thanks are also given to Rodney Stock for comments on an early draft which forced the authors to clarify the major assumptions.

PANEL

THE STORAGE, RETRIEVAL AND DISPLAY OF INTEGRATED GRAPHICS AND TEXT

CHAIR: Rae A. Earnshaw - University of Leeds

PANEL: Heather Brown - University of Kent
         William McMunn - Gerber Systems Technology
         William Newman - Consultant
         Steve Pollitt - Huddersfield Polytechnic

CHAIRMAN'S INTRODUCTION:

Methodologies, techniques and applications for the storage, retrieval and display of integrated graphics and text will be discussed. Current areas of interest include engineering drawings, CAD, publishing, graphics and databases, business graphics, office systems, cartography, typography and high quality text. This topic is at the leading edge of current developments and cost-effective applications will be examined.

Dr. Rae Earnshaw, Chairman of the BCS Displays Group, will outline current needs and objectives for integrating graphics and text in the context of information processing and display, and indicate progress towards the long term goal of "what you see is what you print".

Dr. William McMunn, Manager, Technical Publications at Gerber Systems Technology, Inc. will review emerging commercial systems capable of combining high quality typography with complex high-resolution graphic illustrations, with improved user-friendliness and ease of interactive editing capability. Anticipated future trends in commercial systems will be outlined.

Dr. Heather Brown, Chairperson of the BCS Electronic Publishing Group will discuss the problems involved in the transformation of device-independent output from high quality document preparation systems into printed copy. Problems with the use of varied fonts and the lack of standards will be outline. Incorporation of graphical commands, such as GKS primitives, into text and word-processing systems will be discussed.

Dr. William Newman, Consultant, is co-author of "Principles of Interactive Computer Graphics" and has recently completed a book on designing integrated systems. He will discuss integration of text and graphics in the wider context of multi-function, multi-window, integrated systems. He will present some ideas on how to approach integration and what benefits to expect from integrated systems.

Mr. Steve Pollitt, Chairman of the BCS Information Retrieval Group, will examine user-interface issues, knowledge-engineering aspects and information retrieval problems of multi-disciplinary systems. The anticipated future of integrated systems in the light of the Japanese Fifth Generation and the Alvey Programme for Advanced Information Technology, will be reviewed.

A Programmer's Interface to Graphics Dynamics

Joshua U. Turner

IBM Corporation
Poughkeepsie, NY 12602

ABSTRACT

The term "graphics dynamics" is used in this paper to describe a capability which permits the application programmer to specify a relationship between various graphics input devices and aspects of the graphics output presentation. Subsequent use of the input devices results in continuous real-time changes to the picture. An experimental graphics system is described, in which a powerful programmer's interface to graphics dynamics was implemented. This interface appears suitable for use as an extension to any of the existing standards and standards proposals, including, CORE, GKS, and PHIGS.

CR Categories and Subject Descriptors: I.3.4 [Computer Graphics]: Graphics Utilities -- graphics packages; I.3.6 [Computer Graphics]: Methodology and Techniques -- device independence; K.1 [Computing Milieux]: The Computer Industry -- standards

General Terms: Design, Programmer Interfaces

Additional Key Words and Phrases: graphics dynamics, graphics standards, CORE, GKS, PHIGS

1. INTRODUCTION

Within the last few years, graphics hardware has evolved to the stage where it is now possible to achieve a number of real-time effects within the graphics terminal. Examples range from the programming of a simple rubber band line, to the dynamic rotation, translation, and scaling of a three dimensional object. The term "graphics dynamics" is used in this paper to describe such effects. The programming of the hardware to achieve such effects, requires the application pro-grammer to establish relationships between various input devices and aspects of the output presentation. Subsequent use of the input devices results in continuous real-time changes to the picture.

While many vendors are now providing hardware having a range of graphics dynamics capabilities, the application programmer has not been given an adequate high-level device independent interface with which to program these capabilities.

The earliest and perhaps the most serious attempt to provide such an interface, was the SIGGRAPH CORE proposal [3], which included the ability to specify rubber-band lines and 3D transformations within its "image transformation" capability. This capability suffered two weaknesses: first, it suffered from a lack of generality -- the dynamic capabilities were tied to specific echo types defined for the locator and the valuator devices. Second, the dynamic capabilities which were supported, acted upon the transformed image. This could result in some disturbing anomalies, as when a 3D picture subject to perspective was rotated. The successor standards-making activities have largely ignored the issue of graphics dynamics.

As a learning exercise, a group within IBM's Data Systems Division, implemented an experimental graphics system, having as its objective, the provision of a complete high-level device-independent application programmer's interface to a comprehensive range of state-of-the-art graphics capabilities. For this experiment, an Evans and Sutherland PS300 was used. As part of this effort, a general facility was provided in support of graphics dynamics. This facility attempted to provide a compatible and consistent extension to the style of programming used within existing graphics standards, and standards proposals. The SIGGRAPH CORE specification was used as a basis for this work. However, the concepts and capabilities which were developed for the CORE, apply without difficulty to the GKS [2], or the PHIGS [6] standards as well. Part of this paper provides an outline of a GKS/PHIGS implementation of the facility.

It is to be hoped that this exercise will have relevance for the standards makers, as well as for those vendors and users seeking to provide graphics software in support of terminals having graphics dynamics capabilities.

Permission to copy without fee all or part of this material is granted provided that the copies are not made or distributed for direct commercial advantage, the ACM copyright notice and the title of the publication and its date appear, and notice is given that copying is by permission of the Association for Computing Machinery. To copy otherwise, or to republish, requires a fee and/or specific permission.

© 1984   ACM   0-89791-138-5/84/007/0263 $00.75

2. OVERVIEW OF THE APPROACH

In order to provide a programmer's interface to graphics dynamics, a facility is required which allows the application programmer to establish relationships between the various graphics input devices and various aspects of the graphics output presentation. Subsequently, as the input devices are manipulated, picture changes will be generated.

The instant by instant processing of the input devices and the resultant picture changes take place below the programmer's interface, without the involvement of the application program. The processing may be performed either in the graphics software package, or within the terminal. The experimental implementation described here does not actually dictate how the responsibility is to be divided. However, in order to permit continuous fluid change to the picture, some level of local processing capability is necessary within the terminal. If the real-time processing is not relegated to the terminal, an unacceptable level of performance may be experienced. The term "graphics subsystem" is used in this paper to refer to the combined actions of the terminal and the graphics software package.

The programmer's interface to graphics dynamics makes use of a concept called "graphics variables." Graphics variables are abstractions of the CORE concepts of sampled and event-causing input devices, and they provide an interface which supports the use of these devices to implement graphics dynamics.

Two types of graphic variables, sampled variables and event variables, were defined, corresponding to the sampled and event-causing devices. However, event variables are only useful in cases where the response time associated with application program interaction is very long, and in which rapid response is critical. This paper will focus on the sampled devices and on their support via sampled graphics variables.

In giving a definition of the term "graphics variable", the word "variable" should be interpreted *mathematically* -- not *programmatically*. A "graphics variable" is a named entity which has a value. The value may change continuously from instant to instant, and may be used to effect various picture changes.

Graphics variables may be "basic", or "defined". Basic variables are atomic properties of the logical input devices. The values of valuators and locators are examples of basic graphics variables. Time is another basic graphics variable. The basic graphics variables associated with the various CORE logical input devices are discussed below.

Defined graphics variables are combinations of other graphics variables. A defined graphics variable may change in value from instant to instant in response to changes in the values of the graphics variables upon which it is defined. Thus graphics variables are rather different from the familiar variables of procedural programming languages, which may only change in value following the execution of an assignment statement.

A graphics variable may be viewed as an abstract input device which is used to supply a value. Whereas a basic graphics variable corresponds to some elementary property of the hardware input devices, defined graphics variables provide a means of creating new input devices from existing ones. The defining expression specifies how the existing variables are to be "wired" together to create the new ones.

Graphics variables may be likened to the quantities processed by analog computers. Whenever one of the analog inputs to an expression changes, the output value of the expression changes at once.

Using graphics variables, the application programmer can specify a wide range of dynamic picture modifications. As an example, the CORE allows a color attribute to be set, which determines the color of any lines which are subsequently drawn. The value of the attribute is a graphics constant. By setting the color attribute to a graphics variable rather than a constant, the input devices can be used to dynamically alter the color of any lines which are given that attribute.

For example, the CORE would permit the following:

    SET_COLOR (120.0)

    LINE_ABS_2 (1.0, 1.0)

The color attribute is set to a hue corresponding to 120 degrees in the HLS color model, which is the color red. The line which is then drawn, is assigned this color. The line retains this color, and the color may not be changed.

With graphics variables, the following could be coded instead:

    SET_VAR ('COLR .=. 360 * VAL (1)')

    SET_COLOR (/COLR/)

    LINE_ABS_2 (1.0, 1.0)

The first command, the "SET_VAR" command, defines a graphics variable named "COLR". This variable is defined as equal to the value of the expression "360 * VAL (1)" where VAL (1) is a basic graphics variable taking on the value of Valuator 1. The symbol ".=." should be read "is defined as". This symbol is used to emphasize that this statement constitutes a definition rather than an assignment statement.

The second command is the CORE SET_COLOR command. This time, the hue is specified as a graphics variable. The slashes surrounding the name of the graphics variable are used in this paper wherever an argument of a command is specified as a graphics variable rather than as a program variable or constant. This notation is not proposed as an actual programming syntax. The form of the syntax would depend on the language binding.

Finally, the third command, draws a line. The color attribute of this line will be determined according to the most recent SET_COLOR command, and in this case, the hue will vary according to the value of the variable "COLR". Again, the line retains this color attribute, and the attribute may not be changed. However, the value of the graphics variable changes whenever the valuator changes, and this will cause the color of the line to change as well.

As a second example, the sequence:

    SET_VAR ('X1 .=. 2 * VAL (1)')

    SET_VAR ('Y1 .=. 20 * VAL (2)')

    LINE_ABS_2 (/X1/, /Y1/)

defines a "rubber-band" line, whose end-point is determined by the current values of Valuator 1 and Valuator 2, scaled by different scaling factors.

Four types of graphics variables are allowed:

1. Real Variables

2. Integer Variables

3. Boolean Variables

4. Character String Variables

In general, real and integer variables may be mixed in arithmetic expressions. The other types may not be mixed.

The following facilities for defining and manipulating graphics variables were developed:

2.1. SETTING GRAPHIC VARIABLES

A new graphics variable is defined using the SET_VAR command:

    SET_VAR ('Var .=. Expr')

        or

    SET_VAR ('Var .=. IF (Cond)
       THEN Exp1 ELSE Exp2')

If the variable has been previously defined, then this new definition supersedes the previous one. Thus the definition of a graphics variable may be changed at any time. A graphics variable may also be defined as a dynamic expression, and later re-defined as a constant, or vice versa.

The IF form allows a graphics variable to be defined as equal to one of two expressions based on a logical condition. The condition may be expressed in terms of graphic variables. It is evaluated dynamically, and may change from instant to instant. Consequently, the defined variable may take on the value of either expression at any given instant.

A partial list of the operations which may be used in the defining expression of a graphics variable includes the following, given in a FORTRAN syntax.

1. Arithmetic: +, -, *, /.

2. Logical: .AND., .OR., .NOT.

3. Arithmetic Comparison: .GT., .GE., .EQ., .NE., .LT., .LE.

4. Concatenation: //.

5. Library Functions: INT, MOD, FLOAT, SIN, COS, SQRT, MIN, MAX, CHAR, INDEX.

The INT function allows a real-valued graphics variable to be converted to an integer-valued graphics variable.

The CHAR function produces a character string suitable for display, from a real, integer, or boolean value.

Here are a few examples of graphics variable definitions:

    SET_VAR ('R .=. 5*P + 3*Q - 7')

    SET_VAR ('ABC .=. (X.GT.7).AND.(Y.LT.2)')

    SET_VAR ('Z .=. IF (ABC) THEN 4 ELSE Y + 2')

2.2. READING GRAPHIC VARIABLES

Sometimes the application program may want to obtain the current value of one of the graphics variables. This is done using the READ_VAR command:

    READ_VAR ('Variable', VALUE)

This command causes the current value of the designated graphics variable to be placed in the designated program variable.

3. BASIC GRAPHIC VARIABLES

The following sections describe the basic graphics variables which were defined for each of the various types of CORE input devices. Note: pick devices, and button devices were defined to be available for local processing only through graphics event variables. Stroke devices were not implemented.

3.1. KEYBOARD DEVICES

Keyboard devices are defined in the CORE as event-causing devices, which cause an

ⒶⒸⓂ SIGGRAPH'84

"INPUT_STRING" to be built and then queued for processing by the application. The CORE also provides a default echo for this INPUT_STRING.

As a generalization of this capability, "INPUT_STRING" was defined as a basic graphics variable of data type character string. This graphics variable may be displayed in any way desired by the application programmer.

3.2. LOCATOR DEVICES

Locators are referenced using up to three separate graphics variables: "LOCX (n)", "LOCY (n)", and "LOCZ (n)", where n is the device number of the particular locator of interest, and the X, Y, and Z components of the locator position are available as separate variables.

3.3. VALUATOR DEVICES

Valuators are referenced as "VAL (n)" where n is the device number of the particular valuator of interest.

4. USE IN CORE COMMANDS

In CORE, a number of commands are provided which permit the establishment of a viewing transformation, and the drawing of lines, markers, and text, subject to a collection of segment and primitive attributes. All of the arguments of these commands are graphics constants. However, most of these arguments may be meaningfully specified as graphics variables. This section reviews the various CORE commands and points out cases where it is valuable to be able to specify arguments as graphics variables.

4.1. OUTPUT PRIMITIVES

In general, any of the X-Y-Z coordinates used to define the endpoints of lines, or the locations of text or marker symbols, may meaningfully be specified as graphics variables. By using graphics variables to supply the world coordinates locations of various entities, the world coordinates definition of the picture can dynamically change as the values of the graphics variables are changed. The example of a rubber-band line has already been given. In general, the shape of any three dimensional wire-frame object may be dynamically manipulated, when its coordinates have been specified as graphics variables. What is more, when used in conjunction with a graphics package supporting circles, arcs, spline curves, and the like, graphics vari-

ables could be used to permit dynamic changes to these primitives as well. Note, that in each case the picture is manipulated by altering its <u>world coordinates</u> definition, not the corresponding transformed image.

Text primitives may also be graphics variables. In particular, by specifying the graphics variable "INPUT_STRING" as the argument to a TEXT command, the keyboard may be made to echo at any desired position, and with any desired size, orientation, or color.

4.2. ATTRIBUTES

Generally, attributes are used to control the appearance and detectability of graphical objects. At the time a segment or primitive is defined, it is automatically given the current setting of all applicable attributes.

In CORE, GKS, and PHIGS, these attribute settings are graphics constants. The constant attribute values which are assigned to a segment or primitive, may not change dynamically.

With the use of graphics variables, however, it is possible to permit dynamic changes to the values of these attributes. If an attribute is set to a graphics variable, then as that graphics variable changes in value from moment to moment, the segments or primitives which have been given that attribute setting will change as well.

In the case of primitive attributes, once an attribute setting has been assigned to a given primitive, that assignment may not change. But if the attribute has been set to a graphics variable, then the value of the attribute may change dynamically as the graphics variable changes. An example has already been given showing the use of a graphics variable to permit dynamic changes in line color. Other real-valued primitive attributes which might meaningfully be specified as graphics variables, include line intensity, line width, and character size. The graphics variable concept would also permit integer-valued attributes such as line style, font, and marker symbol to be specified as graphics variables.

When used in conjunction with a graphics package supporting the generation of shaded pictures, graphic variables could be used to support the dynamic color blending of such pictures. An example of this application is given in Warn [7]. Graphics variables can provide a friendly programmer interface for such an application. In this interface, graphics variables would be used to specify the colors to be assigned to the various surfaces of the shaded objects. For instance,

    SET_VAR ('COLR .=. 360*VAL(1)')

    SET_POLYGON_COLOR (/COLR/)

    POLYGON_3 (polygon definition)

If the graphics terminal includes a color look-up table (LUT), the graphics package can implement the dynamic color blending capability by establishing appropriate dynamic connections to the LUT. The application programmer is shielded from the hardware specifics. Several vendors are providing graphics terminals today which permit such color blending of shaded pictures, but a device-independent application programmer interface has been lacking.

Segment attributes such as visibility, detectability, and highlighting, may also be meaningfully specified as graphics variables. For example,

```
SET_SEGMENT_VISIBILITY (7, /V7/)

SET_VAR ('V7 .=. IF (VAL(1).GT.3)
   THEN .TRUE. ELSE .FALSE.')
```

The first command specifies the visibility attribute setting of segment 7 as the value of the boolean graphics variable V7. The second command defines V7 to be .TRUE. whenever Valuator 1 is greater than 3, and .FALSE., otherwise. The visibility of the segment will be controlled by the valuator.

One application of such a facility would be the dynamic "dialing in" of levels of picture detail. By properly structuring the picture data, one of the valuators could be specified to gradually cause more and more of the picture detail to become visible.

4.3. VIEWING OPERATIONS

The CORE proposal supports a static "synthetic camera" viewing model. A viewing transformation is specified, and subsequently, a series of segments are specified. The graphics primitives within these segments are immediately transformed, at the time they are specified, and positioned on the viewing surface. The original world-coordinate specification of the graphics primitives is not retained, and the viewing parameters which apply to a given segment may not be changed once the segment has been created.

With graphics variables, however, any of the viewing parameters such as center of projection, view plane normal, window boundaries, and front and back distance, may be graphics variables. By using the input devices to alter the values of the graphics variables, the user may dynamically alter his viewing position relative to the objects on the screen. To achieve the dynamic effect, the original world coordinates of the graphics primitives must be retained in the graphics subsystem, and the primitives must be dynamically re-transformed, subject to the new values of the viewing parameters, whenever these change.

4.4. MODELLING TRANSFORMATIONS

Although the CORE specification does not support modelling transformations, such capabilities were implemented in this experiment as an extension of the CORE. Foley and Van Dam [1], was used as a basis for this extension. This reference proposes a coherent set of capabilities for modelling transformations including commands which permit pieces of a picture to be ROTATE'ed, TRANSLATE'ed, and SCALE'ed. With graphics variables, it is natural to permit the arguments to these commands to be specified as graphics variables.

5. EXTENDED EXAMPLES

To get a feeling for the full power of the capability, the following are provided as extended examples of the use of graphics variables for local dynamics.

5.1. RUBBER BAND RECTANGLE

A rubber-band rectangle is to be drawn using graphics variables. The lower-left corner of the rectangle is at (0, 0) and the upper-right corner is to be determined by the X-Y values of Locator 1:

```
MOVE_ABS_2 (0, 0)

LINE_ABS_2 (/LOCX (1)/, 0)

LINE_ABS_2 (/LOCX (1)/, /LOCY (1)/)

LINE_ABS_2 (0, /LOCY (1)/)

LINE_ABS_2 (0, 0)
```

In GKS or PHIGS, the above could be accomplished with a single POLYLINE command.

5.2. LOCAL 3D TRANSFORMATIONS

It is desired to define an object, and to use the valuators to translate, rotate, and scale it. Two valuators are to be used to translate the object relative to the X and Y coordinate axes. Three more valuators are to be used to cause rotations of the object about the X, Y, and Z axes. Three more valuators are to be used to scale the object relative to the X, Y, and Z axes.

Modelling transformations having graphics variables as arguments will be applied to the object to achieve the desired effect. The following commands establish the required modelling transformations:

```
TRANSLATE_2 (/VAL (1)/, /VAL (2)/)

ROTATE_3 (/VAL (3)/, /VAL (4)/, /VAL (5)/)

SCALE_3 (/VAL (6)/, /VAL (7)/, /VAL (8)/)
```

Now, any output primitives which are created beyond this point, and to which these modelling transformations apply, will be transformed accordingly.

5.3. DEPTH CLIPPING

It is desired to use two of the dials to control the positions of front and back clipping planes.

In the CORE, the position of the clipping planes is controlled by the SET_VIEW_DEPTH command. The two arguments to this command may be specified as graphics variables:

```
SET_VIEW_DEPTH (/VAL (1)/, /VAL (2)/)
```

5.4. PERSPECTIVE ANGLE

It is desired to use one of the dials to control the perspective angle governing the perspective view of an object.

The SET_VALUATOR command will be used to specify that Valuator 1 is to have an initial value of 1 degree, and take on values in the range 1 degree to 45 degrees.

In the CORE, the perspective angle is not specified directly. Rather, a window is specified, and a center of projection is specified at some distance from the center of the window. The perspective angle is the angle at the center of projection formed by projectors drawn to the center of the top edge of the window and to the window center. If we assume that the window height is 2*W, then the distance from the center of projection to the window center is given by the expression W*COS(Q)/SIN(Q) where Q is the perspective angle. Thus the following commands will achieve the desired effect:

```
SET_VALUATOR (1, 1, 1, 45)

SET_VAR ('D .=. -W*COS(VAL (1))/SIN(VAL (1))')

SET_PROJECTION (1, 0, 0, /D/)
```

5.5. VALUATOR READOUT

It is desired to be able to display a digital read-out of the value of one of the valuators on the display screen. The value displayed is to be updated as the valuator changes. The following will achieve the desired effect:

```
SET_VAR('VT .=. CHAR (VAL (1))')

TEXT (/VT/)
```

The CHAR built-in function is used to convert the valuator into a character string. It is then displayed on the screen at the current position using the TEXT command.

5.6. TIME AS A GRAPHIC VARIABLE

In addition to the input devices provided in the CORE, a facility may be provided to allow access to the system clock function provided by some terminals. Such a facility would permit continuous changes to the picture to be programmed. The clock function is provided by means of a family of basic graphics variables named CLOCK (n). A SET_CLOCK command is provided which allows a given clock to be set to a desired initial value:

```
SET_CLOCK (n, INITIAL_VALUE)
```

A clock may be used like any other graphics variable. For instance, the following commands:

```
SET_VAR ('DZ .=. 360.0 * VAL (1) * CLOCK (1)')

ROTATE_2 (/DZ/)

TEXT ('SIGGRAPH')
```

cause the text string 'SIGGRAPH' to be rotated around the Z axis continuously, at a rate of one full revolution per second, assuming Valuator 1 has an initial value of 1. By manipulating Valuator 1, the user could speed up or slow down the rate of revolution.

6. GKS/PHIGS IMPLEMENTATION

The adaptation of the graphics variables concept to the GKS or the PHIGS standard, is largely straightforward. Since these two standards are very similar in those aspects relevant to this discussion, they will be dealt with together. The intent is merely to outline how such an implementation might be achieved. Only the differences from the CORE implementation are discussed.

6.1. LOGICAL MODEL

The first consideration must be the logical model for the association of basic graphics variables with the physical input devices.

In GKS and PHIGS, the notion of the logical input devices is developed as a model for application interaction. The logical input devices are defined as combinations of various lower-level measures and triggers. The various operating modes which apply to the logical input devices (REQUEST, SAMPLE, and EVENT mode), as well as the deferral mode, specify the protocol governing the application interaction. As such, the logical input device model does not appear appropriate for use in specifying graphics dynamics, since an application program is not involved.

Therefore, a separate logical model is proposed. Specifically, it is suggested that one basic graphics variable be provided at a logical level, for each of the lower-level measures and triggers. These measure and trigger "variables" would be on a par with, and independent of the logical input devices defined for application interaction, and would have their own state information and controls.

In keeping with the argument presented earlier, the trigger variables probably have very little use. However the following basic measure variables seem desirable:

String Devices: STRING(n) -- current value of string device "n" (data type is character string).

Locator Devices: LOCX(n), LOCY(n)

Valuator Devices: VAL(n)

Choice Devices: CHOICE(n) -- most recent choice number (data type is integer).

Stroke Devices: STROKECT(n) -- current number of defined points; STROKEX(n,i), STROKEY(n,i) -- coordinates of the i th defined point.

In addition to identifying the above basic measure variables, facilities must be defined to provide controls similar to those provided for the logical input devices. For instance, for the VAL(n) basic measure variables, controls over low value, high value, and initial value would be required. These controls would be independent of those provided for the logical input devices. Furthermore, it would be desirable to provide these controls in the form of basic graphics variables -- for example, VAL_LOW(n), VAL_HIGH(n), and VAL(n) respectively, thus permitting these controls to be set either by the application, or directly through local processing.

6.2. USE OF MEASURE VARIABLES

Basic and defined measure variables could sensibly be used in most of the ways already discussed:

Output Functions: As coordinate values, and as text strings.

Output Attributes: The following workstation-independent attributes could be graphics variables: highlighting and visibility (boolean variables), bundle table indices and indices of indirectly-specified individual attributes (integer variables), values of directly-specified individual attributes (data type according to the particular attribute, for instance, LINEWIDTH SCALE FACTOR would be a real variable).

The above are all workstation-independent. In addition, the values of the entries in the color table, which is workstation-dependent, would profitably be specifiable as graphics variables. Implications of multiple workstations are discussed in the next sub-section.

Normalization/Viewing Transformation: Window and viewport boundaries, and for PHIGS, the near and far distance, and the elements of the view matrix.

Note: the GKS normalization transformation is workstation-independent. The PHIGS viewing transformation is workstation-dependent.

Modelling Transformations (PHIGS): Elements of the modelling transformation matrix.

It is unfortunate that for both the above types of transformations, PHIGS specifies the higher-level functions, such as SET VIEW REFERENCE POINT and ROTATE, as utility functions, which convert their input arguments into a matrix returned to the application. This approach prevents the direct specification of these arguments as graphic variables. As it stands, a compound expression must be specified for each matrix element to achieve simple effects (such as rotation). It would be preferable to provide higher-level transformation functions, which would be directly interpreted by the graphics package, whose arguments could be specified as graphic variables.

6.3. EFFECT OF MULTIPLE WORKSTATIONS

In the majority of the uses outlined above, graphic variables are employed as arguments to functions which are workstation-independent. Consequently, when an argument is specified as a graphic variable, this specification applies to all target workstations. It is necessary, however, to permit the interpretation of a picture definition to vary from one workstation to the next, depending, possibly on workstation capabilities. To allow for this, it is reasonable to give each workstation its own definition of each defined graphic variable, by adding "workstation-id" as an argument to the SET_VAR function. A separate definition of a particular variable could then be given for each workstation. A graphics variable could be defined to be a constant for a workstation without dynamic capability.

For those cases where a graphics variable is used as an argument to a workstation-dependent function, as in setting the color table, and in the PHIGS viewing transformation functions, the application programmer has a choice. If the same graphic variable is used across different workstations, then the workstation-id specified in the SET_VAR function, serves to qualify the variable name.

To permit retrieval of the current value of a particular graphics variable for a particular workstation, the READ_VAR function would also require the addition of "workstation-id" as an argument.

The operation of the GKS and PHIGS inquiry functions would be affected as well, in that where an argument had been specified as a graphic variable, the inquiry function would return only the name of the graphic variable. The READ_VAR function could then be used to retrieve the value of the graphics variable for a given workstation.

The above has not attempted to tie up all the loose ends, but does demonstrate a reasonable approach to extending the GKS or PHIGS specifications to include the graphics variable concept. In practice, graphics variables would probably make more sense as an extension to PHIGS rather than to GKS.

7. EVALUATION OF THE APPROACH

It has been noted that the graphics variables concept provides a non-procedural model for the programming of graphic dynamics. Starting from the basic graphic variables, existing variables are "wired" together to form new ones. These are ultimately used to control various dynamic properties of the picture. As the values of the basic graphic variables change over time, the picture changes along with them, continuously, and if the graphic subsystem provides sufficient power, with a sense of real-time control. It is hoped that the graphics variables concept provides a natural and intuitively comfortable conceptual model for the programming of graphic dynamics, and that it mirrors the experiential model of the terminal user.

It should also be noted, that graphic variables are not intended to permit graphic editing of the picture definition in the sense of adding or deleting primitives. The provision of such capabilities for the editing of picture content appears to be of questionable merit in general purpose programmer's interface, since the visible picture is merely a reflection of a portion of the application data base. In many cases it makes no sense to change the picture content without first changing this data base, and in most cases, the style of the dialog used to specify such changes is application-specific.

8. CONCLUSIONS

Within the last few years, graphics hardware has evolved to the stage where it is now possible to achieve a number of local real-time effects within the graphics terminal.

While many vendors are now providing equipment having a range of graphics dynamics capabilities, these capabilities have so far gone without a high-level device-independent programmer interface.

An experimental graphics system has been described which permits the applications programmer to specify non-procedural relationships between the input devices of a graphics terminal, and various aspects of the output presentation, permitting the picture to be dynamically modified. The relationship between the input devices and the output presentation is specified by means of graphics variables. The objective of the experimental implementation was to identify a high-level device-independent programmer interface. The graphics variables capability was implemented as an extension to the SIGGRAPH CORE specification. However, the approach is applicable to GKS, PHIGS, or any other graphics system having a similar philosophical basis.

It is to be hoped that this exercise will have relevance for the standards-making community, as well as for those terminal vendors and users seeking to provide their own graphics software support of the dynamics capabilities of such terminals.

REFERENCES

1. Foley, J. D., and Van Dam, A. *Fundamentals of Interactive Computer Graphics*. Addison-Wesley, Reading, Massachusetts, 1982.

2. *dpANS GKS* (Graphical Kernel System). American National Standards Institute. X3H3/83-25R1. July 19, 1983.

3. Status report of the Graphics Standards Planning Committee. *Computer Graphics 13*, 3 (Aug. 1979).

4. Michener, James C., and Van Dam, Andries. A functional overview of the Core system. *Computing Surveys 10*, 4, (Dec. 1978). McGraw-Hill, New York, 1979.

5. Newman, William M., and Sproull, Robert F. *Principles of Interactive Computer Graphics*. McGraw-Hill, New York, 1979.

6. *American National Standard for the Functional Specification of the Programmer's Hierarchical Interactive Graphics Standard (PHIGS)*. American National Standards Institute. X3H3/84-40. February 29, 1984.

7. Warn, David R. Lighting controls for synthetic images. *Computer Graphics 17*, 3, (Aug. 1983).

GKS for Imaging

Cliff Stoll
Space Telescope Science Institute
Johns Hopkins University
Baltimore, MD 21218

ABSTRACT: By adopting the Graphical Kernel System (GKS), groups who manipulate pixelated images can take advantage of device independent graphics without giving up the functions which have traditionally been hardware dependent. Most of these functions, including image I/O, zoom, pan, lookup table manipulation, and cursor reading, are supported within GKS; several other functions, such as the use of multiple image planes and multiple look up tables, are accomodated by the GKS Escape and the Generalized Drawing Primitive (GDP). Because GKS has powerful inquire capabilities, it's possible to tightly customize applications code to a particular hardware display device. The inquire functions also can be used by an applications program to determine the hardware display size and thus avoid resampling of a pixelated image.

GKS thoroughly separates applications programs from device-dependencies; however, device drivers must still be written. The time and effort of writing device drivers can be largely eliminated by using a single programmable device driver, which is tailored to each device by a GRAPHCAP configuration file, in much the same way as TERMCAP is used by Berkeley Unix implementations.

CR Categories and Subject Descriptors: I.3.4 [Computer Graphics]: Computer Utilities - Graphics Packages I.3.6 [Computer Graphics]: Methodology & Techniques

General terms: Image Display, Standardization

Additional Keywords & Phrases: Graphical Kernel System, GKS

Permission to copy without fee all or part of this material is granted provided that the copies are not made or distributed for direct commercial advantage, the ACM copyright notice and the title of the publication and its date appear, and notice is given that copying is by permission of the Association for Computing Machinery. To copy otherwise, or to republish, requires a fee and/or specific permission.

© 1984   ACM   0-89791-138-5/84/007/0271 $00.75

INTRODUCTION:

Groups who display images -- as opposed to vector graphics -- have traditionally used homebrew software which is heavily dependent upon a single type of display hardware. Such device-dependent software is notoriously difficult to transport to other devices, and is usually expensive to support and maintain.

Contrasted with this is device-independent software, exemplified by two well-known graphics systems, GSPC/CORE [3], and GKS [2]. Such software isolates applications programs from the actual plotting commands; these, in turn, are generic plotting commands which work on any graphics device.

Because the GSPC/CORE system only explicitly supports vector graphics, those who specialize in image display systems have tended to ignore the benefits of device-independent graphics software. GKS is attractive to these groups because it supports the display of pixel graphics as a distinct primitive; this allows pixelated images to work alongside vector graphics with all the advantages of device independence [11]. Early subset releases of GKS have not fully supported pixelated images [6], but more recent implementations have the necessary pixel-directed features.

Displaying pre-existing pixelated images is quite challenging. Such images, stored as pixel arrays, can each easily exceed a quarter megabyte. Clearly, any image display software must minimize computational overhead when dealing with such large blocks of data. On the other hand, the software must support a wide diversity of display devices: some devices with extensive image manipulation capabilities, others with almost none. GKS provides a terse set of image primitives which satisfy most of the traditional needs of imaging shops, without imposing the heavy computational burden of a more diverse set.

IMAGE COORDINATE SYSTEMS UNDER GKS

Presently, image display systems use a pixel-based coordinate system, while vector graphics use a world- or user-chosen coordinate system. This makes it difficult to superimpose vector graphics on top of images, or to mix the two types of graphics. This problem has been recognized [11], but seldom solved on a practical implementation. Because GKS provides a single coordinate system for both vector graphics and image displays, it's easy to overlay line drawings on top of images. Since the same coordinate system is used for a 1024x1024 display and a 512x512 display, image display software can be written without regard for the ultimate device. This, of course, is the essence of device-independence.

IMAGE DISPLAY WITHOUT RESAMPLING

The main reason why world coordinates aren't commonly used for image displays is that the wrong choice of coordinates will force the software to resample images. For example, if a display screen is 512 x 512 pixels and an image is 800 x 800 pixels, asking the software to display the entire image will force the image to be resampled. Under GKS, the user has the choice: if she decides to display the entire image, the GKS system will resample the image to fit onto the display. Alternatively, her application program can determine the size of the display screen (in pixels) by using the GKS inquire functions, and choose a subsection of the image to be displayed without resampling. In this way, one can force GKS to avoid resampling an image, without affecting the normalization transforms. Using the inquire function, along with the pixel readback functions, one can read an image out of a display device and into an array, or even read out a single chosen pixel.

LOOKUP TABLES, ZOOMING AND PANNING

Look up tables within an image display device translate each pixel value into either a black and white intensity, or into a combination of red, green, and blue intensities. Traditionally, device-dependent image display software treats look up tables as byte- or integer- translation tables from non-normalized color values into an integer value of color. Each device has a different translation table, making display software very device-dependent.

Since GKS uses normalized, real-valued color values, look up tables are device-independent, and can be implemented on widely differing devices. Setting a particular pixel value to 0.5 red, 0.0 green and 0.5 blue will always yield a violet pixel, independent of the internal word length of the display station. Contrast this with a typical device-dependent specification of 128 red, 0 green, 128 blue -- one doesn't know what effect such a setting will have on an arbitrary display station, since one doesn't know how long each lookup table entry is.

Image display devices often allow an image to be zoomed, usually by factors of 2. This can be done cheaply in hardware, by pixel replication. Under GKS, a zoom is seen as a change in the workstation normalization transform. The problem is to permit only factor-of-2 zooms to be passed on to the hardware, and to do all other zooms in software (by re-sampling). The applications program can filter all zoom commands, so as to permit only fast, hardware supplied zooms. Panning across an image can be seen as a change in the normalization transformations, and is easily accomodated by GKS.

GRAPHICS INPUT FROM GKS

It's become clear that graphics input is a much more challenging problem than graphics display [5]. For many interactive display systems, a simple non-hierarchical, non-segmented input mechanism is adequate, although we recognize the need for a more universal management of graphics input devices [4]. Although GKS (and CORE) provide both synchronous and asynchronous input streams, most implementors appear to support only synchronous graphics input, due to the difficulties of porting interrupt driven software.

Graphical input from a GKS package will have been transformed from the device coordinates into the user coordinates, saving the applications programmer from this task. However, because of the diversity in hardware and operating system interfaces, the user interface may be quite different from one implementation to another. As with graphics output, it is wise to thoroughly isolate graphics input routines into modules which can be easily changed when porting software to new display devices or operating systems.

MOVING TO GKS

Image display software which has isolated the actual graphics commands from the applications code can be directly layered onto GKS. Usually this will require writing a layer to change the existing graphics commands to map into GKS commands. Under these conditions, existing software can quickly be ported to GKS; new devices can easily be added, and local efforts in support of graphics can be minimized. This is the approach which we are taking at Space Telescope Institute -- it essentially preserves the existing software investment while providing a device interface which can grow in the future.

Software which is tightly tied to a single device, or which has graphics commands imbedded throughout applications code tends to be more difficult to port [8]. Often, such systems will need general rewriting anyway, since they tend to be very dependent upon local operating systems or near-obsolete display devices.

Astronomical institutions have long been heavy users of graphics systems and are very interested in program portability and minimizing software costs. Several major astronomical centers have informally agreed to cooperate in using GKS as the graphics interface for astronomical display devices [9]. In this way, we hope to reduce the costs of maintaining the low-level graphics systems, and let us work more on astronomy and astronomical computation.

HOW TO AVOID WRITING DEVICE DRIVERS

In most device-independent plotting packages, a separate device driver must be written for each graphics device. This is a considerable amount of work, and oftentimes, these device drivers are non-portable. Usually, the major effort in supporting a plotting package is in the device drivers. Any way to minimize this work will save many groups a considerable amount of time and trouble.

NCAR, the National Center for Atmospheric Research, is developing a non-interactive GKS system which will be in the public domain [1]. One attractive feature of this system is the concept of GRAPHCAP -- a single, programmable device driver which is configured to a particular device at run-time. This is a logical extention of the Berkeley Unix TERMCAP idea. Instead of writing a new device driver for every graphics terminal and workstation, one merely alters a configuration file which describes the terminal's capabilities to the device driver. In this way, driver writing is minimized, and new devices can be quickly supported.

LIMITATIONS OF GKS FOR IMAGING

Because GKS has such a terse set of pixel directed commands, it must be extended to cover certain applications. The GKS virtual device for image display is surprisingly similiar to several middle-priced hardware display devices, most notably the AED 512 and Jupiter Systems model 7. More advanced graphics display hardware devices tend to have capabilities which GKS does not explicitly support, such as multiple display planes, multiple look up tables, window/rasterop command sets, image wraparound, etc.

With presently available hardware, users will find functions which require extentions to GKS. These should be implemented through the GKS escape function, or via the Generalized Drawing Primitive (GDP). For example, one might wish to toggle between two images which have been loaded into a display device. Other image functions which are needed include viewing surface priority, image boolean algebra, multiple lookup table manipulation, etc.

Graphics standards groups should reserve blocks of escapes and GDP's for commonality amongst graphics groups. This would allow GKS to grow with future needs, while remaining a standard with well defined interfaces.

CONCLUSIONS

For pixelated image display, as well as vector graphics displays, GKS offers a reasonable environment which covers virtually all of the commonly used functions. Since most image display groups transform 3-dimensional scenes into 2-dimensional arrays, the support of 3-dimensional graphics primitives is not a pressing issue for image display software. Presently, the PHIGS [7] graphics standard proposes that images be projected onto billboards located within a 3-dimensional space; this is generally not essential for the display of most captured images. Imaging groups have not heavily used graphics segments, although we can expect more of this as it becomes available.

Of much greater utility is a generally available graphics standard with rigorously defined interfaces and language bindings. The wide adoption of GKS should help relieve many problems at the low level, and permit groups to devote their attention to solving the more difficult, high-level problems.

REFERENCES

[1] Clare, F. and Humbrecht, J. Private Communication from NCAR: National Center for Atmospheric Research, Scientific Computing Division, Boulder, Colorado.

[2] Graphical Kernel System, ANSI X3H3/83-25r3; Special Issue, Computer Graphics, February 1984

[3] GSPC. Status report of the Graphics Standards Planning Committee. Computer Graphics 13, 3 (August, 1979).

[4] Kamran, Abid, and Feldman, Michal B. Graphics Programming Independent of Interaction Techniques and Styles. Computer Graphics 17,1 (January 1983)

[5] Rosenthal, David S. H. Managing Graphical Resources. Computer Graphics 17,1 (January 1983)

[6] Simons, Randall W.; Minimal GKS Computer Graphics 17,3 (July 1983)

[7] Sondregger, E. L.; Comparison of Proposed 3D Graphics Standards. Computer Graphics 17,4 (October, 1983)

[8] Straayer, D. H. in Developing Applications Using GKS. SIGGRAPH Tutorial July 1983.

[9] Stoll, C. Astronomical Image Display Systems Bulletin of the American Astronomical Society, June 1984 (in press).

[10] Stoll, C. Image Display Systems using GKS. NCGA Proceedings, May 1984.

[11] Warnock, J. and Wyatt, D.; A Device Independent Graphics Imaging Model for Use with Raster Devices; Computer Graphics 16,3 (July 1982)

NOVA*GKS, A Distributed Implementation of the Graphical Kernel System

Clinton N. Waggoner, Charles Tucker & Christopher J. Nelson
Nova Graphics International Corporation
1015 Bee Cave Woods
Austin, Texas 78746

ABSTRACT

NOVA*GKS is an implementation of the Draft International Standard Graphical Kernel System (GKS), built using a distributed architecture. The specifications for GKS present an implementor with many design tradeoff decisions. The implementors of NOVA*GKS have analyzed those tradeoffs and created a distributed design which allows users of the package to design applications which can perform efficiently on many different graphics hardware configurations.

CR Categories and Subject Descriptors: I.3.2 [Computer Graphics]:   Graphics Systems – distributed/network graphics; I.3.4 [Computer Graphics]: Graphics/Utilities –   graphics packages; software support

General Terms: Design, Standardization

Additional Key Words and Phrases: GKS, virtual device interface, device independence, ANSI X3H3, ISO

1.0 INTRODUCTION

The Graphical Kernel System (GKS) is a Draft International Standard now being ratified by both the American National Standards Institute (ANSI) and the International Standards Organization (ISO) [1, 2]. This paper assumes a basic familiarity with GKS and device-independent graphics software systems. Hopgood [3] provides an excellent exposition of the history and main technical features of GKS.

GKS defines a standard interface between a graphics application program and a collection of functions which can be realized on a graphics workstation. These functions are specified in GKS in a way that is completely independent of both programming languages and graphics devices. Because of the high level of abstraction assumed by GKS, a graphics application programmer can write software which is highly portable over many graphics devices and computer systems. By building on the pioneering work in graphics programming standards which resulted in the GSPC CORE specification of the late 1970s [4], GKS provides a very important foundation for the computer graphics industry at a relatively early stage in its development.

Although the functionality of GKS is specified in detail, great latitude is left to its implementors. This is as it should be given the complex tradeoffs faced by an implementor when taking into account the sometimes conflicting issues of programming language interfaces, graphics device independence, computer and operating system portability, and hardware configurations.

This paper describes an implementation of GKS which allows major functional components of GKS to reside on distributed processors. The main technical issues which led to this distributed design and the tradeoffs encountered in implementing a distributed GKS architecture are described.

2.0 DESIGN MOTIVATION

Before describing the technical considerations leading to the development of a distributed implementation of GKS, it is useful to discuss the motivation and perspective of the design team. The designers are part of a newly-founded software development company whose initial product is an implementation of GKS called NOVA*GKS. Future products of the company will use NOVA*GKS as a foundation providing full graphics device independence and portability. Because of this, the designers were first of all strongly motivated by the need to produce a practical, efficient, maintainable, and commercially viable product. Second, the designers of NOVA*GKS had previously participated in the design of an interactive contour mapping system, built using a CORE-based graphics package. The limitations encountered in trying to build a very complex graphics application using a CORE package made the designers keenly aware of certain important design factors. In particular,

Permission to copy without fee all or part of this material is granted provided that the copies are not made or distributed for direct commercial advantage, the ACM copyright notice and the title of the publication and its date appear, and notice is given that copying is by permission of the Association for Computing Machinery. To copy otherwise, or to republish, requires a fee and/or specific permission.

© 1984   ACM   0-89791-138-5/84/007/0275 $00.75

there was a very clear need for a device-independent graphics package which is highly efficient in its use of computing resources.

3.0 DESIGN CONSIDERATIONS

This section discusses the design considerations which evolved as a result of this perspective of the design team, and which led to the choice of a distributed architecture for NOVA*GKS.

3.1 Graphics Hardware Configurations

Graphics hardware manufacturers are now making available equipment with an increasingly wide range of characteristics. The advent of microprocessors and inexpensive memory components allows the incorporation of impressive amounts of processing power into a graphics workstation. However, there is still a large market for graphics devices with little or no local processing capability. Furthermore, the nature of the local processing capability, if it exists, can range from a system which can only be programmed via microcode to one providing a full operating system including high level language support. Thus the implementor of a device-independent graphics package such as NOVA*GKS is faced with a complex task in attempting to cleanly interface to the facilities of such a wide range of devices.

However, it is very frustrating to the manufacturer of an "intelligent" graphics device to find his terminal limited by the graphics software package to the performance of a "dumb" terminal. The only way an applications programmer can take advantage of advanced hardware features is to bypass the graphics software package, thus defeating the reason for using it in the first place. The large number of possible processor/graphics device configurations makes it all the more important that designers of packages such as NOVA*GKS find a solution to this problem.

Therefore, considerable attention was given to devising a model for graphics software to enable it to be as flexible as possible in adapting to various processor configurations. Figure 1 shows a variety of typical graphics system configurations which must be addressed by a device independent graphics package. Although the configurations shown are physically considerably different, they differ logically only in the number of processors and the capabilities of each processor. By properly organizing the software modules in a graphics package, it is possible to allocate portions of the software to different processors. Section 4.0 describes how NOVA*GKS is organized to handle the widely varying configurations shown in Figure 1.

FIGURE 1

TYPICAL GRAPHICS SYSTEM CONFIGURATIONS

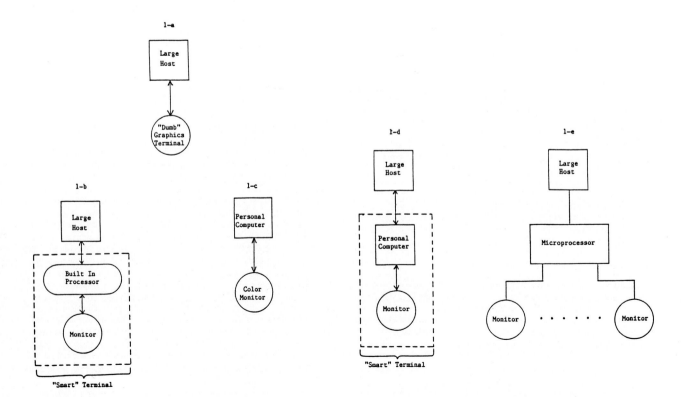

3.2 Memory Utilization

A major problem encountered in using the CORE-based package to implement the interactive contour mapping system mentioned in Section 2 was the excessive amount of storage that it required. Even though only minimal capabilities of the package were used it was not possible to gain any corresponding significant reduction in memory. The organization of the package was such that it did not permit effective overlaying.

Despite the widespread availability of virtual memory systems, there is still a large class of customers for which memory efficiency considerations are important. The specification of GKS goes a long way toward solving this problem by providing several levels of functional capability which are proportional to the needs of an application program. For example, the contour mapping system could have been written using a level mb (minimal) GKS system. The primary need of the designers of that package was simply output device independence. Simons [5] describes a minimal GKS system which requires on the order of 12,000 bytes of program space. In contrast, the CORE-based package mentioned above required approximately 200,000 bytes of storage. Therefore, a major design goal for NOVA*GKS was efficient and appropriate memory utilization.

3.3 Communications Efficiency

A large class of graphics users work in an environment where graphics devices are connected remotely with at best 9600 baud communication lines. Interactive graphics can become very difficult in this environment because of the bottleneck imposed by the communication line. Those who enjoy the luxury of large budgets might say that one should not attempt interactive graphics in such an environment but rather should use dedicated processors with high speed interfaces. However, that solution ignores the realities of the situation for many applications. Therefore, another major design goal for NOVA*GKS was to find an inexpensive solution to the problem of slow communications.

The "least common denominator" approach to device drivers ignores the capabilities of devices such as the Sanders Vistagraphic 4000 [6]. The Vistagraphic 4000 has a powerful processor capable of running high level programming languages. A distributed design allows offloading significant parts of GKS to the workstation, thereby allowing a significant reduction in communications overhead.

A second practical issue related to communications is the problem of interfacing graphics devices to large mainframe computers which often add or delete characters being sent to or received from remote terminals. Such protocols cause severe problems in interfacing graphics devices communicating in binary mode. Some hardware devices get around this problem by using encoding schemes which map all possible bit patterns onto a restricted character set. However, these encoding algorithms usually

result in increased communications overhead. This problem is one of the most difficult problems faced by developers of device- and computer-independent graphics packages. For "dumb" graphics devices there is little that can be done to solve the problem. However, with intelligent devices the same software package can control both ends of the communication line, allowing efficient encoding schemes adapted to the characteristics of a particular host/device combination.

4.0 DESIGN AND TRADEOFFS

This section presents a summary of the NOVA*GKS design. It presents example configurations to show how the distributed design can be adapted to typical configurations. Finally, it describes the major technical tradeoffs faced by the designers. Space does not permit addressing all the tradeoffs which result from the design considerations discussed in the previous sections. In particular, the discussion of tradeoffs is limited to areas directly related to a distributed design.

4.1 Summary of NOVA*GKS Design

Figure 2 illustrates the final architectural design of NOVA*GKS which resulted from the motivations and considerations discussed in the preceding sections. The system consists of four layers. All four layers can reside on a single processor or the layers can be distributed among processors. In practice it is likely that a specific installation will not be distributed among more than two processors. However, the distribution point will very likely be different for different installations.

FIGURE 2

*NOVA*GKS SYSTEM ARCHITECTURE*

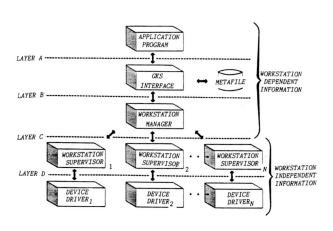

Layer A is the interface between the user and NOVA*GKS. It consists of the functional modules defined by the GKS specification. Layer B is the workstation manager, which manages multiple graphics workstations and handles workstation independent segment storage (WISS). Layers A and B are completely device independent. Layer C is the software layer required to convert a graphics device into a GKS workstation by software simulation of GKS functions not directly supported by the device. Layer D, the device interface, is more or less equivalent to the "device driver" component of other graphics software packages.

The initial implementation of NOVA*GKS is written in ANSI FORTRAN and conforms to the proposed GKS FORTRAN language binding, expected to become part of the final ANSI/ISO GKS standard. It is written in a minimal dialect of FORTRAN 66 to allow maximum portability of the system amonghost computer systems.

A second version, written in C, is now under development, and will be completed by May of 1984.

4.2   Example Configurations

Figures 3 through 5 show a few example configurations and illustrate how the NOVA*GKS layers can be distributed. The configurations shown represent only a few of the possible configurations.

In the configuration shown in Figure 3, the graphics device has no intelligence. In this case all of NOVA*GKS resides on the host processor. The host could be a large mainframe or it could be a microprocessor or personal computer.

In the configuration of Figure 4, there is a host computer connected to a microprocessor. The microprocessor has sufficient processing power to drive multiple unintelligent graphics devices. The host computer contains only the user interface, layer A of NOVA*GKS. The rest of NOVA*GKS resides on the microprocessor. Segment storage (WISS and WDSS) is on the microprocessor.

Figure 5 shows a configuration in which the graphics device has a processor as well as sufficient storage to implement workstation dependent segment storage. Storage can take the form of either random access memory or an attached disk. In this configuration the remote processor and graphics device taken together form a GKS workstation. Physical realization of this configuration could be a personal computer with a monitor, a microprocessor with a monitor, or a graphics terminal with an incorporated microprocessor. NOVA*GKS can be provided in two forms: for this type of configuration it can be used in distributed applications requiring access to a central host-based data base or it can be used in stand-alone mode on the local workstation processor.

FIGURE 3

HOST/UNINTELLIGENT GRAPHICS DEVICE

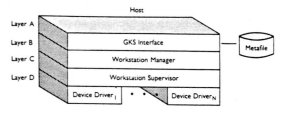

FIGURE 4

HOST/GRAPHICS PROCESSOR/UNINTELLIGENT GRAPHICS DEVICE

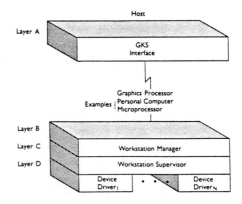

FIGURE 5

HOST/INTELLIGENT GRAPHICS DEVICE

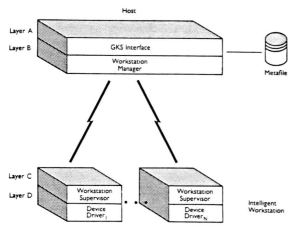

Note: Examples of Intelligent Workstations
(1) Personal Computer
(2) Microprocessor (M68000)
(3) Graphics Terminal with a Microprocessor

4.3 Inter-Layer Coupling

Figure 6 shows the inter-layer coupling for non-distributed and distributed versions of NOVA*GKS. The figure represents any two adjacent layers (A/B, B/C or C/D); the same structure is repeated for all layers. The upper layer may consist of many modules. For example, at layer A there is one module for each GKS function. However, every upper level function must call the same lower level supervisor in order to gain access to the next layer below. Thus, all upper layer functions funnel down to a single module. The lower layer supervisor is then in effect a large "case" statement which fans out to the appropriate lower layer module. In general for NOVA*GKS, only the output primitives and input functions descend all the way to the lowest layer. Most other functions, such as control or inquiry functions, can be satisfied above the device level.

The alternative to the coupling scheme shown in Figure 6 would have been a more traditional direct call to lower level routines. However, that approach would not be appropriate for a distributed system because of the many paths of communication (tight coupling) between routines. With the approach shown in Figure 6 there is almost complete independence between layers. Each layer could even be implemented in different languages, since information is passed between layers in encoded packets.

4.4 Inter-Layer Communications

Figure 6 also shows how NOVA*GKS can be changed from a non-distributed to a distributed environment effort. It is only necessary to insert two communication modules between any two layers, one at each end of the communication line. The rest of the code remains unchanged. One communication module is substituted for the lower layer supervisor at the upper layer. It

has the same name as the lower layer supervisor and thus the upper layer routines are unaware they are invoking software which resides on another processor.

The function of the upper layer communication module is to send packets to the lower layer and receive a reply packet. In reality there are three "pseudo-channels" between layers. One channel handles downward bound packets, one handles return packets, and another handles error packets. The communication module also handles the bookkeeping chores associated with particular communication protocols.

The lower layer communication module receives packets from the upper layer and passes them on to the lower layer supervisor (which, again, is unaware the information came from a separate processor). The lower layer processor also sends return packets containing requested information and error packets generated by routines detecting errors at the lower layer.

The modular nature of the communications approach also makes it possible to change out communications protocols as necessary, with minimum impact to the system.

4.5 Placement of Data Structures

The GKS standard defines several key data structures to control the operation of GKS. The most important of these are the GKS state list, workstation state lists, and the workstation description tables. The thorniest issue associated with a distributed design is the placement of these data structures. In a distributed architecture, a data structure must be placed only on one side of a distribution point. That is not a problem as long as one layer does not need access to a data structure residing on another layer. In general, it is appropriate to place the GKS state list at layer A or B, the workstation state list at layer C, and the workstation description table at layer D. However, there are many cases where this placement results in information being inaccessible from a layer not containing a data structure with needed information.

There are three basic approaches to solving this problem. One solution is to define a set of functions for passing information between layers. Thus, if a layer requires a data item it generates an internal inter-layer inquiry request. A second solution is to redundantly maintain all data structures at every layer. The third method is to duplicate only those portions of the data structures which require inter-layer access.

The third method was the one chosen for NOVA*GKS. The first and second methods were rejected because they would generate excessive additional communications overhead. The selected approach generates less communications traffic than either of the other two. The issue of attribute binding, discussed next, illustrates these points.

FIGURE 6

INTER-LAYER COUPLING AND COMMUNICATION

NON-DISTRIBUTED

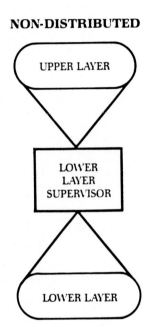

DISTRIBUTED

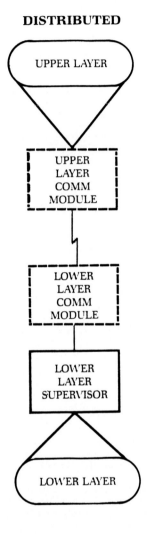

4.6 Binding of Attributes

GKS defines a basic set of five output primitives: POLYLINE, POLYMARKER, TEXT, FILL AREA and CELL ARRAY. Each of these primitives has an associated set of attributes. For example, POLYLINE has the attributes of LINE STYLE, LINE WIDTH and COLOR, while FILL AREA has the attributes of INTERIOR STYLE and COLOR. Figures 7 and 8 illustrate several possible values of these attributes.

Attributes can be defined either individually, or within "bundles" defined for each workstation, indicated by a bundle index or number. Individually set attribute values are maintained within the GKS state list, while bundled attributes are maintained within the workstation state lists, which are in turn initialized from pre-defined bundle tables in the workstation description tables. Whether attributes are set individually or retrieved from a bundle, current attribute values must be associated with, or "bound" to, a primitive before it can be displayed.

In order to reduce communications overhead it was decided to bind attributes to output primitives at layer C. This implies that the portion of the GKS state list containing individual attribute values must be available in at layer C. That in turn requires all functions which set primitive attribute values in that portion of the GKS state list to pass data down to layer C. However, in a typical application it is probable that the frequency of output functions will be much greater than the frequency of attribute setting functions. Since some of the GKS output primitives, especially TEXT, have a large number of attributes which must be bound it is felt that there will be a net reduction in communications traffic.

Workstation independent segment storage (WISS) complicates the decision to bind attributes at layer C. Attributes are bound to output primitives comprising a segment at the time the segment is created and cannot be changed subsequently. When a primitive originating from WISS is sent to a workstation (as a result of the function COPY SEGMENTS TO WORKSTATION, for example), all of its associated attribute values must be "sent ahead" in a separate communication transaction.

This transaction must also take place without disturbing the values of the individual attributes stored in (the copy of) the GKS state list at layer C.

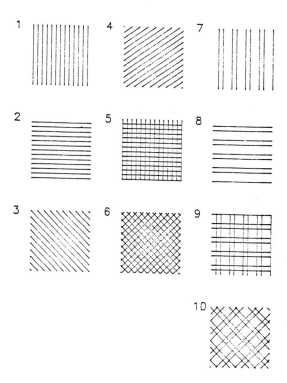

FIGURE 7

EXAMPLES OF FILL AREA INTERIOR STYLE ATTRIBUTE

FIGURE 8

EXAMPLES OF POLYLINE LINE STYLE ATTRIBUTE

5.0 SUMMARY

The adoption of GKS as an international standard will provide a valuable tool for implementors of graphics software applications. It will enable software developers to concentrate on high quality applications for the rapidly growing graphics software market without having to be concerned with the details of a wide array of graphics devices. The GKS specification helps address the efficiency and resource utilization problem by providing a logical structure with several levels of functionality. The applications programmer can select the level of GKS appropriate to his application.

The GKS implementor must consider many tradeoff issues within the latitude allowed by the GKS standard. The tradeoffs can have a significant bearing on the efficiency, resource requirements, and flexibility of the implementation. The designers of NOVA*GKS have investigated the tradeoffs and selected a distributed design approach resulting in a practical system allowing considerable flexibility in designing applications software for a wide variety of hardware configurations and application environments.

REFERENCES:

1. "dpANS GKS X3H3/83-2541", ANSI X3H3 Project 362, New York, New York (1983).

2. "ISO/DIS 7942 Information Processing - Graphical Kernel System (GKS) Functional Description: GKS Version 7.2", ISO/TC97/SC5/WG2 N163 (1982).

3. Hopgood, F. R. A., D. A. Duce, J. R. Gallop and D. C. Sutcliffe. Introduction to the Graphical Kernel System (GKS), Academic Press, London (1983).

4. GSPC. "Status Report of the Graphics Standards Planning Committee", Computer Graphics 13, 3 (August 1979).

5. Simons, Randall W. "Minimal GKS", Computer Graphics 17, 3, pp. 183-189 (July 1983).

6. Vistagraphic 4000 Series Graphic Processor Programmer's Reference Manual. Sanders and Associates, Nashua New Hampshire (1983).

PANEL

COMPUTER GRAPHICS RESEARCH IN JAPANESE UNIVERSITIES

CHAIR: Laurin Herr - Pacific Interface

PANEL: Eihachiro Nakamae - Hiroshima University
        Makoto Nagao, Kyoto University
        Norio Okino, Hokkaido University

There is considerable research activity related to computer graphics within the Japanese academic community. However, little is known about it outside of Japan. Another problem is that some of the most interesting work being done is not called "Computer Graphics" and is therefore only reported in other fields such as "Precision Engineering" or "Image Processing." Interpreting "Computer Graphics" broadly, this panel will survey the work of three leading Japanese researchers who will each briefly describe the history of computer graphics at their institutions, outline the level of staffing and equipment resources in their laboratories and report on their current areas of research activity. These presentations will be preceeded by the chairman's overview discussion about Japanese University research, in general. The panel will conclude with a question and answer period.

Professor Makoto Nagao, Department of Electrical Engineering, Kyoto University, Sakyo, Kyoto, Japan - The main thrust of research at Kyoto University has been in the field of digital image processing systems. Work began in 1965 on the problem of Japanese character recognition. One of the earliest digital processing systems in Japan was also designed. Working from beliefs about the human pattern recognition process, efforts were directed towards the development of a structural approach rather than mathematical theories which were popular during the early days of character recognition research. Current topics of interest include the modeling of more human-like image understanding functions, such as trial and error processes, knowledge-driven analysis processes and declaritive representation for image understanding. These can be summarized under the theme "Image Interpretation by Knowledge Presentation".

The image processing laboratory at Kyoto University uses a variety of image processing systems functioning largely as remote display stations linked to the university's central mainframe computer. The research team includes 4 faculty members, 8 graduate students, 6 under-graduates and 15 researches.

Professor Eihachiro Nakamae, Department of Electrical Machinery, Hiroshima University, Higuahi Hiroshima, 724 Japan - Research in computer graphics at Hiroshima University began in 1968. By 1973, basic solutions had been developed for the problems of hidden lines, hidden surfaces and convex polyhedra shading. After a year abroad at Clarkson University, Professor Nakamae returned to continue research in such areas as hidden lines on curved surfaces, solid modelling and the depiction of magnetic flux lines derived from FEM analysis. Since the installation of their first color raster display in 1979, the Hiroshima group has focused its efforts on the graphic display of various simulation results, such as lighting simulations and magnetic field simulations. Other areas of current research interest include operation of visual montages for environ-mental/architectural evaluations, various non-linear splines, semi-transparent stereographic anatomical displays and 3D analysis with display of electrical and magnetic fields.

Currently, the computer graphics team at Hiroshima University consists of 5 faculty members, 6 graduate students, and 7 under-graduate students.

Professor Norio Okino, Department of Precision Engineering, Hokkaido University, Sapporo, 060 Japan - The CAD/CAM working group at Hokkaido University began development of the TIPS-1 solid modeler in 1967 and first reported the results of this research in the second

prolumat in 1973. Considerable work based
on TIPS-1 has been done in a variety of
CAD/CAM fields, such as Computer Graphics,
CAD Database, CAE, process planning, NC
tape generation and robotics. There is
now a TIPS research association comprised
of more than 50 companies and several
universities, some of which are in the
United States and Europe.

Current research topics include:

1. Geometric simulator project which
    includes 4 kinds of simulators: engin-
    eering, assembly, NC and robot
    simulators. Advanced computer
    graphics techniques are being utilized
    in the development of this project.
2. Shading display techniques for solid
    modelling which involves development
    of new raster display techniques.
3. Robotics software which involves basic
    study of robot planning, especially
    graphic simulation of robot motion.

The TIPS working group at Hokkaido
University consists of about 25 people,
including 10 graduate students and 5 under
graduate. The laboratory is equipped with
its own Prime 550 II and 6 Graphics
Terminals, including a Lexidata Solidview.
The main frame computer in the Central
University Computer Center can alo be
accessed from terminals in the Lab.

Author Index

Omnimax Film Contributors

Art Center College of Design
Caltech Computer Graphics Group
John Beidenharn
Tom Brown
Chuck Esrock
Susan Gipson
Ted Owens
Vibeke Sorensen
Rebecca Wilmot

Bowling Green State University
Thomas A. Hern

California Institute of Technology
James F. Blinn
Jeffrey Goldsmith
James T. Kajiya
Timothy L. Kay
John Platt
Bob Schaff
Brian Von Herzen

Chromatics
James A. Squires

Control Data Corporation
John R. Jackson
Richard M. Mueller

Cray Research, Inc.
John Aldag
Bill Samayoa

DICOMED Corporation
Cal Kirchhof
Bruce Lindbloom

Digital Effects Inc.
C. Robert Hoffmann
Donald Leich
Judson Rosebush

Dynamic Graphics Inc.
Art Paradis

Earth Satellite Corporation
Kawana Estep
Max Miller

Fifth Generation Graphics, Inc.
Richard A. Weinberg

Geometric Productions
Charles E. Henderson
Agnis Kaugers

Intelligent Light at Austin Electronics
John Butler
Stan Cohen
Rick Fitzpatrick
Dan Hiepler
Roland Johnson
Charles Lamb
Steve Legensky
Tod Rogers
Dan Stripe
George Tsakas

Lawrence Livermore National Laboratory
Nelson Max

New York Institue of Technology
Computer Graphics Lab
Jules Bloomenthal
Ned Greene
Paul Heckbert
Dick Lundin
Robert McDermott
Lance Williams
Paul Xander Jr.

Purdue University CADLAB
Michael Bailey
Bill Charlesworth
Rich Crawford
Joe Cychosz
Dave Plunkett
Steve Van Frank

Rensselaer Polytechnic Institute
Gray Lorig

Research Institute of Scripps Clinic
Arthur J. Olson

Scripps Clinic
Michael Connolly
John A. Tainer

Skidmore, Owings & Merrill
Peter Jurgenson

University of California, Los Angeles
Francois Antier
Dahna Butnik
Phillip Cizewski
Philippe Daniel
Diane Feingold
Bernard Servoulle
John Whitney

University of California, San Francisco
Peter A. Kollman
Paul K. Weiner

University of Minnesota Computer Center
John Sell
Bob Williams

University of North Carolina at Chapel Hill
Anne C. Andersen
James S. Lipscomb
Michael E. Pique

Duke University
Karl Beem
Elizabeth D. Getzoff
David Richardson
Jane Richardson
Byron Rubin
John A. Tainer
Kenneth Thomas

Ian Macleod
Richard Moszkowski
Jerry Reed
Ron Resch

Image Credits

Cover Image

Ned Greene
New York Institute of Technology Computer Graphics Lab
Frame from "Inside a Quark" (animation)

This three dimensional environment was modeled entirely from polygons and rendered with Paul Heckbert's POLY program. The vines, which trace the edges of a diamond lattice, were modeled using tree modeling software written by Jules Bloomenthal and rendered with bump mapping. Flowers, sepals, and leaves were modeled using a program written by Lance Williams which creates a polygon mesh from a depth image and hand drawn boundary curves. Depth cueing simulates homogeneous fog; contrast falls off as an exponential function of distance from the eye (software: Ned Greene). Picture resolution is 1536x1536, 24 bits per pixel. Design, modeling, and animation by Ned Greene.

Title Page Image

Hank Weghorst/Gary Hooper
Program of Computer Graphics, Cornell University
"Hank's Bar and Grill"

This environment was modelled and rendered using the testbed image synthesis system developed at Cornell University. The environment contains items of polygonal, spherical, and cylindrical descriptions, rendered using a modified ray tracing technique. Modelling, viewing, and rendering software was developed by Gary Hooper and Hank Weghorst. Special thanks to Roy Hall for the original groundwork, Chan Verbeck for lighting descriptions, and Gary Meyer for color consultation. The image was produced at 512x480 on a VAX 11/750 running under VAX/VMS.

Back Cover Images

1. Franz Herbert
Swiss Federal Institute of Technology
" oral Bank"

    l design of a coral bank using an octree data

           don
         ter Imagery Inc.

Data for JACKS was generated from spheres and hyperboloids using a recursive growth process. The image was rendered on a VAX 11/780 with the program VQUSP. The image was displayed on an AED 767 at a resolution of 640 X 484 X 8 and photographed directly from the monitor.

3. Patricia Search
Rensselaer Polytechnic Institute
"Spirit Two"

The image was created with a ray tracing algorithm. The image was generated on a DATA GENERAL MV4000 and photographed with a MATRIX QCR. Objects were created with superquadrics.

4. Darwyn Peachey
University of Saskatchewan
"Jetport"

The objects in the scene were modelled using constructive solid geometry with quadric primitives. The image was generated by a ray tracing program that supports multiple light sources, reflection, refraction, and texture mapping. The photograph was produced on a Matrix Instruments Model 3000 film recorder.

5. William Reeves
Computer Division, Lucasfilm Ltd.
"Andre's Forest"

The trees, grass, and flowers in this scene were stochastically generated using particle systems. A specialized shading function was used to cast sunlight on the trees and to simulate self-shadowing. The shadows on the grass were generated using a shadow mask derived from the trees. Thanks to John Lasseter who helped design the scene and Eben Ostby who wrote the region splitting software.

6. Hank Christiansen/Rob Zundel/Don Jones
Brigham Young University
"Pear to Apple Geometry Transformation"

Produced using the modeling, transformation, and display capabilities of MOVIE.BYU. Displayed on a Ramtek 9460 frame buffer and recorded on film using a Log E/Dunn 632 system.